WITHDRAWN 8/6/21

Total Customer Satisfaction

Lessons from 50 companies with top quality customer service

JACQUES HOROVITZ
MICHELE JURGENS-PANAK

FINANCIAL TIMES
PITMAN PUBLISHING

Pitman Publishing
128 Long Acre, London WC2E 9AN

A Division of Longman Group UK Limited

First published in 1992
Reprinted 1992 (three times), 1993 (three times), 1994

© Jacques Horovitz and Michele Jurgens Panak 1992

British Library Cataloguing in Publication Data
A CIP catalogue record for this book can be obtained
from the British Library

ISBN 0 273 03447 2

Phototypeset in Linotron Times Roman by
Northern Phototypesetting Co. Ltd, Bolton
Printed and bound in Great Britain by
Biddles Ltd, Guildford and King's Lynn

CONTENTS

PREFACE

Why this book?

As consultants in service quality, we encounter many companies that are interested in becoming service quality leaders. While in some measure, we are able to assist these companies using our past experience, the core question for both us and our clients is 'What makes a service quality leader different from other companies?'

This is the question which this book will attempt to answer. We have spent two years researching European companies recognised for the quality of service they provide. We have looked at their service strategy, their management, their structure and organisation, the way they train, the way they hire and how they motivate their employees. We feel that we've covered these companies from A to Z.

What we have learned has not only helped us shed some light on what differentiates service quality companies from others, but also what management techniques can help other companies to improve their service quality. We now present this information to you, the reader, and hope that you come away with ideas for improving customer service in your own company.

How we did our research

We began our research with the notion that learning about good service companies had to be done directly from the source. This meant approaching major service leaders in Europe and spending time with them to learn how they treat their customers and how they run their business to ensure that their customers are satisfied.

Top service leaders are well known and appreciated. Normally, the reputation of a good service company extends far beyond its geographic sector of operations and sometimes around the world. To identify the companies to be included in this book, we relied on word-of-mouth, information from experts, the advice of customers and the comments (sometimes envious) of competitors. We also used documentary research, particularly to enhance or enlarge our view of a company already recommended to us. The voice of one expert or competitor alone did not determine our choice. Only the combined voices of many convinced us that a company had a strong reputation as a service leader.

We also tested the service quality orientation of the companies ourselves. In some cases, we used the services of the company. We looked to see if it matched our expectations every time we used it and in every location. In other cases, we tested the quality of the service in the reception that we received when we contacted them for our research. We evaluated the way in which the company responded to our request and the ease with which the research could be carried out.

As a final acid test for every company, we scored their service orientation, based on the information obtained from our interviews. We used a pre-established list of criteria based on what we already know about good service quality management. Our list covered issues such as the company's research on customers' expectations, training, employee incentives and motivation, measurement and monitoring systems, standards and handling customer complaints.

Only those companies that passed the full battery of tests appear in this book. They represent many industry sectors and can be practically any size – from a single location to a large world-wide network. We focused on companies originating from the northern part of continental Europe and the UK, where the demand for better service quality has been more pronounced.

We originally intended to include only firms of European origin, leaving out even the well-established American and Japanese firms, for example. Our research showed, however, that some of the foreign firms were setting the standard for good service throughout Europe and that their operations, run by European managers, were so extensive that they could hardly be considered to be just American or Japanese off-shoots. We definitely changed our minds when we reminded ourselves of our original objective: to learn about managing service quality in Europe, an activity pursued equally by all firms, European, American and Japanese alike.

Within each company we interviewed at least 3 different managers and sometimes as many as 8 or 10. Each interview lasted for between one and four hours, during which time our objective was to learn how each manager ensured good service provision by his company.

We didn't limit ourselves to a superficial examination of the company's organisational chart or to polite exchanges about business cycles. At the risk of offending, we drilled our interviewees about how they organise and motivate their personnel on a daily, even hourly basis. We looked at how they communicate, how they integrate new employees and how they adapt the company's service to changing customer expectations.

We dug for clues to explain how an employee on the frontline knows just what to say and do for an angry customer, and why what he does is virtually the same as what is done by another company employee halfway across the planet.

In the end, we can't say that we've uncovered every key to good service management, but what we have found proves that managing for good service quality requires special skills and special attention in the soft tools of management – culture, leadership, motivation and communication.

What we learned

What we learned from two years' research is presented in this book. Each of the following chapters deals with an area which we found particularly important for good service quality management in the companies we interviewed.

At the beginning of each chapter we give a brief introduction highlighting the trends we saw in all the companies we researched. Each introduction is followed by a case study showing how particular companies managed in the area in question. While we have used certain companies to illustrate particular points in the book, it should be kept in mind that these companies not only manage service quality well in the areas discussed, but in all areas – otherwise they wouldn't have been included.

Finally, the Chapter concludes with some general lessons which can be applied to improving service quality in almost any company. Highlighting the lessons we learned, we can say that:

- It's not just a question of putting in the right structure, pushing the motivational 'buttons' and waiting for results. A company that is a service quality leader is in a constant state of 'up'. It's perpetually 'turned-on' for the customer. Corporate culture is crucial.
- Maintaining that kind of hype demands leaders (not just managers) with tremendous energy and enthusiasm for their work – even spiritual or inspirational leaders.
- Inspired employees need to be helped to go towards a goal; if the goal is to provide excellent customer service, then a company's strategy should be based on a good analysis of customers' expectations.
- Motivating frontline employees is important, but motivating middle management is even more important and that means empowering them. Good service companies give middle managers their independence and count on their own self-motivation to create successes.
- Progress should be measured. Knowing where they stand and where they have to go motivates employees and helps them keep their priorities straight.
- Technology was created to be used to serve the customer better, not to be a 'white elephant'.
- Training in hard skills is important, but training in soft skills is equally so. Besides mastering their trade, employees should learn how to greet

customers, handle customer complaints, respond to enquiries etc.
- Communication is non-stop.

Managing for service quality is, thus, a judicious mix of hard and soft management tools. The hard tools are needed for structure and control. The soft tools are needed to create an environment which inspires employees with emotional devotion for their company and its goal in order to serve the customer better.

Rational thinking is not what makes these companies tick. While in the end, decisions taken may be rational, the process taken to arrive at them is dominated by inspirational brainstorming.

A service quality company is an emotional place to work. Its employees don't just punch in and punch out. Employees have a certain sentimental attachment to the company or to what they do; they find it impossible to be indifferent.

Philosophy is a more powerful motivator than business logic. Successful change in these companies achieved by the former, but by the latter.

Above all, what we learnt from the companies we researched is that managing for service quality is not easy.

ACKNOWLEDGEMENTS

In carrying out the research for this book, these authors were grateful for the assistance of a number of individuals without whose help none of this would have been accomplished.

First, we would like to thank all of the companies and their staff who have taken the time and effort to explain and teach us about the management of service quality in their companies. It has been a pleasure to work with all of them and we were extremely grateful to be able to learn from them.

We would also like to thank some of the experts in the field which we contacted for advice and recommendations. In addition to many others, we would like to cite in particular, Dr. Willi Fischer from the Kundendienstleiterverbank in Germany, Richard Tille, 'Administrateur' of the company Ombre Porte in Switzerland and Mr. Kees J. van Ham (today retired) and his team at the European Foundation for Quality Management.

In addition, we would also like to thank the msr consulting teams lead by the msr Partners; Eberhard Peill and Moritz Spilker in Germany, Laurence Ducharne and Pierre Castera in France, Juan Quijano and Jorge Mendosa in Spain and Olivier Saurais in Switzerland. These individuals provided invaluable assistance for the identification and contacting of service leaders and for the carrying out of interviews with the companies when these authors were unavailable.

Finally, we would like to thank our families who were, as always, patient and understanding.

INTRODUCTION

Why Service Quality?

If you've bought this book, you are probably familiar with companies that owe their success to good service quality and are already convinced that it can make a difference in your business. In fact, companies that differentiate on the basis of service can ask higher prices for comparative products or services and achieve superior profit margins. These same companies are more resistent in economic downturns and experience greater growth in economic boom periods. They also have, on average, lower advertising costs, lower sick-leave rates and higher employee retention rates.

For these and other similar reasons, service quality excellence has become the most recent 'buzz' phrase in management circles and the strategic objective of many major firms. Adopting service quality as a basis for a business strategy is an attractive option for companies finding it increasingly difficult to compete on the basis of price or technology alone, or for any company willing to make the long-term commitment needed to create a service-oriented culture.

It is an attractive option because the long-term commitment to create the appropriate culture can pay off in the form of an even longer-term sustainable advantage over the competition. Unlike most strategies, a strategy based on excellent service quality is nearly impossible to imitate or reproduce. How can a competitor recreate the good relationship established between a client and supplier or the experience of a customer who has had a memorable dinner? Service quality converts a company from an anonymous object into a familiar face. A good service company has a personality in its customers' eyes and every good service company has a personality which is unique and different from any other.

Because service quality is difficult to imitate, a company with good service is less open to attacks by 'clone' competitors or 'heavyweight' multinationals. Even when the clones or the heavyweights finally do arrive, customers resist change. Customer loyalty is based as much on sentimental attachment and habit, as on objective evaluations of the price/quality ratio. Most customers who have already experienced good service with a company will not want to take the risk of experiencing bad service with a new company. Within a certain limits, they will be willing to pay a slightly superior price for a guarantee of good service.

Yet, few companies really do provide excellent service. Quality products are readily available, but what about quality service? An enlightening exercise is to try to think of five firms from which you, personally, have received fault-free service more than twice. If you can think of three, you're probably receiving better service than the average European. Now, compare that with the number of firms from which you have purchased quality products – you should be able to name 10, 15, perhaps.

Service quality is hard to achieve. It's hard because service is complex and multidimensional. Selling a service means not only selling a commitment to do something, it also means selling the way in which it is done. Thus, the service quality battle is fought on two fronts – design and delivery. Companies must do both well in order to become a service leader.

Two kinds of service

Providing well-designed service means 'doing the right job' for the customer

Service design concerns the basic or 'billable' service offered to customers. For both product and service companies, it is determined by the company's marketing strategy and is, in short, the 'package' presented for sale to the customer.

In the case of a product company, it is the set of services provided with the product – the before, during and after-sales service, whether or not they are available and what they include. Can I have a free trial? Will my machine come installed? Is an owner's manual provided? Is after-sale service available on a 24-hour basis? Are parts included? Is there a repair shop in my neighbourhood? If not, who pays for the travel or postal expenses? Does the company reimburse for down-time?

In the case of a service company, it is the basic service to be offered. For a hotel, this means the number of stars, the style of the décor, the inclusion of breakfast in the price or not, the availability of laundry service, room service, a restaurant or bar etc. For a department store, it is the range of products available, the availability of salespeople, the access to lavatories, the ability to use credit cards or the possibility to return unsuitable merchandise.

Providing well-delivered service means 'doing the job right'

Service delivery concerns the 'non-billable' aspect of the service or how the job was done. In the case of a product company, it is the reliability, or the timeliness or efficiency of the service, in short, the degree to which the service is hassle-free.

With the purchase of a washing machine, it is whether or not the repair man can come on time. Can he answer my questions? Do I feel reassured? Does he have the parts on hand and can he fix the machine the first time around?

With the purchase of baby food, it is whether the flavour my baby likes best is always on the shelf. And do I always have ample time in which to consume the product before the expiry date? Are my questions answered quickly and completely when I have a problem? Can I return the product easily if I need to?

For a service company, service delivery concerns the experience the customer has when he uses the service, and whether or not he appreciated doing business with that firm. Was I waited on as rapidly as promised? Could I change my hotel room without any fuss? Was the salesperson polite and courteous? Did I feel at ease? Could I have my purchase gift-wrapped without feeling that I was bothering them? Do I feel that they care about me and my purchase? And so on.

Service must be both well designed and well delivered before customers perceive a company as a good service provider. One aspect alone is not sufficient. We often encounter well-designed service which is poorly delivered:

The Sleepy Time Inn is the most beautiful little hotel that Mr Smith ever saw at that price, but the bar girl ignored him and the laundry service returned his suit half a day late; next time he'll stay at the Holiday Inn across the street.

But, we can also see well-delivered service which is poorly designed.

Mrs Bridge's bank has the nicest, most helpful bank tellers in town, but the computer isn't programmed to produce an account balance daily and the interest rate on the savings account is three points lower than other banks; Mrs Bridge will transfer her account next month.

Both designing and delivering service right means mastering two different kinds of management skills, strategic and operational.

Two kinds of skills

The strategic or 'Doing the Right Job'

Offering a well-designed service means having correctly evaluated what your customers expect in terms of service and creating service 'packages' which reflect those expectations.

A customer does not enter into contact with a company with a completely open mind. He has certain expectations or pre-established ideas about what he will receive. His expectations are determined by a number of factors, including the advertising of the company, his/her previous experience with the same or similar services, the price he believes he will pay for the service, what he has heard from friends or the press about the company, his own capacity to do the same service and his underlying objective (the client that dines in a chic restaurant because he wants to be 'seen'). A returning customer also has further expectations coloured by his previous experiences with that company.

Customers generally have expectations on a number of aspects of the service. For a hotel, customer expectations could concern the cleanliness of the hotel, the degree of intimacy, the ease of access, the rapidity of the check-in/check-out etc.

The service aspects which your customers value most can be identified. For a bank, do customers place premium importance on the bank's ability to consult them in financial affairs or on the rapidity with which they can respond to a balance enquiry? For a restaurant, is it the atmosphere or the attentiveness of the service which is more important to their overall satisfaction with the restaurant?

Customers' perceptions of good service for each aspect can also be determined. If the bank's customers place a priority on responding rapidly to a balance enquiry, what does the customer consider to be 'rapid', two minutes or five? For a four-star restaurant, how attentive do customers expect the waiter to be?

A company should adjust or fine-tune its service to match its customer expectations. If a company says that it provides 'perfectly customised' service, then that is what its customers expect to receive – to the letter. 'Perfectly customised' service in computer software means creation from scratch; it does not mean the judicious adaptation of a program developed for another client.

Woe betide the company that promises what it can't or doesn't intend to provide. Besides losing the customer, it gives him a wonderful opportunity to tell others how he was misled. Studies show that, on average, a customer will tell 11 people about a bad service experience. And, we all know someone who will repeat endlessly the story about The Company that promised 24-hour emergency service and showed up three days late.

A customer is satisfied if his expectations are met. Knowing what the customer's expectations are permits a company to create a desirable service 'package'. We talk about creating a *service package* because a service represents a combination of different offerings to the customer. When you buy dry cleaning services, for example, you are buying the reception which you receive at the counter, the use of the cleaning machines, the accuracy of the bill, the atmosphere of the shop, the advice you receive (or don't receive) about clothing care etc.

Being able to create a good 'package' of services or a product/service package (in the case of a product company) is extremely important. A service package should be well balanced – a poorly-balanced service package can disappoint customers and discourage them from repurchasing. Take, for example, the case of the designer clothing boutique that doesn't put chairs in its dressing room or hands you your purchases in a plain plastic bag. The client who comes in expecting to receive 'designer'-level service throughout his or her visit is understandably disappointed when he or she leaves with a nondescript plastic bag in his or her hands.

An unbalanced service package can also confuse customers. The use of an elegant marble entrance into a fast-food restaurant is likely to intimidate potential customers and mistakenly draw the attention of other clients looking for a more sophisticated eating environment.

Service packages can be not only satisfactory, they can also be innovative. A good example is IKEA, the Swedish home furnishings retailer, which sells furniture unassembled, direct from the warehouse. In other aspects, IKEA's service is exemplary. Advice on furniture arrangement and assembly is readily available, assembly instructions are easy to understand and printed in many languages, and their showroom is spacious and well-designed with restaurant and bathroom facilities and even a changing room for visiting babies.

The best service 'package' reflects the strengths of the company. Certain customers may want 24-hour delivery, but if the company's logistical system is 10-years out of date, it is more reasonable to offer a package which emphasises other aspects. Customers who are willing to settle for three-day delivery may find it absolutely vital to receive weekly invoices, something which the company's new financial accounting system can reliably supply.

The operational or 'Doing the Job Right'

Customer expectations must not only be met in service design, but also in service delivery. Providing well-delivered service means being able to ensure that the service package is provided without fault, wherever and whenever the customer comes into contact with the company. We refer to this as zero-default service.

Good service delivery also means creating an environment in which the customer will experience a positive 'fit' with the company – the special emotional plus that keeps him coming back time and time again. This we refer to as service zest.

Zero-default concerns the consistency of the service. Customers who have experienced good service once come back hoping to receive the same good treatment. There are three ways in which customers expect to receive consistent service. They expect to receive consistent service between visits, between different geographical locations and between different employees.

Consistency in service between visits primarily involves influencing the behaviour of employees. If the first time a customer found the sales clerk in the boutique helpful and cheerful, then the next time she comes to the boutique, she expects the same degree of helpfulness or cheerfulness. Bouts of humour on the part of the sales clerk will be poorly received by the customer who is the innocent victim.

Consistency between locations involves not only influencing employees' behaviour, but also ensuring that the company and its products or services are presented in the same manner. For example, the company's logo in Italy may be navy blue; if it's also navy blue in France then that's fine, however, if it's blue-green, then you can be sure that more than one customer will be dismayed or confused.

Consistency in service between locations also means ensuring that the same advantages are offered in each location. The car rental customer from London who is used to paying by credit card will naturally assume he can pay by credit card in every location, including Athens or Ankara. The car rental company's job is to ensure that he can.

Most of all, service consistency must be assured between people. There is nothing more irritating than to be told by one employee that you can have something and, five minutes later, to be told by his boss or colleague that you can't. Furthermore, this kind of situation generally gives way to a sometimes rather heated discussion between the two employees while you, the customer, wait impatiently on the sidelines. Few things will discourage a repeat visit more than that!

While managing for zero-default service involves the standardisation of behaviour and practices, managing for service zest involves the development of employee creativity and independence. Zest, in general, concerns people. Employees who offer customers zest in service are confident, competent, motivated and people-oriented.

Confidence and competence go hand in hand. Confident employees are that way because they know their job and they are prepared to handle any situation that might be presented to them. Confident employees mean reassurred customers. That's important because customers want to be reassured; they don't want to worry that what they are buying is substandard or unreliable. Contact with a confident and seemingly competent employee reduces the insecurity of the purchase.

Zesty service also means having motivated employees. Motivated employees increase the pleasure of the purchase. The positive energy which they generate can make a purchase become an adventure or a novelty for the customer. Such employees are the initiators of the emotional attachment which customers develop for certain companies and which keeps them loyal.

Motivated employees are also more ready to respond to customers and will make greater efforts to ensure that they are truly satisfied. The competent but non-motivated employee may be perfectly able to resolve the customer's problem, but will not execute it with the same enthusiasm as will a motivated employee. The motivated employee often responds with such alacrity that customers feel grateful, even indebted, to the company, despite the company being the source of the problem.

Motivated employees mean employees who are prepared to take special initiatives to give customers a service plus. It's a motivated employee who will think to procure and offer a walking stick to an elderly tourist trailing behind the rest of the group. It's also a motivated employee who will propose to write to the manufacturer for care instructions on behalf of a customer who purchased an expensive stereo system. Taking initiatives on behalf of customers comes down to thoughtfulness and today a company that can demonstrate that it thinks about the individual needs of its customers has a considerable advantage over its competitors.

Motivation, confidence and competence are still not enough. A good employee can have all those things, but if he's not directing his skills towards the satisfaction of customers, then he's doing as much damage as a poor employee.

A good service employee should be people-oriented or be able to put himself 'in the shoes of his customer'. Short of that, he should be prepared to listen to his customer, accept his explanation and act with the same rapidity and enthusiasm. Being people-oriented means sympathising, if not empathising with the customer.

1 CORPORATE CULTURE IS ESSENTIAL

Introduction

Having the right corporate culture is crucial to achieving good service quality. In all the companies we looked at, this was the element that managers cited as contributing the most to good customer service. It directed employees' efforts when no points of references were available, it motivated them towards ever greater achievements and it kept them thinking of the customer.

The simplest way to understand corporate culture is to understand it as being the character of the company. Just as individuals have characters which are unique and different, so do corporations. As an obvious consequence, they are described in the same way as individuals. 'We are seen as being a young, dynamic organisation,' says Patrick Odier of Lombard, Odier. 'Migros is a company with a social conscience,' explains Mr Haller, Director, Migros Vaud.

Corporate characters or cultures can be strong or weak, just as people can, and they can be customer service oriented or not, just like people. 'The customer is everything' at Schlumberger. 'All Tetra Pak staff must be committed to the task of customer service.'

The textbook definition of corporate culture goes something like this: 'The set of values, behaviours and ways of communicating which are mutually accepted by all individuals in the company.' For the purpose of our work and in so far as corporate culture concerns service quality, we have defined corporate culture as being the philosophy of the company, the way in which the individuals communicate with one another and the way in which they work together.

The philosophy is the dominant set of beliefs on which everyone agrees and it can be at any level. Employees can agree about the the business of the company and what its objectives in that business should be ('We develop, produce and market complete packaging systems for the distribution of food products. . . . Our most important goal is to have an increased amount of food products distributed in Tetra Pak packages.') or they can agree on a broad set of ethical issues such as honesty or aid towards mankind 'We don't work so that someone else can get rich; we must make a profit, but it's for the benefit of the co-operatives', says Mr Rentsch of Migros St Gallen.

Corporate culture is also the way people communicate with one another and the type of information which is communicated. For service quality, this is important, because it provides an indication of how much importance the customer plays in the daily life of the company. At Citicorp, discussions centre around target customers; at other banks, customers are 'just accounts'. Clues to look at are how often the customer is featured in verbal and written communications, and in what way, for example, he is featured as a grumpy gorilla or a lovable teddy bear'.

The area of work relations is the third aspect of corporate culture we chose to look at. By work relations, we mean the work habits and patterns people have, as well as the nature of the relationship between colleagues. 'People work hard in this company . . .' (Lombard, Odier).

For service quality, work relations are an important issue, because they are generally mirrored in employees' relationships with their customers. An employee who is often rude with fellow workers is likely to be rude with customers as well. 'In the trial period, we look at the way that trainees deal with fellow employees; this will have an impact on how they work with customers,' says Thierry Lombard, of Lombard, Odier.

The issue of work relations also provides a clue to the general level of quality which is pursued by the company as a whole and to what is considered to be a priority. This is true internally, 'We have a 100 per cent "help others" rate; it's part of our culture' and with customers, 'Our customers' problems are our problems. We are always available to assist' (Tetra Pak).

Inherent in any culture is a way of viewing the customer. Sometimes this is stated, 'We want to be partners with our customers,' says Mr Krähenbühl of Ciba Geigy; at other times it is implicit, 'To our mind, every person in every department works for client satisfaction,' says Mr Bonna of Lombard, Odier.

The philosophy provides a general idea of the obligations which the company feels that it has to the customer. Likewise, it provides an indication to employees of what is expected of them *vis-à-vis* the customer, 'We aim for 100 per cent customer satisfaction' (Kwik-Fit).

How corporate culture contributes to service quality

Good service happens when you have employees who are committed to quality in their own work and are willing to go out of their way to deliver that same level of quality to customers. They do so either because they care for customers as individuals or because they care for the company and what others think about it. Different company cultures emphasise either one or both approaches to good service.

Caring for the company: the case of Migros

Whatever they might appear to be on paper, companies are not inanimate objects to their employees. Employees can become emotionally attached to the company they work for and ready to go beyond the minimum expected for the company or for its customers.

Having an appealing company philosophy is a good way to tie employees emotionally to the company. Individuals join a company because they agree with its philosophy; they stay with the company because they believe in it and have gradually become advocates of it.

Just as the philosophy ties the employee to the company, it also ties the employee to behaviour which is consistent with it. It shows employees where special efforts must be made. 'An engineer must be always ready to go to the aid of his client' (Schlumberger). Even without a particular rule, regulation or standard, an employee knows where priorities lie – if a company's philosophy emphasises customer satisfaction, then so do employees. 'Our company objective is, in our stores, to achieve the highest standards of cleanliness and hygiene, efficiency of operation, convenience and customer service' (Sainsbury's).

Some companies have a lot of emotionally attached employees, who believe in the company and share its objectives wholeheartedly. Migros provides a good example of one of these.

Migros is Switzerland's leading food retail chain. It is organised as a federation of 12 co-operatives. Through the members of the federation, it controls roughly one-third of all food sold in Switzerland.

Migros employees respect and appreciate the Migros philosophy. Most Migros managers say that they could not work with the same level of devotion anywhere else. The Migros philosophy emphasises a fair deal, the common man and the importance of defending the consumer's interests. Above all, Migros wants to mean more to the society than just a commercial enterprise. 'Our value-added is in what we do for society beyond our commercial activities,' says Mr Haller (MigrosVaud).

Perhaps because of its status as a co-operative, profit takes on a different meaning in the Migros organisation. With profits going back to consumers, top management is not motivated by self-interest or greed, but by the possibility of increasing the company's contribution to the general welfare. 'We feel that we're doing something that we can be proud of. When I stand in front of St Peter, I'll be able to say honestly that I did something in my life to help other people,' says Mr Rentsch (Migros St Gallen).

By statute, the Migros Federation must contribute one per cent and the co-operatives one half of a per cent of sales to cultural, social and socio-economic expenditures for the general public. The 'contribution', as it could be called, is a focal source of pride for all employees; what is done with the 'contribution' is a major source of discussion. The fundamental criterion is that the events sponsored must be 'available to the greatest number'.

Reflected therein is also the concept of doing things for the 'common man'.

At Migros, services are not conceived to meet the 'particular' needs of anybody. If it can't be useful to a large section of the population, then it's not something that Migros offers. Migros managers speak with great pride about the events sponsored with the 'contribution'. 'We try to offer something for everyone, so that everyone can profit,' says Mr Forrer (Migros St Gallen).

Within each Migros co-operative a department has been created to manage the 'contribution'. The manager of the department is on the management board and reports directly to the co-operative director. 'We manage the contribution with as much care as we manage any other part of the company,' says Mr Haller.

When it came to developing the Säntis Park shopping/recreation complex, 'it had to be a fair deal – good value for money,' says Mr Forrer. The notion of offering the consumer a fair deal is also part of the Migros philosophy. Migros was Switzerland's first food discounter and the company's history is filled with battles fought to win the right to offer customers that discount. 'We fought to defend the philosophy,' explains Mr Gugelmann, Marketing Director (Migros Federation).

Another tenet of the Migros philosophy is its role as the consumer's advocate. In stark contrast to the policy of most companies, Migros takes active positions on political questions that they feel impact on the consumer. They are particularly active on farm policy and, more recently, on environmental questions. While most employees are not expected to defend the firm's political policies, most are ready to because of their commitment to the company. 'In the past, we were social outcasts in society if we went to work for Migros. That created a special bond between employer and employee.'

Taken as a whole, the Migros philosophy is a powerful motivator for employees. They are devoted to the philosophy and they do their best to execute it – as the consumer's advocate and as 'capitalists with a social conscience'. Each Migros employee is prepared to respond to consumers' questions about the quality of the goods in his department and about sensitive consumer issues. Migros's internal newsletter and its letter to co-operative members is full of high-quality information about food, consumer issues and cultural events.

If a customer buys Migros-grown fruit, he can be sure that Migros employees have carefully considered the usage of pesticides; if he buys washing-up liquid, then he can be sure that its impact on the environment has been studied and that Migros has a report available on request. 'It's a question of self-discipline; we do everything with a social conscience.'

At Säntis Park, energy usage, water usage, land usage and even the bus routes were all studied to choose the best ones and the ones which were of low cost to the consumer. Migros had to pay the city council for an addition to the bus route, so that consumers would have easy access to the centre.

Migros employees know what level of commitment is required of them;

they're ready to do the maximum in order to live the philosophy on a daily basis and with customers. 'We ask a lot of our employees, but we try to be fair and correct.' Nobody at Migros is paid according to financial results. Employees are expected to devote themselves entirely to Migros. 'One should feel 24, hours out of 24, a Migros man or woman.'

'Migros is like a church and the philosophy like a religion.' Each new Migros trainee attends at least one cultural event (paid for by the company). New store employees frequently receive flowers on their first day. Within each co-operative, there is a family atmosphere. 'There is little difference between people according to hierarchy.' Employees party together – retirements, anniversaries, weddings, etc. 'I remember in 1955, Mr Duttweiler bought a big white American convertible; he used to lend out the car to employees to go out in on Sundays,' says Mr Haller.

At Migros, one never forgets the customer; in any case he is not really a customer, but a co-operative member. 'Our employees feel responsible to the customer. We work hard to provide them with the best quality possible at the lowest price.' The customer could be your grandmother, neighbour or the coach of the children's ski team. 'When you supply one-third of Switzerland, you can't be indifferent,' says Dr Battaglia (Director, Laboratories).

Caring for the customer: the case of Club Med

In some cases, a corporate culture will focus less on creating an emotional attachment between the employee and the company, and more on creating an exchange of rights between the employee and the customer. In such cases, the culture will bring the customer into the company and present him as a friend or partner in the achievement of common goals. Club Med is a good example of this type of corporate culture.

Club Med is the innovator of the village vacation concept in which vacationers pass their time in a location where everything is provided. Food, lodging, entertainment and access to sports facilities are all included in the price and are paid for in advance.

At Club Med the team are oriented towards achieving total customer satisfaction. The Club Med philosophy of customer service comes from its history. When Club Med started up in the 1950s, it was truly a club and had a non-profit status as a company. The objective was for members to enjoy a vacation together in a beautiful location. 'The spirit of the Club in the 1950s was to live side by side with our guests; we wanted them to be happy,' explains Michel Perchet, who is responsible for the development of human resources for the company as a whole.

The Club's organisers became so involved in the managing of the Club that they became full-time organisers, calling themselves *'gentil organisateurs'* or nice organisers. The other participants and their guests subsequently became the *'gentil membres'* or nice members. Because many of the GMs were personal friends of the GOs, the GOs worked hard to make the GMs visits pleasant; their reception could be compared to the one given to a friend visiting the family's house in the country.

The circle of GMs continued to get wider and wider over the years – vacationers continue to pay a yearly Club fee when they buy their holiday – but the philosophy of GMs being personal friends on vacation has remained. Take, for example, the way GOs speak to GMs. To start with, everyone is on a first-name basis, regardless of age or status. Moreover, GOs are very relaxed with GMs: they joke with them, openly express their likes and dislikes, and encourage GMs to divulge their own opinions. 'GMs need autonomy to give good service; they have to be able to step out of a mould sometimes and treat each customer as an individual.'

The way that GOs speak about GMs is also important. It's not 'a client . . .', it's 'George . . .' or, at the worst, 'the funny guy in the red bathing suit'. In any case, the customer is not an anonymous individual; he is a person with a character and a physical presence which can be described and identified. GOs frequently talk about the GMs among themselves. They exchange their impressions of different individuals and describe experiences they had with the GMs. Conversations like this are regular fare at the Club,

'It was great yesterday . . . the guy in the red suit just got a good wind up when . . . and there was Mira, you know, the redhead from Ireland, . . . she really learned fast . . . there was a great atmosphere'.

'I've got Mira today in my windsurfing class; it would be fun to. . . . She would enjoy that.'.

To reinforce the GO's tie to the customer, Club Med has a policy that no GO is ever off duty. As long as he's at the Club, he is always available to the GMs and prepared to help them, play with them or party with them.

In terms of customer service, the principal advantage of having a customer-oriented culture like Club Med's is that change to improve service occurs rapidly, i.e. the closer the GOs are to the guests, the better they can evaluate their needs and expectations in terms of service, and the quicker they can adapt the service to meet those expectations. 'It is a serious error not to give a GM what was promised to him. If ever anything goes wrong, we act very fast; the decision is made by the village chief and immediately acted upon by everyone in the village,' says Mr St Jean. 'We don't wait for standards to be changed; even so the standards are changed at least once a year to integrate what we've discovered from the villages.'

To find out what's happening in the village and to make sure he gets the information he needs about customer satisfaction, the village chief holds a weekly meeting to discuss how the week went and what could have been done to improve upon it. Details about exactly 'who liked what' are discussed. GOs often ask GMs for their opinions on ways to improve things and pass this information on to their peers and superiors through these meetings. 'Information is always coming up from the village; we listen to everybody in quality circles, above all, the new ideas coming from the customers via the

GOs,' explains Michel St Jean, who is in charge of recruitment.

There is also plenty of one-on-one communication between the chief and individuals in his team. 'There is a relation of confidence between the chief and the GOs. The GOs know that they can come to me with everything; I'm always ready to listen.'

A customer-oriented culture can help companies adapt quickly: the case of Marks & Spencer

Whether or not employees are bound emotionally to their company or to the customer, they can find themselves in a corporate culture which encourages either slow, thoughtful behaviour or more rapid responses to decisions or events.

When people are of one mind on a particular issue, they are capable of making rapid decisions and acting rapidly. When that issue happens to be the imperative to meet customer expectations, then you have an organisation which is infinitely flexible and highly capable of responding to a rapidly changing market. That's just what Marks & Spencer is.

Marks & Spencer (M&S) is a large UK-based chain of retail department stores. They sell primarily household goods and clothing, and are the largest group of their kind in the country. M&S has a corporate culture which embraces the notion of adapting rapidly to changes in customer tastes. The philosophy of the company, the lines and methods of communication, and the way people work with one another all reflect this imperative for quick response and flexibility.

The M&S philosophy is an extension of the corner-shop approach to business – if the customer doesn't buy it, get it off the shelf. M&S doesn't believe in carrying merchandise that is hard to sell. Everything M&S puts on its shelves should be readily accepted by the public and have a high rate of turnover. Mr Poppleton, Director, explains 'Our approach is purely pragmatic, even in this day and age. We make an entrepreneurial guess with our fashion experts or our food experts and then make a judgement [about what to put out]. . . . If the customer doesn't want it, we get rid of it.'

The customer doesn't have long to make up his mind. In some M&S pilot stores, 24 hours is enough to determine whether a product will sell or not. If it doesn't, it's taken off the shelf the next day and replaced. M&S doesn't try to be innovative. Innovators try to push a product; M&S doesn't believe in this. What is more important is whether the customer will buy the product without being pushed. 'The customer is the ultimate arbitrator. If she wants it, we'll give her a lot more of it; if she doesn't, we get rid of it quickly,' explains Mr Poppleton.

All M&S employees generally agree with the principle that 'the customer is always right' and that his or her wishes can be gauged by monitoring purchases on the shop floor. Consequently, discussion at M&S centres around customer acceptance of given products. All the way up and down the hierarchy, people talk about whether 'the new line of wool cardigans was well received' or whether 'blue silk socks were a popular item' last week.

Sales staff on the floor talk about 'restocking or not restocking' and whether a new model will replace the present line which 'hasn't been selling very well'. They are also aware of exactly which items are being discontinued or 'restocked' and can give the date on which that will happen, if it's not tomorrow. 'Lilac is a typical colour; we get seduced by lilac about every five years; we practically never restock in lilac.'

In most large department stores, time frames for merchandise are discussed in terms of seasons, i.e. 'that item sold well last season'. At M&S the time frame is much shorter and, unless an item has become a classic, time frames for stock rotation can be weekly.

Top management survey personally the success or failure of particular products. Stories abound at M&S about directors testing the merchandise and overseeing the product's success with customers. Mr Poppleton, who we interviewed for this book, gave us an excellent demonstration of the kind of exchange which occurs between employees and managers: 'I was just up for a cup of coffee and I saw the man who had just launched a new line of hosiery. It's gone very well. It was a trial and we'd bought a one-off quantity. The stock is now getting low, but we know exactly what's missing and where. . . . '

'M&S's strength is in monitoring and reacting.' M&S work relations and the methods of communication between employees facilitates the quick response which is necessary once customer reception of a product is known. A key point is that M&S employees respect authority. Managers are 'Mr' or 'Mrs' and inferiors are 'Jane' or 'Samuel'. If a decision is made on top and comes down, that decision is obeyed absolutely. There is no hesitation in the response of employees to their managers' requests. Just as the customer's judgement is absolute, so is the boss's.

While work relations up and down the hierarchy are somewhat formal, relations between individuals at roughly the same level in the hierarchy are informal and friendly. Many store managers know one another personally. Practically 100 per cent of the staff worked their way up the ranks and in the process have developed a strong sense of camaraderie with those at the same level. As the result, information passes rapidly from store to store about product successes or failures with customers.

Buying or marketing managers have an important role and help facilitate the passage of information; they are constantly on the phone with the stores, receiving practically hourly reports on the sales of their merchandise. Others are actually on the floor observing their products' progress which they then telephone in to their managers. 'We have an excellent system of management reporting. We know every night what the stores have done. If we wish, we can find out exactly how many of what colour and what size sold that day.'

When decisions are made to remove products, staff respond quickly and efficiently at every level. Buyers arrange for another item to appear on the shelves, logistics staff arrange for its delivery to the pilot store, the clerks clear and refill the shelves the very same evening and a new product appears the next day. Employees are accustomed to rapid changes and are geared up to respond.

M&S's response can be extremely rapid, especially when the stakes are high. In 1989, the company set up its first store in Madrid. 'It was a huge success; we sold out in less than a week in 'crisps', in ladies' lingerie, etc. . . . by week's end, we were flying stuff in daily in order to fill the shelves. We had already planned an expansion of two floors and are looking at other stores throughout the country.'

A culture acts as a regulator, encouraging certain types of behaviour and discouraging others: the case of Tetra Pak

Some companies rely on an extensive list of rules and regulations to control their employees' behaviour. Most of the companies we looked at did not. When we asked them how they managed to ensure that their employees were doing the right things, they said, 'That is just the ways thing are done here, there is no other possibility'.

By digging a bit, we discovered that managers spoke and behaved in a very similar fashion. That is not to say that they were clones, but in certain key ways behaviour was identical from one manager to the next. Because managers serve as role models for all employees, their behaviour was mirrored at the lower levels. Anyone whose behaviour deviates from the norm on the key points would not be considered to be part of the team and would eventually be encouraged to leave, but in other aspects a different approach was generally well received and highly appreciated.

At Tetra Pak, we encountered this type of culture. Tetra Pak is highly specialised in the production and sale of packaging systems for the distribution of consumable liquids – mostly milk. They were one of the first companies to develop packaging for the use of UHT long-life milk; today, a high proportion of European consumers buy their long-life milk in a Tetra Pak container (called Tetra Brik).

The company has its roots in Sweden with corporate headquarters located in Lund. At the same time, Tetra Pak has a national identity in each of the markets in which it has established a local company. Tetra Pak could most appropriately be called a 'multi-domestic' organisation, implying assimilation, integration and decentralisation in each market where it has a presence.

The business approach of the company is quite clear. The company is firmly entrenched in the packaging industry and believes that, 'A package should save more than it costs'. Within this statement of Dr Ruben Rausing, the founder, is a broader concern for the use of the package which is produced. A more inclusive statement of the company's philosophy might be 'Tetra Pak promotes, wherever possible, the use of extremely hygienic liquid packaging systems and the development of that industry'.

As such, Tetra Pak actively assists the customer to improve the entirety of their packaging system and provides a large number of services with the packaging systems they sell. Tetra Pak is also very active in community affairs and in assisting in the development of the milk industries in countries where this is needed.

Tetra Pak employees have described Tetra Pak's corporate culture as being 'open, interested, engaged, energetic, responsibility seeking, friendly, communicative'. Above all, Tetra Pak employees are professionals and they treat one another as such, with managers setting the example. Relations are cordial and friendly. Tetra Pak people are not the kind of employees one would see running up and patting each other on the back. Nor could one imagine them joking boisterously at a convention. In general, they maintain their composure and a certain polite reserve.

Commitments from one employee to another are meticulously respected. If someone says that he will pass a document over to a co-worker within an hour, the document is there within the hour. Likewise appointments are respected. An appointment made with a fellow employee is second only to an appointment with a customer. 'We're a very professional organisation.'

Tetra Pak employees are also professional in the way they present themselves. Tetra Pak is a 'well-dressed' company. Every manager had a suit and even the most informal suit (there were not many) is impeccably neat and clean. Employees observe rigorously all of the proper forms of business address and behaviour. There is always a 'Thank you', 'Could I be of assistance?', 'I apologise for the inconvenience, but . . .' and a 'Could I offer you some coffee?'.

Tetra Pak people are precise in the way they communicate. They do not just say whatever comes to mind; instead they consider carefully what they will say, knowing that it will be considered with equal care by the person with whom they are speaking. This attention to precision in communication is reinforced by the fact that Tetra Pak has defined specific standards for communication. Only certain terminology may be used when describing Tetra Pak's products or technologies. For visual or written communications, there are guidelines for signs, presentations and even for typefaces to be used in the various types of written documents.

Employees themselves say that Tetra Pak makes a point of receiving visitors well. As visitors we can confirm this; all the managers with whom we spoke, up to Board level, were found to be equally calm, attentive, interested and open. One manager, who fell ill just before our visit, offered to receive us at the hospital!

The kind of professionalism that they expect from one another is the same kind of professionalism that they want to offer to their customers. 'We "live together" with our customers.' It is vital that the forms of behaviour and work habits practised inside the company be adopted uniformly by all employees. New employees are judged on the readiness with which they adopt the Tetra Pak way of working with one another as much as on any objective evaluation of their technical competence.

The culture plays its role as a regulator, as the behaviour of fellow employees guides newer employees in the right direction. Managers play a key role, by setting the example for specific behaviour which should be observed. Employees replicate it in their own work and in the way they deal with customers. 'When you join this company, you don't really know how to act. There are no rules, no regulations, no absolute job descriptions. You have to look to those around you and learn the unwritten rules. . . . Once you're in, the lack of rules means greater freedom and greater flexibility; you can do what you believe in and defend it to your manager.'

A culture is also a way of ensuring that everyone is heading in the same direction: the case of Nestlé

Unity in thought and action between individuals permits an organisation to act as one body rather than as a set of conflicting partners. A strong corporate culture brings greater unity to the company by establishing principles upon which all employees agree. The stronger a culture is within a company, the more closely the principles will be adhered to and the stronger the homogeneity in thought and action between individuals is likely to be.

At Nestlé, the culture of the company has always been very strong. Nestlé makes chocolate and coffee, but it is also a worldwide group active in practically every segment of the food goods industry selling under hundreds of different name brands.

Despite a long history of numerous large acquisitions, Nestlé has always remained Nestlé and those companies which are acquired eventually become more Nestlé than anything else. Perhaps it is because the company has had up to now a policy of making only friendly acquisitions – which indicates a certain willingness or desire on the part of those acquired to become part of the Nestlé group – or perhaps it is because the Nestlé culture has inherent in it a philosophy which is universally attractive. In either case, Nestlé remains a corporate entity, distinct and singular.

The first element of the Nestlé culture is the orientation towards the product – not the designing, researching or manufacturing of the product – but the product itself. Nestlé people talk products. The products are not just any products; they must be good. They must be quality products and they have wide recognition with the consumer for their brand name and their quality. When Nestlé acquires a company, it does so with a major interest in the power of the name brand and the products on the market.

Quality products with quality brand names: this is something to which the Nestlé people attach a great deal of importance. They have 420 factories worldwide and in each one there is a quality department with people trained to help the plant staff detect and resolve problems in production. The degree of importance which quality asurance has in the Nestlé group is demonstrated by the fact that in every major country in which the company operates, there is a 'technical director' reporting directly to the managing director of the country, one of whose main functions is to ensure and improve constantly the management of quality within the company.

Proud of the quality of their products, proud of what they represent, Nestlé people are quick to defend the Nestlé name and what it stands for. In one customer complaints handling department, one manager describes her job as 'fulfilling the basic principles of the company to the consumer'. Every problem that could impact the maintenance of the company's high standard of product quality merits the most immediate attention. Hot-lines have been established in practically every Nestlé company which can put a manager in touch with plant directors at home, in the middle of the night and with the director of the company. 'It is part of the philosophy of our company; in such cases, we must act and act quickly.'

An institutionalised concern for product quality has had an overflow effect on service quality. Nestlé sees itself as being a group of 'Quality people, quality products, quality management, quality communication (and service) and quality growth'. Employees are striving continually to improve their individual performance and that of the company. Once an objective or commitment has been established, employees are committed to achieving it. 'At one time we promised to deliver "the right product within 48 hours, with the expected quality",' says Mr Hagman, Technical Director, France. 'Our people would live and die in order to make sure they kept that promise.'

The well-established and structured approach to product quality is contributing to a growing awareness for the need to address quality in a broader sense. 'Our previous promise is no longer considered to be sufficient. Already the definition of quality has broadened; today, it is, "providing the right product at the right time, in the right place." ' The company is also going 'upstream' in the pursuit of better service and product quality. In a number of Nestlé companies, 'partnership' relationships are being established with suppliers in which closer ties are leading to better service and a co-ordinated approach to quality control. 'Our approach with our suppliers is based on an overall approach to quality which includes, in a large way, service quality.'

While service quality with Nestlé's suppliers relates primarily to better communications and more reliability in terms of orders and deliveries, service quality with clients and consumers touches a broad range of topics. With clients, it includes the quality of the relationship with the different individuals in the company, the support services provided to them and a respect of delays and delivery times.

For consumers, it includes the information available to the consumer both at the time of purchase, and before or after the purchase, it includes the degree to which the product is conceived to meet the practical as well as culinary expectations of the buyer, any services which serve to enhance the product in the consumer's eyes and the way in which the company responds to the consumer in case of a problem.

Little by little Nestlé is addressing these service quality issues with ever greater attention. For clients of Nestlé Rowntree, the company is developing a centralised service for market and merchandising information. The department will be able to provide specialised advice to customers on how better to merchandise their products. Elsewhere, the individuals responsible for managing a client's account have become a servicing team and are co-ordinating their efforts, between themselves and with their counterparts in the client's company.

Consumers are also benefiting from closer attention to service quality. At Gloria Pet Food, a Minitel service has been introduced which provides customers with practically everything they need to know about the care and raising of dogs and cats. The company has also created a cat club called 'Club Gourmet' which organises events, and sends out a monthly newsletter and a magazine *Moustaches*. The customer with young children also benefited last summer when Nestlé set up Baby Stops on some of the major autoroutes in Europe. With free nappies, water and friendly, helpful assistance, the programme went a long way towards gaining the loyalty of practically everyone who stopped and used the services.

Nestlé's objective in the future is to broaden its quality approach to encompass service quality. Another aspect of Nestlé's culture is that change doesn't happen overnight. There is first the building up of a consensus of opinion and thought within the company and only after that is there a move to action. 'We prefer to construct little by little with the co-operation of everyone.'

Creating a corporate culture: the case of Mercury Communications

One of the companies we looked at had the unique opportunity consciously to build a corporate culture from scratch. Mercury Communications was created in 1982 as part of a consortium of companies owned by British Petroleum, Barclays Bank and Cable and Wireless. It has been the only company to obtain a licence to compete directly with British Telecom in the telecommunications market. In 1984, when it became the 100 per cent-owned subsidiary of Cable and Wireless, the company had 200 employees. Today, it has nearly 9000.

The management of the company has been fully conscious from the beginning of the impact which a corporate culture can have on the level of customer service and thus upon the success of the company in a competitive situation. Because of that recognition, management look upon its goal as the creation of customer service and quality-oriented culture. 'It was clear that as the company had to be competitive in an existing monopoly situation it had to develop a cultural framework for quality and customer service,' explained Fiona Colquhoun, Director of Personnel, in a speech at a major conference in February 1990.

The company chose to accomplish its objective by working in two major areas: human relations management and internal communications. Work in the area of human relations management began quite early and was focused upon 'personalising' its relationships with employees. At Mercury, that means, 'dealing with people as individuals'.

This is in contrast to the approach of most UK companies in the telecommunications industry that evaluate and pay people according to their grade, and not necessarily according to their performance on the job. 'Mercury is non-unionised and there are advantages to being non-unionised. We have been able to be more radical and progressive in our employment policies and style. . . . Mercury is non-unionised, but arguably getting the best out of people's contribution in terms of what they do for the organisation.'

With pay as a function of each individual's performance, employees are encouraged to achieve in those areas which are considered to be a priority for the company. Mercury has established customer service as one of the seven most important categories of evaluation. It is defined as, 'The way that the employee has demonstrated his awareness of customer needs'. The complete list includes other items which contribute to good customer service, such as initiative, attitude, commitment and leadership. 'We really want to link people's performance to how they develop and have regular reviews. Again, we have emphasised the customer aspect. We try to bring everything as close to the customer as possible.'

With two of the major criteria for employee motivation – pay and performance evaluation – firmly reflecting the importance the company places on good customer service, Mercury already has taken a major step towards creating a customer service culture in the company. To help employees understand more exactly what is expected of them in terms of serving customers, Mercury created a one-day training module which each new employee must pass. The training module explains just what quality customer service is at Mercury and covers basic service standards such as telephone practices and handling customer complaints. Employees are also taught how to participate in the local quality action teams which are organised to identify problems in quality or service and propose solutions.

In terms of their impact on creating a service quality culture in the company, the local action teams contribute by making customer service and service quality daily topics within the company. Employees are actively involved in discussing issues which can detract or enhance the company's service to customers and thereby are less likely to 'solve service quality issues under the table'. In practical terms, the local action teams are designed to yield positive results. 'Overall, the objective is to facilitate a quality culture in the company. Already, the culture is customer driven; now, we want functional change as well,' explains John Dawson, who is manager of the programme.

The local action teams are actually part of a larger effort within the company to create a service quality culture. In 1988, Mercury launched the quality customer service programme. The aim of the programme is to push Mercury's efforts to establish such a culture just one step further. The major thrust of the programme is in internal communication. The company designed a very attractive and rather humorous brochure which was given out to all employees to introduce the quality customer service programme. It's called the *Quality Assurance Handbook for Employees* and is subtitled, 'How we're making Mercury the best telecommunications company in the world'.

Inside the *Quality Assurance Handbook* is a discussion of what quality is, what it means for the company and its customers and what it means for the employees. Each new employee to Mercury also receives the *Handbook* along with a short guide on how to use the telephone entitled, 'How we'll sound like the best telecommunications company in the world.'

Every single brochure that the company produces on quality is backed up by regular communication through the employee newspaper with reports on the progress that is being made in the programme. The results of the local action teams are reported. Stories about employees providing excellent customer service are also reported. Talks by top management discuss systematically the company's objective to make customer orientation and service quality a part of the company's culture. 'We want a total quality culture that routinely improves everything we do.'

Ongoing, relentless internal communication about quality serves to focus employees' attention. The more that service quality is discussed within the company, the greater the understanding will be of what it means in the day-to-day work environment and the better the company will become at achieving it. 'We are still a long way from saying that the quality customer service approach has been completely integrated into the company. We are culturally getting there, but bear in mind that we are like a new university or a new school. It takes time to get there.'

Communicating about the customer service orientation of the company doesn't stop with the internal newsletter. Mercury believes in reinforcing the message by telling customers and the public about its aims to be the most customer-service-oriented telecommunications company in the world. The first way it has done that is in its recruitment ads. 'Ensure customer satisfaction', says one. 'Work on the system with fewer bugs', says another. Posted on the underground, on the streets or printed in newspapers and magazines, such ads are a clear message to employees, future employees and the public about Mercury's customer-oriented culture.

Mercury's brochures for customers also talk about its concern for customer service: 'Mercury's customer-oriented approach', as the guide to Mercury's services describes it. 'Mercury was created to provide the most competitive service possible at lower costs, placing the needs of the customer first.'

Perhaps the most convincing thing Mercury management has done to create a customer-oriented and service-quality culture is to set the example for good service by serving internal customers well. 'The quality customer programme is also about us being leaders in how we behave to customers externally, but also internally – so that people have a strong, positive, internal service behaviour. As Personnel Director, I make sure that my department provides the expected service to the customer, i.e. managers and employees,' says Fiona Colquhoun.

To illustrate just how much they were committed to serving their internal customer well, the personnel department asked an external research company to conduct a satisfaction survey within the company to find out what employees thought about their work and the company. In addition to asking about various aspects of the work environment, the survey looked at the company's present customer and quality orientation. Out of a list of 12 items including 'profitability', 'new services', 'technological innovation' etc., 87 per cent of employees named 'responsiveness to customer' as the aspect of Mercury's business that was most critical to its success. Next in line was 'reliability' with 82 per cent. Mercury's efforts to create a quality customer service culture don't seem to have been entirely in vain!

Note: Mercury was one of the first companies we researched two years ago. Since then the company has continued to experience enormous growth, both in size and customer base.

The figures included in the text have been up-dated to reflect this continued growth. The personalities and specific documents referred to in these sections have been left unchanged, although the company has moved on since they were written.

For example, the Quality Customer Service initiative has now been absorbed into Mercury's Total Quality process, which was launched in 1990. Total Quality is empowering employees to change and improve the business processes on which the company is built. The Total Quality Culture, which is now emerging in Mercury, places customer requirements at the heart of the organisation and aims to achieve zero defects through a process of continuous improvement.

How to develop a corporate culture that fosters customer service

Some key success factors include defining shared values, allowing time to do its work, using culture leverage to make an organisation change, and finally reinforcing values constantly through examples, legends, symbols and patterns; changing the structure to release energy.

Defining shared values

When companies have grown to a large, mature stage they have often more difficulty in adapting to external market changes than the newly formed company which is more flexible, more energetic and enthusiastic to go ahead. This is partly due to loss of culture, which is often witnesses by a loss of touch with frontline people, customers and operational issues. IBM challenged by Apple, Caterpillar by Komatsu, TI by NEC, Sears by factory outlets – every day the international news tells us how big corporations have lost touch and how younger companies develop an enthusiasm and energy which can make them move the earth. Everyone in the young company is still in touch with someone who was involved at the beginning and so understands its values, whereas in the mature companies, the first generation is gone.

A special conscious effort is necessary to familiarise everyone with the values of the company. The effort is even more important and more formalized when the company has grown to a size where oral tradition is not enough. There are too many ways to do it. One is from the top down, where through a cascade system the hierarchy defines and shares the values with their teams, starting with the executive committee, until a consensus is reached. The second is bottom up, where all employees are asked to sit down and formalise what they see as the values to be put forward, depended upon, and used for daily behaviour. The top-down approach is more effective when a company is older, has lost touch and feels it is important to restate its values. The second is more effective when it is a rather newer company in which the entrepreneur/founder is still in charge and would like to make sure everyone shares the beliefs he has held since the beginning and crystalise them for the time when his company reaches a size where he cannot carry those values alone.

Whatever the mode used, values have to be shared through internal communication. Disney does a marvellous job at instilling its values to new employees through training. At Motorola, everyone must carry a card in his pocket which spells out essential values and objectives. Continental tyres has used as a communication device throughout its hierarchy a tool called BASICS:

- **B**eware (make people aware of programme)
- **A**cceptance (discuss to make people accept)
- **S**ituation (analysis of issues at hand to be solid)
- **I**nitiative (list of initiatives to be taken)
- **C**ooperation (who will do what, with whom)
- **S**upport (help from heirarchy and structure needed to solve problems)

where every manager, using prepared slides, instils in his team the values of the company then opens a forum for discussion, action plans and decision.

Let time do its work

The CEO of the Royal Bank of Canada told us how comfortable he felt, that in its tenth year of effort, the customer service revolution was now well ingrained and irreversible. Xerox started its customer satisfaction programme in 1980. The first six years were essentially oriented towards improving internal quality (both products and administration).

At Xerox in 1985/6, the programme shifted its focus towards service quality and customer satisfaction management, to culminate in 1990 with the launch of the total customer satisfaction guarantee. Honda, who had started quality circles in the 1970s, started to measure intensively and focus attention on customer satisfaction in 1986. They have been consistently number one, year after year in customer satisfaction for the last five years. In 1991, they even established a customer satisfaction office at the highest level to promote and foster total customer satisfaction both inside and outside. American Airlines started its programme in 1978. It got the award for the best airline food finally in 1991. All these examples show that changes towards customer service do not happen overnight.

For change to be permanent, action has to be taken, not only to change the system but also to change behaviour. That is where culture can impact negatively or positively on the change. However marvellous new service delivery systems can be, if behaviour has not improved as well, nothing much will happen. For instance, one large tour operator put a new reservation system into place whereby a computer is available to help the reservation agent give alternative choices for travel. This was introduced in a company which has always been product oriented rather than sales oriented, with experience in taking orders rather than actively selling. As a result, two years after its development, the system is hardly ever used – especially by the agents who have been in the company for a long time. It will probably take another two years both to adapt the system to make it more palatable to agents and to train everyone not just to use it, but to make them feel more in charge of the system. Since it took two years to develop the system in the first place, we are talking about six years from inception to application!

Unfortunately, many CEOs do not have this long-term view. They want action now, when what is most needed is to install a strong culture that is oriented towards the customer. It is a process of continual improvement and full employee involvement, and changes in patterns of behaviour that takes three to five years. Being too impatient for results is as bad as wanting cost reductions without a budgetary process was in the 1950s. Now that every company has budgets (which is management process), it is relatively easy to reduce costs, do profit improvement programmes, because there is a set information base, a method to establish cost and profits, responsibility for achieving objectives, relationships between means and ends. The same applies to customer satisfaction. For management to establish such a process means passing through four phases: 1) analytical and psychological preparation to understand what customers need and want, what the company thinks customers need and want, an evaluation of potential gain, road blocks to change, and a preparation of a master plan for change (1 year).

2) Launch the programme: either by mounting a pilot operation or by

launching the programme throughout the company. In this phase objectives are set and communicated to everyone and enthusiasm is built.

3) The implementation phase consists mainly of defining what the company will give to its customers and how it will manage uniformity. This is where projects for improvement are defined, project teams or quality teams are set up, training is made to reward recognition, and communication systems are designed (1 to 3 years).

Finally in the fourth phase – follow up – the pilot operation is expanded to the whole company, measures of progress and results are made, changes of emphasis or concentration of efforts on one or two key points are made, and updates on customer wishes, employee involvement or project teams are reviewed and refined to better meet their purpose.

Use culture levers to foster change

There are at least two levers that companies will use to demonstrate what their values are: figureheads and communication.

Figureheads are people within the company that best represent the values and culture the company wants to adopt for the long term. They need not be high-ranking executives of long standing with the company. They are people whose behaviour, point of view and work habit can be used to emphasise a certain orientation. It can be a person taken on a management contract basis who will bring the new values needed to bring the change. It can be people who have been with the company for 20 years, who represent best the basic values of the company, it can be people who have the best knowledge in the field. It can be a retired executive who still serves on the board or in a consulting capacity to bring the historical perspective. What is key in using these figureheads with success, is having people within the organisation who are considered to be the leaders of today and tomorrow so that others will learn from them and duplicate the values emphasised.

The second lever is communication. Chapter 3 is devoted to this issue. For now, simply put, companies who succeed in installing values and a culture in their employees spend more money than average on internal communication. In addition they emphasise heavily the role of the hierarchy in developing those arguments (either through forums, opening or closing training sessions, or special sessions). Take the example of a Swiss pharmaceutical company which had started a programme one year earlier and which seemed to be falling apart. The essential reason was that the three division managers were not convinced and enthusiastic about it. They were put together to design a set of three one-hour sessions with their team to discuss the past, the present and the future. They were helped to communicate with a pre-design tool. Resistance to the process disappeared and things started to happen.

Reinforce the message through patterns, legends, examples and symbols

Show you put the customer first. When the largest mail-order business in France wanted to emphasise that deliveries will be made in 48-hours, it created a mascot: a cute little figure who is dressed like a racing bicycle rider. He is photographed in all the catalogues. He is sold as a souvenir. He is given to all employees and they give him to their kids, since most of them are housewives. He represents the service in three dimensions. He *is* the service.

The list of things that can be done daily to show that you care for the customers and that the service orientation of the company is constantly reinforced is endless. The key is not words, speeches, written beliefs or credos. The key is a consistent set of actions, behaviour and symbols which demonstrate daily that you mean it. Let's review an example of such a consistent pattern.

A one-hour glasses retail chain – Grand Optical – has put a mirror in the employee lounge, so that employees can see themselves before they go into the shop. There is a sign below the mirror which says: 'Are you ready for the customer?'. The CEO got his inspiration from a police station, where policemen have to pass in front of such a mirror before they go out in the street to see if they are ready to go out. The employee lounge itself is as clean and comfortable as the stores themselves. This shows respect for the employees. Every potential new employee is taken to a three-hour meeting where the values they want in their employees are emphasised – 25 per cent leave. The remaining 75 per cent become committed. If, at any time, a customer feels he did not get what he wanted, there is no discussion. Exchange, repair or a refund is automatic, even if the company knows the customer made a mistake. Openness is also used as a means of showing respect for the employees: All of them know the results of the month; how the money is spent, where it comes from. At seminars, employees are greeted like customers.

This example is typical of those companies who want to develop a strong service culture. It has two arms: putting customers first and putting people first. Show respect for the customer and show respect for the employees. Showing respect for the customer can be done in several different ways and you can check within your company to see if you do them or not.

- Is their viewpoint taken into account?
- Are they listened to?
- Is their satisfaction measured and known by everyone?
- Are they known to back office people (data processing, accounting etc)?
- Are they welcomed at reception?
- Are they shown, pictured, symbolised throughout the company?
- Are they celebrated (1 millionth customer)?
- When unsatisfied are they treated as if they are always right?
- Do they get initial responses to problems within 48 hours? . . .

Take two contrasting examples: a consulting firm decides to decorate its walls only with its clients' posters. A bank says customer service is important. However, on its office walls you see modern art and in the annual report pictures of the board members and executive team. Who believes more in customer service?

Respect for employees can also take different forms.

- Do they feel welcome when they join?
- Are they treated as well as customers in internal offices, (especially by personnel officers)?
- Do they get enough training to be competent to meet customers' expectations?
- On every occasion where they meet, is enough effort given to welcomeing them?
- Are customer-oriented employees recognised for their contribution?
- Is openness used to show respect?
- Are they treated well when they leave? . . .

Patterns of behaviour such as those described above have to permeate the organisation at all levels especially middle management (*see* Chapter 7). This is where you will make or break it.

Symbols such as mascots can help in creating legends of extraordinary service. Many companies provide extraordinary service, but they are never enhanced or pushed, as if the company was ashamed to have done something special for the customer. One symbol which emphasises a company's commitment to its customers is the service guarantee. These ensure a company's commitment to the customers, as well as saving employees the pain of not satisfying a customer. It's on time or it is free. It's good or you return it. It's perfect or it's $100 for each item which is not (seminars at SAS Hotels). It does not break down or its 10 per cent off the maintenance contract. It works or it's free (Interent in Sweden). More and more companies are using service guarantees today in the same way the product guarantees were used in the 1950s and 1960s to enhance the level of quality as non-quality became an issue.

The stronger the culture and its daily demonstration through behaviour, actions and symbols is, the easier it will be to give consistent service to customers. However, the stronger the culture, the more difficult it will be to adapt to changes in the environment, including customers, unless change, listening to the customers, adaptation, flexibility, risk taking and trying are also part of the philosophy of the organisation!

2 POWER LEADERSHIP

Introduction

Service quality companies are not led by managers, but by dynamic leaders; people who demonstrate tremendous conviction in what they are doing and utter commitment to doing the right thing for the customer.

Two main characteristics were present in all of the leaders we came in contact with:

- they were inflexible when it came to the way that customers were to be handled;
- they were perfectionists when it came to service delivery in one or more aspects of the service.

These individuals' style of leadership is not what one might expect. We observed very little of what could be called 'management by consensus'. Because of the dominant personalities of these individuals, the prevailing leadership style in these organisations is, authoritarian, top down, sometimes paternalistic or dictatorial.

At the same time, these styles of leadership encouraged the development of other conditions which are very positive for the organisations concerned.

- *Strong team spirit* – everyone is pulling towards the same goal, i.e. that of the boss.
- *Recognition/back patting* – because the standards are so high, employees encourage each other to try to achieve them. The highest honour is the approval of the leader. He's generally aware of it and uses it to guide people in the direction he wants them to go.
- *Initiative-taking* – people are willing to take risks because they need to receive recognition from the boss and they know that is a good way to do it, i.e. they want a place in the sun.

Overall, these companies are very well run and appear to have many happy employees. It has often been remarked that the vast majority of people in this world do not like to assume full responsibility for their environment; they would prefer to be led.

Moreover, it appears to be very rewarding for individuals to achieve their objectives within the parameters of an ethic and philosophy established by such a leader. We can, therefore, question the universal applicability of modern management methods which proclaim the necessity for consensus management, management by committee etc.; which are probably only substitutes when no real leader is available.

The leaders

Enforcing quality standards: the case of Castel Novel hotel

Albert Parveaux is a man of about 40 years old, whose father was a well-known pastry maker and caterer in Brive in France. Castel Novel, a lovely medieval castle sitting on 40 h of green, rolling pasture land, was purchased by the elder Mr Parveaux in 1956. Mr Parveaux Jr took over the management of the hotel in the 1970s and additionally expanded his family's hotel activities with the acquisition of four other establishments – one in Brive, one in Montignac (a nearby town) and two in Courcheval in the Alps.

Mr Parveaux runs these establishments with unquestionable concern for the standard of quality to be maintained and for the welfare of his customers. Good service at Castel Novel focuses on two things – the 'Hello', 'Goodbye', the quality of the food and the price/quality ratio provided by the entire package. 'With these things, we don't fool around.'

For Mr Parveaux, the 'Hello' and 'Goodbye' is every employee's business. It starts from the moment the customer enters the establishment – the welcoming sign at the bottom of the long winding path up to the hotel, the first 'Hello', assistance with the baggage, and the greeting at the reception desk – and ends with the very courteous 'Thank you for staying with us' that the guest is given as he is escorted personally to his car. The objective is to put the customer at ease and to ensure that each contact the customer has with the staff is a pleasant one.

The quality of food is an important aspect of the establishment's service package. Castel Novel is situated just on the borders of the Périgord, a region of France famous for its excellent cuisine. There are even tourists who visit this region simply to partake of the pleasures of the table. Mr Parveaux makes sure that Castel Novel does not disappoint even the most demanding traveller. Whether it is the fruit basket and the croissant or *pain au chocolat* in the room or the enormous buffet one can enjoy in the castle's elegant restaurant, Mr Parveaux's guest's day begins in style. During the rest of the day, the choice is the guest's, from a large menu featuring all of the region's specialities.

Maintaining the price/quality ratio of the hotel means ensuring that every customer goes away satisfied. Mr Parveaux believes in emphasising adherence to certain consistent standards of service which, if they are maintained, provide the customer with a stay which more than satisfies him.

Managing his establishments so that these standards are maintained requires continual vigilance and reinforcement by Mr Parveaux himself.

To say that Mr Parveaux rules with an iron rod is not putting his management style in the right perspective; to say that he is a perfectionist is more exact. But, before he demands perfection of others, he demands it of himself. It is his policy never to ask an employee to do something that Mr Parveaux cannot or has not already done himself. Moreover, he prefers to give tasks to those employees who can do them best.

At the same time he insists upon the flexibility of all employees. Like Mr Parveaux, all employees must be ready to do any task which needs to be done for the client. In this sense, Mr Parveaux points out that there is very little hierarchy.

Mr Parveaux surveys everything personally himself. His day begins with a full tour of the establishment in which he examines the exact condition of every part of it. The tour is then followed by the preparation of a number of memos to the department heads, drawing their attention to a number of items to improve or complimenting them on improvements already made.

Mr Parveaux also sets an example as concerns the 'Hello', 'Goodbye'. He greets as many guests as possible or bids them 'Goodbye'. While he cannot be present at every meal, he is present at most of them and makes a point of touring the tables to gauge the customers' satisfaction with the food and with their visit as a whole. He expects his employees to follow his example and, thus, to greet every guest with the greatest of consideration and with a smile.

Balancing this demanding attitude is a paternalistic approach to employees to whom he refers as 'my young ones' (*mes jeunes*). He is a father figure within the enterprise and looks out for the welfare of all of his employees. Moreover, he fully recognises and accepts his hotel's role as an educational experience for many of his employees.

Most of his younger staff are from the surrounding area and are presented by their parents for employment with Mr Parveaux. In many cases, it is their very first professional experience. For some, it is followed by a formal education from one of the hotel schools. Mr Parveaux regularly assists aspiring employees or children of employees to enter one of these schools, from which he graduated himself.

Mr Parveaux accepts responsibility, not only for his younger staff's professional lives, but to some degree their personal lives as well. He is very open and friendly with his staff and supports his attitude by generous policies. Employees have full use of the premises – as long as they don't disturb the guests – and are housed on the premises. There is a great deal of camaraderie between the staff which Mr Parveaux encourages to a certain degree because it improves the work atmosphere.

Staying close to customers: the case of Superquinn

When you meet Mr Feargal Quinn, you just want to smile. He is the living image itself of the cheerful, energetic and witty Irishman. Despite the effect, Mr Quinn is a very adept and successful businessman. He was asked not too long ago by the Irish post office to come and be their chairman for a while – to give the administration a boost of customer concern.

He is also a wonderful speaker; and one of his favourite topics is how to stay close to customers. Most of all, Mr Quinn is the founder/director of Superquinn, a chain of 12 supermarkets serving greater Dublin. At Superquinn, staying close to the customer is not the topic of a recent speech, but an everyday practice for Mr Quinn and his staff.

Mr Quinn's magical management technique could be summarised by saying that he stays close to employees and close to customers. As far as employees are concerned, Mr Quinn is a leader who deserves devotion. His employees respect and appreciate Mr Quinn, and his beliefs and convictions.

Once employees come to Superquinn, they don't leave very quickly, unless it is to create their own companies. 'We breed entrepreneurs', says one of the managers. The company is a good training ground for entrepreneurs, because although Mr Quinn runs the company by his beliefs and convictions, from a practical point of view, the company is highly decentralised. As one manager explained, 'The stores call the shots; head office is the "support office".' Once, when an employee asked Mr Quinn what his 'capital authorisation limit' was, Mr Quinn answered, 'Go ahead and spend it and then I'll tell you if you spent too much'.

Head office is made up principally of the 'Monday morning meeting group', which is what Superquinn calls its board of directors. They are responsible for setting general policies; in practice, the most important thing this group does is to keep in constant contact with the stores, act as advisers to store managers and cheerleaders to employees.

One way they do this is by 'going over the figures'. This is done on a weekly basis with each one of the store managers and every 13 weeks with the entire staff of each store. The information flow is as much top down as bottom up and all kinds of information get passed on to employees. 'Be open with employees', says Mr Quinn. 'Disclose huge amounts of information; let everybody see the figures.' He believes that it's a great way to gain commitment and to motivate everybody.

Another way Mr Quinn and his management team stay close to their employees is by physically being there with them – on the store floor.' The managers regularly tour the stores and talk with employees to find out 'how things are going'. They also pick up and do store chores themselves. Mr Quinn, who is energy itself, is the best at setting the example. If there is something that needs doing and he sees it, he'll do it. 'The young boy packing groceries just might be me,' says Mr Quinn. This is what one manager means when he says that Superquinn's management is very 'hands-on'. Hands-on also means that everybody at Superquinn has had experience working in the store before he or she was promoted to another post. They are told that at the outset.

Staying close to employees is the next step to staying close to customers. Feargal Quinn began practising the reversed pyramid method before there ever was one. As one manager said, 'We do everything backwards – we reversed the pyramid, before there ever was a model.'

Feargal Quinn's favourite way of staying close to customers is through his customer panels. There is one every week in one of the company's 12 stores. Customers are invited to come and 'talk to the boss'. Generally about 10 to 15 shoppers take Feargal Quinn up on the offer. One manager calls it a 'wonderful crystal ball' into the minds of shoppers. For Feargal Quinn, it's his 'secret weapon' in his listening campaign.

Feargal Quinn's listening campaign is nothing other than a continuous reminder to employees that the best way to succeed in the business is to 'Listen carefully and open your eyes'. Feargal Quinn practises what he says very well, when he's down on the shop floor. He not only listens to what customers are saying, but he also listens to employees who have ideas for him. Because the company is fairly small, everyone knows who Feargal Quinn is and, because he's such a friendly, approachable fellow, everybody talks to him.

Feargal Quinn believes that it's more important for his company to stay small and friendly than to be big and successful, so he has made it a policy not to grow too fast or too big. He believes that adding one store every two years is quite fast enough. That way he and his staff can stay close to the customer. He describes this policy as YCDBSOYA or, 'You can't do business by sitting on your . . . armchair'. Feargal Quinn either spends his time on the shop floor, with employees on the store floor or with his store managers.

Feargal Quinn doesn't spend an inordinate amount of time in his office – although he does have one. It's sparklingly neat and clean. Feargal Quinn's principle is that when there's a problem, 'You deal with it, you don't make a report on it,' says one of his managers. Likewise, he is not too keen on using customer service measurement tools unless they are complimented with direct customer contact. 'The danger is that you get caught up looking at the measurements and you forget the customer.'

Bringing about change: the case of British Airways

When Sir Colin Marshall took over as Chief Executive of British Airways in early 1983, a disaster had been averted, but British Airways was by no means in good shape. The disaster that had been avoided was financial bankruptcy; through a series of accounting and financial manoeuvres, Sir John (now Lord) King, Chairman since 1981, and Gordon Dunlop, Chief Financial Officer since 1982, cleared away the company's rotting financial situation. It was left in a situation of manageable poverty.

Between 1983 and today, British Airways has been completely turned around, principally by Sir Colin's very tough, but effective management methods. It is now one of the most profitable and customer-oriented airlines in the world. There were three areas of the company's culture where the greatest amount of change was needed. The first concerned the management practice of managing by committees and by consensus. It took too long.

When Sir Colin arrived, he replaced the company's traditional method of management by commmittee and consensus to individual management with high responsibility. He assigned responsibility for ensuring that the planes were clean to one person, for example. That person could cut across lines of authority to get the job done. And he was totally accountable.

Today, managers are responsible and success oriented. Sir Colin made sure that his employees understood that 'if we don't put the customer first someone else will'. Concerning service standard measurement methods, for example, Sir Colin has made sure that what needs to be measured is getting measured, then, they are published for managers, who 'proceed according to their own best judgement'.

Sir Colin doesn't really believe in quality groups or problem-solving groups, '. . . because then problems become the group's responsibility and not the individual's'. The authority to solve problems should exist at every level. 'The authority to solve problems is everyone's responsibility,' says Sir Colin.

He believes that the principle is particularly apt at the frontline, no matter who's working on it. Sir Colin himself spends as much time as he can with staff on the frontline. He expects his managers to do likewise. Many of the managers we spoke to claimed that the best information about what is happening with customers comes from walking around. The manager of the Shuttle service operation spends at least five hours a week out in the customer service area alongside staff to get direct feedback. 'Sir Colin Marshall feels strongly about getting involved on the front line, so this kind of involvement goes all the way to the top.'

Sir Colin also demonstrates frontline involvement by reading complaint letters daily himself. He also gets directly involved in responding to customer complaints. 'If I overhear a customer comment, I will go and talk to the customer directly. It's a good thing because it's possible to deal with the real problem right then and there on the spot. One time I heard a customer register a complaint with the cabin services about the food. He said that he was going to write to me. I went right over and told him not to bother – but to tell me what was concerning him there and then; he was quite surprised.'

The fact that Sir Colin was personally involved at every level and personally demonstrated what it meant to be customer-oriented made changes easier within the company. Another thing that helped was the internal and external communication which came out of the top office. Sir Colin made it clear that his goal was to make British Airways 'the best' and to make it provide the tops in customer service. He used the company's high profile with the press to his advantage. He announced that change would happen, that it had happened and that British Airways now offered top service quality. The impact that had within the company was to increase employees' commitment to delivering what had been promised to the public.

At the same time that Sir Colin communicated change to the outside, he was preaching the value of customer service within the company. 'Today, we use the word 'customer' in daily language. From planning to administration, everything should reflect the desires of the customer, whether the customer be internal or external. When this ethic is pulled all the way through the organisation, the customer becomes part of the daily life – that is the ultimate mission,' explains one of Sir Colin's managers. Sir Colin preached a strong customer orientation and he also let a series of training programmes speak for him as well. In total, there were three or four different customer service training seminars which have run over the last eight years attended by the airline's entire worldwide workforce. First, there was 'Putting People First', then there was 'A Day in the Life', 'Being the Best' and most recently 'Winners'. Management development programmes have run hand-in-hand with these staff programmes.

Sir Colin's biggest challenge has been to change British Airways's culture from being operationally driven to being customer driven. 'We started with people who like aircraft. It took quite some time to understand that we were a customer service industry.' He has used all of the management methods described above, over and over again. As he explains himself, 'The most difficult part is to get people past the status quo and to get them to do things differently, to get them to accept that in the increasingly global and competitive environment, they have got to respond to the challenge.'

Generating employee motivation and commitment: the case of Movenpick

Movenpick was created by Ueli Prager, a citizen of Zurich. Today, Movenpick is an empire with 5 large divisions, with over 300 restaurants, nearly 40 hotels and a whole selection of Movenpick brand consumer goods sold to distributors all over Europe. The first thing that is often said about Ueli Prager is that he is a marketing genius. The second thing is that he is a great leader. In fact, he is both, but each skill has dominated in a different period of the company's history. It was largely his skill as a marketeer that permitted the company's initial and rapid development in the 1940s, '50s and '60s.

It is largely his skill as a leader that has permitted the company to grow and diversify while still maintaining coherence between all of its businesses. Despite its geographical and product diversity, Movenpick today is an extremely tight-knit and homogeneous organisation. As a leader, his greatest contribution has been the creation of a philosophy which generates tremendous motivation and commitment on the part of over 10,000 employees.

Mr Prager is no longer with the organisation – he retired in 1989 and was replaced by his wife – but his management style and business philosophy is as much a part of the organisation as it ever was. The fundamentals of Mr Prager's philosophy appear in two books. The first which covers the Movenpick business approach, is called *Business Principles of the Movenpick Group*. It talks about portion sizes, freshness, the product range, the menu design, the decor and the way of serving.

Mr Prager's philosophy about how to manage a business is written down in another book called, *Guidelines for Co-operation and Management in Movenpick Companies*. Here, he talks about 'Suggestions for improvements and changing of rules, loyalty, conflicts, teamwork and other general principles of management'.

Throughout both books, Mr Prager talks about Movenpick's concern for quality. When it came to quality of either service or products, Mr Prager's standards were very high and rigidly enforced. There was no quarter given, no slice to be taken away; the customer was to receive the full benefits of the best quality of service and the best quality products his money could buy. Mr Prager's ethics concerning quality are well documented: 'I can say one thing here, in this declaration signed by me: for my colleagues in management and for me personally, quality is the yardstick with which we measure everything. Quality and not profit.'

As Mr Prager himself wrote in an article, 'It took many mistakes before I learned that there is a definite correlation between quality and price. . . . In most restaurants the coffee-cream has 15 per cent butter content. My colleagues tried to convince me that there was no difference between coffee with whole cream and coffee with coffee-cream. Whole cream is, of course, twice as expensive. By serving coffee-cream instead of full cream we could save SF50,000 a year. Nevertheless, we continued to serve whole cream with our coffee in the conviction that quality is our best advertisement.'

Quality is only one topic touched upon in the Movenpick books. There are many, many others.

What is truly notable in Mr Prager's approach is the mix of policy with ethics. In the *Guidelines*, under the title 'Information', there is the following, '. . . our policy is to provide as much information as reasonably possible'. Then, 'Only people who are informed can think clearly and constructively, offer useful advice and recognise the broad issues involved'.

A page later under the title 'Allocation of assignments, responsibility and competence', you find, 'Our policy is that all employees, within the limits of their competence, should have as much independence as possible in their decisions and actions.' Two paragraphs down, you see, 'However, anyone demanding competence must consider carefully whether he is really capable of accepting the responsibility involved. . . . Being happy in a job means having neither too little nor too much competence.'

The balance between policy and ethics is not less than 30 to 70. In some cases, one would have difficulty saying whether there is any policy at all. On

'Supervision' he says, 'Supervision is one of the responsibilities of every superior. It cannot be delegated. Inadequate supervision is a sign of indifference on the part of the superior. Supervision makes a constructive contribution towards the attaining of objectives and does not in any sense imply a lack of confidence.'

On 'Motivation' he says, 'Our employees are people, and people have moods and feelings which they cannot simply divest in the cloakroom when they arrive in the morning to start work. . . . The expression "motivation" comes from the word "motive", which means having a reason for doing something. By motivating the employee the superior generates the drive, the will and the enthusiasm necessary for good performance. . . . If employees are to perform well, they must have the feeling that they are acknowledged and accepted as people. They must feel that they are accomplishing something and that their achievement is being recognised.'

There is page after page about ethics applied to business practice throughout both books. Mr Prager's policies are appealing because of the ethics which stand behind them. Conforming to policies is no longer a means to an end, but rather the adherence to a philosophy. As one manager described it, 'Movenpick gets under your skin. There is a strong identification between Movenpick and Mr Prager. It's Mr Prager's ethics. He was a pioneer, an innovator, a risk-taker.'

Ueli Prager's *Guidelines* are for internal use only, but he also wanted customers to understand some of the basics of his philosophy. So, Mr Prager developed a statement of 10 basic principles of Movenpick which summarise what makes Movenpick different from other restaurants and the standard of service the company is trying to achieve. The Movenpick principles hang in every Movenpick restaurant.

For each of the concept restaurants in the Movenpick group and for the hotels, a special statement of principles has been developed which resembles the basic Movenpick statement of principles. Mr Prager believed that it was important to explain to customers what was different about each new restaurant concept.

Today, the statements are used as working documents for the development of specific policies and principles for each activity. The hotel group, for example, reviews its statement and the associated policies every year to find out what has changed within the year, what evolutions must be reflected, and what standards must be raised to match new heights in customer expectations.

In the Marché Restaurants concept group, the statement is discussed on an ongoing basis, because the business is so new and is still under development. The 10 basic principles of the Movenpick group, however, apply everywhere. They are philosophical enough not to need to be changed extensively over the years. They summarise what Movenpick stands for and, as Ueli Prager himself says, 'Movenpick is not a chain of restaurants; it is a philosophy.'

Making staff exceed customer expectations: Feinkost Käfer

Gerd Käfer, the son of a small food retailer in Munich, realised in the late 1950s that with increasing labour costs large households would not be able to keep all their domestic staff. From this realisation was born the idea of an 'out-of-house' service company whose goal would be to act as the perfect replacement for in-house staff when they were really needed.

Today, Feinkost Käfer is a name synonymous with luxury in catering in Germany. Revenues from his activities now exceed DM120 million per year. In addition to the group's activities in catering, Käfer also owns deli-shops, restaurants and eight theatre restaurants. It also collects royalties from Käfer licensed products such as pizza, coffee, chocolate etc. It employs over 600 people a week and even has a restaurant in the Munich Opera House.

Gerd Käfer has flair. With a boyish grin, a crop of blondish hair and a kind of dare-devil 'try-me' look, he gives the impression of someone ready to conquor the world. The success of the business is the success of Käfer himself. He is the owner/manager of the business and the creator/implementor of practically every event.

To say that Gerd Käfer is a 'hands-on' manager is to put it mildly. Käfer is present at practically 70 per cent of all events that place all over Germany. He owns a fleet of cars, helicopters and planes so that he can move from one place to another. His omnipresence is itself almost magical. It is an image which inspires employees to greater and greater feats of service and creativity in their work.

Käfer has a reputation – the reputation of being the Rolls-Royce of the catering industry. Gerd Käfer has numerous candidates for each job opening; he only hires the best and they are expected to uphold that reputation. To do that, Käfer says that they should 'see in my customer's eyes what they want'. That means talking to the customer at length before the event, as well as after the event to know and understand what the customer liked and didn't like.

Käfer places a premium on doing exactly what the customer expects in a creative and sometimes surprising way. He has a warehouse full of the best china and silver, and the most outrageous party entertainment props. His staff are trained and prepared to use them to their best advantage.

As a result, employees are not remunerated as much by senority as by their service orientation and creative initiative. For example, in one of Käfer's Munich restaurants, waiters receive a percentage of the restaurant's turnover. In addition, the tips are not split according to hierarchy; each waiter keeps the tips he receives. As a result, Käfer's waiters earn more than double what waiters in comparable three-star restaurants would earn. It's Käfer's belief that personal effort should be encouraged and rewarded.

Käfer manages as much by sheer dynamism as anything else. Because of his success, his creativity and his personality, he is a star himself; his employees, like his customers, are his fans. It is part of what has made him the caterer to the stars, the politicians and the very rich. To document the point, personal thank you letters and signed photos cover the walls in the directors' floor of Feinkost Käfer's office.

How to be a service leader

It is difficult to give lessons to top management about what they can do to demonstrate their commitment. The reason is simple. Either they believe that customers and service are the most important thing for their company's success and, in that case, they will naturally act in that direction. Or they don't and whatever can be said, written or proven won't make them change their minds as far as the decisions they take, their behaviour and daily demonstration of commitment goes. Below we address the issues of service leadership, not just for top managers, but also for any manager in charge of others.

Set an example

Managers often do things which do not seem important to them, but which are examined with magnifying glasses by their subordinates. Not to say 'Hello' one day to your secretary because you are worried is just a detail to you. For her it is a pain. To spend only 10 per cent of your time with customers seems enough. For your team it shows commitment to other matters. To go and see all your staff members every day in their offices is different from just seeing them once in a while in your office in terms of how they feel about how much you care about them.

In fact, what you do counts more that what you say. So what are the core signs of the customer satisfaction orientation of the CEO, or the service leader? Here are a few.

- Attitude *vis-à-vis* your team: do they also feel well received?
- Time spent with customers / on customers' issues
- Who gets rewarded (promotion, new jobs) in relation to what they have done with respect to customers and service.
- Questioning done when your team presents their plans. How explicitly do you push issues of customer service and challenge them to go further?
- Decisions on resource allocation: does it feel like customer services gets a fair share of resources or not? Or is the answer always 'not' because of other priorities
- Personal appearance where something is going on with respect to customer service.

The higher you go in the hierarchy, the harder it becomes for you to demonstrate commitment. The managers (see chapter 7) you supervise can often transform your good intentions into anti-service decisions and actions by misinterpreting your intentions or not thinking how they can themselves contribute to reinforcing them. Let us look at the following real-life example. A regional manager in charge of 15 restaurant units was telling us how he felt his CEO was not so committed to improving quality service, and that in fact it was just all words and beautiful speeches rather than concrete results. When asked why, this is what we got. The CEO had decided to introduce a new free service to the existing product in order to add value to the product they sold rather than fight on price, which was what was happening in the rest of the industry. It was expected that it would result in a 25 per cent increase in volume. The added service was a free Caesar salad every Monday. To achieve this result, the regional manager had asked for money to invest in the kitchen ($150 000) to help cooks make the salads. He feared otherwise that the cooks would leave if they did not get the means to do the job right. He was surprise to hear the CEO say they would not invest until the idea proved right (a month), but that he had to do with current means. That's why he was angry and feeling top management was not committed. However, he had found a substitute solution to help the cook: hire students for two weeks (as you can see, sometimes people get imaginative if you say no). But looking at his own behaviour, it was not any more quality oriented. The programme was to start a week later and he had not yet trained his waiters to present the new offer, to respond to objections, criticisms 'I don't want a salad, give me a reduction'. So, although blaming his boss, he was not looking closely enough at himself! As has often been said, with no reinforcement of the programme at point of sale, the bright idea of the CEO could become a failure. It was not a problem of means. It was more a problem of outlook.

Before you put the blame on someone else, first take a look at yourself.

The second most important way a leader can use to show his commitment is to use the structure in the direction in which he wants to go

Using the structure can entail the following

- Putting the right people in the right place. Are key managers who run the show customer oriented.
- Having a quality director that reports directly to the CEO. Is it the case in our company that there are quality directors in each major function, division or business unit? You should have about 1 for 500 employees at the least, which should be co-ordinated by the quality director that reports to the CEO.
- Having a head of quality or customer satisfaction who is a figurehead, someone that everybody respects rather than someone who has been put there for lack of other opportunities.
- Having a structure that is more market oriented than product oriented. Have you selected to divide into units per market served rather than per

product. Continental Tyres just made the move to have a automobile tyre division and lorry division. It might cost more in terms of back office resources, but if you look at market needs they are completely different.

- Having ownership of customer problems clearly identified. Who owns problems. GE, in a bold move in 1987, created the role of the customer service manager to co-ordinate the sales and after-sales effort so that customers knew who to call to solve their problem. In many cases, nobody owns the problem.
- Creating cross-functional horizontal task forces and project teams to solve customer problems. Not everything can be solved by going up and down the hierarchy. Leaders who are customer oriented foster the creation of such teams to treat customer issues. At Club Med, the international village concept emerged from such a project team and customer satisfaction went up by seven points. The same was done to define service norms in a large distribution chain with 300 out of 4000 employees participating in defining service norms. It was the decision of the top to create those teams.

Apart from those two aspects, we can also say that powerful leaders are the ones who are going to use all the tools and processes described in the other chapters. So, let us move on.

3 COMMUNICATE – INTERNALLY AND EXTERNALLY

Introduction

Companies with good service records are, on the whole, companies that communicate a great deal. They commmunicate internally in order to motivate people, to keep them abreast of the company's successes and failures, and to ensure that the goals and objectives of the company are well understood by everyone.

These companies communicate externally to make sure that customers understand what the company is offering in terms of service and so as to manage customers expectations. They also keep a running dialogue open with customers in order to keep ahead of changes in customer expectations and to integrate customers' suggestions or ideas into their organisation's service offering.

Communication plays a particularly important role when a company is in the midst of change. Companies in the process of introducing a service quality programme or a new strategy had to inform employees and customers constantly of objectives and developments. This reassures customers that progress is being made and it reassures employees by reducing the level of uncertainty within the company.

Successful communicators

Promoting challenge: the case of TNT

TNT is in the delivery business in the UK. This is a highly competitive market which has known tremendous growth and expansion over the last ten years. None has grown as fast and as big as TNT, which is now the UK's leading express letter, package and parcel deliverer.

TNT is an Australian company that established itself in the UK in 1978 with the purchase of InterCounty Express, a small parcel transportation company with 6 depots and 500 people. For over 10 years, nearly every year the company launched a new form of delivery service to customers. Some of the most notable include TNT Newsfast, a distribution service for newspapers and magazines, TNT Garment Express, which transports hanging clothing stock and TNT AM Express which provides overnight letter and package delivery before noon or earlier.

Because of the company's rapid expansion and its need continually to outdo the competition, TNT has relied heavily on internal communication to boost employees to ever greater feats of excellence. The company has used two main types of communication continuously.

The first of these is 'posted' communication. That means messages posted throughout the company on the walls for all employees to see. The second method of communication is verbal, either in meeting or in speeches by Alan Jones and other executives.

Posted communication is generally used as a reminder or encouragement tool. Company objectives or themes are made into messages and posted on the walls. One of the first things that TNT did in this domain, under the leadership of Alan Jones, was to create a mission statement.

It all fits on one page. It shows the company's values – enthusiastic people, customer matched services and excellence in performance – the company's guiding principles – teamwork, expertise, technology and leadership – and the company's culture – caring for customers, quality, accountability, innovation, profit growth. The very last statement is 'Service is our only product'. Alan Jones's signature appears in the bottom left-hand corner of the mission statement. The mission statement is posted in the entry hall of the company's headquarters and appears in every office throughout the company.

In 1988, TNT launched a service quality continuous improvement programme. The first campaign was called 'Who Cares – Wins!'. The objectives of the programme were communicated throughout the company. Some of the major themes were also communicated. Posters with the name of the campaign appeared on the walls. Alan Jones has been a figurehead for all of the company's internal communication associated with the service quality programmes because of his dynamic character and his speaking ability.

A more recent campaign is called 'Driving for Quality'. The communication programme associated with this effort is even more extensive. A video has been made with Alan Jones and other executives who speak about the company's objectives and its concern for quality and customer care. In addition, a full range of posters have been developed with messages like, 'Care for your customers', 'Your smiling voice makes your customer's day', 'We deliver on Time', 'The big idea is service' and 'We are the Quality Carrier'.

Posters are also being used to remind employees of the company's service standards that have been developed. A poster now exists, for example, with the company's telephone policy. One by one each of the 10 standards appears on the poster. 'Incoming telephone calls must be answered promptly and always within no more than six rings', 'A caller must never be asked to call another TNT number' etc.

Verbal communication is the main means of communication at TNT. While posted communication aims to remind employees of the key objectives of the company, verbal communication is used to agree objectives, report progress and to encourage premium performance.

In connection with the quality programme, every department has established work standards which fix a minimum quality of work that should be completed within a certain time. One example is the financial administration department's 'five-fives'. One 'five' is that overdue debt should not exceed 5 per cent of the ledger balance. The progress on work standards is monitored on a daily and weekly basis. At the department level there are weekly meetings to announce the progress made on each standard and discuss how it can be improved upon. Profit accountable managers throughout the business chair weekly meetings called the 'Friday Bleaching' in which all of the figures for the week are examined and discussed with depot and divisional management teams.

So that employees keep their progress in mind all week as they work, the results from the previous week are posted on the walls. Management constantly sets new challenges for employees by tightening the standards which must be met. In financial administration, for example, Alan Jones is now looking to tackle the 'four-fours'. There is now a saying at TNT that 'You're only as good as your next week's figures'.

Alan Jones's aim has been to make service quality a part of the company's culture, an aim which he hopes he has partially achieved today. 'Throughout TNT UK over the last decade a culture has developed as a direct result of our constantly analysing trends and always striving to improve our pervious best result. This practice creates a 'climate for commitment' which has an ongoing and positive influence on the attitude of all people within TNT.'

Selling service quality internally: the case of Vergölst

One of the most effective methods of communication is person to person and yet it is seldom used to its greatest advantage. Vergolst provides an example of a company where personal communication was used to help change the entire culture and customer orientation of the organisation over a period of four years.

Vergölst is a subsidiary of Continental A6, a producer of re-tread tyres and a distributor of new tyres, primarily Continental Group brands, such as Continental, Uniroyal and Semperit. Seventy-five per cent of its sales are to individuals and 25 per cent through other wholesalers.

In 1986, Vergölst was a very product-oriented, industry-dominated company with centralised management. 'Employees showed signs of apathy and resignation.' The company was losing money and an increasingly greater percentage of the company's sales were going to discount wholesalers. The top management team believed that the company should adopt a strategy of being more than just a tyre dealer and become a full-service company for the customer. The key to the entire process was to convince a very staid and product-oriented management that service quality was the way to go.

Top management began to convince the leading people at Vergölst one by one that the company had to change its strategy. For a period of at least one year, they did nothing but sell the idea to managers inside the company. As their primary argument they used the results of customer focus groups and customer surveys which showed that customers weren't getting the service they expected. A great deal of time was spent learning about how other top service companies managed, i.e. Maredo, SAS etc.

At the same time, senior managers were brought into the change process and revitalised their engagement to the company by asking their advice continually and asking their opinion about how best to accomplish the different objectives set for the company. Many personal letters to managers from top management encourage them to support their effort and explain exactly what it meant for them.

A large and important presentation of the entire strategy and vision was made by top management to the staff at headquarters. In this presentation, it was made clear that managing a service quality company means managing people well, not products; and that achieving excellence as a service company means adopting a customer orientation without compromise.

It was also emphasised that service management means an investment in people and an investment in customer-contact locations. The theory of the reversed pyramid, which places the customer at the top of the pile and management at the bottom, was explained.

From 1986 to 1988, top management visited every single one of the company's 160 outlets and presented their ideas personally to employees and managers alike. As the strategy gained greater and greater acceptance within the company, management developed a 'Service Bible' for all employees. It is a document which relates customers' service expectations to the kind of customer service Vergölst management believed the company should be providing . A copy was handed out to each and every employee. On the left-hand side of each page, there is what Vergölst asks from its employees in terms of service; on the right-hand side of the page, there is the desired customer reaction.

Positive service stories began to be published on a regular basis in the in-house magazine to demonstrate what effect good service had on customers. A mascot was also created and was used as a symbol of identification for anything concerning customer service within the company. It is used both for internal and external communication, and shows a friendly, round tyre face with hands and no feet. A Vergölst song was written and a service award was created which is given to employees who provide extremely good customer service. The company now also has a mission statement. It is 'The most customer-friendly service company around the wheel'.

'Walking and talking' management methods were encouraged within the company in order to foster communication and generate ideas about how to improve service to customers. Bureaucratic behaviour was strongly discouraged. No actual adaptations in the organisational structure were made in order to reassure employees who were fearful of the effects of the changes going on within the company. Yet, after just four years, 'The style of management within the company from being directive and centralised to being co-operative and decentralised.'

The company has increased sales and revenues by around 25 per cent from four years earlier and it is making a profit. The sales of new services increased substantially and started to cover part of the former investments in the programme. Much of the success was attributed to the direct person to person approach that management adopted.

Bringing cultures together: the case of Novo Nordisk

One of the most difficult situations a company can face is a complete merger of its operations with another company in the same or a similar business. The problem becomes all the more acute if the merger is between two rivals. Novo faced this problem following its 1989 merger with Nordisk, its arch rival.

One of the most important measures that the new company has taken to fuse these two entities is the launch of an important communications programme. With the programme, the company has been able to create a homogeneous image *vis-à-vis* customers and to create greater internal understanding and co-operation.

Both Novo and Nordisk were Danish companies whose primary business was the production and sale of insulin for the treatment of diabetes patients. Prior to their merger, Novo was ranked number two in the world and Nordisk number three; today, the company is the world's leading producer of insulin.

Both companies were originally family-owned companies. Novo has been a public limited company for some years; Nordisk became one following the merger with Novo. And both companies have a historical background of pioneering discoveries at the forefront of insulin technology.

Insulin products are sold primarily to general doctors, practitioners and to diabetes clinics. Both Novo and Nordisk have in the past targeted primarily the specialists and the clinics, making the most of their complementary services. Novo and Nordisk offered seminars, educational and technical brochures, videos and advice to customers on product use and storage.

While there were a great number of similarities between Novo and Nordisk before their merger, there were also a large number of differences, particularly in terms of management style. Novo has a strong consensus style of management, whereas Nordisk kept a more top-down style of management.

At Novo, there was the 'Novo way of doing things'. 'Opinions are welcome and everyone was involved in the decision-making process. A great deal of time was spent in discussing and explaining within the company.' Nordisk had great pride in their scientific strength and technological achievements, while Novo was more marketing oriented. Nordisk was once known as being almost a non-profit organisation – by design.'

Both Novo and Nordisk were doing well at the time of the merger. They merged primarily because the costs of research and development required more resources. 'In order to move away from our dependence on insulin products, both companies needed to spend more on research and development; neither could do so effectively with their prior size.'

The Scenario Novo Nordisk 2000 was developed to communicate to customers and internally what the new company represented. 'Keeping in mind that 2000 out of 8000 people had a change in their job situation, one of the principal aims of the communication programme was to minimise insecurity.' One way this was done was through the provision of weekly updates. Employees were kept up to date on developments through special bulletins which told exactly what was happening. The same kind of information was repeated in the company newsletter. 'One of the main messages was that this was a non-aggressive merger, the main aim of which is not cost-trimming but rather a wish to make the most of existing costs'.

The thrust of Scenario Novo Nordisk 2000 is the creation of a new corporate identity and a new philosophy of management. The new company is an ethical company with a pride in being in a 'people-helping business'. There continues to be a strong scientific emphasis and an emphasis on quality both in products and services. 'Service is important all the way down because we want to stay ahead of the competition in every way.'

Novo Nordisk's communications department created three separate documents for internal communication. The first explains the history of Novo and Nordisk, the reasons for their merger and a description of the new company as it stands today. The document is presented in the form of a book in which each page has an associated transparency which can be used for internal slide presentations. The second document is presented using the same format. It presents the company's new corporate visual identity and explains its use.

The largest and most important document is called *Rationale and Management Philosophies*. In it are the business goals, business policies and management philosophies of the company. Its business goal, for example is 'to be an international leader . . . and the company which serves our customers' needs in the most competitive way'. Under 'Management Philosophies', there is, 'We shall, whenever possible, decentralise responsibilities to provide the best possible and swiftest service to our customers . . .'.

The entire set of documents has been translated and distributed throughout the company worldwide and has been presented to groups of employees by managers already briefed on developments within the company. It goes with a video which is used as a support tool. 'The package was designed to help managers communicate to employees about the changes.' The packet also comes with documents to be used to explain the merger to customers. Employees are instructed about how to present it to customers. Novo Nordisk also created a brochure entitled 'Our merger adds up to better care for diabetics', which presents the new company to its customers. It explains the reasons for the merger, presents the advantages to the customer and the advantages in terms of service.

'At Novo-Nordisk we're well aware of the fact that even the most impressive new products can't stand alone. . . . As a result of our merger, we're in a stronger position than ever before to provide that assistance.'

Testing innovation with customers: the case of 3M

3M is a company that has gained a worldwide reputation for its capacity to innovate and apply new technologies to the creation of new products. 3M is widespread in Europe with operations and development labs in every major country. The company has been successful in Europe because it has adapted its products to the European market and to the needs of European customers.

One aspect of service quality is the capacity to listen to customers and to create products according to what customers say. We approached 3M to discover what process they used to get the most out of their contacts with customers and how this information makes its way into 3M's laboratories for product development or adaptation.

3M have four types of laboratories. In the US, at the heart of the company, 3M has its 'dream labs'. These are labs where the basic technologies of the future are developed. The time-span before these technologies appear on the market in the form of products is 20 years. Next there are the 'sector labs'. These are labs that take the basic technologies developed in the 'dream' labs and convert them into applicable technologies. A new formula identifed in the 'dream' lab will be sent to the sector labs to be made into a formula for an adhesive, for example. Technologies under development in these labs will appear on the market in 5 to 10 years.

Then there are the 'division labs'. The jobs of these labs is to convert the technologies into products. A product under production in a division lab can appear on the market in anywhere from six months to three years. Lastly, there are the local technical services labs. They are particular to the European environment and are responsible for gathering the information and technical feedback from the market place and translating it, both in terms of language and application, for use by the division labs, which are located in different countries throughout Europe.

Information between the customers and the labs goes back and forth in both directions in the 3M organisation. Those who are responsible for making this communication possible are known as technical services staff and they are part of the division labs organisation, as well as part of the technical services lab.

In a typical divisional lab, there are three types of engineers: the product developers, who are those individuals responsible for creating the composition of a new product; the product engineers, who work with the manufacturing division to make it possible to produce the product; and the technical services people. 'The technical services engineers are the eyes and ears of the product developers. They are the ones that make the link between the company and the customer,' explains Jan Pinkster, Director of Technical Services for 3M France.

The technical service people's job is to travel with the salespeople and to discuss with customers. They try to find out if customers are satisfied with the existing products, to find out what could be modified to make the product meet the customers' need better and to find out what additional needs a customer might have that 3M can meet.

'When we first went to see Airbus, for example, we found out that they had a need for a very strong sealant for their planes. The product had to block out any kinds of toxic gases, smoke or anything that would endanger the lives of the passengers or the crew. They told us that two to three years before they needed the product to put into their planes. We went back to the divisional lab for adhesives with that idea and we worked on the product that would fit Airbus's need.'

Sometimes it is not the technical services division that identifies a new customer need; it could also be marketing or sales. If the company doesn't have an existing technology that can be adapted to meet a particular need and if it is important, the company goes back first to the divisional lab, and then to the sector lab and the 'dream' lab to develop a new basic technology. 'These kinds of requests are called market development requests or product development requests.'

For ideas which come from the labs and which the company would like to sell in the form of a product to the market, the technical service engineer again serves as an intermediary. 'He must know all of the products and technologies very well. In his contacts with customers and with the marketing people, he must be looking for ways to apply a new technology.'

Once a potential use for a new technology is identified, the lab goes to the marketing department, which is capable of evaluating whether or not the product will be well received or not in the market. Suggestions for changes are then received and incorporated into the product development. The product is then tested in the market with customers and, again, adaptations are made if necessary. Only then does the product appear on the market for sale. 'We never go out with a product that customers don't want.'

One of the keys to the success of the 3M development system is the listening which is done by the technical services engineer when he's with the customer. 'When I go to hire an engineer, I look for an engineer with the personality of a salesman. He has to be an extrovert.' In addition, the engineer doesn't just go to the customer to carry out a casual conversation. 3M's technical services people go with a full list of questions about every aspect of the customer's operation to identify exactly what is needed in each area to meet his needs best. The manufacturing process of the client is examined in detail, for example, to be sure that the product developed for the customer is easy to apply in his line of production.

The other key to the success of the system is the voluntary exchange of information. 3M doesn't just receive information from the customer and let it stop at that; they go back to the customer once the development has been done to make sure that what has been created is really what the customer wants. And the dialogue continues – all the way through to the moment when a new product ideally adapted to its functions, is created, tested and delivered to a very satisfied customer.

Communicating internally for greater external quality: the case of Hoffmann La Roche

Hoffmann La Roche is one of Switzerland's leading groups in the pharmaceuticals and chemicals industries. Its operations are worldwide, while the central headquarters for all of the company's four divisions is located in Basle, along with the central service functions and part of the company's research and development activities. A restructuring took place over the past two years which permitted the company to streamline its central operations and position the company for future growth.

New strategic goals were established and the next step was to address the question of what was needed to achieve the company's strategic goals. 'We felt that the customer focus was not enough in the forefront. We wanted to orient the company further toward the outside and toward the market', explains Dr Markus Altwegg, Director and member of the Executive Committee. The decision to launch the customer focus programme was taken at a meeting of the executive committee in 1988.

Hoffmann La Roche has four major divisions: Pharmaceuticals, Vitamins and Fine Chemicals, Fragrances and Flavors; and Diagnostics. The management policy of the company is that of high decentralisation. From an operational perspective, divisional managers are given the freedom to develop their business and invest as they see fit. The launching of the customer focus programme could not, therefore, impose any particular approach upon the divisions. 'To centrally develop a programme that runs throughout the group would be against our culture; each division was left on its own to develop an approach best adapted to its business.'

Since 1989, the Diagnostics Division ('Roche Diagnostic Systems') has gone the furthest in terms of setting up a structured approach to increasing the customer focus within the company. A major part of their approach has been an ongoing communications programme. From its origins, the programme has represented a cultural revolution within the company. 'It implies a change in values and, thus, it has been one of the most marked changes in the division in its recent history.'

The Diagnostics Division 'saw the programme as a way to change the attitude in the whole organisation'. The major issue was to improve the service provided by headquarters to the subsidiaries in the field. That included the delivery of products, information on new products, brochures, training, support and feedback for research and development. 'We tied head office improvements directly to the quality of service to the end customer,' explains Mr Claude Schmutz, co-ordinator of the programme within the diagnostics division. 'It was the first time service to the affiliates had become an issue. . . . It was the first time we started to call the subsidiaries "customers".'

The launch of the customer focus programme was a big event within Roche Diagnostic Systems which, in communication terms, had a significant impact on the success of the programme. Prior to the the launch, quality animators (quality group leaders) had been chosen. They were to be responsible for leading the inter-departmental teams that would work on improving service quality problems. They were trained to perform that function and were already motivated by the concepts behind the programme.

The launch was a half-day event held in a large congress hall. It was something between a show and a participative event. All of the employees of the Diagnostics Division were invited. Each had received a special invitation letter which informed them of the event, reminded them of the importance of the programme to the company's future and was signed by the head of the division.

The event was for the Diagnostics Division only; to demonstrate the importance of the customer focus programme, members of the executive committee of Hoffmann La Roche attended and spoke. At one point, the quality animators were called on stage and were applauded.

To gain the active participation of all of the people in the auditorium, there was a customer service quiz and prizes were awarded. Volunteers to the quality groups were also asked to come forward and give their names. The highlight of the event was the presentation of the diagnostics' headquarter division's promise and commitments to the subsidiaries.

This event, so foreign to the culture of Hoffmann La Roche which is a somewhat reserved company, made a huge impact upon the personnel. 'We had never done anything like this before. It drew a great deal of attention.' The result was that employees understood the level of commitment that the company was willing to make to the programme, which was underlined by the presence of members of the Hoffmann La Roche Executive Committee. They were also motivated by the enthusiasm shown by those who organised the event.

The event was preceded and followed by an ongoing communications effort through the company newspaper and with the use of banners, posters and regular information on the progress made in the quality groups.

Roche Diagnostic Systems has recently introduced a customer satisfaction survey which questions their customers – the subsidiaries – to find out whether genuine progress is being made in terms of the service quality headquarters is providing them with. The results have been most encouraging and have given everyone in headquarters just one more reason to continue their efforts. 'We are in the process of dramatically improving our service to the subsidiaries so that they can offer a maximum level of service to their customers.'

Gaining a personality in the customer's eyes: the case of Damart

Damart, a French company, has gained a reputation in the market as the 'anti-cold specialist'. It is a producer and retailer by mail order and through its own chain of Damart shops which sell clothing and underclothing of exceptional wearability and comfort. In the early 1950s when the company was established, it specialised in cold-weather undergarments. Today, the company's clothing range has been expanded into fashion items and a full range of accessories.

The company has defined two very specific target client segments. The first are individuals over 60 years of age who 'have time and like to take their time and want to be taken care of by the company'. A second group of target clients include individuals between 45 and 60 – 'the new generation' which is both more time and more fashion-conscious than the older group. Both groups, however, represent the 'Damart customer', an imaginary person around which all of the efforts of the company are focused. Damart's objective is to provide the best possible service to this individual and to ensure that he becomes 'our very best publicity agent'.

Because the company is targeting a very precise and well-defined market segment, communication to the customer is a very important aspect of the company's business. It is important in order to create an image for the company in a market where there are a large number of competitors, and it is important in order to position Damart clearly as a supplier to its target customer segment.

Over the years, Damart has been very successful in creating an image for itself in the market. Practically any French consumer, when asked, could tell you exactly what Damart sells and to whom they sell it. The two principle reasons for its success in communication are, first, the consistency of the message and, secondly, the degree to which the message has been visualised – in the style of the shops, in the logo, in the catalogue, even in the way that the clothing is packaged in the boxes to be sent out. The advantage of such a consistent approach from the customers' perspective is that they know what to expect. There are no surprises; in every respect Damart is true to its image and, over time, it is as reliable as an old clock.

In recent years, Damart has been particularly successful at creating an atmosphere in its shops which meets the expectations of its target customers and clearly communicates to everyone who the target customers are and the kind of service that Damart is trying to provide.

Unlike the windows of most clothing shops, Damart's are not cluttered with a vast variety of the season's latest offerings. In some Damart windows, there are not clothes at all – just a large sign with a message like, 'Cold? Me? . . . never'. In windows where clothing is displayed, it is never in great numbers and is generally a display of the company's best sellers – cold-weather underwear.

The shop itself is a combination of a mail order pick-up centre and shop floor display. The first thing one notices upon entering is the predominance of seats arranged throughout the store, just begging the passer-by to sit down and take a rest. This is in sharp contrast to the practice in every other retail store in France where seats are a 'no-no'! ('They take up display space and are an invitation to people who just want to look and not buy.') Damart think of the 70-year-old customer who would love to buy if only her feet would hold out!

The next thing to notice is the age of the sales staff – no young girls to be found! Their average age is around 35 years. They are 'the accomplished daughters' of their customers. 'The Damart customer prefers to be taken in charge by the adviser who represents for her, her mature and responsible daughter.' Their neat, clean, knee length uniform wouldn't shock anybody's grandmother and their name tags read 'Miss' or 'Mrs' and never 'Sally' or 'Jane'.

A Damart store is not aggressive, brash or even elegant. It's clean, comfortable and unintimidating. In clear, clean, neutral colours like light brown, beige and blue, the store is neatly arranged with the welcome desk, the purchase pick-up and payment desk, and the fitting rooms clearly marked with big, large-lettered signs that even people with bad eyesight can read. Clean, bright lighting helps the shopper feel welcome and unhurried. There is no loud music nor any video shows, no spotlights or theatrical effects.

The welcome desk is positioned directly in front of the door without blocking it and serves as a focal point in the store. A smiling hostess – generally the store manager – is at the welcome desk and from there can keep an eye on the welfare of all of her customers. Every customer entering the store can count on receiving her greeting.

The pick-up and purchase desk, positioned in another part of the store, is always clean and never cluttered with merchandise or crowded with impatient customers. A ticket system controls the order of customers approaching the desk. Customers knowing what they want to buy are given a numbered ticket right away upon entering the store. They can either sit or browse while they wait their turn. Customers who want to browse and then make their choice are given numbers by the person helping them once their choice is made.

Sales staff are always available and ready to help. They are trained to have a receptive attitude *vis-à-vis* their customers and to help them make decisions. 'At Damart, we do not sell, we advise. Our commitment to the customer is to find the article which is best adapted to his needs.' The behaviour of the sales staff is consistent with the company's philosophy. In the store they are present, attentive, but never pushy.

The combined impact of all of the small details above is a clear message about the kind of service Damart is trying to offer its customers and for whom those services have been designed. The greatest strength of Damart's approach is that practically no other retailer in France has gone to such lengths to communicate its commitment to serve the elderly. The result is truly notable.

How to use communication for reinforcement of quality service

As the previous examples show, communication can be used internally to convince and/or involve employees in the service drive. It can also be used externally to convince customers to buy and to know what to expect. When the internal and external elements concur they have the perfect conditions for going forward. This is why we see, for instance, more advertising which features employees: it shows to customers the importance of service through people. It also demonstrates to employees how important their role is in service. Thus, when British Airways launched its programme, its advertising relied heavily on its 'putting people first' programme featuring how its staff were taking care of people.

However, reducing external communication to advertising alone is reducing greatly what external communication can do for improving customer expectations. There are other means which are sometimes more effective than advertising. So let us review first how different kinds of external communication can help.

External communication helps managers and reduces the gap between what customers could expect and what the company can deliver.

There are three mains ways in which this can be done.

- **Reduce perceived risks** When using a new supplier, be it a new service or product, it is always a risk for the customer. How much better will they be? Can they deliver what they promise? How do I know it is wise to use them? Why should I change? The tools that reduce perceived risk are multiple. They are not usually related to advertising and are sometimes overlooked. They range from references, testimonials, documentation, salesman contact, preparedness and responses to objections, quality and speed of proposals or estimates, if any (including the format), a trial period, if any, and finally a very new tool which has emerged in the last five years: service guarantees. For instance Interrent in Sweden says if the car you have rented is not there within five minutes you don't pay the rent. Otis says that if a lift breaks down twice during the same week you get a 10 per cent discount on the maintenance contract. The 1990s are going to be the decade of service guarantees.

- **Give attention to peripheral clues to facilitate customers' choice** In many instances, evaluating service quality cannot be done until you have tried it and it may be too late by then. You will only know if the hairdresser was good after he has cut your hair, a vacation only after you have come home, delivery of a package only after it has been sent. So, from the customer's point of view, the evaluation of such services can only be done *a priori* on peripheral clues, i.e., elements which surround the service which might seem to indicate that it is good. A clean restaurant window will indicate safe cooking more than a dirty one. An express mail company which answers the phone after a single ring will seem more serious than one which answers after 10 rings. Many clues exist to form customer expectations and help him choose. These are not always given enough attention. As a result customers don't buy.

- **Keep promises just below your capability to deliver while being sufficiently attractive** Advertising is changing dramatically. The 1970s and '80s were years of dreams, exaggerations, wild promises, seduction. The challenge of the 1990s will be to use simplicity and truth, while still being attractive. When Air France launched its new business class in 1990, they compared their seat to one you might have in a beautifully decorated – like Versailles – living room. Who do they think they can fool? In fact, a year later, the advertising has changed to say simply that they have the most convenient departure points from France to the rest of Europe!

Give the opportunity to your loyal customers to reinforce word of mouth

All market research studies on service show that between 50 and 70 per cent of purchases are made through the advice of friends. Studies also show that negative word of mouth travels three to five times faster than positive. So the competition is hard! A communication tool that will improve the spread of positive word of mouth can mean big results. Naturally, fewer people are inclined to talk of their good experiences with a supplier than their bad ones. That is why it is often said that a service will always be evaluated on its weakest link! There are ways to make positive word of mouth travel. Making your customers feel proud about using your company is one way. Advertising is sometimes done for this purpose, i.e. keep the image high so that current customers can continue to justify their purchases. This is why when computing the cost of acquiring a new customer versus keeping one – even if the purchase rate is very infrequent – at least 30 per cent of the advertising budget should be kept for the 'key customer category'. Other ways to make a customer speak positively of you are to invite him to discuss you with others:

at the launching of new products or services to the press; at users' clubs, where current customers can be the best ambassadors to sell a company.

A third way used by companies is to give to customers signs of recognition which can be used in public. Building caretakers or hotel lobby receptionists carry the Otis badge for Otis. If they meet another caretaker who has had a problem with his elevator, they are sure to remark how good Otis's service is.

Co-branded credit-cards are used more and more. When an Alitalia customer pays with his credit card on which is largely featured an Alitalia plane, his business associates are sure to ask about Alitalia (it had better be good!!).

Another scheme used is to involve customers in the management of your service quality: ask them to be on a jury for quality prices, as Texas Instruments does. Ask them to be on the jury for the award for the best ideas on quality, as Motorola does. Ask them to be a part of new employee recruiting process as this consulting company has done. Or, ask them to be part of a panel to give inputs for new products or services as pharmaceutical companies do with doctors or car manufacturers do with taxi drivers.

All these methods of 'recognition' transform your satisfied customers into committed customers and committed people love to talk about their commitments!

Internal communication is the fuel for launching and helping the service quality 'rocket' maintain its course over the long term

As with any fuel, it must be adapted to the vehicle and used differently depending on the speed of the engine. The process of a good internal communication campaign is as follows.

First, identify the objectives of communication which fit the stage the programme has reached: usually a programme has four stages of preparation (one year), launch (three months), implementation, follow up and improvement (or reorientation), as described in Chapter 1. For each stage the objectives of communication are not the same, as is shown in Table 3.1.

In addition, as a programme evolves over time, the messages that will work best also change. This is shown in Fig. 3.1.

If at preparation stage, it is useful to talk about the drive and show the results of market studies, at the follow-up stage only tangible results will make the programme move forward.

Given these premises, it is not difficult to see that the means of communication cannot be the same, depending on the objective and stage of a programme. When visiting one of the largest telephone companies in the world, we were asked to help make their customer service people (250 of them) be 'passionate for their customers from 9 a.m. to 5 p.m. We tried out a list of the methods described in this book. They seemed to have done it all. They had started their programme six years before and had gone through

	preparation	launching	implementation	follow up
make tangible		– welcome people as customers – article in the press	– invite 'customers' into factory	– have quality groups present at work
involve		– 'breaking of the bread' in a ritual – card game to identify service dimensions	– have phone answered by those who don't do it normally	– so they know what they are talking about, spread best practices
convivial	– link of satisfaction to customer behaviour market share – videos on customers	– 'necessity of service to compete', as theme in convention management	– 'the promise and service standards' have been enriched by all employees	
inform	– analysis of customer expectations – results of diffuse satisfaction survey	– tell why – tell workers why	– distribute service standards	

Table 3.1

most of the stages of implementation. Still, management felt it was not enough.

We did not have anything left in our bag, until we asked to see the place where the staff worked. It was a vast area with little cubicles for each employee, a screen and a telephone, and grey walls all around. There was a gigantic black-and-white banner saying 'be passionate to the customers'. The carpet was orange (bleached!). In short an awful place to be in. So we drew a rabbit from our bag: make this office a place of celebration so that employees can see what you mean by passion. Change the colours, put in balloons, have games and challenges – in a word be happy – like the reservation centre of Club Med which is full of beautiful colours and pictures.

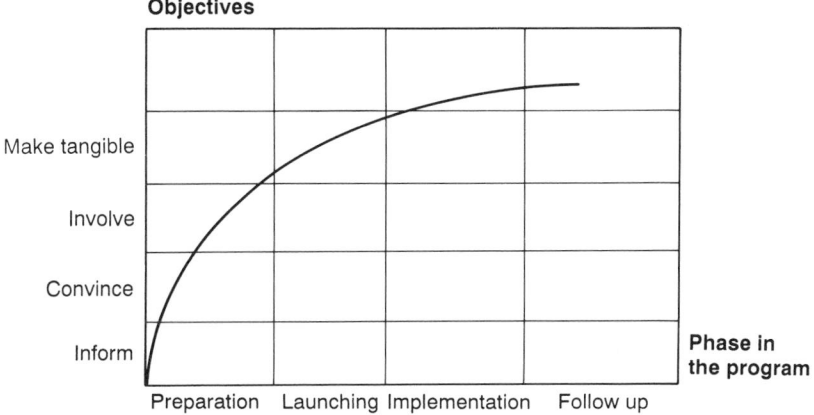

Figure 3.1

Choose messages and media to appeal selectively to different targets within the company and be coherent with company culture

The worst internal communication campaign is the one which says the same thing with the same creative approach to everyone with words and drawings that come from standard kits! People see it as artificial, and they believe that it is just another manifestation of a common disease: BOHICA (Bend Over Here It Comes Again). Management has a new idea every year – this year, it's quality!

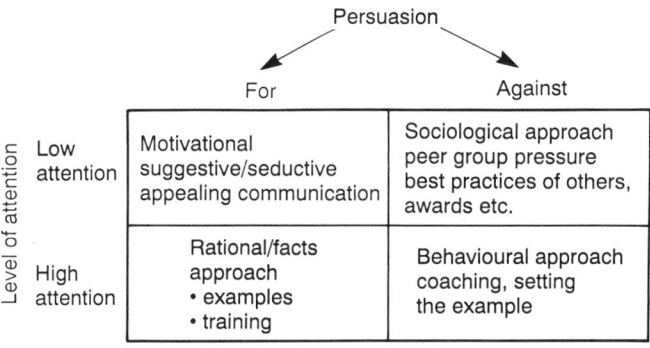

Figure 3.2

Another point to keep in mind, you cannot address senior executives in the same way as employees. You cannot approach people who feel threatened with a programme of employee empowerment, in the same way as you approach salespeople who at last see they have been heard. We have found it useful to use two terms to describe successful communication: attention and persuasion. The way to get attention and persuasion will differ depending on the target. As a result the way to communicate will differ.

For instance, in one multinational company, a study showed the two items that bothered the 50 or so world subsidiaries the most: wrong products delivered and wrong documentation. We used the motivational approach: we said we would put oversized toilet paper at HQ for a week and say at the end: this is what happens when you get the wrong product – We put a menu at HQ restaurant with foreign words and after a week said: this is what happen when you get the wrong documents.

At French Rail, where people are very proud of belonging to the French public service system and think they have always been quality oriented (after all trains do not get in accidents and arrive on time!) a more sociological approach was used. A convention took place in each of the regions (600 to 1000 participants), where quality teams presented their current work on improving service to their peers. The best ideas were selected and presented at a national convention of two days where over 200 experiences were presented on videos, by witnesses in one-to-four minute well-rehearsed presentations. These conventions, held within the first year of the programme, helped greatly to continue its implementation.

Use the current work environment to reinforce the message continuously

If quality or customer satisfaction messages are communicated using tools that are too foreign to the everyday working environment, they risk appearing artificial. This is why – especially when the objective is to make service quality as concrete as possible – companies use tools that can be found in the existing working environment. For instance, service standards for the maid of a hotel will appear in illustrated form on her daily work sheets rather than be listed in a book on quality which the maid will not – or perhaps cannot – read!

Restaurant managers will be reminded of service standards when they look at their diary or agenda – which they are required to do on a daily basis. For a maintenance engineer, it could be on his job checklist, etc. Thus, one should assure that there is constant reinforcement in a natural way.

Another way to reinforce service quality objectives naturally is to take into consideration the current situation the unit is facing. It is useless to communicate all the unit's weak points if the objective is to improve only one or two. This is why successful companies selectively choose to address improvements to service standards as the unit manager sees fit, depending upon the existing situation in the unit.

Here is a complete example of a communication campaign which was aimed at the HQ of a large multinational company. It was based on the following hypothesis:

● the notion of customer was not a top priority at HQ;
● among HQ function, nobody felt he was supplying another person;
● nobody saw what he/she could gain from such a programme.

Three objectives with three messages were set:

Objective 1: 'open your eyes'

messages:
everyone has a customer
we all belong to a service chain

Objective 2: 'forge ahead' (do something)

discover your customer
have the service reflex
do your service check-up

Objective 3: 'want to do more'

messages:
enlist now in the service quality seminars

'Open your eyes'

● An urgent first objective is to awake and alert personnel to the fact that everyone has a customer.
● Without this internal link-up binding each department person to another, service to the final customer can be utopic. Those who do not serve final customers serve someone who serves someone who does.
● As the dust settles and people become fixed in their own job and their own priorities, they become blinded and lose sight of this internal customer service chain.
● Who links up with whom in what order, with what priorities, and with what results is key to good service.
● This unsettles the dust, wakes up everyday routine, and allows for surprises and eye opening moments.
● To open the eyes on the customer chain a mix of teaser campaigns and actions that show what lack of service does, or what new service does, will be used.

☐ Two messages will be used for this first phase:
  √ 'everyone has a customer'
  √ 'we all belong to the service chain'

'Forge ahead' or 'lift yourself up and walk'

- Once the environment is ready, we can move ahead from thought to actions.
- The keys here are that accountability and personal responsibility are required.
- For this to happen the scapegoats need to disappear and the people need to replace it. What do people do or not do?
- This phase will essentially be action-oriented for each individual, rather than concern actions that are done by the environment.

Have the service reflex

What?	Why?	How?
15 weeks' service reflex campaign	Change behaviour on fifteen major service dimensions, show how one can even anchor the habit	Tracts distributed on each desk explaining what the reflex is
16th week super serve campaign	Forge ahead – try to go beyond the reflex	Reminder note of 15 service reflexes with a grid. Ask each to try and do all 15 each day and report on a grid
17th week beyond forge campaign	Spread the customer virus everywhere	Each one use a few reflexes, but great ones and beyond what is expected from the customers.
Customer virus		A reward when a service has gone beyond expectations, given by someone at HQ who feels someone else has done some exceptional work

Table 3.2

Discover your customer:

What	Why?	How?
Invite a customer to lunch	To understand their position	Invitation card
Take your customer's place		Spend 1 hour with the customer; you are invited on his work site
Are they satisfied?	Push people to want to know	Evaluation grid on the 15 services reflexes
Customer debate	anticipate	+ if not good why? bringing sandwich lunch, a customer is invited to debate informally at my work place (with debate agenda and questions answers panel)

Table 3.3

Do your check up

What?	Why?	How?
Self check up	See how individuals rate on service quality and suggest remedy (i.e. training programme)	Princess quality – story with princess quality book
Company check up	See how each department hierarchical level sees quality	Quality check up showing which seminar he/she should take Take a representative sample of levels/functions to see outlook *vis-à-vis* quality, service, customers, and publish results

Table 3.4

Themes: weekly service reflexes

- Responsiveness
- Competence
- Openness
- Courtesy
- Information
- Credibility
- Security
- Personal attention
- Fun
- Accountability
- Availability
- Keep your word
- Keep in touch
- Punctuality
- Initiative

'Want to do more/enlist now'

- As the campaign ends, each will have made a check-up, inducing him to follow one of two seminars.
- the discovery programme 1/2 day programme on the principles
- the 'focus now programme': a five day programme on the tools of quality to be used on the job.
- The programme will have been developed and tested (100 trainers trained to train every employee who wants to attend (these 100 trainers will be volunteers who will also lead the first quality groups; thus, they will be part of the hierarchy).

4 SERVICE STRATEGY: CREATING ARTFUL DIFFERENCES

Introduction

Today, in this world full of consultants and multinational corporations, there are strategies for everything. There are marketing strategies, product strategies, advertising strategies, strategies for development, for invest-ment, for industrial production . . . There is even a strategy for international technological joint ventures. The reader may be asking himself what he needs with yet another strategy, and . . . what on earth *is* a strategy anyway?

Let's go back to the basics; we looked up the word 'strategy' in the dictionary. *Webster's New World Dictionary* (2nd College edn.) gives the following definition.

Strategy, noun (coming from the French *stratégie* and the Greek *stratégia* or generalship)
1 (a) the science of planning and directing large-scale military operations, specifically (as distinguished from tactic) of maneuvering forces into the most advantageous position prior to actual engagement with the enemy.
(b) a plan or action based on this.
2 (a) skill in managing or planning, especially by using strategem.
(b) a strategem or artful means to some ends.

And for 'strategem':

1 a trick, scheme, or plan for deceiving an enemy in war.
2 any trick or scheme for achieving some purpose.
see synonym – trick.

If we are willing to accept the proposal that military combat in the developed world has been largely replaced by economic battles for market share, then we can apply the definition in its entirety. A service strategy is, then, *an artful means to provide service and, thereby, outdo your enemy*, oops, sorry, *competitor*.

The key word in the phrase is 'artful', because if a strategy isn't artful, it isn't likely to be better than your competitor's 'trick' so the battle is not yet won and you're back at square one.

So, now you ask, 'Why a *service* strategy. Won't a good development or marketing strategy be enough?' It depends; if you're a company that's got a good strategy in another domain which it believes will maintain the company's competitive advantage over the long term, maybe it won't matter so much. On the other hand, if you're a company, no matter what the field is, that is reasonably sure that its competitors will be hot on its trail tomorrow, if they aren't already there today, then, a service strategy is a good thing to consider.

A service strategy can give your company a differential advantage, because most people underestimate the importance of the service part in the total package they sell. High-technology companies, for example, are notorious for telling you that the reason customer A bought their product in preference to a competitor's is because of their technological advance. When you are customer A and you know that you bought it because the salesman took an extra half-hour to explain how the machine works, then you are in a better position than the company to evaluate the importance of service.

In general, product companies underestimate the impact which service can have on their level of competitiveness. Most product companies attribute a maximum of 30 per cent importance to service in the total service/product package they offer to customers. Companies we interviewed for this book placed it at between 40 and 50 per cent; some said it was even more.

Some service companies also forget the importance of the pure service aspects of what they offer. At one restaurant where we know the owner, he thinks we keep coming back because he serves good food. Not in the least (his steak tartar is lousy) – we keep coming back because he organised a super party for a friend of ours at his own expense; we had such fun that every time we go there, we have a good laugh about the event with one of the waiters.

In those rare companies that do recognise the importance of their service quality, it is seldom presented as a benefit to the customer; the customer is expected to 'discover' it all on his own. For those of you who do not spend precious time searching for good service as we do, such a company just might slip your notice. Apart from the unusual event, customers don't take a note of the quality of the service until the second or third time around – good service is expected to be the norm in this day and age, and it's only bad service that makes us take notice.

Once you've got an 'artful' strategy, don't hide it in the cupboard. Service strategies, like clothes, are made to be modelled in front of others. A service strategy is an artful means of outdoing your competitors, but if you don't give your competitor and your customers a demonstration of just how artful it really is, it's not going to improve your position in anyone's eyes.

To get the full benefits of an artful service strategy, a company should announce its strategy far and wide. It gives the customer the opportunity to see the value-added which the company is offering. A good way of announcing your strategy is to put it in the form of a customer promise or guarantee. If, for example, a computer software development company promises the customer it will never go back on an estimate, always deliver on time, provide training on how to use the new program and deliver the program with a user-friendly operating manual, its customers know where to focus their expectations for top-quality service. They will not necessarily expect the company to provide a completely customised programme, created from scratch; it's not part of the promise and is probably not something that the company does well.

Another reason to consider a service strategy is that service is now a hot item and an important issue. Perhaps because the world is becoming too automated, computerised, chronometrised, synthesised and most importantly, impersonalised, we find that customers are crying out for better service. The importance of customer service is not likely to diminish. A recent study by the Management Centre Europe showed that European managers cited service excellence as the key differentiator in the battle for market share in the 1990s and beyond. If your company isn't doing something about service, you can be sure that your competitor is.

A service strategy helps companies allocate resources. Whether or not service is going to be the company's principle point of differentiation from its competitors, it is still likely to represent an important element of what it provides to the customer. A service strategy permits one to define priorities and manage that element in a way that enhances the rest of the product/service package.

FNAC, a French chain of book, record and electronic equipment shops, differentiates itself from the competition in part by the competence and knowledge of their sales personnel. When it comes to hiring staff, they set priorities to fit with that positioning; FNAC favours individuals who have previous experience in the technical fields, over those who have experience of selling.

Hoffmann La Roche's Diagnostics Division sells medical diagnostic instruments and materials to clinics and hospitals. The company has defined a service strategy which, among other things, focuses on fast response to customers in the case of a breakdown. Not surprisely, funds that previously might have been used on sales training, for example, are now going towards the setting up of hot-lines and towards improvements in its logistics system from headquarters to the subsidiaries.

Strategies in action

The creation of practically any service strategy involves deciding: what to serve, i.e. identifying customer service needs and expectations; who to serve, i.e. the creation of customer groups based on similar needs and expectations; and who to serve with what and how, i.e. choosing target customer groups and creating services adapted to each group, taking into account the company's strengths and weaknesses.

Beyond this very simple guideline, the service strategy inventor is completely free to exercise his imagination. Artfulness generally appears most in the third phase – deciding 'who with what and how'. It doesn't take much imagination to create five star service if you also plan to charge through the nose for it. What is interesting (and artful), is a service which makes the customer feel that he is getting something from you that he can't get somewhere else for the same price, i.e. your service should have a higher perceived value to him than somebody else's.

The theory sounds deceptively simple, because, in reality, it's hard to develop a good service strategy. In this chapter you will find some examples of typical service strategies and why they were chosen. These examples should provide you with some ideas of how to approach your own service strategy creation.

Targeting niches; the case of Kuoni

In any target customer population there are niches, or subsets, of that population which have specific needs in terms of service. One strategy is to create services which meet the specific requirements of one or more of these niches.

Kuoni Travel has chosen such a strategy. Within the large population of travellers and holidaymakers which it targets for its services, are a number of niche groups which have specific interests or requirements. For each niche, Kuoni identifies the requirements and creates services which match the expectations of these customers. The strategy is successful because nowhere else can customers in these niche groups find services which, for the same price, meet their expectations better than at Kuoni.

Kuoni is a major European tour operator and the owner of a chain of retail travel agents. In terms of its international representation, it comes third after American Express and Thomas Cook. The group offers a wide variety of packaged tours for various upmarket segments.

Kuoni has identified four major clients segments for targeting – the business traveller; long-distance tourist; short- and medium-distance young tourist; and the teen/sport-oriented tourist group. Traditionally, its market was in the long-distance older tourist group. Today, it has developed services to meet the other groups as well.

Targeting is either done at the retail level and/or through the creation and marketing of tour packages. For the business travel sector, separate offices are being established. In some cases, these offices serve only one client company and are located on that client's premises. In addition, Kuoni has created a range of support services to offer to business travellers. They include travel insurance and detailed information on hotels or restaurants, presented in the form of a guidebook.

To meet the needs of niches within the business segment, Kuoni has created a special advisory service, which has packages on particular types of business travel, trade fairs or conventions, or information on special business travel issues, such as bonus mileage on air travel.

Helvetic Tours, a separate name brand of package tours, caters to the short, medium and long distance young tourist group. They are sold through Kuoni agencies and through agencies handling Kuoni products, and consist of a set of tours specifically designed for this group. Particular attention is paid to price as this niche of clients tends to be very price-conscious.

Kuoni's traditional sector is the long-distance, older traveller. Packages are created to meet niches within this large category in terms of destinations and activities. The emphasis in all the Kuoni brand packages is on quality accommodation, and the experience and knowledge of the tour guides. Kuoni name brand travel is sold through Kuoni retail agencies, as well as through other agencies throughout the world.

Within the traditional target sector, the company has been particularly successful with its packages to the Far East, as well as with its packages for Far Eastern travellers to Europe. Roughly 58 per cent of all of the incoming tourist business that it handles is made up of travellers from this region. 'We have tremendous growth in incoming travellers from the Far East. We provide a high standard of service in terms of the tour guide and the companies or hotels with which we work; this is what they come to us for', says Mr Bosshard, Director.

In addition, the company is targeting certain younger, up-market niche markets. Packages for these customer groups include, for example, sports holidays to attend major competitive events and a series of 'nostalgia tours' aimed at French travellers with visits through Africa by amphibious plane. 'We are now working on developing adventure holidays, like treks through the Saudi Arabian desert or mountain hikes through the Himalayas.'

The key to its strategy is the ongoing identification and reidentification of service niches for which no product yet exists. 'You need to have a lot of experience in this business – a "feeling" for what will work.' Then when creating the package, 'you must see everything from the client's point of view'. For each package, the services are carefully adapted to the customers who will be using them. A tour package aimed at senior citizens won't include the same hotel accommodations as that of a package destined for young people, even if the price or the rating of the two hotels on the tours is the same.

Kuoni must always stay on top of trends in travel. Most holiday packages have a very short life and therefore Kuoni innovates on a continuous basis. To be successful, a new package must attract the interest of a segment large enough to justify its creation. There is, therefore, an endless balancing act to be done between targeting narrow enough to meet the needs of a new niche and targeting wide enough to attract the business necessary to make the package profitable. 'It's a high-risk business because the gap between making and losing money on a package is very narrow.'

Outpacing the competition: the case of IKEA

IKEA provides one of the classic examples of a strategy called 'outpacing' in books on management. Outpacing is the concept of achieving lower costs and high differentiation from competitors at the same time. It is generally done by deviating from a classical set of service offerings to a new, innovative set whose perceived value to the customer is greater. IKEA's concept of 'anti-service' does just that.

IKEA is a retailer of home furnishings of Swedish origin. Ingvar Kampard is the founder of IKEA and the IKEA concept. At the time that Mr Kampard began doing business in the 1940s, most of the nation's furniture was sold out of furniture shops. The owner or the salesperson 'assisted' the client in his choice from the somewhat limited selection generally available. The furniture was then ordered and delivered anywhere from four weeks to three months later.

Mr Kampard did not start out as a furniture dealer. His primary business at the time he added furniture sales to his range was selling small items like Christmas tree ornaments, pens, etc. door to door. Kampard soon had the idea to replace door-to-door sales with catalogue sales. When he tried out the idea and provided customers with a very detailed and attractive catalogue, he discovered that his clients were just as happy or happier purchasing by catalogue. It was more convenient for them and gave them more time to make their choice. And, thus, Kampard replaced the first of a series of traditional services in furniture sales – consultation with a salesman.

Mr Kampard replaced the second 'service' when he discovered that customers were prepared to assemble their own furniture. Rather then sending the furniture already constructed, which made it difficult to package and hazardous to ship because of frequent damage, he started shipping his goods unassembled. Once again, the customer felt that he was better off overall – he was more sure that his furniture would arrive intact and, because Kampard lowered his prices, the customer was getting more for less.

A third 'service' – delivery – was replaced at the time Kampard created a central depot for customers. His original thought was to offer customers a chance to see the furniture before buying. That it did; however, as he placed the showroom right next to the warehouse, customers could also take the furniture with them when they left. Customers were again more satisfied than before because they had the furniture they wanted right away and didn't have to pay for delivery.

A fifth 'service', that of collecting the items from the warehouse for the customers, was also finally replaced. The customers collected their own goods in the warehouse and didn't have to wait for store personnel to go get it for them.

The replacement of all of the traditional furniture dealer services – consultation, elegant shop displays, delivery, assembly and credit payment – created opportunities to provide yet other services which are unique and attractive. Imaginative posters and information materials, do-it-yourself decorating aids, baby strollers and an enormous children's play-pen are some of the services now offered.

At the same time prices have remained low. In terms of a price/quality ratio, IKEA is ahead of its competitors. It is also ahead of them in terms of differentiation. IKEA has a strong image as being an original company with an attractive, original product. That image itself is a strong drawing point today. While other companies can now copy the concept, taking away some of the originality of the approach, they will be at a disadvantage as late starters. They will be facing many of the problems that IKEA has already resolved or will resolve very soon.

Because it is generally a novelty, to be successful, an outpacing strategy must offer a clear significant advantage to customers for them to be willing to try it. There are generally two barriers, 1) the customer has to give up a service or many services which he is accustomed to receiving as a matter of course, and 2) most customers have an innate fear of trying something new.

It is said that only 3 per cent of the population is willing to try a new product when it comes out. To compensate them for their temerity, the innovator must provide some form of reassurance in the purchase decision. In the case of IKEA, it is the money-back guarantee within 30 days. It is also the Swedish quality label which IKEA puts on its products at a very early stage to be sure that customers know that IKEA's products maintain good standards of quality despite their price. The catalogue also is a form of reassurance for those who have not yet visited the store and are hesitant to do so.

At IKEA, the customer began by giving up services in order to save money. Today, we can say that what the customer originally gave up to save money has been more than replaced by a new attractive and interesting set of services', . . . and the customer is still saving money. Table 4.1 summarises for the reader what exactly has been given up and what has been gained.

The customer now sees the home-assembly process, for example, as a fun challenge rather than a dangerous or complicated chore. IKEA has always encouraged that by selling furniture which is fairly easy to put together and which looks easy to put together as well. Clear instructions are always provided with the furniture.

Consultation on furniture choice was also given up, yet customers feel more than compensated by the written documentation which answers most of their questions. If they still have questions, staff are available to answer them. In the end, what has the customer really given up, the discomfort of being pressured by a pushy salesperson?

Services – Traditional Furniture Dealer	The replacement – IKEA
Service 1 • Elaborate shop, usually small • Little display flexibility • Limited merchandise on display	• Large, attractive warehouse, with modular displays that change regularly • Large selection of merchandise on display – every item in catalogue plus more
Service 2 • Consultation by salesperson; sometimes aggressive • Little opportunity to browse	• No systematic consultation; detailed, user-friendly information in catalogue • A tag with information on fabric, care instructions, origin etc. on *every* item • Additional comparative information for certain products – kitchens, sofas etc. • Consultation with sales staff if desired
Service 3 • Furniture with choice of materials – available in four to six weeks at best	• Furniture with choice of materials – available immediately except for certain sofa materials
Service 4 • Delivery – only between 8 a.m. and 6 p.m. generally; not at weekends (must make an appointment and miss work)	• Delivery with extra charge if desired, otherwise goods available immediately
Service 5 • Assembly: still high possibility of damage to furniture in transit	• Assembly possible with extra charge; if not can Do-it-Yourself with clear, easy instructions
Other Advantages • ? ? ?	• Easy parking • Long opening hours • Activities for children • Toilet facilities, baby changing facilities • Restaurant • 'Outing'

Table 4.1

Not just after-sales service: the case of Bobst

For many product companies, good service means good after-sales service. They forget that there are many service aspects to what they provide and that they can focus on one or many of them to obtain a differential advantage.

Bobst is recognised for the total service package it offers customers. The company manufactures top-of-the-line printing and packaging machines.

Most of the machines it produces represent an important investment for the purchaser. Bobst was an entrepreneur in the industry and in its early years developed a full service approach to its business. Today, the company features a seven-point product/service package.

The central part of the package is the machine itself. It could be a printer which prints the design on the package, an autoplatine which cuts and makes the folds in the carton, a folder/gluer which folds and glues the boxes or any variety of auxiliary machines. For the most part, they are very large machines or product lines, which must be integrated into a manufacturing concept of packaging.

The other six parts of the package are service elements. The first of these is sales consultation; it ensures that the client doesn't make a mistake about the machine he is buying. A Bobst is an essential asset and a client shouldn't feel rushed or pressured into purchasing one. A poor decision reflects as much on Bobst as on the buyer, because an unhappy client will lay the blame at the company's door.

Consultation on installation is the second part of the package. This step is designed to ensure that the client can integrate the machine rapidly into his production concept. The installation and sales team co-ordinate with the client and verify that the client's production line will be correctly adapted to include the new machine and to assure an efficient material flow.

Thirdly, Bobst co-ordinates the installation of the machine. In this way the client is relieved of the task of organising transport, electrical connections, import documents etc.

Fourth, once the machine is in place, Bobst technicians install and commission it and train the customer to achieve optimum capacity, not just of the machine but of the entire production line.

Fifth, Bobst also provides additional training to the client's personnel to run and maintain the machines. Training is provided on-site, as well as at Bobst technical services centres.

Sixth, Bobst provides after-sales service. Their after-sales service is far more attractive than that provided by most companies because they guarantee the supply of parts for the entire life of the machine. Some of these machine last 40 or 50 years. If a client needs a piece which is no longer held in stock, Bobst manufactures it for him.

Bobst charges, for its machines, a fully justifiable but high price. The company has the reputation of being the 'Rolls Royce' of the industry in respect to quality, performance and reliability of its products. Their reputation is based as much on their service as on the technological advancement of their products. The value-added that Bobst offers its customers is an ongoing partnership. Regardless of the situation, the problem, the complications, Bobst is there to handle it.

Many a four-star hotel would like to claim that they do as much for their customers. The customer in negotiation in one of these hotel's meeting rooms rings for the waiter, 'I have a problem; we will not be finished in time for me to make my plane to Vienna. Can you please book me on the next flight?' The hotel that deserves its four stars, will have it done in a wink; another will either say they can't or will interrupt the customer five times for more details.

The importance of a 'partnership' approach from the customer's point of view is that he does not have to concern himself with the issue; his mind is free to devote himself to other pressing problems. Below is a list of the typical problems a Bobst machine buyer might have to concern himself with if Bobst weren't there to take things in charge. There are 19 different problems to be resolved, involving 14 different persons. With Bobst, the comparative list shrinks to zero problems, involving only 3 people – the plant director, the technical director and the line production manager.

When a Bobst customer buys the Bobst service, he is buying peace of mind; he's buying the ability not to have to concern himself with the details of buying and installing such a complicated machine. Moreover, he is buying peace of mind for the future too, because Bobst's 'partnership' approach doesn't stop once the machine is up and running; it's available as long as the customer has the machine.

Bobst markets its product/service package actively so that customers know what they will be getting when they buy Bobst. Many companies simply sell a technologically sophisticated machine and assume that that is enough. In the end, they provide some of the same things that Bobst provides, like consulting, transportation, installation and training, because they are obliged to provide them, by their customers or by competitive pressure. Unfortunately, they don't see the value to the customer of offering a good set of auxiliary services – the customer does not get engaged in a 'partnership' and has very little peace of mind.

Customisation: the cases of ABB and Endress & Hauser

The objective of a customisation strategy is to satisfy the demands of more customers by offering a choice of options, one of which meets their particular need.The customisation strategy works equally well for services provided with a product, as for services alone. In the case of services provided with a product, as is true with ABB and Endress & Hauser which are discussed below, the product can be standardised while the service is customised to meet the expectations of different customer groups.

One major issue with a customisation strategy is the degree of customisation. Complete customisation means adapting the service completely to the individual customer's requirements in every case. Some companies make the mistake of customising the entire service, supposing that the more they customise, the happier the customer will be. In most cases, this does not prove to be true. One the one hand, the customer bears the cost of full customisation and, on the other, he must take the time to set parameters for the work to be done. Figure 4.1 gives a good

Figure 4.1

description of a typical customer's demand curve for customisation in terms of price.

Not all aspects of the company's service need to be customised. If the two primary dimensions of a laundry service company's service are the frequency of the pick up and the degree to which the clothes are sorted and treated separately before washing, the company doesn't have to customise on both dimensions. It may be sufficient from the customer's point of view to customise the treatment of clothes; the company then offers standard pick-up times which are the most cost-efficient for its own operations.

The demand curve shows that it is clearly more desirable to the customer (as he is willing to pay more) that the clothes are sorted and treated on a customised basis, than if there were customised pick-up times.

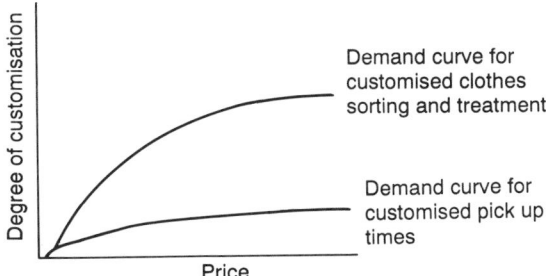

Figure 4.2

ABB Turbochargers

As part of our research, we looked at ABB Turbochargers who have developed a service strategy which focuses on customising their approach to

Step of the process	'Issue'	'Number of people to involve'
Step 1 Purchase decision	1 Production capacity of machine 2 Choice of auxiliaries necessary 3 Adaptability of the existing line to the machine	Plant manager Marketing Director Technical Director
Step 2 Installation preparation	1 Electrical installation necessary 2 Configuration of new production line 3 Adaptation to existing machines	Line Production Manager Plant Manager Technical Director Architect Electrician Public utilities Consultant on production line productivity
Step 3 Installation	1 Transportation 2 Installation of machine 3 Set up of new line configuration 4 Preparation of administrative documents 5 Downtime for installation	Plant Manager Transport company Technical Director Electrician Consultant on production line productivity Customs authorities Personnel Manager
Step 4 'Up and running'	1 Training of staff 2 Optimisation of productivity	Outside training company Plant Manager Consultant on production line productivity Technical Director Line Production Manager
Step 5 Maintenance	1 Downtime 2 Availability of off-site technicians 3 Lack of qualified personnel on-site	Plant Manager Technical Director Line Production Manager Independent maintenance companies Machine producer
Step 6 Parts & service in case of breakdown	1 Down time 2 Lack of parts availability 3 Lack of qualified technicians, on-site or off	Plant Manager Technical Director Line Production Manager Machine producer Independent maintenance companies
Total	19 different problems to be handled	14 different people to coordinate

Table 4.2
Example: non-Bobst purchase

the different needs of their clients, according to the relative importance of speed to each client.

ABB Turbochargers produces turbochargers which are integrated into large engines for ocean-going freighters and train locomotives. The company has an important aspect of its business in after-sales service because of the long life of the products, their technical complexity and the implications for customers when the product isn't working properly. For ABB Turbochargers, a breakdown means that a ship is stopped practically dead in the water: without a functioning turbocharger an engine is reduced to 25 per cent of its capacity.

ABB's clients differ in their requirements for the speediness of repairs and their willingness to support the high cost of an extremely rapid repair. Shipping clients are generally very anxious to have rapid servicing and repairs. Locomotive clients, many of whom are public companies and are more price sensitive, require less speedy assistance.

ABB Turbochargers has a strategy of customisation by speed of response. Up to last year, ABB guaranteed a 48-hour delay; however, that kind of speed is generally expensive. For the client who doesn't require that kind of speed, the 48-hour service is a disadvantage. A 48-hour response is also a great strain on ABB resources if they have to respond to every call in such a manner.

The solution has been to propose three scales of service which correspond to the degree of urgency of the call. For clients for whom even 24 hours seems like a century, ABB has improved its response time. For those who can accept a modest delay of up to a week, ABB has a lower price. Finally, for clients who are prepared to wait for up to a month, ABB has introduced a very low price. In this way, it has customised its service and met the service requirements of a larger percentage of its clients. ABB has also created greater flexibility in its own operations, which will permit it to assure its deadlines with great accuracy.

The major advantage of any customised approach for service is that it blocks out competition by meeting the needs of a wider variety of customers with only slight variations to the original product or service. The case of ABB Turbochargers illustrates the point well. Their original service was 48 hours guaranteed. That service offer only met half-way the expectations of the client who needed immediate assistance and was too expensive for those who didn't need the speed, but who were more price conscious. Those price-conscious clients were probably going to the competition to have their machinery repaired. The new approach, adapted to meet the needs of these customers as well as the less price-conscious ones, will make it more difficult in the future for competitive companies to make inroads into ABB's client base.

Endress & Hauser

Endress & Hauser is another company which has developed a service strategy of customisation. The company was founded in 1953 and first focused on the development and production of level instruments. Subsequently, measurement instruments for throughput, temperature, humidity and pressure were added to the product line, as well as tools to analyse water and gas levels.

Today, the company has over 30 sales companies and production facilities throughout the world, and is an international leader in some of its markets.The company claims that one of the reasons for its success is a good understanding of customer needs. Its clients are typically in the food industry.

The company offers installation assistance to its clients and after-sales service. Such servicing requires the active participation of the technician in the measurement and testing of the chemical mixtures. Chemical companies or those handling the production of Coca Cola, for example, are reluctant to give outsiders information about the exact mixtures in their product.

Water treatment plants, on the other hand, are more than happy to subcontract all of their maintenance work to Endress & Hauser. Based on these differences in their clients and their clients' businesses, Endress & Hauser created distinctly different services approaches.

Whereas ABB Turbochargers' strategy of customisation was based on the degree of service urgency, Endress & Hauser has a customised strategy based on the degree of service implication.

For companies that object to the presence of Endress & Hauser technicians for reasons of secrecy, the company has created a package by which maintenance and repairs are assured but without the imposition of the company on the customer's property; the company's own technicians are trained to perform the work. Endress & Hauser provide extensive training and support on-site or at Endress & Hauser training centres to ensure that their work is up to standard. The training involves a high degree of customer involvement.

For companies that do not want to take on maintenance and repair responsibility, the company has the opposite approach; it takes full charge of the maintenance to be performed on a contract basis, and ensures all repairs and parts supply.

Variations are also possible – in each case the objective being to meet the particular needs of the client for servicing – with, for example, repairs being handled by the company and the client being trained to perform standard maintenance.

Redefine your business to create new opportunities: the case of Europ Assistance

Being in the wooden nail industry doesn't condemn a company to selling wooden nails eternally. Companies can redefine their business to create new opportunities for growth. Europ Assistance did that and successfully expanded their business as a result.

In 1963, Europ Assistance was created to provide rapid, on-site medical aid to French travellers going out of the country. The company's assistance was sold like an insurance policy in that individuals subscribed to Europ Assistance prior to their departure. In the case of an accident or severe medical problem, the subscriber contacts Europ Assistance which arranges for him/her to be transported to a regionally located hospital or clinic for treatment. In some cases, the patient is repatriated.

At the time of its creation, no such service existed in France. The creation of Europ Assistance represented the creation of a new profession – the profession of assistance to travellers by subscription. Because of the way the service is sold it has always been closely identified with the insurance industry. It has not stayed like this over time.

Twenty years later, in 1981, the company redefined its business by creating a new field – assistance to persons in difficulty. The company introduced a range of new products oriented towards the individual at home, including information/advice on legal and administrative matters, assistance in the case of home accidents, damage or repairs and assistance for the elderly including urgent medical care, pet care and child care in the case of an emergency.

Today, the company is again in the process of redefining its business. As the Director of Marketing and Sales puts it, 'In the past, we had the responsibility for providing the assistance; today, instead of being providers, we are organisers – we're evolving towards a pure service function, that of putting the subscriber in contact with reliable suppliers of the assistance they require'.

Europ Assistance has recently introduced Settler, a subsidiary of the company, whose goal is to assist employees sent by their company on foreign assignments, in the process of integration. They help them find housing, enroll their children in school, meet the country's administration requirements etc. The new company fits the new definition of Europ Assistance's business and takes advantage of one of the company's greatest strengths – its international network of contacts.

To identify new opportunities, Europ Assistance started by looking at its service strengths. In 1981, the service they provided best was fast access to help. Such a service didn't have to be limited to medical or transportation assistance and, thus, the company created a range of home services.

In 1990, the company considerably expanded its network overseas. It still provided fast access to help, but had become more an intermediary than a provider. It thus created Settler, which takes advantage of the international network and is a pure service provider.

In terms of competition, Europ Assistance has, at once, very many and very few competitors. Very many, because the company provides a wide range of services which are provided elsewhere either by individuals (independent plumbers, electricians etc.) or by companies (hospitals, towing companies, insurance companies, specialists). Very few, because no one company provides the range of services Europ Assistance provides with the same expertise.

Make a customer, not a sale: the case of Ciba-Geigy

Ciba-Geigy recently took on a service strategy which focuses on the creation of 'partnership' relationships with customers. The decision to pursue such a strategy came out of the results of a thorough study and analysis of customer expectations. The study showed that a certain segment of customers were very interested in receiving a range of support services. The focus of their interest was on greater co-operation and communication in the area of product applications technology which implied increasing ties between the two co-operating companies.

Based on this study, the partnership strategy was developed. It is an attempt to create a durable, long-term relationship with a target segment of the market. For the most part, the segment represents companies which are technically sophisticated and which, in terms of product and service quality, are in the upper range in their own markets.

Under the partnership relationship, Ciba-Geigy and its customer would co-operate closely on product development and on product application. The partnership company would also obtain certain advantages, such as quicker delivery times or access to certain market information, which other, less regular, clients would not receive. The partnership relationship implies a certain degree of dependence on another. As the Director of Marketing puts it:

'Not every company is prepared to accept a degree of dependence on one of its suppliers, and the reverse, of course, also applies. Because, although for the customer, partnership does not mean that from now on he deals with one supplier only, most of his business will none the less go to the chosen partner. Our resources – and here I would purposely foremost mention human resources – are not unlimited, and have to be shared carefully and systematically among the partners who promise the greatest return in the long term. So we have to be selective.'

Selectivity is one of the characteristics of a partnership strategy; dependence is another. For the latter, we can draw comparisons between Ciba-Geigy's partnership strategy and the supplier/client relationship practised by the Japanese, in which the supplier is highly dependent upon the client company for its business.

A partnership strategy can give strong advantages to both parties. Closer co-operation means more effective communication. It also means less time lost at the development stage because customers will be actively involved in determining what is being created for their use. It also minimises the risk of misunderstanding, and increases trust and moves the two companies closer to a true 'win-win' situation.

For companies with the profile of Ciba-Geigy, it is an excellent option. Ciba-Geigy is in a mature market. Competition based on innovations or on cost is becoming more difficult and less desirable. And the company does not wish to expand its operations to the point where it can meet the demands of the entire market, because the market is no longer growing significantly.

Moreover, Ciba-Geigy has positioned itself as a top-quality supplier. Because it operates in a mature market, there is a growing section of the market that prefers quality to price. The 'extras' which Ciba-Geigy supplies are attractive to this market segment. The partnership strategy, which by its nature is a focused strategy, permits the company to make the most of its resources with the customers which will appreciate them the most. At the same time, Ciba-Geigy makes life difficult for the competition into the segment it serves by meeting these customers' expectations as completely and thoroughly as possible.

Once a company has embarked on a partnership strategy, the key to its success is the continual creation of linkages. A linkage is an activity or a service by the company to the customer which draws these two parties' interests more closely together. The closer the linkages, the more parallel the interests of the company and its client are likely to be and the more solid the relationship will become.

Below is a simple graph which visualises the concept of linkages – the more linkages there are, the closer the two companies get to achieving a 100 per cent 'win-win' situation. A 100 per cent win-win situation occurs when neither side perceives any disadvantage to the relationship, i.e. both sides win all around.

Ciba-Geigy is creating linkages through its joint development efforts, through its sharing of market know-how, through its assistance in product adaptation etc. Using the same conceptual graph, we can plot some of major linkages that Ciba-Geigy is making with its customers.

Perhaps the best method the company is using to create linkages is its non-product-specific differentiation programme. In just one booklet, the company presents to its employees over 70 linkages which it can create with customers. The use of each one of these 'services for differentiation' can increase communication between the company and the customer, create

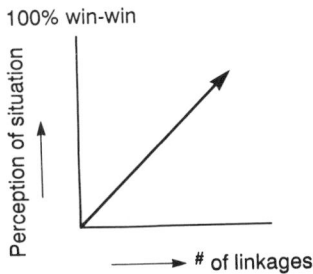

Figure 4.3

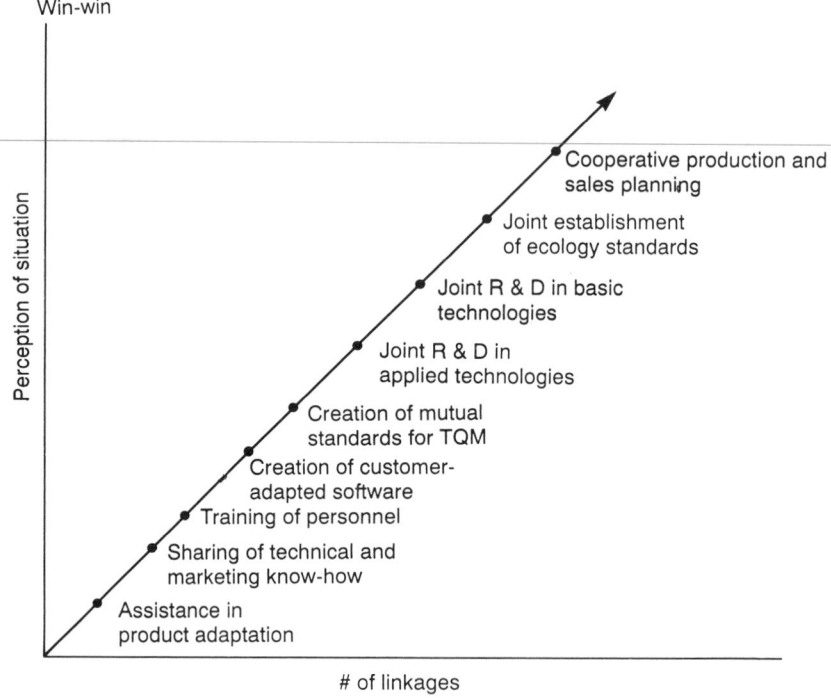

Figure 4.4

common ground for co-operation, and increase each one's understanding of the other's business and objectives for the future. The continued promulgation of these kinds of linkages will bring the company and customer as close as they can get to a long-term 'win-win' situation.

Keeping your customer after he's signed on the dotted line: the case of Quelle

Quelle is Germany's largest mail order house as well as the largest in Europe. It is a household name to most German consumers and sells a complete variety of products from clothing to household goods, to white and brown goods. Customers purchasing its products on a regular basis come from primarily low and middle-income families.

Quelle cares about the service it provides its customers both before *and* *after* the sale, and as a result, Quelle's management has been able to use its after-sales service as a point of strategic differentiation for the company.

Generally, in the mail order business, once a product is sold and delivered, the contact with the customer ceases. The customer is recorded in the company's very large and important database, is coded to receive a catalogue once, twice or more times per year, and is not heard from again until the next purchase is made.

The exception occurs when the customer has a problem with his product, particularly a problem with a mechanical product. Few mail order houses have taken the time and effort to prepare themselves for such event; yet, the ability to assist the customer rapidly and efficiently when he has a problem is one of the best ways to gain that customer's loyalty for the future.

Quelle is prepared to assist its customer with after-sales service problems. Quelle has 67 decentralised service centres located throughout Germany. These centres are not run as a cost centre depending upon the profits of other divisions within Quelle, but as profit centres in their own right.

Each service centre is run under the relatively autonomous leadership of its managers who can operate practically as an entrepreneur. The ultimate objective for these centres is to become an after-sales service centre for all white and brown goods, and not just for those goods sold through Quelle's mail order operations. 'The after-sales service operation represents a marketing tool for Quelle; it is to be run as a profit-making profit centre,' says Mr Beckmann who heads up Quelle's after-sales service.

Quelle's after-sales service policy is to provide a repair service as near to the customer as possible. That means in his home for all white goods and for 50 per cent of brown goods. Smaller items – radios, hair-dryers etc. – are often brought spontaneously to the service centre by the customer. The idea is to cause the customer as little disruption as possible.

Quelle also adjusts its service according to the customer and the urgency of the repair. Repairs of washing machines for families with children receive priority over other repairs. Customers expressing an urgent need receive top priority. During major televised events (Olympics, football matches etc.), Quelle prepares special top-speed service to repair televisions the same evening.

The first contact with Quelle's after-sales service generally occurs over the phone. Management considers this to be a vital moment in the relationship with the customer. All of Quelle's service staff are therefore trained on how to deal with customers over the phone. They are also trained to do a first diagnosis over the phone. This permits them to evaluate the gravity of the problem and to bring the appropriate tools and parts with them to the customer's home. Quelle believes that good service means that the repairman comes once and only once. As such, one of its most important internal indicators is the percentage of calls on which the repair was done on the first visit.

Service technicians are not just trained to perform good repair at Quelle; they are also trained on how to behave with customers. For Quelle, its repairmen are the 'ambassadors of the company' and it is important that they know how to deal with difficult situations. No new employee is ever put in contact with a customer before at least 10 days of training have been completed. Over the period of the first year, a repairman receives in excess of one month of training, of which roughly half represents training in dealing with customers. A repairman is not considered to be prepared to work alone before six to nine months. Before that time, he makes customer visits in the company of a more experienced technician. 'When a customer calls us, he has a problem; top service is absolutely necessary in order to satisfy their expectations', says Mr Beckmann.

Quelle managers are not the only ones motivated to keep customers happy with the service they provide. Both managers and service technicians are paid on the basis of fixed salaries with large bonuses according to the level of customer satisfaction, the number of complaints and the sales for their unit. Both complaints and satisfaction are measured on a regular basis. Overall, Quelle's customers are very satisfied and 96 per cent would recommend Quelle's after-sales service to others.

How to develop a strategy

In this section we will look at how to develop a strategy that fosters good customer service, while making it the most profitable for the company. In our experience and through our observations, it seems that three ingredients contribute to a successful service strategy: redefining the business to think in terms of customer benefits; identifying service dimensions to position the company as a leader; and reducing costs while increasing service and segmenting according to service.

Think of your business in terms of customer benefits rather than in terms of products or technology

It is a illuminating exercise to ask all divisions, strategic business units and top management to redefine their business only in terms of customer benefit, and not in terms of the product or technology. Are you in the air-filter business or in the clean air business (Danfoss in Denmark); are you in the ball-bearing business or in the hassle-free operations business (SKF of Sweden). Are you in the leasing business or in the technological flexibility business (NMB Bank of Holland)? Are you in the hotel business or in the 'wonderful experience' business (Hyatt USA), are you in tourism or in the holiday business. Are you in the holiday business or in the happiness business (Club Med, France)? Are you in the delicatessen business or in the last minute solution business (Deli in Phoenix, Arizona)? . . . The more you express your business in terms of customer benefits, the more it will enlarge the vision with which you do business. Selling filters is selling hardware and replacements. Selling clean air is selling maintenance contracts. It gives a different way to compete, and better long-term relationships with the customer.

In addition to enlarging the vision of your business, speaking in terms of customer benefits forces you to add value to existing products, services or technologies. As a bank, thinking of yourself as being in the 'technological flexibility business' might lead you to create a second-hand market for the exchange of out-dated equipment.

How does a company go about redefining its business in terms of benefits? Here are a few hints.

- Identify how your product or service competes in the mind-set of your customer. With what does he compare it? When he spends time with you what does he give up? What alternatives does he have? Toyota has understood very well that buying a car takes up their customers' leisure time. This is why their showroom in Tokyo looks like a complete recreation park or leisure complex (restaurants, shows, shops, 3Ds, computer-assisted car design for the freaks etc.).
- In a completely different domain – Tectronics, a major components company identified that its customers were industrial buyers. Those buyers had two critera: price and no hassle for users. The company has devised software that will help the buyers evaluate not just the price of buying but the total carrying costs, so they can compare buying from them or from their competitors (total cost includes price plus inventory cost, description costs, return cost, quality control costs . . .). By enlarging the criteria, they set themselves apart. They used the mind-set of the buyer to give themselves an advantage.
- A second useful way to rethink one's business in terms of customer benefits is to use analogies. If you describe in key terms what a garage does in terms of after-sales service and what the customer wants out of it you will very quickly come to the conclusion that it is like McDonalds: fast service, low cost, you do not want to go twice for the same problem, you want to talk to the mechanic. It has been used on a pilot basis by Ford ('McFords') to serve its customers better: small, efficient operations; the stake is high. When a customer is satisfied with after-sales service in the automobile industry, its brand loyalty is increased by 60 per cent. In addition, dealers are becoming multibranded. So if the manufacturer does not keep a foot in the service door, he will have as little power as food manufacturers have *vis-à-vis* hypermarket chains!
- A third way is to think in terms of know-how rather than in terms of product. What is the relationship between one-hour spectacles and one-hour photo development? Optics and photos are two different businesses? Are they? The same know-how applies: it consists of knowing how to select high-density traffic spots in shopping malls, buying the latest technology to be cost-efficient, speedy and high quality, managing highly decentralised units of 5 to 10 people. That was the reflection of the GPS Group (France), which in 10 years grew to 120 photo stores and in 2 years 24 optical stores! Think of what could be your next move with the same know-how in mind.

Identify service dimensions to position yourself as a leader

There are two main ways to differentiate today. The are price or service. In today's business world the rate of innovation and new product development is fast. But the rate of imitation is also fast and leaves less and less scope for innovative companies to be innovative. Product quality is assumed to be a differentiating factor but is not necessarily so. Customers will be unaware of manufacturers experiencing manufacturing/design problems, and will assume the quality of a product is good. However, good product quality can only help to keep you in the market, it will not make you different in any way. The third way, image, is becoming less and less a differentiating factor if the image does not relate to the reality of good products and service. The 1990s are seeing a return to simplicity and truthfulness in advertising. Those who oversell and raise their promise above what they can deliver won't make it. The best example is the Lexus car in the US: one-thrid cheaper than Mercedes and BMW, which have a high brand image, but with equal features and better quality, and sell like hotcakes. All this is doen without the image-making that was necessary in the 1970s and 80s, which sold cars on dreams.

If we take service and price, a company has more chances to be a leader in service than on price for a simple reason: service has several dimensions. One can be leader in one or two key elements. With price there is only one element. You are number one or you are not a leader. We call it the Christopher Columbus syndrome. If we ask you who was the first person to discover America, you will answer immediately. If we ask you who was the second, you have difficulty. The same goes with differentiation through price. Nobody remembers the second one!

That's positioning!

How to select the one, two or three key service dimensions on which to compete and become the leader requires a careful analysis of all contact points with the customer ('customer contact analysis'). For each point you need to make an analysis of what you do right or wrong, compared with what customers want, need and expect: what competitors do and don't do; and your own intuition of what would please customers most.

Let's take the case of an insurance company. The main contacts with such a company are when a customer buys and when he has a claim. Most insurance companies try to be nice when you buy, but never try to be nice, efficient and hassle-free when you claim. Within the buying segment, you can also be leader in risk diagnosis (very few companies will do an annual assessment of what you have, don't have, how well protected you are and remind you of it), or in salesman contact and speed. Regarding claims you can be the leader in speed, hassle-free, value-added (legal help, transition help in case of a loss in the family) or no questions asked . . . I have yet to see such a claim in advertising of insurance cost! As you see, positioning through service offers a wealth of opportunity. It is not just true for the service sector. It also works in the industrial field. Thus, an international chemical company made all its differentiation by selling with cross-functional teams. 'We build our relationships with you to prevent any mistakes from day one.' To sell to a customer, the salesman, logistics manager, production manager, quality manager, administrative and billing go together to make sure everything is discussed before. Not after.

In selecting the key service dimensions on which to compete and try to become leader, be careful not to apply the same dimensions when changing customer targets. The Ikea case illustrates this. Their leadership in the consumer market – its first customer target segment – is based on immediate delivery, easy access to goods in the store, stores with lots of space and activities for families. When, however, they attacked the office furniture market – their second customer target segment – none of the above held true except price. Office managers do not come to the stores, they want their furniture to be delivered. They are buying pieces of furniture and not parts of furniture. How can you receive furniture in an office and sign off that everything is in order when the receipt describes legs and arms rather than chairs and tables! Subcontract shipping, which is not well received since the shipper rarely has the same quality that IKEA offers. And finally, how can a business take advantage of the IKEA return policy (100 per cent exchange or reimbursement; but 70 per cent only if it is not in its package), since the first thing you ask the shipper to do is to get rid of the package for you!

Reduce costs of operation while increasing service

The true challenge for most companies is to be able to be service leaders while keeping their costs down or ever be cost leaders (outpacing), as shown below (Fig. 4.5).

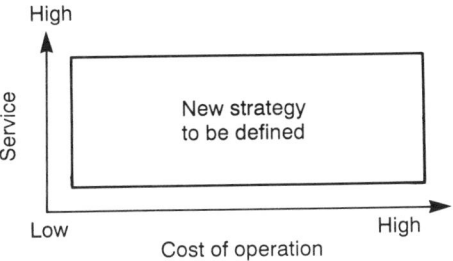

Figure 4.5

Unfortunately, in most cases cost reduction leads to service reduction rather than enhancement. The reason is simple, it is easier to reduce service costs rather than decrease central staff or structure.

Since service economies of scale are often minimal, one of the keys to successful cost reduction, as exemplified by IKEA, is analysis of the value-added chain: what are the elements we add to make a complete product or service and how can we reduce costs while keeping service high? The second key is perceived value. How can we reduce cost while not increasing perceived value by the customer? If perception moves upward and costs decrease, the customer will feel he has the best value for money. The company will get the best profitability, and/or be ready for price wars.

This reasoning – how can cost reduction protect or even enhance perceived value – has to become a reflex action for all managers within the company. Table 4.3 gives some widely used devices.

Unfortunately, in cases using the cost reductions we have just described the perceived value of the service is often reduced. For instance, French banks' ATM machines only permit 3000 francs to be distributed every 7 days. French Telecom's beautifully named 'pastel' card cannot be used abroad unless you have a special code number, which must be kept separate from the card; the number on the card serves no purpose.

Segment your market according to service

The year ahead of us will not be the year of striving for customer satisfaction, but the year of customers' satisfaction. Within each market the company tries to reach there are different segments. All of these have common core needs and expectations, but the most successful company is one which will be able to cater to each segment and at the same time keep a good core service. Two factors are necessary in order to be service oriented as well as segment specific: identify the segments and recognise who belongs to what in the service delivery process.

Identify the segments. Segmentation is model building. Model building is simplification of reality which is used in order to make decisions. Marketing segmentation is usually done to decide on price, product, place, promotion and objectives. A marketing model may not fit service decisions. For example, which dimensions should I use to emphasise within the same market to be as close as possible to customers?

We will take an example. In studying airport bars and restaurant service in Europe, we asked management to identify for us which segments they catered for so we could interview customers. Four were listed: businessmen; tourists; groups; employees of the airport. This segmentation made sense from a product, price or promotion standpoint (light meals for businessmen, special direct marketing effort for groups, price specials for local employees . . .), but from a service viewpoint we found that everybody had a common need: the bars or restaurants have to be a place for relaxation (busy place, fear of missing the plane, loudness of airports . . .). Besides this, there were two segments, whatever the length of stay or the price or type of menu (bar versus self-service versus Maxim's type): people in a hurry and people not in

Cost reduction device	Higher perceived value
home (rather than distribution centre)	repairman closer to customer
dispatching (used for installation and repair of system)	increased speed of intervention
remote service (hot-line)	immediate access – one call does it all expertise reassurance
self-service	speed – convenience – personaliza-tion – help to choose
packaging of service (such as insurance investments, maintenance contracts . . .)	adapted to needs; easy to choose from
automated transaction (just in time automatic reorder system . . .)	information sharing; flexibility; risk reduction (tell me when you come!)

Table 4.3

a hurry. Satisfaction meant recognising those two segments and catering to each.

As another example, with garages you have two segments: the car lover and the utilitarian. Good service, besides doing a reasonably priced complete repair on time, means for the car lover to talk about his car, show signs that you did something special to the car (such as cleaning the wheels when you check the brakes), even inviting the customer to watch, proposing to give the customer the old parts to show it was really changed . . . For the utilitarian, good service means taking the car (when it breaks down), bringing it back with no question asked . . . and building a relationship with the driver rather than speaking about the car!

As nice as it is to identify segments, this is not enough to provide good service. What is needed is a way to identify which customer belongs to what segment so that the salespeople and administrative or production staff, adapt their style, behaviour or environment to each segment.

Type of identification / Type of encounters	Self	By company
Transactional		
Interactional		
Environmental		

Figure 4.6

There are three types of adaptation which are needed. Adaptation has to be made for each type of encounter between the customer and the company in all functions: transactions encounters (I order, you deliver); interaction encounters (I have problems, you help me); environmental encounters (I come to reception – it is clean and warm). And there are two main ways in which a customer can be identified as belonging to one segment or another: self, or the company (see Fig. 4.6).

In our previous examples a garage can recognise the car lover by the fact that his car is usually clean and he only comes to the garage when his maintenance book says that a check-up is necessary. In the airport, a restaurant can have 'express' menus or dishes which will probably be chosen by those who are in a hurry. Thus, the table would look like this (see Fig. 4.7 we have only done it for one segment – test yourself by doing it for the other).

Bars and restaurants for the person in a hurry

Bars and restaurants for the person in a hurry

Type of iden-tification / Type of encounters	Self	By company
Transaction	Express dish	Bill brought with coffee
Interaction		Don't worry you still have 10 min
Environment		The fast-service bar is located on the 2nd floor

Figure 4.7

And the garage might look like this.

Garage for the utilitarian

Garage for the utilitarian

Type of iden- tification Type of encounters	Self	By company
Transactional		Dirty car Bring car back
Interactional		'How is business'...
Environmental		

Figure 4.8

5 TAKING
ADVANTAGE OF
TECHNOLOGY

Introduction

Information technology (IT) has long been a tool used in product development to gain a competitive advantage; now it is being ever more effectively applied in service conception and delivery.

There are two principal ways in which technology is used to bring value-added to services:

1　gathering and structuring information to put it at the service of customers;
2　gaining efficiency and speed in transactions.

Either one or both methods can be used. In most cases, they are combined.

The following are examples which illustrate both uses of IT to create value-added service for the customer. The cases of Robeco, Colirail and Lombard Odier show principally how information is put at the service of customers; the cases of Anacomp, Convent and Galenica show principally how information technology is used to increase efficiency.

Using information technology

Personalising with technology; the case of Lombard Odier

The blame for the move away from personalised service towards more automised service is often attributed to the expanded use of IT. Detractors claim that because companies want to reduce costs, they eliminate the human element and replace it with a machine. The classic example is the automated teller machine; the customer no longer carries on a discourse with a flesh-and-blood individual, but rather with a push-button machine. Besides not being programmed to smile, the machine is rather limited in its repertoire and is totally incapable of dealing with the unusual or exceptional.

We were pleased to find a case to the contrary, where the use of IT has markedly increased a company's ability to personalise its service. The case in point is Lombard Odier & Cie, one of the top Swiss private banking institutions and a leader in its industry in the use of IT.

Lombard Odier began introducing IT into its business in the 1950s; it was originally introduced in order to improve internal bank efficiency, particularly in the execution of financial transactions. Very quickly, however, it became apparent that the new technologies could be applied in different ways throughout the bank. In the early 1980s, the company embarked on a programme of development to create one unified system which would be at the service of the portfolio managers for all of their needs. The software was developed in-house to run on the company's network of over 600 Digital Equipment terminals and printers.

The result is a 'unique work tool', highly appreciated by staff, managers and customers alike. It is an on-line, multiple access system connected to a database following over 12,000 instruments daily. It is highly user-friendly, is up-dated daily and has a message system incorporated. Every portfolio manager has access to the accounts of his clients only, which guarantees privacy. With the numerous programs incorporated into the system, the portfolio manager can test rapidly different financial scenarios. He can also have access to a large range of general financial information on market movements and conditions through the same system. 'As a work tool and a support for decision-making, it's extraordinary!'

Lombard Odier is in the business of investment management for private individuals and institutions. Historically, a large percentage of their clients have been wealthy families that needed a safe and politically stable place to invest their fortune. More recently, the Bank has expanded its client base to include institutions which are less attracted by the security of the investment and more attracted by the fact that Lombard Odier are specialists in asset management. For both client groups, individual and institutional, the personalisation of the service remains an important factor in their choice of Lombard Odier.

There are two ways that service is personalised at Lombard Odier. The first is in the structuring of the portfolio. Each customer's portfolio is composed individually by the portfolio manager; no two portfolios are exactly alike. This is in contrast to the practice at some other institutions where the client's money is placed into a pool with that of other investors and is invested in a set selection of shares – the same way as is done with a mutual fund. The second way in which the service is personalised is in the handling of the relationship. The way the information is presented to the customer, the quality of the contact and the nature of the relationship all reflect a concern for treating each customer as an individual.

The company's IT system is a strong tool, aiding the company to offer a highly personalised service. The system permits the portfolio manager individually to choose the securities to be included in the portfolio and to follow the evolution of each security, as well as the portfolio as a whole. Should the portfolio analyst be asked to explain its performance, he has at his immediate disposal all the information he needs to respond to the customer's questions on the spot. 'If, for example, we receive a call from a client asking us to explain performance on his portfolio, we can immediately identify each security that is pulling the portfolio up or down and try to analyse whether it is temporary or permanent.'

He can also compare performance on his customer's portfolio with data about movements in the market place and can find out, on a daily basis, the performance of the portfolio, as compared with a certain benchmark. 'The system is a source of information: I can pull out analyses of performance over different periods in real terms or relative terms.'

To make the information more readily understandable to the customer, the system can present it in a number of different graphic forms. There are a total of 19 different display options. 'There are some ways of presenting information that will be comprehensible to some clients and totally incomprehensible to others.' The portfolio analyst can immediately adjust the presentation according to the customer and his own personal way of understanding financial information.

The system also allows the bank to personalise its approach in terms of the way information is presented to the customer. The same reporting formats which are used to explain financial information to customers at the bank are available for the communication of monthly, quarterly or yearly results on the portfolio. The customer can choose the information he would like to have communicated and how it is to be communicated.

Lombard Odier's information system also allows portfolio managers to be more personal in their relationship with the customer. Following each customer contact a report on that contact is written up by the portfolio manager and recorded in the customer's file. At any moment, a manager in the same team can access that report (and others made before it), to gain information on the customer and the development of the relationship. Managers make a point of recording not only financial information, but also some personal data which would be necessary to someone else who might have to follow up on the relationship in the portfolio manager's absence.

In general, the information system permits managers to focus on their relationship with the customer and not on the explanation of financial details. Every meeting room has a terminal. The customer and the portfolio manager can carry on a conversation with the terminal serving as a support tool. Rather than shuffling through his papers, the portfolio manager calls up the information he needs on the computer rapidly. Its accuracy, the variety of presentations available and the immediacy of the information, relieves the portfolio manager of tedious calculations on paper or long explanations, and allows him to listen more attentively and more carefully to what the customer is saying. 'We are very transparent in our relationship with customers. It's one of the reasons that we are very much appreciated.'

The system also allows portfolio managers to be more efficient. 'The system permits us to have a better quality of analysis and an immediate correction of errors if they occur. . . . The quantity of information is such today that a broker can, within certain limits, sell just about anything. With this system, we are in a position to take the right decisions.'

Efficiency is also improved through better internal co-ordination and communication. The customer file, accessible to members of the team, permits better co-ordination within each unit. Throughout the bank, communication is enhanced through the continual use of the message system. Lombard Odier's head office recently split into two separate locations. A large part of the bank's support services were moved to a new building on the outskirts of Geneva. The client reception activities remained in the traditional building in the centre of the city. The message system permits the different departments to communicate rapidly and efficiently amongst one another.

Last, but not least, the information system represents, for the company, a differential advantage which the company has *vis-à-vis* its competitors and which can be presented as such to prospective customers. Besides all the advantages the system offers to its users, which can be explained to customers as yielding benefits for them, the system makes money management more real.

When selling the bank to potential new customers, portfolio managers use the system to make the services provided by the bank more tangible. The portfolio manager can show the customer a mock portfolio on the screen and demonstrate how the company would manage those funds. It makes a very intangible service – the management of money – more solid.

Making information useful to customers; the case of Colirail

In many companies, information is a dead thing. They are data that are recorded and shifted from one filing unit to another. Only very seldom is the time taken to organise the information to be used by managers or other employees. Even less seldom is information put at the disposal of customers.

Our research identified two companies that do use information technology to organise and present information to customers – Colirail and Robeco (we will look at Robeco below). In these companies, information is not only made available to customers, it is also presented in ways that make it both useful and understandable.

Colirail is a French company providing rapid delivery services of packages under 30 kilos to all parts of France; it's the Federal Express of the French Republic. Its customers are primarily high-technology companies or medical suppliers that need to have packages of parts or medicine delivered urgently to other divisions or to their customers.

Colirail noticed some time ago that it had a credibility problem; customers didn't seem to believe that the package would arrive at its destination on time, despite all the company's promises and its excellent rate of reliability. They wanted to be told that it had actually arrived.

It wasn't that customers didn't have faith in the company. The problem was of a more psychological origin: customers needed to be reassured. As many of the packages were destined to be delivered to customers of Colirail's customers, it wasn't only Colirail's reputation that was at stake, but also the reputation of their customer. The client that used Colirail, then, liked to know that the package had indeed arrived at its destination. So, to meet this very real and important customer expectation, Colirail developed, as a part of its package tracking system, a way to put information on the status of the package at the disposal of the customer.

From the moment that the package is picked up from the customer to the moment that it is delivered to its destination, the package is followed using an electronic reading system that monitors the presence of the package at each stage of its journey. The information on the package's location is recorded on the company's central computer system, where it can be accessed at any moment by staff.

The objective, however, is not to provide the customer with information on the path which the package takes to get to its destination. The customer couldn't care less whether the package passes by the North or South Pole, as long at it arrives where it is going on time. So, travel route information remains in-house. Colirail communicates just the essentials to customers – to whom the package was delivered and at exactly what time.

The company doesn't, however, telephone each customer personally to tell him that his package has arrived. With over 7500 packages a day, 97 per cent of which arrive between 8 a.m. and 9 a.m., such a service is neither practical nor desirable. The company adopted an alternative and more efficient approach: each customer can connect to the Minitel machine and find the information he needs.

Minitel is the French telecommunications video system which permits the general public to be connected to a large variety of information providers, just by a click of the keyboard. Colirail customers can connect into the Minitel using the code given to them by the company when they sent the package. They connect directly to the file with information on their package by using the delivery reference number. By 10.45 a.m. every morning, information is available to the customer on whether his package reached its destination or not. The person who signed for the package is shown on the file. If there is ever any problem, it is indicated, i.e. intemperate weather; delivery delayed by one hour.

This information isn't only available on Minitel. Colirail can also arrange to have the information transferred directly on to the customer's own information system, if he prefers.

Once having recognised the importance which access to certain information represents for the customer, Colirail did not hesitate to package other information and offer it as a value-added service to the customer. For example, one service that has been well received is the provision of information concerning all of the transactions made by the customer during the year.

The information is presented by destination, by time or by type of delivery service (the company has five different services) and is used by customers to monitor deliveries to certain destinations. It is provided free of charge. The information can, for example, be used to make a price comparison between sending spare parts by delivery service, with the cost of maintaining an on-site warehouse facility.

Collecting and packaging information for the benefit of the customer: the case of Robeco Group

The Robeco Group is a Dutch company which sells participations in a variety of mutual funds. Its value-added as compared with other mutual fund management companies is that, in addition, it provides a telephone-based information and consultancy service to its customers. Its customers are frequently small investors who do not have the large amounts of capital that, in the eyes of investment managers, merit particular attention. At Robeco, that extra attention is available by telephone.

Opening an account at Robeco gives a customer access to Robeco's customer service department. The department was conceived as a support unit to customers to answer whatever questions they might have about their account. It is necessary because participation in the mutual funds are sold and customers have no face-to-face contact with the company.

The customer service department is, today, a full-fledged investment advisory service. Customers can call in between the hours of 8 a.m. and 9 p.m. They are received by any one of a number of qualified investment advisers on duty. Using his own dedicated terminal, the investment adviser has immediate access to all information on the customer's account, including the type of investment he has chosen and the growth of those investments over the last three years.

The investment adviser is also equipped to provide full information on each of the company's different investment funds. The return to date, the return over the last year, the selection of shares into which the fund has invested and other similar data are immediately available to the adviser from his terminal and to the customer by telephone.

Information on market developments and stock indices can also be brought on to the screen and used to respond to the wide variety of customer questions. 'The customer can ask us all kinds of questions . . . "Should I sell my stocks; what happened on Wall Street today?" '

Investment advisers are trained to respond not just by repeating the information, but also by interpreting the information for the customer. A customer might ask, 'What implications does the end of the Gulf War have on my investments?' or 'I heard that the property market in London has experienced a fall in prices of nearly 20 per cent; what effect will that have on the Rodamco fund?'. Investment advisers are not entirely left on their own to respond to these kinds of questions. Their training permits them to know what kind of information is needed to answer the question; the computer system then gives it to them.

The investment adviser responding to the question about London housing will, for example, first look for information about the Rodamco fund; there he might find a full list of items impacting the fund and their estimated degree of impact; he will also find what percentage of the entire portfolio is invested in the London market. He will then look under another subject heading concerning the property market in London to find forecasts concerning the direction it is expected to take in the short and long term. Putting the two together, he will then be able to respond to the question.

The company has developed an expert system which permits the investment advisers to be even more efficient when it comes to responding to these kinds of questions. It will increase both the accuracy and consistency of the responses. 'The expert system is for us to give better advice, quicker advice, but the customer will not notice there is an expert assisting the investment advisors. He will just see that he is getting better service.'

With over 350,000 telephone calls coming into each of the company's offices every year, Robeco is already very efficient at providing good service rapidly. Some of these telephone calls must be responded to in writing. The computer helps there too. The investment adviser prepares the letter to the customer. It is immediately registered in his file and transferred by computer with the name and address already on it to the documents department where the necessary documents are stored. The appropriate documents are attached to the now printed-out letter, put in an envelope and popped into the mail. The entire process is accomplished in less than a day.

For the customer who is used to being ignored or forgotten by investment managers, Robeco's service is a welcome change. Because it is by telephone, it provides the additional advantage of being more easily accessible. The customer doesn't have to skip work to keep an appointment with an investment manager who doesn't really care to meet with him, nor does he have to 'go into their offices' simply to make a transfer of his investments from one fund to another. Because the information is interpreted by the investment adviser, he is getting as much advice as he would ever get from an investment manager. He can also call as many times as he wishes and never feel that he is abusing of the information service – Robeco is there for that.

Knowing customers better; the case of Anacomp

In practically every service activity, customers want to be known and recognised. They don't want to be a number or just another nameless face. There are hundreds of ways to show a customer that he is known: call him by his name, refer to something he said on his last visit, compliment him on his suit etc.

In a business-to-business relationship, customers expect more than individual recognition, they also expect their supplier to have a general understanding of their company's business and a recognition of its recurring problems. And the more complex the relationship and the more people who are responsible for handling the relationship, the harder it becomes to show customers that they are known and appreciated by the company. When it's not one-on-one, but 20, 30 or more different people between 2 companies or when the contact is irregular or infrequent, there is no longer a personal reference point. In such cases, IT technology can really help. It makes the process of information gathering and information sharing as efficient as it can be.

Anacomp is a company manufacturing, selling equipment and COM service for the transfer of information to microfilm. A small percentage of its contacts with customers occurs at the time of sale; a much greater percentage occurs once the customer has the machine up and running. After-sales at Anacomp is provided either under a maintenance contract or in the case of a machine breakdown.

Contacts between the customer and the after-sales staff are fairly infrequent or irregular – generally not more than once a month. In order to provide efficient service and to 'recognise' the customer, Anacomp's staff must be well-briefed on the company before they respond to a call or go on a maintenance visit.

For some time, Anacomp's German and Austrian subsidiary has been gathering information on its customers in its central database. Anacomp's files on its customers are very complete. The sales engineer can have at his fingertips the customer's history, information on the type of machine the customer has, the spare parts he should bring with him, the problems the customers has had previously with the machine, the date of the last service call, the names of the individuals who serviced the company last, the name of the service engineer responsible for the account (if it is not himself), the individuals to contact within the company and any other precise data which would better equip him for his visit.

The delay, however, between the time that the service engineer or salesman submitted his visit report and the report was entered into the computer, was much too long for the information to be used fully. A customer who had a problem on day one and called back with the same problem on day three, for example, would be obliged to explain to the engineer what happened two days earlier.

There were also problems with the availability of spare parts. Part 'X' was no longer in stock because there was no way of knowing that the part had been used in repairs five times the week before and thus it hadn't been reordered quickly enough.

In 1987, Anacomp found a solution to this. They equipped all of their service engineers with Toshiba T1100 laptop portable computers. The Toshiba is programmed to stock entire customer files from the central databank and to record the reports of the visits of the service engineer carrying the computer during a given day. In addition, it records expense account information and spare parts usage.

At the end of every day, the entire set of information added during the day on each service engineer's computer is transferred by telephone connection via modem to the main computer which updates the files during the night. The next morning, the portable computers are updated with all the information from the previous day. Spare parts stock replacements are automatically ordered and the bills are automatically sent by the main computer.

Because customer data is transportable, the service engineer can study the data on his customer anywhere – in the car, in a restaurant, in the park etc. No matter how far away from home the engineer finds himself, nor how unexpected the service call, he has immediate access to information on the customer.

From the customer's perspective, he is known and recognised. The service engineer knows the history of the two company's relationship; he knows the machine and its problems, and he knows his customers by name. Because he is better informed, he is in a better position to know what might be wrong with the machine. He comes prepared with the right spare parts – not those for another model, for instance. He also knows who to ask about what while he is there. With the operating technician, whose name is probably noted in the file, he can discuss maintenance issues; with the technological manager, he can discuss the advantages of a maintenance contract etc. Overall, the service engineer is more relaxed and efficient with the appropriate knowledge in hand to do his job.

Packaging flexibility; the case of Convent

Most companies don't give their customers very many service options; i.e. you can either have the hotdog with mustard or without. Generally, a lack of options reflects the rigidity of the company's logistics system and a slow feedback from the frontline.

At Convent, a producer/distributor of snack foods, the use of IT and a highly efficient logistics system permits the company to respond rapidly to changes in end-customer demands. Low stock levels are maintained because reliable sales figures are rapidly available from the frontline. High standards for product freshness are maintained because the stocks in the store are monitored very frequently.

Convent is Germany's leading producer of crisps and salted snacks. It has a 35 per cent market share which has grown regularly since the company was created in 1972. Customers number over 30,000 a year and represent a wide cross-section of the buying public. Convent's products are sold under two brand names, Funny Frisch and Chio, for which the company has two parallel sales distribution networks. Intermediary customers include a range of supermarkets, hypermarkets, corner shops, petrol stations, kiosks etc. In its relations with its intermediary customers, Convent's objective is to obtain the greatest amount of shelf space in the store and to achieve the highest amount of sales possible from that space. To do that it relies upon the advantages of its service strategy.

The company's service strategy is based upon its *fischdienst* system, meaning freshness service. In short, the *'frischdienst'* service is the direct delivery of products from the factory to the shops. This is done by the salesman who is also responsible for handling the customer relationship. He visits the store on a very regular basis, depending on the store's turnover, checks the products on the shelf and those in the store room, sorts out products with expired freshness dates, refills the shelves and puts price tags on the products, if necessary.

Intermediary customers are happy because they do not have to concern themselves with the stocking and upkeep of that portion of their shelf space. The system has also been shown to increase sales because the products are generally better presented and more fresh than if the supermarket maintains the shelf itself.

The key to the success of the *'frischdienst'* system is the rapid feedback and application of information from the frontline. Hand-held data-recording sets are used to record and monitor changes in each customer's stock levels. The salesman enters into the set data-recording information about the number of packages replaced because of expired freshness dates, the number of products added in each product line and any other pertinent changes.

The accumulated information is used by headquarters to program production and control stock levels. Because the feedback from the line to headquarters on sales is very fast – the same day – the company can rapidly adjust production and stock levels as necessary. As a result, the stores are seldom, if ever, out of stock of popular items, even in peak periods of the year.

In addition, the information is used to determine how much of each product should be charged in the delivery truck of each salesman prior to his sales circuit. Restockage quantities for each customer is calculated in advance. Unloading and shelf sorting is completed more rapidly, leaving more time for the salesman with the store manager.

The information coming up from the frontline is also used by the marketing department to test new products and receive rapid results. Sales figures on different product lines are available for each store and can be grouped by region or type of shop, to find out exactly what type of products sell best in which regions. Salesmen can then propose an assortment of products to a customer which correspond best to the profile of his store.

The biggest benefit which this system offers to retailers is the possibility to maximise the use of their shelf space. End customers buy more because what they find on the shelf has been exactly adapted to their demands. As demand changes, Convent's offerings change with it. The *fischdienst* approach, then, allows for the maximum flexibility and, thus, the maximum return for both the retailer and Convent alike.

Increasing efficiency; the case of Galenica

In many cases, good service boils down to getting the right product to the right person at the right time. In short, it's a question of efficiency.

For Galenica, efficiency has life-and-death implications. As a supplier of medicines and medical suppliers to pharmacies, Galenica is often in the position of delivering urgently needed supplies in very short time-frames. Delays or errors in preparation of the order can have very negative consequences. Galenica's first and foremost mission is, thus, to be precise and reliable.

Galenica is a Swiss company supplying pharmaceutical products throughout Switzerland. It has six central stocking centres from which the company can deliver anywhere in the country, within a day, over 98 per cent of the items asked for. In total, over 40,000 items are stocked on a regular basis. These are furnished to around 1300 pharmacies. To do so, the company maintains relationships with over 1500 suppliers.

Its competitors are mainly small, local suppliers which provide a slightly more flexible and more personalised service because of their size. In terms of efficiency, however, Galenica is extremely proficient, more so than its local competition and more so than most comparable firms worldwide. Its order preparation rate is less than 3 for 10,000 (0.003 per cent). None of its Swiss competitors can match the figure.

The company has used a combination of good organisation, excellent logistics, IT and a good bit of creativity to develop its exceptionally efficient order taking, order processing and delivery service. The most highly perfected example of Galenica's operations is at the Berne Warehouse, which functions as follows.

The customer is contacted by the receptionists at almost exactly the same hour every day. The calling schedule is determined by a computer program which is available through the terminal on her desk. The entire file appears before her eyes. Besides the telephone number and the name of the person to contact, it also indicates the times at which he should be called.

The receptionist dials the number and the client answers. After the greeting and the exchange about the weather, the client puts in his order. For 80 per cent of the time this is done automatically through a card system which permits the pharmacist to prepare his order in advance and then simply 'punch a button' to send it through the system. Because the order passes directly, there is little chance of error. For the remaining 20 per cent, the order is received verbally.

The minute the receptionist is done with the customer, the order is automatically transferred to the other side of the building to the warehouse where the order prints out in the form of a computer print-out. In addition, it is transferred, together with other orders, into a receiving unit which is attached to a collection trolley. A collection trolley is an electrically controlled cart that makes the circuit of the warehouse on a fixed rail – like the amusement rides at Disneyland.

Once the trolley has received the programming from the central computer which tells it which items must go into which orders, the trolley knows exactly where to stop in the warehouse for the orders to be collected. It won't advance until all the items have been loaded into the correct order bin. The trolley takes 14 orders at once through the warehouse. The trolley is manned by an individual whose primary task is to take the right items off the shelf and put them into the bins. He is aided by the trolley whose miniature computer screen indicates on which shelf the product is to be found.

Having completed the tour, the order is placed into the truck with the computer print-out of that order. The same print-out also indicates the destination of the order and the address. The entire process from the time that the order is registered takes 35 minutes. This permits Galenica to deliver to practically any pharmacy in Switzerland within one to three hours.

The company developed the collection trolleys themselves. The central information system, which controls the order recording and processing, is held on a 35 gigabyte system which is also responsible for the monthly billing of customers. With experience and extreme attention to detail, the company has refined its delivery schedules to co-ordinate as well as possible with the various telephone ordering hours.

A system as efficient as Galenica's is of great interest to customers. It gives them great peace of mind and the assurance of no hassles. Together with the company's many other services – documentation, training, management consulting etc. – Galenica offers its customers an unbeatable package.

How to develop information technology to improve customer satisfaction

Take a hard look at your internal development of IT and get rid of price commodity investments

How many times do managers feel frustrated because data processing is busy developing programs to improve internal efficiency and thus postponing applications which will give them better information to decide on and/or improve service? Everyone wants his own pay system, accounting system, production planning system, logistics management system. It takes for ever to develop systems that can be subcontracted or bought on the shelf! If we look at Fig. 5.1 it is easy for you to assess where you have put your emphasis versus where you should be putting it:

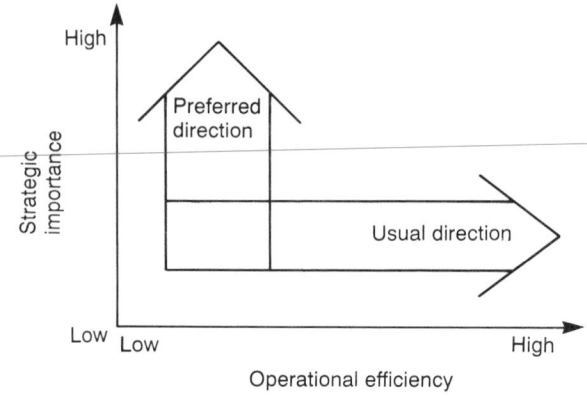

Figure 5.1

In order to devote more time and effort to strategic issues, which will set you apart, an audit of where the money has gone and where you intend to put it tomorrow is key. And don't be shy or weak in front of hard-nosed technical experts. Today it is possible to buy out or subcontract what it is not strategic. One of the ways people are starting to handle this question is to appoint as head of data processing someone who does not know anything about it, but who has good business sense. It is better to adapt a company procedure by 10 per cent to a standard software package on a pay system rather than to spend three years developing your own!

Another way companies are shifting their data processing priorities is to make it a separate entity. Instead of having this arrogant 'I know it all' attitude, they become more service oriented (and not only to the financial controllers), because otherwise they have no customers and no income. Boeing has just gone in this direction by creating Boeing Services. People can even buy IT outside if they wish to!

A third way progressive companies use is having internal customers select priorities for data processing/telecom projects. Every year data processing asks its customers what project they would like to see as priorities. They are evaluated in terms of costs and time, and proposed to the units (and later on are charged for) as well as top management approval. Other companies have changed the name of the data processing or computer department to 'new technologies' to show a) that not only can the computer help (Telecom is a big helper in service), b) that you don't necessarily have to come from data processing to qualify for the job and c) it is for *new* things. All these means have been used to avoid what happens to government: new things are not possible since most of the budget is either spent to reimburse the debt or to continue or maintain current programs!

Select your priorities for the use of technology that will put you ahead of the competition

Once you have at last been able to get some time and money together to spend on really important issues, the job is just starting. You have seen above that there are different ways in which information can be used to improve service. We can classify them in four ways: enhancement of customer, enhancement of value for the customer, reduction of hassles for the customer, feedback to improve service.

- Enhancement of the customer has to do with all the means that will make the customer feel he is recognised, his needs individualised, service personalised. It goes all the way from a machine being able to say 'Hello' with your name when you put in your cashpoint card, to mailing you only offers that fit your needs and experience, to avoiding mailing a standard packaged offer when you complained about it a week before, thus not recognising your recent problem. It has to do with an insurance diagnosis made just for you or with putting you in the same room as last time in a hotel because you liked it. It also feels nice when you ring the front desk in a hotel and they call you by your name without you even having to give your room number. It often leads to a complete change in the database management of a company which is often made by product sold rather that by customer. Customer enhancement through technology is, of course, the best priority for the use of technology. If your business is characterised by frequent and regular customer purchases, which create opportunities to sell more or new items.
- Enhancement of value is different. It is not so much caressing the ego of the customer as improving his perception of the value of the product or service he buys. When one calls LL Bean, a mail order house, to order a sweater, the lady on the phone will tell you that you should order a size 2 rather than 3 since she has on her terminal that all size 3s have been returned because they are too large. Augmenting the value of a product or service is the name of the game in this instance.
- If you undertake – on their terms – the quality control tests on your drugs which are going to be used in the food industry, they don't have to redo the quality control. It is not so much database management which is necessary here, but more information sharing within a company among different functions and, as importantly, between the supplier and the customer. It is used in teledistance diagnosis and repair, automatic reorder systems in industry, or in on-line phone information to select a vacation or videotext information to select investment.
- Another use of IT is reduction of hassles and costs for the customer. In automatic reorder, sometimes customers fear they are going to get their delivery late. A telecommunication system might reduce their perceived risk by telling them in advance when the delivery will be made. The same idea applies when Federal Express or DHL can trace your parcel within 30

to 60 minutes. Technology is also used in some German hotels where when you dial to obtain a wake-up call, it repeats in your language the time you have set. When American Express decided that no customer would have to repeat their problem twice, it meant millions of dollars of investments to enable operations everywhere to have on screen in front of them why a customer called, so that in subsequent calls he would not have to repeat his problem. Complaints cannot be handled properly if the person who answers does not have access to the information required to help the customer, reduce his anxiety, solve his problems. Equally, a lot of thinking is necessary to make sure that when a customer calls, the message gets properly routed and on time to the person who will handle it (especially when he is not in). Danish or Swiss taxis which have micro-computers on board both reduce hassles to the customer and increase perceived value. On one side, instead of having the telecommunications calls bothering the customer through loud speakers, you have silent displays for next possible calls. On the other side the perception is that taxis can be reached more easily and you get a printed bill fast! The same idea prevails when Honda put into the memory of your car card all past repairs so when you go to the garage, the car history is visible to the mechanic rather than forcing you to remember it.

- Feedback to improve service. The best example I have seen of this is Kao of Japan. Kao is the leader in toiletries, cosmetics, household products. Its brand names sell through all distribution channels. They started to develop a customer service department in 1979. Today, it receives 40,000 enquiries per year. It is fully computerised using a system with three components:
  - a technical information screen containing more than 17,000 document pages to answer any queries on technical information;
  - a PC which will select the menu depending on the customer enquiry or complaint;
  - a video text which will show the operator what the customer is talking about: package, advertising, model advertised (useful if customer says she wants the same make-up), product itself, types of buttons or material or the shirt closest to one the customer purchased, parts of products (such as a vacuum cleaner, if one customer asks about a filter which Kao sells) . . . Not only are customer service people prepared to answer customers' questions, but all enquiries, suggestions, remarks are automatically analysed. They can be printed on paper, or in colour transparencies for presentations (such as complaints per month, per day, per type . . .). One hundred and fifty such PC screens are dis-played in all functions of the company (R&D, marketing, production) so as to help better product, launch new ones, etc.

Sixty per cent of enquiries are product related, 20 per cent on health, 10 per cent mix, 10 per cent on distribution. Ninety per cent of questions come from consumers, 10 per cent from retailers.

The training of customer relations employees is three months (four days on the system, the rest on Kao products), plus some experience in selling. All have a bachelor's degree, some a master's. To answer 40 000 enquiries, they have 13 workstations, disc and computer (disc updated every night). The current system has been working since 1989. Prior to 1983, they were using microfilms. The current system cost 5 billion yen. It takes 2.5 people to maintain.

To support the consumer system, Kao gives lectures at universities, holds seminars for opinion formers and consumers (500 per year), and produces document and videos for distributors.

As an example of feedback for production and for maximum customer satisfaction, on a kitchen detergent, they received 40 complaints: as the bottle was opened by consumers, bubbles would come out. In six months, improvements were made to suppress the bubbles. In addition 110 consumers who had complained received a new product.

Every day such feedback is made by type and by product. Access to a database can be by brand, size, factory, age group, customer address, customer relations.

Information captured from the customers can be a fantastic tool for improvement if the information is shared throughout the company. The biggest success comes when all these systems are integrated: at DHL a telesales person will see what complaints a customer had on his screen before making a salescall. At Club Med, the 'white list', i.e. customers who have had problems are treated differently when they make a reservation.

Use information technology through people

At Kao, the customer service department is staffed with nine people. All have university degrees. All have had sales experience before taking the job. All have had a three-month training course, out of which only three days were devoted to using the computer (user-friendly, of course) and the rest devoted to trying all products and answering customers' queries. In most companies, customer service people are put there because no one knows what else to do with them!

It is a fantastic observation post from which to discover customer likes and dislikes. It should be a compulsory part of training for all young marketers and factory managers.

6 MEASURING AND MONITORING

Introduction

Measuring permits a company to do a number of things:

- increase service quality awareness;
- know where you stand according to a certain benchmark;
- test homogeneity;
- identify strengths and weaknesses;
- focus efforts;
- monitor progress; and
- quantify achievements.

In most of the companies we looked at measuring systems were used to achieve one or more of these objectives – be it increasing service quality awareness or identifying weaknesses. What follows are examples of some of these companies, the objective they wished to achieve and the way a measuring tool was used to achieve that objective.

Measuring systems

Gauging progress: the case of National Westminster

One of the most important roles of a measurement system is to permit managers to know whether improvements are being realised as compared with a certain objective. National Westminster, one of the four leading clearing banks in the UK with over 110,000 employees and 6 million customers, has used measuring systems to gauge progress, ever since it introduced its service quality programme in 1983.

National Westminster's first step in the service quality improvement process was the launch of a 'standards of service campaign'. Among other aims, the programme was designed to provide top management with an idea of where it stood in terms of local customer service satisfaction, and to provide data on the nature and frequency of customer complaints.

To measure overall satisfaction, the local branches were asked to hand out short questionnaires to customers concerning their satisfaction with, for example, the waiting time in line, the courtesy of the staff, the efficiency of statement processing and other transactions.

To collect data on customer complaints, employees were asked to record all complaints coming in over a four-week period – verbal and written. 'A major benefit was that it opened up the quality debate for branch staff to get involved in service aspects locally, and also demonstrated that up to 60 per cent of the causes of customer complaints could be obviated most effectively by branch staff.'

In addition, these initial results provided a benchmark against which the impact of future actions could be measured. The next step was to broaden the programme and, likewise, broaden and refine the measuring instruments used. In 1986, National Westminster officially launched the service quality process which had the support of top management and their commitment to make it a long-term effort.

Four principal objectives were established, one of which was 'to install, maintain and monitor performance'. Performance is monitored according to established standards of service. National Westminster's ongoing research into customer expectations permitted it to establish service standards in areas such as processing times for loans, response times for customer enquiries, degree of accuracy for new accounts etc.

Monitoring is initially done to verify the feasibility of the standard and the functioning of the monitoring mechanism. The branches have six months to put the standard in place, after which, a random sample of 100 branches is chosen to complete a questionnaire and submit the data collected in their local monitoring activities. The results permit adjustments to be made, if needed, and realistic short-term objectives to be established by each branch.

Monitoring then becomes a permanent tool to measure improvement against the initial performance and the ultimate target: a different set of 100 branches are approached every six months. The monitoring process is eventually used for all of the standards and is conducted on a permanent basis.

A permanent system to measure customer satisfaction on an ongoing basis has also been introduced. Every year, the bank measures customer satisfaction throughout the UK. With titles like, *Can you Spare a Minute?*, and *Help us to Help You*, short, one-page multiple choice pamphlets in bright colours are either being handed out or made available to customers to complete during roughly a one-month period.

The results are available by branch, by region and for the whole bank. Top management uses the survey to judge the effectiveness of the service quality programme and the performance of middle managers. Branch and regional managers are now being evaluated, in part, according to improvements made in customer satisfaction.

One observation that was made is that the service quality effort has brought about a good deal of improvement in some branches and very little in others. In part, this is due to the degree of commitment of each of the branch or regional managers to the programme. This, in turn, explains the decision to include improvement measured by the customer satisfaction survey in their performance evaluations.

Permanent measurements of internal service quality have also been introduced. Under the title *The Cost of Making Mistakes*, a programme for identifying, monitoring and improving problem areas was launched in 1990. Each branch takes an average of five problem areas to address at one time.

The first step in the process is to record over a 10-day period how long it takes to perform a task and the accuracy with which the task is performed, for example, how long it takes to find out whether a new customer's credit cards or cheque books have arrived, and the number of times the cheque books were not ordered is also recorded. The time spent correcting or identifying errors can also be monitored, i.e. how long does it take to correct a faulty debit to an account?

The second step is to develop an improvement plan which targets improvement over a period of six months to a year. Advancement according to the plan is then monitored on a monthly basis in terms of minutes saved per problem area. National Westminster provides all its branches with a kit with instructions as to how to follow through the process and two charts – one to record the time and accuracy at day 1 and the eventual targeted level, and a second chart to post internally which shows the month-to-month progress made on each problem.

This programme was extremely well received in the bank because it allowed managers to realise tangible improvements and to chart those improvements over time. 'In terms of results, looking at just the first 100 branches, there has been a sizeable improvement.'

Keeping in touch with customers: the case of Nederlandse Spoorwegen

Measuring to achieve or improve upon a certain benchmark level is valid in so far as that benchmark accurately reflects the service expectations of customers. If not, a company is creating perfection with no purpose – the proverbial white elephant.

Nederlandse Spoorwegen has a set of interrelated internal and external measurements which avoid this problem. It permits the company internally to measure progress against a benchmark and then to adjust the benchmark on a continuous basis to the real expectations of their customers. 'No measure has value in and of itself. It only has meaning when compared to the results of customer satisfaction surveys. For example, you can clean all the trains and have them meet internal levels of cleanliness, but the customer may not perceive that the trains are clean.'

Nederlandse Spoorwegen, or NS for short, is the national railway company in the Netherlands. It is one of the smallest of its European counterparts, but is one of the most service oriented and most efficient. The company began focusing on service quality in 1981 and has expanded and refined its approach continuously: today, service quality is one of the leitmotifs of the company.

Measurement and monitoring is one of the most important aspects of the company's quality effort. Even as one of the smallest European railways, it serves over 600,000 passengers a day. Measurement systems allow management to know more precisely what is happening on any given day throughout the system. Specifically, they allow the company to know whether the service and operating standards which have been established are being met.

Following extensive research into customer's service expectations, NS established service standards, expressed in terms of what should be provided to the customer at every moment of his interface with the company. These, in turn, have been translated into internal operating standards. A single individual is assigned responsibility for the meeting of a certain standard. 'What we learned is that specifying requirements without linking them to responsible personnel members and feasible measuring methods is an impossibility. Specification then becomes an empty gesture.'

Research into customer service expectations has also permitted the company to prioritise the aspects of the service in terms of their importance to the customer. Original research established that punctuality, information and seat capacity were the most important service aspects to the customer.

NS has also prioritised the various steps in the customer's contact with the company, i.e. the customer buys a ticket, the customer tries to find the train etc., according to the degree of influence which any particular step is likely to have on the customer's satisfaction. By prioritising, NS can focus on those aspects of its service which have the greatest impact on customer satisfaction.

Measurement tools were created to monitor performance on the service standards. Customer service expectations research permitted NS initially to ascertain what the appropriate benchmark for a measurement should be. Results from a yearly customer satisfaction survey taken in November permit NS to judge whether the benchmark is still at the appropriate level or whether customer expectations have increased, requiring an adjustment.

Starting in 1982, 20,000 passengers were asked to participate in the customer satisfaction survey, called the Thermograaf; per year roughly 50 per cent actually did. For the large stations and overall service provided by the company, the survey was conducted twice a year. Because of the need for more specific customer satisfaction rating on station facilities, an additional survey was introduced in 1986 at the local stations. Another 20,000 questionnaires were distributed every year in connection with this survey. Since June 1991, the Thermograaf has been changed. Instead of asking customers their opinion once a year, NS started asking for customer views on a weekly basis. At the same time, another change was introduced. The forms are handed out to customers on the train and collected during the journey. By using this method, the return rate has jumped from 50 per cent to ninety-five per cent. The disadvantage which a break in the continuity of the approach presents, is more than compensated for by the possibility of having continuous quality monitoring and the swiftness of the results. The results of the Thermograaf today are produced within three weeks! From these studies the company knows, for example, that the tolerable waiting time for buying a train ticket is three minutes; beyond that, customer satisfaction drops sharply.

By monitoring the results from the customer satisfaction surveys over time, NS can determine, for example, whether three minutes' waiting time is still an acceptable benchmark or whether the benchmark does not need to be moved upwards, in order to achieve the same level of customer satisfaction on quality items related directly to the staff (friendliness, availability, service. . . .).

NS targets customer satisfaction at 85 per cent. That is to say that in the surveys it undertakes, at least 85 per cent of the customers responding should rate the company at 7 or above (on a scale of 10), in order for NS to consider that its targeted level of customer satisfaction has been met. The company is also trying to do better than 85 per cent whenever possible; only 5 per cent of the customers should be dissatisfied (give a rating of 5 or below).

Once the benchmark for a standard has been established, the company measures internally whether the benchmark is being maintained, for example, whether indeed in over 85 per cent of the cases, the waiting time is under three minutes. These internal indicators are monitored on a monthly basis and, in the case of a particular problem, more often.

For non-staff related quality areas, satisfaction is targetted for a minimum of 50 per cent. A maximum of 15 per cent of the customers should not be satisfied.

Progress on internal indicators and the results of the customer satisfaction surveys are distributed throughout the company. The results of the customer satisfaction surveys are printed in a booklet form called the *Thermograaf*. The results of the internal indicators are also available in book form. Looking at the two together, one can find, for example, the item 'punctuality' under both. In the *Thermograaf*, customers give a rating of their perception of the punctuality of the NS train service: for one month in 1990 it was 45 per cent, i.e. only 45 per cent of the respondents rated the NS over '7' on punctuality. An internal indicator on the same topic – punctuality – might show that 95 per cent of the trains are on time within five minutes.

This example clearly shows the importance of setting benchmarks according to customer expectations. Still greater improvements are clearly necessary in punctuality before customer satisfaction will reach the 85 per cent benchmark, despite the fact that actual punctuality, at 95 per cent, appears fairly good. Actual performance on any given standard could be 98 per cent and still not be enough to meet minimum levels of customer expectations. Likewise, performance could be at 40 per cent in another area and more than amply meet customer expectations.

Tools permitting this kind of comparative analysis are extremely useful to NS, which, by the nature and history of its business, has a strong technical orientation, as opposed to a customer orientation. By providing the two kinds of measures, the company can relate all of the very intricate and elaborate organisations within the company to produce tangible and measurable results for customers. 'The essential point is that one knows what the customer appreciates, . . . quality control means customer orientation and control for and within the railway company.'

Global measurement for global service: the case of American Express

One of the principal difficulties facing multinational companies in the management of service quality is the inequality of customer expectations between different cultures. On the one hand, the multinational must be able to adjust its approach in order to be accepted into local markets; on the other hand, it must be able to guarantee a certain homogeneity of service quality to those customers whose own activities and contacts with the company transcend borders.

American Express, as a provider of travel and financial services to customers worldwide, is a multinational in precisely this situation. An American company from its origins, its rapid expansion over the last 20 or 30 years, has made the company into a true multinational group with 1700 offices in 130 countries.

Because of the nature of its services – travel services and charge card – customers use American Express's services quite heavily in countries other than their own. An American Express office in Rome, for example, will be required to adapt to meet the expectations of an American from Idaho (on his first visit to Europe) and those of a local businessman wanting information on his up-coming weekend in Portofino. The service expectations of these two customers are clearly quite different in many respects.

To respond to this situation, American Express has developed service standards and a corresponding measuring system that reflects culture differences, while at the same time enforcing a common approach in certain key service aspects.

American Express first began measuring its service quality on a systematic basis in 1978. Research was conducted into customers' service expectations; based on the results, standards were established. American Express learned that good customer service in their business revolved principally around three aspects: timeliness; accuracy; and responsiveness. 'People wanted error-free bills and they want questions answered promptly. But just as important, they expect company representatives to be knowledgeable, caring and polite. This is the third element of service quality, which we call responsiveness.'

A large number of standards were created in the first two categories:

timeliness and accuracy. There is, for example, a standard stating that a new account application should be completed within two days and that there should be no errors in recoding the information from the form.

Another group of standards was created in the third category: responsiveness. One measure is called fraud responsiveness, 'If you have reported that your card has been used fraudulently we have to be responsive to you as a cardmember and we have to credit your account and start the research. And you should not suffer as a cardmember.' There is also award responsiveness. The establishment that identifies cards that are lost or stolen and returns them receives an award and is paid for their trouble.

Operational standards about how to deal with customers also exist. All employees in responding on the telephone, for example, must say their name, the name of the company and 'Hello'. In this category, however, no formal measurement exists to test whether this is actually done. It is up to the individual manager to supervise his staff in the way he sees fit.

Not all of the standards of service apply in every market in which the company operates. Only certain standards are expected to be maintained on a worldwide basis. Likewise, the measurement system only measures performance on standards in the regions in which they apply. In this way, American Express adapts its approach to local conditions.

'In total, we have three sorts of measures. We have what we call worldwide measures which are being monitored by our head office in New York. Our worldwide standards are set for certain worldwide type services. And, then we have what we call European measures specifically for European markets. And, then we have local area measures.'

American Express's measurement system measures timeliness and accuracy on a large variety of services. It measures responsiveness by measuring whether or not the standard has been fulfilled, i.e. in what percentage of cases was an award given to the establishment identifying a lost or stolen card?

The measurement system which applies on a worldwide basis is called the STR (service tracking report). 'There are 24 types of measurement. One of them is the 24-hour emergency delivery. . . . Another one concerns the payments to establishments following charge card purchases.' All are tested on timeliness and accuracy. The same standards of service are expected to be met on a worldwide basis. The 24-hour emergency service, for example, is a promise given to customers worldwide, regardless of where they are travelling. To keep its promise, that standard of 24 hours must also be met on a worldwide basis.

Certain standards need not be applied on a worldwide basis and can be adjusted to fit local conditions. One example is the telephone-answering time delay. In the US, the standard is higher than it is in Europe. In Europe a standard exists of seven seconds. It is one of the European standards which is measured every month. Another is the 'member get member'. 'If you as a member bring in a new member then you can select one of the rewards and we send it to you in a certain time frame. That's only done in Europe. It could be one of the worldwide measures in the future.'

In some cases, a standard which is applied in a local market or in Europe is eventually made into an international standard. A local standard would be for a particular country or region. 'A local measure can be a measure that we are starting to test and that eventually becomes a European measure and maybe even a worldwide measure.' American Express is presently testing the level of service that can be delivered with the point-of-sale terminals, which permit automatic transmission of the purchase request to American Express and the automatic approval thereof by computer. 'What's important is the speed. . . . It's difficult to judge at first for the world. It may be completely impossible for one country and completely easy for another.'

In some cases, service standards are adapted locally to correspond to the team's immediate ability to reach them; they are then moved forward as the team's efficiency increases. Progress is monitored monthly. 'It's a monthly quality assurance report. We have so many measures in place – in one month we reached so many measures and we missed so many – so we had an overall performance level of, say, 60 per cent or 70 per cent of the 100 per cent. . . . It has a lot of focus during monthly meetings and if certain departments have reached their standards, we celebrate it.'

A new or poor performing unit is not expected to try to reach all of the standards, all at once. Standards are addressed group by group. 'We start off slowly and build up – if, for instance we want a count of 20 – then we take it step by step, a reachable 5, a reachable 10, a reachable 15, . . . to reach the objective. . . . It's a way to have a positive reachable target for the people. They know that if they deliver more effort they will reach the 100 per cent or the ultimate goal.'

Overall, American Express delivers a very consistent level of service to its customers in key areas like charge card loss recovery time. In other areas, it permits greater flexibility within the organisation to respond to local conditions and different local standards determined by the culture and the local infrastructure. Developed with care and sensitivity, it is a model that many multinational firms could follow.

Increasing quality awareness internally: the case of Hippopotamus

Selling service quality internally is not always an easy job. Among the many counter-arguments given by managers is the argument that service quality is already being delivered. It probably is, but perhaps not the right kind and not enough in the areas that count to the customer.

One good way to show managers that improvements can still be made, is to go direct to customers and ask them to evaluate the company's service quality using a customer satisfaction survey. When the survey can provide a measurement of the manager's own particular scope of responsibility, it can have an even greater impact.

Measurement of customer satisfaction at Hippotamus was introduced in 1987 as one of the initial steps in the launch of a service quality programme for the group. Hippopotamus is a successful chain of grill-style restaurants located in a number of locations in Paris and in some of the major French towns. The group experienced rapid growth in the late 1970s and early '80s and began to lose focus. It was at this point that the founder and CEO decided to revitalise the company's original service quality focus with the programme.

While, in part, the aim of the customer satisfaction survey was to discover where the company stood with customers, the primary aim was to draw staff and manager's attention to the need to focus on service quality as a way to increase customer loyalty. The restaurant business in Paris and major French cities is a very competitive business and it is primarily through the establishment of a stable clientele that a restaurant can survive.

Customer satisfaction was measured on a restaurant-by-restaurant basis. It was conducted by external consultants during one week at different times of the day and with over 5000 customers – a minimum of 500 per restaurant. Forty questions appeared on the original questionnaire dealing with all aspects of the restaurant's service to customers – décor, cleanliness, waiting time, politeness of staff, dress of the staff, etc. The results were then communicated throughout the company. Satisfaction ratings were established for each restaurant and could be compared between the 16 restaurants. Within the first year, the survey was conducted every three months. Today, it is conducted twice a year.

Initial satisfaction ran at an average of 77 per cent for the group as a whole. Research shows that, in general, an 85 per cent rating is necessary; below that level, the impact of negative word-of-mouth communication by dissatisfied customers outweighs the impact of positive word of mouth. Given that fact, Hippopotamus targeted to reach an overall level of 85 per cent or above.

The results for the company showed managers and staff that there was room for improvement. Because the survey was very detailed and dealt with each aspect of the service, it was also possible to identify exactly in what areas the greatest effort has to be made, whether it be in the speed of service, the quality of the food or the attitude of the hostesses.

It was also possible to identify those restaurants where the greatest efforts were needed. While the score overall was around 75 per cent, there were considerable variations between restaurants – some were up at 85 per cent and others were only at 60 per cent.

This brought an element of competition into play. Once all managers knew their scores and knew that customer satisfaction would henceforth be measured on an ongoing basis, they felt obliged to make an effort to improve their performance *vis-à-vis* their counterparts. Managers increased their efforts in all aspects of their service, which brought about an improvement of the scores for the group as a whole. Satisfaction in 1988, at the end of the service quality programme, stood at 87 per cent.

This barometer has continued to have an important impact on the management of the group. It is used as a reference point to verify that there are no slippages in service quality and, as it was originally, to convince managers or staff of the importance of service quality to the success of the group.

Customer satisfaction continues to average 87 per cent, a little less in November and a little more in July. Christian Guignard, the founder and CEO summarises what he felt the barometer brought to the group. 'Most of the managers were service quality oriented by spirit, but not always in practice. In the beginning, they thought that they were doing a good job and couldn't believe there was a way to evaluate service quality objectively. The barometer showed what there was to do and it permitted us to do an analysis by restaurant. The managers' mentality has changed. . . . They now welcome the barometer because it's a way to listen to customers' thoughts.'

Measurement for better customer feedback: the case of London International Group (Colour Care)

Measurement tools don't always have to be something uniquely used by management to control or monitor service quality. They can also be used to create value-added for the customer.

Colour Care, part of the London International Group, is one of Europe's leading photoprocessing companies.

The company's service strategy is to differentiate itself by the quality of service it offers. On the one hand, they work with the retailers to improve the quality of advice and assistance they provide to customers coming into the store; on the other hand, they try to add value to the end-product given to the customers – the processed photos or prints.

A way in which Colour Care adds value to their product is through the provision of a "*Photo Tips Booklet*" with each processing job, which gives examples of mistakes in photography and explanations of how they can be avoided in the future. The booklet does not, however, stand alone. In addition, Colour Care indicates on each unsuccessful photo processed, with little advice labels on each photo, exactly what the problem was. Using the book together with the labels, the photographer is in an excellent position to improve his photographic skills with the help of Colour Care. 'We try to develop relations with warm and personal service feedback and advice for how to take better pictures.'

While it may not appear obvious at first glance, this advice service offered to customers is a direct result of a quality monitoring system which the company uses today in its own lab. Colour Care has a very extensive service quality monitoring system which measures errors in the photoprocessing process, as well as in other aspects of the service delivered to customers, such as photo pick-ups and deliveries.

In terms of processing service quality 'all prints are individually graded for quality assurance. The lab then tests to see what the nature of the error is. If it is the fault of the lab, it is reprocessed; if the fault appears to be with the quality of the photo itself, it is given an advice label reflecting the exact problem which has been identified.

The approach is quite new to the company and was initiated, along with the introduction of a customer service quality programme, which not only improves service to Colour Care's direct customers, the retailers, but also to end customers in the form of a more thoughtful, conscientious approach in the photo development process. 'We constantly remind the labs who see millions of films a year, that each print is a special, priceless memory. . . . Before it was taken for granted that there would be variations in colour prints; now we measure and ask why.'

Using measurement as a tool for customer communication: the case of Equity & Law

Just telling customers that the company provides good service quality is often not enough; tangible evidence needs to be given in a communication campaign focused on service quality. Equity & Law is a company which used its measuring and monitoring systems as a concrete example to show how the company was implementing improvements in service quality.

Equity & Law is a life insurance society in the UK providing mortagages, investment opportunities and insurance – life, health etc. It has been in existence since 1844 and has for a long time had an excellent investment management record within the industry. Since 1987, the company has been part of the AXA Group of insurance companies.

A complete re-evaluation of the company's marketing approach was conducted in 1990. Market research was carried out on the perception of the company with end customers and with financial advisers who are responsible for selling their products on to end customers. One of the conclusions was that the company had little or no name recognition.

A second conclusion was that the company had a possibility to differentiate itself in the market on the basis of the quality of its support services to financial advisers, which was already evaluated to be quite good.

The decision was then taken to focus on service quality to financial advisers and to develop a large communications and advertising campaign which would increase name recognition of the company in the market. 'Equity & Law is to become a company known and recognised with the general public for the quality of products and services it provides.'

In the customer servicing department, changes were being made which would improve the quality of the service providers to the financial advisers and to end customers. Customer Servicing is the branch of the company that handles the administration of the business. They respond to the enquiries of financial advisers concerning various investments or policies; they process applications or changes in policies; they produce statements and reports on the status of individuals' accounts or of an investment fund. 'The first step we took was to change the department's name from "policy servicing" to "client servicing".' Further steps were taken to reorganise the department to serve customers better, including the introduction of a new computer system, the elaboration of new standards of written and telephone communication, the introduction of a system of analysis to identify where the greatest number of customer complaints were coming from etc.

The most important step was the introduction of service standards. In this initial phase, the department has limited itself to standards that can be measured in terms of response times to customers. The standards were set as objectives to be attained with challenging, but realistic delays of from 1 to 10 days.

Adherence to the standards could be measured using the new computer system. In the past, the measurement of processing or response times for documents would have been a very time-consuming exercise. The new system permits processing times to be measured which then simplified the rest of the measuring process.

Adherence to the standards chosen was measured over a period of one year to verify the feasibility. 'We wanted to check if they were realistic in the market place or if customers would be happy with these delays . . .'. According to the company, there is no established level of 'acceptable service' in their market. The delays were established based on experience of what their customers accept to be reasonable.

Once the standards had been tested, Equity & Law did a very innovative thing. It decided to publish its standards in the form of a communication/ publicity brochure for financial advisers and customers alike. Thus, in October 1989, every financial adviser with which the company dealt received a very elegant and glossy brochure called *Commitment to Excellence*, which listed by product area, the delays that were expected for most types of activities. Under the title 'Personal and Executive Pension Plans', for example, one finds:

Job Title	Description	Target Turnaround in Working Days
Policy production	Production of all multipension series policies including increments	5
Quotations	Quotations of all types of policy values for existing policies	5
General post	Items covering premium collection queries and interim correspondence for claims and changes	3
	Other types of post including general queries, change of address etc.	5

Table 6.1

'This move was completely innovative in the insurance market; nobody had done it previously and nobody since. We had feedback from other companies that, "Well, you are very brave to put those out, we wouldn't dare publish our standards".'

The brochure also explained exactly what the company was doing in the area of service quality and what the next step would be. 'We elaborated a little bit on our philosophy and what we were trying to do.' The standards printed were ones which the company was sure that it could meet in practically all instances, based on the information gained from measuring the standards over one year. The next step was to demonstrate to customers that the standards are being maintained.

In 1991, the company published a follow-up document which stated exactly how the company performed according to those standards over the previous year. Again, a very open and systematic approach was used; each standard is addressed separately with the percentage of times that the company had met the targeted response time in each case. Reporting the results of standards monitoring is now a permanent feature of the company's communication campaign and will be done on a yearly basis. 'We are fairly public on what we do now.'

From a strategic perspective, the communication of standards and the results of measurements reinforces Equity & Law's positioning as a company providing top-quality service and products; it was extremely successful in this, because the move was an innovative one.

From the perspective of the financial adviser, the publication of standards and the results of standards measurement demonstrates a tangible commitment to the maintenance of service quality within the company. In addition, the document itself provides an excellent reference tool for advising end customers exactly when they can expect to receive certain information or policy changes.

Monitoring customers' evolving expectations qualitatively: the case of Hilti

Hilti is the world's leading manufacturer and distributor of fastening systems. For those unfamiliar with the product, fastening systems are used in the construction industry for the joining of two objects of metal or concrete. These systems first appeared on the market in the early 1950s and have since become an indispensable part of the construction of any major structure.

Because of the originality of the product, Hilti began by selling its products direct to end-users. This gave the sales force an opportunity to demonstrate their use and application on-site which increased customers' appreciation of them and their potential. The company continues to market the products in the same way today, because although there is widespread acceptance of the products, the technology and complexity of the products has increased. Customers still need to have them demonstrated in order to use them to their maximum potential.

The company's service strategy is therefore to offer a complete package of advice, service and after sales assistance. Essential to the success of this strategy is the ongoing monitoring of customer's needs and expectations. On the one hand, Hilti needs to know exactly the developments in the industry in order to anticipate in the design of their products, the future needs of customers. On the other hand, Hilti needs to gauge customers' present level of satisfaction with their products and service in order to adapt them better to what the customer expects.

Hilti therefore has an extensive system of customer satisfaction monitoring, which includes customer satisfaction studies, customer complaints analysis and a value-added information system which tracks customers and their purchases to identify potentially dissatisfied customers before they drift away from the company completely. The most successful tool which the company has developed to discover the needs and opinions of customers has been its 'lead user' groups.

A 'lead user' is defined as a potential customer who 'critically looks at the performance of the company, who has a clear idea of what he needs, and who is able to express the gap between need and performance'. Lead users are being identified by the whole Hilti organisation. Hilti customers are sorted out and the critical non-users are selected and invited to a weekend seminar during which highly professional discussions lead to new technological developments and help to identify perspectives for future market needs. The 'lead user' approach has been so successful in Hilti's German company that it won the company an innovation award from Hilti's worldwide headquarters.

From the experience described above, as well as from the experience of working with more than 60 companies in designing and measuring systems for service quality improvement, it seems to us that the following steps are key to successful use in a service improvement process.

Keys to successful use in a service improvements process

What does not get measured does not get done – and do not hesitate to invest in selecting the right elements you want to measure

Beyond simply measuring customer satisfaction, which many companies have started to do, other measurements are necessary either to assess the situation before starting a service improvement process or to monitor progress and results. Other indications include the following.

- Measurement and analysis of lost customers. Their profile and the sources of dissatisfaction which made them leave allows us in many cases to identify and predict how many and which of our current customers are likely to leave us in the future because their sources of dissatisfaction are similar to those who left.

- The measurement of the gain that would be created by improving service is often underscored. Many companies engage in a service quality improvement process without having clearly identified what they can gain from it, whether it be in reduced costs (marketing costs are cheaper to keep a customer than to get a new one), or additional sales (pleased customers buy more) or additional profits (an increased retention of a customer base of 5 per cent can increase profits between 50 and 85 per cent!). As a result of this lack of evalution, the investment costs associated with launching and sustaining a new level of service quality are rapidly absorbed.

- Equally important both to assess the current situation correctly and pinpoint the priorities for action is an assessment of what is the relative importance of different items on customer satisfaction, as well as key factors which contribute to good or bad customer service. This form of analysis can usually come from analysing customer complaints, relating overall customer dissatisfaction with specific items the customer is not happy about, as well as measuring internally key failures in the service delivery process. Benchmarking, which consists of comparing a company to best practices, is done either internally (Who has the best service results? What do they do best?) or externally (Who are our best competitors?) or even more interesting with world-class leaders (Who has the best practice in sectors which could be used by our customers as points of comparison).

Take as an example a company which provides sophisticated systems for the printing industry. Such a process might tell them that over 50 per cent of its customer satisfaction is due to service and not to product. A surprise for a product/innovation-driven company. It might also tell them that within service the most two important dimensions are good service at sales (40 per cent) and within that the way it helps reduce the uncertainty and doubts of its customers to switch systems and the support (30 per cent) to help make the best use of the systems. In addition, measuring internally delivery dates, time to make proposals, speed of reaction to a customer's problem will tell how often the company is late, how fast it responds to customers' requests. Finally, since their customers are only using one supplier at a time, and they are market leaders, it is useless to benchmark against their competitors. However, they know that their German operation has had the best results. What factors contribute to that success? amount of training, staff support size etc. In addition, their customers also regularly buy microcomputers from world leaders and naturally it will be impossible for their customers not to make comparisons although they sell them different products. Why for instance does a microcomputer have a hot-line and they don't? Why can the customer get an answer in six hours from those market leaders and not from them? . . . Whenever, in fact, the company is a leader and has a customer who does not use competitors products or services, it is better to use the 'mind-set' or 'comparison map' of the customer in selecting companies to benchmark rather than comparing oneself stupidly with competitors who are behind.

All these elements just described will help this company identify which elements to work on as well as revolutionise the internal culture from a product to a more market-driven organisation.

Use measurement as a factor for change: don't keep it secret!

Nothing is so sterile as speeches made by top management about quality and service without concrete measures behind them showing what is good and less good, and showing possible root causes. People feel hurt that their work is questioned without hard facts or causes. The priority areas for improvement are often cosmetic changes or selected not on the basis of where it hurts the customers . . . but what top management has seen or observed. In a grilled meat restaurant chain people work continuously on improving the quality of the French fries because the CEO does not like them. However, a close analysis of lost customers shows in fact that by far the number one reason for customer dissatisfaction is the waiting time before being seated! In order to change the cultural 'mind-set' of management and employees, measurement systems have to be used extensively as fact-finding therapy. It usually requires a cascade (progressive top-down) diffusion of the results of taken measurements at all levels of the hierarchy and discussions about the results. Many companies unfortunately pay little attention to sharing this information with everyone. The knowledge is theirs. It is not shared. An acid test for your company of whether customer satisfaction has become a shared concern and supposing you do measure it – is to ask people at different levels and functions whether they know what the current rate of customer satisfaction is and what it was last year. If nobody knows – and the information exists – your current customer satisfaction programme is like a mayonnaise where the oil and egg did not mix! Companies who want to progress spend a great deal of time diffusing the information on results from measurements throughout the organisation on a regular basis. Take the example of this large chain stores of books and records in which all stores managers have been trained for three days to understand and communicate to their staff the results of quarterly customer satisfaction surveys. Those two days of training consist not only of presenting the measurement tool, its design, method, its results but also help management communicate (not just inform) with numbers, respond to objections, pinpoint key areas for progress. Role playing is used to improve communication skills and skills in conveying messages that should lead to action.

So please don't leave the data in the marketing or quality department, even if it comes as a shock to learn – like in this pharmaceutical company, that service accounts for 62 per cent of customer satisfaction and product only for 38 per cent.

Use measurement as a motivation tool: thus measure by unit

Not only can measures be used to make people realise what goes well and what goes less well, and thus change their perceptions of the change required, but they can also be used to motivate people to act upon it. In this purpose, measurements have to be done as many times as there are operational units which provide the service. How useful an overall customer satisfaction survey will be if it is not made by region, country, function, units, district, or branch. What will management do if people say that it is always done here, so the problem must be elsewhere. How will people know where the best practices are, learn from and use them as possible references if they cannot be identified? How will it be possible to set specific objectives for improvement in a particular area and link the reward system to good service performance? Having just corporate wide data would be as meaningless as having a corporate wide budget without detailed budgets per departments, units functions.

Companies today link bonuses or portions of employees' salaries to customer satisfaction results. For instance, at Xerox, 20 per cent of management compensation is linked to achieving a set of service targets (sales, delivery quality, aftersales service).

Other companies will use the results of measurements not just to reward employees on levels attained or progress made since the last measurement, but also to identify specific actions a unit can take. Measurements can be created to find out more about how quality teams or task forces are resolving problems which they have tackled. If this kind of measurement is done, a company knows where everyone stands with respect to problems solved (how many ideas we have developed, at what phase of the problem resolution process each team is, how many solutions have been generated, with what potential gain etc).

Some companies have made the results easily accessible to everyone through a computer networking system that permits each employee to look at the latest results at his leisure. In this way, teams do not work in isolation. They can get help from others, avoid duplicating the efforts of others or get tips from teams ahead of them. The approach also fosters cross-fertilisation and a positive sense of competition among teams. Lastly, such a monitoring system can help top management to intervene at the right moment to help groups that are stuck (working on the same problem for too long) or spur forward those that are not achieving.

In order for measurements to be successfully used to motivate employees, a couple of guidelines must be observed.

First, balance rewards between those on results and those on progress. If rewards are uniquely based on results, poorer performing units will be de-motivated because they will feel that they will never be able to make it. On the other hand, if rewards are uniquely based on progress, then the top scorers will not feel the necessity to make additional efforts as they are already at the limit. A good blend is possible by breaking the awards into two or more categories that correspond either to different objectives and/or different service dimensions.

Take the case of a bank with different branches: one reward could be for the highest level of customer satisfaction at the branch level (overall results). Another could be for the best transaction speed or the best responsiveness to problems as perceived by customers (a specific service dimension) and finally, another could be for the agency or account officer that has 20 per cent or more of its accounts using all services of the bank. Eventually, for those companies whose employees have a good sense of humour, creating an award for the worst achiever might set the spotlight on the unit which is not performing well and thereby motivate that unit to do its best to improve.

The second factor has to do with the acceptance of the measurement system by all units. Since comparisons are rapidly made either implicitly (because people want to evaluate themselves against their peers) or explicitly (for challenges or competition), it is important to avoid any 'noise' that might discredit the system. In our Bank example, customers' perception of the ATM's transaction speed might give different results than cronometered speed. As a result, some managers (particularly those with low ratings) might challenge the fact that they are measured on speed as perceived by customers, by pointing out that they are in areas where people are more in a hurry (business centres rather than residential areas). In addition, they might argue that the way that the information was collected (cashiers asking customers to fill out a questionnaire) is subject to bias (beautiful cashiers, special efforts on the week the survey is being taken etc.)

This is why it is key to measure units against themselves (progress) as well as results, and on variables they can control, and use as little as possible biased information collection procedures, even if it increases the cost of the measure.

The third factor has a lot to do with the relative importance of service quality objectives and measurements in the overall evaluation of unit managers. Unfortunately, too often, managers of units have too many conflicting objectives to achieve at the same time. Take for example the sales department of an industrial company selling industrial control to factories. Once a system is sold, responsibility is passed to the delivery installation and to the after sales service Department. Salesmen go on to new customers and try to get new contracts, rather than do a good follow up job on current customers. Why? Probably because they are measured on sales volume and perhaps on customer satisfaction with the purchasing process, and not on a mix of factors including sales volume with current customers/new customers, lost customers and the satisfaction of customers with the total process sales, delivery, billing, start up, new development. Too many or conflicting objectives can kill the intent. Club Med has been very successful partly because for 40 years, village managers have been measured on only one criterion: customer satisfaction.

7 MIDDLE MANAGEMENT: THE KEYSTONE IN THE CORPORATE STRUCTURE

Introduction

Middle management are often accused of being responsible for the failure of top management policies: 'middle management didn't push the project enough', 'middle management are reluctant to change', 'middle management don't take initiative', 'middle management have distorted our original aims'. Yet, in companies where things do get done, middle managers are often the people to be thanked for those achievements.

Where does the difference come in? How can a top manager be sure that his middle managers will do their utmost to achieve his aims for the company and not waste their time in useless debates about who is responsible for not having done what.

This chapter explores the role of middle management in the achievement of service quality. It will look at the various roles that middle managers have in the organisation, the ways those roles are managed in good service quality companies and, finally, at specific examples of middle managers in action in some of the companies we researched.

The role of middle managers

In the structure and organisation of a typical company middle managers play three predominant roles as:

- translators;
- implementors; and
- motivators.

Translators

As translators, middle management translate top management policies and aims into language which means something in an operational context for employees and other managers down the line. This is probably the most difficult and controversial of all of middle management's different roles.

By being given the authority to translate top management's policies and thereby influence employees' behaviour at the frontline, middle managers wield tremendous power. As translators, they use their own discretionary judgement, according to what they believe to be the interest of the company, to choose what should be translated and in what way.

Moreover, as human beings, they can only translate what they have heard. Like the old expression 'the story got lost in the telling', even with the best efforts, the likelihood that middle management will translate all of top management's message is very unlikely. Some of the message is bound to get distorted or lost.

For example, top management says, 'We want to be a top service quality company'. Middle management's translation could be, 'Our division must deliver products on time, every single time', or 'Our division must give a priority to receiving customers with the greatest possible consideration', or, yet again, 'Our division must be sure that everything we give customers is 100 per cent fault-free'.

In the first case, middle management defined service quality as being timeliness, in the second case, consideration for customers, in the third case, zero-defect. All of the translations could be correct or none of them.

Implementors

Middle managers' second role is as implementors. In this role their job is to put top management's ideas into action. To do so, they become resource allocators, prioritisers and task masters.

Take, for example, the case where top management decides that, 'We should create a new range of information services to help our customers understand our products better'. Joe Blow, a middle manager responsible for putting top management's words into action, is given a budget and is then sent off on his own. He must:

- justify the project to his employees;
- set specific objectives;
- choose a project team;
- organise the necessary resources;
- establish a schedule;
- establish a calling order to indicate in what instances the achievement of this project has precedence over the achievement of other objectives;
- control progress on the project, and institute disciplinary action if necessary.

The ultimate achievement of the project depends greatly upon the calling order Joe Blow establishes, and upon his willingness and enthusiasm to dedicate resources to the project at the expense of others. If he gives it too great a priority, large sacrifices will be made in other areas; if he gives it too little priority, nothing will be accomplished.

Motivators

Middle managers' third role is as motivators, encouraging employees to achieve the objectives set by top management. The battery of tools which they have at their disposal include:

- their own enthusiasm and charisma;
- financial compensation in the form of salaries, bonuses etc.;
- delegation of responsibility;
- the setting of clear personal and group objectives;
- training;
- rewards other than financial – dinners, awards, personal or group recognition prices, salesperson of the month etc.

A middle manager's skill is reflected in his ability to use all of these tools alternatively and to know what tools he should use, when and with whom.

Take once again, for example, Joe Blow and his project. He might motivate his team by promising them a financial bonus if they achieve the set objectives in less than the time allotted. He might also use the group to set the example for other project groups by asking them to present their project at a meeting or convention; he might also choose to delegate entire responsibility for achievement of the project to the group and announce it to them as such. The group would then report directly to Joe Blow's, boss with Joe Blow standing in as an observer.

The thing Joe Blow would not want to do, for example, is to reward one individual of the group more than the others, or in any way imply that the success of the project was due more to one person's efforts than another. The result would be to destroy the team spirit and create competitive animosities within the group, that would be detrimental to its functioning.

Looking at all of middle manager's roles taken together, it is clear that these individuals do not have an easy task. There is plenty of room for mistakes and there is a thin line between good middle management and bad.

What middle managers from top service quality companies do differently from other middle managers

Perhaps the most crucial difference one notices between ordinary companies and a top service quality company is the relative importance which each of middle management's three roles has in the life of the company.

In the ordinary company, middle management plays all three roles in relatively equal portions – 33 per cent all the way round. In a top service quality company, middle management's role as translator is minimised, while the motivator role takes greater precedence. The balance shifts from 33 per cent all the way round to, perhaps, 15 per cent, 33 per cent, 62 per cent for translator, implementor and motivator, respectively.

The switch is possible and desirable for two reasons: first, most top service quality companies are big communicators. They make it a policy to have a strong internal communication programme whose aim is to communicate on a continuous basis, the objectives of top management. As such, middle management's role as translators of top management's policies and objectives is no longer vital. The majority of the information which employees need can be obtained from other channels. Middle management's translator role is converted into an explanatory role.

The second reason for the shift in balance away from translating is to permit middle managers to play a greater role as motivators. Middle managers in top service quality companies are expected to be dynamic individuals who are good at people management. From top managements' point of view, they play a vital role in the achievement of the company's objectives and they are counted for their enthusiasm and dedication to carry the company through difficult periods.

As such, middle managers' own personal enthusiasm for the achievement of the company's objectives is a major tool for motivating other employees. When Davy Smith gets depressed and tired serving customers on the front-line, he can count on his boss, Jerry Gotoit, to be right there next to him, setting the example with his own endless energy, dedication and willingness to take it all in hand. The scenario is not at all fictitious. In our interviews with the companies for this book, we heard numerous versions of the same dynamic behaviour. 'Mr Lake is always down on the store floor; he really keeps us moving' (Sainsbury's). 'We count on our agency managers to create a really exciting work environment for employees' (OK Service).

Middle managers are also given great freedom to exercise the other tools listed earlier. A number of middle managers we spoke with said that they literally had no budget restrictions when it came to training employees. SVP was one of these; 'Training is given when and where it was needed', explains Mrs Cazabanpere.

In others, the delegation of responsibility was used as a motivator. 'I challenge employees to come to me with ideas for improving things; when it looks like a good one, I let them implement it', says Norman Lake, (Sainsbury's). Objective setting is another way middle management motivates employees, 'Commitment to the customer can only work if the staff buy into the ideas in the yearly plan. So, everyone in my division contributed to the elaboration of the plan', says Mervyn Davies, Citicorp.

Beyond the changes in middle management's role as translator and motivator, there is also a change in their role as implementor. The middle manager does little prioritising or resource allocation and more taskmastering. The explanation is simple; top management, through clear policy setting or goal setting take away most of the responsibility of middle management in the allocation of resources or the prioritisation of their employees' efforts.

Take the case of Kwik-fit, whose corporate aim is 100 per cent customer satisfaction. If the manager of a service centre has a customer who needs a tyre the centre doesn't have in stock, what does he do? Does he place the customer's satisfaction before the company's profitability and go and buy the tyre from a competitor and fit it (at a loss), or, does he simply explain to the customer that he is unable to supply that tyre at the present time and thereby save his centre valuable time, energy and money?

In the ordinary company, the manager would probably opt for the second solution. Even if he was aware that the company's goal was 100 per cent customer satisfaction, he wouldn't be sure that his managers would expect him to put customer satisfaction before profitability. At Kwik-fit the choice is clear and it's already made, customer satisfaction comes before anything; it's company policy.

Club Med offers another example. It has a policy of being totally available to the customer at all times – given the choice between responding to a customer's request and completing an important document for internal use, the option is clear.

Migros has a policy of only taking on projects which have a social benefit. Given the choice between a project with little social benefit and large profits, and one with large social benefits and little profit, the option for them is also clear.

Maximising personal commitment: the case of Kwik-Fit

One of the biggest problems top management has when it comes to managing middle management is this group's reluctance to commit themselves personally to the achievement of a given goal. Most middle managers prefer to remain somewhat removed from the 'battlefield'; from this position they are able to place the blame 'elsewhere' in case of a failure. As a result, most actions do not benefit from middle management's full enthusiasm and devotion, and suffer as a consequence. For service quality mangement, it's a sure killer.

At Kwik-Fit, Tom Farmer, the CEO, has combined a unique financial remuneration scheme and a well-thought-out managerial structure to get the kind of top commitment from middle management that he wants.

Kwik-Fit is a Edinburgh-based chain of over 600 rapid service repair centres for tyre changes, oil changes, lubricator and shock absorber changes. In this business sector renowned for poor quality service, Kwik-Fit has made a name for itself by promising (and delivering) 100 per cent customer satisfaction. Tom Farmer is the founder and dynamic CEO who still runs Kwik-Fit.

In terms of managing middle management, Kwik-Fit's problem is very simple. They have over 600 separate outlets, each of which must be managed by a tremendously energetic individual, totally committed to Kwik-Fit and top quality customer service. If the company breaks these 600 centres into 10 or so smaller groups of centres, each with a separate boss, and then again into 10 or so smaller groups each with its separate boss, it quickly created a self-perpetuating hierarchy big enough to rival the public administration. Boredom could rapidly set in.

If, on the other hand, Kwik-Fit keeps its structure lean and mean, it must, none the less, have a way of controlling and motivating all of these managers simultaneously. The structure which Kwik-Fit chose focuses on the 'magic number 3'. The structure is called the 'partnership scheme' and was developed by Tom Farmer who remembered the days when he had just three Kwik-Fit centres to manage. 'Three centres was great. The guys used to get together once a week for beers at a local pub. Everybody was really up and felt that they had a piece of the action', explains Mr Farmer. 'When we went to four it was different. The guys weren't so excited and I had trouble getting them all to come every week.'

From this he deduced that a manager's capacity to direct and to engage the enthusiasm of his employees sharply declined when he had more than three centres to manage – thus the magic number was three.

Today, all Kwik-Fit centres are grouped into units of three, called partnerships. Each partnership is headed up by a partner who is at once a director of a centre and responsible for the well-being of the three centres. He ensures that the staff in all three centres are sufficiently motivated, trained, supervised etc. He ensures that all centres are keeping up the standards of service quality set by the company. He is also the individual who explains to managers how to turn 'leads' – potential new customers – into loyal customers and how to use the service quality monitoring systems provided by the company. He also acts as the liaison between the centres he managers and the regional director.

There are 17 regional directors at Kwik-Fit. Their role is 'to provide the hype'. 'Customer service has to be an obsession; it needs hype', says Tom Farmer. Regional managers are there to support the partners and managers. They also provide the procedures and the discipline. It is these individuals who pass the message about the company's commitment to customer satisfaction and its objective to be number one.

Above the regional managers are the three divisional managers, for Scotland ('which includes a bit of England'), middle England and south England, and, above them, Tom Farmer.

To make sure that partners don't stay in their own centre and neglect what's happening in the other two centres they manage, there is a set programme of visits which is co-ordinated with the rotation system controlling the work schedules of all employees. Centres are classified as A, B, or C. All the partners in the country visit A centres on Monday, B centres on Tuesday etc. They work in each centre twice a week; on one of those days, they work directly with the manager, on the other they replace him, so that he has a day off.

The rotation system provides for all employees to work a five-day week, but the system provides for a six-day work week. For one week in four, employees work a six day week, but in another week they get three days off in a row.

For Tom Farmer, it's the centre manager who is the pivotal person in the organisation, 'The kingpin at Kwik-Fit is the centre manager.' Centre managers tend to be very young, between 20 and 25 years old. Partners are around 30 to 35 years old. They are highly motivated by the financial remuneration scheme that makes it possible for them to earn twice the industry norm.

An average Kwik-Fit centre takes in, say, £40,000 a month. Of that 50 per cent – £20,000 – goes to headquarters to cover costs; such as training, computerisation, stock purchases, advertising etc., the other £20,000 goes to cover the centre's controllable costs such as heating, lighting, telephones, labour, small maintenance costs etc. The centre manager gets a five per cent profit share, after these costs have been deducted from his five per cent, and the partner a slightly larger percentage (of all the three centres).

There are also profit sharing schemes for all the staff in the centre according to their seniority/experience in the company – staff are classified as being either one, two, three or four star, the last being the most senior. All the stars of the staff are added up and divided into the profits, and distributed according to how many stars each employee has.

The end result is a middle manager who is totally committed to running his centre, or his three centres in the case of a partner, in the most efficient and most customer-conscious manner possible. These middle managers are committed to ensuring profitability of the centres because of the remuneration system. They are committed to achieving customer satisfaction because that is what they are evaluated on and because they are convinced that that is what ensures the continuity of sales in their centre. 'We balance the customer loyalty concept with the remuneration policy based on profits', says Tom Farmer.

Guiding middle management forward: the case of OK Service

Some top managers would claim that training middle management is a waste of effort. It doesn't improve their performance; the company makes an expensive investment for little return. It's just a motivation exercise, they say, 10 per cent knowledge improvement and 90 per cent entertainment.

In a lot of cases, those top managers are probably right. Middle managers don't often themselves see the applicability of most of the courses designed to improve their performance on the job. 'How to communicate better', 'Managing your time', 'Performing employee evaluations' – the titles are enticing, but what do they really offer to the middle manager in his daily work. He is not stupid; most of the theories at the base of these courses he has already heard of or read about. Worse, he's been trying to apply them for years and is not getting any better. Enrolling in the course doesn't help. It's not concrete enough. It gives him a better understanding of how the theory should work, but it doesn't help him *do* it.

At OK Service, training has another face. It's results oriented and it's interactive. Employees don't devote their training time to learning management theories, they devote it to applying them on their own business using real-life numbers.

OK Service is a French company in the business of supplying urgent handyman services to primarily city dwellers. The business is operated out of agencies located in major cities. The company has 14 owned agencies and 26 franchise agencies. The company's services are available on a subscription basis to individuals and small businesses, and the company focuses upon providing a high quality of service to its customers.

The key player at OK Service is the agency manager. Whether franchise or company-owned, the agency director has a great deal of autonomy from headquarters and few directives. His salary is tied to the profitability of the agency and to customer satisfaction through the customer retention rate which is calculated on a monthly basis.

Headquarters sees its role as a support unit, providing managers with the tools they need to manage their agencies and training in their use. None of the agency managers are obliged to use any of the tools or training headquarters offers. They have only two obligations: turn over a profit and attend the monthly managers' meeting in Marseilles.

Mr Kirichian, Chief Operating Officer, describes the monthly managers' meeting as being, '20 per cent analysis of the month's results, 20 per cent marketing information and 60 per cent training'. All of it takes place in the same location in the form of an enormous work session. Part of the benefit of the meeting is the exchange which occurs between managers from different parts of the country, with different levels of experience and different operating problems to resolve.

Headquarters has fixed the training part of the session to a rotational programme. Three topics are covered on a recurring basis every six months to a year. Service quality, financial and personnel management, and marketing/sales are the three topics covered. The objective of the training in each one of these subject areas is to master a set of management tools which permit the agency managers to run their agencies better.

For each of the three topics, the approach is the same. Management establishes an indicator which is 'measurable, objective, pertinent and rapidly available'. This could be the monthly operating profit, the number of clients discontinuing their service each month, the number of new clients each month, the employee turnover rate or any number of other indicators of business health in the agency.

Headquarters, then, establishes a benchmark standard for each indicator based on past experience with healthy agencies. The objective of each agency is to meet, and hopefully improve on, the benchmark figure.

More precise objectives are established for each manager. For example, a new manager's first task will be progressively to learn to forecast the indicator for his agency. At first, he will try to match his mid-month forecast to the end-of-month reality. Later, he will try to forecast the indicator at the beginning of the month. Finally, he will try to move both his forecast and his real figures up to the benchmark level set by the company.

A more experienced manager's goal might be to forecast an improvement on the benchmark indicator and consistently to realise his forecast. Regardless of whether a manager has been with the company for 5 months or 10 years, the economic conditions in the market, the labour situation, evolutions in customer expectations will always make it worth while for agency managers to share their views about how to improve their performance using the indicator system.

To permit agency managers more easily to monitor their performance against their own forecasts and against the performance of other agencies, headquarters calculates them for the manager and 'posts' them via their private Minitel (the French telecommunication interactive video system) line at the end of each month.

Headquarters' job is to ensure regular innovations in the indicator system. While some indicators are a permanent part of the management system; others are developed according to evolutions in the market or in response to the problems managers are facing. For example, one indicator that was developed in service quality is the customer satisfaction survey. It is a sheet sent directly from headquarters to customers asking for their feedback on the service provided and for a confirmation of the sum charged to them by the technician. The survey was developed with a two-fold objective in mind; first, to have real feedback on the standard of service the company was maintaining and, secondly, to ensure that technicians were aware that their work (and what they charged for it) was being double-checked by the company.

The beauty in OK Service's training system is that it allows for a never-ending period of apprenticeship on the part of each agency manager. One day a month, he has the glorious experience of receiving feedback on what he did right and wrong on the basis of objective indicators, together with suggestions from a very varied source – other agency managers – on ways to improve his performance.

Because of the judicious blend of theory and real-life practice, the middle manager recognises the immediate value of what he is learning and has a reason to improve, be it only in the total of his own paycheque at the end of the month.

Because the management lessons are taught using measurable and objective indicators, the agency managers can gain an immediate sense of accomplishment with the application of the methods and their subsequent reflection in the indicators.

Because the situation facing managers is real and is thus never identical, and because headquarters ensures a certain degree of innovation in the indicators, the training is always applicable, regardless of the manager's length of experience in the company.

Lastly, because the use of the indicators is never imposed, agency managers don't feel forced by 'big brother' to apply the training; they do it of their own will and in their own interest. 'We call it training by self-discovery', says Mr Kirichian.

Promoting the entrepreneurial spirit: the case of Citicorp

Large, mammoth-sized companies are usually those that have the greatest difficulties with motivating employees. By necessity, these companies compartmentalise their activities, limiting the scope and range of most employees' activities to that which is available in their own department. 'The division', 'the company' are simply ambiguous terms on a piece of paper.

The case is all the more serious with middle management. Their job is to fill slots in little compartments shown on an organisation chart. Each compartment needs a name in it, so there you are; as long as all the slots in the compartments are filled, everything's OK. No one is really aware of what the individuals filling these slots do or of their value, if any, to the corporation.

Many companies have dealt with the problem of compartmentalisation by making each compartment into a separate business – strategic business units, these are called. There are a lot of them around. They operate as independent profit centres and are run by 'SBU' (Strategic Business Unit) managers who, for one reason or another, don't seem to feel that they are much better off than when they were filling slots.

Somehow, somewhere, someone should be able to make business units a little less like compartments and middle managements a little less like slot-fillers. Although we can't promise to have found the miracle solution, Citicorp's way of managing its organisation comes a little bit closer. At Citicorp, 'SBU' units (although the term was never actually used) have become enclaves of entrepreneurial effort and middle managers have become entrepreneurs, their own boss and masters of their own destiny.

In general, Citicorp has always encouraged the entrepreneurial spirit in their employees – they encourage them to 'take the ball and run with it'. Now, the company has gone a step further. Today, whenever possible, managers are being actively encouraged to run their departments or divisions as separate companies. 'Within a big multinational, we try to manage it (our division) as a small family firm,' says Mervyn Davies, Corporate Banking.

Citicorp is one of the world's largest banks. It is active in all major banking sectors, including retail banking, corporate lending, investment banking and foreign exchange. It has operations worldwide with major subsidiaries in Europe, Asia and South America. For many years, it has been a recognised leader in the retail sector in the US for the quality of service to customers. Our research looked at the group's European operations in the investment banking and corporate lending areas.

Citicorp is a good company in which to create 'entrepreneurial enclaves' for two major reasons. First, practically every department of the bank has some form of contact with the external customer. 'There are not many people in this Bank that don't in some way manage a customer relationship.' In terms of managing in an entrepreneurial fashion, that's important because the manager and his team can thereby gauge the results of their efforts in terms of its impact on customers.

The second reason is because the bank today has a lot of different activities that can be developed separately by groups of qualified individuals. Foreign exchange is a good example, cash management is another, assistance to developing businesses (venture capital) is a third, portfolio management a fourth . . . the list is quite long. Some of the bank's greatest successes have, in fact, been made by middle managers running this department for a particular country or sector, as if they were their own company. Citicorp's retail strategy for Asia is based on the concept of targeting high net-worth individuals. Rana Talwar created the programme and manages it. He said of it in a recent interview in *Fortune*, 'We are building one of Citibank's most successful franchises' (*Fortune* magazine).

In our research for this book, we met the managers from three of Citicorp's European-based entrepreneurial enclaves – Corporate Banking, Investment Management, and World Corporate Group. All of these divisions' managers were motivated and committed to what they were doing for the bank. Three factors in particular seemed to motivate them.

The first of these was transparency. As managers of an 'entrepreneurial enclave', the results of their work and their specific achievements are well known in the organisation. It is less a question of operating a profitable unit, as might be the case with an SBU manager, and more the expansion of the business into something bigger and better. 'We are not an established player and we're looking at a horizon of three to five years', says Mervyn Davies.

The second motivating factor was the possibility to manage one's enclave as one sees fit. There are no restrictions from the big bosses or any particular methods of management imposed upon middle managers; they are free to apply what works best. 'Everyone is pretty much left to his own devices'.

Mr Davies, for example, used that freedom to create standards for client presentations and proposals; in Investment Management they used it to increase training and changing the way the unit called on customers. 'When we talk about entrepreneurial spirit at Citicorp, this is what we mean: nobody tells you to do it that way, you just do it. Each unit is like a small business. It's your baby.'

The third big motivator is the possibility each manager has to develop and promote his business with clients. All Citicorp personnel are focused on improving the bank's penetration in the market place, but managers of entrepreneurial enclaves, particularly so. Target clients and market share are the topics of daily discussion. Being responsible for increasing that market share or gaining a big, new customer is a source of considerable satisfaction. 'We recognise efforts beyond purely financial achievement.

Our purpose is to emphasise global teamwork and interdependence and the fact that we are working for the client', says Linc Hoffman.

While it's true that top management delegates a great deal of responsibility to the managers of the various units, they still guide the direction of their efforts, primarily through the review of the yearly business plan which each manager does for his unit. It is as thorough and detailed as any ever presented by an entrepreneur to his venture capitalist or banker.

Each entrepreneurial enclave has the right to its own marketing research from the marketing research department, in addition to what he has already provided; he also has the right to create his own market strategy, in co-ordination with the other world units and those units with which his activities overlap, and to do his own planning for the unit on a medium-term basis. Assuming his plan is accepted, he's on his own.

'Every year, I do a plan. There's a definition of our business, a very complete synopsis of the market including an analysis of the strengths and weaknesses of our competitors, objectives for the next year, including target clients, competitive advantages, marketing approach and areas for improvement, a financial projection of the business over the medium term and for the next year'.

In most cases, the entrepreneurial enclaves seem to work. In the rare cases where they don't, it's a question of the quality of the middle manager and his readiness to assume the level of responsibility that was given to him. In general, the advantages of the approach outweigh the disadvantages.

First, the entrepreneurial enclaves are a good way to obtain the full commitment of middle managers to the achievement of the business. Because they are solely responsible for what happens to the unit, most managers feel obliged to live up to the responsibility that has been entrusted to them.

Secondly, it encourages whatever creative or innovative tendencies these managers might have. The possibility to organise and run things as they see fit permits them to experiment with new methods which can later be taken and used elsewhere in the bank. The Asian high net-worth market approach is a good example.

Thirdly, it makes managers more flexible. Because they are more committed and tied to the satisfaction of their customer, they are more aware of market and business realities, and more ready to adapt to them when necessary.

Lastly, the positive effects which this kind of structure has on the level of motivation and commitment of middle managers cascade down to the lower levels, encouraging similar kinds of behaviour with frontline or more junior managers. 'Commitment to the customer can only work if all the staff buy into the ideas in [the yearly] plan. Everyone contributed to the elaboration of our plan.'

Leaving managers with freedom to motivate: the case of Sainsbury's

Sainsbury's is the largest UK food retailer. It has been in business for over a century and today operates over 300 stores throughout the country.

Sainsbury's believes in providing service quality to its customers. Not only do they believe in it, they have also committed themselves to it, in writing, in the company's corporate objectives printed in every annual report and financial statement (*see* company description). For Sainsbury's, good service in the food retail business means good service at the store level. Beyond the pleasant shopping environment, the company places a priority on the quality of the personal interaction between customers and staff.

To ensure that good interaction they need staff who are committed to service quality and happy about providing it to their customers, and, most of all, they need good store managers. A good store manager, according to Sainsbury's, is not necessarily a good accountant, nor is he necessarily good at merchandising or at store displays. He certainly doesn't have to be capable of making heads or tails of an electrical refrigeration system and wouldn't know what to tell the landscaping companies about his share of the £½ million worth of plants and shrubs growing on Sainsbury's property. If, by chance, he knows something about cooking, then it's just that – by chance. Sainsbury's store managers are asked to do one thing and only one thing really well, and that is to manage and motivate people.

The strategy is clear; it's a question of creating a system which allows people to do what they do best. The Sainbury's corporate structure with its army of experts in every conceivable domain is must better equipped to concern itself with the intricacies of managing the store. By taking on all of these responsibilities, the corporate centre leaves store managers free to spend time on the floor with their staff and customers. 'I manage from the shop floor', says Norman Lake, store manager.

The system works well. Sainsbury's has created a model store which virtually runs itself. The heat, electricity and refrigerator units are all controlled by a central unit, programmed and maintained by an outside company. If anything goes wrong, the machine itself notifies the company which has a contract to be there within one hour. In most cases, the manager doesn't even know that something has gone wrong before the problem is fixed.

The programming of the machine controls the heat so that it is never below or above, by more than $3°$, the optimum $20°$. It also ensures that the lights are at just the right level all day long and all season long.

Sainsbury's efficient systems also control food ordering and price checks to ensure that low stock items are automatically delivered to the store and that there is no difference between the price recorded at the check-out stand and in the company's advertising.

Sainsbury's central management also ensures that store managers don't have to worry about the store layout, the merchandising policy or the sales policy – it's all standardised and it's all controlled by headquarters.

Worries about staffing are a thing of the past; that, too, is controlled by computer and comes out each week for every employee in the store.

The shrubs are watered, the grass is mown and the windows are washed all without the store manager lifting a hand.

A store manager in a large Sainsbury's store manages over 350 line staff and nearly 50 managers – it's the same size as a small factory! His job is to maintain a personal contact with all of these individuals throughout the day. Because the structure is relatively flat he is personally looked up to to set the example for the appropriate behaviour, particularly *vis-à-vis* customers.

To understand a little better how it works, let's follow Norman Lake through a typical day in his store. His actions will include at least some or all of the following:

- a talk with the local vicar to make sure that the special bread that Sainsbury's supplies them is as appreciated as much this year as last year;
- a wipe-test to make sure that the top of the refrigerator case is perfectly clean for store opening;
- a look at the vegetable counters; he picks up any green leaves on the ground;
- a discussion with the beverage department manager to have his reaction on the new line of soft drinks. 'Last year my beverage man came up with an excellent idea about how the beer should be laid out; it was against company standard, but I let him try it. It turned out so well that it's now being used elsewhere.';
- a look at the staff information board to find out what social events are scheduled for the week;
- a stop to chat with one of the cleaning staff; he asks about a new baby, adding that nothing would be the same around the store if it weren't for the vigilance of the cleaning staff;
- a brief visit to his office when he signs a birthday card for one of his staff members 'Every member of staff at this store gets a birthday card from the manager';
- a talk with one of the girls handling the ordering 'There's something good in everybody; I just need to find it and develop it';
- up to the lunch room for the daily 'snaps' meeting – it's like bridge 'All the managers have a snaps meeting every day; it's a game of cards at lunch and teatime; it's a big motivator';
- back down on the store floor, he hands out a star; stars are for employees that have done something really special that week; 'They're always asking me, "Do I get a gold for that?"';
- later, he hands out the 'plonker of the week' award for something really stupid done by an employee;
- for an hour or so he just chats to customers; some of them he already knows personally;

- on his way to the training room, he passes by the mirror which says, 'See yourself as the customer sees you', which he put up a month earlier;
- in the training room he checks the training log to see who has and who hasn't done their training;
- for the rest of the evening before closing time he circulates, reminding staff of his theme of the month, 'Be one step ahead of the manager'.

At no point in the typical day of a Sainsbury's manager is it necessary for him to plunge into the operational details of making the store run. His entire focus is on ensuring that his employees are motivated and satisfied, that his store is kept neat, clean and well stocked (by these same employees), and that his customers feel that they are receiving a good quality, personalised service. Sainsbury's managers are chosen and promoted on this basis and, thanks to Sainsbury's corporate support structure, they are free to do their job well.

What, then, are the lessons we can learn from this example about how top management could better manage middle managers? There are two. First, if you're a top manager, before handing down multiple directives to middle managers, decide for yourself what you want them to do with their time. Choose people that fit that description and then don't expect them to be strong in every field. Second, once you've decided what middle managers in your company should be doing, take away all of the peripheral tasks. Don't clutter up a manager's day with things that others can do better. Instead, set up a system which permits your middle managers to apply their creative talents and enthusiasm where they are likely to yield the best results.

Fighting the public servant syndrome – the metamorphosis of an engineer: the case of Schlumberger

Today, in practically any public administration the world round, one encounters the same thing – 'It's not my job; you have to go to the office down the hall', 'I register deaths; I don't know anything about births'. It's the public servant syndrome, i.e. the inability of an employee to step out of his assigned role to assume another responsibility, however small.

While the public servant syndrome can be found to some extent everywhere, in private corporations, it affects primarily middle management. After 10 or so years in their 'chosen' field, middle managers are often unwilling or unable to assume responsibilties in areas which are unfamilar to them. They become rigid into their role and are, as a group, the least flexible part of the whole organisation. In a corporation under change – which most corporations are these days – a middle management suffering from the public service syndrome is a real handicap.

Schlumberger has managed to avoid the public servant syndrome and is instead blessed with a middle management which is, by contrast, not the least, but the most adaptable part of the organisation.

Schlumberger was started in the beginning of this century by two brothers. One of these brothers, a professor in physics, invented a method for describing the configuration of the earth's subsurface by dropping a line into a well pit and recording electrical resistances. The technique was refined and later used primarily by the oil and gas industry to obtain information about the producing power of a well. Today, the company is the primary company worldwide practising the technique, with a major market share.

In terms of its personnel, Schlumberger employs only engineers. Besides secretaries and the occasional financial accountant, Schlumberger employees only engineers. Most engineers are hired into the company right out of school. They go through a three-month intensive training course before they are allowed to go to a customer's well site. Even so, they have another nine months of apprenticeship-type training before they are ready to go out alone. Another five years with the company and most of these engineers are at middle management level.

Since Schlumberger has essentially engineers, functions which are normally assumed by other specialists are assumed by engineers. More accurately put, Schlumberger adopted a deliberate policy, from the very beginning, of encouraging the versatility of its engineers. In our interviews, we spoke with a product manager in Paris who had previously been a field engineer in Saudia Arabia, and with the group training manager, who had assumed the function only two months ago and had only one previous training post. Today, despite the complexities inherent in running a modern corporation the size of Schlumberger and the widely acclaimed need for specialised knowledge in all domains, these engineers do a very good job of running their organisation.

There are three things that make this possible. The first is training. Schlumberger's one year introductory programme which all engineers go through is only the first step. Training is a continuous process. Each person has his own development plan with "areas to be enhanced". Training is given to help the employee to progress in those areas.

Schlumberger has a very large series of self-managed training programmes. The employee is provided with materials for the course; he co-ordinates with his supervision to set a schedule for its completion. There are six tests for each topic, and when the individual completes the material for that level, he takes the test. Assuming he passes the test, he finally attends a week-long seminar in Paris for which specialists in the given field are brought in to lecture. There is training available on any range of topics, from communication and sales to financial management. Most of the course topics are not in engineering, but in those areas of managerial functions with which the engineers are unfamiliar. In total, the engineers get a minimum of about three weeks of formal training a year.

A second element that makes the system work is the constant mobility that is practised throughout the firm. No one engineer stays in a given post for more than three to four years. While the beginning of his career is dominated by time spent at the well site, in his later years he is transferred between different geographic locations and different functions. As a result, he learns to adapt himself quickly to new environments and to meet new job challenges as they arise.

The third element that makes middle managers so flexible is the culture of the company. There is no shame in not knowing how to do something. Because everyone starts at the same level and is, at one time or another, equally inexperienced in a certain task, employees do not demand of one another a great degree of 'technical skills' in their function. There is little competition among managers to 'prove' their expertise to one another and the most highly demanded skills are those of good general management, such as communication, team spirit, good co-ordination etc. In terms of managing middle management, the advantages of the system are many.

The system gives the company greater flexibility. No one individual is attached to a post or to a geographic location. This is particularly true of middle managers who, with their more extensive experience, can fill any number of positions within the company. No one is irreplaceable either. If the company needs to cut staff , it can, right across the board.

The system provides better preparation for top management. In comparison with companies that are obliged to choose from the ranks of either marketing, finance or production for their top executives, Schlumberger can choose from a wide selection of managers who, by their 15th or so year with the company, have had experience in every function that exists. They are less likely to have built-in biases or prejudices, or to have built up a 'clique' of managers in their speciality area which would prevent them from making objective business decisions.

The Schlumberger approach also permits the company constantly to re-evaluate what it is doing. Each new engineer occupying a post sees things with new eyes; he has the same position as a consultant does when he comes in from the outside to help a company. Policies and structures which have existed for some time and which no one thought to reconsider can be examined in a new light.

Lastly, the approach encourages better team spirit and co-ordination between departments. Because no one stays in any function or any post for any length of time they do not have the opportunity to develop deep rivalries. An engineer who is a salesman today, may be in research and development tomorrow; it is in his interest to foster the best possible relations with everyone.

How to transform middle management into quality leaders

Every company we meet where top management wants to change the service orientation always has the same complaints: middle management is blocking the road to improving service. Some of the causes are well known.

- Often, promotion to middle management positions has been based on good performance at the frontline rather than good potential to take the role as coach, trainers, communications.
- Middle management often has conflicting roles. On one side they are told that customer service is important, on the other side that their peformance continues to be based on economic terms only (sales volume through new clients rather than sales increase through increased loyalty).
- Organisations have a tendancy to increase fat by adding layers in the hierarchy. This is especially true when companies focus their quality effort on quality control rather than *ex ante* prevention. It is particularly visible in service; supervisors are led by district managers who are themselves

Pay for supervision or pay for service?
(Average pay)

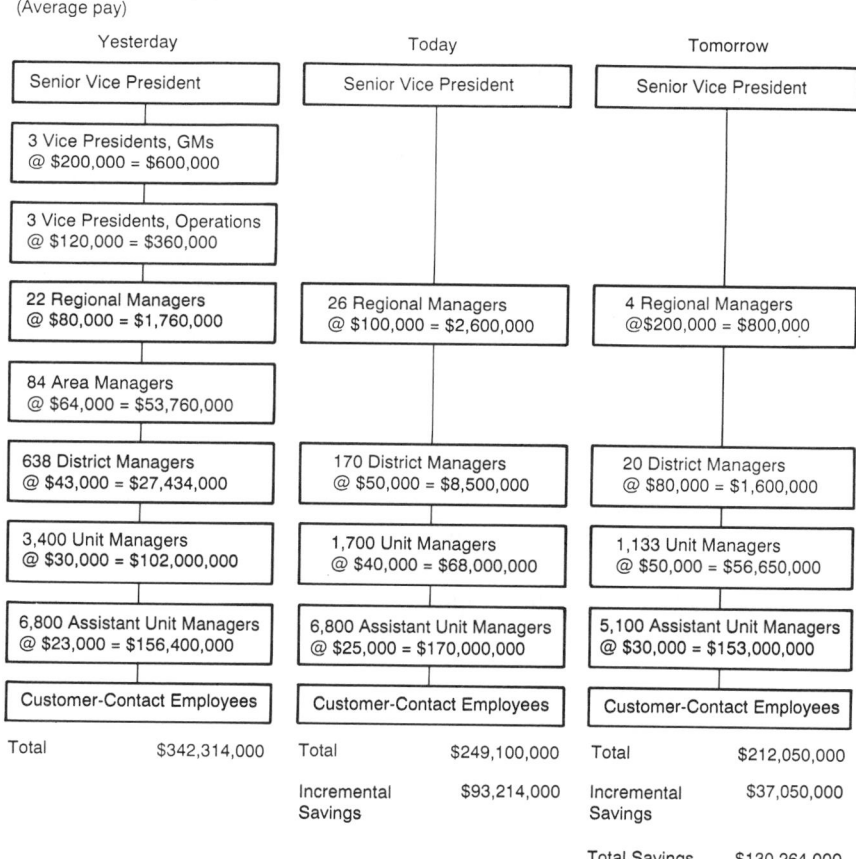

	Yesterday	Today	Tomorrow
	Senior Vice President	Senior Vice President	Senior Vice President
	3 Vice Presidents, GMs @ $200,000 = $600,000		
	3 Vice Presidents, Operations @ $120,000 = $360,000		
	22 Regional Managers @ $80,000 = $1,760,000	26 Regional Managers @ $100,000 = $2,600,000	4 Regional Managers @$200,000 = $800,000
	84 Area Managers @ $64,000 = $53,760,000		
	638 District Managers @ $43,000 = $27,434,000	170 District Managers @ $50,000 = $8,500,000	20 District Managers @ $80,000 = $1,600,000
	3,400 Unit Managers @ $30,000 = $102,000,000	1,700 Unit Managers @ $40,000 = $68,000,000	1,133 Unit Managers @ $50,000 = $56,650,000
	6,800 Assistant Unit Managers @ $23,000 = $156,400,000	6,800 Assistant Unit Managers @ $25,000 = $170,000,000	5,100 Assistant Unit Managers @ $30,000 = $153,000,000
	Customer-Contact Employees	Customer-Contact Employees	Customer-Contact Employees

Total	$342,314,000	Total	$249,100,000	Total	$212,050,000
		Incremental Savings	$93,214,000	Incremental Savings	$37,050,000
				Total Savings	$130,264,000

This hypothetical example reflects the experience of actual companies that are redesigning their organisations according to the new logic of service. By cutting out layers of management and redefining frontline jobs, they are generating labour cost savings that allow price reductions, higher wages, and human-resource investments – and thus yield better service and higher profits.

Figure 7.1 Source: Harvard Business Review, *Sept–Oct 1991*

managed by regional managers who report to operations managers. The more layers there are, the more everyone is playing the role of quality controller rather than giving initiative, training, coaching and helping the front line to operate satisfactorily for the customer. In an issue of *Harvard Business Review* a mock-up calculator was given which shows in fact it can be less costly and more effective to reduce the number of layers and give more responsibility and initiative to front line supervisors and site managers. This is not to say that the hierarchies are useless. After reorganising to reduce the layers, there will still be unit managers, supervisors and regional managers. Companies which have been very quick to understand the need to put customers first, put frontline people first. Middle managers are there to help the process. Below are a few ways companies are helping middle management take care of customer service.

Restructure by outsourcing or subcontracting what a company cannot do best internally

From pay to data processing, to maintenance, to documentation, to training personnel, companies are not only reducing costs but also reducing the amount of pressure a permanent structure puts on the field because it has to invent its own justification every day. This means controls, procedures, more compulsory ways of doing business. Support functions are minimised and find their original role: to 'support' the business. Boeing, for instance, has put all its functions into a separate service company of 5000 employees!

If the line is not happy with their service they can outsource.

Transform head office into a service centre

This requires a change of both mind-set and culture. It usually starts with measuring the degree of satisfaction of the field (sites, national subsidiaries, regions) with head office services.It then goes on to define what service to give to the field using this simple matrix:

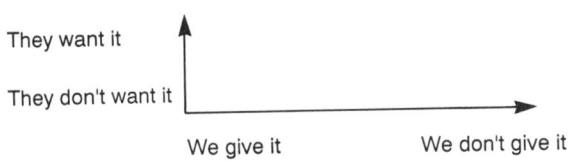

It also means a lot of sensitizing to change the mind-set of headquarters employees going from changing the name (thus a restaurant chain, Hippopotamus, has renamed its HQ 'hippo advice') to training on customer/supplier relationship, to big campaigns to show what it means not to be treated like a customer seen from a subsidiary 20,000 km away. An example of such a campaign is described in the chapter on communication.

Finally, often it means rewording the work flow process of each HQ service completely to fit internal customer needs. Companies would typically define what product or services they produce for internal customers how it is currently done, how important it is for internal customers and either eliminate or improve efficiency of the work flow process in order to maximise effectiveness and minimise costs.

Change planning and control systems

Unless service is fully integrated with the planning and control process of a company, it has virtually no chance of success. Below is an example of how Xerox UK incorporates service into its business objectives, action plans and performance evaluation.

1991 Goals	*Objectives*	*Measurements*
Customer Satisfaction (Applies to both internal and External Customers)	● Become No 1 Vendor in the industry for customer satisfaction	● 3% dissatisfaction as measured by 90 day post install survey
		● CSMS target at 86% overall satisfaction
		● 10% XF Order Reject target – DOP Reject rate TBD
		● Accommodations target at $677.3mk
	● Account Management process implemented	● Sales Returns TBD by 19th Oct
	● Sales Tenure	● 100% Account Plans completed for Key Accounts
		● Targets by category
Business Results (applies to achievement of revenue, profit, cash goals, and/or reduction in expense and utilisation of RX(UK) assets and resources)	● Plan Achieved	
	Direct and Indirect ORS	● 100% achieved
	Rev Plan Achieved	● 100% achieved
	Direct and Indirect ORS	● 100% achieved
	Profit Plan Achieved	● 100%
	Achieved price levels attained	● 100%
	Activity Plan Achieved by PDU	
	● Marketing programmes achieved (balanced participation)	

Figure 7.2

Figure 7.2 continued

	• Marketing programmes implemented	• 100% plan achieved
	• Coverage Strategy implemented	• 3% vacant territories
	• Sales Management Process Implemented – 30 60 90 day prospect cycle managed	• Outlook accuracy +5%
	• Expenses Managed	• Plan met
	• Assets Managed	• 80% Free trial conversion within 30 days
Employee Motivation (applies to improvements in employee motivation; objectives required for all managers, self-development objective required for all employees)	• EO Programmes and Goals • ESS overall satisfaction at benchmark • HRM process implemented	• Trend towards 1992 Functional Goal achievement • Employee survey results at 50% satisfied • PP&A 100%
Quality (applies to the utilisation of Leadership Through Quality tools and processes to reduce errors and improve business results)	• Policy Deployment implemented • Quality Behaviour and Practices Role Modelled • Ethical Business Conduct • LTQ Refresher Cascade implemented	• Partnerships and function with Processes implemented • 100% Quality RROs • MPS conducted • No of Policy Violations • Implemented by end Q2/91 and 80% positive feedback achieved

Look at your planning and control manuals. Where does the customer fit in? Where is service incorporated? Where does it ask what you intend to do to improve a customer satisfaction next year?

We are not talking only about long-term planning here. Creating project teams of managers whose purpose is to devise action plans to increase service while reducing cost is also part of the process of transforming the role of middle managers. We have found it useful and effective, for example to finish any training seminar by asking each manager to write his action plans for the next 3 months right after the seminar, week by week. It forces them to think hard on priorities and really incorporate their new role into daily life.

Help individuals at every level in the hierarchy become service quality leaders

This is an another task taken on by service companies. The level of investment in an individual's training is usually inversely proportional to his or her level in the hierarchy. The higher you are, the less training you get on customer service! World class leaders have understood that you have to do the reverse! For two simple reasons.

In many cases, these individuals are part of the permanent structure (it is the case in tourism, hotel distribution, leisure, restaurant, industries for instance). If they do not feel comfortable with quality, service, customer satisfaction issues, they won't transmit the message to employees whose turnover can go as high as 300 per cent! Disney has understood this phenomenon very well. A student who comes for Christmas to work in the park gets 4 days of training on how to answer all customer questions. But his boss who is a permanent employee gets 10 weeks. A new GO at Club Med gets 3 to 8 days of training. A chief of village gets 5 months! If the changing role of managers is from telling to showing, from ordering to persuading, from deciding to facilitating, in a nutshell from manager to leader, it requires fundamentally new skills that cannot be taught overnight. As an example, in a large distribution chain of leisure products, it took 2 days just to train store managers to use the results of customer satisfaction surveys as a leadership tool (not just putting the result on the information board): how to read it and understand, how to communicate it to the team, what points to stress, which points to use for improvement challenges for the team, how to answer employee questions . . .

Working with 20 managers of a bank, all of equal rank, all responsible for a branch or a product division, I asked them to indicate why a customer should go to their bank rather than another one. I got 20 different stories! In another company with over 100 sites of 500 employees and 20 managers, a survey showed 50 per cent of managers did not know about the company's history, culture and main strategy.

How can you satisfy customers, if your managers do not even know how to sell your company!

Help managers learn management by signals

All managers are looked at by their teams with magnifying glasses. Whatever they do or say is magnified 10 times. And many times what seemed trivial to a manager is seen as being of great importance to his team. Every day, managers send positive or negative signals about how much they believe in customer service. The sum of those signals will tell more surely than any policy, event, or presidential speech whether commitment to quality of service is there or not. Leaving how to supress negative signals and increase positive signals requires some doing. In seminars with managers, I often ask the following questions:

- if you were a little mouse and heard what they say about your commitment to service, what would you hear. If it was a true one,
how can you improve by actions, or behaviour so that you will hear what you want to?

It is only after hearing a long list of actions that we arrive at the suggestion that a manager should say thank you when someone brings him something he asked for! In fact there is a famous case – the Paul Revere Insurance Co – which had to launch a thank you campaign to push the managers to say thank you to their secretaries.

Redesign top-down communication

The mere fact that we call it communication and not information is to emphasise a key element that is missing in many organisations: two-way feedback. World-class leaders have their employees rate their management. World leaders also make sure that whatever gets sent out, has been received and fully understood. Take the very simple example of memos: all top-down memos have virtually the same style, the same format, whether they are for action, for information, for response, or for an emergency. In a study we did with a retail chain we found out that 80 per cent of what was sent out by headquarters had not been 'received' by unit managers and 90 per cent of the information received was not diffused within the stores! Using such trivial devices as having different colours for each type of memo (red for emergency!) helps. Less trivial is training managers to become communicators rather then lecturers or, as with the Continental example in the chapter on measuring, it is the furnishing of support material both to make sure messages sent are coherent and to make middle management more at ease with their staff when communicating the information.

Reorganize to reduce layers and refocus on the customer

It is often necessary for companies to change their organisation structure either to reduce the number of layers or to refocus the structure around the customer.

A local manager supported by a staff of trainers, communication and public relations experts, marketing managers and top flight team of specialists trained to lend a hand to operational units or to replace people on vacation or sick will be more effective and less costly than a regional structure in which all district managers do is control and audit the work of others – when they are not driving around in their cars.

Reorganising by market segment is a big task but it is a necessary one if one wants both to change the outlook of management, their perspective and the way they think about customers. Club Med's success in Asia and North America improved dramatically when the organisational structure changed from a funcitional set up to a structure by zone. The product became better adapted to local needs, marketing became sharper. In 1987, when SKF realised that the needs of OEM, automotive and industrial markets were different, they moved from worldwide product divisions to market divisions. It was a fantastic success and a major turnaround against the Japanese competition. Most resistance to such structure changes come from two directions: duplication of resources are necessary (but the pay offs are bigger) and middle management does not want to move or change their roles. These issues should be addressed prior to the change for example, what common resources will be shared and which will be duplicated? How will managers change roles, and with what training? In the end, some disruptions are necessary; it is difficult to make omelettes without breaking eggs.

Change performance evaluation

Again if the role of middle manager goes from saying no to saying try, from telling to training from ordering to persuading, from selling volume to getting customers it should be reflected in the way they are evaluated. Since it is a revolution, evaluation should not be done in the classical way, using a dimension followed by a rating system such as outstanding, good or to be improved. We recommend companies to use a subtler approach.

Table 7.1

Outstanding Service	Good	Fair	Insufficient
– helps front line people serve when there is a crowd			
– sets the example by welcoming and orientating customers			– spends too much time in his office
– does more than is usual to make a customer happy			– does not talk to customers directly
– takes into account his staff ideas to improve service			– prefers to do inquiries before responding to customers
– encourages initiatives to be taken by his staff			
– never doubts a customer's good faith			

- To define the mission of each manager in four parts: quality, economics social relations and cooperation with other departments.
- To set up objectives for each.
- To identify the competences necessary to accomplish the mission.
- To evaluate current competences in three categories (outstanding role model, good, to be improved through . . .).
- To evaluate performance on criteria which describes good behaviour. Such a scale might appear as one of those shown in Table 7.1 (only two extreme points are filled).

  As the list of 'how-to's' suggests, there are many facets which can help middle management grow and change. No simple one will do. It is the biggest investment and it is also the biggest risk.

8 RECRUIT RIGHT, TRAIN WELL

Introduction

Recruiting the correct employees into the organisation proved to be an important aspect of service management for many of the companies we looked at. For the most part companies we talked to wanted employees who were open-minded, flexible and people oriented. For all of the companies, training was even more important than recruitment and was a crucial success factor.

Training was a split between practical on-the-job training and what could be called philosophical training which presented the company's business ethics and how they should be applied to each employee's work environment.

Most of the companies didn't train people right away upon entering the company; they gave them a one or two-day introductory course. After that they were on the job, closely supervised by their manager or a godfather. Real training came later, between one month and three months later, but generally within the first three months.

This training was extensive and customer orientation was an integral part of most training programmes. In fewer cases, customer handling was separated, but generally only when applied to a specific situation, i.e. a return or complaint.

Ongoing training was primarily used as a motivational tool and refresher courses were preferred for skills used every day – including those concerning customer contact.

Training and recruiting

Training for motivation: the case of ISS

ISS is a Danish company with international operations in professional cleaning, security services, linen services, building maintenance, building automation and catering – practically any service which a large office building or complex could need. In professional cleaning, which represents roughly 80 per cent of the company's revenues, it is the leader in practically every market in which it operates.

Its services are provided primarily by what is called 'unskilled labour'. It employs 115,000 individuals worldwide, roughly 80 per cent of which fall into this category. 'We work in the low end of the labour market. We employ people who speak other languages, immigrants or workers who are not necessarily educated.' With 73 per cent of its revenues going towards saleries, wages and related expenses, ISS points out that, 'People are our most important asset.'

Its strategy is to provide service excellence and that includes, in a very large way, the behaviour of their employees on the job. 'We are a pure service company, service is not an add-on, service is our core product. The technology we use is located between the ears of 115,000 people.'

ISS's policy is to nurture employees in order to develop their skills and to motivate them in their work. Training and education plays a principal role in this nurturing process. For ISS, training represents the principal factor of job motivation for its employees. By working through the company's training and development programme, an employee can gain skills and status which are recognised within the company and on the open market.

There are basically three kinds of training being done at ISS. The first kind is introductory training, done when the employee first joins the company. Secondly, there is speciality skills training, done to prepare an employee for a specific and specialised task. Thirdly, there is promotional and managerial training which qualifies employees to advance on to higher levels of responsibility within the company. Overall, ISS sees training as an absolute necessity. 'If you don't train people, you don't deliver the product. It's as simple as that.'

'Our induction training is very formalised', explained one manager. In fact, the same basic two half-day session course is followed by every employee in Europe upon joining the company. The course introduces the employee to the company and presents its business principles, including its customer service orientation. The same basic minimum of training must be observed throughout the company regardless of whether it's for employees in Brazil, the US or Sweden.

Once the employee is on the job, he is being trained on a daily basis by his supervisor. Within the first year, an employee receives between three and four days of additional classroom training. In some countries, the employee will be sent to a special school where they will receive three weeks of commercial cleaning experience before going on the customer site. Roughly 50 per cent of any cleaning course is on how to clean and the other 50 per cent is on how to behave with customers. Employees are trained on how to handle customer complaints and what to do in uncomfortable situations with the customer.

Specialised training is offered to prepare staff for special cleaning functions or situations. such as hospitals, industry, hotels etc. Each requires a specific skill or know-how. ISS prepares employees for working in these situations and has had very positive results in terms of employee motivation. 'The key is professionalising the job. . . . Every time we have professionalised an area or when people are transferred to a specialised area like that, [employee] turnover rates and absenteeism rates go way down.'

Overall, ISS has lower employee turnover rates than the majority of the competition. Managers at ISS believe that this is at least partly due to their training programmes. 'I think that this is due to the fact that we get people into training programmes.'

While training of frontline staff is very important, the training of their supervisors is considered to be vital. 'The main focus of all training activities will be on the supervisory level, training them to train, giving them all the knowledge that is required by their people. This is the only way that we can get all the knowledge out to the worksite.'

The training which is provided for supervisors falls under the general category of training which the company offers for career advancement. This programme is considered to be a major motivator. The training increases employees' overall competence on the job and increases their self-esteem. 'In order for us to give quality to our customers, we need to raise the whole level of esteem of the job.'

The training is organised as a five-step career development programme. As the employee moves from the first to the fifth star he gradually gains more responsibility. By completing the first star level, the employee attains the bottom rung supervisor position. It takes two to five years to go from the first to the fifth star.

Training is offered on a yearly basis and it is a series of sets of training – first a classroom course followed by an on-the-job evaluation, followed again by more classroom training. As employees move up, they become responsible for larger and more demanding projects. 'You don't motivate people very much by money, you motivate them with programmes like this.'

Training by monitoring progress; the case of SVP

SVP stands for 'If you please' in French; it is also the name of a company providing information and advice by telephone. It was created as early as 1935 and has survived wars and boom periods to become the largest provider of its service in the world with subsidiaries in 24 countries.

SVP has been managed by Brigitte de Gastines since 1976. For her, the heart of their business is, 'to provide the information that is necessary for management in order to take decisions'. SVP's target clientèle are small to medium-sized businesses that do not have the resources to maintain an in-house information or reference library. SVP is equipped to answer questions and provide advice on a full range of topics including law, finance, taxation, accounting, international expansion, labour issues and social and cultural aspects.

The SVP service is available on a subscription basis. Subscribers pay a fee for the year and can use the service as often as they like. Presently, SVP has a 90 per cent fidelity rate. 'My objective is zero-departure,' (subscription cancellation) says Mrs de Gastines.

To keep that 90 per cent fidelity rate, her company must provide an extremely high quality of service. 'The originality of SVP is in its capacity to treat information, to advise the customer well and to be always available and always at the disposition of the customer.' The principal individual responsible for doing that is the consultant whose receives the customer over the phone. An average discussion lasts 16 minutes and during that time, the customer must become convinced of the value of SVP's service. 'What is the most important is for our consultants to understand that success in this business depends upon service.'

SVP's management puts supreme importance upon the training and preparation of consultants for their job. All of their consultants have university degrees and previous work experience in the area in which they are consulting. From the time that the person is recruited into the company, it takes at least three months to train a consultant and within that period the consultant passes through three distinct phases.

Each new consultant is assigned to a godmother or godfather with whom he or she shares an office. During the first period of apprenticeship, the consultant spends the day listening to the godparent speaking with clients over the phone. This is done with a telephone with two receivers. The new consultant says nothing. This lasts for one month.

In the second phase of the training, the consultant does the speaking while the godparent listens in. Once the conversation is finished, each time the godparent gives some tips on how to improve. This second phase lasts another month.

The third month, the new consultant is more or less on their own. He or she remains next to the godparent who is immediately available to respond to questions or to save a situation, if there is ever any problem.

SVP trains its consultants extensively because it doesn't want its consultant just answering questions. SVP consultants are just what the title says and they are expected to provide advice. The true role of an SVP consultant then is to 'find the real problem behind the question'. 'Our job is a bit like that of a doctor: it begins with a dialogue. The doctor's job is to listen and to ask questions in order to find the specific disease troubling the customer. He then makes a diagnosis . . . [and] gives a prescription. . . . We must always go beyond the question to provide good service.'

The most useful training tool which the company has developed to train its consultants how to 'go beyond the question' is a system of telephone recording. The technique is used extensively, not only for new consultants, but also for senior consultants. At any given moment a consultant's conversation with a customer can be recorded by the company. This is done at least twice a year for senior consultants and once every month for new consultants for a period of up to nine months.

In a private session with the manager of the department, the consultant and his or her boss listen to the recording. The evaluation is almost entirely upon the way the consultant dealt with the customer and very little upon the technical aspects. Specifically, two things are examined: 1) the quality of the communication; and 2) the adaptability of the response to the true concern of the customer, i.e. to what degree has the consultant identified and responded to the 'question behind the question'?

'I have very little problem with new recruits not being technically competent. My biggest problem is to train people in the 'technique' of communication', says Mrs Cazaban-Peyre. With the recording technique, consultants are generally capable of evaluating their own performance. 'They can hear when it's not good', explains Mrs Cazaban-Peyre. If they cannot, it's a bad sign. 'For a new consultant, it doesn't matter if the first few times are not very good. What matters is that they understand that they are not good.'

Training for multi-functionality; the case of Hotel Vier Jahreszeiten

This is one of the best hotels in the world. It has been ranked consistently number one in Europe for the last five years. It is located in Hamburg, Germany, overlooking the Binnen-Alster and is an old and glorious building dating from the end of the 19th century. Its present owners, the Japanese Aoki Group, and its past owners, the Haerklin family, have preserved the building and its interior in excellent condition. It is a virtual museum from its entry hall to its furthest bedroom.

The hotel's primary customer is the businessman; in particular the German, American or Scandinavian businessman. A large percentage of its customers are loyal customers who return regularly twice or more a year.

The hotel emphasises personalised service. By that, they mean the adaptation of every aspect of the hotel's service to the customer's wishes and the noting down of customer's preferences so that the service can be adjusted accordingly in the future. Detailed customer records are kept in which one can find a note that, for example, Mrs Benedict likes white roses in her room.

Providing personalised service to a large variety of customers from different countries, cultures and backgrounds requires a great deal of flexibility on the part of the hotel's staff. Recruitment and training at the hotel take on a very important and very practical role in this respect. The Vier Jahreszeitan wants its staff to be able to fulfil many functions within the hotel and they like to have a large number of staff who know the hotel very well.

The objective of the hotel's recruitment process is, thus, not to hire an employee for the next three years, but to hire an employee for life. Likewise, an employee is not trained to work at one job, but for all the jobs that he might be required to do immediately or in the future.

The first step is in the recruitment process. Being the best, Hotel Vier Jahreszeitan has the pick of the best. It, nevertherless, is careful to hire employees that meet certain criteria. For customer contact staff, candidates are evaluated on their attitude towards customers and on their ability to communicate with others. For non-customer contact staff, the hotel looks for creativity and the ability to manage complexity.

Recruiting and employee integration is the responsibility of the personnel department: 'What the reception is for the guests in the hotel, the personnel department is for employees and with the same level of attention.' The personnel department also assists employees with administrative procedures and to find a flat in the city, for example.

An employee's induction does not start in a customer contact position. Most new employees work in several back office functions before they are put in contact with customers. 'He gets to know the hotel from the inside out.' Ongoing training is offered for all employees in order to increase expertise or to broaden their experience within the hotel. Several seminars are offered every month to staff which deal with a specific topic – bartending, banquets, answering the telephone etc. Participation is not mandatory, but many employees are anxious to take advantage of the opportunity.

The Vier Jahreszeiten's belief in giving its employees the broadest experience possible extends beyond the hotel limits. It also helps employees gain experience in other hotels. They assist employees in career planning and development and arrange traineeship for employees in other hotels.

As a result, employees who start out on their career with Vier Jahreszeiten often return to the hotel after having gained experience in a variety of different situations and environments. From the hotel's point of view that makes them more versatile and more flexible in their functions, and better equipped to deal with the diversity of customers which the hotel has.

Recruiting for customer orientation and initiative taking; the case of Sixt Budget

Sixt Budget is Germany's second-largest car-rental company. Owed and run by the Sixt family since 1912, the company gained its top position in the industry in the early 1980s with the launch of a campaign called 'Rent a Mercedes for the Price of a Golf.'

The campaign reflected a new service strategy of the company which was to focus on the rental of exciting cars at prices comparable to what other companies were charging to rent standard, 'boring' cars. A businessman who, by company policy, could normally not afford to rent anything other than a car in the simplest category could look forward to driving a 'dream car'.

Today, Erich Sixt, grandson of the company's founder, describes his business as 'fulfilling customers' dreams while keeping them mobile'. The company has 171 rental car offices throughout the country and a fleet of 20,000 cars. In its fleet there are a full range of Mercedes, BMWs, Porches and Ferraris.

The company has a reputation for being one of the most creative and customer service-oriented companies in Germany. In addition to offering the most exciting cars, he also offers the most exciting selection of extras. Most cars are already equipped with telephones. Faxes are available for rent. The cars are also equipped with a joke-line that customers can call to hear the latest joke. Customers can also choose from a wide selection of cassette tapes.

Many of the ideas for services like these have come from employees. Erich Sixt attributes the success of his company in large part to the personnel who work for it. The company attracts young people who have an entre-preneurial spirit and are able to work autonomously.

To make sure that the company continues to attract these kinds of people, Sixt has introduced a recruitment process which selects and tests people according to their attitude towards customers, and their creativity and initiative. To begin with, Sixt prefers people who have had little previous experience. They don't want people who might be 'spoiled by working in a heavy administration'. In addition, 'we prefer it if they've never worked for another car rental company at all'.

The recruitment process itself has three phases. First, there is a general interview. Customer orientation is the first thing that interviewers look for. The employees' skills and level of studies comes after. Next is a 'counter test'. Candidates work on the counter for a day and experience what it's really like. Their behaviour, initiative and customer orientation are all observed closely by the manager who assists the candidate through the process. In the third phase the candidate is asked to write a one-page report on what could be improved about the company's service. Candidates who don't write anything are out. The candidate then meets again with the manager to discuss his ideas.

The same process is repeated for the middle management level recruitment. The only difference is that the last interview takes place with the Erich Sixt and not with other middle managers.

The objective is to identify candidates who are 'entrepreneurs'. Sixt Budget wants 'individual fighters' rather than 'team workers' and they must be able to take decisions on the spot that will satisfy customers. These kind of individuals tend to manage better with many of the company's policies, such as the one whereby the rental price of cars is not fixed. Each employee knows the break-even point for each car and is free to negotiate the rental price in order to please the customer.

Once hired, the employee begins immediately by working on the frontline. There are supporting training courses available, but the company believes in accustoming employees first to the job.

Employees are relatively well paid and even frontline staff have the use of a car with their employment.

Long-distance training; the case of Saab

Saab Automobiles is a Swedish company that produces cars for the domestic market and for export since 1949. Today, 73 per cent of Saab cars are sold to the export market, mostly in the US and Europe.

The Saab car, of which there are never more than three or four models on the market at any one time, is positioned in the premium sector of the market. A Saab car is for the individualist. It is for the customer who wants an exclusive car which surpasses its competitors in terms of safety, road-handling and performance. It is for the customer who wants quality in an original package.

For many years, Saab's objective was to increase the brand awareness with the car buying public and to gain new customers. Technical developments and a successful marketing campaign more or less achieved the company's goals in this respect by the early 1980s. Since that time a major push is being made to retain Saab customers with high quality personalised service.

'Saab's goal is to get Saab owners to repurchase a Saab when they buy their next car. To do this we need to take such good care of our customers that they come back and buy a Saab next time. And by that we do not mean [only] when they trade in their car for a new one, but also when they come in and come back for service and repairs. . . . It is much more expensive to find new customers, so it is more important to care for old customers.'

Because of the large percentage of export sales, Saab must work through its importers to reach the car dealer who is actually the person who has a direct contact with the customer. Saab must, therefore, not only convince individuals of the need to provide good service quality at one level, but at two. 'In the parent company, we are working through our importers and our dealers; they have the most contact with the customer. We have to make the weakest link stronger. The importers should support the dealers and we should support the importers.'

The programme which it developed to do that is called FAST (forming after-sales together). In addition to a major communications effort and the development of service standards and which must be met by every Saab dealer, the programme also calls for the comprehensive training of importers, dealers and all of their personnel. This is part of a training structure which has been developed for the whole company and which it calls its total training concept.

The total training concept is designed to give employees a good background in the philosophy and general policies of the company – including its concern for the customer – as well as prepare them to fulfil specific job functions according to the standards established. Saab has structured the training in a way that it can be carried out either by the importers or by the dealers themselves.

New employees will receive at a dealership, for example, a 'workplace' introduction of half a day, a 'general company introduction' course of one day after three weeks of employment, and a 'personal development interview' of one to two hours after three months of employment.

In some cases, the dealer is provided with support tools, videos, worksheets and booklets, generally in others he has a checklist which he can use to ensure that all of the important points are covered – salary, benefits etc.

In terms of content, Saab believes that 'The starting point must be with the customer'. In the general company introduction, the employee learns about the parent company Saab and its goals, strategies etc., the importer and his goals, policies etc., and about the dealership. In particular, he learns about the business objective in various customer situations – purchase of a new car, of a used car, of accessories and auto servicing.

All employees also receive instruction in the basic features of the product, using a formal training module and training in communication, customer handling and selling awareness using another formal module.

The communication, customer handling and selling awareness modules' principal goal is to sensitise employees about the expectations of customers. One video and workbook is entitled *In the Eyes of the Customer*. The module also gives specific instruction to employees in areas such as telephone techniques, body language, handling customer complaints, and correspondence – how to communicate with your customer.

Beyond these basic modules, every employee in the company gets specific training for their function: parts people, technicians, service consultants (receptionists, salespeople etc.). These sets of training are again done using modules and are divided into three parts – Saab selling, Saab parts and Saab service (auto servicing). Within each there is an aspect of 'Sales and marketing', which provides specific information on 'customer analysis, customer contact and correspondence', as it relates to the activity in question.

Advanced training is generally carried out through the importer who co-ordinates training sessions. When this is not possible or feasible, the training is carried out at the dealership. Most modules are accompanied by videos and by workbooks which the employee should complete as he goes along. There are a total of 15 advanced training modules, each of which runs for between one to four days.

'When it comes to winning the battle in the market place, we are sharing the possibilities with the product itself, the salesman and the after-sales service. We see the customer for services, for repairs, for buying parts etc. We see the customer an average of 12 times between his car purchases. If we do that well, we have a positive influence on the customer. Every time we meet the customer we have to satisfy him. . . . The total training concept helps employees get a good understanding of the company and its approach to servicing the customer.'

Achieving self-advancement; the case of SupaSnaps

SupaSnaps is a chain of around 360 retail stores which handle photo-processing and sell related products such as frames, bags and cameras. The company was established in 1978 by Gratispool International Holdings, bought by 3M in 1981 and sold by 3M to the Dixons group in 1986. Throughout its history, the company's employees retained a strong customer-service orientation and a great deal of enthusiasm for the business and the company.

Located in the central shopping areas with a staff of 95 per cent women, SupaSnap shops became known for their excellent customer service and for their important contribution to community life. However, when Dixons took over, the company was losing money. Shop space was underutilised and revenues were coming almost uniquely from the company's photo-processing activities – the stores had become simply depots for leaving off film for development.

Despite the company's difficulties, the frontline staff had maintained their reputation for excellent customer service which was now recognized by the new owners as a major company asset. SupaSnaps employees had never been extensively trained in how to offer good service; their reputation was gained from a sincere and genuine concern for customers.

SupaSnaps decided to use the goodwill which the staff had generated with customers to expand the sales per customer. For this, new products and services were developed. In addition, employees' service skills were to be further enhanced and they had to be trained in how to offer good service and sell at the same time.

SupaSnaps developed a training programme with a series of modules which permitted employees to pass successively from one level to the other, always developing a new skill at each step. All of the modules could be done in the stores. They are supplemented by the training done by trainers from head office who regularly work in the field.

Each module allows the employee to cover a set amount of work per week. Her work is then checked over with her Branch Manager. Once the entire module has been successfully completed, she can pass on to the next one.

While the training modules help achieve the company-wide objectives mentioned above, from the staff point of view, the training modules offer a unique opportunity to improve themselves and improve the service they offer to customers. For most staff, being able to help customers well is a major factor of motivation in the job. 'The greatest benefit of providing good customer service? . . . It's the satisfaction of customers coming back. It's a form of recognition to our staff.'

SupaSnaps's training, which gives sales staff greater knowledge about how to advise customers and more information about products and services, makes the staff feel more efficient and capable on the job. That, in turn, makes it possible for them to offer better service to customers. '. . . It's a good feeling going out to the customer. It's a good feeling coming back to the members of the staff. . . . It's like a meeting house sometimes, but that's good because that's what generates photographs – these children and babies.'

SupaSnaps's modules deal with specific aspects of serving customers. One module deals with how to answer customer complaints. The company's policy is gone over in detail and exact situations are discussed. The 10 most common complaints are presented and the right responses to those questions are given, with the reasons why.

There is also a sales module with new additions each year. The approach is again to provide examples of real questions and answers in situations which the staff are likely to find themselves. The objective is to teach the staff how to recognise key moments in the conversation with the customer when a complementary product can be introduced. Once introduced, the sales module explains exactly what to say to convince the customer.

For example, at step four in the customer – sales staff discussion (when the customer's film processing slip is being filed out at the counter), the employee is advised to say, 'By the way, we've still got our special offer on film.If you buy two you get one free.' While the sales module is very explicit, employees are encouraged to adopt their own language once they master the basic selling technique.

New sales approaches are introduced on a regular basis in order to give staff selling arguments for each new product which is introduced. In addition, the staff can rely on the 'Features and Benefits' sheets produced for each product and kept in a book in every store for reference. The 'Features and Benefits' sheets describe the major features of every product or service, and the benefits which the customer can derive from each feature.

Of all the modules, the company's sales module was particularly successful and contributed to a substantial increase in non-processing related sales the first year it was introduced.

With any of SupaSnaps's training modules, there are two key success factors. The first is the extensive use of very graphic and explicit examples to communicate any message. All of the training modules have videos which go with them with examples of 'real-life' situations in which the employee might find herself. In some cases, personalities are characterised to make them easier to remember – well-known television personalities are used to describe different types of sales staff; friendly, helpful, or intimidating, embarrassing.

The second success factor is the support tools which are kept in the stores or given to staff and used as reminders about what has been taught. The most notable are the SupaCards, a set of five small, plasticised cards which hang next to the cash register. SupaCard 1 gives the features and benefits of the most popular cameras, Card 2 gives a chart of the most popular camera features and the cameras which have them, Card 3 lists the most important factors contributing to good customer service ('Start with a Smile', Use the Customer's Name', 'Make Eye Contact When You Speak' etc.) and lists the company's procedures for handling complaints, Card 4 lists the most common problems with prints and what they are caused by, and Card 5 presents common questions and their answers. The SupaCards provide a handbook of good service 'in a nutshell'.

Godfathering: the case of Ideal Job

Ideal Job provides temporary employment placement, and the identification and placement of permanent staff to the Swiss market. The company is young, established in 1965, and has, over the last 15 years, experienced rapid growth and expansion. Today, the company has 28 agencies throughout Switzerland and roughly 12 per cent of the Swiss market for temporary placement.

Its success is due in part to a very clear philosophy of service quality to customers and to employees and fellow workers, alike. For Ideal Job, service quality means 'to accept that one has a responsibility to satisfy others' and 'to manage to achieve things daily in the best team spirit'. When an employee joins Ideal Job, he is taught the philosophy, as much as he is taught about the job.

The integration process at Ideal Job permits the employee to feel that he is welcome in the company and to be quickly operational in a fast-moving business. 'The individual in this company is very important; in our work, we have another objective other than earning money.' One of the most important aspects of the integration process is the role of the godfather or godmother.

A godfather (or godmother) is assigned to each employee once he enters the company. The role of this person is to act as a guide to the employee during his initiation period. Each Ideal Job agency has a designated person who is the godfather for most new employees coming into the company. The person is generally not the new person's immediate supervisor, nor the manager of the agency, though it is someone with extensive experience in the field and with the company. 'This person must transmit to the new employee the *way* we do things, from 'A' to 'Z.''

Keeping very close and constantly with the new employee during the first weeks of employment, the godfather progressively diminishes his role as the employee masters his job better and better. A godfather never, however, completely abandons his role and remains available to the employee for questions and support. 'The godfather is always available to the new employee.'

All new employees at Ideal Job go through a basic course on the company's business during their first three months with the company. In this course, he is grouped with other new employees for three days of formal training. In addition, during the first six months to a year, the employee passes two additional courses: on sales training and telephone training. In all of the courses, the attitude and behaviour of employees with customers is covered in detail.

The godfather's role in relation to these courses is that of assisting the employee to pass from theoretical knowledge to practical application. The new employee accompanies his or her godfather on client visits, helps him or her prepare files or internal reports and, with the help of a telephone-listening device, the new employee can hear how the godfather discusses with clients or candidates over the phone. On average, during the first month, a new employee passes at least half an hour per day with his godfather.

The godfather also acts as a sociological crutch for the new employee and is responsible for presenting him or her to the rest of the office. He also takes the new employee to lunch and ensures that he or she is well installed in the working environment. All new employees visit the administration building in Pully, near Lausanne, 'to get a feeling of what happens in the back office'.

A tool which is used to help the employee learn the business is a book, known internally as 'the Bible'. The document addresses each aspect of the business separately and presents exactly what is expected of the employee in order to satisfy the customer. While the employee is learning about his work with his godfather in the field, the book serves as a back-up source of information and reference. What the employee hasn't understood in his discussions with his godfather, he can have clarified for him in the book, and vice versa.

Ideal Job's integration process for new employees is very important to the company 'Our employees are our greatest asset', explains Mr Philippe Grunder, Managing Director.

How to have effective organisational learning

Singapore Airlines expends 9 man hours to recruit a flight attendant and 12 weeks of training to be sure they are number 1 in service quality. Air France expends 2 hours and 3 weeks respectively. They are number 11. In general, European companies prefer to put in inspectors and correct mistakes rather than investing in preventing mistakes from happening. The amount of effort devoted to recruiting and training is the first tangible sign that the company means business in satisfying customers.

Recruiting serves to select people who have the potential to do the job. Training adds value and transforms the potential into reality. No amount of training will do the job, if the potential is not there. No potential will be easily transformed if the training does not add value to the human invest-ment. The Japanese have become the masters of human investment. At Ricoh, it takes three years to train a customer service engineer (here in Europe we would call him a repairman!) and every year, thereafter, he has to pass an exam to check that his product/maintenance knowledge has not eroded. If he passes, he gets a diploma . . . from manufacturing. In Nikko, 150 km north of Tokyo, it takes five years to train a maid well! One must add, there is one maid per bedroom and the toughest job to learn is how to handle drunken businessmen without being offended or offending them!

What seems to work is fourfold: recruit at the top to get biggest potential; train not just on customer service but also on the company, do not think training only happens in the classroom and finally, to make training effective, emphasise organisational learning rather than individual training. We will now review them one by one.

Recruit at the top

The cycle of failure described in a recent article in the *Sloan Management Review* tells how companies get bad service from their employees when they hire people in at the last minute to replace someone who's leaving. They get in (people with no potential) because the company is unwilling to pay higher salaries for people in customer contact jobs to correct the mistakes and avoid catastrophes, they hire lots of inspectors and supervisors, whose only role is to control, inspect and fire!

The cycle of success is to pay good salaries to customer contact people who have potential, make economies in the superstructure if necessary so that training can become beneficial.

Another issue which often arises in the cycle of failure comes from the bad management of new employees' expectations. The fact that they have to work on Saturdays, wear certain gear and help each other is not well specified at entrance ('We are in a hurry to replace someone who left'). These misunderstandings rapidly transform themselves into resignation or dismissal.

In fact, most of the jobs which deal with the future quality of the economy, or health teachers and nurses, do not get well paid! It is a cycle of failure. Nobody with potential wants the job!

In contrast, think again of the customer service department at Kao which recruits university graduates with sales experience for repairmen positions. They are surely more expensive. But they also have more potential to solve customer problems and take initiatives.

Enlarge the scope of training to company knowledge and problem-solving, as well as competence on the job

Many companies have invested lots of money in Europe in the last five years to have employees trained on service and customers. It has been successful training. A creative success and, with poor results, a commercial failure. Besides not training management before training employees, one of the suggested reasons for failure has been the limited scope of training. Limited, in fact, because its objective is to increase employees' customer awareness rather than developing their customer service skills or knowledge.

In addition to teaching actual skills, training should also focus attention on increasing employees' knowledge of the company: who we are, what we do, how different we are from competitors, who does what in our organisation. This is an important part of any serious customer oriented training – known as sales training. Know how to sell your company! Competence should not be forgotten in training either. Being just nice is not enough. Over the years we have developed the concept of helpful vs thoughtful. Helpful is being nice – Thoughtful is being nice plus anticipating and finding solutions to customers' problems. Helpfulness alone cannot do the job. Thoughtfulness requires good people who take initiative as well as technical knowledge based learning. What we want to avoid is a nice hostess in restaurant telling you 'have a nice day' when you leave, when in fact it is midnight outside!

Finally, if a process is to be implemented in a company, a lot of time is to be devoted to developing problem solving skills.

Training does not happen only in the classroom . . . far from it

If you were to aks yourself honestly where you learned what you know today, most of you would probably find that you learned the most from mentors, from observing others, from sharing experiences, from inductive reasoning, etc.

The same can be said of your employees. By giving your employees a mentor, by rotating jobs, by creating forums to exchange experiences or good service practices, by having to teach or to train, your employees will learn as much as in the classroom . . . on one condition: everything must be carefully prepared. Trainers have to learn how to train, mentors have to be briefed on their role, forum leaders have to know how to animate a discussion and sharing experience sessions have to be organised. Otherwise, it will all be seen as being a waste of time.

Organisation learning

How many times do we have a poor impression of training because the training was great but after the session people have gone back to old behaviour? How many times also do we feel there are great individuals within the organisation who know a lot but are unable or have not been asked to transmit their knowledge to others. How many times also knowledge and skills exist in one part of the organisation but is not shared by others. Finally, in other cases, knowledge exists but people are not convinced of its use. Formal training will not help much. Other means must be found to create a learning organization. Take the example of the new strategy of Club Med training. It includes the following principles:

Before any training is done, individuals will be evaluated to see what is missing in their competence so that there is no waste in sending people to the wrong place. In addition, every boss will get an overview of what his team member will get in training and why. Extensive use will be made of 'pilots' , i.e. individuals within the company who are regarded as having the best knowledge on their subject. To help them articulate their personal knowledge however, the internal training department will be responsible for developing their teaching support and material and rehearsing it with them. After every training course, all participants will receive a concrete set of tools so they can practise and apply the freshly acquired knowledge rather than receiving a heavy manual, which they will either throw or file away.

A 'delegation contract' will be agreed upon between the person that was trained and his boss. It will set forth what the superior is willing to delegate to the person and over what period, now that his subordinate knows more.

As in General Electric, the 'best practices' of Club Med as well as those of world class companies in other industries will be identified, recorded, transmitted and shared among all the GO's. In addition, all technical know-how will be put into interactive videodisks and updated every year. The same will apply to service standards and work procedures, so that everyone is updated on the latest ways to do business rather than having to be trained for what is, in fact, information that should be readily available on the job.

All of these elements put together will reinforce the learning process of the organisation as much as training employees on service. It will assure a better return on invested money rather than fooling oneself with well-organised, well-presented seminars of which people remember very little.

CONCLUSION

The best conclusion we think we could offer you is for you to test yourself against the top service practices just described above – some people call it benchmaking. Simply add up the number of 'yes's' to the questionnaire below. When this is done, you will know how far you are from the best practices, and what are your weakest points.

This questionnaire includes the same questions that we used to judge the companies in this book. If you are interested in service quality in general, and in knowing where you stand as compared with these companies, please complete the questionnaire below and send it to us. We will send back your overall score, showing your areas of strength and weakness in each category, and give you a ranking as compared with the companies in this book.

Even supposing you answer 'yes' to all questions and are better than any company in this book, you still have a challenge in front of you to go further than total customer satisfaction; this is to go beyond the customer's expectations: what the Japanese call customer delight. In this case, do not worry about competition or time. You are well ahead. You do not need a crash programme to become quality oriented. You are probably five to ten years ahead of others and should not have any difficulty reaching the ISO 9000 European Quality Standards . . .

Corporate culture

	YES	NO
Is there a clear definition of values?	☐	☐
Are they shared by everyone?	☐	☐
Are they given when an employee enters the company?	☐	☐
Is customer care one of the values?	☐	☐
Do you have 'legends' about customer service?	☐	☐
Do you have a quality process in place?	☐	☐
Do more than 45 per cent of employees participate in the process?	☐	☐
Did your process start more than five years ago?	☐	☐
Do you use pilots to show the way?	☐	☐
Is the customer considered to be always right?	☐	☐
Do you have a mascot to represent customers?	☐	☐
Are you more market than product oriented?	☐	☐

TOTAL FOR PAGE
NUMBER OF YES AND NO ANSWERS   ☐   ☐

Power leadership

	YES	NO
Do you have a quality director?	☐	☐
Do you have a customer satisfaction director?	☐	☐
Do they report to the CEO?	☐	☐
Is there a quality or customer satisfaction manager in each division?	☐	☐
Do you consider the key managers of your company customer oriented?	☐	☐
Does the permanent quality team have more than 1 member for every 500 employees?	☐	☐
Are customer problems clearly identified?	☐	☐
Do you have horizontal crossfunctional project teams working on improving service?	☐	☐
Do managers of 'back offices' spend time with customers?	☐	☐
Are managers who improve service quality more likely to be rewarded than others?	☐	☐
Is top management commitment to service quality clearly stated/witnessed?	☐	☐
Do you have clearly identified service quality priorities for next year?	☐	☐
Do you systematically ask your managers to answer 'what will he/she do for service quality' in your planning and resource allocation process?	☐	☐

Are managers always available to the customer when and where he/she wants? ☐ ☐

Do managers regularly enquire about customers and their level of satisfaction? ☐ ☐

Do managers drop everything to attend to a frontline employee who has a question/enquiry concerning a customer? ☐ ☐

Do managers systematically initiate quality groups with employees? ☐ ☐

Are more than 50 per cent of the solutions proposed by these groups implemented per year? ☐ ☐

TOTAL FOR PAGE
NUMBERS OF YES AND NO ANSWERS ☐ ☐

Do managers have to systematically spend a day or more on the front line doing the job? ☐ ☐

Do managers systematically read complaint letters from customers? ☐ ☐

Did the top management sit down and talk with a customer last week? ☐ ☐

TOTAL FOR PAGE
NUMBERS OF YES AND NO ANSWERS ☐ ☐

Communication   YES   NO

Does your company's communication strategy stress the importance of customer service quality? ☐ ☐

Do your advertisements, brochures, etc. specifically address service quality and what your company is doing about it? ☐ ☐

Are they 'honest' about the level of service quality your company offers its customers? ☐ ☐

Does your company involve frontline people in the development of your communication strategy? ☐ ☐

Is information and documentation about your company's services readily available to clients when and where they need it? ☐ ☐

Have you a process to measure whether the language is clear and easy to understand by customers? ☐ ☐

Do you have someone in your communication department who is specifically in charge of service quality? ☐ ☐

Do you systematically thank customers for doing business with you? ☐ ☐

	YES	NO
Do you measure customers' perceptions of the accurateness of your advertising message in relation to service delivered?	☐	☐
Do you involve customers in the development of your communication plan?	☐	☐
Is your public relations department evaluated by the percentage of dissatisfied customers it is able to turn into satisfied customers?	☐	☐
Do you always answer the phone within 3 rings or less?	☐	☐
Does everything in your company visible to your customer (phone service, premises, vehicles, documentation, uniform . . .) carry the same 'message content' as your advertising?	☐	☐
Does every employee (even if not frontline) know about company service quality definition per customer segment?	☐	☐
Is each employee clear about their role in service quality?	☐	☐
Do employees know the company's customer satisfaction rate?	☐	☐
Are the results known by everyone in the company?	☐	☐
Are your customers regularly invited to your non-commercial premises?	☐	☐
Do you formally ask your frontline people to tell you about customers' needs and expectations at least once a year?	☐	☐
Do you systematically encourage customer suggestions?	☐	☐
Do you reward customer loyalty?	☐	☐
Do you inform your customers loud and clear of where to call or write to complain?	☐	☐
Does it take less than 2 days for a letter of complaint to get a first response?	☐	☐
Do you reward customers' recommendations of new customers?	☐	☐
Do you have customers' clubs or users' clubs?	☐	☐
Do you stay in touch with all your customers?	☐	☐
Do you have a service quality guarantee?	☐	☐
Do you post/circulate customers' compliment letters?	☐	☐
Do you publicly reward the employees with the best performance in customer service?	☐	☐
Is there a hot-line for your customers who need help fast?	☐	☐
Do you give a 'no-questions asked' refund?	☐	☐

TOTAL FOR PAGE
NUMBER OF YES AND NO ANSWERS   ☐   ☐

Service strategy

	YES	NO
Have you defined your target customers?	☐	☐
Is your business defined in terms of customer benefits?	☐	☐
Have you studied the service expectations of your customers?	☐	☐

	YES	NO
Do you know why lost customers went to the competition?	☐	☐
Do you know how many customers you have?	☐	☐
Do your service standards also apply to pre-selling?	☐	☐
Have you identified 3 to 5 service dimensions in which you want to be a leader?	☐	☐
Have you clearly identified your market segment in terms of service?	☐	☐
Do you know the relative importance of service in overall customer satisfaction?	☐	☐
Is the customer a top priority in your company?	☐	☐
Is the service quality a separate item in planning (or budgeting or resource allocation)?	☐	☐
Does your budget process allow you to balance an increase in cost by an increase in customer satisfaction?	☐	☐
Do you have a clear definition of the service quality you provide to your primary customer, stating your competitive advantage in writing?	☐	☐
Is this definition written in terms of customer benefits rather than describing your organisation process?	☐	☐
Is this definition distributed to employees?	☐	☐
Is this definition shown to customers'?	☐	☐
Is each task and process in your organisation defined in relation to these customer benefits?	☐	☐
Are these customer benefits measurable?	☐	☐
Does your company analyse customer complaint letters to identify problems?	☐	☐
Have you defined service standards which state what customers should receive in terms of service?	☐	☐
If yes, do these service standards apply to everyone in the company?	☐	☐

TOTAL FOR PAGE NUMBER OF YES AND NO ANSWERS	☐	☐

Middle management

	YES	NO
Do managers and frontline people work together to establish goals for service quality?	☐	☐
Do frontline people come to managers to discuss solutions to customer complaints?	☐	☐
Is there a systematic process for the review of managers by frontline people in terms of customer care and service quality?	☐	☐
Do these results play a role in the salary review process of management?	☐	☐

Do frontline employees have measurable target objectives in terms of customer service quality? ☐ ☐

Are your sales people rewarded for maintaining long term customer relationships (i.e. sales persons with low customer turnover ratios)? ☐ ☐

Are employees who do the best job serving customers more likely to be rewarded than other employees? ☐ ☐

Do employees who make a special effort to serve customers receive special rewards /recognition? ☐ ☐

Do you promote challenges/competition between regions, departments or branch offices based on customer satisfaction? ☐ ☐

Do frontline people participate in suggestions about service improvement? ☐ ☐

Does a frontline employee know how much he can spend without permission to satisfy an angry/unsatisfied customer on the spot? ☐ ☐

Is this allowance more than 10 times the damage caused? ☐ ☐

Do frontline employees have complete freedom to spend whatever they think necessary to recover from a mistake made to a customer? ☐ ☐

Do frontline employees spend at least 80% of their time with customers? ☐ ☐

TOTAL FOR PAGE
NUMBER OF YES AND NO ANSWERS ☐ ☐

Taking advantage of information technology   YES   NO

Does most of your budget go on information technology or a value added system? ☐ ☐

Does the system track details of the company/customer relationship, such as individual customer preferences? ☐ ☐

Does data processing ask its internal clients what they want to achieve each year? ☐ ☐

Do you have technology to enhance customers? ☐ ☐

Does your information technology reduce hassles for customers? ☐ ☐

Do you have a customer service department? ☐ ☐

Does it answer all customer enquiries/complaints at once? ☐ ☐

Are you able to give special treatment to unsatisfied customers? ☐ ☐

Do your factories, marketing and R&D get systematic feedback on customer complaints? ☐ ☐

Can your information technology system personalise information for each customer? ☐ ☐

TOTAL FOR PAGE
NUMBER OF YES AND NO ANSWERS ☐ ☐

Measuring and Monitoring

	YES	NO
Do you know how much business you lose each year from disatisfied customers?	☐	☐
Do you regularly undertake customer satisfaction surveys?	☐	☐
Is customer satisfaction measured at least twice a year?	☐	☐
Do you personally know the level of satisfaction of your customers?	☐	☐
Do you know the weight of each subdimension of service on overall customer satisfaction?	☐	☐
Do you know the cost of losing a customer?	☐	☐
Do you know the cost of acquiring a new customer?	☐	☐
Do you know the level of customer complaints in your company?	☐	☐
Do you measure in some way the ROI of complaint handling?	☐	☐
Do you systematically enquire why certain customers do not buy from you anymore? (once a year).	☐	☐
Do you have a method for tracking your best customers (loyalty, frequency of buying?)	☐	☐
Do your support departments have a measure of their quality of work for internal customers?	☐	☐
Do your customers get the same minimum level of service at different locations of your business?	☐	☐
Internally, do you systematically monitor more than 10 quality service aspects visible to the customer?	☐	☐
Is service quality monitored on a monthly basis?	☐	☐
Do you regularly play at being a customer to test your company's service quality?	☐	☐
Do you use outside firms to do 'mystery shopping'?	☐	☐
Do you know your customer loyalty rate?	☐	☐

TOTAL FOR PAGE
NUMBER OF YES AND NO ANSWERS   ☐   ☐

Recruitment and training

	YES	NO
Does management receive the same training about service quality as frontline employees?	☐	☐
Have supervisors (or middle managers) received a formal training or coaching?	☐	☐
Have supervisors received a formal training on how to communicate service quality to their teams?	☐	☐
Have supervisors received a formal training on how to sell the company to a customer?	☐	☐

Have supervisors had training on how to communicate results of customer satisfaction surveys/customer expectation studies/ answering complaints etc.? ☐ ☐

Is your salesforce trained to be customer oriented? ☐ ☐

Is customer service training mandatory for everyone? ☐ ☐

Does your hiring process for frontline employees include a systematic evaluation of their sensitivity to service quality? ☐ ☐

Do you have a brochure specially designed for recruiting? ☐ ☐

Are frontline employees clearly instructed of their role in service quality? ☐ ☐

Do frontline employees receive at least eight days of training before they can serve customers? ☐ ☐

Do you have a training programme to teach new employees about the company's commitment to quality? ☐ ☐

Do you consider service attitude more important than knowledge at the hiring stage? ☐ ☐

Is supplementary training available for employees who need improvement in customer relations? ☐ ☐

Is this instruction systematically up-dated as changes in the level of service quality occur? ☐ ☐

Does the employee welcome book include the company's service promise, company history and customer service standards? ☐ ☐

TOTAL FOR PAGE
NUMBER OF YES AND NO ANSWERS ☐ ☐

Fifty Examples of Total Customer Satisfaction Management in Action

ABB

The kind of service one can expect to receive at ABB is well illustrated by these authors' experiences during our interviews. Our German colleague, who had been to visit ABB Metrawatt, described his experience, 'It was amazing!! Imagine a freezing cold morning ($-12°$) in Germany. There I am at 8:30 a.m., one hour early for my appointment, in front of the ABB Metrawatt gate. I didn't want to wait until I got frostbite, so I went up to the guard at the gate. There must be a hundred guys a day coming up to that gate; he looks up and smiles and says, "Now, you must be Mr. Spilker, aren't you; we've been expecting you, welcome to ABB Metrawatt." And the rest of the visit went just like that!'

Warm welcomes seem to be the norm at ABB. Despite a somewhat austere and overwhelming exterior, ABB is a very people-oriented company. They emphasise the importance of a personal, 'customised' relationship with clients and take an interest in customers' individual needs. For some ABB companies, the 'customised' customer approach is new; for others it is very old and an important reason for their success.

ABB is not *a* company but a group of 1150 companies. Before it was 1150 companies, it was ASEA, a Swedish group and Brown Boveri, a Swiss group. In 1988, the two joined. Both were, and still are, 'into' electrical engineering. It is a stated goal of the company to be customer focused and to improve the group's level of service to customers. This important task is the responsibility of all line managers supported by a quality team.

Managing service quality at a group like ABB is not easy. By policy, each ABB company shall manage quality in the way best suited to its business and market. The holding company, located in Zurich, has a total staff of 140. Of that, two people are devoted full time to quality co-ordination. They are backed up by a team of regional quality managers who report, at once, to the holding and to the regional functional managers. For the present, the quality team is concentrating on increasing customer focus.

ABB defines the customer as being 'the most important person in any business'. They have developed a customer mission statement which has been sent out to every company and which represents ABB's commitment to the customer.

The quality team is helping ABB companies in two principal ways. First, they provide support tools and information for the communication of the customer focus ideas. These include customer service videos, brochures, slide sets and posters. A quarterly quality newsletter informs on good practices of other ABB companies.

Secondly, they provide training and guidelines for implementing customer oriented improvements. In just over six months, the corporate quality department ran over 30 seminars on customer awareness and 12 executive workshops on managing for greater customer focus. There are also seminars designed to train internal trainers.

In addition, the corporate quality department has 'kits' prepared which assist managers to implement certain quality measures. For example, one kit provides guidelines on how to conduct a useful customer satisfaction survey. It provides instructions and examples from point 'A to Z', including the type of questions that should or shouldn't be asked.

The efforts of the ABB quality team have yielded results. By encouraging employees to think more about their customers and their expectations, the level of service quality has risen. While there continues to be variation in the levels of service provided by the various ABB companies, the results of a survey done last year for practically the entire group showed that ABB was seen as providing better service quality than the competitions in most industries.

For certain ABB companies, where service quality is a strategic issue, the quality team's assistance has yielded even more important results. Some companies now lead in their respective industry sectors in terms of the service quality they provide. ABB Metrawatt and ABB Turbo Chargers are two of those companies.

ABB Metrawatt
History

ABB Metrawatt was originally the Dr Siegfried Guggenheimer Company. It was established in 1906 to produce soft-iron and moving-coil electrical measuring instruments. In 1909, the first precision thermomillivoltmeters and ammeters were developed, permitting 'lab-test' measurements of alternating currents with very high accuracy. Developments in the company's technology and scope of activities has expanded from this date through to today.

Over the years, the name changed; the Dr Siegfried Company became Metrawatt AG in 1933, BBC Metrawatt in the 1960s and finally ABB Metrawatt in 1988.

Today, ABB Metrawatt produces electric meters and control circuits for two major customer groups: electricians, representing 35 per cent of revenues and industry, 65 per cent of revenues. For electricians, the bulk of the products are portable items; for industry, they are fixed or installed products. They are number 1 in Europe in the electrician segment and among the top companies for the industrial segment.

Service strategy

Although the service element is only 5–10 per cent of the purchase price of a measurement tool over its lifetime, ABB Metrawatt is a very service-oriented company, whose service philosophy is, 'to deliver fast solutions to clients at high standards of quality.'

The company's service strategy is different for fixed installations – destined for industrial clients – than for portable products, which are sold to electricians. Typically in portable items, service is not as crucial as in fixed installations.

For fixed installation clients, the availability of parts and the speed with which they can be serviced by a technician can be crucial. Many clients use Metrawatt for the control and measurement of industrial flow processes. When there is a technical problem, ABB Metrawatt service technicians have to be fast to avoid halting production. Written standards exist for frontline technicians, which ensure that certain time deadlines are respected.

For electricians, after sales service is carried out over the phone, with replacement parts being sent by mail. Electricians normally have two or more tools and therefore

ABB 169

there is seldom any urgency for repairs.

ABB Metrawatt is particularly proud of its cooperation with clients for product development; many of its major breakthroughs have been the result of close cooperation with clients. One way in which the company is kept in tune with its clients is through surveys done each year to measure satisfaction. In addition to questions relating to satisfaction, customers are asked for their opinion on various options for future product developments.

The feedback from customers leads to innovations, which are rewarded in the company with bonuses. In 1990, 5–10 per cent of all employees received a bonus for technical improvements to which they contributed

Service strengths

Metrawatt demonstrates that staying close to one's customers isn't something done only by service companies. Top management sets the example. Department heads and members of the management board are all expected to see customers on a weekly basis; the CEO himself visits customers every week.

To keep down the bureaucracy, which tends to reduce a company's customer orientation, Metrawatt has stayed a very flat organisation. There are only three levels: the sales force and the sales technicians, the department heads and top management.

It's clear that just visiting the customer isn't generally enough to satisfy them. Being customer oriented also means providing the right services. To know what customers expect, Metrawatt conducts satisfaction surveys on a regular basis. On the latest one, they were pleased to note that they ranked above their competitors in service quality.

Data gained from the surveys is fed into Metrawatt's extensive customer training programme. Everyone up and down the organisation is trained, from the secretaries to the the CEO. Switchboard and lobby receptionists, secretaries and sales and service staff receive 3 to 5 days of telephone training per year. Out of the company's total training budget 40 to 60 per cent is devoted to customer service training.

An indication of the importance that good customer service has in the organisation is that promotion is determined to a large part by the employee's customer service skills. One doesn't have to be an engineer to make a career at ABB Metrawatt. Employees are tested at the time of recruitment for their customer service orientation by presenting them with scenarios of real life situations and asking what their reaction would be.

Implementation

A tool which Metrawatt relies on heavily to improve service is its quality circles or error-chasing groups. Errors are identified when one of the company's standards – a delivery deadline or the rate of first visit repairs – is missed or when dissatisfaction with a particular aspect of the service is expressed through the customer satisfaction survey. An error-chasing group is formed to tackle the problem. The company's philosophy is to chase errors and not employees. Employees openly discuss errors in order to learn from them. Using this method, the groups have achieved substantial results in the form of a reduction in response time, work-in-progress and development time for new products.

A second valuable tool for service quality management at Metrawatt is the company's computer database. It records all relevant data on each client including key contacts, type of purchase, frequency of purchase and maintenance required. Among other things, the information is used to keep track of preventive maintenance schedules, even if the client does not have a maintenance contract. The company can then contact the client, before the client calls in distress. The same information is also used to forecast periods when maintenance activities will be the heaviest and extra help needed.

ABB Turbo Chargers

This subsidiary of ABB produces markets and services heavy duty turbo chargers. For those readers who don't know what a turbo charger is or does, the historical review in the company's *Turbo Magazine* provides a good description 'the [original idea] was to use the hitherto useless exhaust gas of the diesel engine to power a turbine, which in turn drives a compressor wheel to compress air into the diesel engine's combustion chambers, thus boosting engine power and efficiency'. This was the idea of Alfred Büchi from Winterthur in 1905 when he went to see Brown Boveri in nearby Baden. Refinements have since occurred, but the concept remains the same.

Brown Boveri liked Büchi's idea and development of the product began immediately. In 1923, the first turbo chargers left Baden for Germany to be installed in the ships MS *Preussen* and MS *Hansestadt Danzig*. The turbo chargers boosted engine power by one-third. In the 1950s, the company was creating turbo chargers that boosted engine power by 50 to 55 per cent. Today, a turbo charger provides an additional 75 per cent to engine capacity, making it an indispensable part of a correctly functioning engine.

Turbo chargers were originally designed to be used in ship engines and that remains a major client group for the company. In addition, turbo chargers are used on locomotive engines, on large tractors and other small engine-powered machinery. ABB Turbo Chargers remain concentrated on the heavy duty segments of the market. They have roughly 45 per cent of the world market in this category, nearly half of which is in the marine sector.

Service strategy

ABB differentiates itself from the competition principally on the basis of service quality. The company's service package involves before and after-sales service.

Before-sales service focuses on the company's relationship with the engine manufacturers. ABB does not sell its turbo chargers directly to the end-user, but rather to engine manufacturers who then sell the engine and the turbo chargers as a package to ship or machine constructors. Some engine manufacturers make their own turbo chargers. Many both manufacture their own and buy from ABB Turbo Chargers. As a result, engine manufacturers are both the clients and the competition for ABB.

Keeping a customer who is also a competitor satisfied is not always easy. ABB Turbo Chargers' principal point of approach is to involve their client/competitors in the development of new products to better serve the needs of end-customers. Being close to the market, the engine manufacturers are in a valuable position to know what best meets customers' needs.

ABB 171

When it was first proposed, this concept of close co-ordination was received with some scepticism on the part of engine constructors. Today, the relationships are a success, allowing both parties to benefit from greater sales to happy customers.

After-sales service is provided to end customers and is the more critical part of the company's service package. A typical scenario is one where technicians rush to aid a ship practically dead in the water due to a breakdown of its turbo charger. Time is crucial because each day lost for an ocean-going freighter can mean millions of dollars of loss for its owners.

ABB guarantees service in 24 hours. The company has 78 service stations located throughout the world. All stations are equipped with 96 per cent of the parts that might be needed for a repair and with trained technicians prepared to move at a moment's notice. Even with 78 locations, employees must move very fast when a call comes in in order to arrive on time. An employee from the Baden plant must be out of the door and headed for the airport with the replacement piece in less than an hour to arrive in time at any destination outside Switzerland.

Some clients don't need or want 24-hour service. To make its service more adapted to a wide range of companies, ABB now offers a three-tiered service option. The less rapid the service, the lower the price.

At the top of the range is the guaranteed 24-hour service. This is destined for clients for whom 24 hours can mean a substantial loss in time and money. At the middle range is service in under a week. This is destined for the company which needs rapid repairs, but not immediate repairs. Lastly, there is service within two weeks to a month. This is for the price-sensitive client for whom time is not a crucial factor. A typical example is a national rail company.

Service strengths/implementation

ABB's service strength is the efficiency of its after-sales service organisation.

If you're the chief ship engineer and it's your job to organise the repair of the engine's turbo charger while the ship sits dead in the water, odds are you are not a very happy person. ABB makes your life a bit easier.

Like most ABB turbo chargers that are sold, yours is probably not registered with ABB. However, if you call ABB with the number engraved into the side of the machine, they'll know just which one of the over 150,000 turbo chargers worldwide it is. They will also be able to identify with exactitude the piece you need to replace and tell you instantly whether it's available – in 96 per cent of the cases it is.

If you called into Zurich and you're just off the Venezuelan coast, Zurich will arrange to have technicians sent out from their southern Caribbean service station within the hour. If necessary and if you agree, they'll even take a helicopter or speed boat to get to you.

If your ship's owner is in Greece, the southern Caribbean station will arrange for him to be billed through Athens rather than from the American continent, so that he can pay at the centre closest to him.

The next time you call, ABB will know who you are. An ABB turbo charger has a life-span of roughly 12 to 20 years, so the company likes to keep track of who its owners are over time. They will have noted what the repair was last time and be able to recommend follow-up maintenance. You might also receive reminders every couple of years when your turbo charger is likely to require the replacement of major parts.

To be able to provide this kind of service, ABB has a computer database which tracks both customers and products sold. For the moment, the company can only track customers from the moment when they enter into contact with the company, because the engine manufacturers do not pass on the information about which turbo chargers were sold to whom. Once the customer contacts the company, however, he is matched up with his turbo chargers and the relationship can begin.

ABB's system notes the contact person in the client company, the ship name and the 'flag' (country of origin) on which the turbo charger is located, breakdowns, operating hours, particularities of the product and much more. Once the newest wave of improvements on the database system is completed, regular maintenance work and replaced parts will also be recorded.

ABB also must have the parts on hand in each of its 78 service locations in order to respond to an emergency. The company target is to ensure 96 per cent availability of parts. Another computer system is managing this aspect of the service, backed up by an extremely efficient team of on-site technicians who are trained in Switzerland before being posted to all parts of the world.

What can be learned

1 Giving more attention to customers has rub-off effects on service quality

ABB Holding's quality team is helping the 1150 ABB companies to focus on the customer. By reminding employees about customer expectations and the need to try to meet those expectations, the group has seen a boost in the level of service quality they offer. Thinking about customers means that one takes the extra minute to serve them better.

2 Logistics is a strategic issue

ABB Turbo Chargers' after-sales service cannot function without the support of the company's database systems, spare parts stock and customer/product tracking and the tie-in of those systems to the rest of the company.

Without the customer and product tracking system which gives the mechanic superior information about the type of machine and its condition, there is little difference between ABB's service and that which could be obtained from any machine shop that has a skilled turbo charger mechanic. The added knowledge about the turbo charger – its age, its past repairs, its date of fabrication and model type etc. permits them to provide truly competent after-sales service.

The data processing support system for the company's stock control means that the right parts are in the right place when they are needed. Managing 78 different stock depots for 96 per cent parts availability using a less efficient system would mean keeping stock levels extremely high, thereby increasing the cost to the customer.

AMERICAN EXPRESS

'An unequalled leader in service quality', says the November 1991 *Fortune* article that criticises practically everything at American Express except service quality. The point is rightly taken. Over 10 years after the initiation of the company's service quality drive, the company remains unequalled in its ability to provide consistently accurate, timely and responsive service to its customers. No company which our research examined had as thorough a system of service quality management and monitoring as American Express.

Background

American Express is a company which goes back nearly 140 years. Over the entirety of its history, the company has offered products and services involving 'a promise to pay'. From its first product – the letter of credit – to one of its most successful – the travellers cheque, invented by the company in 1891, to one of its most recent – the Optima Card, American Express has offered its products on a worldwide basis to some of the most demanding customers of financial and travel services.

While the company has always been recognised for the quality of the services it provides, in the last decade, the company has truly excelled in its management of service excellence. The first step was taken in the late 1970s. 'In 1978, we made the critical decision to launch a new quality assurance methodology. Its purpose was to track, evaluate and correct the weak spots in our service delivery.'

A task force was created and given US$750,000 to get the programme up and running. The group began by tackling the card operations centre in Phoenix. 'Not surprisingly, because we were introducing change, we met with some resistance and resentment from some of our employees. Employees had thought they were doing a top-notch job and we did, too. Our results, however, proved that the picture was not altogether rosy.'

A major step was getting across the point that what counted was not what American Express thought of its service quality, but what its customers thought of it. 'Once we saw the gap between our old way of thinking and measuring, and the correct, customer-perspective way of thinking and measuring, we knew we were on the right track.'

Market research showed that, for customers, 'quality in the card business revolved around three service characteristics – timeliness, accuracy and responsiveness, that is being knowledgeable, caring and polite.' Service standards were developed which largely surpassed customers' expectations in these three service characteristics.

With the service standards established, the company implemented a system 'to measure and monitor performance on an ongoing basis'. The foundation of the system is the 'STR (Service Tracking Report)', a set of measurements applied on a worldwide basis. Over 100 service measures and statistics are collected and analysed each month.

At the Phoenix centre, the change over took one year to accomplish. During that period, Jim Robinson, Chairman and CEO of American Express, personally followed the progress and visited Phoenix to talk to employees and receive first-hand feedback. After that year, the programme was extended to other centres and then overseas.

'Our bottom line results were dramatic! On a consolidated basis, over three years, we achieved the following:

—we improved the quality of our service delivery 78 per cent;
—we reduced expenses per transaction 21 percent;

To cite one example of improved service: within two years after we started quality assurance, we had reduced our cardmember application process time by 37 per cent. We have since reduced it even further, a 50 per cent total reduction in processing time has made our customers and our shareholders happy. This single fact has meant more than 70 million dollars in increased revenues over the past 10 years. . . . We no longer have to sell quality. Our results speak for themselves.'

(Raymond Larkin, Speech given 14 July 1987)

Service strategy

American Express's strategy is to provide top-quality travel and charge card services to business travellers and upper middle income individuals. Their intent is to provide top-quality service in every sense – in the products and services made available to the customer, as well as in the way those services are delivered. Service quality is American Express's strongest point of differentiation.

American Express target customers are a well-defined group – an up-market group. Typically, an American Express customer has an above-average income, works as a liberal professional, as a senior manager or has his/her own business. They travel more than the average citizen and often for business. They also take more than one holiday a year abroad. This profile fits as well for European customers as it does for American or Asian customers.

The company's products and services in the travel related services division, which represents the company's core business, can be grouped around two product categories: travellers cheques and charge cards. To service both businesses, the company has over 1700 locations in 130 countries. Some of those locations act primarily as traveller assistance and travel agent bureau. Others provide more extensive support in tandem with the credit card operations, including corporate travel servicing or cash advance or currency change facilities.

The company's success in Europe in its charge card business has been less phenomenal than in the US. In part, this is due to the retarded growth of the charge card market as a whole. In addition, the company faces very stiff competition from the banks which in some markets, notably France, have been issuing their own cards for some time. Because of interbank agreements, the bank cards permit the holder to withdraw money from the automatic teller of practically any bank or savings association. The banks have blocked American Express's access to this aspect of the business. American Express's response has been to re-emphasise the exclusivity of the card and the quality service that goes with it.

In all markets, American Express products and services are positioned to be top quality products and services. Its charge cards, for example, come with more services overall than cards offered by competitors. An American Express card not only permits one to make purchases at over three million locations; it can also guarantee retail purchases against loss, theft, or damage for 90 days with Purchase Protection and/or extend a manufacturers' warranty with Buyer's Assurance.

Customers can also have their room reservation assured, no matter what hour they arrive, their baggage guaranteed and carried for them with valet service. American Express also offers Global Assist in the case of difficulties while travelling. The range of the company's services is, in fact, quite extensive; in each case, the company's aim is to create a service which clearly provides more than that of the competition. 'Quality service is about adding value. Not just 'perceived value', but real value:

practical, relevant and credible. It means making the card more than just a card . . . more than just a payment instrument . . . more than just a lifestyle accessory' (Jürgen Aumüller).

The company's aim is not just to offer quality products and services, but also to deliver them with equal concern for quality. 'Quality service has two elements: first, you have to decide what services you will provide; then you must ensure that your quality of delivery makes those services truly worth having' (Jürgen Aumüller). American Express is one of the very few companies to position itself and advertise on the basis of the quality delivered in all aspects of its service. It is a strong statement because it is equivalent to guaranteeing the smile on the face of every American Express employee.

As a natural complement to its positioning as a quality service company, American Express has always pursued a strategy of exclusivity. It has never been the company's aim to have the American Express card accepted in every establishment worldwide. Its objective has been to have it represented in those exclusive places where its cardmembers are most likely to go. The sticker on the door indicating the cards' acceptance was designed to be a status enhancer, both for the establishment and for the card user alike.

Its merchant fee on American Express card purchases is correspondingly high. The establishment pays two to three per cent more per dollar purchase by American Express customers than by Visa or Mastercard customers.

Cardholders are intended to have the feeling of belonging to an exclusive club. In 1987, the company launched its worldwide advertising campaign around the concept 'Membership has its Privileges'. The phrase embodies to a large degree the company's positioning for the card over the next 10 years.

Service strengths

American Express's goal is to offer its customers timely, accurate and responsive service. They have succeeded in achieving that goal.

The company began by establishing a set of standards which are valid throughout the world. As a result of these standards, customers receive the same high standard of service in these key areas wherever in the world they use American Express. There are 24 worldwide standards which are tracked on a monthly basis to ensure that they are being uniformly applied. They are measured for timeliness and for accuracy which makes a total of 48 different measures.

Worldwide standards include, for example, the promise to replace a lost or stolen credit card within 24 hours. Another worldwide standard is 100 per cent accuracy on new card applications.'If a customer sends in an application, we have to capture the information given by the customer on the application correct 100 per cent,' explained Mr. Renfrew, Manager Operations, France. Yet others are the speed and accuracy of remitted payments from cardmembers and of payments to establishments.

Customers not only receive good service because of measured standards, but also because of standards created to make American Express more accessible to the customer. American Express offers 24-hour service which means that in any given country in which it is represented, a customer can speak to someone at American Express. It could either concern a lost card or charge authorisations; the receptionist who mans the phone is generally capable of responding to a large variety of basic questions with the support of an on-line computer. 'You have to be available 24 hours a day, not only for cardmembers, but for establishments and other service centres around the world who should be able to contact us even with the time differences,' adds Mr Renfrew.

During the day, most calls go into the telephone service centre. In France, that represents an organisation of 85–90 people. Their objective is to be able to resolve 96 per cent of the problems and questions of customers on the spot. In the remaining 4 per cent, follow-up work is required. Unless it involves researching a charge which occurred in another country, the follow up is accomplished within 48 hours by phone, or 72 hours by mail. Cases involving research in another country – international enquiries – must be resolved within 55 days; that's the standard.

American Express also has standards of service which apply just for the European market. One of those concerns the telephone answering rate. Customers in Europe can be assured to wait no more than seven seconds before someone picks up the phone. 'In France, that translates to about two to two and a half rings,' says Mr Renfrew. A customer won't find the line busy very often either. That is measured and controlled as well.

Within the telephone services department is a unit called 'authorisations'. 'It is a very sensitive area because of the speed of the transaction. It is very simple; the shopholder wants to finish the transaction and the customer wants to get his goods and leave. So, we have to be very sensitive in our authorisation process.' All of the telephone services department staff are trained for at least two weeks before they begin to handle calls. Their training includes courses on how to handle customer enquiries and how to speak over the phone.

While the majority of American Express's service quality is focused on timeliness and accuracy issues, the company also encourages employees to be responsive and sensitive in their contacts with customers. One way in which this is demonstrated is how the company responds to complaints.

A number of complaints come through the 'Ask the President' programme. On a regular basis, the company advertises in their mailing the possibility to write to the CEO, Jim Robinson, or to a local director with comments, suggestions or complaints about the service. All the letters eventually go to New York and are answered from there; however, they are first seen by the local directors who have the option to respond personally to any or all of them.

Mr Renfrew, the Operations Director in France, was previously working in Holland when he received a letter to which he felt he had to respond personally . . . and not just in writing. 'I took my car and drove 65 kilometres to see a customer. I surprised him; he did not expect me to come personally and discuss the letter that he wrote. But I cared enough to do it and he appreciated it.'

Each receptionist responsible for handling enquiries over the phone has a limit of FFr300 at his discretion to use to resolve a customer's problem or to compensate for an error. Employees are encouraged to go to the next level, however, if greater sums are needed. In one instance a customer in Hong Kong contacted the insurance division of American Express in order to have assistance covering costs she was incurring as the result of the unexpected death of her husband. 'The reaction of the insurance company was very poor, so she wrote a seven page letter to me. I immediately authorised an extension of her limit of FFr24,000. The second step I took was to call the insurance company and say, "What happened?" ' explained Mr Renfrew.

The same close attention to complaints and enquiries is given by the Swiss office as by the French office. Mr Dietzi, Director of Operations personally reads every complaint letter that comes through his office. 'I respond personally in some cases, because it's justified,' he adds.

In the Swiss office, enquiries that can't be handled by the telephone services unit are referred to the 'back office' which is manned by specialists who have extensive experience in handling customers and customers' problems. Each specialist is responsible for a certain set of accounts which permits him or her to have a certain degree of familiarity with the account and customer. Irate customers are switched almost directly through to the 'back office'. In general, the rule about when to transfer a call is, 'When in doubt, pass the call through,' explains Mr Dietzi.

Implementation

Crucial to one's understanding of service quality at American Express is an understanding of how the company deals with cultural and geographic differences. The company does not impose the same approach to quality management in every single country regardless of local conditions and local cultures. While there are specific standards and methods which are completely standardised, others are left to the discretion of the local management.

On a global basis, American Express applies its Blue Box Values. Reproduced below, there are seven items which express in a condensed form the philosophy of the company. They act as an important reference point for policy decisions and for the handling of interpersonal relationships within the company.

American Express also imposes a standardised quality review process, which if it is not completely comprehensive, it permits a worldwide comparison on a vast number of elements in the service package provided to customers. There are two parts to the quality review, as follows.

The first part, the Service Tracking Report (the STR mentioned above), is a measurement system designed to follow statistics relative to service quality on a monthly basis. Over 100 statistics are followed. A portion of the 100, 48 to be exact, are worldwide standards, i.e. they represent standards which must be the same worldwide. The remaining 100 are tracked on a worldwide basis, but are adapted to meet local requirements – the telephone response rate, set at seven seconds for Europe, is an example of one of these.

If performance on the STR is not satisfactory, country management generally receives assistance from the head office quality team. Action plans are developed which are designed to put employees on the right track towards correcting the problem. The STR report is circulated on a monthly basis throughout the world. Solutions developed by one country are shared with other countries, using the STR as a forum for discussion. The European operations managers, for example, meet at least once a year to discuss and review quality problems encountered by all of them.

The second major part of the worldwide quality review is the on-site business review. Such a review lasts between two to four weeks per country and 'takes a holistic view of what is going on. We look at the marketplace, at competition, as well as at operations and systems' (MaryAnne Rasmussen). The outcome of this is recommendations and action programmes to support the company's strategy for superior service delivery.

Another globally applied quality management tool is the transaction-based customer satisfaction survey. The survey is sent out to customers just following the completion of a transaction with the company. A transaction could be 'a customer was contacted concerning a late payment', 'a customer was asked to speak to an American Express agent over the phone prior to approving a charge', or 'a customer called the company with a complaint or an enquiry'. The objective of this type of survey is to receive precise information from the customer concerning his satisfaction with the way that the company handled the situation. A key question in the survey is, for example, 'At the outcome of this contact, has your opinion of American Express, 1) improved, 2) stayed the same, or 3) declined?'.

Also on a global basis, American Express organises and supports service quality training and motivation programmes. In terms of training, 'Putting People First' is one of the core courses offered in service quality. In two days, 'the focus is as much on the personal as on the professional'.

Employees are also motivated to strive for top quality by two worldwide recognition programmes, 'Great Performers' and the 'Chairman's Awards for Quality Improvement'. The first rewards individual employees who have gone out of their way to assist customers in need or to provide exceptional service. Each year, the results are printed in a book with a photo of the individual and a description of the outstanding service that was performed.

The Chairman's Quality Improvement Awards are given to teams which have made significant improvements in terms of productivity or innovations which improved service to customers. In 1990, one team, for example, 'created a "one-stop" service environment which increased card member satisfaction levels by 6 per cent and improved the response time to establishments . . .'

Just as significant are the initiatives taken at the local level to manage service quality. Our research looked at the operations in two European centres, France and Switzerland. While standards in each local market can be different, the method which is used to establish them is similar. A standard can be internal, that is between departments, or external, between the company and the customer. External standards are set, based on marketing research results done on the local market. They are controlled using a locally controlled measure.

Internal standards begin as a service level agreement. Service level agreements are reached between departments. 'One department might go to another department and say, "I want a service level agreement with you," and then they set up an agreement and they have to stick to it.' France, for example, developed a service level agreement with the statement processing department in Brighton, England. 'I have certain service standards which I must deliver in France, so a service level agreement was established between ourselves and France concerning the delay with which statements are mailed at the end of the month.'

With a service level agreement in place, a measurement system is then installed which measures on a weekly or monthly basis adherence to the agreement. Once the agreement is being reached on a consistent basis, the service level agreement is considered to be fulfilled and the measurement process stops. 'It's a strong programme. Certain departments use it, especially if you have a new programme going. You can do it for a period of time until you're satisfied that everything is correct. Then you can stop the service level agreement. It doesn't have to continue to have a life of its own.'

Local quality control methods can be oriented towards different areas, depending on the country's individual strengths or weaknesses. In France, the greatest emphasis at the present time is placed upon adherence to timeliness and accuracy standards.

Mr Renfrew not only uses the STR on a monthly basis, but also uses internal indicators of service quality which are compiled on a monthly basis and, in some cases, on a daily basis.

'I have a manual report that I produce every month from the various departments. In that report I can identify the number of people who have called in for a statement enquiry, for instance. . . . Certain indicators I get on a daily basis. I know exactly how many telephone calls come in my telephone services department, and then I can follow the trend and see whether I need to do some more research. I can also get on a daily basis the average speed of answering rate and the lost call rate. It could be an early signal for me that there could be some problems,' says Mr Renfrew.

In Mr Dietzi's Swiss office, one department has a system of group evaluation. Measures are taken regularly to see how the group is performing; then the employees meet together to discuss how they might improve their performance. In another department, employees evaluate one another using a set of criteria. A major support tool is the recordings which have been made of employees' conversations with customers over the phone. The recordings are anonymous and are used as a training tool rather than a performance evaluation tool.

The Swiss office has very high performance records on the STR and in its recent development has begun to focus more on the relationship aspects of its service with customers. 'In the past, employees were rewarded when a job was well done – it was transaction oriented. Now, we are putting more emphasis on the interactional aspects of our service.'

As a result, the Swiss group is increasing meetings among staff to discuss how to improve customer contacts and may soon establish its own customer promise which would reflect some of these considerations as well as the traditional concerns for accuracy and timeliness.

What can be learned

1 Make money with service quality

American Express shows that service quality doesn't just improve employee morale, increase customer satisfaction and foster better internal communication. It also yields cold hard cash gains. American Express calculated the gains from reducing cardmember application processing time by 37 per cent; in 10 years they add up to over US$70 million!

2 Manage service quality on a needs basis

Managing service quality at American Express is not a rigid process. Standards are developed according to need. They are also monitored according to need. With the exception of the unified worldwide standards, standards are created and monitored only when and where there is a perceived service weakness and thus a need to focus efforts on achieving a certain measurable objective. Monitoring stops when the group is achieving the standard on a consistent basis. This allows the company to focus on resolving weaknesses, and not to waste time and effort in heavy paperwork and procedures.

3 Focus in on customer perceptions

American Express measures customer satisfaction on a 'transactional basis'. That means that it measures satisfaction with each contact with the company. The advantage is that satisfaction or dissatisfaction can be more closely related to a particular experience or action than it can be with broader customer satisfaction surveys. Thus, improvement can be more pinpointed and more effective.

4 Go from high efficiency to greater personalisation

For the past 10 years, American Express has focused upon improving the timeliness, accuracy and efficiency of their service – and they have succeeded very well. The company is now going the important one step further: they are working on managing service quality for greater personalisation.

ANACOMP

Multi-million pound legal battles are sometimes won or lost on the basis of thin, wobbly, plastic sheets of film. Microfilm they call it. It was invented 100 or so years ago and is capable of storing up to 1000 pages of information on postcard-size microfilm. It can determine the outcome of important legal battles because the people who use it for storage are generally organisations such as banks or administrative bodies that store records of financial or legal transactions for 30 or more years.

Anacomp is a company that produces and services equipment that transfers information from a computer or paper document to the microfilm. They are the world leader in this very precise market with over 50 per cent share. Their success they attribute to the quality of service they have provided customers since 1968.

Background

Anacomp is an American company. It has been established in Germany since 1972 and over the period has increased its market share in the industry in Germany and Austria to over 60 per cent.

Like Anacomp worldwide, the company's prime target customers are banks, administrations and other institutions which are obliged to keep extensive records of their activities. In Germany and Austria, it has over 600 customers. Anacomp's clients typically need microfilm as a long-term storage medium (microfilm doesn't deteriorate before 100 years); all the larger banks in Germany are obliged to store records of individual bank transactions for more than 30 years.

The company employs 120 employees in Germany, 80 of which work in the after-sales service segment. Of Anacomp's 600 customers, 200 clients have large, long-lasting service contracts with the company. The other 400 do not have service contracts, but call on the company whenever there is a breakdown in the machine.

The after-sales service aspect of the business is highly important and highly successful. Anacomp machines transfer information at the rate of nearly 900 pages per minute. A breakdown of one hour can severely delay the process of transfer, most of which takes place on a daily basis. The machines themselves are also very expensive – up to DM600,000 – and represent a considerable investment which companies do not like to see sitting idle. The efficiency and high level of service quality maintained in its after-sales service has permitted the company to have a very profitable operation.

Service strategy

Anacomp defines its business as 'solving customers' filing problems'. The company sees itself in the role of a long-term collaborator of its customers. The actual sale is only the beginning of the relationship and the majority of the company's contact with its customers takes place after a sale has occurred. Because the company is targeting a particular market niche, it cannot afford to lose a customer.

The company's after-sales service organisation plays a very important role. For the reasons described above and because of the need for complete machine availability, the quality of Anacomp's service is primarily judged on the basis of the after-sales service it provides. Anacomp describes service quality in after-sales service as 'knowing the customer and providing top quality response times to calls for assistance.'

For Anacomp, 'knowing the customer' means having top quality information available to each service engineer prior to seeing the customer. He is expected to know the frequency with which the customer calls for assistance, the type of agreement it has with the company, the outcome of the last contact with the customer, the nature of the problems, if any, that the customer generally has with his machine, and any other pertinent data. With this information in hand, the engineer is in a much better position to diagnose the machine problem rapidly, and answer the customer's questions completely and with greater assurance.

The second important aspect of the company's service quality is the response time to calls. Because machine downtime is such a crucial factor for the company, Anacomp has made every effort to reduce its response delay to emergency calls to an absolute minimum. It has gone one step further by offering a guarantee to its maintenance contract holders that the 'machine is available and functioning over 95 per cent of the time during a 16-hour day.' If the guarantee is not met, the company refunds the customer 50 per cent of the price of the maintenance contract. As maintenance contracts cost between DM250,000 and DM1,200,000 per year/customer, the guarantee is a powerful one.

The positive service orientation of the service engineer is an important part of the service quality provided by Anacomp. On the one hand, it ensures that the engineer will conscientiously fulfil the company's commitment's to the customer in terms of response time and customer knowledge; on the other, it is a key point in the creation of a good working relationship between the company and the customer. In management's eyes, it has such a degree of importance that the company considers it, 'a strategic point in the maintenance of the company's competitive edge *vis-à-vis* the competition.'

Service strengths

'Our competitors are equipment vendors, being this as well, we see ourselves as a service-oriented team.' This statement summarises the strengths in Anacomp's service as compared with others in the industry. Anacomp sees its primary mission as providing good service to customers who have purchased its machines. Its service engineers are equipped to do just that.

Calls coming in for assistance pass through the company's hot-line, open 16 hours a day. Service engineers, generally in the field, are notified immediately by the central dispatching department, by Euro-signal, that a customer has a problem. He already has all the historical information on the client logged into a portable computer which he carries with him throughout the day and receives the customer's malfunction report either over the phone or directly from the dispatcher in person.

Based on the report and on the historical information he has on the company and its machine, the engineer can determine what are the likely spare parts he will be needing. He can decide to take the likely parts with him to the customer's and can stop on the way at the company's stock depot where they are immediately available. The company monitors stock levels and has a goal of 100 per cent stock availability.

Within two hours the service engineer is normally at the customer's premises. While the company guarantees up-time on its machines over a 16-hour day, in practice, the company assures a response time to customer calls of under two hours. This also is monitored, which is why the company can be sure that its objective of two hours is consistently achieved.

Once having arrived at the customer's, the engineer is already prepared to devote himself to listening to the customer and his description of the problem; he has already reviewed the company's past history and knows the type, age and peculiarities of the machine. He might spend 15 minutes to repair the machine and half an hour discussing with the customer how to avoid the problem in the future and about general maintenance issues.

Once the engineer leaves, he immediately enters a report of his visit into his portable computer. The report will be immediately entered by telephone connection via modem into the company's general databank. The next morning, the engineer's own computer will be updated with the information from all the engineers' visits of the previous day.

If, within 24 hours, the same customer calls back with a problem, the repair becomes top priority and is responded to immediately. If he calls back within 48 or 72 hours, it is a priority repair and is responded to before others. The central databank monitors the time delay between the first call and the second and sets the priority for the engineers. Any engineer who responds to the call on the second day will already have in hand the report of the engineer who dealt with the customer the day before.

While quick response and high efficiency are a strong point of Anacomp's service; they are not the only ones. Anacomp encourages its engineers to open communication channels with customers. To do this, the company helps by providing training in dealing with customers and a budget for relationship development. Roughly 20 per cent of the total training budget is devoted solely to training in customer service. An estimated 80 per cent of all video-based training deals with customer service. The result is that engineers are tuned into listening for changes in customers' needs and are on the lookout for areas of dissatisfaction. 'Our engineers are trained to follow every rumour about a potential complaint . . .' and are expected to solve it during their visit before it turns into a real complaint to headquarters.

Engineers also have a discretionary budget to be used to deal with problems encountered with customers or for general relationship development. Dinner with a customer's engineers, a bottle of whisky at Christmas and other treats are all acceptable expenses to be made at the discretion of the engineer for the advancement of the relationship.

Implementation

Anacomp has 17 service stations in 6 districts located throughout Germany and Austria. The company's service activities are centralised at Wiesbaden, the company headquarters. Located at Wiesbaden is the company's central computer system. It contains and manages all of the company's information concerning customers from all of the company's 17 service centres. This computer and its communication with all of the portable computers carried by the service engineers provides a vital service of logistics and monitoring without which Anacomp would be incapable of assuring the same level of service quality.

The computer receives all information on a daily basis about what has occurred on behalf of the customer. Repairs and general maintenance are all recorded along with detailed information about the quality of the relationship with the customer. It also co-ordinates this with information stored in the computer about the terms of the contract with the customer.

Based on the information, the computer schedules maintenance visits and auto-matically bills the customer for repairs or maintenance if and when necessary. It also uses the information to control the stock levels of spare parts for each of the warehouses. If, for example, an engineer in Hamburg reports having used a chipboard on April 27, the computer automatically orders a second to replace it. This permits the optimum control of stock levels and permits the company to offer nearly 100 per cent availability to customers.

The system also permits Anacomp to monitor its service quality on a large number of parameters. As is indicated above, it monitors response time, breakdown frequency, spare parts availability, machine down-time to the customer, repair efficiency levels etc. With this information, the company can target improvements in its service quality and control that quality standards and the guarantees to customers are met.

Targets are monitored at least on a monthly basis. Some key indicators are monitored on a daily basis – like the response rate to customer calls. The company's standing on the indicators is made available to all employees up and down the hierarchy in order to make employees sensitive to the need for improvement in key areas.

The company doesn't just monitor service quality using internal measures. It also believes in going direct to the customer to have his impression on the service quality delivered, not only on quantitative factors – response delays, down-time etc. – but also on qualitative factors such as the helpfulness of the repair staff.

A customer satisfaction survey has been conducted by the company on a yearly basis since 1983. While response to the enquiry is voluntary, the return rate is, nevertheless, extremely high – 70–80 per cent. It deals with the full range of the company's service from the sale to the after-sale. Questions include, 'How pleased are you with the technical expertise demonstrated by the repair engineer?', 'How would you rate the behaviour and appearance of the service engineer?', and 'Based on your experience, what are the positive expectations that you would have of a technical salesman? What are the negative expectations?'.

Results are available by service team, district or for the whole company. The results are published in the company's internal newspaper, *Compost* (printed four times a year) and are used to determine the winning team for the Best Technical Service Award. It is either the team that has the best score or the one that has made the most improvement from the previous year. Interesting gifts and money awards are given to the winners.

The results of the customer satisfaction survey are also used as a starting point for error-chasing groups which are formed four times a year to deal with specific problems identified by the survey. The outcome of the groups is often the intro-duction of improvements to the existing service or new services. One of the improve-ments that came out of this kind of group was the assignment of each service engineer to a particular customer account. In the satisfaction survey, customers had expressed concern about not having an identified person to contact about serving problems. The company now has one service engineer responsible for each account. Although he may not be the person who responds to a customer's call in every instance, he is the co-ordinator for the account and is responsible for the service relationship.

The company is aware of the richness of information which each service engineer has about the expectations of customers in the domain of service. Rather than let this information rest idle, the company tries to bring it out and use it to improve the company's overall service. The principal way in which the company does this is by performing an internal employee survey, once a year. The survey response can be anonymous or identifiable, as desired and the questionnaires are collected and analysed by the marketing department. The questions include, for example, 'Can you please rate the various departments on their speed of response to enquiries?', 'Can you please rate the quality of information provided to you on company developments, . . . on new products?', 'Putting yourself in the customer's shoes, how would you rate the company on quality, reliability, products, and the degree to which we meet client's needs?' and, very important, 'How would you rate our image with the clients . . . and what is it?'.

To help employees develop or improve their service orientation, Anacomp offers extensive training in customer service. Each employee has a six months' initiation period during which he receives six weeks of product training and one week of pure customer service training. For further advancement, the company has created a video library with 30 or more training videos for self-improvement. Eighty per cent of those videos concern attitude and behaviour training for employees *vis-à-vis* the customer.

The company's present push is in the area of sales training for every employee. They have a programme running called 'Everybody helps to sell' which is designed to improve employees' capability to recognise opportunities to sell to customers. From a less ambitious standpoint the programme is designed to improve employees' knowledge about the company's products and services, and to help them present and explain them well to customers.

What can be learned

1 Define your business according to the value-added you offer to your customer

Anacomp is not in the business of selling machines that put information on micro-film, although that's what they do. Anacomp is in the business of 'solving customers' filing problems'. With this definition, the company identified the most pertinent customer targets – banks, saving banks, administrations etc. – and the most vital customer expectation – machine availability – to create a sustainable competitive advantage over its competitors – 'Our competitors are just equipment vendors; we see ourselves as a service-oriented team.'

2 Use information technology for more personalised service

Using information technology doesn't always decrease personalisation while it increases efficiency. At Anacomp, it permitted the service staff to increase the personal touch. With more administrative paperwork eliminated, the service staff had more time to spend with the customer. With the computer providing ready-at-hand information to prepare the employee for his customer visit, he was more relaxed and confident when he arrived and got off to a better start with the client.

3 Train your after sales-staff to sell

Most companies might find it strange to give sales training to staff that only meet the customer after the product's sold. At Anacomp, they'd say it's normal. No customer is ever 'sold'. There is always something more to do to convince the customer of the high quality of your services and products. Anacomp trains its after-sales people to sell so that they will better understand customer expectations, will be better prepared to respond to customers' questions and to present the company in its best light.

4 Use your employees' databank of knowledge about customers

Anacomp recognises that the continual contact with customers that employees have gives them a privileged knowledge about customers' expectations and an insight into trends in customer demands. They tapped into this knowledge source by conducting an internal employee survey.

BOBST

Bobst is one of the companies that makes it possible to buy Chivas Regal Scotch whisky in a fancy silver-embossed box. Bobst produces machines which print, emboss, cut, glue and fold cartons, cardboard, and plastic boxes and packaging. Bobst is the world's leading producer of these types of machines, some of which, for example, are capable of producing an astonishing 200,000 cut and creased cartons per hour.

The production of boxes and packaging requires three distinct processes. The first is a high-speed, high-accuracy printing unit. The second is a converting unit which cuts the printed sheets into the shape required, strips the waste, creases the sheets at the corners and embosses or stamps them, if required. Lastly, the sheets are passed to a folder–gluer unit which folds and glues each box in preparation for filling. The three processes can be associated in the same machine or can be purchased on a stand-alone basis with auxiliaries which expands their capabilities or permits them to be associated with other machines in a production process.

These machines are by no means a light investment for the company purchasing them. Each one is the size of a small house and can cost up to SF1,000,000, for a folder–gluer, for example. The technical complexity of the machines has increased vastly since their introduction in the 1940s, and even more so with the development of new processes and CAD–CAM. They must not only be able to be installed on a stand-alone basis, but also integrated into an entire production process on the client's premises. A mistake can have implications on the client's productivity as well as on the overall adaptability of the production line to different products.

History

The Bobst company celebrated its centenary in 1990. It began its existence selling graphical art supplies. The first store was in Lausanne, owned and managed by Mr Joseph Bobst. By the 1920s, Henri Bobst, Joseph's son, had gone into the production of printing machines following the request of a hospital for a machine that printed in braille.

In 1940, the first prototype of the 'autoplaten' was ready. This machine permitted the industry to pass from an artisan state to an industrial one and from the production of 1200 pieces per hour to 4000 per hour. Rapid growth for the company followed on a worldwide basis. Today the company has subsidiaries or is represented in over 90 countries. A mere 5 per cent of all sales is in Switzerland.

Service strategy

A Bobst machine is the 'Rolls-Royce' of its kind, not in the sense of luxury, but rather as a quality label. It is the top of the line and has a reputation for excellent productivity and reliability. If a client buys a Bobst, he does so believing that the extra price he pays is more than justified in the greater productivity levels which the machine will allow him to attain.

The machines' reputation is not explained entirely by their technical attributes. Bobst sells a very elaborate product/service package.The product/service package has seven parts. At the centre one finds the machine, a high-quality machine at the forefront of technology. Around the machine, one finds six service axes which make it possible for the machine to achieve the purpose for which it was designed – to increase the productivity of the client's production line. The service part of the Bobst package is such a vital aspect that one could say that the company doesn't sell a product but rather a service – increased productivity.

Sales consultation

The first of the six service axes concerns the sale. Bobst salespeople are trained consultants in the production of packaging products. Their objective is to ensure that the client chooses the machine best adapted to his situation and to the development of his business.

Bobst recruits engineers from the best schools for sales positions and, even so, no salesperson at Bobst goes out the door alone until he has had six months training. Extensive schoolroom as well as practical training is provided in production processes and in the workings of Bobst machines. Trainees also spend time on the shop floor with the technicians responsible for installing and maintaining the machines.

Extra care is taken to ensure that the client chooses the right machine and not the most expensive machine, because Bobst's present and future success is based on client loyalty. Worldwide there are only 10,500 potential buyers for Bobst machines; a lost client is not easily replaced.

Because of its reputation, clients are proud to own a Bobst machine. It is a sign of accomplishment for many smaller companies to be able to buy a Bobst. Yet most Bobst machines are positioned at the top of the line in technicality and in price; they sometimes cannot meet the needs of smaller producers in the West or in the Third World. To attain these markets, Bobst has been repurchasing machines, refitting them to simplify the operations and selling them to companies that fall into this category. Furthermore, Bobst has recently designed simpler machines for these markets.

Even if it might happen that, due to Bobst success, machines are not available as quickly as needed by the customer, Bobst always finds a solution by, for example, lending a used, rebuilt machine in the meantime.

Consultation on installation

Another service axis concerns machine installation and delivery. The salesperson remains the primary contact of the client, although he is now joined by a team of three to five specialists whose job is to consult on the best method of integrating the machine into the client's production line. There are teams of specialists for each line of machine. Again, training is key and a Bobst service technician receives a year and a half of training on the product complemented by on-the-job training with more experienced personnel.

Installation co-ordination

Installing teams are not just trained to perform the technical aspects of their jobs correctly, but also to communicate well with the client. This permits Bobst to offer yet another service to its clients – that of co-ordination of the installation process. Bobst handles all aspects of the transportation and installing right up to and including the machine start up.

Machine optimisation

Keeping in mind that the ultimate objective is to improve clients' productivity, Bobst also offers clients assistance in minimising changeover times between different product runs. With machines that produce 100,000 to 250,000 boxes per hour, down-time is vitally important. Changes from one box model to another require some down-time. The installations specialists are prepared and trained to assist clients to reduce down-time.

Training

Bobst trains clients' personnel on how to operate the machines installed. Most Bobst trainers are former service technicians with extensive experience and additional training in production processes. They are also trained in languages; the most senior can speak several fluently. Most training sessions at the client's premises include a series of different instructions at different levels, as well as a general presentation before the entire factory personnel.

After-sales service

Once having purchased a Bobst machine, the client is initiated into the fold of Bobst users. A Bobst machine user is assured of the reliability of his machine and of the devoted attention of the Bobst team of maintenance and parts service people. Bobst's implicit promise to its customers is to ensure that its machines maintain their level of productivity. Technical updating of existing machines is also an important part of this service.

If a Bobst machine is out of order, help is on its way within the hour, regardless of where the company is located in the world. In most cases the machine is up and running within 24 hours.

Perhaps the most comforting news for clients is that no matter how old a Bobst machine is, the company will continue to provide spare parts to its owner. Ninety per cent or 35,000 of the parts for Bobst machine are kept in stock. The other 10 per cent is manufactured on demand.

A recent example was a call that came in for a machine which was over 40 years old. Within two days, Bobst was able to identify the piece which was necessary, manufacture and deliver it half-way across the world.

Service strengths

Henri Bobst's philosophy 'was to never let a client down'. Right from the start, Bobst positioned itself as a company which not only furnished machines, but also the services and technical support needed to make them run the way they were intended.

Today, that approach remains the dominant concern of the company. The company's client services department is one of the most vital in the company and puts together some of the most experienced individuals the company has.

A key point in the strategy has been the guaranteed replacement of parts. Bobst ensures its clients that no matter the age of the machine, Bobst will continue to supply the parts and technical assistance needed to keep it running in major markets such as, for example, the USA. A 24-hour hot-line is available for the re-ordering of spare parts or for technical advice in the case of a breakdown. Parts are sent out by air to points worldwide and generally arrive within 48 hours. Over 140 calls for spare parts are received a day and handled by a staff of 30.

In the technical services section, individuals with many years of experience receive the calls from clients needing advice on how to run the machines or deal with problems. They have been trained in handling technical enquiries over the phone, in handling emergency situations and, in most cases, are able to provide the necessary advice over the phone to get the machine up and running.

If help by telephone is insufficient, someone is sent immediately to the location. Bobst has a travel agent office within the company and all formalities are rapidly dealt with. Two hundred 'super service technicians' are located in Switzerland, another 200 are located in strategic locations throughout the world.

The individuals manning posts in client services are given a great deal of autonomy and are encouraged to take the initiative to respond to a client in the way in which they see fit, depending upon the gravity of the situation. In one instance, on a Saturday night when the factory had stopped production, an employee received an emergency call for a spare part. He got the part from the factory, went to the airport and took a plane to the US to deliver the part personally.

Implementation

Bobst is notably strong in two areas of service management – training and customer responsiveness. Their strengths in customer responsiveness stems directly from their concern for keeping the client productivity levels at the top. The client expresses a problem or a concern and Bobst responds.

The capacity to respond to clients rapidly is increased by the company's information system which logs information on clients and on major events in the relationship. Information is also kept on client satisfaction at the moment of the machine installation and start-up or in response to a problem. The installer completes a questionnaire following a client visit, the aim of which is to record his impressions on client satisfaction and to note client comments on ways in which the process could be improved.

Receiving a complaint from a client at Bobst is a serious occurrence. Complaints are responded to by the division manager, the manager responsible for the line of product purchased, for example. The objective is to re-establish the relationship through the quality of the response which the company gives.

Bobst is recognised within the Swiss community for the quality of its training. Training represents 5 per cent of the total personnel costs. Training is given in languages and in all aspects of client relations, as well as in the technical aspects. Roughly one-quarter of training is in a classroom and three-quarters on-site.

Part of Bobst training is conducted for apprentices. Ten per cent of the personnel are apprentices and remain in training for a period of four years. At the end of this period, they pass a federal exam. Roughly 60 apprentices a year remain with the company. If they remain, they enter into a new cycle of training; for a service technician, for example, this is a cycle of 18 months.

A good knowledge of the functions of the machines is needed by all staff and Bobst requires that personnel in training have experience at the clients' with the installing and starting up of the machines. All sales staff is required to spend time in the factory under the direction of a mechanic at Bobst and at the clients'.

Knowing how to maintain good client relationships is also considered to be a priority. Sales staff and service technicians alike receive at least a week's training on customer relations.

What can be learned

1 Spare parts policy

One of the key components in Bobst's product/service package is the guarantee of spare parts availability for the lifetime of the machine. It represents additional security for the purchasing company, which is vital because of the importance of the purchase.

In general, the greater an investment the purchase represents, the greater the perceived risk and, thus, the more there is a need to reassure the buyer of the essential quality of the purchase and of the company's willingness to stand behind what they produce. Bobst's spare parts policy was historically designed with this consideration in mind and it continues to be as important today as it was 50 years ago.

2 The value of complementary services to customers

Bobst also provides a good example of the standard of service which is required by purchasers of large investment items. Bobst is willing to fly anywhere in the world to repair their machines and will custom-produce a piece for a client if it's not available. Its clients expect that standard of service. A company that thinks that a quality design is enough to justify the price of an expensive machine is forgetting that the value of complementary services to customers is greater than its incremental cost.

3 Initiating clients to the technical complexities of the Product

Bobst's product and services are complex. They require a considerable degree of technical expertise to sell and even more to operate. By initiating clients to the technical complexities of the product as early as possible in the sales process Bobst reassures them and avoids uncomfortable incidents later in the sale when the client doesn't understand either a step in the process or underestimates the importance of a certain step, on-site training for example.

BRITISH AIRWAYS

A dusty, unwieldy organisation sinking slowly, but surely, into the murky waters of high debt and poor return . . . possibly eventually to disappear. That would have been a good description of British Airways in 1980.

Today, the description is somewhat different – a dynamic, profitable company tuned into customer needs and a quickly changing marketplace. In just over 10 years British Airways has done better than most movie stars. It's had more than a face-lift; it's had a new lease on life.

A great deal has been written about how Lord King, Sir Colin Marshall and their team achieved that turnaround. Today, the question is less 'How did we get where we are today?' and more, 'Where do we go now that we've reached the top?' Perhaps the answer to the first question is that British Airways has not yet reached the top. Despite regularly being voted the top airline in the world by travellers, British Airways is still convinced that there is more to do.

'Integration of service quality into the quality approach is still the biggest challenge after eight years of the [customer service] programme. The most difficult part is to get people past the status quo and to get them to do things differently – to get them to accept that in the increasingly global and competitive environment that they have got to respond to the challenge', says Sir Colin Marshall.

Background

The turnaround began in 1981 with the appointment of Lord King (then Sir John King) to the post of Chairman of British Airways. In short, his mission was to make the state-owned company profitable and prepare it to be privatised.

Examination of the situation showed that British Airways' most immediate problems were heavy overstaffing and insufficient capitalisation. The company was the result of the merger of two corporations, British European Airways and British Overseas Airways, completed in 1974. Little rationalisation had been done following the merger and little effort had been made to bring the two widely different cultures closer to one another.

Lord King cut the staff of 58,000 to 38,000; he also cut unprofitable air routes and revalued more realistically some of the company's fleet. The severance costs for staff cuts were charged off in the same year, fiscal 1981/2. With these actions, the company was ready to tackle some of the most fundamental management issues.

Sir Colin Marshall was brought into the company in 1983. He had had wide experience in the management of service industries. He had worked for both Avis and Hertz and had most recently been deputy chief executive of Sears Holdings plc. 'The real problem . . . was basically quite easy to identify. The airline had forgotten that it was a service industry' (Sir Colin Marshall, *Turnaround*).

The year 1983/4 saw major changes in the management team. Marshall has a more directive style than what was practised in the past and he wanted people who were capable of making and implementing decisions rapidly. British Airways had previously had a culture of collective decision-making which meant that it took a long time before anything happened.

Intensive market research was also begun during this period. Sir Colin was determined to bring a more coherent marketing approach to the company and to make customer satisfaction a primary objective.

Also in 1983, the company began to put a third of the staff, those in contact with the customer, through a training course called 'Putting People First'. 'In it, we set out to show people how their own attitudes towards the customer, and towards their own colleagues, affected the way in which customers saw them' (Sir Colin Marshall, *Turnaround*).

In the end, the course was so popular that practically every employee at British Airways passed through it. A follow-up programme was launched in 1986/7 called 'A Day in the Life'. This was designed to give employees an understanding and appreciation for the work done by others in different parts of the organisation. This programme was also a great success. It was also succeeded by 'To Be the Best', which focussed on competition.

Following on from 'Putting People First' was 'Managing People First', a course for managers to help them learn how to motivate, take responsibility, delegate responsibility, plan and create a vision. It also was designed to develop a consensus among managers about where British Airways was heading.

The whole set of training programmes fell under a general theme of 'Putting the customer first – if we don't, someone else will'. More recently it has given away to a new corporate initiative, 'Winning for Customers'.

To back up what was being said in the training programmes, Sir Colin and his staff worked full time on operational issues, such as punctuality, cleanliness, material maintenance and support services. Sir Colin believes in keeping the 'shine' on the product on a daily basis – something that had been neglected when the company was having profit and cash-flow problems.

And, to mark the changes being made, a new visual identity was introduced. There was a new colour scheme, a polished new logo, new uniforms, new seat covers, and refurbished passenger lounges. To complete the effect, a new advertising campaign was also launched.

In 1986, following the management seminars, a corporate mission statement was developed which set forth the company's goals for itself in key areas. The main goal statement to which all the others contribute is, 'To be the best and most successful company in the airline industry.'

Eight years later, a great deal has been accomplished. As one manager we spoke with put it, 'We've moved a hell of a long way . . .'.

Service strategy

When Sir Colin Marshall joined the company in 1983, there was no market strategy and little attention paid to market research. As part of the changes implemented, he created the present marketing structure and turned a very passive organisation into one which not only follows, but also anticipates customer demands.

The core of the present service strategy is 'branding' – the notion of attaching a name, an image and a precise set of services to a particular class of travel. The first segments to receive this treatment in 1988 were the business classes – Club World, on intercontinental flights, and Club Europe to European destinations. Reviews of all other market segments followed: Super Shuttle, Super Shuttle Executive, First Class, World Traveller and Euro Traveller (formerly Economy) and Skyflyers (for children).

The branding strategy represents a way of more fully meeting the needs and expectations of specific customer groups, i.e. targeting customer segments and then developing services especially for that segment. Central to this philosophy is a regular review of what is offered, to ensure it still meets customers' requirements.

British Airways' service strategy today is actually the result of British Airways' new focus on listening to its customers. Customer satisfaction on key indicators is monitored on a monthly basis. Research is conducted on an ongoing basis to identitfy customer segments and their expectations. Over 150,000 interviews are conducted per year with passengers as well as focus groups and ongoing dialogues with regular passengers. A truly innovative way to receive customer comments was the Video Point, located at Heathrow, which gave customers the opportunity to make comments about the airline on video.

Staying close to its customers has not only permitted the company to develop a successful service strategy, but is permitting the company to develop an image as the airline that 'listens best to its customers'. In 1989, when *Business Traveller* magazine announced that British Airways had won the prize for the Best Airline Overall, it commented that, 'Its success reflects the enormous and continuing progress the airline has made in listening and responding to its customers, as well as its rapid expansion in terms of routes, frequency and new products.'

Today, an airline cannot survive alone on good 'products'; it must also position itself as a provider of good, helpful and friendly personal service. British Airways' close to the customer image is doing that for them. 'We use the word "customer" in daily language. From planning to administration, everything should reflect the desires of the customer. When this ethic is pulled all the way through the organisation, the customer becomes part of the daily life; that is the ultimate mission' (Shaune Shaw, Ground Operations).

Service strengths

Perhaps the most impressive thing about the changes at British Airways is that customers are experiencing better service at every step and at every level.

First and foremost, flying with British Airways is a whole lot more hassle free than it ever used to be. The airline has made dramatic improvements in punctuality, for example, and that's in a travelling environment in which punctuality on the whole has suffered.

There is also a much speedier check-in at British Airways. In some cases, this is simply the result of better organisation. In other cases, the airline has developed express check-in and its 'Turn up and Take off' Super Shuttle system on key UK domestic routes, which uses a Time Saver 'self-service' system enabling customers to purchase their tickets and be issued a boarding card in as little as 40 seconds.

Investment in information technology has also seen the development of touch screens, multilingual information points for passengers at UK international airports. Stewardesses are also now equipped with portable computers which make on-board duty-free purchases easier and more rapid.

Other on-board equipment such as ovens and serving trolleys have also been improved or replaced with some of the most efficient models in the industry. The in-flight magazine, *Highlife*, has even been revised and regularly wins awards for the best in-flight magazine in the industry from the World Airline Entertainment Association.

Improvements in in-flight food and drink have also been recognised with a whole host of awards.

If you are the lucky fellow travelling in first class, you will have a six-course meal, a 20-inch wide seat with 5ft in front of you and the chance to try out the world's first personalised video system. Each passenger can choose from 50 or so tapes of movies or television shows. The screen is about 15cm wide and 10cm high and carries digital sound quality.

For those under 12, travelling is simply more fun. Special lounges for children with toys and appropriate refreshments have been set up in some of British Airways' airports. On the plane, children's meals are now available: they don't have to eat the 'icky black stuff' called caviar any more.

Last, but not least, British Airways has become more environmentally-conscious. Besides bringing into the company specialists whose sole function is to find ways to improve the company's green approach, the airline has already transferred its entire automobile fleet over to non-lead fuel and is in the process of installing a super energy-efficient climate and lighting control system in its buildings.

Implementation

To arrive at where the company is today, it had to implement major structural and organisational changes such as a trimming of the workforce investing in new equip-ment and technologies and the creation of an important marketing function. In addition, it had to train staff to understand why the changes were being made and which direction the company was heading.

The airline is today at a stage where most of the 'visual' changes have been achieved. But change is not, by any means, a thing of the past. The most important step facing Sir Colin Marshall and his team is to complete what has been started – a revolution in the corporate culture.

'We started with people who liked aircraft. We were an operationally driven culture and that means "we are the professionals and we know best". This is very different from a customer service culture; it's a fundamentally different philosophy: "we are only here to deliver good value customer service and the customer knows best." . . . It is the culture that is difficult to change,' explains Shaune Shaw.

In the coming years efforts will be focused on two areas: solidifying the progress that has already been made and adding to it; and becoming yet more customer oriented. Certain tools of service quality management are proving to be the most useful to the company in achieving its present aims. The first of these is a system of quality measurement and communication.

'We work with over 200 separate performance targets in the business, both quantitative and qualitative which are published for the managers who then proceed according to their own best judgement,' says Sir Colin. Progress on some of the key measurements appear every month in an internal journal. The document has charts and clear explanations of what's happening within the company in key service areas.

'We're measuring from the customer's viewpoint all the time,' says Ms. Shaw. As part of a formal audit, customers are sampled and interviewed every day at Heathrow Airport. Information is constantly coming through complaints and suggestion letters which are systematically analysed. 'In the letters, we look for trends and analyse information for ideas. We share the overall information with staff. If an individual's name is mentioned, he or she will get a copy; this is extremely motivational.'

The company's innovative approach to personnel management has been another factor which has made service quality management easier. Following the major cutbacks in staff and major re-organisations, it became clear that in certain instances or in peak periods additional staff would be needed to meet growing volume and demand. The response on the part of British Airways was to initiate a series of part-time work schemes which permitted it to have the staff it needed without being required to over-staff on a permanent basis. The system applies mostly to women, 'who said that they would like to come back to work after starting a family, but couldn't come back full time,' explains Eva Lauermann, Human Resources.

As a result, the airline has:

job sharing;
job splits;
part-time workers;
twilight shifts (that are short so that the husband can be at home looking after the children);
career breaks; and
a nursery on site.

'This was a response to the labour market and to make sure that we can attract and keep the people that we want or get them back.'

In the same vein, the company has created a secretary self-improvement programme. The programme begins by a skills assessment workshop which helps secretaries to identify the training they think they need for higher posts.

A key turning point in the drive towards better service quality at British Airways was the moment when customer service initiatives began to start coming up the hierarchy instead of always going down. Management has strongly encouraged the development and continues to encourage it.

There is an important staff suggestion scheme called 'Brainwaves', which offers prizes of between £10 and £10,000 to employees who propose suggestions on how to produce efficiency. To back up the environmental effort, 'Greenwaves' was created as a separate category in the scheme.

Customer First teams have also been created with staff volunteers. Their role is to work on proposing ways to improve service to customers. One of the results of the work of these groups was the introduction of the children's services as described above.

A big contribution in the past, and probably a big contribution in the future, to the evolution in the corporate culture has been the example set by Sir Colin himself. He demonstrates personally to his staff that customers come first.

Sir Colin spends as much time as he can with staff at the frontline. He responds personally to customers' complaints when they are brought to his attention 'If I overhear a customer comment, I will go talk to the customer directly. It's a good thing because it's possible to deal with the real problem right then and there on the spot. One time, I heard a customer register a complaint with the cabin crew about the food; he said that he was going to write to me. I went right over and told him not to bother – but to tell me what was concerning him there and then; he was quite surprised' (Sir Colin Marshall).

What can be learned

1 Work on 'shining' your details

Sir Colin Marshall maintains that in any service industry it's essential to keep the product shiny. By that he means paying attention to detail and not permitting imperfections to creep into a company's culture or system of functioning.

2 Break with tradition and turn a constraint into a strength

Some of the greatest discoveries of mankind have been made by individuals who refuse to accept the status quo. Faced with a rigid personnel situation when what he needed was flexibility to respond to rapid fluctuations in demand, Sir Colin simply changed the rules.

Today, British Airways is pioneering an approach to staffing which mixes full-time workers with part-time workers with seasonal workers and flexi-time workers, to name a few of the options available. In addition to meeting Sir Colin's needs, the approach is satisfying the needs of a large number of women workers who for personal reasons do not want full-time employment.

3 Set the example

Employees will do no more than what you as a manager are willing to do. If you will 'drop everything' to help a customer out, then so will they. Sir Colin Marshall is an excellent example, showing how one's own actions can sometimes have some of the greatest impact. Bravo, Sir Colin!

CASTEL NOVEL

The most modern of conveniences with the extreme charm of the Middle Ages – a good description for a hotel in the heart of one of France's most renowned regions for good food and a beautiful landscape.

What can also be found in this lovely location is an appealing style of management which illustrates little of what one learns in management books and a great deal of what one learns from experience. Call it old fashioned if you like, but the results are excellent, and even in this very MBA-dominated world there is much to be learned from a more time-tested approach.

Background

Castel Novel is a renovated medieval castle located on 10 hectares of rolling green landscape in the Coreze, a region just adjacent to the famous Perigord. The Parveaux family has been in the hotel and restaurant business for four generations. The present Mr Parveaux's father was a pastry shop owner and then a caterer in the nearby town of Brive, before he acquired Castel Novel.

It was in 1956 that Mr Parveaux Senior purchased the property and created his dream site – a hotel of charm and prestige. His son Albert graduated from one of the hotel schools and then came to assist his father; he inherited the management of the business upon his father's retirement.

Castel Novel is situated on 40 hectares of green landscape, ever so carefully maintained by two full-time gardeners. The hotel itself consists of five buildings – the original castle and four outlying buildings. One of the outlying buildings houses additional hotel rooms while the rest are facilities for conferences or related activities.

There are 40 staff for the 37 rooms which make up the hotel. There is, in addition a hotel director, the department supervisors (kitchen, dining room etc.) and Mr Parveaux, the owner/director.

Castel Novel represents one of five establishments run by Mr Parveaux. Two are located in a well-known French ski resort, Courcheval, and the two others, not far from Castel Novel in Montignac and Brive. Together the five hotels cover the span from two stars to four stars. The auberge (or country inn) in Brive is a two-star hotel. Crystal 2000 and Montignac are three-star hotels; Pralong 2000 and Castel Novel are four-star hotels. All of the hotels have restaurants.

With the exception of the auberge, all of the hotels have a seasonal activity. The hotels in the south-west are closed in the winter and the hotels in the ski resorts are closed in the summer. The staff follows the seasonal rotation and change residence every six months.

Each hotel, regardless of its location or class, 'should strive to obtain perfection in its category; only the methods to achieve this vary, not the goal' says Mr Parveaux.

Service strategy

In all of Mr Parveaux's establishments, the service strategy is to achieve excellence in three areas: the welcome, the quality of the food and the price/quality ration of the entire package. 'In this respect, we do not cut corners', emphasises Mr Parveaux.

In practical terms this means that no lapses in quality are permitted in these areas; no half measures are taken in order to earn FFr1 more, if it puts at risk the group's reputation. Employees are trained from the very first day they enter the establishments that courtesy and customer recognition, for example, are top priority. To make sure that the message is properly passed, the staff are closely supervised by Mr Parveaux himself, who knows all of his staff personally, by the hotel director and by the department supervisor. And Mr Parveaux doesn't hesitate to insist, just like Walt Disney, that his employees greet every guest with a smile and a hello.

The quality of the hotel's fare is greatly aided by the experience of the Parveaux family in the business of pastries and catering, and by the location of the hotel in a region famous for its excellent cuisine. Besides these 'natural' advantages, Mr Parveaux hires some of the best chefs that the area has to offer and particularly those that demonstrate an interest in the customers. Mr Parveaux and his chefs regularly tour the dining rooms to receive comments both good and bad from customers.

Ensuring that the price/quality ratio of what Mr Parveaux offers is found by customers to be attractive is an ongoing challenge. Many hotels have a service strategy similar to Mr Parveaux's; the quality of the welcome by which he differentiates himself from his competitors is only valid if the price of his basic service remains within a certain range. Keeping it within that range is sometimes difficult, given the rapidity with which customer expectations change and the overall level of competition within the business. Mr Parveaux's 'formula' at price 'X' may be considered to be a good deal in one year and no longer a good deal the year after.

To stay on top of changes in his customers' expectations, Mr Parveaux put into place a satisfaction survey. It is available to restaurant goers and to guests in the hotel. Because of the attractive presentation of the survey, the return rate is relatively high, larger than the standard 5 per cent. In addition, another survey is conducted by the chain of hotels to which Mr Parveaux's hotels are affiliated, Relais & Chateaux. The two sources, together with direct comments from customers, permit Mr Parveaux to make the necessary adaptations to his 'formula' to meet fluctuations in customer demands. The quality of the reception that customers receive at his hotels does the rest.

Service strengths

As one might imagine, given Mr Parveaux's strategy, a major strong point in service for the hotels is the kindness and generosity of his staff. This fact alone has earned Mr Parveaux's largest Courcheval hotel a 50 per cent return rate of customers, year to year. While fidelity at the hotels in the south-west is somewhat less due to the rather remote location, they are still considerably higher than the standard in the region.

These researchers' 'incognito' visit to the hotel included one extremely gratifying experience: each person we passed bid us a good day and gave a true, genuine smile. Mr Parveaux's law of customer consideration worked and it worked so well that employees didn't feel forced or strained.

The genuine warmth and friendliness of the staff is evident in many ways. At meal times, the waitress or waiter always spared a moment to exchange a few words; at the tennis court, staff offered to lend their own equipment to guests in order for them to play. Most guests receive a royal welcome, by Mr Parveaux himself or the director of the hotel. If not, they receive a royal send-off with many thanks and an escort to their car or taxi.

Employees are recruited for their customer service orientation and they are almost all brought in at the same moment – at the beginning of the season. As a result, the group develops a strong team spirit and adopts an identical level of concern for serving customers well from the very beginning.

Besides general courtesy and consideration, the point Mr Parveaux most emphasises is humility. 'The golden rule that must be respected by all our staff is humility,' says Mr Parveaux. Particularly, he means humility in front of the client. Mr Parveaux himself solicits customer comments. He makes a point of exchanging at least a word or two with his customers on their visit and regularly notes suggestions made by customers for future reference.

If there is ever a problem, 'particularly in the restaurant, this can be seen very, very quickly. We go out of our way and propose a solution to replace in some way his disappointment; this could be a present or to invite him for dinner. In all cases, we stay humble,' says Mr Parveaux.

Complaint letters are rare; most complaints are verbal and are dealt with by Mr Parveaux himself. His way of handling the few complaint letters that are received caught these authors by surprise. It is far from what is habitually recommended, but it clearly demonstrates the commitment Mr. Parveaux has to the service quality offered by his establishments. According to policy, all correspondence that comes in is answered the same day, except complaint letters 'We make a point of waiting 24 hours before responding to avoid answering a letter in the heat of fury or disappointment.'

Implementation

Mr Parveaux has brought in around him an excellent management team; however, he remains a very omnipresent figure in the setting of management policies for his establishments. He also sets the example for how customers should be treated and is the last-word enforcer of his policies and practices with his staff. In very concise terms, Mr Parveaux's approach to management focuses on setting the example, establishing a small number of iron-clad policies and providing a supportive environment for young employees.

'I do not believe in asking anyone to do anything that I cannot and would not do myself,' says Mr. Parveaux. Likewise, most employees are expected to be multifunctional and ready to do to the best of their ability any job that needs to be done. Mr Parveaux is regularly seen carrying baggage, just as he is regularly seen doing his accounts for the hotels.

Mr Parveaux works hard to keep the building and the materials of all of his hotels in tip-top shape. Every morning Mr Parveaux makes the tour of the establishment to ensure that everything is running smoothly. Ageing material is often replaced before the employees themselves ask for it to be replaced. Likewise, he expects his employees to keep any material they handle in equally tip-top shape.

In his attitude *vis-à-vis* clients and in his way of dealing with his staff, Mr Parveaux shows that customers always come first. He doesn't believe in rewarding good customer service because 'the satisfaction of our clients is the foundation of our work'.

Whether it's accomplished by setting the example or by communicating directly, Mr. Parveaux's goal is to establish a certain number of principles which guide the management of his establishments. The need to ensure the satisfaction of clients is one of those. Another is that 'the customer welcome is the business of every employee'.

In general, these principles are communicated verbally and repeated again and again by Mr Parveaux, and by his management staff. In addition, many are set forth in a regular series of notes which 'remind each person how best to do his job'. The notes pass through the hands of the department heads and on down to each employee concerned. The end of the season serves as an opportunity to discuss what happened over the season and what could have gone better.

These hotels are considered in the region to be an excellent terrain for training young people interested in hotel careers. In fact, besides the supervisory staff, most of the employees are very young – often under 20 – and are presented to Mr Parveaux by their parents. The hotels act as a home away from home and Mr Parveaux is very conscious of his role as a father figure and educator to most of these young people.

Employees are free to receive training in any section of the hotel that they wish. Desk clerks, if they wish, could be trained in the kitchen, for example. Although training is never mandatory, already many employees are in training in their own departments. If an employee wants to be trained in another function, it is up to him to approach the supervisor of the department where he wishes to go. 'This is a way of encouraging employees to take initiative and responsibility in their own hands.'

One of the principle motivations for employees is the environment in which they work. All of Mr Parveaux's establishments are very attractive; employees are free to use the facilities at their leisure as long as they do not, in any way, disturb customers. As the full team changes location every six months, the variety of the work environment also represents a plus.

Most management level staff remain a long time with the company, first, because of the work environment and, second, because of the salaries which are somewhat above the norm. Mr Parveaux makes a point of looking after his staff. He is often willing to help, for example, employees' children to obtain entrance to the hotel schools if they so desire.

'An employee that deserves it, will have all my confidence and support; but, attention to those that abuse it', says Mr Parveaux.

What can be learned

1 Don't hesitate to crack the whip

A lot of emphasis today is put upon management through teamwork or co-operative management. In our search for ways to gain the voluntary participation of employees towards a common goal, we forget that sometimes clear directives are better suited to the situation. Mr Parveaux's employees have no doubt about where their priorities lie, nor which way to jump when the whip is cracked.

2 Adopt a father (or mother) figure

Again, this is another management style that has been ridiculed in recent years. Yet, Mr Parveaux and many others like him use it to great success. To make it work, it helps if a solid core of the staff has been with the company for many years and if the employer offers something more to the employee than just a nine-to-five job. In the case of Castel Novel, it is the live-in atmosphere and his own character that creates the proper backdrop for Mr Parveaux.

3 Set a precedent and stick to it

Mr Parveaux established a precedent at his hotels that courtesy to the customer comes first. His policy is clear and is strong because he himself never wavers from it; it is applied in every instance, regardless of the circumstance.

CIBA-GEIGY DYES AND CHEMICALS

You may have been under the impression that Ciba-Geigy produced only pharma-ceuticals. In fact, there are seven major divisions of this Swiss company, the oldest of which is dye stuff and chemicals. A dye stuff is what makes a wool sweater red, purple or blue instead of dirty lamb white. A 'chemical' in this sense refers to the products added to make the dye stay in the fabric, or to improve the finish or wearability of the fabric.

The dye stuffs and chemicals business is a mature one. While there are regular improvements in the end-product, the basic technology has been the same for many years. One might even say that dye stuffs and chemicals is a very 'stuffy' business. At Ciba-Geigy, 10 years ago, they might have even agreed. Today, things have changed. The company is full of new ideas and enthusiasm; employees are excited about what they're doing and they're excited about serving their clients better.

Background and history

In 1985, Mr H. Lippuner, then head of the Dye and Chemicals division (now Chairman of the Executive Committee of the Group, i.e. C.E.O.), embarked on a total quality programme. His objective was:

1 to create a point of differentiation *vis-à-vis* competitors;
2 to ensure employee well-being and development.

As Mr Götz, the present division head explains, 'Being Ciba-Geigy and a Swiss company, the quality of the product has always been part of the culture for us. Maybe sometimes too much.

'We have come to realise that from our customers' point of view, when we are up against companies that compete on price, we need a point of differentiation. Today, we can position ourselves as the company that can offer customers superior quality service.'

In the dye stuffs and chemicals business six companies control 75 to 80 per cent of the world market. Those six are known as the 'traditionals', the rest are called the 'non-traditionals'. The non-traditionals are generally nationally based and compete on the basis of price. Ciba-Geigy has 20 to 25 per cent of the world market in dye stuffs.

Historically, innovation was what determined success in the marketplace. In the 1960s and '70s cost issues gained importance. In the last 10 years, marketing has become a determinant factor. In the next 10 years, service quality will be an issue; 'the more mature the business becomes, the more important service will be to our success' (Dr. Götz).

Real change began at Ciba-Geigy when total quality was adopted as a strategic objective, following the launch of the quality programme. It was to be applied on a worldwide basis and at every level. Today, service and product quality targets, with measurable objectives, are set on a yearly basis, not only for managers, but for everyone down to the shop-floor level. In addition, the company is developing a package of incentive schemes which includes financial rewards and rewards for good teamwork.

The achievement of quality goals is already a part of performance appraisals. For managers, 10 to 20 per cent of their evaluation depends upon their results in the quality category.

The first step which the division took as part of the quality process was to perform a very detailed study of customer expectations. Clients throughout the world were included in the study with different customers interviewed at each client – the top executive, the product users, the purchasers, the technicians – whoever had a contact with the product or the company.

The results showed that quality in the very broadest sense had become a major issue. Support in the use of the product was more important; logistical issues (delivery times etc.) were gaining importance. Price was becoming less important.

The company conducted the same survey with employees. Differences between employee conceptions and customer perceptions were highlighted in the company-wide communication which launched the programme.

Today, Mr Lippuner's second objective for the programme is being realised. Employees are highly motivated to achieve quality objectives. Team spirit is fostered in the different quality circles and action teams that have been formed. Training, available to improve personal skills in dealing with the customer as well as to expose employees to techniques for quality management, are developing employees' non-technical skills.

Since Mr Lippuner was made C.E.O., the quality initiative is being supported on a group-wide basis. Employees from the dye stuffs and chemicals division are looked at by the rest of the group as 'the example in terms of quality, not just product quality, but service quality as well'.

Going forward, Mr. Götz says the biggest obstacle he faces is the psychological barrier:

'People believe that they have always been doing a good job and don't accept easily the fact that maybe it wasn't as good as it should have been. It is easier to judge ourselves by our own standards. The ultimate judge is the customer and this is sometimes difficult to accept.'

Service strategy

Using the results of the study on customer expectations, Ciba-Geigy developed a new strategy. In the past, the company had always emphasised product quality and innovation in primary technologies. The new strategy emphasises total quality and innovation in application technologies. The service strategy is summarised by the word 'partnership', a term chosen by the company to describe the kind of relationship it wants to establish with its clients.

One of the reasons that this strategy was chosen is because it permits the company to concentrate on serving one segment of the market rather than on serving the entire market. The strategy is particularly apt as Ciba-Geigy has experienced meeting high world demand for its products due to limited capacity.

Ciba-Geigy's clients represent a vast range. Certain have less need for sophisticated technologies or for the kind of support services that go with them. These customers tend to be more price conscious and less product quality conscious. At the other extreme are clients who place enormous importance on product quality, on product development support and on a whole range of services which could accompany them, including advice on product application and information on product technology. These customers are less price sensitive.

With the partnership strategy, Ciba-Geigy is targeting the less price sensitive, more quality sensitive end of the market. The strategy seems to have been well received. As the marketing director for the division puts it, 'The more sophisticated the buyer, the more they want the partnership relationship.'

Ciba-Geigy's partnership strategy implies the strengthening of ties with clients to create a richer and more open flow of communication. Equality and the recognition of mutual interests is the basis for the relationship. Ciba-Geigy brings to that relationship its expertise in the domain and a desire to increase the quality of its contacts with the client at all levels.

As the focal point of the new approach, Ciba-Geigy is helping clients differentiate themselves from their competitors. The diagram below explains how they view their relationship with clients. A company can be understood in terms of its values, leadership position and its level of innovation. According to Ciba-Geigy, there should be a match between itself and its client on those three dimensions. 'If there is a match, we can assist a client to improve his competitiveness, thereby creating a differential advantage for us as well as for him.' In practical terms, that means that Ciba-Geigy is actively searching for techniques that can improve each client's competitiveness. The result of this search has become a strength in its service package.

Service strengths

Ciba-Geigy has always been a technological leader in its field. Now the company is putting its knowledge to use for its customers. Through an approach called 'non-product-specific differentiation', the company has developed a whole series of new services to help customers differentiate themselves from the competition.

Twenty specific areas of differentiation have been identified. They include things like differentiation through information technology, through training, though ecology consulting, through total quality management and through information.

Area: Ecology Consultancy	
Approach	● Identify problems of customers re treatment of effluent. ● Consult customers when new dyehouses are projected ● Establish contact and co-operate with the community treatment plant.
Action	● Analysis of all dyeing, scouring and bleaching phases and process. ● Optimise recommendations and recipes with the goal to reduce pollution of waste water. ● Co-operate in defining the new layout of the dyeing plant.
Benefits for CG	● Improvement of our product mix. ● Improvement of our contribution/market share. ● Barriers for competitors. ● Long term co-operation in fundamental decisions.
Benefits for customer	● Assistance in technical-chemical decisions ● Long term help from CG.

Example of an ecology consultancy

Units all over the world are contributing ideas about different services that can be offered to customers to help them compete more effectively. The ideas have been assembled by the head office and are presented in the form of a book. There are over 70 ways of differentiating that have been developed and are actively used by Ciba-Geigy for their customers.The book serves as a reference tool for all Ciba-Geigy units and as a source of inspiration for new ideas.

To give an example of some of the services developed, Ciba-Geigy in Austria organised a 'colour matching workshop', France created a computer software for 'memorising lab work' and Hong Kong ran 'technical training' courses for customers.

For each service developed, the benefits for the customer are clearly listed. The benefits for Ciba-Geigy are also cited, in keeping with the company's philosophy about creating differential advantages for both the company and its clients.

One area where the company has traditionally been strong and for which the new approach is creating greater opportunities for its application is in the area of 'technical services'. Product applications assistance or 'technical services', as it is called, relates to the product adaptation process. In the dye business, it is rarely possible to simply hand over the dye formula to customers who then pour it into a bin with water and the cloth to be dyed. Most dyes have to be tested on each new fabric composition and various adjustments made to have the best result. Problems can occur with the way the colour stays in the fabric, with the evenness of the colour, with the colour effect of the texture of the fabric etc. In some cases, an entirely new composition must be created to be used with a particular fabric.

Ciba-Geigy excels in this area, first, because its employees have been coached and trained in how to work with clients to adapt their dyes, but also because the necessary resources are made available: specialists who at one time passed the majority of their time at headquarters are now being sent out to work on-site with clients when necessary. Customers are now invited to headquarters to receive training, and to exchange information and techniques.

Implementation

A vital step which the company took towards improving service quality was to conduct a study of customer expectations. A very complete and thorough study was first conducted in the early 1980s. Over 1000 customers from all over the world were approached and took part.

The study had two parts: a quantitative and a qualitative one. In the quantitative section, the company asked its customers to rank it *vis-à-vis* its competitors on a range of service and product dimensions. Service dimensions represented roughly 70 per cent of the dimensions studied. The customer was not aware that Ciba-Geigy was conducting the study and an outside group handled its organisation.

In the qualitative part of the survey, the company asked open questions about how customers felt about their services and for feedback of ways that service could be improved. From this part, the company was also able to identify future trends and explore the relative importance of the relationship aspects of the service.

Study results permitted the company to segment clients into three parts, to identify which segment's demands most closely corresponded with the company's strengths as perceived by the customers themselves and, then, to choose the segment(s) which to target. The partnership strategy is the concrete result of this market research.

The company has continued to conduct similar studies. Two to three surveys are conducted every year addressing specific points; the same major study is conducted every four years. As a result, the company has developed specific services to meet the individual needs of segments or sub-segments. Many of the services developed under the non-product-specific differentiation programme are a result of this ongoing research.

A second important point for the advancement of service quality has been work done within the company to improve internal service quality. Because Ciba-Geigy is a firm with a fairly large part of its staff in the manufacturing and other non-direct customer contact posts, it is important that all employees serve one another well in order for the customer to be served well.

The internal quality programme is presented to employees at the time of their integration into the company. Beyond the initiation course, most employees will have also received quality specific training, i.e. how to run a quality circle.

The guiding concepts behind the internal quality programme are:

1 'always room for improvement'; and
2 'directed autonomy', meaning that according to his experience and education, every employee has a certain freedom to influence his work and to take initiatives to improve quality.

The director of the Dye and Chemicals Division's quality assurance department says that 'the biggest part of my job is that of trying to change attitudes. Tools like the quality groups help me do that.' Thus, the internal service quality programme has taken form through the creation of quality groups and internal standards.

There are two main types of quality groups. 'Quality circles' run on an ongoing basis and are designed to address problems in the functioning of existing procedures and systems. They are most active in the technical or production area.

'CATs' or Corrective Action Teams are formed in reponse to the identification of a specific issue, frequently one that requires the participation of a number of departments. Interdepartmental service issues are frequently discussed in these groups. A recent CATs group addressed the problem of slow telephone response. The standard in the company was three rings. In actuality, the response was five or six rings. One of the solutions proposed and implemented was the installation of answering machines on individuals' phones. Another was the installation of a system which monitors how many times each phone rings before it is answered.

Standards are used with increasing frequency by the company to ensure good service between departments. Initially service standards were developed for delivery times on products. More recently, the company is developing standards in other areas. The telephone is one. Another is the space of time for a response to a request for a price quote (one day) and the space of time for a request for technical information (10 days). More general standards exist concerning the way to respond to inquiries from other parts of the group.

What can be learned

1 Top management commitment is key

Quality circles at Ciba-Geigy started long before total quality was taken on as a strategic objective by management in 1986. Yet, real progress was only possible after 1986. According to top management the quality programme has become increasingly more active since Mr Lippuner, who supports the programme, was made C.E.O.

Top management support is essential for the allocation of resources and to set the example.

2   *Service quality for mature markets*

It is not exceptional that companies choose to focus more heavily on service quality with the maturing of the industry. A parallel can be drawn between this phenomenon and Mazlow's theory of needs. When a new product innovation appears on the market, it is meeting a basic need. As the product and its technology evolve, it is required to meet the ever more sophisticated requirements of the buyer. In the end, the percentage of product value in the entire package has become quite small with the complementary parts of the package meeting the now highly sophisticated needs of the customer.

3   *Evaluating middle management on service quality*

It is frequently the case that the most resistance to a quality process comes from middle management. One good way to reorient middle management mentality is to change their criteria of evaluation; Ciba-Geigy made a point of including quality objectives in their employee appraisal system.

4   *Focus on customer benefits*

Because of the way it is presented, a key advantage of the company's new 'non-product-specific differentiation' programme is that it encourages all employees to focus on the benefits to customers of any new service before it's created. This reduces the risk of creating 'white elephants' and promotes greater customer orientation.

5   *Not being everything to everyone*

The partnership strategy reflects the determination of Ciba-Geigy to serve certain market segments very well, rather than serving all market segments somewhat well. Given the limitation in their resources, this is a logical choice and also one that will permit them to focus on developing a strong lead over the competition in those market segments.

CITICORP

Citicorp is one of the largest banks in the world and is a multinational organisation with a reputation for innovation and aggressive marketing. It's professional, it's fast moving and it's customer oriented.

History

Citicorp is not a new bank even by European standards. The bank was set up in 1812 by a group of New York merchants at 52 Wall Street. At the time, it was known as the National City Bank of New York. One century later, the bank was recognised as one of the largest American banks. By that time, it had already begun its expansion into Europe and throughout the world. It had branches in Latin America, South America, the Carribean, the Far East and in Europe. The London office was set up in 1902, the Paris office in 1906 and the German office in 1926. Today, the Bank serves 3 per cent of all European households and operates in 11 European countries with 700 branches and 11,300 employees.

Despite its illustrious past, Citicorp (the name adopted in 1974 for its non-consumer operations) has just finished a difficult decade. Massive changes in the banking industry in the 1980s strained the bank's resources as it invested heavily to take advantages of new opportunities, such as the entrance into the electronic information market via the group's subsidiary Quotron.

Non-performing loans (those on which the bank earns no interest) mounted, particularly in Latin and South America where the bank has a heavy exposure, reducing the bank's solid reputation in the market. Rising profits in US consumer banking and in other areas where the bank is strong have been overlooked. The bank now faces a formidable challenge to refocus the market's attention on its historical strengths. As Linc Hoffman, head of World Corporate Group in the UK, puts it, 'To gain back the confidence of clients after the 1980s requires long-term commitment, actions, delivery and interest in things around the world.'

One of the bank's historical strengths has been its ability to pre-empt changes in customer needs. In 1921, it was the first commercial bank to extend its lending activities to individuals. In 1951, it launched the first credit card – the Diner's Club – in co-operation with Bloomingdale's. In the 1970s, it led the industry in the innovation of new services for consumers, including the introduction in 1978 of the first automatic tellers and of interest on checking account deposits. In more recent years, the bank has demonstrated its capacity to adapt itself to the Asian consumer. By focusing on serving high net worth individuals and positioning itself as the BMW of the industry, it has been one of the few foreign banks to gain a foothold in that difficult market. 'Clients are served . . .' says Rana Talwar, (Citibanker in Singapore, who created the programme). 'We are building one of Citibank's most successful franchises.'

In corporate and institutional banking, now know as global finance, the bank has been recognised for its professionalism and its capacity to innovate to meet the requirements of particular clients. Developments in the 1980s have redefined the business which was historically dominated by activities in corporate lending, inter bank lendings and foreign exchange. Now services for corporate and institutional clients range from currency 'swaps', to commercial paper, to hedging, to – the list is endless – all of which represent new mechanisms for managing a financial transaction be it lending or borrowing. The pace of innovation has been so rapid that 50 per cent of the bank's earnings each year was coming from services that didn't exist five years before.

Managing complicated transactions efficiently requires a great deal of experience in the field, wide access to different international and money markets, and a comprehensive understanding of the advantages and disadvantages of each tool, together with the capacity to explain those advantages to the client. Most of the big international banks have the experience and exposure needed to provide such facilities. Where many fall short is in applying these tools to the individual needs of clients. Citibank has excelled in this area, consistently gaining recognition for its professionalism in handling complicated transactions. In 1988 and 1989, institutional investors in the *Euromoney* poll voted Citicorp the most professional bank overall in arranging loan and note facilities. It has also taken the top ranking for arranging finance, developing new financial solutions and pricing sophisticated transactions more than twice in the last decade. In 1990, for the 13th year in a row, the bank was ranked first in handling foreign exchange transactions.

Citicorp's global finance operations in Europe, which our research looked at, was at one point stretched too thinly across many different activities. Today, the bank has, as one internal survey indicates, 'exited from a number of less profitable activities in order to pursue a more focused strategy in Europe'. The result is that the group is concentrating on those areas where it is the strongest – in corporate finance, foreign exchange and capital markets. It will also be making the most of its position as a large global player. Says Linc Hoffman, 'We were the only global player in the 1960s and are one of the few remaining after the consolidation of the market in the late 1980s.'

Service strategy

Regardless of which level of the bank one looks at, the bank's service strategy for the 1990s involves a commitment to customer service. 'Customer service . . . [will] continue as [one of] our central values' (John Reed, Chairman 1989).

The bank's commitment to excellent customer service is not new. It has been a part of the bank's strategy for nearly a century and is integrated into the company's mission statement, a part of which reads:

Our financial objective is to build shareholder value through . . . a continued commitment to building customer-oriented businesses worldwide.

In Global Finance, its customer service approach is being refined to permit the bank to differentiate itself more clearly from the competition on this basis. The bank is now focusing on becoming, first, relationship – and, second, solutions – oriented. As Linc Hoffman puts it, 'It's solutions *vs* products and client *vs* customer. This is not a semantic choice of words; it's a different, new mindset emerging. Customers buy products (widgets); clients buy solutions.'

As Mervyn Davies, Corporate Banking, points out, 'We're a problem-solving unit. If you haven't solved the company's problem, you won't get the repeat business.'

Just what are solutions? Generally they are an amalgam of different financing techniques customised to meet the need of a particular client. Investment management 'makes a concerted effort to understand what the client wants, then we pull in products or bits of products to develop solutions'.

In Europe, each of the divisions has a strategic objective for its business. In Corporate Banking, they are concentrating on relationship development.

'We're focused in terms of industries and in terms of clients. The clients we've targeted are the multinationals, and then at the bottom end, the new emerging companies of the 1990s. In the middle ground, we pick out particular companies.'

In investment management, they are targeting the multinationals and 'leveraging up on relationships established elsewhere in the bank. The World Corporate Group, for example, *knows* their customers; we have to sell them before we can sell to their customers.' The division has identified 200 primary target clients and another 100 secondary target groups with whom they would like to establish a closer relationship.

World Corporate Group (WCG), set up in 1986 to focus on a select group of top flight global players, already has a target list of clients – 250 in total – for which the bank is 'proposing solutions that are appropriate around the world'. To do that the bank has to become a more important partner, 'We work towards a share of their wallet, but equally a share of their mind.'

One reason WCG exists is to take advantage of Citicorp's global reach. 'Globality', as it's called by John Reed, Chairman, has been a long-standing strategic objective and is today a major asset. As is stated, clear as bells, in the 1989 annual report, 'We remain committed to "globality" both within the interlinked world of Europe, North America, Japan, Australia, and New Zealand and the broader world encompassing developing economies from . . .'

Service strengths

Citicorp's strategy is founded in existing strengths. The bank has long been recognised for its capabilities in problem solving for clients. It evaluates with care the requirements of its customers and then innovates or customises a solution to fit the requirement.

At the WCG, the identification of client requirements is part of the relationship development process. Clients are visited on a regular basis, at least once every two months. Visits are made to many individuals within the client company, not just the finance department, and at many levels, not just with the directors. 'We don't generally just go and ask how they are doing? We go there to understand their business and solve their needs,' says Linc Hoffman. 'Calling on individuals not necessarily linked to the banking process helps us to understand the business as an entity.'

Information gained in the client visits is used internally as food for internal brainstorming sessions. For one client, the WCG organised a full day session which brought together relationship managers and product specialists. 'We sat down and thought about the company (after having done our homework) and in the brainstorming session, came up with 32 new ideas. We then tried to narrow them down into categories. Five representatives from the company were invited to dinner that evening and placed at five separate tables corresponding to the five different categories of ideas that we had developed for them. . . . They told us that we had a better understanding of their business strategy than anyone else they'd talked to.'

To do a good job of problem solving for clients, the proposed solutions have to be as good as the analysis. At Citicorp, they usually are 'Ideas are important. When you talk about the quality of service, you talk about the quality of ideas . . . Here, you are playing to Citibank Strengths', says Mervyn Davies.

To underline the point, Citicorp circulates information electronically on examples of client problems which have been resolved with ideas from Citicorpers. Under the title 'An ingenious loan to the Belgian government' one finds,

CLIENT OBJECTIVE: The government's triple objective was to raise substantial funds cheaply, efficiently, within tight budgetary controls and in a short time scale; to keep control of the Berlaymont – an important political consideration; and to establish a financial and organisational structure to permit future renovation of the building as requested by the ECC.

CITIBANK SOLUTION: Citibank's innovative solution involved the establishment of an SPV in which the Belgian government has a 51 per cent stake. This required royal assent. . . .

COMMENTS: Politically, the Berlaymont is the most high-profile building in Belgium, so this was a high-profile transaction. Inevitably, competition was intense and Citibank's proposal was chosen from a large number of others. We were selected because our solution met the Belgian government's financial and political objectives; also because of our underwriting and structuring capabilities. Citibank was also retained as financial adviser and agent bank.

The same format is used for the descriptions of all of the transactions shown and the journal is published on a monthly basis. Between 10 and 15 examples of innovative problem solving appear in every issue, permitting colleagues to draw ideas from situations encountered elsewhere.

Coming up with innovative ideas which meet clients' requirement is one thing, making sure that the clients understand the proposed solutions and its advantages to them is another. In a business in which the complexity and the variety of the offerings is increasing on a daily basis, it is difficult for the average CFO (chief financial officer) to stay on top of developments. He relies upon his bankers to do that for him; he also relies upon them to explain the features of each technique in a way which permits him to make a good decision. Some people would call this consulting, others would call it sales. Citicorp is good at both.

One aspect of sales on which Citicorp places particular importance is presentations. 'Userfriendliness' is important in presentations with customers and so are presentation skills'. Before any presentation goes out, Corporate Banking department has a full dry run before one of the managers. 'We do a lot of internal criticising. That's tough, but we do it.'

A presentation isn't just a verbal description of the financing technique and its advantages to the client. The presentation also provides information about the bank and the people with whom the client would work. Each division has developed certain standards for their presentations. 'We've spent a lot of time on that and we've computerised it. . . . In our presentations, we tell them exactly who will be working on the project, with their names, titles, telephone numbers and addresses. It seems obvious, but nobody ever does it,' says Mervyn Davies.

Presentation skills are just as important internally as externally. In addition to developing their own client base, 'specialist' divisions like treasury, investment management, new issues and foreign exchange must sell their services to relationship managers, including those in the WCG division. This is called cross-selling within the Bank. WCG then on-sells these services to their clients. As Linc Hoffman puts it, 'We are a delivery system for all the product areas of Citicorp.'

Good sales for WCG means good co-ordination – it's the job of current account managers and the relationship manager to ensure that the product areas work together and together with the client. In WCG, a relationship manager generally stays on the account a minimum of five years, so he knows the client well. He organises internal meetings of all those on the account, generally every 60 days. Linc Hoffman, 'We gather, not to discuss problems, but to discuss what we *should* be doing with the client.'

The teams also sit down regularly with the client to make sure that there are no misunderstandings. Sometimes this is part of a biannual review. 'We point out what we're doing in X, Y, and Z countries, set objectives for the next year, find out whether all this is consistent with their objectives (goal congruence).' The results are then summarised in a book which is sent out to the client.

The objective of much of what the bank does in sales is to convince the client of the commitment of the bank to developing a relationship – continuity, they call it. 'You have to prove that you aren't just calling up with an idea, but that you are going to continue calling on that company'.

Continuity at WCG can mean calling on a customer for years before getting his business. 'We recently spent two years to develop a relationship with six presentations in different parts of the world. We focused on the quality of our service and demonstrated that by responding to our client's desire to have the presentation in Texas or Amsterdam, as required.'

The goal at the end of the road is a solid bank–client relationship. 'Managing relationships is a marathon, not a sprint. A relationship properly developed will transcend my lifetime. It takes years to build and seconds to destroy the trust and confidence for a relationship. . . . A short-term point of view just won't work' (Linc Hoffman).

'In general, I think that banks are very poor at telling clients what they're selling. Historically, they go in with the latest product, at such and such a price – one year it's currency options, the next year, it's swaps, etc. etc.', says Mervyn Davies. 'There isn't any point in us giving cheap money to a client. That's just buying a client and that can't last. It's far better to tell the client what you can and can't do. That eliminates the source of a lot of misunderstandings.'

Implementation

Citicorp is strong in marketing. For every business which it enters, it has a systematic approach which involves the extensive investigation of customer expectations, an analysis of the competition, the definition of target clients for each business segment and, finally, the definition of long-term, medium-term and short-term business plans for each business.

From our own experiences we can attest that marketing terminology does run rampant in the halls – upon exiting the lift to go to our interview, we hear a passing duo say, 'We've made our objectives in our target market this year and . . . . Oh yea, you know the Greenwich study came out and . . .'.

Customers have been asked directly what the bank needs to do for them to want to do business with them. Some studies have been done by outside specialists, some by the division heads themselves, 'I've spent a lot of time asking CEOs, "Would you ever use Citicorp and if not, what do I need to do to get you to use us?" '.

The bank also subscribes to the Greenwich studies, an extensive research package which evaluates and compares all the banks in the UK on various products – foreign exchange, corporate lending, hedging etc. – and on the services they offer – managing international relationships, degree of innovation, quality of follow up etc.

WCG, with only 250 target clients, has a special method which helps them allocate resources according to their target client's potential financial attractiveness to the bank and their existing level of appreciation of Citibank. All of its target clients are positioned in the four quadrant schema shown below.

Quadrants 1 and 2 are priority clients for WCG. In quadrant 2 a lot of effort must be made to improve the client's appreciation of Citibank. In quadrant 3 are clients which are not likely to be profitable for the bank and, thus, resource investment should be limited. In quadrant 4 are very low priority clients.

In some cases, the client's headquarters staff is in quadrant 1, but the subsidiaries are in 2; 'We use the quadrants in our discussions between WCG managers to understand and agree on where to focus resources', explains Mr Hoffman. Similar techniques used throughout the Bank.

```
                              2                          1

        high           Invest time            Top priority
                          and
                         effort
    Financial
  attractiveness
    for the
     bank
                              4                          3

        low            Low priority          Limit investment –
                                                 payback is
                                                   limited



                          low                      high
                          Appreciation of Citicorp
```

Using the information gained from market analyses and customer needs evaluation, each of the divisions creates a mission statement for its activities and a plan for the year. Objectives are established in terms of new business, revenues, improvements in service quality and developments in new products..

The customer service expectations identified in the various studies are integrated into all planning. In investment management, for example, studies showed that clients were unhappy with the people calling on them – they felt that they had too little experience. In the plan for the year, extensive training was given to staff; then, younger 'sales' staff was teamed up with product specialists on calls. Customers also wanted more user friendly investment reviews; the format has since been changed to reflect their feedback.

'One of the classic mistakes is to take too many people to a meeting,' says Davies. The client places a high priority on discretion and prefers not to have a pack of people trailing into his office to discuss a potential deal. Citicorp is careful not to have too many people and has cut down extensively on the number of people involved in each deal.

'We've also learned that we have to adapt our approach to different clients. This is spelled out in the yearly plan. If we want to approach a multinational, for example, we're sometimes leveraging up on a relationship the bank already has with the client. In this case, it's important to have a good relationship with the colleague in the bank responsible fo the client', says Mr Davies.

Progress on the yearly objectives are closely monitored. The greatest attention is paid to the progress on relationships. One measurement system used throughout the bank is called tier positioning. If the bank is in tier one, it is a 'trusted adviser', generally one of the client's top three banks. If it is in tier two, it is one of the top six; if the bank is in tier three, it is just one of many banks the client uses. A department in first tier position with 30 of its clients one year and 50 of its clients by year-end has made good progress.

'Revenue is a lagging indicator of performance,' says Linc Hoffman. He looks at a basket of internal indicators to gauge progress. His department measures annually how much time is spent with a client. Calls are tracked, the level of contact at each call is monitored, the depth of discussion is taken into account and the number of calls by client quadrant (see above) is followed. For example, 'Are we calling in quadrant 3 because it's easy (they like us) or are we focusing on the potential business in quadrant 2 (where they like us much less, but where there is more potential)'. Calls are also tracked per product area, i.e. 'the activity around various products to determine if the level is appropriate for the level of business that we want and the clients' needs'.

Customer satisfaction is measured with a yearly survey called a 'relationship review'. The client has the opportunity to express his opinion on how the bank is handling his account according to product area. There is a seven-point scale of satisfaction. WCG employees are evaluated using the results of the review together with the progress made on their own personal objectives for the year.

The foreign exchange division sends out its own satisfaction survey. The response rate was 63 per cent last year. The survey is very targeted and goes out to lost customers, active customers and those with which Citicorp would like to extend its relationship. 'We knew exactly who it was going to and if the person had not responded, the head of the department followed up with a phone call to encourage response.'

The commitment of staff to the bank's objectives and to the client is followed and boosted on a daily basis by each division manager. 'Commitment to the customer can only work if the staff buy into the ideas in the yearly plan. So, everyone in my division contributed to the elaboration of the plan', points out Mervyn Davies.

Improvements in handling clients is also achieved by looking at past mistakes. 'Every Monday at the meeting, we talk about the mandates lost and why they were lost. This is touchy, because you have to do it positively and not negatively.'

The telephone response rate is checked, so is outgoing correspondence, presentations and proposals. 'You can do all the social engagements, all the marketing you want; that's all bullshit, because if the client makes one phone call and he/she is told, "Well, he's not in." "Where is he?" "Well, I don't know.", "Can you ring back." Then, it's a disaster!!'

At Citicorp, employees are evaluated on how they handle relationships. Yearly objectives are established for each employee, on each of his client relationships. 'It doesn't matter what position you are, if you muck up a relationship, you're accountable. You are accountable for relationships. There's not many people in this bank that don't in some way manage a relationship.' (Mervyn Davies).

Employees are also rewarded for what they have accomplished with client relationships. There are internal awards for 'global relationship', awarded to the team which has achieved the greatest growth in client activity. There is also an award for the best partnership – between the relationship manager and the product specialists, for the best transaction – between two or more countries, and for service excellence – awarded on the basis of client satisfaction.

What can be learned

1 Be market oriented

Citibank's big strength is its market orientation. It systematically studies customers, their expectations, and then targets segments and even specific customers. As a result, their services and the way that they are presented match customer expectations and reflect clearly the company's commitment to doing business with those groups.

2 Create human-sized units

Departments of 80 or 100 people rarely bring out the creative and entrepreneurial spirit in people. For people really to be committed and involved in providing service, they have to work in units small enough for their contributions to have an impact. Citibank's concept of creating small entrepreneurial 'enclaves' is a good one and encourages staff to give their best to the company and the customer.

3 Get your units to communicate with each other

You know that you are really dealing with professionals when your counterpart in Hong Kong has already been in touch with his colleague in London and knows what was said at last week's meeting. Good co-ordination between teams in different areas and different locations is essential to good service and yet very difficult to achieve. It's more often the case that 'the right hand doesn't know what the left one is doing'.

Citibank, through policy, concern for good service and the use of good communication techniques does a very good job of co-ordinating relationships between its teams.

CLUB MED

Vacations can mean a lot. The pleasure of a whole year can be concentrated into just one or two weeks of time. There is nothing worse than a spoiled vacation, particularly one spoiled by the actions of other people who don't realise that a vacation should fulfil dreams, not recreate the ugliest nightmare.

Club Med is in the vacation business; it's in the dream business. It's hard work trying to recreate the dreams of every Club Med vacationer, but as many loyal customers will attest, Club Med comes very, very close.

History

Club Méditerranée (Club Med) began its life as a non-profit association in the year 1950. It was started up by Mr Gérard Blitz with the help of Gilbert Trigano; Mr Gilbert Trigano entered the Club in 1954 and became its President in 1963. He continues to manage the group today.

The objective of the Club in these early days was to create a friendly place to receive vacationing friends. As the Club grew, the friends became Club members and the creators of the Club became vacation organisers. The early Club villages were rather rustic – visitors were housed in tents. In 1965, the first bungalows were built for the village in Agadir.

The focus was on the friendly atmosphere. Everyone participated in work and play, and there was little or no division between the GOs (*gentils organisateurs*) and the GMs (*gentils membres*). That spirit of camaraderie has stayed with the Club and remains a key characteristic of its service today.

The Club abandoned its non-profit status in 1957 and was listed on the French Stock Exchange in 1966. In 1984, it was introduced on the New York Stock Exchange.

From the location of the first Club in Alcudia in the Balearic Islands, the Club expanded to other resort locations, in Greece, in Switzerland for winter sports, to Africa and finally to North and South America and Asia. Today, the Club manages over 110 villages in four major parts of the world, Europe and Africa, Asia Pacific and the Indian Ocean, North and Central America and South America.

Service strategy

For many years, Club Med has had a strategy of selling the Club Med concept – this is the Club Med concept focused on the village.

Villages are in beautiful locations. All of the facilities of the Club are located within the village – hotel or cottage, restaurants, sports facilities, fitness centre etc. The tourist pays a flat fee and has access to all the available facilities, the only exception being alcohol which is served in exchange for little coloured beads purchased by the bagful at the reception desk. A variety of sports and entertainment is provided, from which the visitor can choose at his leisure. Nothing is obligatory.

The Club Med visitor is called a GM or nice member (*gentil membre*); the personnel which runs the village are called GOs or nice organisers (*gentil organisateur*). The village is run by the village chief (*chef de village*). The GO's job is to ensure that the GMs have as nice a visit as possible.

In sum, this is what could be called the Club Med formula. It has been adapted over the years to meet the needs of customers with more or less sophisticated or sporting tastes. Today, there are villages which are more rustic than others, some which are more sports oriented, some which can handle conferences, some which cater to older age groups, to families or to young people etc. Despite these modifications, the basic components of the concept remain true for all villages. With over 110 villages worldwide, the 'Club' (as it is called by its friends) has room for these differences.

The Club is in the process of extending the Club Med concept. While the village concept remains, and new villages will continually be added either to respond to a need for new locations or to meet the needs of a particular customer segment, the group is now branching out into other activities.

The Club has begun to offer excursion packages. A fat, 160-page glossy brochure is now available providing detailed descriptions of rather exotic tours done in small groups, numbering no more than 30. Sandwiched into some of the programmes is a visit to a Club village.

The Club has also purchased a sailing cruise boat and is offering three-day to three-week vacation voyages. The price is upmarket and so are the services and ambience provided.

The new Club Med strategy resembles the old in that the group is still selling concepts. The difference is that Club Med is now a trade mark representing many concepts – the Club Med cruise, the Club Med excursion etc., in addition to the classic Club Med village (now called the Trident).

Inherent in the Club Med strategy is a concept of service. It can be described in terms of what it aims to do: put the customer at ease, eliminate hassles and add some extra spice. It is a receipe that is greatly appreciated by its guests. Club Med villages are notorious for their informality. They are hailed far and wide for their excellent organisation. Last, but not least, they are renowned for the giggles, gaities and general fun which is had by all. 'We're always looking for the element of surprise, the something that is just that bit different than what they've experienced elsewhere. Not a gimmick, not a rerun.'

Service strengths

What's great about Club Med is the experience. It's how people treat the customer once he's there – on vacation. Club Med has staff who are always willing to help. In many places, it's hard to find someone to whom to address a simple question. Not at Club Med. The ratio of GOs to GMs is four to one. Moreover, GOs are never 'off-duty'. Every GO wears his badge and is available to help a GM at all times. If the GM is too timid to start the conversation himself, it doesn't matter – GOs come right out and say 'Hi' to every GM they come across.

This isn't just by chance, since GOs are recruited for their outgoing personalities. They are tested on how they are likely to react in certain situations and on their customer service attitude. 'We look for people who have a welcoming way about them. We also want people who can adapt rapidly to different situations, different cultures, different people.' Then they are trained. They are trained even before they are officially hired. Some don't make it through the training; they decide that the Club is not for them. But, even the greenest GOs any GM will meet have been trained for over a month.

Club Med is made easy for its visitors. For one thing, it's an easy place to get around. A GM gets a full-blown guided tour of the entire premises on arrival. Everything is explained by the courteous GO who comes up to introduce him or herself at the reception desk. In most cases, the GO should even be able to speak his language and is perhaps from his or her town back home.

If the GM forgets all that's been said on the tour the next day, it's OK; everything is clearly marked with signs with symbols or in multiple languages. A regular visitor to Club Med will quickly discover that all villages are laid out in pretty much the same fashion. So, after the second or third time, he'll feel at home no matter where he goes.

The GOs are not just present, they are also helpful. If a wandering GM wants to know when the gym opens, a GO is always ready to answer his questions; they'll tell him not just when it's open, but what equipment he's likely to find inside if he wishes to know – with a smile.

Using the facilities is also easy. If the GM wants to take part in sports, then there are always staff there to help and to explain, and they won't 'make fun of a GM' if he's never done it before. If the GM forgot his tennis racket, there is a substitute available; if he doesn't have a partner, the GO does his best to find him one.

Once the GM has become accustomed to a beautiful place in which nothing goes wrong and everyone's polite, he could start to get bored. Club Med doesn't let that happen. It's at this moment that the Club exposes its service quality trump card – the little thoughtful extras.

GOs are trained to keep an eye on the GMs. They are always on the look-out to find the particular likes and dislikes which make each person different – the lemon in the Martini bianco, the almonds on top of the ice cream sundae (no whipped cream, please!), windsurfing at sundown, champagne at breakfast, orange juice with brunch etc.

If a GO doesn't pick up on at least one of these preferences during a GM's visit, then he's not a true Club Med GO. A Club Med GO will not only pick up on them, he will go out of his way to make sure that those preferences are respected. 'It comes from the person. It's a person who likes to give pleasure to others.'

Implementation

Offering an attractive service package in the form of a Club village is one thing; ensuring that the village runs as it should and that the customer gets what he should out of his Club experience is quite another.

When a Club Med vacationer returns home saying that 'Club Med has great sports facilities' or 'Club Med has great entertainment', what he is really saying is not that Club Med employs world renowned singers or that it has the newest thing in windsurfing boards; he's really saying that nothing prevented him from appreciating what was provided.

Good service delivery is that – it's not providing the best, it's simply making sure that customers can enjoy what is provided to the fullest, and it's not so simple to achieve; it means providing 'zero-defect' service. Club Med does this very well.

Club Med has five elements in its promise to customers:

'1 Everything works.
2 It's clean.
3 It's beautiful.
4 There is freedom of choice.
5 To be able to use the village quickly.
6 To make it easy to learn new sports or skills.'

For each one of these items in the promise, Club Med has established standards of conduct for each employee throughout the village which together ensure that the customer's expectations are met. There are standards such as, 'the customer will be always be asked . . .'. In this way employees know exactly what they should be doing for the GMs.

Club Med's standards ensure that GMs encounter the same kind of service quality wherever they go with the group. The GO in the village at Tahiti will greet a GM with the same care and attention as the GO in the village at Corfu. In a large, geographically dispersed group like Club Med, standards like these are key to service management.

Energetic, outgoing individuals like Club Med GOs are not motivated to deliver good quality service simply because there are service standards. Club Med has also developed a system of employee evaluation which pushes GOs to attain ever greater customer satisfaction.

Customer satisfaction is measured. It is measured every week in every village and the results go directly to the village chief. It is called a Barometer. The village chief's performance and those of his staff are measured by these results. Each GO's individual performance is also evaluated, based on the observations of his supervisors and on the feedback from customers. GOs' contributions to improving service are also taken into account, mainly through their participation in error-chasing groups in which employees identify the source and possible solutions to problem incidents.

In terms of personnel management, Club Med places a priority on keeping its staff vitalised. 'We hire lively, personable individuals and then we let them live.' For Club Med's staff, that means keeping them on the move. GOs spend no more than one year in any location; sometimes they stay as little as six months. In between postings or 'seasons', GOs are trained, sometimes for four or six weeks, sometimes for as much as two months. They are trained in one of Club Med's training centres. There used to be centres only around Paris, now there is also a centre in the US.

GOs are told about the evolutions in customer expectations, about the new services which the Club is offering, the new entertainments, the developments in food and sports activities. Information doesn't just flow in one direction; it also comes up from the village in the form of feedback from the GO on what was liked and disliked.

In some cases, it comes up long before the end of the season. Club Med managers are travellers. They spend two-thirds of their time on the road visiting villages to see what's happening at first hand. It's used immediately to adapt the service to the customer at the village. If necessary, service standards are changed, based on verbal communication before they can even be written into the standards guideline. 'We are constantly re-evaluating every part of what we do and what we offer to the customer.'

What can be learned

1 Service quality is measurable

The example of Club Med shows that quality in service delivery can be defined and can be measured. The use of standards permits employees' relations with the customer to correspond to certain norms, without those norms infringing on the ease of contact.

2 Relate responsibilities directly to customer satisfaction

Club Med standards are valuable, not only because they give employees guidelines of behaviour, but because they relate those behaviours to customers and their satisfaction with the service. In that way, no employee is in doubt about the importance of his actions.

COLIRAIL

Colirail is the happy story of a company that entered a new market at the time of its very creation, and has grown with the market to become a successful and healthy company with plenty of opportunity for the future. We are pleased to add that one of the principal reasons for its success has been its ongoing concern for offering top service quality to its customers.

Colirail is in the business of providing express delivery services for packages under 30 kilos – that's about half the weight of an average-sized person. The company operates in France and offers its services exclusively within the boundaries of the French borders. While international competitors have for some time been interested in its market and activities, Colirail remains firmly entrenched in the French marketplace, where it has established an excellent reputation for its personalised service and reliability.

Background

Colirail was founded in Paris in 1977 with 25 people. As Mr Harle d'Ophove explains, 'it was tough going in the beginning'. It was hard to convince customers of the need for overnight delivery services and it took three years before the company could turn an operating profit.

In the early years, Colirail could offer express service to only 70 French cities; that was already more than anyone else was doing. The concept of overnight delivery didn't even exist in France and was just beginning to make waves across the Atlantic in the US with the rapid growth of Federal Express.

Quickly, the French market followed suit; by 1980, Colirail had expanded its service to 90 cities. Overnight service was provided for packages picked up before 4 p.m. the previous day. By 1988, Colirail was serving 200 French cities and had expanded its services to offer same-day delivery.

Today, the company serves all the 36,000 towns in France from 257 main cities and offers same-day service, overnight delivery with pick-up before 20:15, 24-hour service with immediate delivery and Colichange, a service which permits the exchange of defective products for their replacement within 24 hours.

The competition has increased as Colirail has grown with the major international companies now competing on business to the principal French cities and the postal service competing on service throughout France. (Happily for Colirail, the PTT (Post, Telephone and Telecommunications) in France doesn't have a very good reputation for reliability.)

Originally, Colirail's packages travelled by rail, which is where the name comes from ('Coli', short for package in French, and 'rail'). A few years ago the company switched to transportation by truck which made it possible to shrink delivery times even further.

Most of the management team that started the company are still with it, although the total number of employees now tops 200. Its customer list has grown even more; today, it has over 2200 customers for whom the company delivers an average of 7500 packages a day. Seventy-five per cent of those customers are customers with pick-ups on a daily basis.

Service strategy

With growth in the business for overnight delivery, there has been the creation of demand for delivery services which diverge from the basic formula. Colirail has identified and responded to this developing demand by creating new services.

Colirail now offers a total of five separate express delivery services, four of which are clearly presented in the company's brochure, and a fifth, the newest, which is being marketed separately. The first four are as follows.

Coli 9: providing pick-up before 20:15 in the evening and delivery before 9 a.m.
Colijour: providing same-day service with delays of an average of 5 hours.
Colifax: providing urgent, 24-hour service on demand.
Colichange: providing an exchange service which permits defective products to be exchanged and replaced within 24 hours.

Essort, the new service, provides simple repair or replacement services on behalf of a vendor to a client that is experiencing problems with the vendor's machines. It is a step away from a pure delivery service in that Colirail employees intervene to perform simple technical maintenance or installation tasks.

Although the other segments are growing, 60 per-cent of the company's revenues still come from Coli 9. The Coli 9 service itself has changed over time. There has been the continuous extension of the night-time pick-up deadline, now at 19:15 from 16:00 some years ago, and the morning deadline has remained 20:00 since 1977.

While providing an ever-widening line of services, the company's service strategy reposes upon the principles of providing highly personalised service and very reassuring service to customers. Colirail communicates the principles best through their own advertising campaign. One ad features an Arnold Schwarzenegger look-alike with a little blond, white-skinned baby in his arms. The message is that the company *babies* its customers' packages. This kind of message complements an underlying communication theme at Colirail, which emphasizes that speed in delivery means nothing without perfect reliability on a daily basis.

The approach was chosen because it meets the needs of the company's primary customer base. Unlike many express delivery companies, Colirail's principal market is not made up of 'paper producers' like banks, consultants, insurance firms, lawyers etc., who need to have documents transported rapidly from one place to another. A large part of Colirail customers are high technology, medical companies, who need to have valuable products transported rapidly from one place to another, and more recently spare parts producers.

For electronics and computer companies, Colirail is often transporting replacement parts or sensitive material which the company doesn't feel comfortable leaving in the hands of the public postal service. Business from this segment makes up 45 per cent of their revenues for Coli 9.

For medical companies, it is generally medical products which have a short life-span or which are urgently needed. Business with medical companies comprises 25 per cent of the company's revenues for Coli 9. The new market of automotive spare parts contributes 15 per cent of such revenues.

Another major customer segment are those companies that use Colirail to deliver documents with monetary value. Heading the list are temporary employment companies with paycheques for distribution to employees. There are also credit card companies, including American Express, which need to have replacement cards and traveller's cheques delivered rapidly to their destination. Vouchers for employees to use in restaurants or gas stations are also some of the items transported by the company.

Babying is exactly what these kind of packages need and what Colirail wants to provide. Colirail has an objective to continue to target these segments and to 'remain the size we are so that we can still baby our customers' packages'.

Service strengths

Colirail does, in fact, baby its customer's packages. Colirail handles six times less volume than most of their competitors. That permits them to ensure that each package is handled with individual care. With the tracking system the company has created, it is able to know exactly whose hands the package is, at any one moment. The company's rate for late deliveries is correspondingly low: 3 for every 1000 packages.

In addition, Colirail tries to offer a more personalised approach *vis-à-vis* its customers. Most of their business – 75 per cent – is with regular customers which means that they know many of their customers on a personal basis. Whenever possible, the company also encourages the development of personal contacts between its drivers and its customers by scheduling drivers on routes where they have a good contact with the client or are likely to have a good fit depending on the customer contact person's age, personality etc.

During the beaujolais season, with the overnight appearance of 'beaujolais nouveau' on the market, Colirail customers are some of the first to benefit. Colirail sends its drivers around with a bottle of 'beaujolais nouveau' for every customer. On 1 May, it's flowers that customers receive, all with a little note of thanks for their patronage.

In the summer, during the traditional French vacations, customers receive a postcard from their Colirail representative wishing them a pleasant holiday. Colirail makes a point of not doing something on every occasion; the objective is not to inundate customers with signs of affection, but to show concern when it is least expected and most appreciated.

Colirail also keeps its customers informed, but not according to a set routine. Colirail sends out a customer journal, *Precise*, when there is something to say. 'It could appear only five or six times per year or two times on two weeks.'

In addition to providing personalised service, Colirail has positioned itself to be able to provide reassurance to customers about what is happening in the delivery process. The objective is to help customers feel more confident about leaving their packages with Colirail. For some customers, that simply means letting them get a good night's sleep.

The company's tracking system provides the information necessary on the status of the package. It follows the package through every step of the transportation process – from the customers', to the driver, to the sorting centre, into the truck etc. Each step of the process is recorded by electronic readers which transmit the information to Colirail's central office. The information is then made available to the customer via the Minitel – the French visual telecommunications network – into which the customer can connect to know whether his package has reached the hands of the person for whom it was destined. For Coli 9, that means being able to tap into the Minitel at 10:45 and to know to whom and exactly at what time the package was handed over at its destination.

If there is ever a problem, Colirail doesn't wait until 10:45 the next day to notify the customer. The customer is telephoned immediately once the problem is identified. In some cases, this still permits Colirail to keep to its promise to deliver before 9 the next morning. Colirail estimates that its information service is '75 per cent meeting a real need to know that a package has been delivered and 25 per cent meeting a need to be reassured.'

The information recorded on each customer transaction is not discarded once the transaction is complete. Colirail stocks this information, some of it on microfilm, for future reference. On the one hand, it permits the company to know precisely its volume with each customer.

On the other hand, it has permitted the company to offer its customers yet another service – that of providing a breakdown of each customer's transactions. For regular customers who frequently send a large number of packages to the same destinations, this permits them to have useful information about, for example, repeated breakdowns with particular clients or cost data in order to make a precise cost comparison between using Colirail *vs* keeping a fully stocked warehouse.

Implementation

Providing good service quality at Colirail depends greatly upon the company's ability to ensure that packages arrive at their destination as promised. Colirail's headquarters in Paris manages 6 subsidiaries in the main cities and the company's network of 251 exclusive correspondents. While some would claim that such a structure reduces the degree to which quality can be controlled, Colirail is, to the contrary, extremely pleased with the quality provided by its correspondents. 'These are not the kinds of people who would let us down.'

Part of the reason why the system works is that Colirail imposes upon its correspondents the maintenance of a certain quality of performance. The first aspect – delivery on time and to the correct recipient – can be checked and controlled using the company's computer tracking system. Just as Colirail knows to whom the package was delivered, it also knows who delivered it and when.

The second way that the system works is that Colirail managers travel on a constant basis to visit their correspondents to check personally on how they are doing, and provide any assistance and advice which is needed. In addition to visits from the managers, correspondents are also visited by two managers whose sole responsibility is to travel full-time throughout the network training new individuals, assisting in recruitment and advising manager/correspondents.

To motivate this group and make them feel more a part of the company, Colirail organises an annual meeting to which it invites all of the correspondents and frequently their wives (or husbands). 'We try to make it more of a celebration than anything else and use it as a way to strengthen the bond we have with the network.' It generally includes a big dinner with champagne, dancing and orchestra etc.

From what has been said above, it is clear that the company's computer-controlled tracking system contributes greatly to the company's ability to guarantee a certain standard of quality and know that they are achieving it. The system is based upon the use of special labels for the packages which can be read by a laser pen. The information is lifted from the label and used to plot the route the package will take. It is also used to bill the customer automatically.

The label is recorded on microfilm and serves as a reference in the case of a problem. The microfilm copy can be made available to staff within 15 seconds of the demand. As the label has the address and name of the recipient and sender, Colirail refers to the copy if a label has been damaged or lost in transportation.

In terms of creating a strong differentiation *vis-à-vis* its competitors, the Colirail tracking system permitted it to create the Minitel service, which puts the customer in virtually direct contact with his package handlers. For the present time, no other competitor on the French market is offering this service.

Service quality at Colirail isn't only getting the package to its destination on time. It's also about providing service with a personal touch. Most of that is provided by the Colirail driver who has the longest and most significant contact with the customer. Knowing this, Colirail created its 'driver's bible', a guide with service standards about how the driver should behave and perform on the job.

The driver's bible is organised around the four driver's 'S's: *Sympa, Sèrieux, Solide, Sécurisant* (nice, serious, reliable and inspiring confidence). Under 'nice', we find 'Presentation: appropriate dress, trousers and shirt always clean. A neat and cared for appearaence is indispensable to gaining the sympathy of your customers.' We also find, 'A smile with your customers is obliged; our personal or professional problems do not concern them.'

Under 'serious', we find, 'Helpfulness; know how to give a hand when it's needed' and, under 'reliable', 'The Colirail driver knows his company. He is capable of informing the client. He telephones to head office if he cannot answer a question and goes back to the customer with the answer.'

The 'bible' also has information concerning the appearance and care of the driver's vehicle, the procedures to observe when he is at the customers' and what to do in case of a problem with the customer or with his equipment. The bible is used by Colirail correspondents as well as by Colirail's own staff which leads to greater uniformity in the service Colirail provides customers throughout France.

Perhaps one of the most important tasks asked of drivers is to complete a small survey of customers at least two times per year. The questionnaire deals with basic issues such as the frequency with which the customer uses Colirail, the frequency with which he uses the competitors' service, and the customer's overall satisfaction with each. The driver also solicits the customer for general comments or suggestions for improvement.

The survey has three major benefits. The first comes from the information itself which enhances the company's knowledge about customer satisfaction and areas for improvement. The second is that by approaching the customer in this way, the company has clearly demonstrated interest and concern about the ordinary in the customer's opinion. This is complementary for the customer and ties him more closely to the company. The third benefit is that the driver is directly implicated in the search for information on customers' opinions on the company's services; he cannot ignore responses given directly to him by a customer and, as a consequence, is more likely to take concrete steps to improve the service.

On an ongoing basis, the company encourages drivers and other frontline staff to give feedback from customers or suggestions for improvements. All drivers are expected to provide at least three suggestions per month to the company and are given a bonus if they consistently meet the requirement.

Indications on customer satisfaction/expectations do not just come from the frontline staff. Colirail also performs a yearly customer satisfaction survey in which it searches for new ideas for better serving their customers. Three hundred and fifty customers are personally interviewed. Feedback is used to develop new services and to improve existing services. The adaptations made to Coli 9 resulted from this survey, as did the notion for a confirmation of delivery which was later refined by the company into their present tracking system.

Recently, the company adopted a service quality chart. The chart expresses for everyone the principal engagements which Colirail has *vis-à-vis* its customers and serves as a practical as well as philosophical statement of the company's identity. It will be used more in the future to focus on employee efforts for development and improvement. The chart is now published in the company's principal brochure and is being posted throughout the company in different forms. The following is an approximate translation:

Because what we promise clearly is what we deliver, because in terms of rapid transportation speed means nothing without being backed up by perfect reliability, because our range of services has been conceived to correspond exactly to the needs of each of our clients, we have made precision the foundation and the first imperative for every daily action of each one of us at Colirail.

What can be learned

1 Involve your frontline personnel directly in customer satisfaction research

Colirail's drivers question customers personally on their satisfaction with the service they receive and hear his suggestions directly from the customer's mouth. In this way, Colirail gains greater personal commitment on the part of the drivers to improvements in service quality.

2 Don't forget your customer's FUDs

A customer who needs to get a package someplace overnight needs to be reassured that it's actually arrived there. He is full of FUDs (Fear, Uncertainty, Doubt) about the package not getting to its destination. An important part of Colirail's service is to reassure customers that packages have arrived at their destination.

3 Subcontract and gain in service reliability

Colirail subcontracts its delivery and pick-up in smaller French cities and imposes upon its subcontractors strict standards of service quality. It is the responsibility of the subcontractor to meet them, the price of not meeting them being the loss of the business. In this way, Colirail probably ensures better service quality than it would if it employed its own staff on location.

CONVENT

The German consumer of those little salty snacks and treats would probably never have heard of Convent. He most certainly would have heard, however, of Chio or Funny Frisch – the maker of the famous Hungarian flavour crisp in the green and red package! Convent is the company behind these two high-profile brand-name products and the ones that make it possible for Funny Frisch to live up to its name (Frisch means fresh).

Background

Convent, officially known as 'Convent Knabber-Gebäck Gmbh & Co KG', is one of the market leaders in Germany for salty snack products. With both of its two brands, it controls about one-third of the market and has over 30,000 customers purchasing its products every year.

Its products include a whole range of potato or corn based goodies. They can be split into four categories: crisps ('normal' and 'piled' chips; (the ones that are shaped exactly alike and come piled on top of one another in a little cylinder box – like a tennis ball container, says our German colleague)), extrusion products (blown up from grains in an 'extruder', pellet products, which crack or explode when baked, and the standard array of roasted, salted and baked nuts or pretzel sticks.

Convent was founded under the joint ownership of Pfeifer & Langen and Pfanni-Werke in 1972. Both of the parent companies are active in the processing of agriculture produce and distribution of consumable products. Pfeifer & Langen is one of the country's leading sugar producers. It has been heavily involved in contract farming for sugar beet or other food products. Pfanni-Werke, through the Pfanni-Knödel brand, markets ready-to-use and instant potato dishes – dumplings, soups, rösti etc.

Convent's Chio and Funny Frisch products are centrally produced in one of the company's three German factories and marketed separately through the two parallel sales distribution networks – one for each brand. Convent's customers include a large number of large shopping outlets, supermarkets, corner shops, petrol stations, kiosks, cinemas etc.

End customers represent a wide cross-section of the buying public. Traditionally, salted sticks, pretzels and peanuts have been popular in Germany; crisps were introduced in the early 1960s. At that time, the annual per capita consumption of crisps in Germany was 40 grams. In 1990, it was 800 grams and still growing.

Over the last eight years, the total market for salty goodies grew by 8 per cent per year. With the opening up of East Germany, double digit figures have been recorded by all producers. On the whole, Convent's sales are growing faster than the market.

Service strategy

The food retailing business is very competitive and brutal. The buying public wants fresh products, of known quality, well presented, at a low price. A large number of producers and retailers are vying against one another to provide all this.

Retailers fight to win customers' business by stocking a wide variety of goods and a selection of the best-known brands, by providing a pleasant shopping environment and personalised service.

Retailers are producers' customers. Producers compete to do business with retailers and, in practical terms, they compete for shelf space. The more shelf space they get, the more they are likely to sell to end customers.

Retailers are reluctant to give too much shelf space to any one producer, because one of the services they offer consumers is variety in their selection. For producers, the name of the game is to convince retailers that by sacrificing a little of variety they can better achieve the larger goal: that of selling the customer more. The arms available to a producer to do that are price, brand name and, yes, service quality.

Convent has quite clearly chosen to emphasise brand name and service quality. It defines its business as 'selling at best performance with an optimum product in optimum freshness'. With the strong brand names the company has created for itself through advertising and good promotion and packaging, it has created a customer pull effect in the market – that is to say, customers know the name Chio and Funny Frisch, ask for them and will buy them over other brands. End-customer loyalty is estimated to be around 90 per cent.

Beyond that, the company has decided to provide its retailers with exceptional service quality. Its goal is to 'assure an optimum use of space in the shop for the best possible presentation of the individual products'. The service approach it has chosen meets the needs of both its retailer customers and its end customers. It is called 'Frischdienst' meaning freshness service and it focuses on ensuring that products in the market are always fresh and well presented.

In short, the 'Frischdienst' package is the direct delivery of products from the factory to the stores. This is done by the salesman who is also responsible for handling the customer relationship. He visits the store on a very regular basis, depending on the store's turnover, checks the products on the shelf and those in the store room, sorts out old products with old expiry dates, refills the shelf and puts price tags on the products, if necessary.

The particular advantage it offers to retailers is that Convent takes over responsibility from the retailer for the presentation and stocking of the shelf space allotted to Convent's products. For the retailer, that means 1 or 2 or 3 fewer metres of space which his employees must survey and fill. Convent's practice is in contrast to the standard producer practice of delivering to the store the goods in large cardboard boxes and leaving it to the retailer to distribute the goods on the shelf.

The approach has also been shown to increase sales. Because the products are well presented and fresh, customers are more well disposed to purchase them. Bahlsen, Convent's main competitor used to use a 'Frischdienst' type system as well. Since it changed its policy a few years ago, its market share in salty goodies has dramatically dropped.

The advantage which the approach offers end customers is that it represents the fastest way to get the goods from the factory to the shelves. They are fresh and in good condition, and do not remain piled in a back room waiting until a clerk has time to put them on the shelf.

For Convent, it is also important that the goods be well represented on the shelf. A large percentage of purchases for these kinds of products are 'impulse' buys, which means that the consumer purchases them only after seeing them on the shelf and not as a part of his planned purchases. If the products are poorly represented, impulse purchases will fall because the customer is either attracted to another brand or not at all.

Service strengths

The 'Frischdienst' approach is a very expensive one. It requires over twice the normal number of salesmen and a highly efficient itinerary planning and logistics system. Yet, as the Sales Director, points out 'Frischdienst has not been abolished despite its cost'. The company believes that the advantages it offers customers and its success more than justify its cost. 'With Frischdienst, Convent makes the market.'

Convent's service strengths to customers lie in the proper execution of the 'Frischdienst' approach. The principal service which Convent offers its customers is the possibility to maximise the return on the shelf space. This is done principally through the finetuning of the arrangement of the shelf space in accordance with the particular demands of its customers. With the 'Frischdienst' approach Convent closely surveys the sales of each product on each shelf over very short or very long periods of time. The result is that Convent sales staff know exactly which products are selling best at what moments and can rapidly adapt the selection to match the demand.

Products that work well in one store may not work well in another. In addition, products that sell well at Christmas may sell badly in summer and vice versa. Convent identifies trends in the market and in stores by following individual sales figures. It then adapts production and stocking accordingly. A store manager does not have to be concerned that his Funny Frisch or Chio shelf may be empty three days before New Year's Day.

Another benefit of the system for the store manager comes from the freshness guarantee. He is assured that what appears on the shelf is in good shape for his customers and that the full, clean shelves are in keeping with his own high standards of service quality. 'In the past, Convent salesmen meet with strong resistance among retailers who feared that the salesmen were just being pushy with the Frischdienst approach and that they would not be able to sell the products which were "shoved into the shelves", as some put it. Convent's guarantee to take back and refund all products with duration dates expired changed their attitude . . . it gave them greater confidence in the system.'

The approach also permits store managers to benefit the most from new innovations at little or no risk. All new products which appear on a Convent controlled shelf are monitored very closely. Successful new products are instantly restocked with the store benefiting greatly from the success of the new product from the increase in sales. If the product doesn't work, it is quickly removed and replaced with successful merchandise. 'Frischdienst gives the fastest possible feedback if something does not work well.'

Despite all the advantages which the 'Frischdienst' approach offers retailers, some do not need or want the kind of services the system provides. Discounters and some 'hypermarkets' which sell direct from delivery cartons, don't need or want to have the goods arranged on the shelves. For these customers, Convent makes it possible for them to bypass the 'Frischdienst' system. The products are delivered to regional customer warehouses or to the stores in large cases and placed as needed in the stock room or directly on to the shop floor.

Other customers want only some advantages of the 'Frischdienst' service – replacement of expired freshness items, but not shelf placement, for example. Convent makes this possible too. 'Frischdienst' is a service approach '*à la carte*' for those who need it.

Implementation

The 'Frischdienst' service represents a large proportion of the cost of a packet of crisps, on average. Attention to three things permit Convent to implement the approach with success.

The first of these is attention to sales figures. Convent monitors the daily sales figures coming up from the stores. This is done through the use of hand-held units carried by the salesmen to each of the stores. Once at the store, the salesman logs into his hand-held unit the number of packets remaining on the shelves by product line.

He also records those packets which have to be removed after expiry of the freshness date. The information is subsequently processed and compared with data recorded similarly on each visit. The retailer is billed according to the number of packages sold and he is likewise informed of fluctuations in his sales and of general trends.

On its side, Convent uses this information to plan production schedules. Cumulated and monitored over time, these very precise sales figures permit the company to regulate production capacity to match exactly the demand in the market.

The figures are also used as a check on the quality of the salesman's work in the store. If sales figures are consistently low for one salesman, generally it can be a reflection of the care which the salesman is taking in the performance of his job concerning the presentation of goods on the shelves.

Sales figures are also used to schedule salesmen's visits. These visits are very precisely timed and organised according to the number and size of the customers a salesman is expected to see in each region. Each day, the salesman begins his day by presenting himself at the door of one of the company's regional office/warehouses to load his van with the goods needed for the day's visits. The amounts loaded into the van reflects the sales predicted for each particular store. The time allotted for each visit is adjusted according to the amounts of the goods delivered and the size of the store.

In the scheduling of salesmen's visits, as in the planning of production schedules and in the billing and informing of customers of sales figures, Convent relies heavily upon very sophisticated logistics and information technology systems. Together the two permit the information coming up from the stores to be processed rapidly and used as quickly as possible, wherever necessary to ensure the proper functioning of the 'Frischdienst' approach.

The second important area for attention is the company's structure. Convent believes that one of the most important reasons for its success in being able to implement 'Frischdienst' is the very decentralised structure which the company has adopted.

A first point to note is that the company has two parallel sales organisations – one for each brand. While this could be thought to represent some duplication of effort, Convent believes that this is one point that makes it possible for them to respond rapidly to market changes. Because the brands are different, their purchasing publics are different, and developments which are observed in one are not necessarily observable in the other.

In each of the two organisations, Convent puts an emphasis on keeping the structure as light as possible and on creating small team units. The sales organisation is broken into regional units with roughly 30–50 salesmen per unit and a regional sales manager. Regional sales managers have the authority to manage the entirety of the sales relationship with the clients in his region, under the supervision of the sales director. The salesman also operates on a fairly independent basis, co-ordinating primarily with the regional sales office and his customers. 'We believe in giving a great deal of autonomy to individuals. In return, we place high demands on our people and a great deal of responsibility. We don't want "box" thinking and people must be ready to respond to customers in the case of problems.'

The third area to which the company gives a great deal of attention is their salesmen. In the company's view, the salesman is the most important individual in the organisation. There are over 570 salesmen in the Convent organisation, more than three times the number of the principal competitor which does not use the

'Frischdienst' system. To ensure that these individuals get what they need to do their jobs correctly, the company has developed the concept of the internal customer with the salesman being the last internal customer in the chain before getting to the external one. 'Everybody in Convent assures service to the man at the sales front in order to make his work easier.'

The salesman's job at Convent is not an easy one. The job of cleaning out shelves with crisp packets and sorting through price tags and expiry dates does not generally inspire the typical selection of German salesmen. Convent management appreciate this fact – 95 per cent have already worked as Frischdienst salesmen – and do their best to provide other compensation to their staff. Perhaps the most effective programmes for this have been the 'Elite Club' for Funny Frisch and the 'Champion Club' for Chio. Both are honour programmes based on sales figures. The awards are made monthly at the regional level. The staff is extremely involved in the programme; they use it not only as an opportunity to recognise good work, but also as an opportunity to discuss with one another what worked well and what didn't.

Another forum used for this type of discussion is the weekly meeting in the regional headquarters. These meetings are organised by product – there are, thus, 26 meetings per week – with 8 to 35 persons from different units attending each meeting. Service and product problems are all discussed during these meetings in order to help the salesmen be more aware of develoments in the products and of ways to improve the service they provide to their customers.

When we asked the Sales Director what, in his experience, is the best customer compliment he ever received, he answered, 'that one of our customers wants to give more space to Convent because he's happy with the quality of Convent's services and products.'

What can be learned

1 Give good service to all of your customers

Convent's success is to a large extent based on the fact that their products and services have been conceived not just for the end customer, but also for the intermediary customer. The Frischdienst policy, which guarantees fresh, well-presented products, provides good service both to the retailer and the end customer.

2 Use a guarantee when you need a sales clincher

Convent guarantees the freshness of their products and promises to remove any date-expired products at no extra charge to the retailer. For Convent, this guarantee is important in convincing retailers about Convent's Frischdienst approach. Without the guarantee, they saw it as just another marketing ploy to gain extra shelf space for their products.

3 Do your customer's job for him or 'vertically integrate with your customer's co-operation'

Convent's Frischdienst approach is simply an offer to do for the retailer what he should be doing himself. What makes it sellable is that retailers are happy to hand over the extra work. What makes it affordable is that end customers buy more because of it – which makes everyone happy.

DAMART

'Your letter gives me the opportunity to tell you how much I appreciate your products. I am not a very big client – obviously, a priest is not the father of a large family. I spent my entire career as a professor and never took any precautions going from overheated classrooms to rooms with the window wide open and the air rushing through. During the vacations, I went camping in the mountains and I continue to do so despite my 70 years. I believe I owe an enormous thanks to Damart and I am happy to make it. I recommend your products on every occasion possible. Yours very sincerely,

Abbot of Montigny'

Damart handles 5,600,000 purchases per year by mail or in its stores and handles 500,000 letters. A lot of them are just like this one. To say that it has loyal customers is to say the least. Its customers are not only loyal, they are also communicative. They appreciate the consideration and respect which Damart accords its clients and they return that consideration by demonstrations of fidelity such as this one.

Background

Damart is a family-owned French company located in the north of France near the Belgian border. It was established by three brothers by the name of Despature in 1953; today, the company is managed by a directorate of three Despature cousins. It has always been known to the larger French public as the 'antifreeze specialist' for its activities in the manufacture and distribution of thermal underwear and protective clothing.

The present owners maintain that the real genius of the company's founders was the creation of the concept of the 'Damart client'. The 'Damart client' is truly a concept and not just a description of the client the company serves; in every employee's mind, there is the ever-present image of the 'Damart client' to whom he is responsible and for whom he works.

The 'Damart client' is:

a client that wants and expects Damart to take charge;
a client that has time and that likes to take his/her time;
a client that enjoys the personal exchange between individuals.

The profile of the 'Damart client' is constructed around these three basic characteristics. He or she is a person of roughly 60 to 80 years of age, who places greater importance upon the quality of the materials and their intrinsic value than upon their fashion appeal or their popularity. He or she looks upon contact with Damart as a pleasurable activity, an exception to the daily routine. The 'Damart client' is loyal to Damart and is 'our very best publicity agent'.

There has been an evolution in the concept of what Damart provides the 'Damart client'. As explained by Philippe Lachaune, the company managing director, the 50's was the decade of 'the remedy' – Damart provided clients with a way of easing the pain suffered by cold-associated ailments.

In the 60's, the decade of 'health', Damart helped clients stay in good health. In the 70's, Damart's products were a way of keeping clients warm, regardless of their activities. In the 80's, Damart became the synonym of 'comfort', with Damart products providing greater comfort with easy-to-wear clothing in a broad sense.

Today, in the decade of the 90's, Damart is aiming to increase the Damart client's 'well-being', which goes beyond its now wide range of products and covers a complete philosophy.

Damart serves the 'Damart client' in three ways. First, Damart is a manufacturer of knitwear and underclothing. Secondly, Damart is a mail-order house which sells a full range of clothing, underclothing, shoes and household convenience items. Thirdly, Damart has a chain of 51 shops throughout France and 22 shops in Spain in which one can find most of the clothing from the catalogue and all of the shoes are on display. All of the items from the catalogue are also available for pick-up in the store within 24 hours.

Today, the 'Damart client' purchases on average 2.1 times a year; there are over two million customers visiting Damart's 51 French stores. Unlike many textile companies, Damart has kept its textile manufacturing operations in the north of France which produce between 60 and 70 per cent of all the underclothing sold by the company.

Service strategy

Damart's service strategy focuses on creating a relationship of confidence with the customer. There is a high degree of personal exchange between the company and the customer. The company adopts the role of a trusted adviser *vis-à-vis* the customer. The weight of the purchase decision is partially displaced away from the customer to the company. 'At Damart, we do not sell, we advise. Our commitment to the customer is to find the article which is best adapted to his or her needs.'

The consulting act passes through two channels of communication – the catalogue and the adviser in the store. The greatest emphasis is placed upon the advice provided in the shop. 'The Damart client is not a customer who uses the telephone extensively.' The catalogue is expected to be the window of the shop and while Damart does extensive business in catalogue sales, many customers come to the shops to make and collect their purchases.

Within the Damart shops, the sales staff are trained to act as advisers to the customer. There is an emphasis on the quality of the exchange between the adviser and the customer, and not on the speed. 'Our job is to help customers to express their needs.'

The sales staff, mostly women in their mid 30s, are the 'accomplished daughters' of their customers and in a position to provide the kind of information which the customer requires to make a decision. 'The Damart client prefers to be taken charge of by the adviser who represents their mature and responsible daughter.' In the store, the advisers are available, but by no means aggressive. 'We approach them if we feel they require assistance without being aggressive or pushy.'

The shop is arranged in a way which permits customers to take as much time as required to browse and buy. In addition to the information provided by the sales staff and in the catalogue, information is instantly accessible from wall posters or information sheets. With seats readily available, the atmosphere is relaxed and comfortable.

The same service characteristics can be found in the company's catalogue sales activities. There is an emphasis on maintaining a continuous relationship of confidence with the customer. There is high frequency of contact and a high personalisation of that contact. A regular Damart customer receives up to 15 mailings per year. Those could be either catalogues or special offers, including games and discounted products. The name of the customer is used throughout the documentation.

The mailings and catalogues position Damart as a trusted reference. There is an emphasis on the quantity of information provided about each article. A Damart catalogue explains exactly the nature of the fabric used in making its garments and the properties of that fabric in terms of wear and care. Information is provided in order to assist the customer to choose the article best adapted to his or her needs.

Damart's service strategy is designed to appeal to two groups of customers – the traditional customer and the new generation customer. The traditional Damart customer is the one described above – an individual around 60 to 80 years old who places a high priority upon the quality and practicality of the items he or she purchases. Fashion is not really a consideration. Damart's new generation customer is between 45 and 60 years of age and is still fashion-conscious. The new client group is also more time-conscious.

To meet the expectations of this new target clientele, Damart has adopted a two-pronged approach both to service in the shops and to catalogue sales. In catalogue sales, the company is providing a greater fashion emphasis on the articles sold. The company has introduced a new line of clothes, 'Nathalie Andersen', and with it has increased the selection of ready-to-wear items as opposed to lingerie and home-wear garments.

Within the stores, the service is adopted from the moment the customer enters the store. The emphasis is upon reducing the purchase time for those who are time-conscious. Customers who know what they want to purchase and are prepared to purchase without browsing are identified by the reception hostess. The counter service for these individuals is handled differently and more rapidly than for the 'browsing' customer. 'We have developed a separate service approach for those who want to act quickly in our stores.'

Service strengths

Damart has made a tremendous effort to know its customers and their preferences very well. This has made it possible for them to design a sales and service approach which corresponds in every detail to the wishes of their customers. 'At Damart, everyone from the production to the shop is at the service of our customers.'

Unlike many modern shops whose aim seems to be to create an atmosphere which shocks, astonishes and stimulates its customers, Damart's objective is to make the customer feel welcome and comfortable.

There is nothing aggressive or brash about a Damart shop. It is the most respectable reflection of a not too modern shopping environment. In clear, clean, natural colours like light brown and sand, the store is neatly arranged with the welcome desk, the purchase pick-up and payment desk and the fitting rooms clearly marked with large-lettered signs which even people with bad eyesight can see.

Upon entering the store, the customer is immediately greeted by a smiling hostess. She welcomes you to the store and immediately establishes whether you would like to make a purchase of an item seen in the catalogue or would like to browse and then decide. 'The welcome hostess is there to go forward and greet the customer and then direct him or her to the area of their interest.' The smile is an indispensable part of a Damart welcome. 'With a smile, the welcome hostess proves Damart's determination to be kind to its customers.'

The welcome hostess is not just anybody. The director of the store almost always assumes this position and from there manages the entirety of the circulation and activity in the store. Part of that is the 'management of the waiting time'. This is considered to be essential, because of the different objectives which clients might have upon entering the store.

Some clients have already ordered by phone and are coming to pick up and pay for the item chosen. Others have chosen an item from the catalogue and would like to buy it on the spot, or order it and pick it up later. A third group comes to examine the merchandise displayed and the catalogue which is always readily available. There is a rough division of clients between those who 'are in a hurry' and those who 'want to take their time'.

To manage this waiting time, the hostess uses tickets with numbers. Those clients who are in a hurry are not served in the same order as those who aren't. Hurried customers are called to the counter as rapidly as possible, according to the number received. Unhurried customers receive a ticket from the salesperson once his or her choice is made; they are then called to the pick-up counter by name, interspersed between the hurried customers in a way that permits both customer groups to be served at a satisfactory speed.

'When we call the customer, we try to catch the customer's attention and look straight at him or her.' The ticket system is well received by all customers, not only because it permits them to be served at the right pace, but also because they do not have to stand in line in order to assure that they are served in turn. Waiting customers are always reassured during their wait and given the estimated time for which they will have to wait. While they are waiting, the welcome hostess or another salesperson confirms that they have not been forgotten.

Those customers who browse have at their disposition 'advisers' who are there to help them make their choice. They are trained in the 'Damart sales method', the very first principle of which is that 'at Damart, we do not sell, we advise'. The customer's sales adviser is designated by the welcome hostess and the salesperson comes forward to meet the customer and guide him or her through the shop. All sales staff are Mrs or Miss 'X', and never Norma or Nancy, as most people over 45 would prefer.

The first thing the Damart salesperson does for his or her customer is to put him or her at ease. 'The Damart adviser is there to relax the atmosphere.' There is no rush and the Damart adviser is there to listen. He or she then guides the customer's discussion in order to 'let the customer express his or her specific need. Only once the customer has completely communicated his or her thoughts does the Damart salesperson propose not one, but two or more articles which might suit the customer's tastes and need. 'Our goal is always to help the customer choose the item best adapted to his or her needs.'

If the customer prefers just to browse without assistance, that can also be arranged. The hostess can also provide a catalogue and various brochures on the company's products. Sweets are also there for the taking.

Damart is one of the only shops in France in which there are real seats 'inviting' the customer to try them out. There are not just 1 or 2, there are at least 15 in every store. No one glares at the customer or comes to disturb their tranquillity if he or she takes advantage of this rare service and settles down to read the Damart catalogue. A good cup of afternoon tea is the only thing missing.

Damart shops weren't always like the one described above. Because of the product's 'para-medical' history, Damart previously sold their products in a much more austere atmosphere. The Damart product used a special fabric which had particular warmth-keeping attributes. As such it was sold in shops with blinded windows and a high counter to keep the customer from the product, as in a pharmacy. 'Now, the sales staff comes out to meet the customer. . . . Historically, Damart's reputation was based upon three things: the novelty of our product, the recognised effectiveness of our product, and our service approach which means advising the customer.'

Today, the Damart product is no longer unique. Products made of quality fabric with similar attributes are now readily available on the market. To adapt to the new situation, 'we are now trying to enlarge the range of products we provide in order to attract a younger target customer group (45–60 years)'. In addition, the company introduced the new shop and created a two-speed service approach within the shop. The results have been a net increase in shop sales for the company.

Implementation

'The Damart smile to its customers can be found in every box which goes out to the customer.' Employees on the production line fold the garments in a certain way so that they can be worn right from the box; it is one of their contributions to the smile which Damart gives to its customers.

At Damart, the desire to satisfy customers goes throughout the organisation and represents a more important objective than that of making money. 'To satisfy the customer, we organise ourselves well and, as a result, we make money.'

One of the most important elements of this is what customers think about their products. In addition to a battery of customer surveys, Damart goes to its sales staff to obtain feedback on what customers have said to them about their products and services. The marketing department tours the stores twice a year and gathers information in meetings with all of the sales staff. Item by item the group passes through each product in the past season's selection and makes suggestions for improvements for the next season based on customers' comments. 'The information comes back to us and through it the customers contribute to the creation of our products.'

Information also comes direct from the clients. Damart calls its 500,000 letters per year its 'Bible' of information. In addition to writing to Damart to collect presents or change addresses, customers make comments about how to improve the company's products and services. Damart analyses all its letters and uses the information as an 'echo of satisfaction' from customers. To show how much the company appreciates their comments, customers who make good suggestions are sent a small present of thanks for their efforts.

Damart managers also keep in touch with what is going on with internal indicators which permit them to monitor progress on a daily basis. Product availability, for example, is a key factor of satisfaction or dissatisfaction with customers and Damart's management watch developments through daily reports.

By monitoring on a daily basis, management can change production schedules as needed to meet changes in demand as they come in. The production line is specially conceived to make rapid changes. In some cases, the line is changed as much as twice a day in order to fill identified shortages in stock. 'It's more expensive to do short runs, but it costs even more to displease a customer.'

Management also monitors the delay in which letters are answered and in which orders are processed. Orders in process are checked on a daily basis so that management knows that it is keeping its commitment to deliver in under three days. Periodically, Damart goes direct to its customers to verify that packages are being delivered within the established time-frame.

Monitoring is also done at the store level. Each store's sales results are available at the end of every day. Every salesperson has access to the report and can see what he or she sold. Sales figures are available by type of garment or article. The information is used at the end of every month by the store director who sits down with each employee and reviews their strengths and weaknesses and develops objectives for improvement. 'At Damart, information is part of the motivation.'

While employees are not paid commission or bonuses on sales results, all of the company's sales staff have been made aware of the need to contribute to the increase in the company's revenues. The 'notion of profitability' is part of what is taught to salespersons in the 'Damart sales method'. No salesperson can go on the floor before he or she has had at least one week of training in this method.

The method was developed roughly 15 years ago when Damart's notoriety and monopoly position on the market still permitted it to 'sell without selling'. 'At that time, no one really recognised the utility of "selling".'

The method is based on observations made in the field in Damart stores. Store directors have a set plan of formation which each must follow. Day by day, each of the training steps are laid out. Each director is also trained how to train by training specialists who tour the stores. The method also uses video and written support materials which are given to new employees for reference. One part of the training calls for role-playing in which the director plays the customer. Another follows the following format:

The store director 'says',
she 'demonstrates',
she asks the trainee to 'try the same thing',
she 'does it together' with the trainee,
she 'lets the trainee do it herself'.

The format is observed for most of the steps in the sales process which generally ensures that the trainee has truly learned it well enough to repeat it in the future.

Having a customer oriented sales staff starts before the training at Damart. Just as they have a method for training, Damart also has a set method for recruiting which helps store directors choose staff who are the best adapted to the job and to the image of the company. A recruitment book is provided to each store director. In it is a description of the 'ideal candidate' and a step-by-step guide of how to conduct a recruitment interview.

'The Damart adviser differs from a simple salesperson by her ability to learn and practise the Damart training method, that is her abilities in welcoming the customer, in providing advice to the customer and of giving Damart-style service.' The specific characteristics of the ideal candidate are then described in detail under the headings, 'Greeting, morals, intellegence, physical capabilities'.

'The customer should be able to find in the salesperson the qualities of his or her accomplished daughter.'

What can be learned

1 Know your customer and make your customer known

Damart has defined very clearly what its target customer is like. The 'Damart client' is defined not only in terms of age and socio-economic group, but also in terms of service expectations. This clear profile has then been communicated throughout the organisation. Every employee knows what the customer expects and has in his or her mind the image of the 'Damart client' which he or she is serving.

2 Match your profile to your customer

Damart recruits sales staff who correspond to a set profile, a profile designed to fit well with the customer. The Damart salesperson is the 'daughter' to the 'mother' customer. She is the trusted adviser, ready to assist but never pushy. Applied rigidly throughout the company, the policy ensures that customers are at ease dealing with Damart staff and thus more likely to be satisfied with the service provided.

3 Listen to your front line

Damart's marketing team tours the stores every season to have direct feedback from the sales staff about how products were liked or disliked by customers. This occurs in meetings in which all of the sales staff are brought together with the visiting marketing personnel; item by item, they review each Damart product. This is yet another way to bring the customer into the company. It is also an excellent way of showing the frontline how important their work really is.

4 Have a service strategy for each target customer group

Damart has two target customer groups and has created a service strategy for each. The result is a parallel structure which permits each customer to go at his or her own speed within the store and find a sales approach best adapted to his or her expectations.

ENDRESS & HAUSER

Endress & Hauser is a family company with the type of genuine concern for customers' satisfaction that only a family company can have. Started by one generation in 1953 to meet a market need, the company is now being passed on to the second generation. The primary concern that has stayed with it is the need to serve the customer.

'Our company philosophy says, "We are here to serve the customer," ' explains Mr George Endress.

Background

Endress & Hauser is in the business of providing measurement tools and assistance for liquid and solids measurement. These include primarily through-put technologies like those found in the production of chemicals and liquids. The instruments are capable of measuring pressure, volume, mass or bulk flow, water content and trace moisture, gas, temperature as well as other parameters.

Of the German origin, the company was well established in the German market by the early 1970s, at which point it began its expansion overseas. An office in Japan and an office in the United States were the first of the company's overseas branches.

In 1977, Endress & Hauser established a company in Switzerland to manufacture a range of flow meters. Other manufacturing establishments throughout Europe were established for different products. The company is today represented on a worldwide basis with over 30 sales companies and employs around 4000 people.

Inside, the company is structurally divided into two major divisions: sales centres and product centres. The sales centre is the customer of the product centre and it is the job of the product centres to propose products to the sales staff that meet their customers' needs.

The sales centres are expected to concentrate on serving the customer to the best of their ability and to obtain feedback from customers which they can pass over to the product centres for the development of customer-adapted products for the future.

With this approach and with a high service orientation, the company has experienced considerable growth in recent years. Endress & Hauser is now the world's leader in the production and distribution of level measurement instruments. In other areas, it is a major player.

Service strategy

Endress & Hauser has always and continues to put emphasis on the importance of serving its customers well. Always with an ear to customer needs and expectations. Endress & Hauser has been able to develop a service strategy which it believes has gained it its place among the leaders in the industry.

Typical applications for Endress & Hauser measurement systems are chemical plants, food processing and public sewage plants. In sewage plants, clients are more than happy to subcontract the responsibility for the installation and maintenance of measurement systems to Endress & Hauser. The company's products analyse the quality of the water from beginning to end of the process.

In chemical plants, Endress & Hauser discovered that clients were much more reluctant to subcontract the installation and maintenance of measurement systems to the company. By discussing with customers at length, the company discovered that many of its clients did not want outsiders to have access to the exact recipes for all the various chemicals being made. Some are very closely guarded secrets and the process of installing and maintenancing a measurement system properly requires that the individuals performing the work have access to the formulae. As Gunther Dick, head of after-sales service explains, 'Companies like BASF just don't feel comfortable if installation and maintenance of measurement systems that help in analysing and detecting the quality of inputs and outputs are done by foreigners to BASF since they fear that their formulae will become public knowledge.'

With this customer concern in mind, Endress & Hauser developed a segmented approach to their after-sales service. Employees of clients who are concerned about guarding their secrecy are trained by Endress & Hauser to do the installation and maintenance themselves. The company has facilities for the training of these individuals or offers to train them on the customer's site. After the tools are installed, the company acts as an emergency support unit to which the in-house specialists can refer if there is ever a problem that they feel incapable of handling.

For clients who are not sensitive about their business, Endress & Hauser offers a full service approach which means that the customer is relieved of any responsibility for the day-to-day care of the material.

All Endress & Hauser's after-sales service operations operate as independent profit units and are profitable, both with the full service approach and with the back-up support approach.

Service strengths

Endress & Hauser's customer service philosophy is based upon the concept of seeing the client as a partner. As such, discussion face to face with the customer and on-site advice are a very important part of the company's service approach. The key person in this relationship is the service technician. He is the individual responsible for maintaining the relationship with the client and is professionally responsible for the success of the relationship from A to Z.

By policy, there is only one service technician per client. He is the 'master' of all of the technologies that the company offers. It must be so in order for the service technician to be able to identify opportunities for the application of its products in many different instances and in order for the client to benefit to the fullest from the service and products the company offers. Endress & Hauser offer measurement instruments which cost anywhere from DM100 to DM30,000.

A service technician is required to be available to his client around the clock. All of Endress & Hauser's clients have the home phone number of the service technician handling their account or another number in the case of an emergency. This level of service is absolutely necessary, given the fact that a stoppage in a flow process production operation can cost millions of marks per minute. To back up its service and product reliability, the company offers a product guarantee of two to four years and a service guarantee of six months.

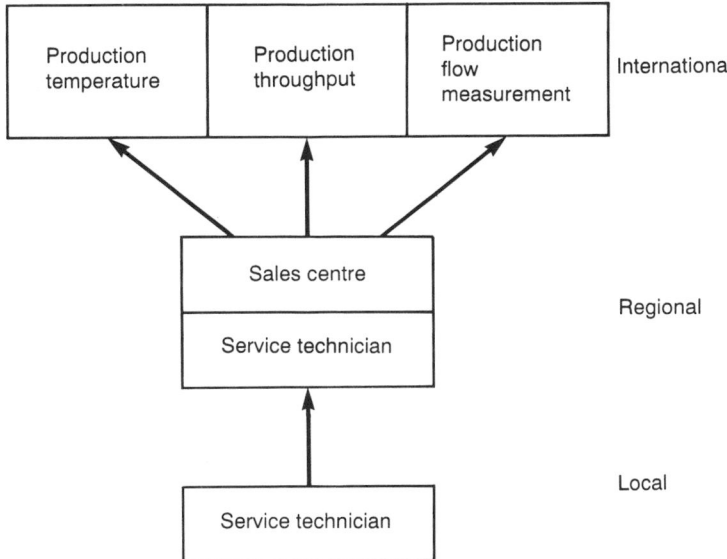

'There are no written standards for our service technicians; they are simply expected always and everywhere to meet the needs of the client.'

The company has gone beyond merely ensuring a good relationship with the customer via the service technician. It has also taken on as an objective the education of the customer concerning its products and technology. 'Informed customers are better equipped to evaluate their measuring requirements.'

There are two ways in which the company does this today. The first is by the organisation of regular training and informational seminars which help customers become conversant with measuring techniques. Real cases and examples are used to illustrate what has been done to resolve particular problems encountered by clients.

In addition, the company has developed a demonstration support unit known as the 'Democar'. It is a mobile exhibition centre which the company can take directly to the customer's premises and use to demonstrate different product and technological approaches.

Combined, the company's approach to its clients has created an environment in which both parties are working together to find solutions to problems. The degree to which its co-operative relationships have resulted in concrete results can be illustrated by the fact that most of the company's new products and systems have resulted from joint development or co-operative projects. The approach is summarised in the first line of the company's creed, 'We serve our customers and learn from them'.

Implementation

Despite the fact that the company sells measuring products, it estimates that in terms of its importance in the total product/service package, service represents 50 per cent to 80 per cent. Among the most important tools which the company uses to control its service quality are the internal error-chasing groups which exist in each production and sales centre.

Problems to be treated by the groups are generally identified by the service technician in his report following a client visit. The problems relate directly to the client in question and are discussed with the head of the department, as well as the service technician. Groups are made up of individuals who have an impact on the problem. For example, in one case there was a problem because the service technician couldn't visit a client because of sickness. The problem was raised and resolved with a second always being available on the account.

Complaints are another area where the company loyalty places a great deal of attention. Active complaint handling is seen as crucial and customer loyalty through good complaint handling has proved very effective. All complaints are answered within 48 hours and are dealt with by the directors of the company. The philosophy is nevertheless to deal with the complaint as close to the customer as possible, which means that once the manager has addressed the problem with the service technician, it is generally the service technician who responds.

The importance of the customer to the organisation is emphasised by the structure which the company has adopted. Internal service quality is judged from the bottom up, i.e. the service technician judges the service/sales department, which in turn judges the production centre.

As a way of monitoring the quality of service that the customer is providing internally, the company has introduced indicators for key services such as shipments and repairs. The number of shipments of tools and spare parts which arrive on time are monitored on a weekly basis. The number of repairs for which the problem was resolved after the first visit are also monitored on a weekly basis.

At the foundation of Endress & Hauser's customer service is the service technician. Management recognises this and follows very strict guidelines for the training and recruitment of these individuals.

In the area of recruitment, Endress & Hauser looks for recruits who can work autonomously, independently from the regional offices and headquarters. To work autonomously means also that technicians draw enough satisfaction out of their daily work that they don't need extensive motivation from their superiors. 'It is harder to manage such individuals, but they are an important factor for the success of the company's service approach.'

Technicians should also be able to communicate well with customers and with other employees in order continuously to enlarge their knowledge about technical problems resolved in other areas or other regions that could be used for his customers.

Technical service training is also considered to be extremely important. New employees receive five weeks of solid training before going out in the field. One week of the five is entirely devoted to training in how to deal with customers. How to handle an angry customer and how to work over the phone are two areas dealt with in depth, particularly as the relationship with many customers frequently takes place over the phone.

New employees are also assigned to a 'godfather' for at least a month and must meet with the head of the after-sales service department in order to discuss how this part of the service is expected to proceed.

What can be learned

1 Handle complaints actively and keep customers

Endress & Hauser has proven from experience that a fast and effective response to problems posed by the customer can regain and even increase the customer's satisfaction with the company. Part of the complaint-handling process at Endress & Hauser permits problems to be discussed in groups which means that problems are addressed from a company-wide perspective and not just from the point of view of the individual service technician.

2 Create a centralised point of contact for the customer

The service technician at Endress & Hauser is the one and only person responsible for dealing with his accounts. He is entirely available to the customer and is completely committed to the customer's satisfaction because of the responsibility he is given. The remaining units in the company are support units and are judged in turn for the quality of service they provide to the service technician.

EQUITY AND LAW

'Our old lady's going . . . but she left something valuable behind.' This is how Equity and Law announced changes in its company from a traditional, discreet provider of insurance products to a more modern, aggressive and service oriented leader in the insurance industry. The company's goal is to become one of the top 10 in the UK by the year 2000. The old lady that has been abandoned was the lady of justice and wisdom with a torch and scales like the Statue of Liberty in New York. She was the company's logo. The new logo, the torch alone, represents much of the same plus more. 'We've been a leading performer in the investment field since 1844 . . . it's about time we shouted about it' (company brochure).

Background

Equity and Law has been around for a long time (since 1844). Historically, the company has had an excellent investment performance record for the funds that they handle. 'An intermediary who recommended the top performer in the 1965 *Economist Survey* for insurance policies taken out in 1940 would be delighted to know that that same society still continues to produce excellent results 25 years on.' Equity and Law figured in the second place in the 1990 league tables published by *Money Marketing* in March and May for bonus declaration on 25-year policies with-profit. In 1989, total funds managed amounted to £5.5 billion.

On the marketing and sales side, the company has kept a low profile. Little or no direct advertising has been done to end customers. Up until quite recently, the company sold all of its policies through the intermediary of independent financial advisers. Today, the company also sells through a network of associated advisers who are more closely tied to the company. The company has 29 regional sales centres through which all contacts are maintained between the financial advisers and the company.

Since 1970, with the establishment of its Dutch office, Equity and Law has had an international presence. Additional offices were established in Germany in 1973, in Belgium in 1982, in the Isle of Man in 1985 and in Spain in 1988. All of these, with the exception of the Dutch, German and Isle of Man offices were either absorbed or disbanded following the 1987 purchase of the company by the AXA-Midi Group, one of the 10th largest insurance organisations in Europe.

Besides the rationalisation of Equity and Law's overseas activities, the acquisition has had little direct affect upon the company's functioning. Its present move towards the repositioning of the group is more accurately a direct result of market research undertaken in 1990, which showed that the company's products were difficult to sell because the company was unknown by the general public and had no major point of differentiation from the competition. 'How can we sell Equity and Law when the public hardly knows who they are?' (documentation for launch of TV campaign).

Service strategy

Equity and Law sells products associated with three activities: insurance including life, pensions and health; mortgages for homes; and Investments including unit trusts, PEPs (personal equity plans), offshore and savings plans.

Independent financial advisers recommend insurance companies, based on an assembly of considerations:

- the financial solidity of the company;
- range of contracts available (insurance and investment);
- investment performance;
- bonus record on with-profit contracts (payout to shareholders based on the performance of money invested);
- service quality.

In the past, the company has emphasised investment performance and its record of with-profit contracts. When compared with other large and highly successful insurance companies, however, Equity and Law was little different.

In 1990, the company conducted extensive market research. Its objective was to know where the company stood with clients and end customers, and to identify concrete measures to achieve the company's objective of becoming one of the top 10 in the year 2000. 'The results of one aspect of our research showed that most were happy with the level of service and support we give them. But, one of the biggest problems facing them was the low public profile of Equity and Law as a company' (David Thorley, Head of Marketing).

The company responded by adopting a three-pronged approach. The first measure was to adopt service quality as a point of differentiation. The marketing research had shown that the company's service quality was reasonably appreciated by the company's customers, financial advisers and end customers alike. The company's objective was to further perfect and enhance upon the quality of service provided, particularly in the after-sales area, and to use this strength to create a strong point of differentiation for the company *vis-à-vis* its competitors. 'Service is only part of the package, but it can be the differentiating factor,' explains Mr Brian Emery, General Manager, Customer Service.

Under corporate philosophy, the new corporate *statement of intent* reads, 'The reputation of Equity and Law is based on the quality of its products and the quality of service to customers and distributors. This reputation will be maintained' (*Statement of Intent*, 1991).

Secondly, Equity and Law took the decision to launch a large communications programme to the general public, designed to create an image of the company in the public's eye. The campaign would emphasise product and service quality and, above all, would attempt to increase name recall of the company with consumers. Just prior to the launch, David Thorley described the campaign in this way, '. . . we are about to go out and tell the public who we are and what we do – in a big way. We have created a dynamic new logo and we are about to launch an exciting TV advertising campaign that will really make us stand out from the crowd.'

Finally, the company reorganised its sales force to create units specialised by type of financial adviser or by product type. The reorganisation was to permit the company to offer better services to the financial adviser and, through them, to end customers.

Some reorganisation had already been done and had been very successful. Two to three years earlier, the company had established its 'mortgage desks' at the sales centres level, backed up by a central support group at headquarters. The result was to increase the company's ability to respond to particular needs in the area of mortgages, and to increase the processing and administration time because of the more direct links. The company attributes its subsequent success in this area – a 20 per cent increase in mortgage-related premiums to record levels despite the worst downturn in the residential market in recent times – to the creation of the mortgage desks which deal directly with the investment advisers uniquely for mortgage management.

In 1990, the company reorganised the rest of its sales force into three units, each dealing with a separate groups of clients. The move was motivated by the recognition that its three primary customer groups – independent financial advisers, large groups like banks or building societies and the company's appointed representatives – had different service needs in order to perform their jobs well and to sell Equity and Law to the general public.

Independent financial advisers represented the core of the company's historical sales base. Up to 1990, roughly 50 per cent of the company's business was generated by these individuals. In 1990, the balance dramatically shifted with independent advisers bringing in only 30 per cent of that business. The difference is being made up by the company's appointed representatives who have been increasingly successful in recent years.

In the past, relations with these two groups were handled by the same sales and marketing group within Equity and Law. The result was that the company provided really top service to neither one customer group nor the other. The new structure allows for the creation of two parallel sales channels at the area sales office level. In addition, the company created a national accounts team which handles the company's relationships with independent national umbrella organizations, independent arms of banks and building societies, and other multilocational intermediaries.

In its 1991 corporate *Statement of Intent*, the company set forth the nature of its commitment to the customer groups, 'We will aim to improve the business of our distributors for mutual benefit. We will treat our tied distributors as an integral part of our business and respect the professional obligations of independent distributors.'

Service strengths

Where Equity and Law is different from their competitors is in their desire to reach out to their customers and make contact. The company maintains close contacts with the financial advisers that sell its products and has a strategic goal of establishing even closer relationships with them. One of the company's 'Key Tasks for 1991' was 'Develop the relationship between Equity and Law and our distributors'.

The company intended to do this by making itself more accesssible. 'Equity and Law would like to grow, but at the same time, maintain a small office approach to their customers,' says Mr Emery. As a small but significant act, Equity and Law recently changed its phone lines. Now, direct dialling to all internal posts is possible. To encourage people to pick up the phone, the company's internal campaign is 'Don't desert it, divert it'.

A more important measure was to make it possible for financial advisers to go directly to headquarters to have their questions answered. Previously, all contacts for regions except the south-east, passed by the local sales office. As a result, financial advisers sometimes had to wait before getting a response to their questions, while Equity and Law personnel went back and forth with questions. Now, financial advisers can contact the head office directly and, as Mr Emery describes it, 'deal directly with the Equity and Law personnel who are servicing his business'.

While most companies consider the administrative part of the business as a 'back-office' activity, Equity and Law has always held the position that administration plays an integral part of the management of the relationship with the intermediary client and the end customer. More than one-third of the company's staff falls under the category of administrative staff; today, their role is more than that of just a support function to sales and marketing. 'A lot of work can be done in what has traditionally been a back-office function to support sales and marketing,' says Mr Emery.

Mr Emery and his staff are focusing upon developing better communication with financial advisers and end customers alike. In addition to more direct telephone contacts, the company is improving its written communication. There is a pilot programme actually to check the presentation, the accuracy and the customer orientation of letters sent out from the department. An internal group samples letters and statistically analyses the contents. 'It is to give us a proper feel and control for what is actually going out of here,' explains Mr Emery.

Mr Emery is also pushing his staff to make letters more customer oriented, 'The challenge is to get them to think before they make any communication with the customer.' He has a checklist of questions for staff to ask about each letter, including:

Is it in layman's terms (no jargon)
Does the phrasing show respect for the customer?
Does the letter really answer the customer's question?
Is it accurate?
Has any information been omitted?

The same review is being done for other types of communication such as documentation on company products. The result has been the identification of new user-friendly tools. The company recently introduced a *Risk Rating Guide*, for use by intermediaries and end customers alike. The guide ranks different types of investments on a scale from 1 to 10, 1 representing an extremely safe investment with a guaranteed return and 10 a highly speculative investment, i.e. commodity futures. All of Equity and Law's funds and trusts are then allocated a position on the scale. The guide helps customers choose which type of investment best corresponds to their need and tastes.

Implementation

The focus of the effort for better service quality has been in the administration department. 'It is one area of service that can differentiate one company from another. We can turn it to our advantage,' says Mr Emery. The department used to be called 'policy servicing' which implied that they 'were servicing policies without regard to the requirements of the customer or policyholder'.

This was considered to be too introspective. 'Though it could develop into an entirely satisfactory standard as far as we were concerned, it bore no relation to what the customer wanted or needed.' The first step in recognising the customer was, then, to change the name of the department from 'policy servicing' to 'client servicing'. Mr Emery changed his title to General Manager of Customer Service and began to look at customer expectations.

Complimentary letters, complaint letters, enquiries from customers, problems which the financial advisers were having were all reviewed and analysed to look for information about where service had to be improved. They are still reviewed on an ongoing basis. 'If customers are consistently asking for additional information in the same areas, that means that our communication is not as good as it should be.'

The department also developed a mission statement: 'We will provide a cost-effective, quality service that recognises the needs of customers and distributors. We will invest in modern technology to provide the necessary products and services cost-effectively.'

Mr Emery's first step was, in fact, to change the company's computer system. The old system did not permit staff to respond to customer's questions with the necessary speed or efficiency. The new Tandem non-stop system has grouped various policies for one customer together under his name and permits rapid answers to a large variety of questions posed by financial advisers and customers about the accounts. The verdict on the system? 'This gives us the ability to address more than ever before the needs of our customers,' says Mr Emery.

The new system also allowed for processing times to be analysed. In turn, this permitted Mr Emery and his staff to set standards to which they would conform across a whole range of activities. All of the standards are set with time objectives and are monitored on a monthly basis. They include, for example, the turnaround time for a customer request for a change in his contract, and the turnaround time for a policy revival.

'There is not yet an established level of acceptable service. We chose the level of standard based on experience, but we also made them somewhat of a challenge.' For the three years that the standards have been in place, the company has improved its performance. The level of the standard will constantly improve as the company becomes more capable of meeting them. 'Equity and Law particularly tries to link service to areas which would improve the financial adviser's view of the company.'

Perhaps the most innovative move made by the company as concerns standards was the publication and distribution of those standards to the financial advisers. The objective was to demonstrate to financial advisers the commitment which the company had undertaken as concerns service quality. 'We believe in the building of business relationships with our supporting financial advisers and that they should know the standards to which we are working. As a demonstration of this, examples of our service standard targets are published in this booklet [*Standards Booklet*].' There were, in fact, no less than 41 standards printed in the booklet. Updates on the company's achievement record on those standards are sent out on a yearly basis.

Things do go wrong sometimes. 'Individuals are bound to make mistakes no matter how much training is available; the goal is to turn those mistakes to your advantage,' says Mr Emery. Equity and Law wants to gain the reputation as being an office which doesn't try to put the responsibility for their own mistakes on to policy holders or the financial advisers. The department guidelines concerning mistakes are:

apologise first of all;
never try to explain why we've done what we've done (we might say that human error has crept in);
take an apologetic tone in any letter;
thank the person for giving Equity and Law the opportunity to examine the problem.

When a customer is unhappy, there are three things that can happen.

He can write in: 'In that case we can actually do something about stopping that person from leaving us.'

He can drift away: 'We will never know when somebody drifts away.'

He can surrender his policy: 'We try to find out why he wants to surrender his policy and win him back.'

Life insurance policies, for example, are 'for life', however, the average span in the industry is 17 years before a case is surrendered. Mr Emery tries to identify surrenders that are about to happen and goes back to the financial adviser with the suggestion that he contact the client to see whether there is something to be done to save the relationship.

What can be learned

1 Provide tangible evidence of service quality to customers

Some companies believe that it's enough to tell customers that they provide service quality. Equity and Law believes in backing up such statements with tangible evidence. The originality in the company's approach was the publication of its internal service standards. Since that time, the company's level of achievement on those standards is measured and communicated to customers on a regular basis.

2 Reduce red tape

At one time, insurance brokers handling Equity and Law policies had to pass through regional offices in order to get in touch with the policy administration department. This increased red tape inside the organisation and increased the time it took for things to get done. It also led to more errors. Equity and Law recently changed this policy; now, insurance brokers go straight to the source.

EUROP ASSISTANCE

Europ Assistance provides immediate assistance to individuals in trouble around the world or at home. They specialise in responding to emergencies and can repatriate travellers needing medical care by plane if necessary. They operate like an insurance company in that their customers subscribe to their services, either on a yearly basis or prior to a departure to a foreign country.

History

Europ Assistance was created in 1963 by Mr Pierre Desnos, at the time a manager of a hardware store in the city of Le Mans, France. There were no such services available to individual travellers; Mr Desnos had the idea to create such an organism following a friend's serious accident in a southern Mediterranean country. He recognised that the consequences of the accident would have been much less serious if his friend could have been brought back to France for the medical treatment he required.

To start up the company, he obtained the assistance and support of Mr André Rosa, Chairman of the Board of Generali, a major Italian insurance company. Further support and assistance was provided by Professor Cara, a pioneer in the domain of medical aid to the injured or sick.

The product reached the public through the intermediary of the banks. BNP (Banque Nationale de Paris) was the first to accept to distribute the product; later other banks followed.

Initially, assistance was assured in only 17 countries. Over the years, the company expanded both its assistance and commercial representation in foreign countries. Today, Europ Assistance intervenes in 210 countries and actively assists in over 200,000 incidents a year.

The range of services offered has also evolved over the years. In addition to providing emergency assistance to travellers in the case of illness or an accident, Europ Assistance now insures foreign expatriates and business travellers on a yearly contractual basis. They have also expanded into the provision of home assistance or assistance to children and teenagers away from their parents. Another large part of their activities involves providing automobile assistance in the case of breakdowns.

Service strategy

Europ Assistance differentiates itself from insurance companies by the nature of the product they sell.

Where insurance companies reimburse the subscriber for expenses related to a certain incident, Europ Assistance intervenes directly and immediately to provide moral and material assistance to the individual in need. From the customer's point of view, this means that he is buying the company's capacity to respond in emergencies, not security against financial ruin in the case of an emergency.

Connected with this point is the fact that Europ Assistance does not try to identify how the accident occurred or who is at fault. Their role is not to be investigators or policemen, but to be firemen. They are thus exonerated from having to sell to customers and later to question the integrity of those same customers.

Europ Assistance is implanted worldwide. This is crucial; the perceived need for these services is greatest in locations poorly serviced by the local authorities. Their capability to serve far removed spots adds credibility to their claim of being able to respond efficiently in less remote locations where visitor frequency is higher.

The most marked point in Europ Assistance's strategy is its commitment to respond in every case. Specifically, they promise always to assist a subscriber in trouble, regardless of whether that assistance is provided for in the contract or not. For a customer purchasing a policy from Europ Assistance, this means real security. No customer will be put in the position of having to go through a dispute to have the aid he requires in an emergency situation. This also means avoiding many subsequent debates about what is covered in the contract, and what is extra and must be paid for separately.

Lastly, the promise reflects the historical background of the company and the beliefs to which it adheres. It is a statement for employees and customers alike of the lengths to which Europ Assistance is prepared to go to aid their customers.

Service strengths

Europ Assistance is remarkably good in two aspects of the customer service it delivers. First, they provide very qualified medical assistance to customers at every level of their contact with the company. Telephone operators receiving calls are given enough medical training to be able to identify the nature and gravity of the medical problem and then to refer the question to the appropriate medical specialist. The specialist taking the call responds to precise customer questions and determines the action that should be taken to treat the problem.

Regardless of the hour of the day or night, medical specialists are available for consultation. Europ Assistance has created a very large and highly qualified network of doctors. The medical team on the staff is made up of 12 doctors. They are backed up by a field staff of 60 doctors and 80 nurses. The qualifications of the entire staff are evaluated carefully before they are brought into the company.

Further support is available from Europ Assistance's council of medical advisers, a body of 50 medical professors covering all major disciplines. They are prepared to intervene for unusual or especially difficult cases and on an ongoing basis act as advisers on medical issues. Professor Cara was the initiator of this group.

The level of medical advice is maintained regardless of where the company intervenes. Qualified medical aid is assured in foreign countries through the company's network. A large proportion of the countries are served by local Europ Assistance employees. Because they are employed by the company, their availability and professionalism can be counted upon.

Emergencies in other countries are served by the company's correspondents. The company has 300 correspondents in 160 countries. Such correspondents are carefully chosen – their qualifications are verified; they are also required to come to France to be trained about the company and in how to respond in difficult situations. Each correspondent has his own network of service suppliers; the subscriber has access to a total of 78,000 suppliers worldwide.

The second element of its service in which Europ Assistance excels is in the rapidity and appropriateness of its response. When there is a serious problem Europ Assistance does not hesitate or furnish half-measure solutions. In over 30 per cent of the cases where an intervention was necessary, Europ Assistance went beyond the terms of the contract to provide appropriate assistance.

The personnel are trained to never say 'no', because the overriding objective is to provide the assistance which is adapted to the problem. If the means deemed necessary cannot be approved by the assistance operator handling the call, then he/she has recourse to top management. Access to top management is assured through a system of 'guards' where each member of the management team takes his turn at responding to night, weekend or holiday calls.

Quick access to the necessary personnel on location is made easier by the company's database which stores all of the information about individuals belonging to the company's network, including home or back-up telephone numbers. Information on the customer himself is also available from the same databank.

Implementation

The key person in the provision of quality service at Europ Assistance is the assistance operator. Assistance operators work in stations or 'platforms'. Each one is equipped with a set of telephones and a computer terminal. Every time a call comes in the operator is required to note down the events and the principal points of discussion between himself and the customer. If he has to refer the customer to a specialist, then he briefs the specialist on the customer's case prior to passing him so that the customer doesn't have to repeat his question or problem again.

Once the gravity of the case is determined, the assistant or the doctor, in the case of a medical problem, decides upon the nature of the response necessary. In this task, he is aided by a guide which indicates for the general case what the response should be and to what point the operator can exceed this response without referring the question to a manager.

Errors do occur with responses which are either above or below what is required by the situation. To ensure that everyone learns from these, monthly meetings are held in which these are discussed.

In general, the assistance operator is well trained before he is allowed to work on a station. Initially, operators receive four days' training on the basic policies of Europ Assistance and on the general structure of the company. Another week is spent within the department, explaining to the new recruitment the responsibilities within the department and his role therein. Finally, training is done through 'godfathering', in which the new employee is assigned to an existing staff member to be coached and observed during his integration period of three months.

Specific courses are required on telephone handling and in the handling of emergency situations, including how to deal with panicky customers or unforeseen hitches. General training on customer relations is also required, and the importance of treating customers with respect and consideration. Most courses use simulation and video training to achieve their objectives.

Recruiting capable assistance operators is as important as training them once they are hired. Europ Assistance tests the adaptability of candidates with psychological testing, mainly to identify those persons which react well in emergencies, and by testing the individual's skills in working over the telephone. As part of the recruitment process, Europ Assistance interviews candidates over the phone.

The importance of the assistance operator to the service quality of the company is underlined by the fact that most employees are required to spend time as an assistance operator and to at least have assisted in an emergency air repatriation before moving on to other services.

What can be learned

1 When your service quality is put to the test, overrespond

Europ Assistance commits itself to respond above and beyond what is stated in the written contract. It is an excellent promise and one that reassures customers, the majority of which will never be able to put the promise to a test.

What is important are the few occasions when Europ Assistance must respond. By overresponding, the company minimises the likelihood that a customer will be unsatisfied and generates positive word of mouth about their service excellence.

2 Be sure that key people have everything they need

The assistance operator is an element crucial to service quality at Europ Assistance. Besides the correspondent on location, most assisted customers are initially in contact with only one person – the assistance operator. He or she represents the first contact with the company and the most important. If his service to the customer is bad, the entire company's service will be judged to be poor. Europ Assistance makes sure that the importance of this position is understood by the entire company and that the entire company stands fully behind its operators.

FEINKOST KÄFER

It's for the occasion which has to be more than a dinner, more than a party, it must be perfect! Guests delivered to the door by a carriage pulled by four white horses, champagne fountains, candelabras, red carpets, black-tie waiters and waitresses galore, . . . please don't hold back on the extras and spare me the details! Can you do it by next Thursday . . . oh, and send the bill to my husband's accountant in New York.

Thursday arrives and, lo and behold, there *are* champagne fountains and white horses, and even more! Swan Lake has been recreated right in the middle of the dance floor – with real swans and lily pads! It's a wonder, it's fabulous, who would have ever thought . . . DO TELL, who's the name of your caterer? Why Gerd Käfer, of course . . .

You may not have heard of Käfer, but anyone in Germany who needs to hear of him has. He is the top of the top, the deluxe of the deluxe, the summit in party entertainment and catering. He cannot only throw a dinner for you; he can make it an event which will keep people raving about it for months – even years!

Background

Käfer does not go back to 1862, nor does it go back to 1910 or even 1915; Gerd Käfer started his very successful business in the promising year of 1960. While it is not 'post-communism', it is 'post-everything else' and, most important, it is post-war(s). Pre-war Germany and 19th-century Germany was dominated by the aristocracy and the Grand Bourgeoisie, who had a tradition of maintaining extensive households with numerous staff. The new economic, social and political era that came into being following the Second World War no longer had a place for those kinds of extended households.

The large buildings themselves remained, however, and people's tastes had changed little; there was still a strong and even growing desire for the kind of elegant and elaborate home entertaining of the past. Short of staff and short of experience, the modern German aristocrats needed help if they were ever going to make a success of any really big or important party. That's when and why Käfer entered into the picture.

Käfer started from scratch and called his business an 'out-of-house service' company. His primary customers were to be large private households and celebrities. Today, he runs a service empire with a revenue of DM210 million in revenues, DM90 million of which come from licences on coffee, chocolate, pizza and other speciality products sold under the Käfer name. In addition to his catering and licence business, he also runs 'Deli-shops', restaurants and eight in-theatre restaurants, including one in the Munich opera house.

Service strategy

To say that Käfer is in the catering and restaurant business is to severely limit the scope and value of what he offers to his customers. The Käfer concept is not just to provide food and drinks to a customer organising a dinner party, it is to take the dinner in hand and make it a success. In Gerd Käfer's opinion, he has not done his job unless, 'my customer has spent a great, memorable moment'.

The Käfer service starts much before the night of the party; it starts with the guest list and the invitations. As a celebrity himself, Käfer is in a good position to advise his customers on attendees. He knows who to invite to what and which swinging bachelor *not* to place next to which elderly matron at the dinner table.

Käfer also takes in hand the decorations, from the design to obtaining all the necessary props to create a true stage-like setting. An enormous warehouse outside Munich serves as storage for all variety of fine china, marble statues, fake fountains – whatever is necessary to create the effect.

Of course, Käfer also helps create the menu, provides food and beverages of every sort imaginable and serves them, impeccably.

Käfer can pick the guests up at the airport, make their hotel reservations, rent their cars, choose their gifts and provide them with costumes, if the occasion calls for it. They also provide costumes to the host and hostess as well as organising the entertainment. Last, and probably most important, they clean up and put the house back the way it was found, to the very last detail.

From start to finish, Käfer offers the most complete and professional service possible. His strategy is quite simply to act as the customer's own staff, and then some. His service is completely customised and no two ideas are used twice; that's the customer's assurance of exclusivity.

Käfer's 'out-of-house service' is the core of his business. If that doesn't go well then the other aspects are not likely to remain strong for long either. His 'out-of-house service' customers are the élite of German society, corporations and celebrities including movie stars and rock stars. Käfer's reputation is made based on the service he provides to these people.

Käfer's principal competitor is Lufthansa which, like Käfer, is active all over Germany. Other competitors are locally based. In total, Käfer estimates that his company has around 30 to 40 per cent of the total business in his market segment.

Service strengths

Gerd Käfer attributes the success of his business to a complete understanding of his customer's wishes. Unlike most modern service companies, he doesn't do it by hiring research companies to do huge studies or analyses; it's all done by Mr Käfer, personally.

Before beginning on any assignment, he meets with the customer and tries to find out what is the customer's real aim – does he want an outrageous, publicity-worthy event or an elegant, discreet evening for friends and relatives. Is the focus to be the food or the company? Are people coming to see new faces or to meet old friends?

The customer can work closely with Käfer to decide how things will be or, as is the case generally, he can leave the entire evening in the hands of the company. Because Käfer himself has spent time in the beginning to understand what is expected, the unexpected is the expected: what Käfer provides corresponds to the spoken and unspoken wishes of his customers.

If thank you letters are any testament of satisfaction then Käfer certainly qualifies as having a large testament. Three long corridors in the director's office are literally covered with thank you letters and photographs from customers – private guests as well as the President of the Federal Republic for whom he organised three dinners for the general secretary in Moscow.

Understanding customer expectations doesn't just apply to private individuals, but also to Käfer's restaurant customers. To theatre or opera-going customers, he offers a dinner that is perfectly adapted to the situation. The customer orders his dinner in advance; at intermission time, he simply turns up at the restaurant where his meal is hot and waiting for him. The service is so good that, if he wishes, he can eat the entire dinner during the intermission. If not, he can come back once the performance is over and complete it at his leisure.

For Käfer, understanding customers means being with customers all the time. Gerd Käfer has the reputation of being omnipresent. In actual fact, he attends 70 per cent of all parties which are organised by the company and personally responds to all complaint letters and most personal correspondence with customers. To accomplish his feat of being in all places at once, he uses a fleet of cars and a helicopter or a plane to move about between parties throughout the country. As he very modestly puts it, 'Good service is very time-consuming.'

Implementation

'If my employees don't see in my customer's eyes what they want, then they are not giving good service.' While 'gut-feeling' is a very important part of Käfer management style, there are some practices which make 'gut-feeling' a little less 'pure intuition' and a lot more 'solid experience'.

After every event, Käfer has dinner with his customers. He wants to hear at first hand what went right and what went wrong. Customers who pay Käfer for the level of service he delivers don't hesitate to tell him what they think. Over such dinners, Käfer receives some of the best and most direct customer feedback any company can ever get.

What's more, he has the opportunity to respond – right away, on the spot. Problems are resolved, the anger is discharged and the relationship can go forward. Even if there wasn't a problem – the food was delicious, the lighting divine, the atmosphere euphoric etc. – Käfer's dinner cements his relationship with his customer. The next year, it's not Lufthansa that will get the business, but Käfer, once again (if he's not already booked up).

Käfer has over 600 people working for him. Half of those are involved in the theatre restaurant, restaurant and the deli business. The other half work in 'out-of-house service'; only 120 of these are regular, full-time staff. Another 200 or so are on standby. While the 120 all work out of Munich, the standbys are located throughout the country. Käfer says that a lot of these are bank or insurance company employees who enjoy working in a more exciting and lucrative field in their free time.

While at first glance the approach seems contradictory with Käfer's determination to offer top service quality, further examination shows that it is not. All of Käfer's staff are heavily experienced and well paid. He believes in 'hiring the best' and then making them perform even better.

The additional advantages that a standby work force provide are flexibility and manageability. Flexibility because Käfer can respond to a greater number of demands without incurring great risk – 10 events per evening can be easily stretched to 30. Greater manageability because it's easier for Käfer to personally manage 120 full-time employees than 300. Moreover, slow seasons of the year aren't likely to produce enough business to support a full-time staff of 300.

Waiters in Käfer's restaurants work only four days a week and can earn double what waiters in local three-star restaurants earn. In addition to their salary, they receive 13.5 per cent of the restaurant's turnover. Tips are not distributed in the usual way – from the headwaiter on down – instead, each employee keeps his own tips. 'This encourages greater personal effort.'

Käfer doesn't have problems recruiting. The name is so well known that everyone in the business would like to have a chance to work for them. So, Käfer hires the cream of the crop, and then he trains them using a godfathering system. New employees are godfathered for three months by experienced staff. That means that they work alongside these individuals and have the opportunity to draw out as much information and guidance as possible. To prevent inexperienced employees having any adverse effects upon customer relations, they start at low-intensive customer contact events and work their way upwards.

The only real problem with Käfer's service is that it doesn't exist in more places. Käfer admits that the success of his business depends upon his presence; any further expansion and Käfer wouldn't be able to keep his omnipresent reputation.

What can be learned

1 Keep going for customer feedback

Many managers, by the time they reach the CEO level, feel that their energy should be spent elsewhere – elsewhere than with customers. Käfer doesn't think so and his success is based on the fact that he has never left the customer's side.

2 Get before and after feedback

By meeting with customers before and after the event, Käfer gets the whole picture. He knows what they said and what he thought they wanted, and can compare it with what they really wanted. It's an excellent education in analysing customer service perceptions against your own conceptions of the service.

3 When you go for luxury, give luxury

Some companies believe that they can provide top-flight service on a shoestring. The example of Käfer shows that when it comes to providing the very best in service, there is no such thing as a shortcut. Shortcuts are the shortest route to a ruined reputation. Customers expect you to go all the way and they come to you for that. So, please, don't hold back on extras!

GALENICA

The word Galenica comes from Galenus in Latin, the name of a famous physician living around AD150. He is considered by modern-day pharmacists to be the father of their practice. Galenica is a Swiss company devoted to providing support and assistance to the profession, notably as a supplier and distributor of pharmaceutical products and drugs and related services.

Background

Galenica was established in 1927 by 16 pharmacists as a central purchasing unit. Its development over the years has led to the expansion of this role. Today, Galenica takes the form of a holding company with activities in three areas: production, representation and distribution. By far the most important focus of the company's efforts is in the area of distribution. The company is still owned by pharmacists and the shares are only available for sale to pharmacists.

It is the largest as well as the youngest of the Swiss pharmaceutical distributors. It has six central warehouses located throughout Switzerland – Berne, Geneva, Lausanne, Lucerne, Neuchâtel and Zurich – and from these delivers, in less than a day to any pharmacy in the country 98 per cent of all items prescribed by doctors and any of the non-prescription products sold in pharmacies – Kleenex included.

In total, over 40,000 items are stocked on a regular basis. The company maintains contacts with over 1500 manufacturers from which it sources all but a small selection of perfusions, injectable solutions and sterile solutions which it manufactures itself, in its production centres. With this organisation, it services over 1300 clients.

The concern for providing good customer service runs deep in the history and philosophy of the company. There is a constant effort on the part of all staff to put themselves in their customers' shoes. Perhaps because the company has always been so close to the market it serves, it has put the concerns of the customer before its own. 'We are everything for the pharmacists; at Galenica, the client is truly king.'

Service strategy

Galenica's mission is 'to provide the pharmacist whatever he needs to do his job well'. In the past, the emphasis throughout the industry was on the efficient and rapid delivery of medical products to pharmacists. Galenica invested enormous time and effort into the development of a system which permits pharmacists to receive their products within, generally, two and a half hours from the time of ordering.

At least once daily from Monday to Saturday, the pharmacists are called by Galenica's staff of receptionists. Thanks to a system of magnetic cards, the pharmacist simply inserts his card in the special slot on the telephone and his order is automatically communicated to Galenica. This is the case for 80 per cent of Galenica's customers. For those who cannot or do not wish to use the card system, the order is communicated verbally. Pharmacists can even order after opening hours. A computer programmed recording system permits pharmacists to pass their orders directly into Galenica's computer system.

Thirty-five minutes later, the first customer order is prepared and placed into a Galenica van for delivery with a printout summary of the items ordered and their price. Depending on the location of the pharmacy and the numbers of orders per neighbourhood, the delivery man appears at the door of the pharmacy anywhere from 45 minutes to 3 hours later. The rate of error in preparation per order is under 3 for 10,000 (0.003 per cent).

This incredibly efficient system permitted Galenica to surpass many of its competitors who were unable to maintain the same level of service at a comparable price. Today, the company has an estimated 58 per cent market share in Switzerland.

The market is changing, however. The majority of Galenica's remaining competitors are small local suppliers. The most competitive of them stocks just two-thirds of what Galenica does, yet, because of their proximity to their customers and their greater flexibility (due to their size), they are able to offer comparative pricing with more personalisation and are, thus, able to retain a certain customer base.

Additional improvements in terms of speed of delivery or greater accuracy are obtainable only with great difficulty. As a result, the focus of competition is switching from the efficiency and rapidity of delivery to the selection of complementary services offered to pharmacists and the quality of the personal contact.

Galenica's service strategy today is to focus on providing an exceptional level of service overall and to excell in meeting the particular needs of its loyal customers. The strategy is expressed in the company's Quality Chart. From the company's perspective, the customer is seen as a partner to whom Galenica provides reliable and reasonably priced distribution services complemented by a full set of services to help the pharmacist practise his profession as well as possible.

Galenica is clarifying and elaborating upon the many complementary services it offers. These include for example:

1 assistance, training and advice to young pharmacists setting up in practice;
2 computer based pharmacy management programmes together with training;
3 documentation and response to requests for information in the field of pharmaceuticals;
4 control systems for ensuring the freshness of the pharmacists stock and for managing product organisation in the store;
5 seminars, conferences and workshops for the exchange of information and industry expertise.

To differentiate between his clients, Galenica has developed a four tiered customer classification system that gives preference to more loyal customers. Preferred customers are delivered on a more frequent basis and receive certain services, such as documentation and training free of charge.

Service strengths

Perhaps where the company excels the most in terms of service beyond its basic business is in the provision of assistance and advice to novice pharmacists. Originally conceived as a service of information on the market, the assistance service for novice pharmacists has expanded into a full-fledged consulting service in the management of pharmacies.The individuals to whom these services are made available has also expanded to include more experienced pharmacists trying to improve their method of management. To get a good understanding of exactly what the company provides its pharmacists in the area of pharmacy management, we will begin at the beginning.

Galenica starts serving its customers even before they become customers. Every year, the company sponsors a free two-day information/training seminar to all graduating pharmacists. The first day provides information on the market and pharmacy customers; the second exposes some of the problems encountered by pharmacists in the management of their business. Habitually, three-quarters of all graduating students attend this valuable seminar.

The first approach leaves the door open for closer contact. Once the pharmacist is ready to set up his practice, Galenica is there as a source of information and practical assistance. The company's staff is available to help the pharmacist prepare his administration papers and his requests for financial assistance. It is also active in assisting pharmacists to identify desirable locations in which to establish their practice.

Galenica is personally involved in financing pharmacists through Pharmaplan, which is connected with the Guarantees Bureau for Swiss Pharmacists, an organisation which supports novice pharmacists.

Once the financing and the location have been established, the pharmacist is in a position to create his 'boutique'. One of the first practical issues facing him is to know how to organise his products in the most practical and useful fashion. There, too, Galenica can help. The company has created a programme which can determine, based on the size and shape of each product, where it should be placed on the shelf and how much space should be allotted to it. This layout plan can be made available to the young pharmacist on request.

To manage his stock on a daily basis, Galenica has created a system that lets him know which items are approaching their expiry date. With the monthly summaries of purchases provided by Galenica, a pharmacist can know exactly which products he's sold during the month and in what quantities. The company is also available to perform inventories for its clients. For those that still need more assistance, Galenica offers courses on a regular basis on stock management – over 600 people attend on every occasion.

Galenica has also created a financial management programme which permits the pharmacist to manage his accounts in a way which maximises the pharmacy's profitability. The programme and the computer can be leased from Galenica. Galenica has trainers on hand who run three day courses for pharmacists in how to operate the machine and the programme.

Beyond all the concrete services Galenica provides, it also provides assistance in the form of 'grey matter'. Galenica's regional managers and assistant managers, most of whom have had experience in the trade and additional experience with Galenica, are available to young pharmacists for advice on any number of matters concerning the management of their business. The company's long-standing tradition as dedicated servants to the pharmaceutical trade ensures their availability and the full commitment of their time to assisting a needy pharmacist.

A needy pharmacist or a not needy pharmacist, Galenica is always ready and extremely anxious to listen to its customers. The company believes that only by maintaining extremely close ties with their customers will they be able to make the rapid and necessary adaptations to their business to meet the ever-evolving expectations of customers. There are a number of methods which the company uses to keep the communication lines open.

If you are a Galenica customer, every year you have a one-in-three chance of being invited to attend a dinner with Galenica management. Galenica conducts 20 such dinners per year throughout Switzerland, at which a maximum of 20 clients are invited.The objective of the dinner is an exchange of information around a certain chosen theme – service quality, new management methods, logistics etc. More precisely, the company's aim is to collect ideas from customers for new services or better ways of offering the same service.

Another way that Galenica's management collects ideas is by visiting their customers personally on a regular basis. This is generally the job of the regional manager and his staff who attend pharmacy openings to maintain a personal contact and keep abreast of developments at a particular pharmacy, or for the region.

Regional directors also invite clients to information sessions. Generally organised as something between a workshop and a seminar, an information session can last for an afternoon or a day. Through these sessions, Galenica gives its clients updates on developments in the industry and at the same time receives information from clients on market demands.

Another way in which the company demonstrates its interest in the comments and suggestions of customers is through its method of handling complaints. A customer's complaint is dealt with in 24 hours and he receives a response to his question or problem. Some complaints or suggestions are handled personally by the President, Mr. Secrétan, who makes direct contact with the customer by phone.

At the end of each year, every customer receives a letter from Mr. Secrétan thanking him for his patronage to the company.

Implementation

Making service quality function at Galenica has historically required two things: systematic setting of measurable goals and objectives for the company and staff alike; and meticulous attention to the organisation of the company for the achievement of those goals.

When the primary need of the pharmacists was for rapid delivery of fresh products, Galenica's goals focused on increasing internal efficiency in order to decrease the delay period between the order placement and delivery. For Galenica, the definition of quality as it relates to that aspect of their service is:

an impeccable order receiving system;
rapid and error-free order preparation;
on-time deliveries.

Today, Galenica has developed a more precise definition through the elaboration of 15 conditions for success. They include:

The client will be informed without delay which products are not immediately deliverable.
The client can obtain outside working hours any medication necessary for an urgent medical treatment.
The client can present in complete confidence his projects and problems to an adviser who will consult him in a personal, objective and neutral manner with the guarantee of the greatest discretion.

The order placing and processing step is a very important one. Receptionists are trained in all of the procedures and on how to achieve the quality objectives for their department. They systematically go through a seminar on how to deal with customers over the 'phone. The course is up-dated regularly, allowing both new and experienced receptionists to benefit from the course. In addition to the best way to communicate with customers, they are also taught how to optimise their time for order taking and to minimise errors. A new telephone training module has just been introduced, which is interactive and runs using disks, video and laser communication. The receptionist can actually carry on a 'dialogue' with the machine.

Just establishing a good definition of service quality is generally not enough to ensure that it is achieved. Thus, Galenica developed ways to measure service quality for each major activity and for the company as a whole. Measuring has permitted the company to focus on its errors and to follow improvements as they have been realised.

Galenica measures, for example, the number of mistakes made by the receptionists in the order-taking process. It also measures the number of errors in the preparation of the order, the punctuality with which the receptionists make their calls and the number of rings before the telephone is answered. They also measure the time it takes on average for an order to be filled, from the time the receptionist hangs up the phone to the moment that the order is put into the van.

The complement of measuring is the setting of standards or norms in accordance with those measures. Galenica has established a standard of 3 errors for 10,000 orders in the preparation stage. It has established a standard of five days for accounts crediting of returned merchandise. The measures are taken on a monthly basis and the results figure on charts which are circulated and posted for staff to see.

Galenica recently used informal qualitative research to get feedback from customers on how they viewed the company's service. Around 10 to 15 customers were interviewed at length by Galenica's staff. The suggestions, ideas and criticism were then used to identify areas of improvement and possible new or expanding services.

There were three parts to the questionnaire filled out by the customer and the company representative. The first and the largest part deals with the pharmacist's own business: 'What place does a pharmacist have in today's society?', 'Is the level of profitability attainable still attractive?', 'Do you know the cost of the services you provide your customers?', etc.

The second part deals with the distributor's role as assistant to the pharmacist: 'What does a supplier bring to you?', 'Can you give some examples of good service you received?', 'Should a distributor help you sell better?', 'What should be the nature of the relationship between pharmacists and their distributor?'.

The third part asks the customer to evaluate Galenica's service: 'How would you rate Galenica as compared with other companies you use?', 'Do you have the feeling that the client is king at Galenica?', 'Are there services that you need that Galenica doesn't provide?'.

Based on the results of the customer interviews, Galenica has also decided to carry out a customer satisfaction survey to be completed on an anonymous basis by customers. Unlike the other survey, this questionnaire deals solely with the customer's perception of Galenica's service to him(her). There are questions such as: 'How would you rate the competence of the telephone receptionists taking your order?', 'How would you judge the quality of the responses given you by the customer services department?', and 'How would you judge the quality of the contact with the driver?'.

'Our objective is to satisfy the customer so that he really wants to come to us', explains Mr Secrétan. In the internal journal, he explains the philosophy as follows, '. . . the client is, above all a man or woman that places a great deal of importance to personal contacts. We will never be able to emphasise enough the importance of the quality of relations between us, the seller and our customer, the buyer. Receptionists, drivers and all the collaborators who have a direct contact with the customer have an important role to play through their contact in influencing the success of our business.'

The company introduced a quality programme in the company over the last three years. One of the first objectives of the programme is to increase the personnel's awareness of the need to provide good service and to create an ingrained quality reflex in the company culture. A Quality Director has been named, whose role is to act as a reference point within the group on quality issues and to centralise ideas on improving service quality. He reports to a Quality committee which meets at least once a month to review the progress that has been made and to identify new actions. A large communication programme has also been undertaken under the name of 'Success through Quality'. Monthly quality messages are sent out, posters have been distributed and a special logo and letterhead were designed to be used for any message in the company concerning the quality effort.

Also part of the communication effort, managers have gone through quality leadership training which will help them to adopt quality concepts in their own work and communicate these on to their staff.

One of the most important steps the company has taken beyond the awareness building programme has been the elaboration of a full set of customer service standards. These state exactly the level and nature of the service the customer can expect to receive from the company. These standards are grouped in the form of a small book, which is used by personnel as a reference point for all of its actions.

The Quality Programme has already achieved concrete results. Galenica identified a problem in the delivery of products that required refrigeration at particular temperatures. Using the quality process, the company developed its 'cold chain', which permits these products to be taken in charge direct from the producer on to the pharmacists, thereby assuring the maintenance of the correct temperature.

At Galenica, management has historically put a great deal of emphasis on the efficient organisation of the company in order to permit the achievement of quality objectives. Improvements in efficiency have, in a large part, been achieved through the introduction of very modern tools in information technology and in logistics. Today, the company is working upon the system of logistics for the year 2000, designed to provide ever greater precision and reliability in pharmaceuticals distribution (see Chapter 5 for further details).

What can be learned

1 Maximise efficiencies in your basic business to create value-added

The efficiency of Galenica's operations for order processing and delivery has permitted the company to dedicate resources to the development of a whole set of service offerings. From the customer's perspective, delivery efficiency is the minimum expected of any supplier; it is, thus, Galenica's services that differentiate it from the competition.

2 Get them when they're ripe

Galenica begins courting its clients very early – even before they're out of pharmaceutical school. This increases name awareness and positions the company clearly as a full-service partner to the pharmaceutical trade.

HILTI

What is service quality when industry sells to industry? Is it after-sales service? Is it a competent and helpful sales technician? Is it fast maintenance or is it fast processing of orders? Or is it good operating instructions on how to use the products?

Hilti, one of the world's leading manufacturers of fastening equipment, has a very good idea of what service quality is in its industry; it's what makes them different from their competitors; it's what brings true value-added to the customer; it's everything that the company does for the customer around the product; it's what Hilti calls its complete customer service package; and it's designed to provide its customers with complete solutions to their problems.

Background

Martin and Eugen Hilti are from Liechtenstein, a small country 'attached' to the German part of Switzerland. The Hilti company was started in 1941 by Martin and his brother in a small workshop in the small town of Schaan. Nothing in these small beginnings in this country in the midst of political and economic turmoil indicated that anything big would ever come out of the Hiltis' enterprises. But Martin Hilti had an engineering degree and, with the manufacturing they were doing on behalf of other companies, Martin and Eugen were gaining experience; it was a beginning.

In 1948, Hilti company came into contact with fastening technology. 'A company in the west of Switzerland, which had a new patent for a gun-like fastening tool, contacted Hilti to have fasteners manufactured.' The specifications for the product were incomplete and the patent was eventually found to be invalid. The Hilti brothers bought the technology from the Swiss company and finished the development work themselves. They then had a technology all their own.

Other related technologies followed and fuelled the company's growth for the next 15 years. Powder-actuated fastening, as the technology was known, is the process of using the power released by a fired cartridge to drive steel nails and studs into hard materials. The objective is to create a bonding mechanism for materials which are used in all different kinds of metal and cement constructions. The related technologies which were developed include hand-drive tools which serve the same purpose, but do so without the use of a cartridge. The technical breakthrough was achieved when Hilti invented the first low-velocity cartridge tool, where a piston drives the pin. This true innovation brought safety for the user and a controllable fastening. This was the innovative basis for Hilti's leadership.

To sell the tools the best method is by demonstration. Very quickly a direct sales system was adopted by which users were contacted directly by the company's salesforce. By 1957, Hilti had 300 employees working in its design and manufacturing facilities, and 300 working on the sales and service support end.

The Hilti company is closely connected to the construction industry, due to the nature of its product. The boom in that industry which occurred over the next 15 years greatly assisted in the company's expansion. Hilti quickly established subsidiaries in the American, French, German and UK markets. Production facilities were also added, with plants being established in the US, Austria, Germany and Great Britain.

In the 1970s Hilti went into the Far East, including Japan. Both production and sales facilities were extended throughout the world. By the beginning of the 1980s, Hilti had over 9000 people working for them. Sales which were Sfr376 million in 1971, had now topped the Sfr1000 million limit. For the first time, Hilti went to the public for financing with a bond issue; non-voting participating bearer shares were issued in 1986, the first entrance of non-family capital into the company.

Today, Hilti's product line covers, in addition to fastening tools, the drilling and electrical tool division, the anchor technology division, the structural protection and restoration division, and the cladding and window systems division. Hilti employs 12,000 people worldwide, two-thirds of whom are in marketing and sales, has 17 production plants, operates in 86 countries and has sales of over 2 billion SF. It just celebrated its 50th anniversary in 1991, at which point in time, Martin Hilti, who had led the company since its founding, passed the chairmanship on to his son Michael.

Service strategy

Hilti readily admits that it owes at least part of its success to its service strategy. In the early years, what later developed into service strategy was merely a sales strategy, the concept of selling direct to end-users. The result of having regular contacts with users, however, meant that Hilti salesmen began to provide customers with more than just a product.

Because it was a new technology, Hilti sales engineers had to advise customers on which product was the best adapted; they had to demonstrate how it was used; they had to supply the customer with clean and concise instructions; they had to be on hand to answer any questions or to respond in case of a problem.

They also had to be able to repair and replace the product quickly if it broke down; they had to be ready to recommend new models or explain new technologies when they became available and they had to listen and note the customers' comments about the products so that they could be incorporated into research and development plans. In sum, because Hilti was constantly at the customer's elbow, he learned to respond to the customer's complete set of expectations both for the product and the service that goes with it.

Today, this complete customer service package approach is Hilti's most important point of differentiation from its competitors. It includes everything mentioned above and a little bit more. The Hilti mission statement expresses it as follows:

The performances we provide in the market are comprehensive solutions to problems, utilising complete systems of machines, insert tools and fasteners which are technically advanced, convenient and safe to use. These systems are supplemented by specialised software, professional advisory personnel and a complete range of of support services. In this way, we create a genuine benefit to customers which is inseparably associated with the Hilti trademark.'

Hilti has just completed creating a new sales and distribution structure for the entire company, to be implemented over the next three to five years. Known as Sales Strategy 2000, it includes a comprehensive description of what Hilti offers to its customers in terms of service.

The first major component is technical advice which is provided on an ongoing basis to potential customers and customers in the process of using Hilti's equipment. Included therein is the demonstration and the thorough explanation of how the Hilti machine systems are to be used. Hilti's machines cannot be sold on an independent basis; the technology requires that they be associated with the correct fastening materials in order to achieve their purpose. They are, therefore, sold as a packaged solution.

Hilti provides rapid and differentiated delivery according to the needs of its customers. In as little as six hours a customer can order and receive a Hilti product, if need be. Hilti offers a repair service which is also rapid with repair turnaround time in as little as one day.

Hilti is equipped to do special product development to meet a customer's specific need or application. For large projects, Hilti is willing to work directly with the engineers to provide ongoing support and planning.

Hilti presently has a telephone ordering service and is in the process of creating a customer service outlet which will be capable of handling all Hilti customers' requests for information and ordering.

There is also the Hilti centre – a complete 'showroom' of Hilti products. Hilti Centres are more than just an over-the-counter operation. The centres are also support facilities for the Hilti sales organisation as a whole. They are demonstration centres where Hilti customers can go with their salesman to see products or new technologies demonstrated. There is a wide selection of brochures and general information readily available.

The whole set of Hilti services are adapted to meet the needs of different categories of Hilti customers. Hilti divides its customers into four categories. There are large clients responsible for the planning and implementation of large construction projects. There are medium-sized clients who are responsible for the organisation of small construction projects. There are construction planning engineers or urban planners, and there are small independent workers.

For the first three categories of clients, Hilti has a mobile salesforce which regularly visits clients on the job-site. Segmentation is done on the basis of industry, market and by size of the customer company.

The sales staff is specialised according to the type of clients and the size. For larger clients and for the planners, Hilti provides more extensive advisory and planning services to determine exactly what the requirements are likely to be for the entire projects.

For the smaller customers, the Hilti Centre is the focal point of contact. In Germany, for example, there are 130 Hilti centres selling Hilti products direct to the customer. The customer can see the products demonstrated and can order direct from the Hilti centre.

The company will soon be moving towards the 'segment-of-one' approach. The ultimate in customised servicing, the new approach will make the salesman on the frontline into a 'Hilti general manager', i.e. responsible for the identification and complete satisfaction of his customer's expectations. He will perform the market research, not by customer group, but on an individual customer basis. He will then use the results to develop an individualised service package to match the customer's full expectations.

Service strengths

Service represents a vital part of what Hilti provides to its customers. Its importance in the total product/service package is considered to be over 80 per cent. 'It's a key success factor.' Hilti is particularly strong in two areas: advice and response.

Appropriate advice depends upon having a good knowledge of one's customer. Most of the Hilti subsidiaries, like the one we looked at in Germany, uses a comprehensive value-added information system which serves as an information and steering instrument for sales. The system stores extensive information on the customer. It records what size of client he is, his industry, the frequency of his purchases, the average quality of purchases and what he purchased.

It shows where he is located – to distinguish between city and countryside customers, the salesman responsible for handling the relationship, the number of times he's used the company's repair services, personal details on the relationship and the different products he buys from competitors.

The salesforce is currently being equipped with lap-top portable computers which permit Hilti to update the information on a permanent basis. The information is available to everybody in the firm permitting salesmen to prepare themselves adequately before going to see customers. On the spot, Hilti employees already have a good idea of what the customers' needs might be.

The close and long-lasting nature of Hilti's contacts with customers have encouraged the company to go beyond the provision of just advice of which product is the best adapted to the customer's situation. For some customers, Hilti uses its own CAD (computer aided design) capacities to plot in more exacting terms the requirements for a certain construction project. Specifically, they determine exactly which pipes, fittings, outlays etc. have to be fitted where and in what quantity and at what price for the entire construction project, based on the construction plans provided by the customer. This service replaces some of the work normally done by the construction engineer and, because the exact prices are also supplied, gives a valuable support to the engineer, allowing him to concentrate on the core issues of his work.

'Advice between Hilti and its customers doesn't just go one way. Hilti provides advice, but it also receives it, particularly for use in product development or service enhancement. Hilti regularly unites its customers in customer panels or lead-user groups (see Chapter 6 for further details) to obtain their opinion on what should be improved. Every three years, face-to-face interviews are conducted. This kind of contact enhances the relationship which Hilti has with its customers and creates a stronger basis for a working partnership.

The second area where Hilti's service is outstandingly strong is in their ability to respond quickly when the customer 'calls'. One way in which the customer 'calls' is when he orders his Hilti products. Because of the nature of the product, most are not stocked on site in the Hilti centre and are not available directly from the salesman. Orders are generally made through the salesman, at the Hilti centre or by phone to the company's service ordering number.

The priority at Hilti is turning that order around as fast as possible. At best, that can be done within 6 hours; the more normal delay is 12 or 24 hours, with 48-hour service being provided for special products or for cases where the customer isn't in a hurry. To make sure they are meeting those delivery delays, Hilti has made the delays into service standards which are measured and monitored at the warehouse on an ongoing basis. The last measurement in Germany showed that they were meeting that standard to the 99th percentile; the tolerance limit had been set at the 97th percentile.

The same system applies when it comes to repairs. The priority is on speed. A customer's tool coming into a Hilti repair plant for an urgent repair leaves the plant the same day. A fast repair leaves three days after it came in. Only in very special cases does the customer receive his tool back from repair in more than four days.

Good and fast response to customers also happens when there are complaints. Hilti wants most complaints handled on the spot. Each salesman has a personal complaint budget which depends on the number and type of machines he has sold. He has full discretion on the use of his budget – if he goes over the budget, he has to pay the difference from his own pocket. With this system, salesmen do their best for the customer and are ready to respond fast if they've made a mistake.

Hilti doesn't just have top service, they also have top quality machines, which they back up with excellent guarantee. Hilti now provides 12, 24 or 36 months of guarantee, leaving the choice to the customer; competitors do not like this, but have not come up with any counter strategy yet.

Hilti's excellent service has not gone unnoticed. In Germany, for example, the customer loyalty rate is over 95 per cent. Of the 240,000 potential customers which are known to Hilti Germany, the company has sold to 180,000 of them in the last 36 months.

Implementation

Hilti places great importance upon its corporate vision and philosophy. They are designed to be important elements of motivation for employees, combined with a strong programme of personal and professional development.

The Hilti vision, published in a separate document, can be summarised in four main points:

we create more value;
we want to be the market leader;
we have successful employees;
we live leadership.

The four items set forth the company's approach to the customer – we create more value – its approach to the market as a whole (including the principal ways of achieving that, i.e. focus on defined segments, maintaining strong bonds with customers, in sum, a complete customer package) – we want to be the market leader – the company's human resources philosophy – we have successful employees, and its management philosophy – we live leadership.

The last item is particularly interesting, because the company has adopted as one of its primary objectives a positive attitude towards change. 'To live leadership means to see change as an opportunity. It means acceptance of common values and goals, personal commitment and teamwork. To live leadership means to have an attitude of openness, creativity, fairness and willingness to strive for continual improvement. It means having a high degree of responsibility for shaping the future.'

In the company's 1991 anniversary issue one finds 'Change, dynamics, flexibility and adaptability while retaining stability – entrepreneurially, all this must become a unit. To pave the way, Hilti developed a strategic plan, a corporate vision and a mission statement. As a result, our employees have a long-term basis for action and communication.'

While there is only one Hilti vision, in some cases individual countries have developed their own mission statements. Hilti Germany developed such a statement and then developed statements of objectives for each department which represent their primary contribution to achieving the overall objective. One of the Hilti Germany mission statements is, 'Our performance in the market must distinguish itself by its high quality . . .' A statement for one of the departments – administration – building from this main objective is 'All payments or receipts of a given day must be processed and registered in the system the same day'. The department statements, then, provide concrete references for the achievement of more theoretical goals.

Total quality has long been a foundation of the company's philosophy. Presently there is an evolution taking place within the company which is changing the focus from 'total quality' to 'total customer satisfaction'. 'It is a move from a somewhat administrative quality management approach to a more active approach centred on the customer. The goal for everyone will be to satisfy every day, in every situation, within the framework of our mission statement, the expectations of external and internal customers to the fullest extent,' explains Mr Egbert Appel, President of Hilti Germany.

Together with this change, Hilti is initiating a change in their employees' training programme. Employees are being taught to focus more heavily on the customer and his needs. One statistical instrument that has been created to help them is a 'regional status' which uses an EDP spreadsheet to show the business situation in a given market to identify sales potentials and market trends.

One new training video begins with and is made up almost entirely of a discussion of the customer, his needs and how they can be met by highly personalised and specialised advice from Hilti's salesforce. It is only at the very end of the tape that some more technical issues of the sales are discussed.

Overall, Hilti has a very progressive personnel development approach. The basis is an MBO (management by objectives) system which sets forth objectives for each employee in terms of things like customer knowledge, regional market knowledge and personal skills. One of the new brochures for the sales personnel deals almost uniquely with personal skills and encourages employees 'to be open to the necessary change processes', and to 'take measures based on your own initiative'. Last and perhaps most important, they encourage employees to 'look at the positive side of things, every day'. Hilti has consistently tried to institutionalise its service quality concept. The company as a whole and most of its subsidiaries have been certified with the Swiss SQS quality standard (based on the international ISO-9000-900Y norms). Thus, not only the production facilities, but also the administrative sectors and the marketing and sales organisation have been centrified – which makes Hilti one of the rare companies in the world to be fully centrified. Today, Hilti strives to go even beyond the SQS norms in its internal quality standards.

What can be learned

1 Sell employees on the concept of change

Hilti has deliberately decided to embrace continual change as a welcome influence on its business. It has then sold that idea to employees. Since change is today such an important factor in business, this strategy is a good one. It permits employees to be ready for changes in the structure or in the market when they come and encourages them to be instigators of change by bringing new and different ideas to management attention.

2 Train your frontline staff to be market researchers

In going more towards a total customer satisfaction approach, Hilti is training staff to be able to identify and adapt to different customer needs and expectations. This goes beyond what any market researcher could do face to face on an individual basis. In addition to providing good customer service, salesmen will also be able to communicate more useful information up the line to management to be integrated into overall product and service improvements.

3 Leave complaints in your salesmen's hands – with a strict central controlling system

Hilti's policy of giving salesmen a proscribed budget for handling complaints is yet another way of making them more sensitive to customer service expectations. One too many complaints hits them where its hurts – in their pocket – and makes them think twice about what they are saying and doing for customers. On the other hand, Hilti installed a very strict centrally-controlled quality monitoring process, with a definition of quality targets in the employees' individual objectives – with direct consequences on their individual remuneration.

HIPPOPOTAMUS

Who can resist a plump, little, smiling hippopotamus! Apparently not many in Paris, Toulouse, Nice and Saint-Etienne. The friendly little hippo is the mascot of a very successful chain of restaurants called Hippopotamus. There are 16 Hippopotamus restaurants in France, 13 in Paris and 1 each in the three smaller French cities. At Hippo (its nickname), the customer is well received, well served, well fed and sure to come back again.

History

The Hippo story begins in 1965 with a young medical student on holiday in the very trendy city of San Francisco. In the process of exploring the city's many ups and downs, he falls upon an 'in' restaurant called Hippopotamus. They serve delicious beef hamburgers in a friendly and animated setting.

The medical student, Christian Guignard, returned to Paris where, three years later with the help of his father, he establishes a new restaurant in avenue Franklin Roosevelt, called Hippopotamus. Hamburgers are not the thing to offer the Parisian restaurant goer in the year 1968. So, after a bit of exploration, Mr Guignard Jr hits upon an alternative formula, that of a grilled meat limited variety menu ('the meat eaters' sanctuary'), destined to be even more successful than the American restaurant of the same name.

With the enthusiasm and natural leadership talent of its owner, the F Roosevelt restaurant flourished. More restaurants are established. By 1975, Mr Guignard had 11 restaurants located throughout the city and was reporting a turnover of nearly FFr10,000,000 per year.

By 1985, revenues had grown to FFr400 million. The exponential growth, however, was beginning to create some problems for the company. Managerial resources were stretched very thin and the large increases in staff had led to a loss of focus for the group. 'The culture of Hippopotamus had always been very oriented towards a high quality of personal contact. We were a very social group of people; it was informal and our success was in the service we gave customers,' explains Mr Guignard 'From 1982 to 1985, we went from 300 to 1000 employees. We needed to recentre the group around the original values.'

In 1987, Hippopotamus launched a service quality programme. The objectives of the programme were to reindoctrinate the company with the basic tenets of the original Hippo service culture, to establish a structure whereby the company's culture and philosophy could be rapidly taught to all new employees, and to create a system by which the service quality delivered by each restaurant could be monitored on an ongoing basis.

On a whole the programme was very successful. Employee motivation was boosted by the programme, customer satisfaction (which was now being monitored) rose by 10 points in one year, and revenues per restaurant rose by 5 per cent. Today, the company's revenues with 16 Hippo restaurants and 3 sandwich shops known as 'Hippolisson' stands at FFr450 million. The company serves 3,986,000 meals per year as opposed to 1,395,000 in 1980 and employs 1300 people versus 367 in 1980.

Service strategy

Since 1986, Hippo has conducted extensive reseach on its customers and their service expectations. Sixty per cent of their customers are men; they come in groups of two or three; over 75 per cent are under 40. They come to Hippo to relax and for the pleasure of a meal out – 64 per cent, or they come to eat quickly and well – 28 per cent in the evening, 45 per cent at lunchtime. Others come for a business lunch or to celebrate.

Overall, the ambience in the restaurant has a big impact on their satisfaction. They appreciate the quality of the welcome they are given and the grilled steak formula. As a measure of how much they appreciate it, 15 per cent eat at Hippo's at least once a week and 31 per cent eat at Hippo's once a month. Overall, Hippo has a customer loyalty rate of 89 per cent. The remaining 11 per cent are new customers that may or may not come back.

Hippo's service strategy is based on attention to three aspects of the company's service: the Hippo product, the Hippo atmosphere; and the Hippo welcome and goodbye. Together, they make a package which strongly differentiates the restaurant from its competitors.

The Hippo product is a limited menu formula based around grilled meat of very high quality and its accompaniments. There are 12 different cuts of either beef or lamb generally served with a sauce and French fries. A choice of appetiser is available and a dessert which, together with the meat plate, are available for one set price. Because of heavy advertising, customers who eat at Hippo generally come knowing that it is a limited menu formula.

The Hippo atmosphere is a second part of the strategy. Hippo colours are red and black, designed to communicate a lively, modern atmosphere. To add chic, there are lithographs on the walls and heavy carpets on the floor. Mirrors, plants (up to 500 per restaurant), and natural brick and stones complete the decor.

Because its clients change from lunchtime to the evening, the atmosphere also changes. The lighting is carefully adjusted. During the day it's fresh and clean, like sunshine; in the evening it's soft and focused to add warmth. The hostesses are more outgoing – more 'ambassadors' – in the evening.

In the evening there are also white linen tablecloths, candles on every table, the wine bottles on silver trays, and the hostesses in black gloves and short fru-fru skirts. For the daytime, it's cotton checked cloths, the wine in a carafe, and hostesses in tailored red suits.

Hippo plans to go even further – the hostesses will become 'actresses' and the restaurant a 'theatre' for the evening. Entertainment, animation and elegance will become the focus. 'In the beginning Hippo was all fantasy; today, we are looking to bring some of that spontaneous, creative atmosphere back in a new form,' says Mr Guignard.

The third part of Hippo's strategy is the 'Hello, Goodbye and See You Soon'. While Hippo believes that every moment of contact with the customer is important, the welcome and the goodbye have a special role. The 'Hello' sets the atmosphere for the customer. If he's received well, he's off to a good start.

The 'Goodbye and See You Soon' are also important; at that moment, the hostess will know if the client enjoyed himself and, if he didn't, do something about it even if it's only to apologise. 'We want to show our customers that we care whether they enjoyed their visit.'

At Hippo, extra effort is taken to make sure that the 'Hello, Goodbye and See You Soon' are perfect. The company even advertises on the basis of the quality of its greeting. 'Grumble, if you didn't get your smile at the entrance' is the theme of one of the company's advertisements.

To reinforce its image with the public, Hippo is a big advertiser. Making the maximum use of its adorable little mascot, the hippopotamus, Hippo publicises the high quality service it offers, the Hippo product formula and the Hippo atmosphere. The 1990/1 advertisement campaign was seen all over Paris; in addition to the statement above, there were others like, 'Complain if you didn't get a chocolate with your coffee', or 'Scream if there were no French fries with your steak'.

Service strengths

Serving customers well at Hippopotamus is part of the culture. 'I believe that my mission is to be a service provider,' states Mr Guignard. Hippo's four million customers a year have this impression the moment they walk in the door. A hostess is there to greet them and to find a place for them in Hippo's busy restaurant. That is all she does and she goes out of her way to do it well.

There is always the 'Hello' and the smile. Hostesses are trained from day one, before they ever appear on the floor of the restaurant, that a smile is part of the Hippo style. 'And right away, a smile' (Hippo introductory brochure). In total, hostesses have four modules which teach them why smiling is important and what to do after you greet customers with a smile.

The next step is to guide customers to the bar and to ask them kindly, ever so politely, to please wait until a place is found. The barman offers no less of a friendly welcome than the hostess. Little snacks arranged on the bar and the invitation to have a drink while you wait are his preoccupation. He also has been trained to treat customers 'extra special'. The 'customer orientation' module and the 'company introduction' module were both part of his initiation course.

The hostess then leads the customer to a table; after being comfortably installed, he is presented to the table hostess (not waitress). She is the 'home entertainer'; the restaurant is her own home and the customers are her personal guests. Her role is to guide them through their dinner experience, making it as pleasant as can be. That also is taught at the beginning – the module on 'advising customers' trains waitresses how to advise customers on what to order, how to respond to customer questions and requests for recommendations. It also helps them know when to interrupt a customer's conversation and when not to, how to deliver the cheque (with the coffee at lunchtime or after the coffee in the evening) and how to show the customer his way out.

According to policy, their dress must be impeccable, their make-up appropriate and their attitude always discreet, but friendly. Hostesses are carefully chosen by Hippo. They are hired for their personality, their team spirit and their enthusiasm for being in a service industry. 'It's a pleasure for me to hire people who enjoy providing good service. They have to have a certain natural generosity,' explains Mr Guignard.

Getting good service at Hippo isn't just a matter of being well received by the staff; it's also a matter of policy. Hippo offers it's customers a guarantee – its called the Hippo Truth and is the promise to tell a client the exact amount of time it will take before he is seated. If it's longer, Hippo pays for the dinner.

Hippo also stands behind the quality of what is in the dish. If a customer's steak is cold, it's taken back, not to be reheated, but to be exchanged. Likewise, if the steak is too fatty or over-cooked, it's exchanged. It's policy at Hippo that customers must be satisfied with the quality of the product provided. In some cases, that means that the customer doesn't pay.

Good service at Hippo also means providing the thoughtful extras – a rose for all the women on Mother's Day, the lily-of-the-valley on the first day of May and the Beaujolais nouveau. To liven the atmosphere, there are sometimes celebrations around a theme – Black Angus Beef, the Challenge Coca Cola, the Special Hagen Daas ice cream.

If ever a customer complains, Hippo does back somersaults to regain his confidence. 'Somebody who writes to us to complain likes Hippo. If we regain these people's confidence, they can be our best ambassadors in the future,' says Mr Wojciechowski, Director of Operations.

A complaining customer receives a kind letter from the manager of the restaurant or Mr Guignard himself, along with an invitation to dine again at Hippo. In addition, complaining customers are invited once a year to have a cocktail with the managing directors of the company.

In the end, it's everyone who benefits: customers give the directors feedback on how to improve their service and customers are thanked for having complained. Customers feel really great when their suggestions are sometimes put into action.

Implementation

'The restaurant manager is a key person,' explains Mr Wojciechowski. He is the principal motivator for the restaurant team and aims to create a team spirit within the restaurant. Hippo is very careful about the people they recruit for these positions. 'We recruit personalities – people with a strong character who can also manage people,' says Dominique Gallo, Director of Human Resources.

All candidates go through at least three interviews. In addition, they spend one day in a restaurant 'in action'. During the day, their behaviour with the staff, with the customers and their general attitude is observed very closely by the restaurant manager and by the director of operations. Out of 300 candidates, Hippo hires only four.

The initial training period lasts two months. In addition to passing all of the standard modules of training which his staff go through, he spends time circulating throughout the various departments and posts within the restaurant to gain first-hand experience on how things operate. Mr Guignard makes a point of dining personally with all new recruits within the first week or 10 days. The recruit then takes up his functions as an assistant restaurant manager. No new recruit is ever put directly in the post of restaurant manager without having at least four months' on the job experience in a Hippo restaurant.

Training doesn't stop once the manager is integrated fully into his post. Within the first year with the company, a manager receives additional training on topics like social legislation and on how to manage his team. Ongoing training is available and is chosen by the manager himself with consideration to the areas where he feels he needs the greatest improvement.

A great deal of the success of Hippo in service quality is attributed to the team spirit which the company fosters within each restaurant. 'We try to create a team spirit.' The restaurant manager guides the team, but the team spirit is further enhanced by certain work practices of the company. The first is perhaps the policy of encouraging employees to take on multiple tasks within the restaurant; they train themselves not only to perform their assigned post, but also to be able to take on other tasks. The policy particularly applies to the kitchen staff where washers are also potato peelers and eventually grill operators, as they increase their skills.

The team spirit is also encouraged by emphasis on qualitative rather than quantitative evaluations of progress. 'We talk about how things are progressing and how things are being done, rather than asking about how much the restaurant turned over in sales last month,' says Mr Wojciechowski.

When customer complaints come in, they are read to all the restaurant staff. Rather than trying to lay blame, the team tries to find solutions and ways to prevent the situation in the future. One tool that has assisted Hippo in this are the error chasing groups which are used to analyse the causes of service errors and to propose solutions. Participation in the groups is open to all staff; the groups are run by individuals from the Hippo School who are trained in the error chasing techniques.

A major contribution to improving service quality at Hippo merits an award. The Quality Cup award is handed out on a yearly basis. In each restaurant an employee is chosen by his team for having contributed the most to offering good service quality to customers. The winners enjoy a super dinner with Mr Guignard – at Maxim's, for example.

The advancement of service quality at Hippo has also been aided by the use of a customer satisfaction survey, done on a yearly basis per restaurant, and by the establishment of the Hippo School. The customer satisfaction survey has permitted management to monitor progress in service quality to customers when it occurs and to identify weaknesses where they exist. 'The customer satisfaction barometer is a good management tool for us,' says Mr Wojciechowski.

The Hippo School was established at the same time that the service quality programme was introduced. At that time, the school focused on training all staff to be more orientated. The School now has a larger role; in addition to training staff in service quality, it also offers training in general management and in skills improvement in key areas such as how to perform employee evaluations and how to recruit. 'Up to now, the Hippo School has been under-utilised. Now, we are trying to encourage staff and managers to use this valuable resource more heavily,' says Dominique Gallo.

What can be learned

1 Don't count on corporate culture to ensure service quality everywhere and all the time

While corporate culture has a powerful impact on employee behaviour, it changes over time and can be lost or transformed. Hippopotamus in 1986 was a company that was in the process of losing some of the key elements of its culture. By introducing the service quality programme, Mr Guignard brought back some of the original elements, particularly those relating to service, and created the Hippo School, which introduced a way to have the culture transmitted to all new employees.

2 Create and use ambience

Part of the Hippo strategy is the creation of an ambience in its restaurants. In addition to providing greater stimulation to its customers' evening, Hippo's ambiance also creates the possibility for employee role-playing. Employees step out of their everyday existence and adopt roles which have been created for them – the table hostess becomes a woman entertaining in her own home, the bar hostess becomes the ambassador of charm etc.

3 Make complainers your best ambassadors

Hippo handles its complaining customers with care. In addition to receiving the most polite and prompt response possible to their complaint, they are also invited to a yearly cocktail to meet the management board of Hippo. The company knows that a complaining customer is one that likes the restaurant, otherwise he wouldn't bother to complain, he would just go somewhere else. A complaining customer whose complaint has been well responded to will not only come back, he will also become a service quality ambassador for the company.

HOFFMANN LA ROCHE

As one of the leading companies in the pharmaceuticals and health care industry, Hoffmann La Roche is a company that is concerned about the impact of its products on its customer. For many years it has been recognised for its innovations, and its strengths in research and development. These strengths have been translated into products which have met and surpassed customers' expectations, a corresponding strength in the market and an orientation toward customers as people.

'Roche is also very much a people and service-oriented company. Key elements built into its business approach include service to customers, respect for the individual, motivating leadership, obligation to shareholders and employees, obligation to society and openness to change.'

Background

The company was founded in 1896 in Basel, Switzerland by Fritz Hoffmann, a pioneer in the manufacture of high-quality medicines, and his wife Adele La Roche.

Today the company has four main divisions of activity: Fragrances and Flavors, Pharmaceuticals, Vitamins and Fine Chemicals and the Diagnostics Division. Together, the three later divisions cover the entire spectrum of health concerns from prevention through to diagnosis and therapy.

Hoffmann La Roche is a world-recognised firm and has operations in over one hundred countries. It employs 55,000 people in those different locations. From the consumers' perspective, Roche is probably best known for its work in psychotropic drugs, or drugs which are used to control the central nervous system. The most famous of these is Valium, which was introduced in 1963.

The company was restructured in 1986 and this was accompanied by a change in strategic objectives and orientation. In the late 1980s, Roche management felt that to achieve those objectives the company needed to reorient in order to be closer to the customer. 'The customer focus was not sufficiently in the forefront. We needed to orient the company towards the outside, towards the market.'

With this goal in mind, the company introduced the Customer Focus Programme, based on the initiative of Mr Andres Levenberger, Vice Chairman of the Board and Deputy Chairman of the Executive Committee. This was to be a company-wide programme, overseen by the executive committee, but operationally managed by each division as it saw fit. The decision to launch the programme was taken officially in an Executive Committee meeting of the company in 1988.

Since that time, each division has addressed the programme from its own perspective. The division that has attached the greatest importance to the programme and that has gone the furthest with implementing measures designed to bring the company closer to the customer and improve service quality, is the Diagnostics Division (known as 'Roche Diagnostic Systems').

'The Diagnostics Division was in a critical phase of its development. It was not sufficiently focused on market needs and saw the programme as a way to change attitudes in the entire organisation.'

Roche is not only structured by division; it is also split up by country. The job of Roche headquarters in Basel is to act as a support unit to the country operations, which are the real centre of commercial activity in the company.

The Customer Focus programme was also intended to impact operations in the various countries. At the beginning, however, it was unclear what would be the best approach for achieving this. Again, managers were free to develop their own approach for achieving the overall aims set by the executive committee.

Service strategy

For the most part, the basic strategies of the divisions changed little. In the Diagnostics Division however, the possibility of focusing on the customer and on the company's service to the customer gave it the means to develop a supplementary element of difference *vis-à-vis* its competitors.

Roche Diagnostics Systems produces diagnostic instruments for blood and other forms of analysis, using various chemicals sold in the form of kits. From a customer's perspective, he buys the diagnostic instrument perhaps once every five to ten years and the diagnostics kits to use with it on a very regular basis.

Roche's competitors are strong companies, as well-placed and well-respected in the market as Roche. They include Abbott, Kodak, Bochringer Mannheim among others. The primary bases upon which competition is waged at present includes price and marketing. Abbott, for example, is known as an aggressive marketer and is gaining business on the basis of its somewhat forward approach.

Roche's strength as compared with its competitors has historically been the quality of the advice and support it provides its customers. It is particularly respected for its technological knowledge and the quality of its informational documents. These advantages had never before been emphasised or given the value that they deserved from the customers' perspective.

The first step in the Customer Focus programme for Roche was to study customer service expectations in many of its major markets. It was at this point that the company identified the value of its strengths in the customers' eyes, and the areas in which their strengths were lacking.

Service in the form of clear and full information on technologies, product and support in the form of good demonstrations, good after sales assistance and delivery service became a focus of the company's new service approach. In addition, the decision was taken to emphasise service more than had previously been the case.

Service strengths

The service issue quickly became the service that was being provided by the headquarters in Basel to the country subsidiaries. 'There was an awareness of the shortcomings of the service provided by headquarters to the subsidiaries.' The company decided to adopt as an objective the dramatic improvement of the quality of service provided by headquarters to the subsidiaries, thereby permitting them to offer a maximum level of service to their customers.

Within the Diagnostics Division, then, this has perhaps been the greatest work in the Customer Focus programme. A recent customer satisfaction survey of the quality of service provided by headquarters to the subsidiaries has shown that there have been substantial improvements in the service since the programme was initiated.

One of the first areas attacked was how the subsidiaries were perceived by headquarters staff. 'For the first time, we started to call the subsidiaries customers'. Certain departments were renamed in order to relate them directly to their function for the subsidiary.

Another area that was tackled was telephone skills and the handling of enquiries coming over the telephone. Through the programme the staff recognised how disagreeable it might be to have to call back three or four times because a person wasn't at their desk and the person who answered didn't offer to take a message.

In the end, 80 commitments were defined, which represented what the headquarters should be delivering to its customers – the subsidiaries. A concise and summarised version of these commitments was written in the form of a promise.

The Customer Focus Programme was not confined to the headquarters however. As indicated above, it was Roche's Executive Committee's wish that the programme touch every part of the company. It was felt, however, that a blanket improvement effort would be too unwieldy and have little real impact. A model for improving the customer focus at the subsidiary level first had to be developed.

Roche's Spanish operation was chosen to be a pilot operation, in which a full programme would be implemented and the results measured. The major focus of the programme has been in the communication of customer focus philosphy, in order to change attitudes and influence behaviour. Dr Klaus Ringer, head of Roche's Spanish subsidiary, says 'People are tremendously more interested in the customer and in the service we provide customers. It has represented an attitude change more than anything else.'

In addition to the communication effort, a quality coordinator was named. It is his job to ensure that the customer focus programme continues to be a major focus in the company. It is also his responsibility to ensure that the new standards of customer service that have been developed in working groups are being implemented. 'People really started to get motivated when they could work on the standards. . . . Since the initiation of the programme, our management decisions have changed somewhat; we have started investing more in marketing. For example, in the Pharmaceuticals Division, we set up a programme to establish better links to decision-makers.'

In the Vitamins Division, 'research into customers' service expectations permitted us to prioritise our work on those areas which were most important to our customers: technical assistance, and logistics.' The division has also now set standards which permit the company to fix definite objectives in terms of delivery times to customers – 24 hours for Madrid, 48 hours in other major cities and 72 hours elsewhere in the country.

'We have always supported the idea that if we had a better customer orientation, we could have a competitive edge.'

Implementation

At the corporate wide level, the Executive Committee established a Steering Com-mitttee, whose job it was to oversee the developments in the Customer Focus programme for the whole group. In addition there is an Executive Task Force, which meets regularly every two to three months and reviews the process made by the division, dealing with specific issues that have been raised and which implicate the group. It was also the group managers' responsibility to pilot the corporate wide communications programme that was part of the Customer Focus Programme.

'It has been a programme for greater customer visibility' and consisted of putting regular articles and reports in the company's internal communication publications. In addition, the activities of the divisions are reported in a special meeting, which managers of the group attend. The communication programme also ensures that the customer is a dominant theme in all of the company's communications for internal or external use.

Within the Diagnostics Division a number of things were done before the pro-gramme was launched and more afterwards. The Customer Focus programme began with a thorough analysis of customers' service expectations in every major company in which the company operates in Europe. The results led the company to adopt the service strategy described above and also highlighted areas where the service had to be improved. In addition to the studies done with the external customers, the subsidiaries' customer expectations were also examined and from there the promise and the 80 commitments of head office to the subsidiaries were devised.

The official launch of the customer focus programme gathered together all employees from the division at headquarters, as well as visitors from the subsidiaries, at a major event held in an auditorium. (see Chapter 3).

The next step was to put the programme into action and to make changes in the behaviour of people at headquarters that would lead to them providing a better service to the subsidiaries. Quality Animators were trained by specialists from outside the company in the leading of Quality groups. These groups had cross-functional representation and were the first attempt by the company to mix individuals from different departments to discuss issues common to all of them.

Twenty-five groups were originally started, which meant that out of 500 individuals in the headquarters staff in Roche's Diagnostics Division, 120 were directly involved in these error-chasing groups. The company uses as a guideline the commitments that had been developed for the division; when a commitment is not being met the group tries to identify the reasons and propose a solution.

The first important solutions proposed by the groups only began to be implemented one year after the groups had been formed. They were presented to the Roche Diagnostics Division board and then implemented. For less complex decisions, solutions were implemented immediately. For example, one problem that the subsidiaries were having was in sending faxes to the logistics department in the headquarters. The solution was to establish a separate fax machine that was to receive only; the solution was immediately implemented.

Another area which the company has been addressing is the assessment of managers. Roche's quality committee would like to have managers evaluated according to their progress in ensuring better service quality to the subsidiaries either by tying it to the satisfaction survey (which is now regularly done with the subsidiaries) or to substantial measures taken to improve service. At present, the managers are being given positive points for notable improvements, but are not yet being penalised for a lack of progress.

The most recent developments at Roche Diagnostic Systems show an increasingly focused approach to service quality improvement. On the one hand, the responsibility for improving affiliates and customers' satisfaction is gradually shifting from interdepartmental quality groups to the line managers, with budgeted service quality objectives on an annual basis.

On the other hand, improvement efforts focus on a smaller number of key commitments, defined yearly from the results of the service satisfaction surveys.

What can be learned

1 Survey internal customers as if they were external

The customer satisfaction survey that is carried out by Roche Diagnostic Systems headquarters of the subsidiaries' satisfaction with the service is a powerful tool for convincing employees that improvements need to be made. When improvements actually occur, it is also a very powerful and necessary tool for convincing management of the value of the investment that has to be made in improving internal service quality.

2 Don't expect progress overnight

Concrete results from Roche's customer focus programme only started to be felt two years after the programme had actually been launched. That is quite normal. It takes some time before people can adjust themselves to new ways of working and become proficient enough for their efforts to have a visible effect on their customers. In the meantime, the momentum has to be kept going.

3 Attack improvements from many angles

Roche's Diagnostics Division was probably the most successful in implementing the Customer Focus Programme because they tried to generate improvement in many areas at once. A single-sided approach to improvements that should rightfully impact the entire company cannot generate the necessary force of change to bring about an overall improvement in service quality.

HOTEL VIER JAHRESZEITEN

Member of 'The leading Hotels of the World', Hotel Vier Jahreszeiten (Four Seasons), ranked consistently at number one in Europe for the last five years. It is truly service quality at its best.

Perhaps it's because human beings so greatly appreciate a good meal, a warm bed and a large dose of pampering that perfection in the hotel industry has attained such heights. At Vier Jahreszeiten, no crease is left unpressed, no 'if you please' is left unsaid, no detail, however small, is unattended to in the hotel's supreme effort to satisfy every need of their client at every minute of the day or night.

Background

The Hotel Vier Jahreszeiten is located in Hamburg, overlooking the beautiful Binnen-Alster which is located in one of the oldest and most beautiful parts of the city. The hotel itself, built at the end of the last century, is a perfect example of one of northern Europe's 'grand hotels' which filled the scenery for much of the period leading up to the First World War.

Any damage which this building has ever suffered has been erased and completely forgotten. Its present state is one of complete perfection with every conceivable amenity in perfect working order and every decoration in optimal condition. The present and past owners have not hesitated to decorate the premises with the same kind of decor which its clients are undoubtably accustomed to: authentic antiques including furniture and paintings adorn the walls, furnish the halls, the restaurants and the bedrooms. Original Gobelin tapestries hang on the walls and original Meissen porcelain is on display for all to admire and appreciate.

Today, this lovely structure, its interior and its business belong to the Japanese Aoki group, who are likewise owners of the Westin and Caesar Park and Camino Real quality hotels. The Aoki group purchased the hotel in 1989 from the Haerklin family, the hotel's original founders and historical owners. Since the purchase, Aoki have made no changes, either to the management or to policies of the hotel. 'Aoki plans to carry forward the traditions and the high quality of this house. One of its principal aims in purchasing this hotel will be to use the management know-how of the hotel to further expand its group of luxury hotels.'

Service strategy

The aim of Vier Jahreszeiten's strategy is to make it the best hotel in the world and to keep it in that position. Thanks to a good service strategy and excellent implementation, the hotel is not very far from achieving its aim.

Hotel Vier Jahreszeiten is targeting the business traveller. Presently 70 per cent of all customers fall into this category. Another 15 per cent are weekend tourists and a final 15 per cent are weekday tourists. Most business visitors stay for no more than one or two nights – the statistical average for all guests is 1.7 nights.

Fifty-five per cent of all the hotel's guests are from Germany. Another 12 per cent come from the US and a second 12 per cent from the Scandinavian countries. The dominant languages heard in the hotel are, thus, German and English.

The hotel's service strategy is to provide a completely individualised service to its primarily German business executive cutomer. A very high percentage of the hotel's guests are regular customers. Their individual wishes and preferences become known to the hotel and are automatically integrated into the service provided to that customer by the hotel. The hotel's objective is to know as rapidly as possible what each customer's service preferences are because the guest stays such a short time in the hotel.

In addition, the hotel has created special services designed to meet the particular needs of the businessperson. The business centre, which provides communications and secretarial assistance is a good example; the fitness centre is another.

Equipped with the most modern of telecommunications technology, a fax, a telex and secretarial services, the business centre provides practically everything a travelling executive needs to carry out his business transactions while travelling. There are staff on hand practically 24 hours to assist him in carrying out his task at hand, rapidly and with no problems.

Service strengths

A customer that doesn't experience notably excellent service during his stay at Vier Jahreszeiten has made a mistake and checked in at the wrong hotel. Hotel Vier Jahreszeiten wants all its customers to go away feeling that they have experienced truly the best in personalised, luxury service, regardless of whether they stay one hour or one month.

One way they do this is by being sensitive to the different countries from which their customers come. All the staff have been briefed on the different service requirement which customers coming from different cultures or religions are likely to have.

Whether due to their culture, their religion or just their character, customers' preferences are of extreme interest to the staff at Vier Jahreszeiten; one could say, moreover, that as with elephants – once learned, it's never forgotten. The hotel staff note down nearly all of their customers' service preferences and whether that customer comes back next month or next year, the hotel staff can still remember and deliver service which matches the customers' tastes in every respect.

'White roses in the room for Mrs Benedict.' 'Mr Meyer must have a horsehair pillow and can't stand soft mattresses.' Keeping details like this in mind is not just thanks to a good memory. The hotel's memory is actually a sophisticated information technology support tool which files information on over 35,000 customers.

The emphasis is on recording personal data – like Mrs Benedict's white roses – so that the hotel can provide the individualised service it promises to customers. It also logs the dates and lengths of the customer's last 10 visits, including the rooms they stayed in and the special comments they made about the service. Before a guest arrives at the hotel, the staff refer to the data system to make sure that everything has been prepared in accordance to his fondest desires. 'In our house every guest is a VIP.'

As many guests will be happy to learn, access to the database is reserved – their preferences are considered top secret information. It's not used for advertising or mailing by the hotel either. No information is ever given to the press unless the customer wishes it to be, so there is no danger of a customer finding personal details or a photo of himself and another business celebrity in the evening paper.

The hotel itself is a celebrity of sorts. Vier Jahreszeiten is a member of the 'Leading Hotels in the World Group'. To guests this means that the hotel has met in full the high standards applied by that group. Beyond its excellent reputation as a hotel, Vier Jahreszeiten is also recognised as a trend-setter in its restaurant and reception service.

When it comes actually to experiencing good service, if nothing else numbers make a difference. At Vier Jahreszeiten, there are at least 2 employees for every customer; the hotel has only 171 rooms for 400 employees. That's two people in any one given moment who are doing practically nothing else but trying to make a guest's stay more enjoyable.

To help those two employees along in their efforts, management has established very strict standards about what all customers should be receiving. They are very specific and very detailed, and have been developed to correspond to the time of day, the event, the number of guests, the season and, of course, the traditions of the hotel. Banquets, for example, are not handled in the same way as receptions or restaurant service – the table setting is different, the flowers are different, the decor is different and the formality or informality of the serving staff is also different.

One standard that never varies is the goodbye. It's a policy of the hotel that on his or her departure every guest should be individually approached, thanked for his visit and asked if he or she enjoyed it to the fullest degree possible. 'It's a way we show we care.'

If ever a customer expresses dissatisfaction, either during his visit or at the end, he receives the most considerate and rapid of responses to his problem. All complaints, regardless of their gravity, are reported immediately to the marketing director, whose job it is to offer an apology immediately in person or by phone (if the person has left) and provide whatever compensation may be required. When the situation calls for it, apology letters are sent, sometimes by the individuals who made the mistake and/or by the hotel director. The customer can always be sure to receive a response dated within 24 hours.

Probably the thing that many guests like best about Vier Jahreszeiten is that they've never heard the words 'No, we can't do it' without first hearing 'I'll see what I can do'. That is not by chance, but by design. 'There is no "No" to a guest's wishes in this hotel. Every employee is expected to do all he can to fulfil the guest's wishes.' If that means personally delivering a package to its destination across the city or waking up the local Italian pizza parlour's Italian chef at 3 a.m. in the morning so that the customer in Room 329 can have a truly Italian pizza, then so be it!

Implementation

'Service in the luxury segment is nothing else but a sum of carefully thought through details. Only highly motivated employees will take care of those details.'

Mr Gert Prantner, Managing Director and CEO of the Hotel Vier Jahreszeiten, is a firm believer in the importance of people in the service process. He believes that all employees deserve the highest respect and the best treatment possible if they are to be motivated in their work.

As a reflection of this belief, Vier Jahreszeiten is a good place to work. Compared to most of their competitors, the hotel offers good salaries, top social benefits and job security. It does not lay staff off in recessions as is the practice in other establishments, nor are any employees dismissed without a full investigation by Mr Prantner himself. Vier Jahreszeiten was the first hotel to offer employees a five-day week, a practice which was later imitated by all of the top hotels.

The management believes in frequent, open communications. And since 'there are no more or less actions in the hotel. A hotel is like a clock, in which all the wheels are equally important,' all of the hotel's employees are kept equally informed. 'For me, it's just as important that the people on the frontline are informed about what's happening as the managers in the back office.'

For many employees, particularly the younger staff, the most motivating factor is the learning experience. Being in an establishment like Vier Jahreszeiten permits them to learn the business from the best source possible. The hotel management enhances the experience by integrating new staff in a very systematic and professional manner.

Day one for a new employee begins with a comprehensive explanation of the house, the management structure, the basic procedures and so forth. The personnel director personally takes each employee in charge; 'What the reception is for the guests in the hotel, the personnel department is for employees and with the same level of attention.' The personnel director's responsibility for employees doesn't stop at the hotel property borders; he also assists employees from out of town to find housing and to get settled in the new city.

During the complete induction period, which lasts three to four weeks, the employee makes the tour of all of the 'back office' functions in the house – housekeeping, the kitchen, etc. 'He is getting to know the hotel from the inside out and learns some basic skills before he is put in contact with the customer.'

Training doesn't stop at the end of the induction period. The hotel runs training and experience building seminars on an ongoing basis. There are two to three internal seminars per month on special service themes: how to answer the telephone, how to be a bar tender, how to wait on receptions etc. While experience is not mandatory, the seminars are extremely popular.

The goal of these training sessions is to give employees an opening to obtaining the broadest experience possible, both within Vier Jahreszeiten and later with other employers. The hotel management goes so far as to arrange apprenticeships for employees in other hotels. It also assists them in their career planning and development. In this way, the hotel establishes long-term relationships with quality people in the industry and sometimes recruits them back after they have gained experience with other companies.

One of the reasons Vier Jahreszeiten feels comfortable pursuing this type of personnel policy is that it is confident that the people it recruits in the first place are of top quality. The main criterion in recruitment is the candidate's attitude towards customers and his or her ability to communicate with others. For non-customer contact staff, the hotel looks for creativity and the ability to manage complexity. The level of education also plays a role in more senior positions. While the hotel has no formal test it uses for employees, management's extensive experience in recruiting permits it to judge candidates with great accuracy in the space of several one-hour discussions.

What can be learned

1 Create data bases that record more than just statistics

Vier Jahreszeiten's database is the key tool for assuring top-quality service. It records more than just names, dates and country of origin; it records the really important things in service – the details. Details like the fact that Mrs Armitage likes rooms with a view and that Mr Blum likes a chocolate with his coffee – even at 8 a.m. The details may not mean very much to someone else, but to the customer, they could be very important – vital even to his or her satisfaction.

2 Never say 'No'

It's a good service rule to keep in mind. Vier Jahreszeiten's staff never says 'No' without first saying 'I'll see what we can do'. Guests don't want to hear a 'No' or a 'We don't do that here', before the question is hardly out of their mouths. By definition service means at least trying to give the customer what would make him happy.

IDEAL JOB

The quality of the service Ideal Job provides to customer is a direct reflection of the spirit and philosophy of the company – and that is a very good one. Ideal Job believes in the importance of the individual to the success of any company and the need to provide the proper environment in which the individual can develop to his or her greatest potential. 'We want to make it possible for the greatest number of our collaborators to feel that they have made a contribution to the company,' says Mr Philippe Grunder.

For customers, that translates into a strong customer service orientation. 'We bend over backwards for our clients,' says Mr Grunder. 'It is the spirit for service that pushes us each day to surpass ourselves, to not give up in face of difficulties, to overcome challenges which appear hopeless' (page 1, Company Brochure).

Background

Ideal Job is a temporary employment agency and a provider of services for the identification and placement of permanent staff. The company was created in 1965 when it was originally known as Suppléance Service SA. The name was changed to the more charismatic 'Ideal Job' in 1974.

In 1980, there was a change in management which brought Mr Grunder to the position of CEO of the group. The Société de Banques Suisses, a former partner, passed their ownership of the company to the Société Fiduciare Suisse, which became the sole owner.

Also during this crucial period, Ideal Job adopted the little green cricket as its mascot and emblem. The personable, dynamic little figure has done a great deal to solidify the company's image on the market. It brought rapid name recognition and has proved to be more or less the embodiment of the spirit and philosophy of the company.

The impact of a solidification of management into the hands of Mr Grunder and the introduction of the green cricket created a great deal of dynamism within the group which permitted it to accelerate its growth. In the early 1980s, it was ranked perhaps 10th or 15th in the Swiss market for temporary agencies; today it is number 3 after Manpower and Adia. 'By 1981, we knew who we were; we knew that we wanted to become an important group.'

In the year of its 25th anniversary, 1990, the group had 28 agencies throughout Switzerland and roughly 12 per cent of the market for temporary employment. Over 5000 clients had worked with Ideal Job during the preceding year and nearly 9000 temporary collaborators. Growth in the group's revenues was 30 per cent over the previous year. Over the previous four years, Ideal Job had grown at between two and three times the rate of the industry as a whole.

Service strategy

The business of temporary employment management is somewhat unique in that there there are two groups of customers to serve: temporary workers and the companies wanting to hire temporary workers. In order to be successful overall, a company must be successful at appealing to both groups of customers.

There are different strategies for doing this. Most companies place greater importance on serving the client companies, believing that the availability of good jobs will in itself draw good candidates. Ideal Job has chosen to favour neither one group of customers nor the other, in every aspect it attempts simultaneously to meet the expectations of candidates and clients alike.

The principal way in which this is accomplished is by following the philosophy of 'the right man for the right job'. This implies that Ideal Job is not in the business of *finding* temporary workers for companies, but in the business of *matching* human skills and personality to a specified need. 'Our job is to find the best adapted solution to a problem facing someone else (client or candidate), says Mr Philippe Meylan, director for the regions of Vaud et Fribourg.

People are not just assigned to a particular job because they happen to be available; Ideal Job attempts to identify the person best adapted for the job, both in terms of their personal characteristics and experience. The client benefits because he or she has an employee who is best equipped to do a good job; the candidate is pleased because he or she will have the opportunity to use his or her skills to best advantage.

Ideal Job does not believe in being a broker of human flesh; there should be a mutual desire by the individual and by the temporary employer to work together. Acceptance by both parties is an important part of the arrangements organised by Ideal Job.

A temporary worker is not an unemployed person trying to fill in the gaps, but is someone who, for personal or professional reasons, has chosen to work through a temporary agency. He or she is therefore, a potential long-term collaborator and a human resource which can be developed during his or her passage at Ideal Job.

Finally, clients are not capitalists looking to exploit human labour on a short-term basis, but rather companies who have a well-defined need for a very precise skill which is not available in their own firm. The contribution the temporary worker makes to the company is often a very valuable one.

Ideal Job's philosophy and service strategy are embodied in the little green cricket which is used in communications with the public and in its publicity. He is 'dynamic, fresh, young, healthy, funny, lively and open', says Mr Grunder. In the field, recognition with the public and word of mouth communications are important factors contributing to the success of a group. 'We live on our notoriety', explains Mr Grunder.

As a whole, Ideal Job's service strategy is particularly well adapted to the Swiss market which has, in contrast to many European markets, a shortage of skilled and unskilled labour. In some fields, the unemployment rate is actually negative – meaning that there is more demand for employees than there is skilled manpower available. Many individuals working for temporary employment agencies are not between jobs, but rather job testing before they commit themselves to a particular company or career specialisation.

Companies who bring in temporary staff often do so because they were not able to find the appropriate labour skills for a permanent position available on the open job market. Ideal Job's approach which emphasises respect, equality and flexibility in its relationship with candidates and clients is more attractive to many Swiss workers and companies than the comparable approaches of the competition which has the reputation of being more aggressive and profit oriented than Ideal Job.

To adapt its service approach to meet the wide variety of demands of its clients and candidates even better, Ideal Job has created a set of employment 'formulae'. 'Your Needs are Varied; Our Services are Many', says the heading in the company brochure. The formulae offered span the horizon from the most transitory and temporary of engagements to a more permanent relationship between the candidate and the hiring company.

The first option is the classical temporary employment arrangement – short-term positions with a variety of companies needing assistance – with an added advantage: Ideal Job guarantees to replace the person if he or she is found to be unsuitable within the first four hours on the job.

The next options is the 'try and hire' formula. After a candidate has worked for three months under the temporary employment arrangement, he or she can be employed at full time by the company with which he or she has been put in contact by Ideal Job. Ideal Job charges neither the candidate nor the client a fee for the transfer.

The last option is the placement of a individual with a client looking to fill a permanent position. For clients needing permanent staff, Ideal Job will attempt to find the appropriate personnel, either with its own group of candidates who are willing to take on a permanent position or from the market place through advertisements and announcements. The fees for the service are paid by the employer who engaged Ideal Job to perform the research for them. However, Ideal Job also guarantees this service; if the employee leaves his or her new job within the first two months, Ideal Job reimburses its client for 50 per cent of the 'finder's fee'.

Service strengths

Ideal Job's approach to its field represents a philosophy of human resources management in temporary employment which, because of inherent respect for the individual, is very service oriented. The fact is not lost upon Mr Grunder, who has, in addition, chosen to emphasise the pursuit of service quality within the company. With candidates and clients alike, 'Ideal Job has a strong spirit of service, at the service of others.'

For Mr Grunder and Ideal Job, service quality means 'to accept that one has a responsibility to satisfy others' and to 'manage to achieve things daily in the best team spirit'. Specifically, service quality at Ideal Job means maintaining impeccable records on candidates and clients, performing in-depth and useful interviews, knowing candidates and clients well, and respecting a consistent approach to their work. The list is very precise because it is set forth in internal training documents.

A great deal of what Ideal Job does well in service is contained in the relationships it develops with candidates and clients alike. 'The difference between Ideal Job and other companies is in the quality of service we provide – it's in the way that we receive the people and in the way that we work with them,' says Philippe Meylan. 'We are honest in everything; we respect our candidates and our clients.'

With candidates, one of the first objectives of the company is to get to know their candidates very well. From the very first interview, an Ideal Job candidate has the undivided attention of the staff of the company. 'Availability; we commit ourselves to being open and approachable for our candidates. 'Each new candidate receives a welcome handbook which, among other things, says on the first page, '. . we attach enormous importance to personal contact. During your time with us, we welcome your comments about your jobs, your experiences, your projects for the future, your problems; the better we know you, the better we can work together.' On the same page, there is a space for the name of the person to contact at Ideal Job.

Candidates also have the possibility to develop their skills through their positions with Ideal Job. Because they have a say in which posts they are offered and in which posts they accept, candidates can choose their experience path through the company. The consultants at Ideal Job are there to help them do that. 'It's part of the company culture to discuss a great deal about the individuals we are placing into jobs and their needs.'

Clients are treated with the same degree of respect and consideration as candidates. Ideal Job is concerned about 'filling a client's need' and therefore does its best to understand the client's business and situation. One thing that helps is the internal specialisation which is done within the company which means that, whenever possible, a consultant who has already worked in a certain field will be handling the account of the client in that field. Another thing that helps is the emphasis placed on the client interview. 'The meeting with the client is always an important moment.'

Once acquired, knowledge about clients is kept. Each agency creates ring binders full of information on its relationships which are available to all the employees in the office. Every visit is recorded by the responsible consultant and a report is created. No client is a bad client; 'we don't have any disagreeable clients'. Nor are there 'less important clients'. In the philosophy of the company, clients are working partners; there is no favouritism and no chauvinism. 'A client is who we work with; they have expressed a need which we must do our very best to fulfil.'

Implementation

For many of its managers, Ideal Job's quality of service is a concrete demonstration of a strong coherence between the philosophy of the company and what it practises.

'The individual in this company is important; in our work we have another objective than earning money.' Service quality externally is made possible by the quality of service which is given to one another internally. The emphasis is on open communication, personal contacts, the respect of others, the development of the individual and the feeling of belonging. 'A person who feels good about himself and about his job will serve clients well. We do our best to bring about that state of well-being.'

The size of the office is an important factor; management has deliberately tried to keep offices down to a 'human size', i.e. around 15 persons per office, in order to promote interpersonal communications and a team spirit. Team spirit is also encouraged through external activities – parties, picnics etc. Mr Grunder also talks about 'creating hype' which he and his managers do by walking around and talking to the staff personally.

'No one has the monopoly on good ideas,' says Mr Grunder. His management is very participative; 'I don't get any real orders,' says Mr Meylan. 'We try to search together to find what would be the best for the company.' As such, there is a constant exchange of ideas. Each week in each one of the agencies, there is a meeting to review how the agency has progressed according to its forecast; there is an exchange about 'what worked well and what didn't'. There are also regular meetings between the agency managers and among the top management team members. 'We talk about the figures, the guidelines, but also about philosophy.'

'Soft' management tools like those above are balanced by some very important hard tools. 'Ideal Job is a company with professional rigour and flexibility.' Those tools include training, service standards and a remuneration system which involves the entire staff.

A new employee at Ideal Job goes through a series of basic training courses within his first three months with the company. The courses represent a combination of practical and philosophical education. The basic course presents the company, its human resources philosophy and the basic rules and regulations of the company; it lasts three days. There is also a sales course of two to three days designed to help the employee present the company in a consistent and positive manner to prospective candidates and clients. For those dealing frequently by telephone, there is a telephone course.

The greatest emphasis is placed on the support provided by the new employee's godfather, an experienced person within the company who takes the employee in hand and is prepared to respond to all his or her questions and to discuss the difficulties that the employee may be having. Godfathers or godmothers are expected to devote on an exclusive basis, up to half an hour per day to the new employee in which they go over together specific training issues.

The most important tool which the company has to manage service quality is what is called 'the Bible'. It is an enormous document given to each employee at the beginning of his or her employment with the company. There are two parts: the first part presents the company philosophy. The new employee is expected to read and go over it carefully with his or her godfather.

The second part is three-quarters empty when it is given to the employee. He or she is expected to complete it within the first three months with the company. Within this section there are a series of exercises representing the practical working knowledge of the company. The employee learns each one in stages, and after completion of his or her basic knowledge about the company's practices and service standards should be complete.

Once complete the document represents a reference book which can be used on a regular basis as a reminder or a support to the individual's memory and daily practising. Items can be added to the book concerning specific skills. For example, Ideal Job believes that it is important for employees to be consistent in their dialogue with clients about the company. To help support that coherence, Ideal Job created a guidebook which presents service standards relating to client relations, together with sets of sales arguments which can typically be used when speaking with a client. The guidebook is given to employees who have regular contact with clients.

Perhaps one of the most important motivation tools at Ideal Job is the re-muneration system. It is important not only because of what it can represent financially to the employee, but also because of its symbolic significance. The system, which rewards employees according to their results for the agency, encourages team work and the taking on of responsibility, both individually and as a group. 'Since we initiated this system, the interpersonal quarrels have been eliminated. We now pull together as a team.

Each agency has a budget which incorporates itemised forecasts for revenues and costs. If the budget is attained, employees and managers alike receive the equivalent of ¹⁄₁₄th annual salary in bonus at the end of the year. If the entire company attains its budget, 15th month's worth of salary is accorded; if, in addition, there has been more than a 5 per cent increase in profits, employees receive an additional 10 per cent increase in their bonus.

'Our employees are our greatest asset,' says Mr Grunder to explain his policies. As for his managers and staff, they are 'proud to work for an organisation which has understood that the human being is at the centre.'

What can be learned

1　Care for your company's inside

Ideal Job has worked hard on developing a good working environment for its employees. Mr Grunder believes that employees who are happy at their job will serve clients better.

He has largely been proved right. The positive attitude of employees is the main difference between Ideal Job and other temporary employment firms. Ideal Job has gained a good reputation with temporary workers; pleasant and cheerful employees also represents a plus for clients who work with Ideal Job.

2　Pamper your image

Ideal Job's success from 1981 onwards is partly attributed to the success of the little green cricket as a mascot in advertising. The cricket embodies the character of the company and communicates to potential collaborators and clients alike the spirit and philosophy of the company.

The cricket is particularly successful because it really does represent the company. If, on the other hand, a less well-adapted symbol has been chosen, it may not have had the same impact.

It is important, then, to chose the external signs of service quality with care. They should be a true reflection of the company's character and strengths, and symbolise the company's main differences from the competition – in the case of Ideal Job, the youth and dynamism of the group.

3 Be generous

There is nothing to be gained by paying employees badly. A badly-paid employee will work poorly and tell everyone how badly he is paid – making poor publicity for his manager and company.

Ideal Job offers the best opportunities to employees to earn good salaries. The remuneration programme motivates them to keep costs low and bring in the revenues. They are all personally motivated and implicated in the results because they are a small team – what one person does rightly or wrongly does have an effect on the results.

IKEA

'Anti-service' was the first thing we were told about the quality of service at IKEA. Service at IKEA stands for no service; that's part of the philosophy. Ingvar Kamprad, IKEA's founder, created an empire by eliminating the service aspect of the furniture business, yet today IKEA is commonly referred to as being a company with top quality service. To explain this apparent anomaly, we had better start at the beginning.

History

The beginning is in the 1940s in a bereft region in southern Sweden called Smaland. Ingvar Kamprad, the son of a farmer, began his illustrious career selling matches, box by box, to the local residents. To his matches business he added fish, then pens, then Christmas tree ornaments and finally furniture.

In 1951, he cut down on his rather time-consuming visits to the local residents by distributing a catalogue of his articles from which customers could order. He then sent the items off by mail to the customer.

The system worked very well for pens or tree ornaments, but much less well for furniture, which was difficult to package and expensive to send. The furniture often arrived broken. His solution was to send the furniture unassembled. Since, for the most part, the furniture was simple and, thus, easy to assemble, this approach was well received by customers, who greatly appreciated the additional cost savings thereby created.

Low cost had always been a major theme of Mr Kamprad. The people he sold to were for the most part farmers like his own family and they lived in the same impoverished region as he did. There was little room in their budgets for luxury items; when they did spend money, they counted every penny. These parsimonious people were his customers. IKEA's objective is:

'to offer a wide range of home furnishing items of good design and function at prices so low that the majority of people can afford to buy them' (IKEA mission statement).

Mr Kamprad was able to ensure low prices to his customers because of the system of catalogue sales and good working relations with his manufacturers. He had reduced his prices to such a low level that in 1952 when he exposed his furniture for the first time at a fair in Stockholm, the other furniture dealers tried to have him ejected from the fair. The contrast between their own prices and IKEA's was too marked.

These same competitors put pressure on IKEA's manufacturers to stop supplying to IKEA. The manufacturers responded by proposing that rather than purchasing the exact same model of furniture as the competitors, IKEA should design their own. No comparisons would then be possible between IKEA's furniture and that of their competitors. By designing his own furniture, Mr Kamprad could also be sure that the models were easy to make and easy to mount.

With the business so defined, IKEA expanded rapidly and passed from SKr1 million in revenues in 1952 to SKr17 million in just five years.

Meanwhile, customers were asking to see models of the merchandise shown in the catalogue. When IKEA opened its showroom in Stockholm, rather than set up in the middle of town where the leases were very expensive, Mr Kamprad built a large, round building just outside town. Rather than buy fancy display materials, he simply set the furniture out. And rather than collecting the furniture from the warehouse for his customers he simply let the customers into the warehouse to pick out the furniture themselves. The first 'self-service' furniture store was thus born.

Today, IKEA operates in 15 countries and has over 95 outlets. Its revenues are in excess of SKr19 billion; in just the last 10 years, revenues have multiplied fivefold. Thus far, IKEA is an astonishing success story.

Perhaps this story doesn't explain to you why IKEA is known for providing good service, . . . or does it. Kamprad took away services which raised the price of the goods and which added little value to the customer. A piece of furniture which arrived assembled, but broken, was not as good as one that arrived unassembled, but intact. A warehouse where furniture is neatly displayed and clearly labelled represents better service than a showroom with a pushy salesman who is frequently busy with other customers. According to the traditional standards of the industry, Kamprad provided fewer services, but from the customers' perspective, they added up to a lot more.

Service strategy

IKEA is a concept. It is the concept of replacing one type of service for another. Because the alternative service approach costs less than the traditional one, it gives customers the opportunity to reduce the purchase price.

IKEA strives to provide the IKEA concept well. To begin with, IKEA works hard to ensure that the service system which has been established functions smoothly. Finding the store, circulating in the store, paying for the merchandise and collecting the merchandise should all occur without hassles or strain on the part of the client.

In addition, IKEA tries to make 'a visit to IKEA pass in the best possible manner in the interest of our clients and ourselves' (*The IKEA Store, The Customer Services Guide*). Over the years, this has turned into a large value-added for the customer. Using this statement as a base, a number of services have been created within the store, designed to make the customer's visit more of an outing or a promenade than a shopping trip.

The concern for unnecessary expense, however, is always present. 'One can do great things with very little' (Ingvar Kamprad). Thus, good service should only be achieved using the most meagre means. The services which IKEA introduces seldom imply a large investment on the part of the company lest they increase costs and thereby the prices of the goods for sale. Perhaps the most costly service the company offers is a playroom for visiting children filled waist-high with little plastic balls in which the children can roll, jump and play without hurting themselves.

Any services created should also correspond to the company's philosophy 'to be at the service of the greatest number' (Ingvar Kamprad). There is no élitism here. IKEA creates services as well as furniture which everyone can use. There are no VIP stands or executive-type restaurants.

Within these parameters, IKEA has created a unique shopping experience. The large warehouse-type buildings are located outside major cities and are generally visible from the main roads. There are enormous parking areas surrounding the buildings. At the exterior of the building, there are sometimes stands selling hot dogs, sweets or flowers, operated by non-IKEA concessionaries. There is only one entrance. At the entrance, there is an information desk for those who have never been to IKEA before. Then, one enters the display area. Furniture is set up in little rooms which associate the whole variety of IKEA products; items which cannot be bought within the store are not exposed. From central desks nearby, the furniture is paid for and the customer receives an itemized receipt which authorises him to pick up the merchandise in the warehouse area.

One passes from the 'showroom' section into the free service section. The goods are no longer displayed in a room environment and can be taken off the shelf. These are generally the smaller items. From here, one passes into the 'self-service' or warehouse section. The goods here are presented in their packages on pallets; the customer can take what he needs. He passes to the check-out counter where he pays for the items he took in the free service and warehouse section. He then leaves the store.

Service strengths

IKEA has an impressive 70–80 per cent loyalty rate. Specifically, that means that out of 10 people entering an IKEA store, 7 or 8 have visited the store within the last year. Customers appreciate the service at IKEA for two reasons: first, because IKEA makes the system easy for customers to understand and use, and secondly, because IKEA has added small, but important services which make an IKEA visit more fun.

As regarding ease of use and understanding, IKEA is guided by the philosophy of simplicity. The IKEA concept is simple and straightforward and it is a stated objective of the company to keep it that way (see *Testament of a Furniture Dealer*). IKEA's approach is to explain the concept to the customers and then to have additional information ready at any time when the customer might have questions.

At IKEA, the customer has access to all the information he needs, not only on the products, but also on the store and the methods of purchase. The guiding principle in terms of information is that 'the merchandise must be presented in a way so that the customer can make the purchase decision himself' (*The IKEA Store*). This is applied in the very broadest sense.

The process of informing the customer starts before he or she enters the store. Signs at the exit of the motorway show one where the store is located. An enormous billboard upon entering the parking area welcomes the visitor to IKEA and gives the opening hours of the store. The parking areas are well marked so that one doesn't get lost, with the driving circuit indicated, the parking places labelled and the entrance and exit to the store clearly marked and visible from a distance.

At the entrance, IKEA has a minimum of seven large-sized posters on which it is clearly indicated how to use the IKEA store and what services are available to customers. For those who are still bewildered, IKEA has a staff member at the information desk ready to answer questions or hand out a small brochure 'IKEA Usage Instructions' (see below).

The catalogue is also available at the entrance. It is a very important communication tool for IKEA. Every item IKEA sells is listed in the catalogue, as well as its price, dimensions and colour or material. It serves as a reference tool for customers before and after their visit to IKEA, as well as during the visit. The order in which the items are presented in the catalogue is similar to the circuit which one follows within the store.

Within the store, information about the merchandise is provided on the ticket. A ticket appears on each item which rigorously indicates the material used, the country of origin, the other colours in which it is available, the dimensions and the price. It also indicates whether or not the item passed the Möbelfakta test, which is the Swedish product quality standards label.

Additional information is also presented in poster form concerning certain product ranges, e.g. mattresses or choose-your-own-fabric sofas. The circuit and the exit are marked throughout the store.

If the visitor still needs help, staff are available at the information desks, at the check-out counters and at the customer service counter. If he can't find them there, he can still easily recognise passing staff from their bright red uniforms with white trim.

The information system which IKEA has established ensures that the customer experiences an efficient and smoothly functioning visit. To make sure that it is also agreeable, IKEA has created a series of extra services.

One of these could be called extra functional services. IKEA has thought about everything that the visiting family might require during the visit and has supplied it. In an IKEA store one always finds toilets, a separate nursery room for washing and changing the baby, free lockers for storing items one doesn't want to carry around, a restaurant, huge sacks and large trolleys for merchandise, and pushchairs for babies who get tired of walking.

Another series of services help customers accomplish their principal task – choosing and purchasing furniture. Available at the information desk, as well as at various points within the store, are, for example, a metre measurement tool, and lined and measured paper for sketching. From IKEA one can also rent cars or vans to take the goods home in or have the goods delivered by an IKEA-approved transport company whose office is on-site.

Lastly, there are the little extras like the free coffee in the early morning, free Swedish ginger biscuits on holidays or the wrapping table at Christmas with free paper and string, which add something more than just functionality or practicality to IKEA's service offering

The result is that customers feel that IKEA provides better service in providing less.

Implementation

Implementing service quality at IKEA means implementing the IKEA concept, precisely and free of errors.

The store must be laid out in exactly the same fashion, regardless of where it is located in the world. It must have the same basic set of services and must be managed so that all of the standards are observed to perfection. For example, if customers are informed at the beginning of the visit that all furniture has tags on it, then all furniture must have tags. If tags are left off, even occasionally, the customer will lose confidence in that aspect of the IKEA system. Instead of looking for the tag, the customer will go to the salesperson every time he has a question. If even $\frac{1}{10}$ of IKEA's customers do that, then the sales staff will be completely swamped.

One way IKEA makes sure that the implementation of the IKEA concept is rigidly followed is with the creation of the 'IKEA Store' book. This is an enormous manual which provides the user with practically every detail about what is needed to mount and run an IKEA store. In terms of an operating tool, it is the company's Bible. In it one can find standards for signage, the arrangement of furniture, the structure of the check-out desk, the number of employees needed to staff each station and guidelines for merchandise selection, depending on the size of the store.

The set-up of each new store is accomplished using this guide. From the time that construction of the site is completed to opening, takes only 13 weeks. A team of roughly 30, called the establishment group, works night and day.

The 'IKEA Store' book is not the only guide given to employees. There are also various policies. The quality policy, found in other publications, calls for 'just' quality in products, in the internal work relations and 'in our services to clients, before, during and after sale'. 'Just' quality is defined as 'at the lowest price possible, meeting the needs and expectations of the majority of people in ourselves, our products and our services at IKEA'.

Among other things, the quality policy specifies that client satisfaction should be regularly studied in a uniform fashion between stores and between different departments within the store, and that measurable quality objectives must be established and managed by each country unit for its store.

As an extension of the quality policy, IKEA is now creating a guidebook on service quality. One of the first versions is being actively used in France. The titles of the first eight chapters are reproduced below; the remaining four involve the layout of the store and its exterior.

1 The IKEA service: Philosophy.
2 Training clients.
3 Signage.
4 Relations.
5 Materials for the customer.
6 Animation.
7 Telephone.
8 Measuring service quality/the role of customer services.

Chapter 2, Training Clients, talks about reducing the customer's fear of purchase by informing him and by reassuring him with the company's return policy (30 days and a full money-back guarantee), the instructions for mounting furniture which come with all items and the quality seal.

Chapter 4 provides guidelines for customer relations; how a customer should be greeted, how his questions should be answered and gives standards for written communication with customers.

Chapter 7 does the same thing for the telephone.

Chapter 8 gives instructions on how to perform customer satisfaction surveys and monitor the length of the check-out queues, the percentage of merchandise out of stock (the standard requires no lower than 98 per cent) and other service quality indicators.

The rigidity with which the IKEA concept must be applied on the international level is balanced by a certain flexible attitude when it comes to managing other aspects of the business to national needs. In practice, as long as the international standards are perfectly observed, a manager of a country can introduce whatever new ideas or policies he sees fit. Each country also handles its own advertising within certain guidelines and its own purchasing.

This flexible approach cascades down and encourages initiative-taking on the part of all employees. New ideas are regularly proposed by staff and can be implemented on just a store-wide basis. If the idea is accepted by staff, it can be adopted by other stores or eventually by other countries. The exchange of ideas is assured through the rotation of personnel between different countries. The manager of France, with whom we met, spoke five languages and had worked in over seven countries.

Although we've implied it, IKEA is not just a concept which is reproduced using the *IKEA Store*, in the same way that one uses a biscuit cutter; it's also a very strong philosophy. The success of IKEA is not just the success of a clever marketing idea, but also the success of the transfer of a corporate culture across borders, to employees and customers alike.

Ingvar Kamprad created the philosophy which is best expressed in his own statement, *Testament of a Furniture Dealer* and is reproduced below. The phililosophy is taught to employees in an important, internal, week-long training programme, called 'The IKEA Way'. It is also reprinted and published in many forms and in many documents throughout the company, and serves as the reference, when none other is available, for decisions and policies taken within the company.

What can be learned

1 Keep it simple

Good service doesn't mean expensive service. If a service strategy is well thought out, it doesn't necessarily have to cost a lot of money which eventually ends up on the customer's bill. IKEA creates little services within the store that cost the customer very little and add a great deal to his shopping experience. A paper metre measure and little pencils provided with notepaper cost very little and are very useful.

2 Use information to seduce your customer

One of the best services IKEA offers is excellent information. Information on the products, information about how to buy, about how to go around the store, about the purchase conditions, all of this is widely available and clearly explained. The customer no longer has nagging doubts or insecurities about his purchase decision. Providing honest, complete information to customers is one of the best ways to increase customers' satisfaction with your product or service.

3 Make your customer's life easy

Providing customers with a take-away catalogue, having plenty of directional signs within the store, providing a changing room for babies, a restaurant, lockers, pushchairs and a play pen for children, all of this makes the customer's life much easier. Some merchants simply forget to put themselves in their customers' shoes; they forget what it is like to carry around a three-year old in your arms when you are shopping for furniture; they forget that theirs may be the 20th shop visited and not the first, and that as far as the customer is concerned, a chair in a quiet corner is more important than a fancy window display. IKEA didn't forget that and their customers are very grateful.

ISS

At ISS you're a person, a person with skills, responsibilities and a career. As a person – and not a dustman, an immigrant or an 'unskilled labourer' – you can feel good about treating others with the same respect which you are given within your own company.

ISS is a company that respects its employees and knows that the satisfaction and motivation of their employees is the ultimate key to their success. An employee who is motivated and has self-respect will treat customers better; he will communicate better with them and he will be proud of his company and what it does for the customer.

Background

ISS is a Danish company turned international. Although today 70–80 per cent of the company's revenues come from its professional cleaning and maintenance services, ISS began its existence as a company providing security services, an activity which remains part of the company's activities.

In 1901, there is the first mention the security company that became ISS. In 1918, this tiny entity merged with another company to become 'De Forenede Vagtselskaber A/S' or United Guard Company. In 1934, a subsidiary providing professional cleaning services was created. There were 43 employees, 1 manager and, most important, 2 customers!

The year represents the beginning of the company's existence as an international group with expansion into its first foreign market – Sweden. At that time the company employed 2000 people. Expansion continued in 1952, with the establishment of an activity in Norway. The West German operation was established in 1965, the Swiss operation two years later, and the UK and Belgian activities in 1968 by acquisition.

The group, as it was by this time no longer a small company but rather a group, adopted the name of ISS – International Service System A/S – in 1973. Thereafter, regardless of the domain of the activities, cleaning, security, catering or something else, the company was known under a single identity and name.

From that time up until the present, the company's history has been marked by an impressive expansion of its activities both by growth and by acquisition. The group now provides services in two well-defined areas: building maintenance, and building automation and service technology. Building maintenance and related services for the occupants of the buildings, which represents 94 per cent of the group's revenues of over DKr10 billion per year, includes professional cleaning services, security services, linen services, supply house services, canteen services, indoor-climate and other special services.

Building automation and service technology concerns the development, production and marketing of systems for the 'effective control of building installation and services'. These systems include energy control systems, heating account systems, security systems and integrated control systems.

The majority of the company's services are provided by so-called 'unskilled labour'. The company has 115,000 employees, of whom roughly 80 per cent would fall into this category.

ISS is well-established in 16 countries worldwide. Forty-two per cent of its revenues come from operations from the Scandinavian countries, 25 per cent from Europe excluding Scandinavia and 33 per cent from North and South America. Cleaning remains the core of its business and is something the company does in each one of the countries in which it has operations.

The four countries making up the Scandinavian Division of the company's activities have just been broken off to create a separate holding company, ISS Scandinavia A/S.

Service strategy

ISS is strongly positioned in the market for professional cleaning; it is the leader in most countries in which it operates. Its customers are either large corporations who own and manage their own premises, or building owners or managers who are responsible for the cleaning and maintenance of a large number of offices.

In the past, many offices preferred to hire and manage their own staff of cleaners and maintenance people. Increasingly, customers are willing to contract this kind of work to outside companies. A study done by ISS in late 1990 showed that customers were not only willing to contract out cleaning work, but also a large variety of other services which ISS is increasingly making available.

Its service strategy for success in all these businesses is the same. It is represented by the provision of a top-quality core service by a professional and customer-oriented staff. In terms of differentiation, it is the latter part of this equation that makes the difference. Most of ISS's competitors have little difficulty in providing reliable cleaning services; very few, however, have employees that are as well trained in customer service and as adept at handling relations with customers as is ISS. ISS employees are professionals – and not just professional cleaners.

Providing a high quality core service means making sure offices are cleaned correctly and on a regular basis. One aspect of that is machinery and equipment. Since 1963, ISS has had an independent company whose sole purpose is to supply machines and materials for the cleaning industries. As such, ISS employees work with some of the best and most well-adapted machines in the business.

A second aspect of providing a core business means making sure that employees know how to operate cleaning machinery and know how to clean when machinery is not being used. ISS has extensive training programmes, both at the time of hiring an employee and throughout his career.

Providing 'customer-oriented service by a professional staff' is the crucial element of ISS's strategy. ISS's staff are customer oriented in three ways. First, employees aren't just trained how to operate machines; they're also trained how to handle customers – their questions, their problems.

Secondly, ISS has uniform standards of visual identity, uniforms etc., which are designed to improve the employee's overall presentation and which must be adhered to by all staff.

Thirdly, employees are motivated to do well in their work; the company counts on that motivation showing through in their relations with customers.

Overall, ISS depends on the quality of its service in every sense. It must be good. 'We are a pure service company, service is not an add-on, services are our core product. The technology we use is located between the ears of 115,000 people'.

For many years, ISS's activities were centralised in primarily two sectors – cleaning and security – each of which was developed virtually independently of the other. This situation has now changed and is changing parts of the company's service strategy.

Increasing enthusiasm on the part of customers to contract various parts of building maintenance has allowed the company to take on a more holistic approach. Instead of marketing each of its services separately, under a different name and by a different channel, ISS is now developing a multi-service supplier, or a one-stop strategy.

This approach allows the company to sell all of its services simultaneously to one client, either as a package or individually. ISS will regroup some of its activities according to customer profiles or by sector, instead of by activity, in order to present a more attractive set of options to the customer.

For example, ISS has already gone ahead and created ISS Supermarket Service. It is an integrated service to supermarkets or department stores which provides cleaning services (through ISS Securisystem), linen services (through ISS Linen Service) and security services (through ISS Securitas) for these customers. Window-polishing services and abattoir services are also available, should the customer so desire.

The advantage of ISS's new strategy to the client is that he deals with only one company for all his needs as concerns building maintenance and building technologies – it's one-stop. In addition, because ISS will be regrouping its activities by customer profile or sector, the customer will eventually be offered a set of services completely adapted to his individual situation and needs.

The survey which the company conducted at the end of 1990 called 'Survey on Europe '92, Strategy for Support Services, Attitudes towards Multi-suppliers in the European Contract Service Market', confirmed the company's hypothesis that for the most part customers are ready and willing to accept a multi-service supplier. Full implementation of the new strategy has started in the Scandinavian countries. 'We're aiming for healthy, safe and intelligent buildings in Denmark' (*ISS News*, 1990).

Service strengths

What does an ISS customer receive? On what basis does he judge the company? There is no product to turn over and take apart. Service quality in this business boils down basically to one thing – customer satisfaction.

ISS sets standards of cleaning designed to reflect the level of cleanliness which makes customers satisfied. Employees use those standards to know exactly how much cleaning is really needed and where.

Standards are adjusted according to the country in which ISS operates. ISS has a highly decentralised management structure precisely in order for standards to be adjusted to meet the requirements of different cultures. 'Cultural differences play a large part in how we service the customer, therefore, we give the local operating companies the power to do the job in the best way possible.'

Experience has shown ISS that cleanliness is a relative thing, not only between different cultures, but also between different customers. Beyond a certain level of cleanliness, it's a question of opinion – the customer's opinion. ISS standards set a threshold minimum; any improvements on that are done on a customer-by-customer basis.

As such, standards are stated in terms of what the employee has to do and not what the customer will receive. 'All of the standards refer to the input standards not output standards, because you can't define what a clean carpet is. We are subject to the opinion of the client. It's his individual assessment that counts.'

ISS knows that it has very rarely lost a customer because of a lack of cleanliness. 'In most cases we have lost customers because of lack of "nurturing". For example, maybe they haven't seen the supervisor for a while.'

ISS is very good at 'nurturing'; the company doesn't lose customers very often. Its contract turnover rate varies from as low as 7–8 per cent to 15–17 per cent depending on the country. 'Nurturing' starts before the client even becomes a client. 'In every proposal, there is a part devoted to what the client can expect from ISS and from our employees.' It sets the limits and at the same time presents all of what ISS is prepared to do.

Once a contract is signed, 'nurturing' becomes primarily the job of the supervisor on each building, and secondarily, the job of each ISS employee working in the building. 'Nurturing' by the supervisor consists of keeping in touch with his customer. 'Supervisors meet with the client every couple of weeks. Through his interaction with the client, he can know whether or not he's satisfied.'

Adjusting cleaning and other service standards to the individual customer's expectations is part of the 'nurturing' process. The more time the supervisor spends with the customer, the more efficient he can be at correcting any laxity in the service or adjusting the service to his customer. It must be a continuous effort because small requests, like one to have a certain office cleaned once every two days rather than every day, can become a big headache if ISS isn't there to respond rapidly.

Keeping tabs on customer's expectations is also done through customer satisfaction survey. In most cases, the supervisor sits down with the customer and goes over every point one by one. The objective is less to obtain statistically valid results and much more to generate a dialogue between the supervisor and the customer on different aspects of the service. The frequency of the survey is a reflection of its objective: 'We send the client a satisfaction questionnaire once a month or once a quarter depending on the country.' In some countries, the return rate is 100 per cent because they are filled out with the help of the supervisor; in other countries like Holland and Belgium, the return rate is about 50 per cent.

Customers can count on seeing not only the supervisor, but a lot of other ISS managerial personnel. It's a practice in the company for all positions to involve a lot of field work. 'Most managerial positions involve a lot of on-site contact, though not necessarily cleaning work, so management stays close to the customer.'

On the whole it's relatively easy for managers to keep the customer's point of view in mind: two-thirds of middle management started as supervisors. Most middle and upper management personnel have taken on their positions only after a stay in cleaning. 'We have an internal recruitment rate of about 60–65 per cent. Part of anyone's introduction is to clean.'

Perhaps the most important players who have contact with the customer are the frontline work staff. It's these people which represent the company to the building tenants and to the customer every day of the week.

ISS's first priority is to make sure they look good. 'All employees are required to have a nice, clean uniform. Uniforms is one of the strictest policy. We start with personal appearance which is extremely important in daytime cleaning.' Last year in the US, ISS won a prize for the best-designed work clothes.

The cleaning materials that employees use are environmentally safe, and safe for the body. The equipment is designed so that the job is performed easily, so that the employees are not bending over all the time or put into awkward positions. 'All these small things add up. It's extremely meaningful.'

Beyond the external is the internal or the 'attitude'. ISS employees treat customers well. They have a positive attitude and are open to dialogue with the customer. It's the result of extensive training. 'Training is 50 per cent how to clean and 50 per cent how to act/how to handle people they might come across in the office environment.'

There is a worldwide minimum standard of training at ISS; beyond that there are variations between countries. In every country, however, at any level, customer care 'is a major part of the curriculum'.

Training includes, for example, how to deal with complaints. As a general policy, ISS wants customers to have their complaints addressed by the supervisors. Therefore, the company has a policy whereby frontline people should not respond directly to the complaint.

Rather than just have a rule which says that all complaints should be passed on to the supervisor, ISS employees are trained how to behave when there is a complaint. They are trained on what to say in the case of a complaint, they're trained on how to deal with an angry customer, how to diffuse his anger, if possible, and on the procedures for the delay and the way in which the complaints should be passed on to the supervisor. In this way, ISS guarantees good service to the person who complains and the right response to the customer who deserves attention at the highest level.

Customers working with ISS often receive an added benefit they might not have expected – the possibility to meet the same cleaning staff day after day. For those unfamiliar with the industry, this may not seem to be such a superb benefit; however, it should be kept in mind that staff turnover rates in this industry are often in excess of 150 per cent. It is not particularly pleasurable to see a new face cleaning one's office every three weeks, which is all too often the case.

ISS can quote to customers a relatively low employee turnover rate of 70–80 per cent per year. 'Sixty per cent of the work force has been with the company for 10 or more years; the other 40 per cent is turning over very rapidly – either by design, people wanting a new TV set etc., so they work for a couple of months and then are out again – or people don't like the work and find another job.'

The benefit for the customer is that he receives better service. The staff are better trained overall and more prepared for the job. 'When the turnover is extremely high, it puts a lot of pressure on the supervisor. It lowers the service quality and the time that can be spent on service quality by the supervisor. Obviously, our personnel policy is aimed at reducing the "non-designed" turnover.'

ISS offers a top-quality customer-oriented service and believes it is worth it. 'We are in the higher price bracket, but it is worth it; we promise good highly-motivated well-trained people who will stay on the job. We've just won the bid for the Sears Tower, in Chicago, USA, the largest building in the world – thanks to our staff.'

Implementation

ISS is a people-oriented company, by design and by need. Seventy-three per cent of the company's revenue goes towards salaries, wages and related items. 'That fact immediately put human resources in the forefront of our concerns. Obviously, people are our most important asset.' Employees are also the key to its service quality.

The company employs 115,000 people in 16 different countries throughout the world. They are widely dispersed over 12,000–14,000 different work sites. For the most part, they are unskilled labour. 'We work in the low end of the labour market. We employ people who speak other languages, immigrants or workers who are not necessarily well educated.'

ISS doesn't apply strict recruitment criteria. 'Skills are not important as regards the machines because we do all the operative training. We look at their personality. The only really meaningful criteria is attitude.'

What is important to the company is the treatment and nurturing employees receive once they are employed. The company's employee care policies are, for the most part, englobed in what the company calls its 'Partner Project'. The programme was introduced in 1986 on a worldwide basis. It has five main principles: co-determination and participation; organisational development; information and communication; training and education; and co-ownership. The last two are the most important aspects of the programme.

Training and education has always been a major focus within the company. For ISS, training represents the principal factor of job motivation within its employees. By working through the company's training and development programme, an employee can gain skills and status which are recognised within the company and on the open market. From a service quality perspective, ISS believes that 'If you don't train people, you don't deliver the product, it's as simple as that.'

ISS offers and requires extensive training both in the classroom and on the job. The greatest emphasis is placed on the induction course. 'Our induction is very formalised.' Every newly hired cleaner in Europe has two half-day sessions in which they are introduced to the company and its principles.

Within the first year, a new cleaner will have four days to three weeks of classroom training depending on the position. 'In many countries, we will send the employee to a special school where they get three weeks of commercial cleaning experience. Workers will also, of course, get a good deal of training on-site from the supervisor.'

In addition to the training given to first-level employees, there is a whole supervisor training programme. The programme is structured so that even the lowest levels of employee, who generally have no formal education, can move up to the supervisor level.

The most impressive results in terms of motivation from training have been obtained in areas which require specialisation. Services for hospitals or hotels require a particular approach; the company trains the staff which gives them a specific skill and know-how. 'The key is professionalising the job. It gives employees a sense, which is absolutely realistic, of some kind of professionalism to their work. Every time we have professionalised an area or when people are transferred to a specialised area like that, turnover rates and absenteeism rates go way down.'

The second, extremely important part of the Partner Project programme was the creation of the employee share plan. Since 1986, all employees at any level can purchase shares of the company. Shares are sold to employees for under the market value. Two years of steady service are required in order to buy shares in the company.

When the programme was first launched, it took a huge communication plan to explain 'shares' to the employees because many do not know what a company share is or how it works. In the end, 62 per cent of eligible employees decided to participate in the programme. Practically 100 per cent of middle and top management bought shares. Currently 8 per cent of the company's stock is owned by employees. 'The Partner Project gives people who are uneducated, and often immigrants, and who have not or cannot succeed through other channels, the opportunity to advance.'

The Partner Project with its training and share ownership plan does a great deal to motivate employees as a whole. Because the company considers that a good deal of its service quality lies in the hands of supervisors and middle managers, ISS also has incentive and bonus programmes.

In Scandinavia, the supervisor has a bonus which is linked to three things: the financial results of the contract with the customer; the turnover of the staff he manages; and the quality of service he provides to the customer. If any one of these three does not meet the standard established at the beginning of the year, the supervisor doesn't get the bonus.

In most countries a bonus, or other incentive, is linked directly to the score received on the monthly or quarterly satisfaction questionnaires. 'We do this because objectively defining objective quality is very difficult; what is important is what the client perceives. . . . It also makes a pretty nice incentive for operational management to take customer satisfaction seriously.'

What can be learned

1 Make your employees customer friendly

The example of ISS shows that it is possible to have an influence on employee's attitudes and behaviour *vis-à-vis* the customers. Thanks to an extensive programme of training, incentives and career planning, employees are motivated and are more customer friendly.

2 Use customer satisfaction surveys as a forum for individual feedback

Unlike most companies ISS doesn't use customer satisfaction surveys as a marketing research tool; it uses them as an opportunity to open up a dialogue with the customer about areas of improvement in the service offered to his company in particular. As ISS points out, 'Most clients are lost for a lack of communication.' This is just one more way of ensuring that the customer has his say.

3 Motivate all the way down the line

ISS offers shares to all employees – managers and cleaners alike. There is no élitism in this system; the lowest cleaner has as much right to own part of the company he works for as does the highest level manager. This is motivating for front-line employees. It's a way of giving them the self-respect that they would seldom get in other companies, given their work experience and their functions.

KUONI TRAVEL

The Kuoni name has stood for good quality in travel for nearly a century. It is recognised worldwide, active in two major areas of the travel industry – in package tours and in the retail travel industry. In both, Kuoni excels through innovation and an endless striving for perfection.

History

Alfred Kuoni's first step into the travel industry was the offer of a round trip tour from Zurich to the Dolder and back for SFr1 (about 20 kilometres). This was in 1906, a time in which the travel industry, as such, hardly existed. He set up his 'Travel Bureau' in the centre of Zurich, as a branch of his brothers' forwarding agency, in what is today a café.

Tourist travel was not a booming activity during the First World War, but took off in the 20 years to follow. The Travel Bureau Alfred Kuoni became the official Swiss general agency for sea passengers and emigration in 1921 and subsequently opened offices in major tourist spots in Switzerland, northern Italy and the French riviera.

Harry Huentobler joined Alfred Kuoni in 1914. In 1939 at the age of 65, Alfred Kuoni handed over management of the company to this former exchange clerk who had proved his devotion to the company and his flair for management. In 1945, Jack Bolli entered the company. He later became the company's most influential manager since Alfred Kuoni himself.

In the post-war period, tourism became a growth industry and Kuoni grew with it. Faithful to their traditions as a pioneer in overseas travel, Kuoni set a series of 'firsts' by offering charter flights to the Belgian Congo, Kenya and Bangkok. It began to be recognised as a first-class tour operator for long-distance travels to places such as Africa and Asia. In 1977, it offered a round-the-world charter flight with the first landing of such a plane in the newly opened China.

In 1980, with the opening of a branch in Sydney, Australia, Kuoni achieved its goal of being represented on all five continents. The group is today third only to Thomas Cook and American Express in terms of its international implantation.

Jack Bolli left the company in 1989, after 44 years with the company and 33 years as chief executive. He was succeeded by Peter Oes, a long time manager at Swissair and the innovator of the Swissair Customers' Service Concept.

Kuoni today is not a nostalgic organisation; it is oriented toward the future and talks little of the past. It operates in an increasingly competitive and cyclical industry. To go forward in its industry, Kuoni plans to continue developing new markets and creating new vacations. The essential, they say, is to put Kuoni's extensive experience at the service of its customers.

Service strategy

Kuoni has always put emphasis on the quality of the services it provides; its service strategy is a direct reflection of this fact. Kuoni's strategy is to offer a wide variety of high quality travel options and services to slightly upmarket segments. On a very systematic basis, Kuoni identifies target segments and then develops quality services to meet the needs of those segments. The strategy is valid both for its activities in the travel retail business and as a tour operator.

In retailing, Kuoni operates 133 travel agencies, 63 of which are in Switzerland. Out of these agencies, the group sells its own catalogue of tours as well as train, plane, car and hotel reservations or tickets, and a variety of tours packaged by other operators. Together with the sales of Kuoni tour packages through nearly 600 other Swiss travel agents, the Swiss market contributes just over 50 per cent of the group's sales.

For the retail activities, Kuoni has created a variety of services adapted to meet the needs of particular target groups. One way in which this is done is through the split between business clients and tourist or individual clients. Separate agencies are gradually being established to cater to business clients. The personnel manning these offices already have experience in dealing with that group of clients. Some agencies are located within a company and service only that company.

For the business traveller, Kuoni's services include assistance to companies in the development of 'incentive travel' packages for their employees and in the organisation of 'trade fair' travel plans connected with the large trade fairs occurring in Europe throughout the year. Kuoni has developed support tools for the business traveller such as, the *Kuoni Air-Guide* magazine, the customer card with its insurance and the hotel specials which give travellers discounts on certain hotels.

Kuoni has also created a set of services to attract young people. Helvetic Tours is a branch of Kuoni which offers mainly seaside holidays at short and medium-term destinations, primarily aimed at a young, active, somewhat price-conscious target group.

High quality in the retail business involves the presentation and the location of the agencies, the quality of the advice provided by the travel agents, the accuracy and speed with which a transaction can be accomplished and the quality of the contact, e.g. the personalisation of the service. Kuoni ensures all four, but is putting particular emphasis on the last of these.

During the past year, the company has had a programme promoting 'the personal touch'. The programme primarily impacts the way in which the customer is served. To make the most of the person-to-person contact, all sales agents are receiving training on how to treat customers as much as possible like separate individuals, and to respect their particular tastes and preferences. At the end of the training, an agent should be better equipped to consult clients on the best travel options available for their specific needs. This training is in addition to a whole series of required in-house courses on various aspects of customer service.

Kuoni service strategy is most strongly pronounced and most successful in the tour operator business. Kuoni has traditionally created innovation packages to meet the needs of particular client segments. Their packages are upmarket, but represent a good price/quality ratio.

Kuoni offers the greatest diversity in terms of activities and travel destinations of any of their Swiss competitors. River cruises, club holidays, sports holidays or adventure holidays are all created and packaged by Kuoni to meet the interests of different travellers. One of the newest developed is a trekking holiday in the Sahara.

Kuoni not only creates packages for segments of the population but also for national markets. Kuoni has packages of particular interest to Japanese travellers,

Australian travellers or American travellers. In addition to a standard range of products, Kuoni offers nostalgic trips by amphibian planes to Africa to the French, trips to Sri Lanka or holidays on the Nile to the British, and visits to Switzerland to the Japanese. In each case the tour is of high quality, both in terms of the accommodation and features of the package, and in terms of the reception and support provided by the tour guide team.

Service strengths

Kuoni agents are specialists in their business. For the most part, all Kuoni agents already have experience in the travel business before they join the company. Beyond that, Kuoni offers extensive ongoing training to ensure that travel agents are well briefed on new market developments and on new products.

As a result, a major strong point in Kuoni's service is the quality of the advice provided to travellers. It is not just that the agent can provide answers, but also the depth and detail of the response. A Kuoni customer doesn't have an agent in front of him, but a travel consultant.

Kuoni agents are particularly prepared to advise customers on the type and destination of their voyage. In many cases, the agent will have had first-hand experience in the country of destination. Kuoni's agents have, on average, more experience than most travel agents: Kuoni considers that it is an important part of an agent's training to travel widely. Educational tours are organised on a regular basis.

Often, the travel agent has the opportunity to 'test' a Kuoni travel package before it's put on the market. The agent travels with a Kuoni tour packager who consults with the agent to receive advice on how better to adapt the tour to the needs of their customers. Tours are systematically followed by briefing presentations by participating agents so that all agents benefit from the visit of just one.

Even when the agent doesn't have first-hand experience himself, the customer can have the majority of his questions answered. Kuoni provides extensive support documentation to its agents, including general information on the climate, the major attractions, and on the social and political conditions in a particular country, as well as more specific data on a particular tour. He can also be provided with answers to crucial questions like 'Is there sand on the beach?', 'In what kind of restaurants will we eat?' etc.

For some questions, the agent can refer to the central library at Kuoni in Zurich. Staff are available to provide information on countries, on accommodation or on foreign contacts in order to answer customer's specific questions or requests.

Once the customer has decided upon his destination, the Kuoni travel agent can facilitate booking. Thanks to ongoing developments in Kuoni's computer system, the traveller can immediately be given information on flight, hotel or package tour availabilities. Client files are also readily available for consultation with data on the client's travel plans and preferences.

While in the retail business, Kuoni has a direct link to the client through its agents, in the tour operator business, Kuoni is only a supplier to other agencies that sell its products. Its network of expert travel agents cannot be there to answer customer questions. To ensure that those answers are there when the customer asks them, Kuoni ensures that the catalogue and brochures that it produces on its vacations provide as much information as possible in a user-friendly fashion.

The tour packaging department at Kuoni puts enormous effort into the creation of

Kuoni travel brochures. The customer knows not only the good aspects of the journey, but also about the shortcomings. Kuoni makes a point of mentioning what some hotels don't provide and what certain destinations don't offer so that customers are neither surprised or disappointed when they arrive.

Outside agents also have access to some of the same sources of information as the internal agent. The Kuoni packaging department is staffed with product managers ready to respond to enquiries about the product or about the destination desired.

Implementation

All Kuoni tours represent a certain level of quality of service, both in the nature of the accommodation provided and in the assistance and care provided to travellers during their trip. The maintenance of that level of quality is the key to Kuoni's success. Quality is assured by the tour packaging department which actively controls quality both before, during and after the tour occurs.

It takes a year and a half, start to finish, for a tour to be created and launched. Kuoni product managers are constantly on the look-out for new ideas for voyages. Most ideas come from comments made by customers and transmitted into the organisation through the travel agents or through the customer surveys system done after each voyage. Ideas are tested in focus groups with clients, and again with the travel agent network.

Once a new idea has been identified and it is determined that it will meet the needs of a certain target group, Kuoni product specialists begin the process of packaging the voyage. They start by visiting the location. They discuss with the company's existing contacts on the spot, with the authorities and with new contacts able to meet the specific needs of the tour.

The product manager must follow certain guidelines. The hotels used should be 3 or 4-Star, the airlines must be Swiss, if possible. All of the service providers must be visited and tested prior to being put on a tour package. Kuoni uses checklists which help its product managers organise the information about each service provider and for each step of the tour. In this way, no details are left out.

Once the tour is launched, the key persons become the hostesses and the local manager. There are hostesses who travel with the group from destination to destination and there are also hostesses on location to assure the service in each country or city. The local manager must manage the entirety of the tour activities which occur in his region.

Kuoni hostesses are highly trained. On entering they receive a minimum of 12 days' of formal training. In addition, they receive training on the job and training for each tour package. They are trained to respond rapidly in the case of a problem and to ensure that customers go away satisfied. The resident manager is positioned to assist the hostess. Both the hostess and the manager have an allocation per person/per situation specifically set aside to resolve problems when they arise. Higher amounts are possible as there is no established limit.

Once a tour is over, Kuoni needs to know whether it was well-received and whether the service experienced matched their customers' expectations. Questionnaires are distributed to tour participants asking for their reaction. Because it is voluntary, the return rate is not enormous, but it is statistically valid and provides enough information from which to judge the general satisfaction with a tour. In addition, Kuoni's packaging department organises meetings twice a year with the sales staff to have their feedback from customers.

Quality control is also conducted on an internal basis. All hostesses complete reports at the end of each tour, commenting on problems encountered and on items particularly well appreciated. The reports can be quite detailed and list errors such as giving a customer a wrong room at a hotel.

What can be learned

1 The interest of specialisation

Kuoni is a good example of a company which has seldom deviated from doing what it does well. Kuoni is in the tour agency and tour operating business and by focusing on these businesses, it has the experience needed to bypass its competitors in the quality of its tours and services.

2 Quality assurance

Quality control is not something done just for factory produced products. The quality of services can be controlled and checked using a similar approach, but adapted methods. Not only can it be controlled, but it should be. Kuoni can assure customers about what will happen half-way across the world, because they have already tested it and checked it many times.

KWIK-FIT

The auto repair business is a nasty business. It was even nastier at the time that Kwik-Fit set up shop over 20 years ago. The industry was made up of small shops and car dealers and, as a whole, was known for shoddy workmanship, endless delays, bills which exceeded the estimation and a general disregard for cleanliness. To make matters worse, the problem was not always resolved the first time around and the customer was often back in the garage the following week.

The industry has since evolved, led by the example of Kwik-Fit that founded its success on top service quality and 100 per cent customer satisfaction. Tom Farmer, the founder, is obsessed with service quality, 'I started a number of businesses before this one. I quickly saw that it was easier to do just what the customer wants . . . the approach to the customer is important. More important than the product or the price. But in order to do this, we must have good quality people with good inter-personal skills'.

History

The history of Kwik-Fit begins with the history of Tom Farmer. Tom Farmer left school at the age of 14 to enter the tyre business. By the age of 24 he had his own store, the Tyre and Accessory Supplies in Edinburgh. By the age of 29, he had made his fortune, sold his business and retired to California. That lasted six months. Today, at the age of 51, Tom Farmer is still far from retiring and 'I am lucky to have a high level of energy and I just love to work' (Tom Nash, 'Fitting into a Niche Market', *Director Drive*, summer 1989).

In 1970, Tom Farmer returned to Scotland to create Kwik-Fit. Kwik-Fit was established in 1971 and is modelled after a company Tom Farmer saw in the US – Midas, the muffler repair specialist. Kwik-Fit provides rapid service for exhaust, tyre, shock absorber repairs, and oil and filter changes.

Growth was relatively slow over the first 10 years. In 1980, there were just over 50 outlets. In the last 10 years, however, the company has grown internally and by acquisition to over 600 outlets. Tom Farmer feels that key factors making the growth possible were the commitment of the Kwik-Fit people and the introduction of a computer management system. The growth is not expected to stop. They are targeting for 850 in the UK alone. In the Netherlands there are presently 122 centres and Tom believes there are opportunities in other European countries.

Service strategy

'Nobody *wants* to come to us. People can be suspicious of car repair companies. In our business customers make a "distress purchase". They don't plan for their car to break down and when it happens, it usually comes at the worst possible time,' says Tom Farmer.

As a result, 'customers want as little hassle as possible; they want to spend as little time as possible, they want their problem solved and they don't want to pay through the nose for it', says Peter Holmes, marketing director. Customers visit a repair shop, on average, only 1.1 times per year. A purchase decision is based primarily upon what minimal price differentials exist between competitors. There is little brand loyalty.

Kwik-Fit's strategy is to emphasise service quality. Why service quality? As Mr Farmer says, 'There's not much differentiation possible in this market. Can't do it on price or on products, so it's got to be on service quality and the most important factor is people'.

The Kwik-Fit concept is based upon customer self-diagnosis of his car problem. That is, 'The customer comes to Kwik-Fit already knowing that he has a problem with his tyres, his shock absorbers, his exhaust etc.', says Peter Holmes.

The principal aims of the company's marketing policy are to increase customer awareness of Kwik-Fit and 'to reassure customers about the reliability and quality of Kwik-Fit stations' (Peter Holmes). Its television advertising campaign has achieved UK-wide recognition. Kwik-Fit has achieved 72 per cent instant name awareness with the logo. 'You can't get better than a Kwik-Fit fitter.'

Service quality at Kwik-Fit is defined in the company's code of practice. It has committed itself to achieving 100 per cent customer satisfaction. The whole is backed up by the guarantee, '*We will move heaven and earth to put things right*', if something does go wrong and the statement '*I am your customer*', (Fig. 1). All its messages are posted, printed and published in every form possible – on the wall, in the welcome brochure, on the television and in internal and external newspapers.

Kwik-Fit is about to enhance its service quality approach. Rather than offering just 100 per cent customer satisfaction ('The customer should have that anyway today; he's more sophisticated, he expects even more', says Mr Farmer), Kwik-Fit is now going for 'Customer delight'. 'The tough part is that "delighted" is different for each customer. One wants to be offered a coffee. Another wants to be able to telephone.

I am your customer

I am your customer. Satisfy my wants – add personal attention and a friendly touch – and I will become a walking advertisement for your products and services. Ignore my wants, show carelessness, inattention and poor manners, and I will simply cease to exist – as far as you are concerned.

I am sophisticated. Much more so than I was a few years ago. My needs are more complex. I have grown accustomed to better things. I have money to spend. I am an egotist. I am sensitive; I am proud. My ego needs the nourishment of a friendly, personal greeting from you. It is important to me that you appreciate my business. After all, when I buy your products and services, my money is feeding you.

I am a perfectionist. I want the best I can get for the money I spend. When I criticise your products or service – and I will, to anyone who will listen, when I am dissatisfied – then take heed. The source of my discontent lies in something you or the products you sell have failed to do. Find that source and eliminate it or you will lose my business and that of my friends as well.

I am fickle. Other businessmen continually beckon to me with offers of "more" for my money. To keep my business, you must offer something better than they. I am your customer now, but you must prove to me again and again that I have made a wise choice in selecting you, your products and services above all others.

We're going to have to be able to identify what will make the customer delighted. We're integrating it into our training. Our staff will be trained to try to identify the one little thing that will make that customer delighted' (Tom Farmer).

To give an example of the care which Kwik-Fit takes to identify correctly the expectations of its customers, we can look at the fleet servicing business, an area the company has recently gone into. They began by studying customer expectations for the three separate types of customers in the business – the driver, the fleet manager and the fleet owner. (The fleet manager and owner are often the same, but in some cases they are different individuals.) Each of the three have separate expectations and separate needs which must be met. Kwik-Fit has developed services to meet the special needs of each.

In terms of expectations, the 'driver' customer is like the driver-owner with one exception. The 'driver' is less price-sensitive because he is not the one who's paying. His expectations are met through the standard guarantee of 100 per cent satisfaction.

The fleet controller, by contrast, is very cost oriented. He wants to approve any work done on the car personally. The service centre must telephone this individual and receive his 'OK' before any work is begun. All Kwik-Fit centres are equipped with a detailed guide providing the names and numbers of the persons to contact, their replacements and any special comments on which type of work can or can't be done by the centre.

Kwik-Fit personnel have also been trained to provide the fleet manager with just the right information over the phone so as not to lose time or have a bad analysis of the work to be done. If, for example, the tyres must be changed, the employee must measure the tread depth of each tyre and communicate this information over the phone to the fleet manager who decides which are to be changed and with what.

The fleet owner needs to be assured that the job has been done correctly. 'Over the long haul, it is the reliability of the work that most impresses the fleet owner,' says Peter Holmes. A system of quality control and quality checklists has been created to meet the expectations of this customer group.

Service strengths

Announcing high and low that service quality is your aim and that you guarantee 100 per cent customer satisfaction leaves a company open to a lot of attacks if customer service isn't just what it's promised to be. Kwik-Fit has made a science out of satisfying its customers' expectations. Kwik-Fit fitters (repairmen) are renowned for their friendliness and willingness to help. Kwik-Fit publishes a weekly internal newspaper in which complimentary letters from customers appear in every issue. To take an example,

Just a quick note to thank you for your excellent service at Southend. The exhaust was changed on my wife's car a week ago. It was a most professional service with helpful and courteous people.

The oil was changed on my car today. Very friendly people and keen to give customer satisfaction.

The price is right, but more important is the way your people dealt with me as a customer. This is the first time I have used Kwik-Fit, but it definitely will not be the last.

K.A. Andrews
Westcliff-on-Sea

and another,

I am writing to you regarding the service I received at the Dalkeith branch of Kwik-Fit. I used the centre following a report from a local garage regarding a variety of work needing attention. I asked for new wheel bearings to be fitted thinking that it did not need to be inspected first. However, upon going to collect my car from Kwik-Fit, I was informed that no new wheel bearings were needed. Obviously annoyed by my own garage, I was greatly impressed by the honesty of your staff and appreciate that I could have been charged for work that was unnecessary.

On all my visits to Kwik-Fit, I have been treated with courtesy and have been given sound advice on all aspects of car maintenance and repair, over and above their otherwise good service.

I am grateful for the excellent service I have received, especially in view of the fact that I have a very old car in constant need of attention.

Hazel Smalley
Dalkeith

Every company receives complimentary letters from time to time; at Kwik-Fit, they get 40 or so like those every week – that's nearly 2000 letters a year!

Tom Farmer admits that the service is not always perfect, so the company gives enormous importance to its after-sales service policy, or its customer complaints handling system, to use the more technical definition. 'We're trying to improve

Help us to give you 100% satisfaction.

Dear Customer

Please help us to give you the best service by giving your frank opinion on this card. Your comments will assist us in maintaining and improving our standards.

Thank you for your co-operation and your custom

Tom Farmer

TOM FARMER, MANAGING DIRECTOR

Centre visited -

Receipt No. ☐☐☐☐☐☐☐☐☐☐

Please ✓ as applicable

Which of the following did you buy on this visit?

Tyres ☐   Exhaust ☐

Battery ☐   Shock Absorbers ☐   Other ☐

What prompted you to visit us on this occasion? Please ✓ the main boxes that you feel apply.

Television ☐   Local Newspaper ☐   Recommended ☐

Passing by ☐

Radio ☐   Yellow Pages ☐   Telephone enquiry ☐

National Newspaper ☐   Past experience ☐   Freefone ☐

Was this your first visit to Kwik-Fit   Yes ☐   No ☐

Now please would you give us your comments on the service you received. Please ✓ each statement if you agree.

My car was treated with respect and seat covers were used ☐

My car was examined in my presence and I was given a frank and honest appraisal of the work required ☐

I requested a quotation before the work started ☐

The finished work was examined in my presence ☐

I requested the parts removed from my vehicle for my retention ☐

The centre was clean and tidy ☐

Finally how would you rate the overall service you received? ☐

Excellent ☐   Good ☐   Satisfactory ☐   Unsatisfactory ☐

Please make further comments:

_____

_____

Name and Address _____

things all the time. It's a constant battle to keep things about 95 per cent. It's got to be 100 per cent in the end; maybe not the first time, but for sure the second time around,' says Tom Farmer.

The company's general policy about handling customer complaints is illustrated by a story that Mr Farmer told us about convincing staff to handle complaints correctly.

'Every year we have a national sales conference. It's a big razzmatazz affair . . . costs us £400,000. At the last one a Divisional Director stood up and told the true story of how back in 1972 he had received a complaint from a customer. Tom asked how much the part cost. £2 was the answer. So Tom explained how much that customer would probably spend every year on his car and how much his wife spends per year on her car, and how much the kids will spend when they grow up. By the time he had finished, he was convinced that he had thrown away about £20,000. The customer was called on, the problem was resolved, and he still comes to Kwik-Fit 21 years later.'

Customer complaint handling falls under the responsibility of Peter Holmes. 'Our objective is to bring the customer back', says Peter. They have, on average, a 90% return rate. That means that out of all customers who have had a problem with the service, 90% said that they would use or recommend Kwik-Fit to others, when asked by an independent survey agency.

There is a staff of ten doing nothing but handling customer enquiries which enter the company in three ways:

by phone (a freephone number);
by letter;
or through the customer satisfaction form handed out to a customer with his bill.

The form asks the customer to rate Kwik-Fit on each point in the code of practice. If any of the ratings are lower than 'satisfied', the customer service team gives them a call.

'We respond to all the complaints by phone on the same day that they are received. Most customers are listed in the telephone directory; for those that aren't, we write them a letter or visit them'.

Once having reached the person, the customer service representative thanks him for his comments, explains that he is calling in order to 'set things right' and asks the individual to explain exactly what occurred. Copious notes are taken.

The representative then contacts the auto service centre. If it's a problem which the centre can fix, the customer is given an appointment to go back in at his convenience.

The same customer service representative handles the customer throughout the transaction. No file is closed before the customer himself has indicated that he is satisfied. Depending upon the situation, Kwik-Fit will reimburse the customer or provide various forms of compensation, if necessary. The auto centre manager can give a refund up to £25. For an excess, the staff can telephone the divisional manager to receive an 'OK' and the cheque is sent out by the customer services department. Total turnaround time for resolving a complaint is generally 48 hours.

Customer service representatives are rated on their ability to turn customers around. Once a month a survey of customers who have complained is made by an outside company. They are asked questions about how their complaints were handled and if they 'would recommend Kwik-Fit to their friends or relatives.'

Twenty customers of each representative are contacted. This yields a customer satisfaction rating for the department as well as for each representative. Advancement and performance reviews are determined by the representative's individual score. The department manager is the person with, on average, the best turnaround score. As is indicated above, the present turnaround rating for the department is 90 per cent. 'Our objective is for 95 per cent to say "yes" right away.'

Implementation

'In some ways we have to be flexible; Kwik-Fit is not flexible when it comes to handling customer service.' That is the answer we got when we asked about how Kwik-Fit deals with 'problem' auto centres. A centre can be experiencing financial difficulties, staff management difficulties or any number of similar problems, and it can expect helpful and patient treatment from head office. If there's a problem with how the centre handles customers, then heads roll.

The level of service quality at the auto centres are monitored in three ways. First, the company analyses results coming in from the customer satisfaction questionnaire attached to the bill (see p. 306). The response rate is about 5 per cent (in normal instances, response rates run about 1 to 2 per cent for this type of questionnaire). On over 3.7 million customers per year, that still gives the company a sizeable amount of information to work with.

Secondly, Kwik-Fit has an independent survey conducted on its behalf. Fifty customers are surveyed per quarter per auto centre, i.e. 20,000 surveys are made per quarter. All centres falling below the threshold limit are noted for follow-up action.

Thirdly, Kwik-Fit has an outside firm conducting 'mysterious customer' check-ups. Eight to ten centres are mystery shopped per month. The results are printed in the internal newspaper with a photo of the centre.

Overall, customer satisfaction is running at 98 per cent. Tom Farmer receives a copy of the report on a monthly basis. The divisional directors receive a copy of the report and a report on each centre. If a particular problem is picked up, it's noted.

Low rated centres, 'get a visit'. A remedial action programme is then initiated which involves the participation of regional and divisional managers. The centre has 30 days to 'clean up its act', before being re-surveyed.

As part of remedial action or in response to a particular type of customer complaint, 'Gripe' sessions are organised at the centre. They require the participation of entire staff, whether or not they are implicated in the particular problem. They are designed to be a learning experience. A 'gripe' session takes place after closing hours, so it is in everyone's interest that the service quality of the centre rise.

A big issue in Kwik-Fit's customer service is keeping the energy level high. 'Customer service has to be an obsession; it needs hype, energy. It's more pleasant to give good service than bad service, but you need people with energy. Our people have energy,' says Tom Farmer.

To make sure its employees have energy, the company hires young and promotes quickly. Many start out on the Youth Training Scheme, a government-supported programme which allows young people to begin working prior to completing their basic education. They get to be centre managers within three to four years. Most centre managers are 23–24 years old. A good manager can make up to £40,000. The average centre manager's salary is £20,000, twice the industry norm.

Because of the level of energy and commitment required, there is a burn-out syndrome. Mr Farmer explains, 'Kwik-Fit is like a Benedictine monastery – you really get into it. Our centre managers are young; they have a certain lifespan. There comes a time when they can't do it anymore. They start to realise that there's life outside Kwik-Fit. They want to change their lifestyle'. Most leave of their own accord; others are promoted into positions elsewhere in the company.

Training is another way in which the company energises staff. The company won a Government National Training Award for its broad and intensive training programme. Mr Farmer places tremendous importance on training; 'Everything stems from training. . . . There needs to be a high element of training to get a good interpersonal relationship going (between the fitter and the customer).'

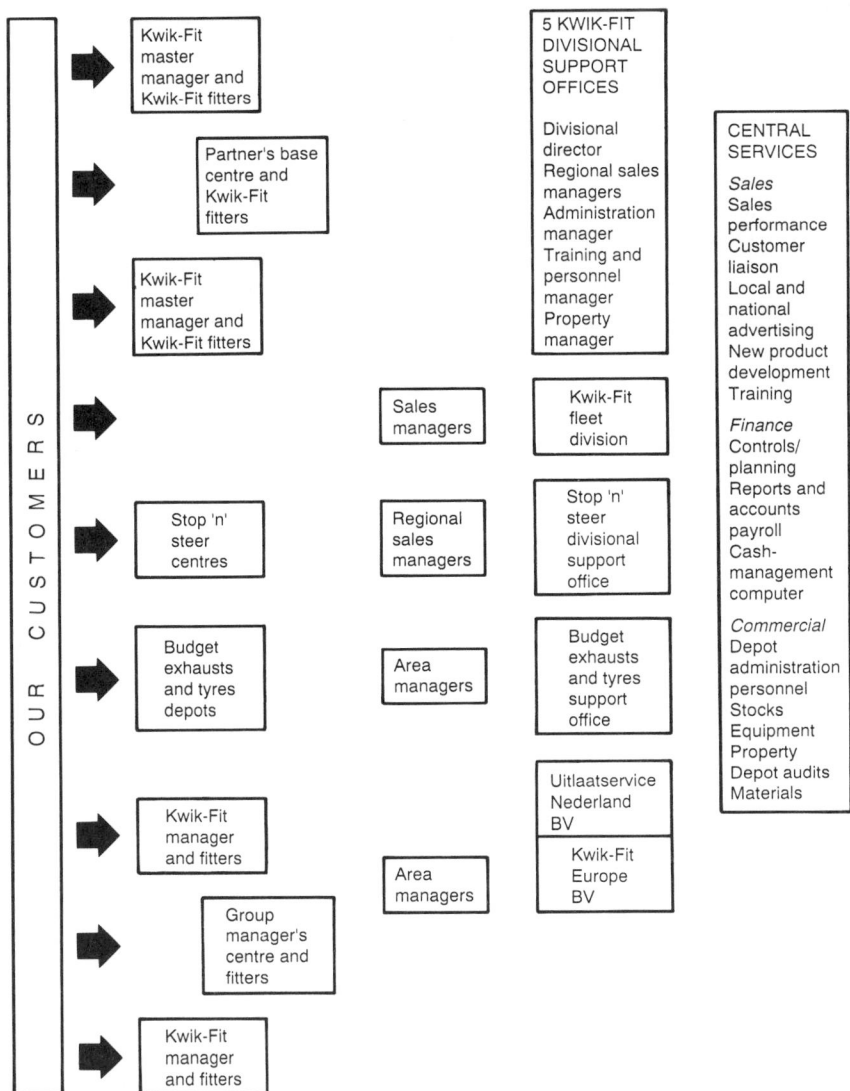

In addition to heavy on-the-job training, Kwik-Fit has two training centres and an entire series of over 60 training modules. All modules cover aspects of customer service. Some cover only customer service issues. The introductory course is a special module on the company's code of practice. There are also courses on 'Meeting the customer', 'Dealing with the customer', 'Leaving the customer' and 'Dealing with complaints'. Every employee has to pass the training module on telephone handling and, at the centre level he cannot answer the phone until he has passed the course! In total, an employee receives over 15 days of training a year.

What does Tom Farmer think contributes most to service quality at Kwik-Fit? 'Me: I started in the centre with the customers; almost all my team started down there too. We know the business; we're the first generation management and we can see instantly when things aren't right.'

Ninety-eight per cent of all managers have experience on the front line. Most worked their way up the ranks. 'Even today, everyone in our company, including the girls, have to work a week a year in the centre. It's a company policy.'

Kwik-Fit has adopted the American management concept of MBWA (management by walking around). 'Videos, audio tapes, posters etc; are all good support materials, but are no replacement for us. We get there and talk to our people.'

Kwik-Fit also believes in the concept of the internal customer. 'For us, the centre manager is the king. He is the one that must get everyone working for the customer.' To reinforce the point, Kwik-Fit's organisation chart, showing the structure of the company, is flipped on its side. It's the customer and the centre manager that sit next to one another in the left-hand column (see p. 309). The rest of the company acts as a service centre to the service manager. There is no head office at Kwik-Fit, just a central services division.

What would happen to Kwik-Fit without Tom Farmer and his team? 'It's true, it wouldn't be the same. This company is an extended family. The only real asset in the organisation is its people.'

What can be learned

1 Deliver what you promise

Kwik-Fit promises 100% customer satisfaction and Tom Farmer makes sure his organisation does everything possible to provide it. The most visible demonstration of this is Kwik-Fit's complaint handling system which responds to customer's complaints instantly and with a personalised approach. Moreover, it's a policy that no file is ever closed until the customer declares himself 'satisfied'.

2 Test the satisfaction of dissatisfied customers

Not only is no file ever closed until a dissatisfied customer declares himself satisfied, but Kwik-Fit also tests the degree of satisfaction of those customers with the way that their problem was handled by the customer service department. It's an excellent way to make sure that the customer service department is doing things the right way.

3 Go for hype

Tom Farmer talks about needing 'hype'. He knows that from his frontline staff's point of view it's not always easy to provide top quality service 5 days a week, 8 and 10 hours a day; sometimes the morale takes a beating. To help his people stay positive, Tom Farmer provides hype and he makes sure all his managers provide hype too. Hype is energy. It's encouragement and it's reminding staff that what they're doing is really appreciated.

4 Set a priority – the customer

At Kwik-Fit, there is no doubt, good customer handling comes first. A centre can experience all kinds of problems – financial, managerial or with its personnel. The only real problem that is unforgivable is poor treatment of customers. It's known and respected throughout the Kwik-Fit organisation. Poor customer treatment and 'heads roll'.

LOMBARD, ODIER & CIE

Imagine fairyland where there are palaces and foreign princesses with pink chiffon evening gowns especially made for floating down marble staircases. There is a beautiful, big lake surrounded by vine-covered hillsides that sparkle at night with a million points of light. There are horses and Rolls-Royces and gardens full of flowers. There are international lawmakers, watchmakers, concert pianists, professors and private bankers . . . private bankers ?! – Ah, you guessed it, we're in Switzerland. More specifically, we're in Geneva, the home of some of the most ancient and prestigious bankers in the world.

Now, imagine a land with high technology, precision machine tools, advanced electronic engineering and aeroplanes that leave on time and arrive on time. We're still in Switzerland, which has forgotten neither a fairytale past nor the time-conscious, technology-driven world of the present.

Lombard, Odier & Cie are private bankers in Geneva. They have not forgotten a rich past nor the necessity to adapt to the present. Among the chandeliers, the pastel rugs thick like plum pudding and the polite but discreet acknowledgements of the staff, one discovers a universe of high technology adapted to the specific financial needs of its clients. Without forgetting the languid charm of an afternoon lunch at the golf club, Lombard, Odier partners still ensure that stock purchase orders are passed within seconds and that investment status reports can be printed within five minutes. For their clients' sake, they have learned how to keep their charm while integrating the best of the 'new world'.

Background

The Genevoise private banking community dates back to the year 1640. In that year, a certain Mr Pierre Gallatin, a correspondent of the Hervant Bank of Lyon, was recognised as the first banker/trader of that city. He was rapidly followed by others. In this small city-state, there was a need for capital to finance the development of industries – watch, silk, lace etc. – that reached out to customers beyond their region and beyond that of the neighbouring countries. Likewise, capital often needed a safe place to go, away from wars and political upheavals. It was only 60 or so years later that gentlemen like Gallatin began to associate themselves by forming partnerships and, yet another 158 years before an enterprising Mr Jean-Gédéon Lombard launched what would later become Lombard, Odier & Cie.

The Lombard family is from the region of Naples, Italy. César Lombard, broker and merchant, emigrated to Geneva and became a citizen in 1589. In 1798, right in the middle of a war, Henri Hentsch and Jean-Gédéon Lombard formed a partnership to engage in the 'commission business' as it was called. The French had invaded Switzerland and the French Republic had just annexed the Republic of Geneva. The bank finally became Lombard, Odier & Cie in 1830.

The bank's business during this period was in placing government bond issues, serving as a deposit base and providing letters of credit. Money invested with the firm over the next hundred years went towards, for example, the development of the railway system in the US and the development of the mining industry. The Geneva bankers created 'trust companies' at the turn of the century which were their version of the modern-day venture capital firm which provides financing to fledgling firms.

In the first half of the 20th century, audacious investments in industry have been replaced, for the most part, by more conservative investments in the stock of large multinationals like IBM and Nestlé. 'There has been a transformation of the bank's activities from support for industrial development to the protection of inheritance and the management of wealth', says Thierry Lombard, Partner.

The strongest period of growth in terms of assets managed has been from the 1960s through to the present day. Today, Lombard, Odier operates in a difficult environment. It has a tradition of surviving wars, economic crises, natural disasters and the like, by applying prudence and measured decision-making. The banking industry today is a fast-moving, competitive environment where quick decision-making and fact action are considered essential. Whereas before it was primarily a nationally based activity, today banking is, by necessity, international.

The bank's competitors are many and varied. The large commercial banks have spent the last 15 years expanding into other activities, including 'private banking'. They don't offer their clients entry into the luxurious Genevoise banking community, but they can provide access to many international markets and can provide a wide range of financial products in which to invest.

Beyond the commercial banks, there are the other private banks or banks which are like private banks. A private bank, in the strictest sense of the word, is a Swiss legal institution which is organized as a private partnership. This means that the firm's owners are its executives – its managing partners. At Lombard Odier eight managing partners direct the firm on a collegiate basis and assume unlimited joint and several liability to the full extent of their personal assets. 'Because of our legal structure, every decision must respect a certain degree of prudence; in this business, one must never forget that we have a fudiciary responsibility – we work with the assets of others,' says Mr Lombard.

A number of banks have positioned themselves as private bankers, but do not operate under that legal denomination. Frequently, these competitors are the Swiss subsidiaries of the commercial banks or of large investment banks. They tend to be more aggressive in their investment policy as well as in their commercial approach to clients.

Other banks include mainly those in Zurich and those in Geneva. The Zurich private banks have a little less illustrious and long history and many today have changed their legal structure to become corporations. As they are Zurich-based they have an advantage when it comes to serving German or German-speaking clientèle.

Last, but not least are the other private banks in Geneva. Four of these, together with Lombard, Odier have formed the Association of Geneva Private Bankers (Groupement des Banquiers Privés Genevois). In the true spirit of Swiss confederation and in consideration of the competitive forces facing these banks from other sources, these five banks have agreed to pool their efforts in certain areas, rather than dispersing limited resources on fighting one another. Points out Patrick Odier, 'Our type of bank could be bypassed by other larger, more powerful institutions. We have, therefore, a greater interest to live in harmony with those banks in the same position as ourselves.'

This eminently sensible policy has led to co-operative advertising campaigns which promote Geneva private banking, in general, and to the establishment of a joint training centre, used by all of the five banks to train their staff. In addition, the partners of these five institutions have taken on the responsibility to meet at least twice a month, with the aim of co-ordinating their approach to the community and *vis-à-vis* the rest of the world.

A good indication of their level of comradeship, is that it is difficult to convince these gentlemen to say anything derogatory about one another. 'Our competitors are, like ourselves, a company made up of individuals. We can have friendships of long duration and, thus, a good understanding of the situation of the others; we must respect certain norms of friendly competition,' says Patrick Odier.

This co-operative approach has not by any means killed the competitive spirit and merely increased mutual respect between the competitors. 'If we are up against one of the other private banks for the same business and we win it, this represents a greater success for us than if we had won the business from one of the big institutions,' explains Thierry Lombard.

Service strategy

At Lombard, Odier, a service strategy has evolved over time that focuses upon three characteristics of the bank – tradition, innovation and personalization. The strategy reflects changes within the composition of the bank's clientèle and represents a concerted effort on the part of the bank to respond to the expectations of all of its clients in the level and type of service it offers.

The bank has a strong traditional base of clients. Over the past three centuries, money has come to Geneva to be sheltered in a stable political environment, with a group of specialists adept at finding investments throughout the world.

To this base, has been added a new group of clients many of whom are institutional clients.

While the bank intends to 'remain loyal to its traditional clients they are also positioning themselves to meet the demands of their newer clientèle. In general, the institutional new clients tend to be very demanding. They expect a very high level of professionalism and competence on the part of their bankers.

They are are more demanding concerning the performance of their portfolio and are quicker to move if what they receive doesn't please them. Mr de Tscharner, very active in the management of individual portfolio accounts, explains, 'They are well informed because of their own experience and are highly professional. They expect to receive the same level of professionalism from us as they themselves provide to their customers.'

The service expectations of all clients are influenced by the reputation which the Genevoise private banks have in the world financial community. It is a reputation which serves more to the Bank's advantage than to their disadvantage as it appeals to the majority of their clients, regardless of their background. This reputation is, thus, fostered and cultivated.

The Genevoise banks are reputed to be bastions of luxury and privilege. Merely one's presence inside such a bank, however temporary, can enhance one's personal image. All the private banks are located in some of the most discreet, but elegant buildings in the city; they are furnished with the greatest consideration to comfort and beauty with antiques and rich fabrics in abundance.

The Genevoise private banks are also reputed for security and discretion in the handling of investments. In the current banking environment, this has its drawbacks. They are sometimes thought to be too conservative and to miss opportunities for gain from important market innovations or events. The issue of conservatism is handled differently by each of the Genevoise banks as regards international expansion, diversification into new businesses and the application of new technologies to their business. While all of the private banks are opening themselves to some degree, Lombard, Odier has clearly chosen to position itself as the trail blazer.

'Tradition and innovation are the two words that best characterise the bank,' says Messrs Lombard and Odier, the sixth-generation descendants of the founding partners. 'Tradition in the sense that we are specialised in asset management and have two centuries of experience in service to our customers. Innovation in the sense that we feel that we are representative of a new generation of private bankers, that we have new talent and are open to the international banking community.' 'Lombard, Odier does not fall into the same category as the other old, established banks, that believes that "we are good because we are old". We want to be good and old.'

The practical implications of its positioning as a traditional, but innovative private bank are that the bank has actively pursued a policy of international expansion. Lombard, Odier was the first private bank in Geneva to internationalise and has had an office in North America since 1950. They were the first European bank to acquire a seat on the New York Stock Exchange in 1979. They have offices in New York, London, The Netherlands, Montreal, Bermuda and Gibraltar. A year ago, they established an office in Zurich, and have had an office in Vevey for over three years.

Private banks are not like commercial banks in that the number of branches one has overseas is a direct reflection of the degree of internationalisation. In the case of private banks, the objective is to be present in the major investment markets. This presence has permitted the bank to develop a specialisation in the international diversification of portfolios. 'We discovered very early that our clients' portfolios could yield a higher return with the same amount of risk if we followed a policy of international diversification of investments,' says Philippe Sarasin, Partner. The bank is well recognised in the international investment market for the performance of some of the asset funds they have created for international investors, one of which has been the top performing Pacific Rim fund.

Lombard, Odier's 'innovation' is sometimes equivalent to a kind of avant-gardism in the private banking sector. As such, it was one of the first private banks to introduce information technology into its midst and one of the only banks to pursue an active policy of investment in continual upgrading. Marcel Odier (father of the present-day partner, Patrick) took the first step in the 1950s. In 1957, the bank's first computer, an IBM punch-card system, was installed at his initiative. In 1963, the bank replaced the machine with an IBM1440 and three years later, they added the first IBM360. This has been followed by other large investments which permit the bank to have one of the most modern and user-friendly, interactive, on-line networks presently in use by any bank. Today, the bank's flagship system is a Digital Equipment, with in-house developed software, said by some to be a portfolio manager's 'dream machine'.

The bank has also been avant-garde in its approach to new markets. As the historical result of managing the pension fund of their own employees, Lombard, Odier developed an expertise in pension fund management which they began to market actively in the late 1960s. It is now aggressively pursuing the quickly growing market of asset management for institutional investors and is well placed despite stiff competition. Institutional investors are generally company pension funds, insurance companies, large trust funds etc. Already over 40 per cent of the bank's assets managed are coming from these sources.

By being a specialist in asset management, the bank can assure clients that there is no conflict of interest between its activities, i.e. the bank is not going to push clients to invest in a company to which it lends money, because corporate lending is not one of the bank's activities. The quality of the bank's research is good for the same reason. A company is more open with a bank that will not later use the information given by the company to advance their own case for corporate lending or other types. 'The fact that we are specialised gives us greater credibility in our approach to clients,' says Mr Mivelaz, Senior Vice President, Institutional Clients. 'It's an important point of differentiation, particularly in the international market-place.'

The third major aspect of the bank's strategy is personalisation. While private banks have always stressed the personal aspects of their services, in recent years there has been a trend towards the creation of 'products' from which the client chooses for his investments. A product, for example, might be a fund for investments into a set group of US high technology companies or a group of large multinationals in the food industry.

One advantage to such funds is that they permit smaller investors to group their money with that of other investors in order to avoid large transactional costs. A major disadvantage is that it doesn't permit the investor to choose the companies in which his money is invested, nor to adapt the portfolio to his specific requirements in terms of risk/return.

Lombard, Odier has resisted this trend towards products and has limited its creation of products to those which are highly specialised. Today, the bank has positioned itself as a supplier of a service; the service in this case being the creation of an individual portfolio according to the specific requests or requirements of their client. As Mr Bonna, Partner, points out, 'When you go to a big institution, they sell you a product; us, we sell a service.'

The bank's strategy of personalisation holds true for both individual and institutional clients. In the case of institutional clients, personalisation can sometimes take the form of innovation, as the bank attempts to develop solutions which meet the specific needs of their clients. 'We have the spirit of initiative necessary to develop new solutions for our clients; we have the flexibility and adaptability that the larger banks don't have,' points out Mr Mivelaz.

Service strengths

Lombard, Odier's key strength is that it offers a personalised service in every sense of the word. From the reception to the financial advising to the way that performance is reported to the client, at every step, the bank makes the client feel that he is recognised and appreciated.

Recognition begins at the front door. Lombard, Odier has a staff of nine 'concierges' responsible for greeting and welcoming the clients to the bank. We specify 'welcoming', because it is not just a question of assuring that the automatic wrought-iron door opens just as the person approaches it, but also a question of making eye contact with the guest, assuring that the bank representative is properly informed, that the client is escorted personally into a meeting room and that he is systematically offered something to drink in a spotlessly clean, fresh (and elegant) setting. To accomplish this in a fashion which is neither rushed nor military-like requires training and a true concern for the welfare of the client.

Not surprisingly, all of the concierges at Lombard, Odier have previous experience working in the grand and luxurious hotels of Geneva. The bank compares its welcome service to that of a 5-Star hotel with the concierges having the important role of being 'the visit card, the flag holder, and the first smile of the house' as it is described in the bank's internal newspaper *Hello*. As the concierges themselves explain it, 'Nothing must be overlooked in our attempts to ensure that the client has the impression that he is unique.'

Personalisation at Lombard, Odier goes beyond the welcoming stage; it goes in the 'sales' phase. The greatest concern of all of the bankers at Lombard, Odier is that they understand exactly what their client's needs are. As Patrick Odier explains, 'We have to inspire confidence in our clients. To do that, the person that the client meets must understand the client and what he wants of the bank. We have to pass the message, 'Madam, Sir, you are the most important person to us at this moment; we have well understood you and your objectives; for a case like yours, this is how we would proceed.' According to Mr de Tscharner, 'The relationship must be well defined by the first conversation. All risk of a misunderstanding must be eliminated; our job is to translate the ideas of our clients into numbers (rate of return desired, degree of preservation of capital needed) .''You cannot imagine how many hours we spend to find out two things – risk tolerence and the intended use of the money invested,' says Mr Sarasin.

To get this level of understanding, the private bankers search for information beyond just the financial concerns of their clients. They attempt to understand their client as an individual in his entirety. 'We are interested in our clients, not only in the perspective of what we know how to do, but also in order to assist them in areas which are important to them, but not necessarily in our domain,' says Patrick Odier.

'Once our client feels that we understand them and their position, then when historical events happen – the Gulf War, the stock crash etc. – we know what to do for our clients and they know that we know.' 'Take, for example, the Gulf War. When the Gulf War happened, some clients were ready to play on the events; others were not. We had to know this, and we had to know it before, not three days later. So, part of the service at Lombard, Odier is to really understand our clients and know how they would want us to react,' explains Philippe Sarasin.

Personalisation is also present in the ongoing relationship. Clients at Lombard, Odier know that their bankers are thinking of them and they're given concrete demonstrations of that concern. 'Part of the service is to call them and say, "This is what we've done and this is why we've done it." The argument is very important, just as important as the action,' says Philippe Sarasin. 'They don't want to feel that we are people across the ocean from which they receive a piece of paper. It may be a very beautiful piece of paper, but what really reassures them is the contact, the telephone call.'

The relationship is often personalised to the point where the client becomes a friend. The portfolio manager plays the role of a personal financial adviser to his client. The contact extends beyond the boundaries of the bank meeting room and develops on a more personal basis, and over time. Being from well-recognised families themselves, many of the private bankers circulate easily in the social environment of their clients. This is taken into account in the recruitment process. 'We need people who have "bagage" [character and personal experience] – young people who fit into our culture,' explains Mr de Tscharner.

Aware of the fact that the bank is somewhat unique in the attention it pays to its clients, the Bank's management has allocated resources to keep that degree of personalisation. In London, for example, their team of analysts/portfolio managers is quite large in comparison with the total funds managed. 'It was a business decision. Yes, we have a nice portfolio performance; yes, we have a technological advance with our system, but we don't know how long either of those will last. What does give us a competitive edge is the bond that we created with our clients,' says Mr Sarasin.

Personalisation is also taken into account in the way information about his account is reported to the client. As a general rule, the choice is the client's. To use the expression of one client, it is '*à la carte*'. The choice of options is generally presented to the client at the beginning of the relationship. First, he chooses between different visual formats. 'There are some ways of presenting information that will be comprehensible to some clients and totally incomprehensible to others,' says Patrick Odier. Models of the visual presentation are shown to the client on the computer screen and also on paper. Once the reporting format has been chosen, the client chooses the 'When, where and by whom'. But, it's not always just a matter of presenting options. 'Sometimes our clients bring us ideas and we try to realise them as they would wish,' says Patrick Odier.

In certain cases, the bank goes beyond the paper or verbal communication of results; they also 'go live' with a visual/computer colour presentation to groups of clients. This technique is most frequently used with institutional clients who come in numbers. The conference-like effect stimulates conversation and permits the bank to provide a very complete explanation of portfolio activity.

Implementation

'The quality of service in this business necessarily reflects the human element – the quality of our people and their professionalism,' says Patrick Odier. For Lombard, Odier the principle point is to hire the highest quality of individual possible and those that are best adapted to the business. 'We look for a certain homogeneity among our people,' says Mr Lombard.

In terms of service quality, 'Do we want people who feel bad about bad service and good about good service?' explains Mr Odier. Their level of ethics and sense of service are tested in the recruitment phase and during the three-month trial period. In general, it's done by observing the individual's behaviour or reaction in certain key situations or to key questions. Since the bank demands an exceptionally high level of customer orientation, the response provided by the candidate must be perfect in every instance.

To ensure the cultural 'fit' of the candidate to the bank, every candidate is seen by more than one partner for a customer contact post and often by more than two. In addition, they are seen not just on one occasion, but on many occasions so that the impact of fluctuations in the mood of the interviewer or interviewee are mitigated. 'This week we already saw one candidate three times. He's seen five partners and two managers,' says Mr Odier. 'Our decision on people is very slow; we like to see them a lot of times before taking a decision. Once that's done, however, the feedback is very fast, sometimes the next day,' says Mr Odier.

Ninety-five per cent of all trainees admitted to the bank stay with the bank. They begin their apprenticeship by a 'tour of the house', i.e. a tour of the different services. That lasts from six weeks to two years depending on the function for which they were hired and their previous experience. Young portfolio managers almost always spend time in the research department. 'Typically they stay in the department for about nine months,' says Mr Zupponi, head of that department.

Each new employee has a godfather responsible for overseeing his development during his period of integration into the bank. In some cases, the godfather is a senior individual in the activity for which the individual was hired; in many cases he is not. Partners are regularly godfathers for young portfolio managers.

In addition to the in-house and 'on-the-job' training which recruits receive, there is also more formalised training from the training centre. This is a centre jointly sponsored by the five Geneva private banks which provides technical and ongoing education for every level. Courses are offered in legislation or new financial techniques, as well as in management or communication skills. Even with such a heavy programme of training, a good portfolio management is not created overnight. 'From our experience, it takes over 10 years before becoming a top, qualified portfolio manager,' says Mr Lombard.

Dynamic and professional are the two words that came back again and again in our conversations with clients, observers and employees about Lombard, Odier. How does one get to be a dynamic and professional company? 'It's a question of motivation and the pleasure which we all take in responding to the needs of our clients,' explains Thierry Lombard. 'We're motivated by the fact that everyone in the company does the same job and has the same conception of service quality to clients.' Adds Patrick Odier, 'There are few companies in which there is no difference between those that manage the company and those that serve customers.' 'From the day that we stop receiving clients and managing portfolios, we won't have long to live,' underlines Mr Lombard.

So, it's the lack of difference in hierarchy, the fact that everyone is listening to clients that makes Lombard, Odier a dynamic company. It's also because, 'we're a young company; we have the image of a firm on the move,' says Mr Odier. The average age at Lombard, Odier is 37; the average age of the partners is 49, and the average age of partners on the board of management is 42. These authors were particularly impressed upon meeting Patrick Odier, who at the ripe old age of 36, still manages to convince his listener of the bank's prudent, professional approach to portfolio management. This is a considerable feat given the fact that, physically, he resembles more a professional tennis player than a banker.

There is also the motivation provided by the work itself. As Mr Bonna points out, 'There is in our bank additional motivation provided by the impact which an employee's contribution can have on the success of the bank.' For Mr Zupponi, 'It's the interest in the job and the responsibility that we can have that makes the difference.'

Employees are given freedom to exercise their judgement. 'There's a great deal of delegation. Once we feel that a person is competent, we let him go,' says Mr Bonna. 'There's no Big Brother looking over your shoulder,' points out Mr Zupponi. Employees can easily be responsible for millions of Swiss francs of the clients; for employees this in itself is a source of motivation. At the same time there is no room for incompetence. 'There's only room for those who succeed and who are hard workers,' says Mr Zupponi.

Employees' retention is high. As compared with other banks, even other Swiss banks, the low turnover is an advantage *vis-à-vis* clients who are tired of seeing the person handling their account change every two or three years. At Lombard, Odier there is 'the notion of longevity – longevity of the relationship with the client, the longevity in the relationship with collaborators and the longevity of the bank itself,' explains Thierry Lombard.

The partners explain the level of motivation and service quality in part by the size of the bank. Roughly 700 people work for Lombard, Odier. 'Our present size is a good size; we want to stay at this size,' says Mr Lombard. It's above the 'critical mass' and below the point where communication becomes difficult and inefficiencies start occurring. 'Above 1000 people for this kind of activity, we couldn't offer the same level of personalised service we presently offer,' says Thierry Lombard.

To illustrate the point, Mr. Odier adds, 'You're an American client and you need references in Paris for the creation of a company. If I don't have them, then somebody else in our organisation might be able to provide them. Because we're a small company this kind of information circulates easily, on a personal basis. We can do this for our clients because of our size.'

Another important factor to service quality is the team structure which the bank has adopted. In the past, each portfolio manager had an assistant and a secretary. He operated independently; the disadvantage was that if he wasn't available, there was no one who was totally equipped to replace him. Today, portfolio managers operate in teams. A partner heads up each team which has two or three portfolio managers each, and two or three younger trainees and staff. 'This way the client has contact with a number of people and recourse to more than one or two, if he has a question,' points out Mr Odier. It also gives the client a choice. 'Sometimes each of us feels that we are not necessarily the best contact for the client and that another person might be better,' says Mr Odier. With the team system, they can easily introduce the client to another manager, without the risk of losing any continuity in the relationship.

The practice of introducing the client to more than one banker begins at the very first contact. Two portfolio managers, generally a partner and a manager, see a client on the first visit. The one that has the best 'fit' with the client follows up on the relationship.

Lastly, service quality at Lombard, Odier can also be explained by the way in which resources are allocated within the bank. Management follows a long-standing policy presented in allegorical terms: 'There are certain trains which we prefer not to take because we don't know where they are going. Once we know the destination of the train, we'll take the "express" to get there.' In less allegorical terms, once the bank takes a decision to pursue a certain course of action, they do not hesitate or waver in the commitment of resources or time to the achievement of that objective. While there are many small examples that could be used, the two most outstanding are the bank's decisions to pursue the use of information technology in the bank and to enter the institutional investment market. In both cases, the bank has committed itself to a policy and has not wavered, despite the considerable time that has been required before these two investments began to be advantageous for the bank. 'We don't change our policies in the heat of the moment. Sometimes we take a route which may not seem ideal at the moment, but we keep to it and do not waver because we believe that it will be in the long-term interests of our clients and the Bank,' says Thierry Lombard.

What can be learned

1 When selling services, 'tangibilise'

Lombard, Odier is selling a very intangible service – money management. There is nothing to touch or see besides a report at the end of the year with numbers on it. To increase customers' confidence in the service provided, Lombard, Odier must give them concrete references. They cannot present potential customers with a list of existing customers for reasons of confidentiality. Instead, the bank uses the elegance of its premises, the furnishings in the meeting rooms and the company's computer system. They also tangibilise by presenting a senior partner to each potential customer. The customer verifies in a sense that there is indeed a 'Lombard', an 'Odier' or another reliable reference point besides the individual he just met sitting across the desk.

2 Make sure that the first impression is one of the best

It is often said that first impressions are the lasting ones. There is probably some truth in it. Lombard, Odier goes out of its way to make sure that the first impression is a good one. It gets customers off to a good start.

3 Be aware of size

Lombard, Odier believes that an important element in their success is the maintenance of the appropriate size of the company according to its activities. A smaller operation would not give the company sufficient resources to operate efficiently; a larger operation would also reduce efficiencies by making communication and co-ordination more difficult and would decrease the human element both within the bank and with the customer.

4 Make time for customers

Mr Lombard clearly points out that the bank wouldn't stay where it is for very long if the partner stopped receiving customers. Contact with customers is, thus, an essential element. Many CEOs don't seem to have time any more for customers; perhaps they would be better off by following the example of Lombard, Odier.

LONDON INTERNATIONAL GROUP

London International Group is a large, diverse company providing products and services to industry and consumers alike. It is somewhat rare for such a diverse group to adopt a homogeneous philosophy towards its businesses as London International has done, particularly when that business philosophy includes a strong commitment to customer care.

In 1987, the company developed its mission statement and at the same time announced a strong ongoing commitment to a broad-based customer orientation in all its businesses. 'Today, we're dedicated to good customer service. In 1979, when Mr Woltz (CEO) joined us, we weren't enough customer oriented. He has brought in strong leadership and today we are committed to providing quality products and services to customers in our core businesses' (Victor O'Shaughnessy, 1990).

Background

London International Group was founded in 1924, as The London Rubber Company. Over the years the Group has expanded both organically and by acquisition, throughout Europe, North America and the Far East.

Whilst over the years, many of the Group's activities have been sold or discontinued, the Group now concentrates on five core businesses. These are barrier contraceptives; surgical gloves; consumer and industrial gloves; over the counter medicines and toiletries; and photoprocessing.

The manufacturing and marketing of condoms has been a core business for over 68 years. London International Group is the world's largest producer of branded condoms and has a leading position in most of the markets in which it operates. The condoms business represents approximately 24 per cent of the Group's total sales.

In addition the Group manufactures and markets high quality latex surgeons' gloves; industrial gloves for use in the workplace when in contact with harsh chemicals or sensitive products; and household gloves sold through retail channels to the needy housewife or househusband. These activities amount to around 17 per cent of the Group's sales.

The Group's over the counter medicines and toiletries comprise a number of products with strong brand heritages, sold through pharmacies or supermarkets. Included therein are 'Wright's' Coal Tar Soap, 'Buttercup' cough syrup, the 'Sauber' range of toiletries and tights, 'Mister Baby' products and 'Cook Bates' manicure implements. This sector of the business represents around 28 per cent of the Group's revenues.

The remaining 31 per cent of the Group's total sales comes from its activities in the photoprocessing business. London International Group is the parent company of ColourCare International, one of Europe's leading photoprocessing companies. Most of its UK activities are carried out through the intermediary of large retailing groups like Boots, which use ColourCare mainstream laboratories, or on-site minilabs. On mainland Europe ColourCare operates a mail order photoprocessing business under respected brand names such as: Trifca, Maxicolor, Norsk Foto.

Operating in over 120 countries, the Group has an annual turnover of approximately £370 million and employs around 8,000 people. A common factor between most of the businesses is their leadership position in their respective markets. 'When you have such a strong position in a market, you have to work doubly hard to convince people that you really deserve to be where you are. They have a tendency to regard you as being very arrogant.'

'We've done a lot of work in this area over the last two years or so. It starts on the shop floor, we try to make the product to a standard that is better than the recognised standard that is required and it must be capable of meeting any standard in the world. Then we try to instill in our people the standards of customer service and we monitor everything by computer and show managers exactly where they are performing,' explains Nick Hodges, Managing Director European Division.

At ColourCare service quality plays a more crucial role than it does at LRC. It is the guarantee of a high quality result to the customer and a way to set oneself apart from the competition.

To provide a high quality result to the customer, ColourCare has instituted very rigorous quality control procedures to ensure that the result coming out of a processing machine can stand up to the most stringent standards. Quality control has an important role because the company does not see itself as just a processor, 'We are not producing photos, we are producing memories.'

ColourCare competitors are in most cases the other large photoprocessing companies like Kodak. They market their services in much the same way as ColourCare – through associated retail outlets, minilabs and by mail.

Over the years, ColourCare has gained market share from its competitors. What has visibly set the company apart is the degree of support and information which it provides to intermediary and end-customers.

Like most photoprocessers, ColourCare uses a retail outlet for most of its business; as a result, it has little name recognition with the consumer. The consumer is more likely to choose his photoprocessing outlet on the basis of the store in which it is located rather than on the quality of the photoprocessing, i.e. if the consumer likes to shop at Boots, he will go to Boots. 'The customer's perception of the photo servicing offered is more likely to be determined by the perception of the individual outlet than by the actual services offered.'

ColourCare has largely overcome this structural disadvantage and, thus gained market share, by providing strong support to the retail outlets in order to enhance their professionalism in photographic assistance, and by furnishing information and assistance to the consumer with his processed photos.

Intermediary customers benefit from extensive training programmes offered by the company to improve retailers' ability to advise customers how to take better pictures. To make administrative processes easier, Colour Care provides extensive explanatory support materials.

For the end-customer, booklets, brochures and special offers help the customer better understand what the photoprocessing company is supplying him in terms of service and how better to take advantage of that assistance.

Service strengths

In all of its businesses, London International demonstrates strong concern and a great deal of expertise in the provision of information to customers. Three types of information are being provided, depending on the business and the particular customer need.

There is information for education. This gives consumers valuable background information about the social, health and legal context in which the product is sold. It is generally directed at consumers and the public at large.

There is information for better use. This gives customers the information they need to use the product to its maximum efficiency. And, there is information for better service. This is specifically information and assistance provided to distributors and retailers to better prepare them to serve end-customers.

'As a corporation, London International has a genuine concern for the business sectors in which it operates; we feel a sense of responsibility and a need to inform the business community and the general public,' explains Clive Kitchener, Group Director of Marketing and Communications.

At ColourCare, the information is provided to customers as an added service. For instance ColourCare produces a booklet called the *"Photo Tips Booklet"*. In it are examples of photography mistakes along with instructions about how to avoid such mistakes in the future. On the photos themselves, customers can find little advice labels on the unsuccessful photos which tell them just where he or she went wrong. Should photoprocessing be delayed, the store receives a Customer Information Card from ColourCare which apologises, explains why it's delayed and gives a new date when the pictures will be ready.

ColourCare also uses information and training as a way to help distributors improve their service to end-customers. A manual, *The Winning Partnership*, is provided which advises retail personnel how to handle certain customer problems and how to complete the various forms necessary for photoprocessing. The manual also sets forth very clear pricing instructions, processing delay guidelines and information on promotions occurring within the year. In addition, the retail staff are trained by ColourCare staff during visits on all aspects of customer handling. On a yearly basis, retailers' photoprocessing staff are invited to 'open days' in the laboratories to see how they function.

Implementation

At ColourCare, measurement and monitoring also takes on an important role, but before beginning to measure, the company performs extensive research to find out exactly what customers' and retailers' service expectations are.

Such research permits the company to identify convenience, reliability, speed and value for money as being the most important expectations customers have of a photoprocessing company. 'Ours is also a highly emotional business, where customers require understanding and security.'

Similar studies for retailers are undertaken. 'We must understand the objectives of each particular retailer, then underline that with systems and procedures.' Product quality requirements don't vary between retailers, although service requirements do. Hobby camera chains want more training and more support materials, for example, than do general retailers.

To follow evolutions in retailer expectations, the salesforce calls on retailers regularly with a checklist to get feedback on the quality of service from the labs and to hear from them the comments they have received from customers. The checklist goes back to the lab manager who uses it both to identify problems and as a reference tool in internal meetings.

Lab staff also regularly tour the stores with the sales staff in order to get feedback first-hand on how their service is perceived by retail staff.

One of the improvements that resulted from its research with customers was the restatement of delivery times. When delivery times were quoted from the lab's point of view and didn't take into account retail store 'administration' time, the films were often late from the customer's point of view. 'Shop to shop times are now quoted in all of ColourCare's literature.'

In the future, ColourCare will be doing even more targeted research with end-customers. Following an agreement reached with some of its retailers, it will approach customers that use its services on a regular basis through the store.

Knowing what customers expect permits ColourCare to measure service quality with greater pertinency. 'We took the business apart and addressed it in terms of the customer instead of the process. We spent one year researching the procedures and systems.' Delivery times, processing quality and exact error types are all measured and monitored on a continuous basis. The company has set national standards for quality indicator levels. 'Everything is measured nationally, regionally and locally.'

'Measuring is an important motivational tool. The labs need to know that they are the best.' The results are graphed, plotted and published weekly. The results are used for incentive schemes, quality challenges and awards, including the performance lab of the year.'Quality in terms of prints is subjective to some extent so we're always looking for new ways to measure quality.'

What can be learned

1 Inform to show you care

One of the best ways to show concern or interest in another person is to share information with them. London International applies this axiom group-wide. It shows its concern for customers by providing them with as much information as possible about the products and about the legal or medical environment surrounding them.

2 Give away your expertise

ColourCare produces the "*Photo Tips Booklet*". In it are examples of photography mistakes, along with instructions about how to avoid such mistakes in the future.

3 Reach out to your customers

Some companies products are so well camouflaged behind other firm's retail labels, that end-customers never know who they are; that's not the case with ColourCare. ColourCare's advice labels on unsuccessful photos are just one way that the company reaches out to make a direct contact with customers. Customers appreciate the extra information and, with the "*Photo Tips Booklet*", are made aware who is providing that service to them.

MARKS & SPENCER

Marks & Spencer is a household name in the UK and is the country's leading retailer. Sales from its department stores represent 16 per cent of total UK clothing sales and 20 per cent of UK clothing production. It has 281 stores and employs over 62,125 employees.

Background

Marks & Spencer is not a new name on the market and has been in existence since the 1880s. Michael Marks, a Lithuanian refugee, set up a stand in the local market selling buttons, pins, socks etc. He put up a large sign which read 'Don't ask the price, it's a penny'. The notion of selling everything at a fixed price was new to the market and was a great success. He ensured that he sold good quality products for the price and the business grew rapidly.

In 1894, he had eight penny bazaars and needed help to run them. He brought into the business Tom Spencer, a cashier in Marks's major supplier's store. Together, the two partners ran the business until their deaths, in 1905 and 1907 respectively. At that point there were over 60 penny bazaars belonging to the company.

The management of Marks & Spencer was passed on to Marks's son Simon, who managed the company until his death in 1964. Simon also brought into the business a partner, Israel Sieff, a long-time friend of the family. The Sieff family continue to be major shareholders in the group, although management of the company passed to a non-family member, Lord Raynor, in 1984.

Today Marks & Spencer is a UK institution. It represents the traditional values of the UK family and the British commitment to simple, practical, quality products and service. Little of what we see in a Marks & Spencer's store could be called 'avant-garde' or 'revolutionary'. It is known to be an excellent place for tourists to shop because of its ready selection of traditional British goods.

Service strategy

Marks & Spencer represents the mainstream. It sells to the average British consumer. It is the store that today's British housewife shops at, that her mother shopped at and that maybe even her grandmother shopped at. When they go into a Marks & Spencer store, the British know what to expect.

What they expect is, first, a no-frills presentation. Marks & Spencer stores could be described as austere by today's usual standards for department stores. There are no elaborate window dressings, no oriental rugs, no fancy lighting and no boutique-type arrangements in the corner. Everything is simply arranged on racks or box stands. There is homogeneous daylight-quality lighting throughout the store. One can find the occasional mannequin, but generally, clothing is displayed alone or is shown in a photograph which decorates the wall.

The British also expect to see clearly labelled products and they do. Above each stand there is a description of what the product is and its price. All the garments are arranged by style, colour and size. On each garment, the price, size, origin and fabric content is indicated. The same format for display and labelling is rigorously observed throughout the store.

The Marks & Spencer client has the right to browse. He is not disturbed by aggressive salespeople nor pushed to buy when asking for information. Salespeople at Marks & Spencer are trained to be friendly, helpful and competent – nothing more, nothing less. When addressed a question about a particular garment, they are expected to know the answer. If not, they should know to whom to address the question and be able to provide a rapid response to the customer.

The British do not go to Marks & Spencer to buy the latest fashions; they go for 'timeless' clothing. A Marks & Spencer garment is the kind that you can pull out of the wardrobe five years after you bought it and still wear it. It won't resemble what you see in the latest fashion magazine, but it didn't when you bought it either. It's a guarantee of wearability and of conformity to a classic look.

Lastly, the company has a reputation for honesty and fair-trading practices. This is backed up by their return policy. Unlike customers of many major European department stores, the Marks & Spencer customer has the right to change his mind. No fuss, no nasty looks and last week's purchase is exchanged or refunded on the spot.

Marks & Spencer has a statement of corporate principles which clearly expresses the major elements of the company's service strategy for all to see. Marks & Spencer strives to:

> 'create an attractive, efficient shopping environment for customers';
> 'provide a friendly, helpful service from well-trained staff'; and to
> 'sell clothing . . ., fashions . . ., and . . . fine foods – all representing high standards of quality and value'.

Particular attention should be paid to the exact words used in each of these phrases. Marks & Spencer does not promise an 'elegant' or 'beautiful' shopping environment, but merely an attractive one. Moreover, it should be efficient. That means that attractiveness must be weighed against efficiency in each instance, which it is.

Staff are helpful and friendly, they are not 'responsive' or there to 'advise'. Clothing and food represents 'high standards of quality and value'. Nothing is said about it being 'fashionable' or 'reflecting trends'.

Service quality strengths

Marks & Spencer's commitment to service quality grew out of the basic fundamentals of the business which were established over the years. Good service at Marks & Spencer is most pronounced in three areas:

> in the environment in which one browses and buys;
> in the support provided by the staff to the shopping experience; and
> in the security which the shopper has in the quality of goods purchased.

A Marks & Spencer store is very clearly laid out. Even if a truly inexperienced shopper happens to wander in, he can easily find where each department is located and what is sold in each one. The number of departments is kept to a minimum and there is an ample number of signs showing the store layout.

A Marks & Spencer store is not a cluttered place. Unlke many stores, there is no attempt to bombard the shopper with a vast array of gaudy items for sale. Each item has its space and can be seen from some distance away as it is not blocked by 20 other displays showing similar items.

A shopper can quickly find the size and colour he is looking for. Moreover, it is practically never out of stock. It is rapidly paid for at a close-by checking counter and tucked away in a bag which, for many years, said 'Buy British' (except in France).

Should the shopper have a problem, then the staff are available to help. Marks & Spencer ensures that there are sufficient staff on the floor so that they are rarely pressured or rushed. It also ensures that they are well trained and regularly briefed on developments with the merchandise.

As an example, one of the authors was shopping one day for some lingerie. 'Finding a model which pleased me, I wanted to know whether I would be able to repurchase the same model at a later date. The salesgirl was able to tell me not only the exact date on which the item would be removed, but also that it would be replaced by a similar model within three months. Despite the fact that the item I chose was about to be discontinued, she did not push me to buy nor push me to buy the item's future replacement.'

Sales assistants are rarely aggressive or disagreeable. They treat customers with respect and are friendly, but not overly helpful. Marks & Spencer offers extensive training in customer service, some of which is mandatory. Among the 16 courses offered there is 'dealing with customer enquiries', the 'customer's point of view' and 'good connections – telephone manners'.

Lastly, Marks & Spencer provides quality products for value. In service terms, what is important is the confidence which the shopper can place in his purchase. If a retailer manages to convince the shopper of the quality of the product he sells, then the fear associated with the purchase is reduced; the buyer is reassured that he has 'done a good thing'.

Few retailers really manage to convince buyers of their commitment to quality for value; Marks & Spencer is one of the few that has, thanks to strict policies with product suppliers, to the money-back guarantee and to a genuine concern for quality demonstrated repeatedly over the years.

A small item which sticks in my mind most clearly from one of our visits was seeing a poster-size sign clearly displayed at the top of the lifts. It said, 'It has come to our attention that the pink ribbon on the children's fleece pyjamas, model number X, is not securely attached. Should you have purchased these pyjamas, please contact us. We would be most pleased to be able to refund or exchange this item at your convenience.'

Implementation

Marks & Spencer's success stems directly from what it calls the 'gut-feeling' or 'trial-and-error' approach to management. Historically, Marks & Spencer did no marketing research. Their fundamental principle for products and services alike is 'If it sells, stock up; if it doesn't, remove it'. Up until very recently, no marketing surveys were done, no customer profiles were developed and the decision about what customers should be receiving was determined by a combination of 'gut feeling' and 'trial and error'.

The 'gut feeling' came from the top. Simon Marks was known personally to 'test' goods before they were put on the shelf and demanded that his management staff do the same. A frequently repeated story is the one in which Marks hails a passing director into his office to try on a pair of pyjamas. Five minutes later, the director was scooted back into the hall – still wearing the pyjamas.

'Trial and error' means putting an item out on the shelf to sell and taking it away immediately when it doesn't. Certain stores are used as pilots for the introduction of new items to the line. The most frequently used is the Marble Arch store in London. The stock turnover is said to be the fastest in the world, so if a new item is not sold out within the day, it is not renewed. A Marks & Spencer supplier has to be ready for either utter failure or total success.

While it may seem that Marks & Spencer is insensitive to customer needs because of their approach to marketing research, one can argue that, in fact, they are ultra-sensitive. The fact that no item is kept on the shelf unless it receives immediate customer acceptance, means that the company does not attempt in any way to impose its tastes upon the consumer. What one sees in the store is a direct reflection of what customers want and are ready to buy.

The same can be said of the way in which the company delivers its goods. The group's commitment to ensuring that customers receive friendly, helpful and efficient service reflects the customer's desire to have helpful, but not overly servile or insistent staff.

The fact that the company's goods are presented in a seemingly 'austere' environment reflects the customer's preference for purchasing products at a low price rather than paying for the window-dressing or elegant presentations. The emphasis upon homogeneous and detailed labelling reflects a similar concern – customers don't want to take the time to ask staff to find their size or the fabric content, so clear labelling is key.

The Marks & Spencer success formula did not then develop by chance. Nor is the formula changed on a whim. Changes are made only once management is absolutely sure that such a change reflects the wishes of its customers. Dressing rooms were added at the request of customers, but only after many years and after the company was sure that the generous return policy was not sufficient consolation for customers unsure of how a garment would fit.

Managing by 'gut feeling' is equivalent to managing by keeping in touch with the customer. By testing the products to be sold personally and personally visiting stores on a nearly daily basis, Simon Marks was putting himself in his customer's shoes. For each new product, he asked himself whether it met the standard of value for money which he himself had established. The chairman's so-called 'gut feeling' was actually an endless reformulation of the same question, 'Is this what the customer wants today?'

'Trial-and-error' management contributes to an even greater degree to the company's success. It permits the company to be open to trying new products as well as new ways of doing things. Once it is established that the new product or service is appealing to customers, the company rapidly adapts. Demonstrated acceptance by customers acts as a justification for any changes made inside the company.

Sometimes the changes required are quite considerable. The flip side to Marks & Spencer's success with customers is its method of internal management which permits the company to adapt rapidly to meet new imperatives.

For the most part, management at Marks & Spencer is top-down. It is not participative nor is it gentle and understanding. This is an organisation that respects the authority of its managers and rapidly and rigidly adheres to the orders sent down from above.

Modern management theory claims that this is bad news, especially for service-minded organisations. Marks & Spencer is one of the many examples to the contrary. A military-like organisation means that once a decision is made, it can be implemented very rapidly. This is particularly advantageous in a large organisation like Marks & Spencer in which any change involves many different locations and a lot of people.

A military-like organisation for the execution of decisions does not exclude taking into account staff's views in the decision-making process. Marks and other managers frequently visited stores and demanded directly the opinion of sales assistants on the floor. This behaviour is frequently imitated by store or department managers.

Communication at Marks & Spencer is also good and news about what works in one department or at one branch is rapidly communicated vertically, as well as horizontally. Official channels include the internal newspaper and circulars. More frequently used are the unofficial channels – visits from head office staff and cross-store communications.

The capacity to manage by 'gut feeling' is not the exclusive domain of the chairman. At Marks & Spencer, all staff are expected to be able to develop a feeling for what the customer wants. In practice, employees are their own best customers and each manager regularly puts himself in his customers' shoes. The company's uncanny ability to 'hit it right' on most occasions is due to the extensive experience which all management staff have on the frontline.

It is a Marks & Spencer policy to promote from within and it is one which has stood the company in good stead. All management staff are expected to have worked on the frontline and to have many years of experience in the stores before being able to move on to other posts or head office. An astonishing 90 per cent of all management positions are filled by individuals having been with the company for over five years, at least two of which were on the store floor. As a result, not only are managers able to determine what their customers are likely to appreciate, but also what the company is ready and capable of providing.

Adapting to customers' rapidly changing tastes requires responsiveness, not only on the part of Marks & Spencer, but also on the part of its suppliers. A key to the company's success since the early days has been its close relationship with its suppliers. Marks & Spencer insists upon adherence to very specific and rigorous standards for the products it sells. It also insists that suppliers are able and willing to cut or expand production rapidly to respond to market conditions.

Many suppliers are not able to keep up and the company is known to be ruthless in its relations with its suppliers. Because of the market power which it wields in the UK, it can make or break most small or medium-sized producers.

On the upside, once a relationship has been established and the supplier regularly meets the standards set by Marks & Spencer, the company can be very supportive and loyal to its suppliers. Out of 700 suppliers, more than 200 have been with the company for over 25 years. In some cases, the supplier depends on Marks & Spencer for 70–100 per cent of their sales.

A major tenet of the company's marketing strategy is to use a British supplier whenever possible. This also creates benefits for those companies. One story is about a large British textile manufacturer who would have gone bankrupt in the textile recession of the 1970s were it not for the support of Marks & Spencer.

What can be learned

1 Keep your exterior presentation consistent with your internal objectives

The example of Marks & Spencer illustrates the importance of the physical environment to the buying process. Their motto is good value for money. If they had chosen to sell their goods in highly decorated or elegant stores, the buyer would have had difficulty believing in their claim. Most shoppers are aware of just how much it costs today to create an elegant shopping environment and know that that money comes directly from their purse. The fact that they have kept a very modest presentation reinforces their honest image. In this instance more would not have been better.

2 Good service is no service

Marks & Spencer is the archetypal example of a self-service store. There are no high pressure sales tactics and, while they're there if you need them, no one is jumping out to help you. Most service quality books today talk about wonderful service in the form of smiling salespeople ready to respond to the customer's every whim. Marks & Spencer shows that it can also pay to leave customers alone.

3 If you can, use test sites

A frequently cited key element in management at Marks & Spencer is its reliance on 'trial and error' marketing methods, e.g. putting a new item out on the shelf and watching what happens. Taking this to heart, one could conclude that all modern marketing techniques are 'for the birds'. 'It works for Marks & Spencer, so it'll work for me.'

The problem is that it won't work in every situation. It works at Marks & Spencer, because they are able to use some of their large stores as consumer testing sites. Because of the large frequency of purchase in these stores – remember, Marble Arch has the largest turnover in the world – management can get a very accurate indication of whether a product will be well received or not by introducing goods on a small scale in these stores. The technique won't necessarily work if the volume isn't high enough or if the store's customers are not representative of the entire target population. The latter was true when Marks & Spencer expanded overseas and encountered difficulties when it tried to sell exactly the same merchandise in its foreign stores as at home.

4 Go for quality down the line

Marks & Spencer is known for service quality and product quality. Providing both well depends upon having suppliers which do the same.

To adapt quickly to changing consumer tastes, for example, means having suppliers which are prepared to change over from one product to another rapidly and deliver rapidly. To offer zero-defect products means having suppliers who are as commited to quality as Marks & Spencer is, and which will provide appropriate compensation if anything should go wrong.

Marks & Spencer's tough supplier policy is, thus, clearly justified; the company is a good example of the frequently cited quality chain practised by the Japanese.

MERCURY COMMUNICATIONS

Even the name implies change – lightning-fast change. Mercury skyrocketed into the UK as a direct outcome of the change in legislation of the telecommunications industry by the Thatcher Government. One day, there was British Telecom, a state-owned monopoly. Like most monopolies, it was a sleepy bureaucracy with little feeling for its customers.

The next day, there was Mercury Communications, a subsidiary of Cable and Wireless, already challenging the Goliath. Mercury not only began by offering lower prices, they also wanted to offer better service, to be a company which is responsive to its customers. Despite continual growth and change both inside the company and in the market, eight years later, Mercury Communications' primary goal is still to offer lower cost and more responsive service to its customers. Progress made over the years is permitting it to do that better and better every year.

Background

Mercury Communications began its existence in 1982 as part of a consortium owned by British Petroleum, Barclays Bank and Cable and Wireless. In August of 1984, the company became a totally owned subsidiary of Cable and Wireless. At that time it employed 200 people and was not yet licensed to compete directly against British Telecom.

Less than two months later, however, the company received its first full operating licence under the new Telecommunications Act. Today, it is the only other company authorised to provide a national fixed link public telecommunications service in the UK and, as such, is the only company to compete directly with British Telecom in most of its markets.

One of the principal challenges since 1984 has been to extend the company's service infrastructure fast enough to offer a broad range of services to customers. The company has laid nearly 4300 km of optic fibre cables, opened switching services to most major European countries and North America, put into operation three satellite communication centres and numerous microwave radio links. Mercury now offers services to both business and residential customers, transmitting voice, fax, telex, image and data communications to nearly a quarter of a million households and businesses.

This exponential growth in operations has been paralleled by a similar growth in the number of people employed from 200 employees to nearly 9000 in eight years. As Fiona Colquhoun, Director of Personnel, explains, 'We've probably created, on average, 100 new jobs a month.'

Ten thousand new customers are coming to the company per month, making change and the need to respond to customers' evolving expectations a permanent feature of the company. Mercury's management believes that if it wants to maintain its position as a low-cost supplier of quality service in an environment of continual change, it cannot rely only upon rules, structures and systems to ensure that the company's established standards of service are being adhered to.

In launching a service quality programme, as it did in 1988, one of management's goals was to make a total quality approach become an integral part of the company's culture. 'We want a total quality culture that routinely improves everything we do.' The company sees the quality customer service programme as a long-term effort, but is still very committed to it. 'We are still a long way from saying that the quality customer service approach has been completely integrated into the company. We are culturally getting there, but bear in mind that we are like a new university or a new school. It takes time to get there.'

Service strategy

When Mercury Communications launched itself into the market to compete directly against British Telecom, its first competitive weapon was low price. By using more modern and cost-effective means of communication transmission, such as optic fibre cables, and by taking advantage of its lighter, leaner administrative structure, the company could achieve significant cost savings in the provision of communications services. In turn, these savings could be passed on to its customers giving them a very tangible reason to change from British Telecom to Mercury.

Mercury concentrated initially on providing service in London and the south-eastern part of the country before expanding to other parts of the country. Depending upon the destination of the transmission, Mercury will either transmit the call entirely upon its own network or use a combination of its network, together with British Telecom lines.

A similar procedure is used for international calls. European calls, for example, are switched on Mercury's network under agreements reached individually with the separate national telecommunication carriers, and then connected to the networks of the individual carriers concerned.

While low cost will continue to remain a major feature of Mercury's competitive strategy, the company anticipates it to be a less and less significant factor as British Telecom rationalises and modernises its own network to compete more effectively. This is why, from the very start, Mercury's management has placed great importance upon the quality of service it offers. 'Partly because of being a new, competitive company, the employees always had a strong customer feeling . . . today, the exact balance between quality and low price in what we offer is changing. It's going to be quality and not price where price was the initial focus,' explains Fiona Colquhoun.

Quality service for Mercury means, 'meeting the agreed requirement between the customer and the company now and in the future'. The company has conducted extensive market research to find out exactly what the customer does expect and, in addition, has established 'listening posts' with its customers in order to follow changes in those expectations.

The listening posts for residential customers are user groups, organised regularly, from which Mercury gets feedback on what's going particularly right or wrong with the existing service and on new service ideas for the future.

Mercury's salespeople form the link between the business customer and the company; they perform informal market research to know whether existing systems are meeting the needs or whether adaptations don't need to be made better to serve an individual customer or customers as a whole. Market research done in the field doesn't just look at customers' satisfaction with Mercury systems, but also asks questions about the customer's business and the future trends in his business as they might relate to telecommunications.

Based on this kind of research, together with more formal methods, Mercury has defined four areas in which customers' service expectations are the greatest: provision of service; availability of the service; restoration of service; and customer relations. The last is considered to be the most important. 'We cannot take it for granted that our technological advantages will somehow compensate for lapses in our attitude towards the customer' (the Mercury *Quality Handbook*) 'As well as covering training and sales, it also covers those all-important intangibles – such as the need for courtesy, patience and professionalism.'

Mercury's service strategy, therefore, emphasises heavily the behaviour of each individual in his dealings with customers. In addition to guaranteeing what could be called 'fault-free service', Mercury is ensuring that it is a customer-oriented company which employs customer-responsive individuals, capable and ready to 'pull out the stops' for the customer.

Service strengths

As many Mercury customers would attest, Mercury employees are truly concerned about providing a superior service to their customers. A recent survey inside the company was done to discover what employees thought was most critical to its success. Eighty-seven per cent placed responsiveness to customers above all other options including reliability (second place), quality standards (third place), pricing, technological innovation, profitability or new services.

While the thought and conviction are not always converted into practice, customers do say that they are satisfied with what Mercury is giving them. Phone surveys of customers, done on a regular basis throughout the year, show that over 80 per cent of customers are satisfied with Mercury.

One thing that customers are getting from Mercury is 24-hour, 365-days-a-year availability. That doesn't just mean that Mercury systems are up and running 24 hours a day; it also means that customers can call in any time, from anywhere and report a problem. Once the call comes in, Mercury guarantees that a repair man will be there within four hours to fix the problem.

As the company's own *Quality of Service Report to Customers* shows, in 75 per cent–80 per cent of the cases, service is restored within six hours. In 95 per cent of the cases, service is restored within 48 hours. This report isn't just a monitoring tool for internal use; it is available to customers and is mailed regularly to Mercury 'directly connected' customers, permitting employees and customers alike to know where the company stands in terms of key service standards.

The standards included in the report include those for circuit availability (the target is 99.5 per cent), for the delay before an engineer arrives (the target is 4 hours), the delay before service is restored (the target is 6 hours for simple repairs and 48 hours for major repairs) and the availability of directory assistance (target is 15 seconds), among others.

Mercury isn't afraid to admit when things don't function as they should. In the last quarter of 1989, the company had a severe problem with its directory assistance service – only 1 in 10 calls were getting through to the operator. The company still published its service quality report and explained what was being done to improve the situation. This is in line with Mercury's policy, which is to be as honest as possible with customers and not to promise the moon if they can't deliver it.

That policy is part of a list of seven customer expectations which have been set forth by Mercury management in a *Quality Customer Service Guide*, a one-page document the size of a small address book. The carton-weight card describes exactly what Mercury's customers mean when they say that they want responsive service and exactly what Mercury employees should be doing to meet those expectations. 'Our customers expect to be treated in a courteous, helpful and trustworthy way', 'Our customers expect reliable information to reassure them in areas of worry and concern' and 'Our customers expect meticulous attention to detail in all technical and quality matters' are three statements of the customers' expectations.

Each customer expectation statement is followed by practices which help meet those expectations – 'Present a smart appearance at all times', 'Ensure our advertising proposition becomes a reality for our customers' etc. Statements like 'Use an interested, enthusiastic greeting to the customer' are backed up by training programmes that make sure all employees know how to answer the phone in the same way and underline the importance of the identified points to the company's service approach.

In a statement to the employee newspaper, Peter Moulson, Marketing Director, summarised the company's position as it relates to customer service and the quality customer service programme. 'Everyone working for Mercury projects the face of the company – whether people are digging up the roads, installing equipment or in public meetings. How individuals behave and react to problems speak volumes to actual or potential customers.'

'QCS is about installing confidence in the public by creating an internal work ethic which promotes team spirit and encourages employees to work together. . . . While QCS is an internal issue, it translates directly into better service for our customers. We are now investing in the human quality of our service since we already have the technical lead.'

Implementation

Mercury has a very clear approach to achieving good service for its customers. Beyond the provision of a technically reliable service, Mercury's goal is to create customer-responsive employees who, by themselves and their own self-initiated actions take the responsibility of assuring service quality into their own hands. As Mr van Cuylenburg stated when he first joined the company, 'Success in a very competitive environment like ours depends on continuous improvement. We therefore have to build a total quality culture in which there are structured reporting functions which promote two-way communication throughout the organisation and excellent work practices.'

Regardless of their position, their business or political philosophy, Mercury employees are to become customer aware and customer responsive. The company's quality customer service programme and its personnel policies are key methods of achieving that aim.

Service quality at Mercury centres on the behaviour and attitudes of employees. To motivate the employee to provide good service, Mercury has developed a very complete and integrated approach to employee recruitment, training and performance, and career evaluation. 'It was clear that as the company had to be competitive in an existing monopoly situation, it had to develop a cultural framework for quality and customer service. The best way to achieve this was to recognise individual performance. In growing its business, Mercury has been very dependent on the performance, motivation and morale of its people,' says Fiona Colquhoun.

'Dealing with people as individuals is actually the essential and key approach to our personnel policies. It differs substantially from any sort of collective approach. So, from recruitment onwards, everyone is dealt with as an individual.'

Policies in three areas are particularly important to the creation of a framework which encourages good customer service. The first is the company's policy on pay. The second is its performance evaluation procedures and the third is its recruitment and training policies. 'Mercury is non-unionised and there are advantages in being non-unionised. We have been able to be more radical and progressive in our employment policies and style. . . . Mercury is non-unionised, but arguably getting the best out of people's contribution in terms of what they do for the organisation.'

Pay at Mercury is determined as a function of each employee's own set of experiences and skills that he brings to the job. Unlike the standard practice in the industry which assigns an individual to a grade, and thus to a certain salary range and set of duties, Mercury operates a pay system which rewards employees on their performance and contribution to the company. 'So everybody is paid as an individual and is paid according to market rates. . . . In many ways, Mercury believes that its pay system has been more of a cultural tool than any other management device.'

With pay as a function of each individual's performance, employees are encouraged to achieve in those areas which are considered priority areas for the company. Mercury has established customer service as one of the seven most important categories of evaluation. It is defined as 'The way that the employee has demonstrated his or her awareness of customer needs.' The complete list includes other items which contribute to good customer service such as initiative, attitude and commitment, and leadership skills.

An employee's performance is evaluated once a year between November and February, and career objectives evaluated between June and September. 'We really want to link people's performance to how they develop and have regular reviews. Again, we have emphasised the customer aspect. We try to bring everything as close to the customer as possible.'

The importance of customer service doesn't come as a surprise when a new employee joins the company. Mercury makes its customer orientation clear when recruiting and has advertised using customer service as a feature of its recruiting ads. 'Ensure customer satisfaction' is the title of one recruiting ad. In another, Mercury is described as the 'modern, less troublesome network. One that's not only low on cost, but high on customer satisfaction.' As Ms Colquhoun explains, 'We have done a lot of work on how we advertise opportunities with various advertisements showing the corporate image and the corporate culture. For example, some of our adverts pick up the customer service or quality theme. . . . We tell the market something – that we want to ensure customer satisfaction.'

Employees are also tested during the recruitment process for their customer service orientation, primarily by asking how the candidate might react in certain situations in front of the customer.

Once an employee joins the company, one of the first things he or she does is go through a one-day workshop on quality and customer service. This is the same workshop which every Mercury employee went through in the first days of the programme. 'We took every employee who was in the organisation at that time to the workshop.'

Today, additional training on managing the quality process is offered through the quality customer service department, the group that heads up the programme throughout the company. Participants learn how to manage local action groups, which are quality teams working on resolving specific service problems on-site.

The quality customer service programme, or QCS was set up to increase the awareness of the need to provide good service to customers and to establish a uniform, company-wide definition of what is meant by quality service. 'Many employees who have come into the company have a strong customer feeling, but this hasn't always been totally focused and harnessed. So, one of the objectives of the QCS is actually to focus that and harness it. Largely again because of all these new people coming in with different ideas, we wanted to develop guidelines in how we actually behave to customers, both externally and internally.'

The QCS programme achieves its aims using four approaches: internal communication; the establishment of service standards; the use of quality groups or 'local action teams' to manage change throughout the company; and the introduction of monitoring tools. 'Overall, the objective is to facilitate a quality culture in the company. Already, the culture is customer driven; now, we want functional change as well', explains John Dawson, manager of the programme.

Internal communication for the programme included the introduction of a humorous and illustrated quality handbook which set forth the reasons why Mercury initiated the programme, why top quality service is vital and what is expected of employees in terms of service quality. The guide's 12 pages are a very simple statement of the importance which the company places on customer service quality – a statement which every single employee in the company has received.

Internal communication also included other written material like the telephone guide and the quality customer service guide, described above, which sets forth customer service expectations. Communication isn't only written, however, and for the launch of the programme in every single local district except one, Mercury's managing director was present and began the event with an explanation of the importance of the programme to Mercury's future success.

Mercury has approached standards from two directions. In terms of operating and quality standards, the company is being guided by the structures laid down in the ISO 9000. 'BS 5750 [or ISO 9000] is the standard we've adopted for quality management within the company. It defines a way in which we can reach the required quality we want at an economical cost' (*Quality Handbook*). In terms of standards for customer responsiveness, Mercury has gone beyond ISO 9000, by setting forth patterns of behaviour which help meet customers' expectations. The 7 customer expectations are followed by 26 standards of behaviour which help employees meet those expectations (described above).

Quality groups or 'local action teams' are being used to make changes within departments that will improve either quality or customer service. People are free to participate in the groups and an increasing number of personnel are now involved. Many problems treated by the groups are identified by employees themselves through the company's Error Detection Form. Employees can complete the form themselves and give it to the quality co-ordinator for their area or they can fill it out with the help of their manager and the quality co-ordinator. If accepted by the review committee, the problem will either be assigned to the relevant line manager for action or become the topic of a quality action team.

Ideas for the quality action teams also come from ongoing service quality monitoring activities which identify major areas of customer dissatisfaction or quality failure. Customer dissatisfaction can be identified through telephone satisfaction surveys done regularly with customers.

It can also be identified through the monitoring of customer complaint letters. Mercury records the number of complaint letters they receive on a monthly basis. In addition to analysing the types and gravity of the problems identified by customers, an increase in complaint letters can indicate a significant problem with a particular aspect of the company's service. For example, when the company was experiencing problems with its directory assistance service, complaint letters jumped by around 25 per cent.

Monitoring is also done internally by the company using its sophisticated information systems, which are capable of monitoring service failures in very exact and precise terms. The majority of the problems concern the availability of the company's service lines. Mercury's objective in the first case is to avoid as many such errors as possible 'by doing things right the first time' and, in the second place, by 'being flexible and adaptable'. 'Service is people; if there's a problem, our job is to find a way to solve it. We need to be flexible and responsive', explains John Dawson.

What can be learned

1 Give your customers a chance to appreciate your progress

If you are committed to a service quality programme in your company, but are afraid that advertising it to customers will only remind them how imperfect your service is presently, don't underestimate the support customers can give you. If you and your employees can demonstrate real concern and responsiveness when problems do arise, customers are likely to excuse you your faults and applaud improvements when they are realised.

2 Adopt service quality as a constant factor in a changing environment

Rigid structures and regulations may guarantee your company's service quality today, but it's not likely to help you very much in the future when changes in your business environment will require you to change those structures and rules. The faster that your environment requires you to change, the less useful structures and regulations are in guaranteeing a customer-oriented company.

By making a quality customer service philosophy part of your culture, you can avoid some of the bumps and bruises of constant change. Employees won't require management to provide customer-oriented rules, because they will already be thinking about better ways to serve the customer. As the environment adapts, they themselves will be the initiators in the change process that will permit the company to adapt.

MIGROS

For most visitors to Switzerland, Migros is the name of the supermarket where they bought the ingredients for their picnic lunch. For the Swiss, and for us, Migros represents much, much more. It is a philosophy, it is a set of business ethics, it is a way of life as well as a very large group of people devoted to achieving a set of goals established by Mr Gottlieb Duttweiler over 60 years ago.

Background

It would be difficult to find an individual who has had as much impact as Mr Duttweiler on the social and economic practices of a nation. Mr Duttweiler founded Migros in 1925. He was 37 and had already been successful operating a Brazilian coffee plantation. With Migros, his objective was to sell products direct to the consumer, bypassing the name brand cartels of the period. Initially, sugar, coffee, rice, pasta, vegetable shortening and soap were the only products he sold.

To reach his customers, he used small trucks whose sides opened to present the merchandise already weighed and packaged. This was just the beginning of a long period of hard work and conflict to expand Migros and to convince the Swiss of the worthiness of his socio-economic philosophies.

In the first eight years, Migros grew rapidly. The trucks were abandoned and 28 shops were set up in locations throughout German and French-speaking Switzerland. In 1928, to combat a boycott placed upon him by his competitors, Duttweiler became a producer. He established his own factories to supply his customers with the goods which he was unable to purchase on the Swiss market.

The decision to test his own products had to be taken by Mr Duttweiler at a very early stage in the history of his firm. He established the laboratories which are an important part of the Migros quality management. 'Today, the scientific equipment and the reputation of the laboratories are envied by many scientists and marvelled at by our customers.'

In 1933, under the influence of his opponents, parliament passed a federal resolution permitting the cantons to prevent retail chain shops from building on new sites. The result was to freeze Migros's growth and to push Duttweiler into politics. He created his own party which promoted his own socio-economic philosophies – a mix of Christian ethics and capitalism.

He did not hesitate to put his political philosophies into practice at Migros. In 1941, he and his wife took a step which was to mark the future of the company; they transformed the company into an association of co-operatives, passing their own share ownership on to their customers. Profits are reinvested or passed on to customers, primarily in the form of benefits or discounts.

The most important measure taken at this time was to require that 0.5 per cent of each co-operative's sales be spent for cultural activities or events for the general public. In subsequent years, this had made Migros the biggest sponsor of cultural events in the country. It has also kept managers cost-conscious as these sums come from the co-operatives' operating profits.

In 1946, the majority of the restrictions on growth had been removed and Migros continued to spread. By 1962, at the time of Duttweiler's death, Migros stores were selling a full variety of goods and produce all over the country. The company's activities had also expanded into other areas; Hotelplan, the group's travel agency company, had been created as had the Migros School, one of the largest privately-funded, public service organisations in the world.

Today, Migros activities extend into banking, insurance, transportation, printing and petrol retailing. There are over 550 stores in the country. They sell roughly 30 per cent of all bread bought in the country, 30–40 per cent of all pantihose and under-wear, 25–30 per cent of the coffee, sugar and related dry goods. Seven Swiss in 10 shop at Migros once or more times a week.

'I don't believe in personal cult, like having a picture of the founder bowed to every morning, but it appears that Mr Duttweiler was quite a figure. He was quite somebody. I can remember my parents and grandparents talk about him because he was so much out; he was also a very public and political figure. He was the best hated man for some time. Hated because he had ideas which questioned trade structures, retail trade structures.'

Service strategy

The Migros strategy is an extension of its identity as a company with a social conscience. Migros is committed to providing its customers with good quality pro-ducts for their shopping dollar. It was, in effect, the first Swiss discounter. By bypassing name brand producers, Migros was able to offer its customers better value. The quality of the products sold had to be assured and this was done by the laboratories.

The first laboratory created in 1930, was actively testing the quality of a whole series of food products. Today, the labs are the representative of the customer within the organisation and assume this role in full. The customer has full and open access to reports of their activities. The labs ensure that customers are aware that they are acting in their interests and that the standards which have been established far exceed those adhered to by Migros's competitors or set by law.

'Our role is not only one of assuring that the Migros standards are met, but also of assuring that the justified expectations of customers are fulfilled. . . . This is part of the labs' moral duty to the customer.' The labs are more than a means to an end. They are the tangible demonstration of Migros's commitment to be the 'trustee of the consumer', as Mr Duttweiler called it.

Being a company with a social conscience also means setting policies which it believes to be in the interest of the consumer. Unlike most profit-making institu-tions, Migros does not present a full range of articles and let the consumer pick and choose; it selects for the customer. The best example of this is its policy of not selling tobacco and alcohol. This policy is a left-over from prohibitionist days, but also reflects Duttweiler's conviction that a store which sells to the family should not sell alcohol and tobacco.

Migros also selects for the customer in more subtle ways. Minimum levels of quality are maintained even if cost objectives must be sacrificed. For example, an electric drill that lasts as long as it takes to drill one hole would never be accepted, irrespective of its price; a certain minimum level of quality must be maintained.

For products that do appear on the shelves, Migros ensures that customers know what they are buying so that there are no surprises on returning home. The 'Micasa Guide' is a typical example. This is an information pamphlet which describes the comparative benefits, use and installation characteristics of each set of 'do-it-yourself' type products.

The third pillar of the Migros service strategy is the '½ per cent'. Migros shoppers know that SFr2 spent at Migros means 1 centime spent on the promotion of Swiss culture. Even for the most indifferent Swiss shopper, this represents Migros's commitment to the welfare of the community. 'The ½ per cent is a cultural obligation. In the end, it's a plus.'

The shopper motivated by a social conscience can gain a certain sense of satisfaction from his weekly shopping trolley. Real enthusiasts can take part in the regional co-operative committees which have an impact on the management of the co-operative and of the distribution of the '½ per cent'.

'What makes Migros different from the others? The added-value that comes from being a socially concerned company. Our customers can say to themselves. "There is a company with a true social conscience." '

Service strengths

Service quality at Migros doesn't stop at concepts. The Migros shopper encounters on a daily basis the co-operation's concern for serving its customers and co-operative members well.

One of the clearest ways in which this can be seen is in its effort to provide a 'full service' store. Migros provides more than shelves with low-cost, high-quality goods on them; in the same complex, it provides parking, a bulletin board for announcements and job offers, children-sized shopping trolleys in some stores and self-service restaurants. An information stand is always available.

At the Säntispark complex, a combination shopping/recreational complex, Migros has gone all out. Its objective was to create 'something for both health and fun. A Disneyland idea.' The result is a surprising mix of commercial establishments and publicly available services. In the commercial centre, there is a Migros garden centre and home centre, there is a book store, a real wood-burning bakery, a sports store, sports facilities and a Migros grocery store, among others.

In and around the centre, there is an open play area for children, a copy machine, a posting board for job and other announcements, a hotel, fuel station, and public lavatories so clean that they put the ordinary housewife to shame. There is even a little party house surrounded by trees which can be rented by the public or by Migros's own employees for private gatherings.

The largest building of the complex is a water centre where there are saunas, water slides, indoor and outdoor heated and natural spa-water pools. There is even underwater music and a wave pool. The complex was designed with the idea of providing affordable entertainment for every age, so the prices are kept low and special rates are available to the elderly. 'There is nothing in the area that is so broadly available to the general public.'

In all instances, Migros makes sure that its customers are well informed about what is available to them by providing a wide selection of information. At Säntispark, there is a special newspaper available on all the centre's activities. This is in addition to the Migros newspaper which is distributed weekly to all Migros members. In Migros stores, there are numerous pamphlets available to the shopper on the goods presented in the stores, along with recipes or instructions on usage.

The Migros concept of providing full service to its public extends into the choice and organisation of the co-operative's sponsored cultural activities. Roughly 60 per cent of the '½ per cent' goes towards financing the Migros School. Courses are available in practically every conceivable topic from sewing to ballet to languages. Fifty-one schools are located throughout the country with over 6028 instructors. Last year nearly 10 million hours of instruction were given.

In general, Migros's goal is to sponsor events which are available and of interest to the greatest number of people. It is the main Swiss sponsor of public events. Concerts, exhibitions, theatre events, festivals and other large activities are favoured over the sponsorship of individual persons or small-scale events, for example. 'The ½ per cent is managed with as much care as any other part of the company.'

Implementation

The use of certain key tools ensures that Migros is able to maintain the same level of service over time and throughout all the cantons. The first is the adequate training of personnel. All employees entering the company are exposed to the company's philosophies, as well as to its commitment to the customer. One of the first required courses for supermarket store staff is entitled '(Customer) Service quality and merchandising' – a title which clearly ties the interests of the customer to any sales objectives the company might have. Other courses available include 'The customer = a partner' and 'Consulting – becoming a meat consultant in the assisted self-service department'. The stated objective for nearly one course in two concerns the customer.

To be sure that Migros knows exactly what its customers expect it to be providing, it undertakes market research on service as well as product expectations. Research is performed at the canton level and on the national level. Service issues such as the tolerated wait at the check-out counter and the politeness of personnel are evaluated. 'Compared on a whole, we're better than our competitors; especially as concerns waiting time and the kindness of staff.'

Migros also receives its customers' comments every year in a nationwide survey of co-operative members. Members are free to express their opinion about the company's service and are encouraged to suggest improvements. 'We have thousands of responses which we analyse; people suggest all kinds of things.'

An important aspect of the Migros organisation which differentiates it from all other organisations we looked at, is the relationship between marketing and the research laboratories. Because the research department acts as the conscience of the consumer, it is sometimes obliged to recommend against the commercialisation of certain products or to set certain policies in order to ensure the quality the Migros group aims for. This can be to the benefit of the marketing department in as far as it keeps them from getting into trouble.

As Mr Gugelmann, head of marketing, puts it, 'Our ultimate goal is to provide the optimum for the client; the best relation between price and quality.' By compromising between marketing and the laboratories, the goal is achieved.

Lastly, Migros relies upon the strength of its philosophical message to ensure the uniformity of its service. The idea of being a company with a social conscience is a message which all Migros employees understand and generally adhere to. Inherent in this message is the notion of good customer service or concern for the welfare of customers. For the most part, employees throughout the company are free to apply it as and where they see fit; most are highly motivated by it. Policies such as the '½ per cent' or the reliance on the laboratories serves to reinforce the message, as well as give examples of how the philosophy can be applied.

What can be learned

1 Don't forget the power of ideas

Migros is an excellent example of the power of a philosophy in business management. Many people, particularly those in more economically advanced countries, are
not motivated simply by financial gain. Migros customers and employees alike are
attracted by Mr Duttweiler's socio-economic philosophies as they are applied to
Migros and are ready to do their part.

2 Be the advocate of your customer

Migros has also been able to establish itself as the customer's advocate. Because of
the role of the laboratories and the history of the company, Migros has the enviable
position of, at the same time, representing the customer and selling to it. From a
customer service management position, this is a highly desirable situation to be in. It
increases customer loyalty and gives customers greater confidence in the intrinsic
value of their purchase.

3 Try to establish a privileged dialogue

Migros's position as the advocate of the consumer permits it to carry on a privileged
dialogue with its customers – through the co-operative meeting and the surveys and
referendums required by its co-operative status. This is not the only way to establish
such a dialogue; however, it does illustrate the usefulness of such a communication
channel. The customer freely expresses his likes and dislikes, which can then quickly
be put into action by the company.

MOVENPICK

'Movenpick is not a chain of restaurants; it is a philosophy,' says Ueli Prager, the
energetic and creative founder of Movenpick. It is a philosophy about how food and
services should be provided to customers; it's a philosophy about the atmosphere and
the way in which food and services are provided; it is a philosophy of marketing, a
philosophy of human resources management; it's a philosophy about teamwork,
about communication, about supervision, about motivation – in sum, it's a whole
philosophy about what a business should be and how to run it.

Ueli Prager retired from the company in 1989. Ueli Prager's legacy to those from
the outside will be one of a company of over 11,000 employees, over 300 restaurants
and nearly 40 hotels, but for anybody who has ever worked for Movenpick his
greatest legacy is his philosophy which permeates every aspect of the business –
Movenpick is, above all, a tangible result of Ueli Prager's incredibly imaginative and
fertile brain.

Background

Ueli Prager is the son of the owner/manager of the Carlton-Elite Hotel in Zurich, a
hotel which deserves its name. Rather more of an individualist than a good student,

Mr Prager Jr found himself at the age of 18 learning the hotel trade from the bottom up in London, Paris and Geneva.

The Second World War cut his apprenticeship short. Upon returning to Zurich he found a position with the Swiss Hotel Fiduciary Company as a probationer. His job was to determine whether financial assistance could be provided to one of the many hotels in financial trouble at the time.

'Precisely because Ueli Prager was confronted daily in his job with the less happy aspects of the hotel business, he began to develop in his mind a picture of the ideal establishment. He visualised business without fluctuations over the year, without fluctuations during the 7 days of the week and without fluctuations during the 18 working hours of the day. He planned in his imagination a restaurant which would be dependent neither on the whims and fancies of a particular class of society, nor on the season, the weather or politics.'

His first chance to apply his ideas occurred in 1946 with the construction of an office block, the Claridenhof, capable of accommodating 2500 employees in over 1000 offices; it was the largest such construction in Switzerland at the time. He wrote to the developer and proposed the establishment of a restaurant in its midst.

The restaurant opened in 1948. The architect Otto Zollinger, avant-garde for his time, designed the restaurant's exterior and interior. He is also responsible for the name. Movenpick in German means 'seagull pick'. 'It was intended to symbolise the fact that in this restaurant the guest was able to eat something small but appetising "inflight", just like the seagull . . .' Within five years, Ueli Prager had five Movenpick restaurants – three in Zurich, one in Lucerne and one in Berne.

These original Movenpick restaurants owed their success to Mr Prager's marketing philosophy. He believed that there was a new lifestyle gaining ground which was urban and informal, with a desire for quick, light meals which featured high-quality specialities like seafood and wine. A meal could be very inexpensive or very expensive, depending on how many dishes were ordered. This kind of approach was a major contrast to traditional eating which featured full menus with soup, entrée, dessert and side dishes, all served in enormous silver platters on white linen tablecloths. Mr Prager served wine by the glass and gourmet quality food on individual plates; it was a big success.

An integral part of the Movenpick concept was and still is quality, 'Quality in sparkling variety'. That could be said to be the *leitmotif* for the Movenpick group. Mr Prager explains, 'Quality, that is the constant thread, the inspiring idea running all the way through the many forms in which this philosophy finds its expression. Quality in the kitchen, in our service, in personnel training, quality in our technical equipment and facilities, quality in our printed matter, in the written word, quality in wine and in coffee. In short, total commitment in all areas and complete devotion in all our activities to the concept of quality. Doing the unexceptional exceptionally well: that is a concept of quality to which I have committed myself.'

Variety was also a main tenet of the original Movenpick philosophy. At first, it was variety in the menu with a large choice of appealing snacks. When Movenpick became not one, but two, three and more restaurants, variety meant that each restaurant had its own personality while still respecting the basic tenets of the Movenpick philosophy.

Variety began to have an even greater importance in Movenpick's history when Mr Prager began his expansion into French-speaking Switzerland. The menu and certain dishes were adapted to appeal to the more French-style tastebuds. And, for the first time, Mr Prager introduced the concept of the multi-restaurant which meant that more than one type of restaurant could be found under the same roof.

The 'traditional' Movenpick restaurant was suitable to a certain type of eating – daytime or informal evening meals with friends or family. Many customers appreciated the Movenpick philosophy of light, uncomplicated eating and were anxious to have the Movenpick concept extended to a different kind of restaurant. So, when Movenpick opened in Geneva, it not only had the traditional Movenpick restaurant, but also, under the same roof, incorporated a luxury 'Baron de la Mouette' restaurant which was suitable for more elegant evening dining and business dinners.

There was also a growing demand for a rapid, fast-food type of dining which the traditional Movenpick could not meet. In response, Mr Prager created the 'Silberkugel', a bar-style-stools-only restaurant where the service is very fast and quick.

Today, Movenpick is made up of five divisions, representing fully the concept of 'Quality in sparkling variety'. One division is devoted to the company's growing activities in consumer goods: it manufactures and distributes by itself or through licences ice cream, jam, coffee and other products for which the company is famous. Another division manages the company's worldwide hotel operations.

The remaining three divisions deal with the company's activities in the restaurant field: restaurants, including the traditional Movenpick-style restaurant, standardised restaurants, including the more concept oriented restaurants in the group like the Silberkugel, and Marché restaurants, formerly part of standardised restaurants, but spun off in 1988 to be a separate division due to its growing success.

The common thread between all of Movenpick's businesses is the Ueli Prager philosophy. Some call it the Movenpick philosophy, but excepting slight adaptations, the Movenpick philosophy is the Ueli Prager philosophy.

The entire Movenpick philosophy is very all-encompassing; there is a document dealing with practically every aspect of the business. The central concepts on which the philosophy is based, however, are condensed into 10 short phrases, representing the essence of what Movenpick stands for and what it means to their customers. We produce it here for reference, just as Mr Prager has it hanging in every single Movenpick establishment in the world.

1   In our quest for maximum quality in the goods which we buy and sell we make no compromises.
2   Our wide and carefully balanced range is an expression of true '*joie de vivre*'.
3   Our standards of cleanliness and hygiene are extremely high.
4   The atmosphere in our restaurants is pleasant and relaxing.
5   Anything we can save by improving our organisation must be passed on to the guest in the form of better value for money.
6   We ourselves want to be proud of everything we offer our guests.
7   We want to run our business fairly and reputably.
8   We want to serve our guests attentively and courteously.
9   We want our employees to be aimiable and friendly to one another and to demonstrate at all times a high degree of comradeship.
10 Everything we do must bear the hallmark of our organisation: Young, fresh, good and friendly.

Service strategy

Ueli Prager wanted to create a restaurant for individuals with a certain lifestyle. It didn't matter what the people themselves were like – rich, poor, old, young – none of that mattered. What mattered was what they came to the restaurant for. Movenpick is 'a Swiss solution to a big city restaurant, meeting the demands of the big city lifestyle'.

Movenpick is still meeting the expectations of the same group of customers today. Instead of relying on Mr Prager's instincts, Movenpick today does extensive market research. The appeal of Movenpick has changed; it is still for the young-minded and modern at heart, but it now attracts a much broader category of clients – it's for Mr and Mrs Everybody.

Studies show that Mr and Mrs Everybody are getting more demanding when it comes to the quality of service they receive. In the hotel sector, the main service expectations are for quick, efficient service, a casual approach, straightforward service and a little excitement from time to time. In restaurants, they are looking for more personalised service and more fresh, healthy food options.

Movenpick's strategy has always focused on three principal aspects: atmosphere, the product (or what goes in the dish and in the glass) and customer service. In terms of the product, Mr Prager developed the notion of providing light, but high-quality food options. For the most part, there is no established full-course meal; everything is 'à la carte'. There is a wide variety of items, particularly delicacies like fresh seafood and fresh fruit. All ingredients are of extremely high quality and 'should be perceived by the customers as being of high quality'.

Each dish is served alone with little or no garnish – which, as Mr Prager points out, raise the price and add nothing to the quality of the food. There is a separate menu for children and a separate menu for desserts. Moreover, every day there are specials which the chef has created according to the season or his own spirit of adventure.

Mr Prager's pricing policy is also part of the Movenpick strategy. Unlike many restaurants which, like the government, charge a 'tax' every time one orders a luxury good, Movenpick initiated the policy of charging the same mark-up on luxury products like champagne and oysters as they do on Coca Cola. For the customer, that means that he orders his favourite luxuries at Movenpick's and pays less than practically anywhere in town.

In terms of atmosphere, Movenpick restaurants are to be inviting and informal. They are designed to put people at ease. Each restaurant has its own particular character. That, too, is part of the strategy. One can find Movenpicks which are roadside restaurants, Movenpicks which are elegant business luncheon places, Movenpicks which look like a country inn and others that look like an artist's hangout. On the table of most of these are paper placemats – they could be in the shape of elephants for children or reproductions of works done by famous artists. There is also just one, maybe sometimes two, glasses – no more. Just enough to hold the amount of quality wine served in a carafe. Movenpick's goal is informality and simplicity.

Excellence in customer service is another part of the strategy at Movenpick. According to the 10 principles of Movenpick, guests should be attentively and courteously served. Employees are recruited for their service attitude and they are trained on customer service and on the Movenpick principles. Particularly, service at Movenpick restaurants should be rapid. There is only one waiter for every three or four tables in a Movenpick restaurant. But fast service is not intended to make the customer feel rushed. He is there to relax and his waiter is there to help him relax and enjoy himself.

That is where the little extras come in. At Movenpick, it's a policy to provide the unexpected, the extra touch that makes a visit memorable. Whether it's the chocolate with your coffee, the extra helping of whipped cream that you didn't get charged for or the note on your windscreen that says that the parking attendant washed your windows, it's part of the Movenpick service to think of new and different ways to please their guests every day. And, it's that little bit extra that makes Movenpick at bit different and a bit better.

Service strengths

What really makes Movenpick stand out from the others is the all-round quality delivered to customers in everything it does – like Mr Prager says, '. . . total commitment to the concept of quality'. He has set extremely high standards for the group and they are maintained.

If it's a steak the customer had ordered, it's not just a reasonably good steak he receives, it's a very good steak, with no fat and just the right flavour. For seafood, it's not just fresh, it's very fresh. Likewise with service, the waiters are not just friendly, they are friendly and helpful. A Movenpick brochure is not just informational, it's also descriptive. And on and on; there is no instance in which Movenpick does not place the satisfaction of its customers through the maintenance of quality standards above all other objectives.

'Quality? An overworked word? A worn-out cliché? Undoubtedly true very often. I am well aware of that,' says Mr Prager, 'But I can say one thing here, in this declaration signed by me: for my colleagues in management and for me personally, quality is the yardstick with which we measure everything. Quality and not profit.'

There is not one instance in which Movenpick has sacrificed its commitment to quality in order to improve profits. Item number 32 in the company's Charter for the Movenpick companies says, 'We do not sacrifice any of our principles for profit. Our aim is not maximum profit, but rather the optimum profit consistent with our policy of giving full consideration to the needs of our guests, customers and employees . . .'

Not only is quality something which is a rallying point; it is something which is delivered to the same degree in every Movenpick establishment throughout the world. Quality is, thus, something which is consistent and reliable. It's like the McDonald's hamburger – the same no matter where you go; except that at Movenpick, it's quality in a variety of sizes, shapes, forms or colours – variety which reflects all the different kinds of establishments the company manages. One can find the same level of quality at a Movenpick in Ouchy Lausanne on the border of Lac Leman as one can find in a roadside restaurant in the middle of Germany. Quality at a Silberkugel is the same as the quality at Baron de la Mouette, even though the restaurants themselves are quite different.

What is quality at Movenpick? It's young, fresh, good and friendly and it's everything else that's listed in Movenpick's 10 principles. What is unique and exciting about Movenpick is the consistency of its quality of service throughout every imaginative manifestation of that service in the restaurant and (soon) hotel industry.

If a customer pays SFr10 for a bottle of wine, he can be sure that that wine is truly worth SFr10 and is probably better than the SFr10 wine he would buy himself. If the customer asks for a recommendation from the waiter on what to order, he will not only get good advice, he will get personalised advice: the waiters at Movenpick don't just respond to questions, they attempt to develop a dialogue with the customer in order to identify his or her likes and dislikes so as to provide a better recommendation. No Movenpick waiter would ever recommend a dish because it is the most expensive.

'It took many mistakes before I learned that there is a definite correlation between quality and price. For example, in the beginning, I sold two classes of oysters, one expensive and one less expensive. It was only a matter of time before I gave up the cheaper quality,' explains Mr Prager.

'Another example is the coffee-cream served with the coffee. In most restaurants the coffee-cream has 15 per cent butterfat content. My colleagues tried to convince me that there was no difference between coffee with whole cream and coffee with coffee-cream. Whole cream is, of course, twice as expensive. By serving coffee-cream instead of full cream we could save SFr5000 a year. Nevertheless, we continue to serve whole cream with our coffee in the conviction that quality is our best advertisement.'

Quality for Movenpick also means quality in innovation. Movenpick is creative and imaginative in the services it provides. Worried that construction work in the Zurich airport hotel would disrupt the tranquillity of their guests, Movenpick has earplugs packaged and handed out for every guest. Together with a clever cartoon is the message, 'We are sorry for the inconvenience and hope that these will minimise the discomfort'. Never mind that there was absolutely no work going on during the evening or the early morning – it was the thought that counted.

Innovation is also the regular creation of new dishes – chefs are free to apply their imagination and skills on a daily basis to create new delights. The best of these are offered to guests as the daily special; when they are extraordinarily good, they are integrated into the menu.

Movenpick decorations also reflect a concern for creativity. One of the best-known Movenpick ideas was the use of artist's reproductions to cover the walls or to decorate the placemats.

Movenpick innovation is also the creation of the Confrérie des Gourmets Movenpick club for those loyal customers devoted to the group and its philosophy. There are special offers, elaborate parties for the children, a free copy of the annual report and reductions on hotels and on car rentals. Moreover, the card can be used to make all of the customer's purchases at Movenpick: according to the company, members use the card for 50 per cent of their purchases. Many say that the best perks are the special invitations to dinner and the opportunities to try wine-tasting in the famous Movenpick wine cellar.

Implementation

What makes Movenpick tick? Lest we forget, it's the philosophy. Perhaps what differentiates it from other philosophies encountered in businesses is its omnipresence; it is everywhere and it is set forth and written down for all to see. When one talks about Movenpick's marketing philosophy or its training philosophy, it is not just a conceptual idea, it is a document of anywhere from 10 to 50 pages written primarily by Mr Prager which deals with every vital detail of that topic.

It forms the basis for every single service standard which is created and enforced within the company. There are, in fact, two key documents in which the general philosophy and standards are laid down in terms of principles which must be maintained by the company as a whole. They include, *Guidelines for Co-operation and Management in Movenpick Companies* and *Business Principles of the Movenpick Group.*

Both documents are intended for all employees. In the first document one might expect to find the legal ramifications of the association between the various member companies of the Movenpick group; instead we find, for example, a statement on the desired working atmosphere, the purpose and limits of managerial discipline and a description of the Movenpick management style. Under the heading 'Teamwork', you find, 'The advantage of teamwork as compared with "going it alone" lies above all in mutual encouragement, support and help. . . . We feel that these relationships within the team and the general working atmosphere are right if the members of the team have the confidence to say something which might well be wrong or not properly thought through, without having to fear that such comments might later be used against them or lead to resentment. . . . '

Under conflicts there is

'We believe that whenever people come together, and that includes an organisa-tion such as ours, conflicts are unavoidable. . . . The first requirement is that all concerned must put forward their views frankly and in a courteous, reasonable manner. . . .'

This document is not intended to be a step-by-step description of how to run a company; instead it is a statement of principles about how a company should be run, about how individuals should supervise and manage within a company, and about how individuals should approach their work within the company. The document doesn't bother to go into details; it is not a list of do's and don'ts, just the presentation of how Movenpick and Mr Prager believe things should be.

It is forty pages long and is made up of six parts: What is Movenpick and what does it want? Cooperation, Management, Rights and Obligations of Movenpick Employees, Rights and Obligations of Movenpick Superiors and the Appendix, in which appears the Charter of Movenpick Companies and the 10 Principles of Movenpick (see above in 'Background').

Under Management, Management Style, we find, 'At Movenpick three clear principles apply:

- everyone is expected to use his head
- everyone is entitled to say his piece
- but the decisions must be taken by the person bearing the responsibility.'

Under Rights and Obligations of Movenpick Superiors, Suggestions for Improve-ments and Changing of Rules, there is, 'The Movenpick superior must accept proposals from his employees without any prejudice or bias. He must consider every suggestion objectively and express his thanks for all ideas and proposals, even if some of it may not be feasible. . . . Good proposals put forth by employees must never be "squashed" for prestige reasons.'

Under the Charter of the Movenpick Companies, we find the essentials of all that can be found elsewhere. There again, in the second paragraph we find the reminder, 'Movenpick is not a rigid system – it is a philosophy.'

In the second major document of the Movenpick Group – Business Principles of the Movenpick Restaurant Group – we find a detailed and exacting description of what it means to be a young, fresh, friendly company, with standards of excellence. While there is still a great deal of philosophy, there are also specifics – overall standards of service which must be maintained.

Under the heading Principles of the Product Range, there is, 'Culinary rituals such as brunch, salad buffet, the never-empty coffee cup, sea-food festival, gourmet post, farmer's breakfast, dessert buffet, etc. should be planned and maintained on a long-term basis. . . . A culinary ritual should be something which endures the test of time: consistency in the range of products and no spasmodic alterations.'

Under Thoughts on Portion Size, there is, 'We know very well that we cannot suit everyone's taste. Movenpick is not a restaurant for gluttons (as far as the actual portions are concerned).'

We also find comments like, 'Every client must be convinced of

- an uncompromising quality
- the absolute freshness of the merchandise and the sound price policy'

and, under Presentation and Packaging, there is, 'Presentation must correspond to the standard of quality and price level. . . . We want to avoid tittle-tattle or to be out of date, and instead be unconventional, fresh and dynamic. . . . Every paper bag, every package and every piece of cake on the dining-room table is in itself a form of publicity and an image maker.'

While the *Guidelines for Co-operation and Management* document is only 40 pages long, the *Business Principles* is 44. Together they are, by far, the most comprehensive statement of business philosophy and practice that these authors have seen in all their research.

The setting down of principles doesn't stop with the main documents for the Movenpick Group. For every single restaurant or service concept a separate set of principles and a separate business standards document is established. They are patterned after the 10 Movenpick principles and the *Business Principles* document.

For example, when the Silberkugel restaurant concept was created, a set of seven principles was laid down which summarise the principle advantages which the concept presents to customers. For the Silberkugel, they are, '1 constant high quality, 2 limited selection, 3 quick service, 4 low prices, 5 healthy and appetising, 6 absolute cleanliness and hygiene, 7 no tips'.

For the group's newest concept, the 'Marché', a similar list of six items was drawn up including the principle advantages of the Marché concept – that it offers extremely fresh food – fresh vegetables, fresh meat and fresh fruit which is prepared right in front of the customer. 'Our employees should create an impression of high knowledge about and high identification with our products. The guest must feel that the employees all but love their products. They should communicate intensely with the customers and thereby give them an unparalleled restaurant experience,' says Franz Pichmüller, executive vice president of Marché restaurants.

Starting from Mr Pichmüller's six principles, a guidelines or standards document was created. It is, like all of the comparable documents of the different restaurant groups, not set in stone, but modified and expanded as the concept grows and develops. 'It is discussed time and again by senior management and employees.'

The hotel group has a similar document which is 'living and growing'. Starting from the '10 commandments' of the hotel group, the document deals with each principle separately, expanding on what it means to employees on a daily basis. 'Every six months it is adapted and changed to reflect the new standards and improvements.' There is, for example, a standard that all beds are extra large – 1.4m by 2.05m, that reception desks are no longer desks, but islands, and that all complaints must be followed up personally by the manager

The business guidelines and standards books are only a start. 'Our manuals and standards are very basic. We give employees a great deal of freedom to take the initiative to develop extra services. . . . They come up with ideas, like the butler service we offer between 6 and 8 p.m., the free newspapers and the welcome letter. If we want to be really customer-oriented, we have to make the little extra effort, the little touches.'

Mr Prager believes in giving customers what they want, '... give the client what he wants and not what we think he ought to have' (*Business Principles of the Movenpick Restaurant Group*). To know whether what is being provided is what the customer wants, Movenpick goes direct to customers to ask them what they think of Movenpick's service. This is done in four ways.

First, every hotel or restaurant customer has access to a satisfaction survey card which he can fill out at his leisure. Secondly, test panels of customers are conducted on a regular basis to investigate exactly what customers like or dislike about their services, as compared with competitors.

Thirdly, Movenpick has a survey conducted in every one of its restaurants and hotels two to three times per year. 'Friendliness of the staff, competence, the quality of the food, the degree of attention to customers and many other factors are tested in this survey. Nine thousand customers are approached to participate in Switzerland – roughly 100 per restaurant. We wanted to be sure that we were maintaining the same level of quality everywhere in the group and at all times,' explains Mr Heinz Schurtenberger, EVP of consumer goods and corporate marketing.

The best restaurants or hotels or those making the largest improvements appear on the 'Hit Parade' of Movenpick restaurants. The 'Hit Parade' is communicated throughout the group; there is a great deal of competition between restaurants to get on the 'Hit Parade'.

Lastly, Movenpick uses outside companies to do 'Mystery Customers' tests. Individuals test Movenpick's services and record their impressions. In some cases, the service received is scored according to a checklist of Movenpick's own standards; in other instances, the service is just 'lived' permitting the mystery customer to reflect his spontaneous reactions to things like the atmosphere, the decor, the friendliness of the staff etc. 'We have mystery customer tests done twice a year in all our hotels; when the results come in, they are really examined closely. Each hotel manager assembles all the staff and they analyse the results; there is no hammering down, we just analyse what works and doesn't work.'

With all that the Movenpick Group does to satisfy its customers, one would have to say that, if nowhere else, the customer is king at Movenpick. But no, it's not part of the philosophy. 'At Movenpick, we do not believe that the customer is king, as they say in Switzerland. That saying has something dreadfully undemocratic about it – a flavour of almost prostitution. We want our guests to be our friends in hospitality. We do not want the servile attitude of persons waiting at table. What we want is that the serving of our customers – I'm almost tempted to say our friends – should be our profession and our vocation,' says Mr Ueli Prager.

What can be learned

1 Base your company's success on a philosophy, not a concept

Concepts can go out of date, become old-fashioned; philosophies can be adapted over time. Movenpick is made up of one philosophy, and many concepts – the ones that work best at the moment. The Movenpick philosophy is specific enough to base operating standards upon and general enough to change with customer's tastes or as new concepts are added to the group.

2 Put it down in writing

Mr Prager's philosophy would just be words if someone had not put all of it down in writing. They not only put it in writing, they organised it into a set of Bibles about key aspects of running the company. Today, those books are Mr Prager's greatest legacy and the most powerful tools the company has to help it meet challenges in the future.

3 Tell your customers what you're giving to them

You may think it's obvious, but most of the time customers don't know what you provide better than the competition unless you tell them. Movenpick lays down for each of its restaurant or service concepts, a set of principles which state in no uncertain terms in what way Movenpick is providing a superior service than the competition. In technical terms it's called managing customers' expectations and it helps both you and your customers know where you stand.

4 Do something for your loyal customers

Movenpick, like many very successful businesses, has a very strong following of loyal customers. Rather than letting all of that goodwill sit idle, Movenpick chose to mobilise it through their Confrérie des Gourmets Movenpick club. It offers advantages to members which, in a way, rewards them for their loyalty to the group and increases that loyalty even further. For the company, it gives them direct access to a set of consumers to use to test new ideas or from whom to receive valuable suggestions.

NATIONAL WESTMINSTER BANK

Numbers can sometimes bring things into focus. One number that stands out when one looks at National Westminster Bank is the number 6,000,000 – that's the number of customers the bank serves.

There's another number that stands out – 110,000 – that's roughly the number of people that work for National Westminster Bank and, thus, the number of people that must be convinced that providing top service quality to 6,000,000 customers is an absolute priority.

We say 'must *be* convinced' because in National Westminster's case, the road towards total service quality is a long one and while they are well on the way, they still have a way to go. 'The pursuit of quality,' says Mr Goodstadt, Head of Service Quality, 'is, indeed, a journey without end.'

Background

National Westminster, or NatWest to its friends, is one of the four big English clearing banks. A clearing bank in the English context is a bank that handles the clearing of cheques and all major financial instruments. The four clearing banks, Barclays, Midland, Lloyds and NatWest are all highly active in the retail banking market, in addition to having developed activities in all the major banking domain over the years – trade finance, corporate finance, securities issues, cash management, foreign exchange etc.

All four of the clearing banks have a large network of branches distributed throughout the UK. Competition between the four banks is very stiff. It is getting all the more intense as foreign banks or semi-banks, such as the building societies, are beginning to offer the same services as the clearing banks, i.e. chequing facilities.

In early 1983, it was already clear to NatWest that service quality would become a determining factor in the future for winning customer loyalty. The marketing department had identified it as such and was instrumental in the launching of the initial 'Standards of Service Campaign' in 1984.

The initial campaign merely served to demonstrate how much more needed to be done. Tom Frost, Group Chief Executive, had followed the success of the American operation that had focused on service quality and, in the process, had become convinced that service quality was the direction that the bank should take. The commmitment of resources to achieving top service quality quickly followed.

In 1986, the bank created the service quality department, one of six support units that report directly to the Operations Manager of UK Financial Services. 'There was the recognition that a chain of service existed all the way down to the customer and that there was a need to have performance standards.' Service quality was subsequently adopted as the bank's 'corporate vision' in 1987. (UK Financial Services is one of the four divisions created in a reorganisation of the bank that led to the grouping of all retail activities in one division, and Internation Businesses, Corporate and Institutional Banking and Investment Banking into three other divisions, respectively.)

Also in 1987, a series of communication exercises was launched, designed to advertise throughout the bank the new commitment to service quality and to make people aware of what that implied for them as individuals.

From 1987 onwards, the quality department worked on setting up the systems and structures needed to manage service quality and to instruct staff in the use of these tools. In 1989, the bank organised, 'Making a Difference', a series of management seminars which explained to managers the strategic positioning of the bank in the future and gave them the basic set of tools which they needed to implement change on a branch level.

The follow-on to 'Making a Difference' was 'The Cost of Making Mistakes', introduced in 1990. This programme was aimed at decreasing costs through better service quality; its diffusion was accompanied by a set of tools for implementation at the branch level. A parallel effort was launched in the central departments called the 'Quality Gap Analysis'.

The ultimate objective of the service quality department is for it to phase itself out. This will be possible once the concern for service quality should already have become a built-in reflex of all managers in the company. 'By 1995, my objective is for this department to be phased-out,' says Mr Goodstadt.

Service strategy

National Westminster's present strategy was developed during the period of reflection and intensive market research between 1986 and 1989. The outcome of research conducted during this period showed that greater competition and the effects of an ageing population were going to make it more difficult for the bank to bring in new customers; the emphasis should switch, therefore, from bringing in new customers to retaining existing customers.

To increase loyalty rates and the level of activity with each customer, the bank decided that it must increase customer satisfaction. Satisfied customers 'Buy more, Buy again, and Recommend'. Higher customer satisfaction then became the first point in a strategy to improve the Bank's competitive position.

A second point in the strategy was the reduction of costs through streamlining. It was shown, for example, that 14 per cent of staff's time was being spent on correcting mistakes. Streamlining was translated in practical terms into the programme for reducing errors through improved quality, 'The Cost of Making Mistakes'.

The third point in the strategy was the increase in sales to existing customers. Fifty-five to 60 per cent of the Bank's customers had only a chequing account with the bank. In addition to various lending facilities, the bank could now offer insurance, mortgage loans and savings/investment options.

Better customer satisfaction would already contribute to achieving this goal. The company restructured its insurance and mortgage activities in order to provide better support to the branch staff, i.e. they simplified the paperwork, provided clear explanations of the various products, gave workshops on how to sell to customers etc.

The last point in the strategy was the renovation and improvement of the company's technological support system to make it more user-friendly and customer oriented. One of the first things done, for example, was to change the access system from access by account number to access by customer name. This not only makes the system immediately more personalized and customer oriented, but it will also permit the bank to group all of a customer's facilities under one heading. The situation today is such that a customer who has an account with two NatWest branches cannot, for example, call up one of the branches and know his account number on both accounts.

The ultimate goal of the strategy is to create a perceived difference for the bank in the marketplace on the basis of the quality of its customer service. Eight years into the programme, the bank is already realising considerable improvements in terms of the overall level of customer satisfaction and improvements in efficiency.

Unfortunately, for the moment, there has been no change in the perception of the bank *vis-à-vis* its principal competitors. 'We look particularly at image tracking. There is always a lag effect between change within the bank and the perception of that change by customers. But, what we are seeing is that overall customers are getting better banking services, so we are still no different than the competition.'

Service strengths

The service quality programme at National Westminster has achieved results in one domain in particular: employees now understand what is important to customers in terms of service and are making small, but significant efforts on a daily basis to offer better service.

Through customer research, the bank identified key areas for improvements in service quality. For some service standards were established which permitted the staff to measure their performance according to the standards. For others, progress could be measured by referring to the results of the customer satisfaction survey done each year for each branch.

The length of the queue at the counter was identified as a priority item for customers. Standards are set at the branch level acccording to local conditions (in cities, customers are in more of a hurry so the waiting time must be less). If the branch has trouble meeting the standards, employees meet in a 'Quality Service Action Team' to examine the problem and propose solutions.

The process used, which involves seven steps including cause and effect analysis, fact finding, finding solutions through brainstorming, 'puts the employee in the customer's shoes,' says Terry Deaville, a QSAT co-ordinator for one of the regions. 'In the QSATs, there is a total involvement in thinking about improving service quality for customers.'

The ability with which staff can answer customers' questions is another priority item for customers. No standard has been set in this area, however, improvements at the branch level have still been made through the QSATs. Solutions proposed included more doubling up during initiation training periods, more training in the products the bank sells and the assurance that there is always a senior staff member on duty to which younger staff can go immediately for help.

Results have been achieved. On the whole the QSATs have led to improvements at the branch level through cross-training, training in speaking and answering the telephone, and in scheduling changes to better serve customers in the peak hours. Customer satisfaction ratings are rising in most branches and a recent internal survey showed that 90 per cent of the staff, 'appreciated that service quality is a number one objective'.

Implementation

The service quality process at National Westminster has passed through three big phases. The first phase, let's call it the Adoption Phase, involved the identification of customer service expectations, the sensitising of employees to the need to provide top service quality, and the adoption of service quality as a strategic 'vision' for the bank.

As a part of that phase, there was the 'Standards of Service Campaign' in 1984. The campaign focused on:

courtesy to the customer;
use of customers' names;
a complaints reduction programme;
a customer response programme, i.e. a customer satisfaction survey.

The result of the campaign was to bring service quality to the attention of every employee in the bank. Employees saw through the customer satisfaction survey and through the customer complaints monitoring exercise, the importance of service quality; 'Within the minds of staff we raised a profile of service quality.' The staff were also directly involved in identifying possible improvement areas; 'We encouraged staff participation and thereby identified areas of strengths and weaknesses within individual branches.'

Perhaps the most lasting outcome of the Adoption Phase was the introduction of the customer satisfaction survey. The identification of customer groups, such as service lovers or accuracy fanatics, was made possible by the survey. Since that time, research on customer satisfaction and customer expectations has been conducted every year with results available for each branch and for the whole bank.

The next phase of the process was the 'Tools Phase' which began in 1986 with the establishment of the service quality department and the launch of a full-fledged quality service programme. In this phase, staff were presented with the tools which could be used to manage service quality and were taught how to use them.

Highlighting that phase was the 1987/8 one-day Quality Service Programme Seminar, an enormous bank-wide communications exercise which involved the participation of every employee in the branch banking network – over 60,000 employees. Seven special conference facilities were built throughout the country to host the event.

At the seminar, the organisers presented information on the customers which the bank had and on the expectations of those customers in terms of service. Video-taped passages of interviews with customers were used to make some of the key points. These were then followed by interviews with staff about what they believed customers' needs were. The objective was to show clearly the gap between what employees understood to be good service and what was actually perceived as being good service by customers.

The results were impressive. 'Even those who had rather cynically viewed the day as an opportunity to spend some time away from their normal work were won over and convinced as to the crucial importance of what the bank was trying to achieve.'

Concretely, employees were presented with the concept of service standards and were taught how to organise and run Quality Service Action Teams.

On a bank-wide level, 12 key areas were identified as being the most important contribution to the satisfaction of customers; they were targeted for the creation of standards. For some of these central standards have been set which apply throughout the bank. They include, for example, delays on opening new accounts, the turnaround time for loans, the handling of customer complaints etc.

In other key areas local standards have been set to meet the variations in local conditions. There are, for example, local standards set by each branch for the waiting time at the counter, the level of privacy accorded to customers during discussions, the capacity of employees to answer questions and the handling of the telephone.

With these priority areas in mind, employees then meet in Quality Service Action Teams to identify major problem areas for the branch and propose solutions. The bank has between 3000 and 3500 teams running throughout the bank. In the first three and a half years, the groups proposed over 10,000 solutions, over 50 per cent of which have been implemented.

'Making the Difference' was a communication effort launched in 1989/90 to confirm the bank's commitment to service quality and to outline the four parts of the

Bank's overall service strategy for the coming years (see *Service Strategy*, above). Its follow-on was 'The Cost of Making Mistakes' which provided a new tool to branch managers for the management of service quality.

Employees learned the difference between 'the cost of mistakes (complaints, reworking), the cost of prevention (training etc.) and the cost of appraisal (inspection, checking for errors)'. Employees were given charts which helped them monitor the time it takes to perform certain tasks – investigation time, amending reports, time spent with customers over a complaint etc., and to chart improvements as they are realised.

In a parallel step designed to improve the service quality delivered by one internal department to another, the 'Quality Gap Analysis' was introduced in the head office departments. This tool permitted employees to identify the difference between 'doing the wrong things right', 'doing the right things wrong' and 'doing the right things right'. The first step to the process is the identification of what one's customer department really expects in terms of service. The second step is to streamline and improve internal processes to ensure that the customer department is receiving the value-added he desires.

The third phase of the service quality process at National Westminster came to an end in 1990. 'Now, most staff have grasped the concepts and absorbed it into their functioning . . . it's an accepted norm.'

'We built the structures for Total Quality Management; it's now up to managers and staff to take ownership of service quality issues,' says Mr Goodstadt.

Phase four could be called the 'Ownership Phase'. It involves the integration of service quality concerns into the daily functions and objectives of employees at all levels of the company and, thus, a change in the corporate culture of the bank.

Without putting aside the tools introduced in the past, the bank is placing greater emphasis on bringing about change by building quality incentives into the motivation packages of managers and employees.

In the autumn of 1991, the bank introduced a new procedure concerning customer complaints. Branch managers are now in a position to compensate customers for errors made on their accounts. The funds used for this compensation are taken directly from the manager's budget for the branch. 'It is to give the branch manager another way to try to retain good business; the fact that it comes off the bottom line means that he will be motivated to ensure that less mistakes are made in his branch.'

A portion of branch managers' salaries are being tied to progress made on service quality objectives. Yearly objectives are being established for each branch by the regional director, together with the branch manager. The maintenance of standards and the improvement in the customer satisfaction rate for his branch, for example, can increase a branch manager's salary by between 10 and 20 per cent.

The 22 regional directors are also being evaluated on their achievement of service quality objectives by one of the bank's two regional general managers. While in the past the exact criteria for evaluation has been somewhat indefinite, the bank is in the process of finalising the criteria with improvements in customer satisfaction ratings at the branch level being one of the principal ones to be used.

An important consideration in this phase in the eyes of those managing it in the service quality department is that the change in culture should be implemented with a minimum of backlash effect. 'The culture of the bank in 1980 is not the same as it was in 1990. We have continuously been chipping away at the traditional banking culture that, for example, employs for life, says that if you don't lose money and keep your nose clean, you'll be all right etc. Going from that to a culture based on service quality and competition can create a backlash.'

Since 1989, the bank has been conducting internal employee focus seminars designed to find out what employees' reactions were to the changes taking place within the bank and what aspects they needed to move faster in the right direction. Following the communication of each major new step in the service quality process, a series of panels has been organised throughout the country.

Following the 'Making the Difference' programme 16 different employee panels were organised with 72 staff participating. 'They were asked what they thought the bank had communicated well to them, what the bank had communicated badly, and what they wanted more information or explanations on.'

The regional directors received the results of each panel. Starting in 1991, the panels are being conducted on a regular basis every six months. The positive impact of the panels are that they 'created 72 supportive staff members. It also identified 12 issues that were raised consistently at every location.'

For the future, the bank will concentrate on bringing a greater unity of thought and action within the bank as concerns service quality. 'Today, there is a great variation in achievement between the regions. Geographic issues play a role. The commitment of the regional directors and the branch managers also plays a role: some are totally committed to quality; others less so.'

What can be learned

1 Shoot for the stars; if you are really successful you will make it to the sixth floor

Sad, but true, the standard for good service in the eyes of the customer is always moving upwards. What would be considered outstanding service quality today is only good service quality tomorrow.

National Westminster has made considerable progress in raising its standards of service quality since 1983. Unfortunately, its competitors have also progressed – at least a little. A true differentiation on the basis of service may only be possible if NatWest moves twice as fast as the competition.

2 Make it a process, not a campaign

National Westminster recognised at a very early stage that service quality would not be a short-term but a long term objective that would require the involvement of the entire company if concrete achievements were to be realised. Service quality is, thus, a journey without end as there is always more to do better.

3 Take small steps to make a big difference

One of the greatest successes of NatWest's service quality programme has been the achievement of small improvements at the branch level made by employees through the Quality Service Action Teams. These changes have probably had more direct impact on the quality of service the average customer experiences than many an elegant statement by a bank director.

4 Keep employees focused on service quality

Since adopting service quality as a strategic 'vision' in 1987, the bank has never let up on its effort to convince employees of its commitment to that vision. Employees have received continual reminders in many different forms of the importance of service quality. These reminders have had and will continue to have a positive impact on how employees view and treat customers.

NESTLÉ

Nestlé is a company known to most consumers. It produces and markets quality food products for babies, adults and pets alike. It has operations worldwide and has long practised a policy of providing the best quality goods possible to its customers.

Background

Nestlé was founded in 1867 by Henri Nestlé, a German chemist who came to live in Vevey Switzerland. He was strongly affected by the high rate of infant mortality which existed throughout the world at that time and set about to create an infant formula for infants who, for any reason, need a breastmilk substitute.

By 1867, Mr Nestlé had succeeded in creating an infant formula which had been successfully used by infants. In that year, it was used for the first time with a young infant who was dying because he had rejected his mother's milk. Following this success, Henri Nestlé launched his product into the Swiss market and rapidly into the international market place. By subjecting the product to the approval of doctors, Nestlé achieved rapid acceptance in the different markets.

The firm grew and prospered and under normal circumstances might have been passed on to Mr Nestlé's children upon his retirement, but Mr Nestlé had no children and so in 1875, Mr Nestlé sold the business to three Swiss businessmen from Vevey.

The company continued to grow and expand over the next 30 years under the guidance of these two individuals and their successors. The period was marked, however, by the worldwide competition between Nestlé and another group, the Anglo–Swiss Condensed Milk Company from Cham, in the Canton of Zug. Surprisingly, the end result was the merger of these two groups in 1905.

From that time forward, Nestlé's history has changed regularly by successive mergers which have meant the integration of more than 16 major companies. Many modifications have been made in the business activities of the company as a result. In 1929, chocolate was definitely made part of the company's activities. Soups and other foodstuffs were added thereafter. Nescafé, one of Nestlé's most well known products was launched in 1938.

From the first to the last merger, however, the character of the Nestlé company itself has changed very little. Even with production units in over 60 countries and sales to over 100, Nestlé is still a very Swiss company, although more than 50 per cent of the shares of the company are owned by foreigners. Its headquarters, divided between Cham and Vevey ever since the merger with the Anglo–Swiss Condensed Milk Company, are still in those two towns.

Its initial character as a company resolutely oriented towards the production and sale of nutritious and high-quality foods has remained. So has its practice of having a highly decentralised management and of adapting products to local market tastes. It is a company with a strong marketing orientation that has always believed in promoting the brand names of its products including Nestlé, Carnation, Chambourcy, Findus, Rowntree-Mackintosh, Maggi and many, many others.

It is also a company with a strong research base and extreme concern for the quality of its products in every sense. Nestlé has always maintained research facilities and believed in fostering close relationships with suppliers, just as Henri Nestlé helped local milk producers better to control the quality of the product for his infant formula.

Nestlé is a very decentralised company, and for the most part management is left in the hands of local managers. But, like many Swiss companies, Nestlé believes in careful long-term planning. It believes in setting objectives and in having a strong centralised reporting system for the monitoring of results. It believes in the training and development of personnel, much of which is directed from Switzerland. It has a policy of giving potential general managers and employees in general the possibility of working in other countries. It also believes in bringing local managers to Switzerland to get a feeling for the Nestlé culture at its very heart.

Nestlé is a group which integrates other companies very successfully. It is generally a Nestlé policy to make only friendly acquisitions. Once acquired, Nestlé slowly, but surely, helps the company adapt to the Nestlé mould. Whether through the exchange of personnel, the adaptation in the reporting system, or creation of synergies through research, the new group always succumbs sooner or later and becomes Nestlé.

Nestlé today is 200 operating units, 200,000 employed worldwide, 420 factories on 5 continents and an annual turnover of SFr50 billion. It is the largest food manufacturing group in the world.

Nestlé's logo, a nest of birds, is almost the same as it was in 1867 when Nestlé created it. It stands for 'childhood, the family, motherhood, tradition, food and security', the Nestlé values of today and yesterday.

Service strategy

Nestlé is a product oriented company. It has pursued the aim of providing quality products to consumers since its inception. It has never hesitated in its efforts to ensure that its products meet the nutritive needs of its customers and are of extreme reliability. As a result, it has gained the confidence of thousands of consumers worldwide.

Today, Nestlé continues its pursuit to provide quality products and to be an innovator, creating systems which ensure even greater quality assurance. Yet, new developments are pushing this giant to direct its efforts into other areas, notably into service quality.

Its customers – at once distributors and consumers – are no longer satisfied with just receiving good quality products. Distributors are asking to receive more assistance in merchandising and marketing, greater access to Nestlé's knowledge about the market, quicker delivery times and more flexible delivery schedules.

Consumers are demanding to know more about product contents, to get advice on how best to use it, to receive more detailed responses to their questions on health and nutrition and more personalised attention to their complaints. In sum, Nestlé must now provide complementary quality service to go with its top quality products.

Nestlé's service strategy, unlike that of most companies examined in this book, is not designed to give the company a differential advantage; its product marketing strategy already does this. For Nestlé, its prime aim in pursuing service quality is to reinforce its product strategy.

Nestlé's product strategy is to produce and market high-quality, highly nutritive products under top brand names worldwide. Its service strategy addresses both the needs of consumers and distributors. With consumers, Nestlé has focused on two areas:

> the provision of adequate product information in order that the consumer can evaluate for himself the nutritive value of the product; and
> the creation of services which encourages brand loyalty and permits the consumer to better appreciate the product he buys.

In service quality to distributors, Nestlé is focusing on:

> creating a partnership link with the client; and the provision of complementary information or advice from specialists on market trends, customer expectations, merchandising and marketing issues.

In our research, we looked at six different operating companies at Nestlé, each with a different product line and a different approach to its basic business. One of the primary unifying factors between all of these companies was the common service strategy. Each company is working to achieve the service objectives shown above.

Service strengths

Not all of the Nestlé companies pursued the various service objectives equally. Certain companies focused more on those related to the consumer and others focused more on those relating to the distributor/partner. In our research, we talked to managers in five different Nestlé operating companies in France to see how these objectives were being implemented.

'Providing good consumer information' – at France Glace/Findus, a Nestlé subsidiary making ice cream and frozen dishes, the department of customer services handles enquiries and complaints. Ninety per cent of the communications coming into this department of six people are enquiries. There are questions on how best to cook Findus's frozen quiches, how long to keep frozen food in the freezer section and, even, how to operate microwave ovens. There are also requests for recipes and help on what to serve with what.

Nestlé is encouraging enquiries and has printed on all its packages the number to call whenever information or assistance is needed; the address is also given. Consumers throughout France can call on the freephone number, can connect to the Minitel (France's telephone based communication system) or write. The Minitel is equipped to answer certain basic customer questions. The rest come into the department. Out of 200,000 consultations on the Minitel, only 3000 cannot be answered and are sent on to the department.

Two-thirds of the customer service department's staff are culinary and nutrition specialists, on hand to respond to customer's questions. All requests are answered immediately and the longest turnaround time for any request is one week. The staff are extremely conscientious in their work. Madame Angiboust, who heads the department views her role as 'being the conscience of the company'. She is there to apply the basic principles of the company *vis-à-vis* the consumer, including:

the consumer's right to security;
the consumer's right to information.

One of her greatest worries is that a consumer might phone and say 'you didn't answer my letter'.

Nestlé doesn't just wait for consumers to come to them; a great deal of nutritional information is provided on the packages and booklets or recipes are available in the supermarket. The company regularly produces information designed to improve the consumer's knowledge about the product they buy. Advice on different cooking methods (microwave cooking, light cuisine etc.) is also provided.

Gloria, a Nestlé subsidiary producing pet food, has a full information service about all pets in the Minitel. The service addresses every possible aspect of a pet's life and provides information and practical advice on items such as care and feeding, as well as legal registration. There is also a special section which permits owners to identify particular illnesses, for example. Like France Glace/Findus's Minitel service, any requests that can't be answered by the Minitel are automatically passed on to the company's special department which goes out of its way to find the right response that will satisfy the customer.

'Services to bring the consumer closer to the company – consumers developed an attachment to certain products and are not only loyal purchasers, but strong advocates. This type of consumer appreciates having his loyalty recognised. Nestlé has responded by creating product clubs, journals or special channels of contact for certain types of products.

At Gloria, the producers of Gourmet brand cat food, there is a Club Gourmet. The members of the Club receive a magazine, *Moustaches*, ('*Whiskers*') which provides general information on the cat world. There are articles on famous cats, on the proper feeding and care of cats and stories in which cats feature as heroes. There is also a newsletter, *Infos Club*, with regular features and a calendar of events for Club Gourmet's members. The Club organises dinners and evenings at which members can meet other members and celebrities who are cat lovers like themselves.

Nestlé also brings the product out to the consumer. One of the most appreciated services which Nestlé's baby food division provides is Baby Stops on motorways for summer vacationers. Located at key places on holiday routes, the Baby Stops are full service food, play and nappy-change stops for parents. Everything is thought out and prepared. Changing tables are provided with complementary nappies and assistance in changing baby. A feeding area is also set up with complementary water and food for babies from three months to two years. There is even an area where parents can sit, while the children play. The Baby Stops are impeccably clean and respond to a real need of travelling parents.

'Creating a partnership link with suppliers and distributors' – Nestlé would like to extend its own concern for product and service quality to its suppliers and distributors alike. To do this it has initiated a partnership programme whose aim is to open the dialogue between Nestlé and its business partners to identify the major concerns of each and to allow each to respond to them.

As a result, norms have changed on product delivery times. For many years, Nestlé's promise was to provide 'the right product, within 48 hours, with the expected quality', It was a promise which 'the staff would live or die to complete'. It was presented in the form of a service guarantee.

Today, some distributors do not require such short delivery times, others require an even shorter delay. In yet other cases, it depends upon the product to be delivered. Nestlé is now adapting its approach to meet the specific need of the client.

'For example, dairy products, like Chambourcy, must be delivered in less than 48 hours, whereas other products, like coffee or chocolates, do not require the same short delivery times.'

To create different levels at which dialogues with the client can occur, Nestlé/Rowntree is emphasising the importance of a team of specialists. Nestlé/Sopad is doing the same thing. Each individual on the team is a specialist in his domain – logistics, sales, merchandising etc. – and creates links with his counterparts in the client company. To ensure that the information received by one individual flows to the others in the group, meetings are held in which these individuals exchange what they have learned.

To increase the quality of the relationship with its clients subsidiary company, Davigel's relationship managers provide advice on menus, on food presentation, food preservation and, in some cases, on the management of the client's business. They work hand-in-hand with their clients in order to help them advance their business.

'Providing clients with specialist information' – a key advantage of belonging to such a large group as Nestlé is having access to information about what is happening in many markets for many products. Nestlé puts this knowledge to work for its clients.

At Davigel, customers are given advice on trends in gourmet eating and on what new dishes are likely to best sell with which type of clientèle. The information is available from Davigel's own culinary research which permits it to introduce a large variety of new dishes each season.

At Nestlé/Rowntree, information on marketing trends is being packaged for customers to meet their needs for information on a specific geographic region or a particular product. In some cases, customised studies can be performed.

'We do studies for clients on the best way to merchandise products. This is a service provided by other companies in the industry, but few do it well.' The company has set up a team prepared to respond to requests for merchandising studies. The team is made up of individuals which already have wide experience in the area; 'in terms of the quality of work offered, what we will provide will be ahead of the competition'.

Implementation

Two things contribute the most to Nestlé's good service. The first is that Nestlé knows what its customers want in terms of service; the second is Nestlé's traditional preoccupation with quality that influences the way it serves its customers and clients.

Knowing what customers want

Nestlé performs marketing studies on practically everything. Happily for consumers and clients, Nestlé also performs studies on their service expectations. Such studies revealed that consumers wanted to know more about the food content of what they are buying. It revealed that a club for cat owners would be well received, but that one for dog owners would probably not be. In some instances, studies have shown that the instructions for preparation on packages were insufficient or misleading. The results of such studies at Nestlé are taken seriously and acted upon without delay.

Studies on service expectations with distributors revealed that these clients needed more flexible delivery times, that timeliness on deliveries was becoming a more important issue and that high-quality studies on the markets and merchandising would be greatly appreciated.

Nestlé performs yearly studies of this kind with distributor clients. The results don't just sit in a drawer in the marketing director's office; they are presented at yearly meetings for the sales staff and are used heavily in training exercises for new and experienced staff. They also lead to changes in policy as with Nestlé/Rowntree.

A preoccupation with quality

Nestlé is preoccupied by quality. The word is on the lips of every employee and is the constant concern of every manager. It is demonstrated by the huge investment that the company has made in product quality assurance – there are 18 R&D labs worldwide responsible not only for developing new products, but also creating new systems of production guaranteeing better product quality for the future – and by a company policy that requires every customer complaint on quality to be investigated at the factory level, i.e. the factory manager personally investigates the problem on the production line.

Historically, this preoccupation only concerned product quality. Since some years, the concern for quality has been extended to all forms of quality. Managers now talk about quality in between departments and divisions, quality in the attitude and behaviour of staff, quality of its relations with the community, the quality of its concern for the environment and the quality of service.

The responsibility for the conception and management of the group's approach to quality management still lies largely with the technical department. They themselves, however, believe that a more holistic approach must be adopted. In use in some units is a scheme which they would eventually like to have adopted by the entire company.

A diagram summarising the approach pictures it as a widening conical formation. At the smallest end of the cone is just the product – its conception and its adherence to certain norms of quality. This falls under the title 'quality control'

As the cone widens the product is seen in conjunction with the production process. At this point, quality management systems, specifications, the personnel and the state of the factories contribute to the result. This section is entitled 'quality assurance'.

As the cone widens still further, the product is seen in conjunction with services and person-to-person relations. Marketing, training, logistics and the sales function all contribute to the success of this latter phase of the cone. This is called 'integrated quality'. At the exterior rim of the cone, one finds the distributor, and finally, the consumer. (An abbreviated version is pictured on p. 364.)

Until a holistic approach to quality has been decided upon and adopted, quality at Nestlé remains something that is pursued on an individual basis. Because the company's ethics and culture themselves emphasise quality so heavily in all aspects, quality translates for most employees into 'doing a very good job'. In some cases, distinctive initiatives have been taken by individuals to improve quality.

At Nestlé/Sopad, the accounting department set up error-chasing groups or 'quality groups' to identify way to improve service provided to the other departments. The head of the department, who initiated the idea, said that he saw the groups as 'a way to increase communication and encourage employees to take more initiative in their own work'.

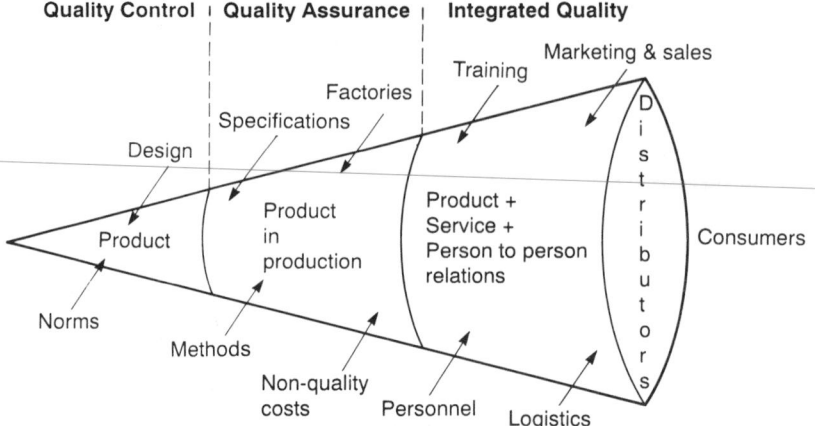

All of the units' heads within the department were trained by specialists on the 'error-chasing' technique for three days. Examples of real problems encountered by the department which had already been resolved were used as examples in the training. Groups were then formed with volunteers to try the technique. They were led by the unit heads that had been trained.

Two out of three early groups that took on major problems were a success. In one of those cases, the solution proposed went beyond the boundaries of the department and thus had to be 'sold' to the other departments implicated. To find, 'sell', organise and implement the change took two years.

What can be learned

1   Integrate service quality into your approach

Service quality is a prerequisite to success in any business today. A company doesn't need to have service quality as a point of differentiation to need to provide its customers with good service quality: Nestlé does not differentiate on the basis of its service quality. However, Nestlé must provide good service because customers are no longer satisfied with just mediocre service. In order to keep their image as a quality company, quality must be total or not at all.

2   Provide an outlet for product loyalty

Nestlé has created clubs for its customers devoted to specific products. It has also created newsletters, information services and sponsored events in which product fans can meet. Many consumers who have no other way of demonstrating their loyalty to the company are grateful to be offered this opportunity.

3   Advice as a support to sales

The only channel of communication between a company and its client doesn't have to be through the sales staff. By creating centralised advisory services to advise

Rowntree-Mackintosh product distributors on the tendencies in the market, Nestlé has created another way to communicate with the customer. Such additional channels underline the point that Nestlé doesn't just want a seller/buyer relationship, but a true partnership relationship with its distributors.

4 Go out to the customer

Nestlé/Sopad's Baby Stops are an excellent example of going out to the customer. A valuable service is provided in an unexpected location. By providing badly needed assistance to travelling parents, Nestlé shows that its logo, that emphasises the importance of motherhood, the family and security, is not just a picture on a piece of paper.

NOVO NORDISK

Novo Nordisk is proud of being in 'the people helping business'. The company is today the largest producer of insulin and diabetes care products and the world's largest producer of industrial enzymes.

What really counts for all of the company employees is that it makes 'products which satisfy needs.' It is with this kind of culture and philosophy that Novo Nordisk has developed a full service approach to its customers.

Background

While today the company is one united 'Novo Nordisk', just a few years ago, these firms were two separate companies and arch rivals. They are both Danish companies and have throughout their history been leaders in the research and development of methods to treat diabetes.

Nordisk's history goes back to 1923 when the Nobel prize winners – August Kroegh, together with H. C. Hagedorn and A. Kongsted – founded the Nordisk Insulin Laboratorium. In 1932 the company founded a hospital that specialised in treating diabetes and continued to be innovators in the area of diabetes treatment up to the time of its merger with Novo. The company's culture was strongly influenced by its scientific background and it even considered itself in many ways to be a 'non-profit organisation' until the early eighties.

The Novo approach to the business is equally based on a strongly ethical standpoint: 'From an ethical standpoint, we run a tight ship.' The company goes back to 1925 when it was founded by two brothers, Harald and Thorvald Pedersen, to produce insulin. A series of innovations followed, paralleling those made by Nordisk, which permitted the company to take the position as the second largest producer of insulin in the world. In 1989, at the time of the merger, Nordisk was number three.

The new company is number one in the world in the production of insulin and has merged the two companies on a completely equal basis. The reasons for the merger are clear. 'The more that our sector of the pharmaceuticals industry grows, the more competition there is. Fighting against one another limited our opportunities for diversification.'

No layoffs have been made – on the contrary – and a tremendous internal effort in terms of communication and coordination was carried out to restructure the two companies in order to be even more competitive in the future. Most employees are convinced that the decision to merge was the right one.

Service strategy

Novo Nordisk Diabetes Care Division describes its service approach as 'providing complete care for all diabetics' needs.'

Because of the company's position as innovators in this new technology, there has always been a need to provide more than just the raw product to the customer. Moreover, insulin is not a product that can be sold or used on its own. It must be accompanied by a kit that helps the diabetic patient measure his sugar level and then calculate the exact dosage necessary. There is, therefore, an aspect of education support necessary to the sale of any insulin product.

Novo Nordisk sells its products to the end-user through the intermediary or pharmacists or diabetes centres. The individuals recommending Novo Nordisk's products to the end-user are doctors. Thus, the company has two layers of customers to satisfy.

For many years, the company has been conducting research into the needs and expectations of end-users, primarily through the use of focus groups. This has led to the creation of easier and more convenient methods of insulin injection. The most recent creations are NovoPen and Novolet created in 1985 and 1989 respectively, which allow the diabetic patient to have a ready to use injector with him or her at all times and to inject the medicine without any measuring out of the insulin, or fuss with glass tubes or needles. The pen represents a complete kit for the patient, grouping a series of different actions into one.

The pen is not the only example of how Novo Nordisk goes beyond the product to take into account the complete needs of the patient. Another need that has been expressed by patients is for information. To meet this need, Novo Nordisk has developed an extensive information library of brochures, booklets and videos, which are made available to the diabetic patients covering all aspects of the disease and its treatment.

Historically, the company has concentrated on distributing its insulin products through diabetes centres. Its support services and sales approach were all targeted to appeal to the somewhat large central facilities. As diabetes increasingly becomes a disease that can be treated by individual physicians, Novo Nordisk is switching some of the emphasis of its efforts to serve doctors.

Helping physicians more means helping them to become more knowledgeable about treating diabetes. Novo Nordisk has thus increased the amount of materials available to this group of customers. The educational and informational support is designed to keep them up-to-date on what is happening in the medical field for diabetes. Novo Nordisk also sponsors conferences and seminars that can help the doctor improve his professional capabilities in the area of diabetes.

Service strengths

Insulin, more so than with most medication, must always be at hand and completely reliable. There is no room for poor product quality or slow deliveries, because the lives of people are at stake. Reliability is therefore the by-word of Novo Nordisk. 'In the context of our business, reliability is essential: reliability of delivery, reliability of the company, reliability and continuity of supply and the reliability of the educational information we provide.'

The reliability of the company is supported to a large extent by its history, both in terms of its financial solidity and in terms of the contributions made by the company's research efforts in the field of diabetes. The reliability and continuity of supply relate in a large part to the solidity of the company and its commitment to the diabetes market segment.

Reliability in terms of delivery is something that has been perfected over the years. To make sure that from the customers' perspective it really always is an inherent part of its image, Novo Nordisk takes precautions by keeping on hand a 'security stock'. One-and-a-half to 3 months' worth of stock is always on hand. 'Beyond the humanitarian considerations, if we don't have that stock and something goes wrong, we lose business that we can never get back. We have to maintain a certain margin.'

Reliability is also something to be found in the company's support literature and communications materials. Novo Nordisk has a medical policy and a promotional policy that sets forth ethical guidelines on what should be made available in terms of information on the products and how it should be presented. An example is what goes on the product package. Another is the way that clinical trials should be handled and communicated.

Reliability also means backing up its products and services. Novo Nordisk provides customers with a two year product guarantee on their pen products. In other areas, a guarantee is not sufficient and the company prefers to handle each problem on a case-by-case basis with the care and attention it deserves. 'In this, we must follow good medical practice.'

From the customer's perspective, probably one of the most valuable things he receives from Novo Nordisk is knowledge. The company's strategy of providing extensive educational support for its products has led to creation of a whole set of services. To begin with, the company has a monthly magazine, which discusses all major developments in the field. Doctors and patients also have access to a special literature service that provides extracts of recent scientific progress reports on request. The company also has videos on the products and on the technology behind them, which it distributes for use in diabetic centres or by doctors for their patients.

Novo Nordisk is also a big sponsor of international conferences. Seminars are conducted to provide educational and technical information to help people to use the product better and to live more normal lives. One extremely successful project was the 'Youth Diabetics' project, which brought together young diabetics and, through exchanges, helped them learn about dealing with the disease. Its activities include a newsletter and regular meetings.

Implementation

At Novo Nordisk, 'people like going to work'. They are proud of their company and they have fun at work. 'It's fun to be able to compete as a world leader and see new products and services come out.' Only 6 per cent of all new employees entering the company hadn't heard of Novo Nordisk before they applied to work there.

The company's management wants employees to be happy working at the company and goes out of its way to ensure that they are happy. As a first step, Novo

Nordisk makes sure that employees work in the best environment possible. Their headquarters in Denmark is an elegant new building especially designed to give the maximum number of employees exposure to sunlight. When employees are not working, they have access to the company's holiday homes, which can be booked for short stays by any employee. Novo Nordisk has virtually no staff turnover in the company. Once an employee is integrated into the company, he is there to stay.

All of this makes Novo Nordisk employees very loyal and hardworking. 'Everyone is very interested in doing their job perfectly; it's quality all the way down.' The internal emphasis on quality is important; Novo Nordisk knows that its customers are perfectionists. One of the measures that was taken to make the merger of the two companies a success was the systematic mixing of staff within most departments. Parallel units from Novo and Nordisk were fused with staff from both put side by side to work. Researchers who previously worked on competing projects sometimes found themselves side by side with their former competitors.

Some of Novo Nordisk's subsidiaries took exceptional measures to make the merger between Novo and Nordisk an easy one. One of the most innovative measures used was the war game. Bringing together employees from both companies, the organisers created two teams, which mixed the individuals. The objective was then to 'kill' the enemy with war paint and squirt guns. Working together as a team helped the former rivals regard each other in a different light. The ridiculousness of the activity brought down formal barriers and increased communication.

In the workplace, relationships between individuals in the company is dominated by the internal customer concept. Each division has defined who its customers are and what they should be providing. This is an exercise that has been done particularly since the reorganisation of the company following the merger. Today, everyone knows who his customer is. 'The internal customer concept is very strong with us.' Headquarters is considered to be a service organisation for the subsidiaries, who regularly evaluate the service they get from headquarters, 'to ensure that they get ideal service from headquarters. All the bases are covered to make sure that the views of the subsidiaries are reflected in headquarters.'

The company's research and development activities remain a vital part of the company's operations. Management, however, wants to ensure that whatever is being done in the labs will serve to increase the satisfaction of customers. As such, the company continues to conduct all kinds of customer and market research. Formal focus group methods are used for end-customers and for doctors to identify trends and overall requirements.

With doctors and clinics, however, the company uses its sales force as a supplementary source of valuable information on customers' expectations. The sales force is expected to develop a dialogue with customers that encourages this information to come out. As a first step, it is recorded on a customer-by-customer basis. Once a month, all of the information collected is brought together and fed into the company's official feedback system. In addition to the reports, which are analysed as a bulk, there are also monthly meetings between sales representatives to make a summary of what has been observed and to discuss ways to improve service. The report of this meeting together with the customer reports goes back to headquarters for analysis.

What can be learned

1 Use dramatic methods to bring about change

Novo Nordisk in the UK needed successfully to mix individuals from companies that for years had been arch rivals. No half measure would have had an impact. By organising a war game, the company diminished many of the animosities that had been hidden and created the basis for a more co-operative future.

2 Create a happy atmosphere

Employees who feel good about where they work will feel good about the company they work for. An employee's working environment is said to be its major factor in job satisfaction. Keeping that in mind, Novo Nordisk goes all out to ensure that employees have what they need to make them happy at work and, thus, enables the customer to get the best out of its employees.

NV NEDERLANDSE SPOORWEGEN

Public rail transportation is not the first place that one would expect to find a group of people committed to service quality, although that is just what we found when visiting the Dutch rail lines, NV Nederlandse Spoorwegen, or NS for short.

Service quality has been this company's daily fare since the early 1980s. With single-minded dedication they have put in place more service quality tools and measures than any of their competitors in Europe. More important, they have achieved results. Concrete improvements have been made in the service quality in the stations and the trains, which have yielded measurable improvements in customer satisfaction.

Background

NS is the official owner and manager of Holland's transportation system by rail. By definition, it is a monopoly. It offers both freight and passenger service to all destinations within the country, great or small. Over 4700 trains run per day with 600,000 passengers and 18 million tonnes of goods. In terms of freight, 75 per cent of the company's revenues come from goods destined for overseas transportation. Providing these services to individuals and companies are 27,000 employees, over three times fewer, for example, than in another company we looked at, National Westminster.

In international terms, the Dutch railway may be relatively small, but it is one of the most efficient. In terms of transport achieved per employee, per rolling stock unit, per track mileage unit, per area unit of railyards, it outweighs the larger European competitors. 'This . . . may have been the very reason why an interest in further improvements by the way of total quality control developed.'

The company's first experience with quality management was in 1981. Between

1979 and 1981, the company has experienced a number of operational and service failures which led it to re-examine its organisation. A special group was established by the board of directors to examine the problems within the context of quality improvement. '. . . by being involved in these actions for quality improvement people started realising that . . . the problems were either not or only in part being solved structually' (Mr. Van Omme)

In 1982, a permanent quality group was established. The group was to carry out its activities separately from the operational divisions. 'The main reasons for a temporary specialization of management were:

> knowledge and know-how of the sitting management are on the whole insufficient; acquisition of extra ability is required;
> better survey of the necessary attuning of departments and divisions;
> a possible greater cogency.'

> > (Speech at 1984 World Quality Congress, Mr Van Omme).

From 1982 to the present day, the quality project at NS has passed through four phases. The first phase is referred to as 'the period of annoyance'. The railway experienced increasing problems during this phase which were studied carefully by the quality group. Definitions for quality were drawn up. No immediate solutions were identified although the level of knowledge of the group about service quality was continually advancing.

In the second phase, 'the period of preaching', the company developed the 'triptych', a creed based on the notion that quality is the result of 1) knowing customers' wishes, 2) the commitment and initiatives of management, and 3) the proper training and preparation of staff to deliver quality. A company-wide service strategy and service quality standards were also developed during this period. Small, but concrete results were achieved. The punctuality of trains departing in the morning, which had been measured carefully since the early 1980s, improved over the period.

In the third phase, 'the all or nothing period', the structural concepts were accepted by the organisation and a number of concrete measures were taken to improve quality. Seminars for over 250 senior managers were organised; over 150 improvement projects were initiated, in general, punctuality improved, information was re-examined to be more user-friendly etc. Efforts and results were sporadic, however; 'many departments could be seen to be working very hard on quality control. . . . Other departments did absolutely nothing' (Mr H.E. Portheine).

Entering into the 1990s marked the beginning of another period called 'Earning the future with quality'. A new company strategy for quality has been developed and a structural approach to quality management adopted. Among others things, the new strategy includes, 'changing the organisational structure from vertical to horizontal, decentralization, setting priorities (first improve the aspects that are most important to the customer) and application of measurement throughout the organisation etc. These strategy proposals are now being practised which means that the organisation is undergoing a complete revolution' (Mr Portheine).

Service strategy

NS offers its customers two types of basic services: regular stopping train transportation and rapid inter-city train transportation. Regular trains service smaller cities and towns, making frequent stops in between. The intercity trains service the larger cities only, making few if any stops in between. In 1993, NS will be able to offer a third type of service – ultra high speed transportation – that will link major Dutch cities with the rest of Europe.

In total, NS estimates that it has only 7 to 8 per cent of the total market for transportation services and that 50 per cent of its customers have the choice not to use the train for transportation. Autos control the largest share of the market with airline and freight, water and bus transportation competing on certain routes. NS wants to double its present volume of traffic by the year 2000. To do that, they say, they need to have satisfied customers who keep coming back. '. . . existing regular customers will have to be retained and we will have to try to make regular customers of the others' (Marketing Plan for 1990–2000).

As a public transportation service, the NS is expected to provide service which matches the expectations of every traveller in the country. In practice, the company is targeting certain segments of the population which represent good growth potential for the company or which are highly profitable. The company's strategy is, thus, to increase overall customer satisfaction, but, particularly, satisfaction in its target customer segments.

NS has divided its customer base into five segments:

leisure market – those who travel in off-peak hours and do so to visit friends, for tourism etc.;
business – those who travel on their employers' account and time;
journey to school;
commuter market;
group travel.

The first two segments are those targeted by the NS. The leisure segment is a priority because the NS wants to use the train's excess capacity in off-hours. The business market is a priority because servicing this market improves the image of the NS overall.

To find out how it can increase customer satisfaction, the NS conducts extensive marketing research on the service expectations in each of its customer segments. In total over 72 relevant aspects of service were studied. They include connections with other forms of public transportation, bicycle stands, the friendliness of the personnel, the comfort of the material, average travelling speed etc.

As a result, NS was able to establish, for example, that the leisure market's satisfaction is based upon the quality of the door-to-door public transportation network. That includes not just the service provided by the train company itself, but also that provided by the bus or taxi service which brought the individual to the station. Aspects influencing customer satisfaction in this case include:

the easy accessibility of train stations;
the ease of connections for journeys to and from the stations;
the quality of the information provided both before and during the journey;
the availability of seating space in the train;
the timeliness of the service.

The business segment is also concerned with the quality of public transportation from door to door, although its concern is focused on slightly different aspects:

the rapidity of the transportation;
the availability of a luxurious first-class compartment in Inter City trains;
a reserved and guaranteed seat in Inter City trains;
additional services such as luggage storage or handling, train catering etc.

This research has allowed the company to prioritise improvements in service quality to correspond. Punctuality, for example, was identified as being the key determinant of customer satisfaction (or dissatisfaction); the company has, therefore, focused resources upon improving this aspect of their service in preference to others.

It has also allowed the NS to go one step further. With this information they are beginning to develop special services designed to meet the expectations of a certain segment. For the leisure segment, for example, which places a priority on having thorough information, NS has started to provide detailed information about what one can do in Holland and how to reach specific locations. In this they are co-operating with entertainment centres or town or tourist authorities. Joint advertising, brochures and directional signage are some of the results of these co-operations.

For the business market, which frequently uses the train to get to the Amsterdam airport, the NS is improving the frequency and the scheduling of trains serving this destination. '. . . NS has done its best to look at its product through the customer's eyes. In order to find out what our customers want, we have organized surveys and carefully studied customer feedback and complaints. . . . Once this is done, the product itself can be determined' (*On the Quality Track* brochure).

Service strengths

NS considers that service is 100 per cent of what they offer customers. As such, the company does not believe in providing good service just at the moment of person-to-person contact, but also at the moment of person-to-system contact: when a customer expects the train at a certain time, it is a satisfactory moment of person-to-system contact when the train comes into the station on time.

No one at NS can say that they don't know what the customer should receive at any moment of their contact with the train company. NS has divided its contact with the customer into distinct phases. It is called the '10 Step model'. This model was developed by analysing the stages through which a customer passes in the ticket purchase and train use process, i.e. the customer tries to get to the station, the customer buys a ticket, the customer tries to find the train and his place on it etc.

Each step is given a letter code which reflects the importance of the step from the customer's viewpoint. These levels are determined by the research on customer expectations done by the company. They are monitored on a yearly basis to be sure that the customer's perceptions have remained the same.

The 10 step model forms the beginning of a book called the *Yellow Book* which presents to employees not only the 10 steps through which the customer passes, but also the expectations of customers at each step. Over 800 copies of the *Yellow Book* have been distributed throughout the company. Excerpts pertaining to their activities are distributed to individuals in each unit. When planning a new station, the book is used as a checklist to see whether they have everything they require.

Norms or standards have been set which provide a measurable expression of customer expectations. For example, one norm would be that 90 per cent of all passengers should be able to receive documentation on schedules and rates for their travel destination upon demand.

To set the levels for the norms, the company looks to the consumer, but also to the marketplace, 'you have to look around to see what are the standards in the market. The standard for waiting in line may be no more than three minutes, but if at the movies and the post office it's only two minutes, then we're the bad ones.'

'The norms/requirements may be objective or subjective. For example, average travelling speed for Inter City trains is 90km/h, is an objective norm. Ninety per cent of all passengers on the platform should be able to understand the central anouncements concerning time-table alterations, is an example of a subjective norm' (Mr Van Omme).

Managers at NS work hard to make sure that the service norms in the *Yellow Book* are maintained. It is considered to be their responsibility. At the ticket counter, there is a norm that no more than seven people should be waiting in line. 'When the line gets too long, the manager has to do something – open more windows or schedule more personnel at busy hours.'

Managers are quicker to respond than they were in the past, because the concern for quality within the company has risen significantly. 'With a certain amount of satisfaction, it can be observed that in NS quality as a notion has come alive,' says Mr Omme.

Managers and staff have been trained in service quality and how to handle difficult situations which frequently arise. 'How to Interact with Customers', 'How to Handle Complaints and Requests' and other topics are now a standard part of all employees' training. Some employees tend to be a bit shy; there is currently a task force training station personnel to give information, especially in the case of irregularities, for instance when the train is late. Even more extensive training is done for managers, including the training of trainers, '. . . how to effectively control the interfaces is important training material. All of the managements teams of the sub top level have had similar seminars and discussion meetings' (Mr Van Omme).

The importance of training in service quality is perhaps best demonstrable in extraordinary situations. 'What is probably also typical [for NS's service] is that the dependence upon "third parties" is relatively great . . . including the effects of other traffic (at level crossings, for instance,), suicide incidents, bomb reports, weather conditions etc. This often calls for ad hoc decisions. The reference framework for quality awareness and the personnel's knowledge of quality control can then mean much to the customer in spite of [his] not being served according to expectations' states Mr Van Omme.

Implementation

NS has passed through many different stages in the movement towards recognising service quality as a top priority objective in the company. Certainly the first major achievement was when the project received the support of top management. That occurred in 1981. At the same time that it decided that quality was to become a major long-term objective, the board of directors set forth a series of quality objectives:

a company-wide awareness of quality;
a clear and optimally tuned quality policy;
quality assurance systems, based on norms, in which responsibilities are as much as possible coupled to persons, and data systems are grafted upon this;

sufficient room for manoeuvre within the process to allow for taking care of inevitable disturbances.

In the two to three years that followed, NS established a set of definitions for quality – in the form of the *Yellow Book* – and a method for monitoring service quality internally and externally. It also created a system of contracted quality between different departments, whereby agreements are reached between internal service providers and customers with respect to the quality to be supplied. These tools, together with extensive training and internal communication, are designed to be the primary management tools of service quality within the company.

The *Yellow Book*, described above, laid the guidelines for what the company had to do to maintain or improve its customer's satisfaction. Just setting the standards, however, wasn't enough. 'What we learned from this is that specifying product requirements without linking them to responsible personnel members and feasible measuring methods is an impossibility. Specification then becomes an empty gesture,' explains Mr Van Omme.

NS's response was, first, to ensure that all norms were measurable. It then created an extensive system of controls and measurement. Two types of measurement are carried out all the time. The objective of the first is to know whether customers' norms or standards for service quality have changed and, if so, to establish their new level and their importance relative to other norms. The objective of the second type of measurement is to know whether the norms which have been established are being maintained.

Measurement is carried out on an internal and external basis – internally, meaning that the company relies upon information available internally and, externally, meaning that the company approaches the customer directly.

Measuring service quality externally with customers is done through yearly surveys. Twenty thousand passengers are approached every year with roughly 55 per cent responding to the voluntary questionnaire. In the same survey, customers answer questions concerning their satisfaction with existing services and questions concerning their desire for future services. Customers rank existing services on a scale of 1 to 10. Using the results, the company cannot only judge its level of adherence to existing standards, but also, through statistical means, monitor changes in standards of customer expectations.

The customer also monitors customer satisfaction and expectations using the complaint and suggestions letters which it receives. Fifty thousand letters are received per year. They encourage customers to write in with comments: on the back of each ticket the address of where to write is printed. They also make a point of handing out pre-stamped cards at the ticket window. This is a reflection of the fact that most complaints, it was discovered, are made verbally at the ticket window. By having a card ready for the customers' comments, the company is more sure to receive any complaints in writing.

Measurement is carried out internally without approaching the customer. For the most part, the objective of internal measurement is to ensure that existing standards are being followed. The NS uses service quality indicators for internal measurements. Like the external measurement, they are based upon the service norms established in the *Yellow Book*. The norm, trains running at an average speed of 90 km/h is monitored by an internal service quality indicator. The company has achieved significant progress by using the measurements, '. . . an example to show what consciousness of quality control may accomplish. In the case of one main line in the Netherlands, it turned out that, when investigated, the destinations panel on the trains was only correct for slightly more than half of all the indications. The requirement is for a 95 per cent accuracy rate. . . . Investigations followed, instructions followed. We now see from investigations that the requirement for 95 per cent has not yet been reached, 91 per cent has been reached.'

The punctuality of trains, for example, is measured internally and externally. Internally the number of trains coming in late to their destination and their degree of lateness are regularly monitored. The company measures punctuality externally, however, to know whether customers' perception of punctuality has changed. For example, in 1981, customers might have said that a train arriving four minutes late didn't pose them a considerable problem; in 1991, the response might be that a train four minutes late poses them a big problem.

Punctuality used to be monitored constantly at the destination stations of trains (about 100 stations). Starting in 1992, NS is measuring punctuality at 30 representative stations along the line. The standard for trains on time has changed from 4 minutes to 2 minutes. That means that trains 2 minutes, oo seconds late are considered to be delayed. By using this method, we comply with the perception of all customers.

NS believes that it learned a lot about service quality management along the way. In one speech given by Mr Van Omme, he describes three lessons ways to convert unbelievers into believers in service quality and expounds on the role of a service quality manager.

How can a manager with the right beliefs begin in a world of unbelief? There, of course, is the core of the problem when starting with quality control . . . there remain ways and means for converting the unbelievers, such as:

1 Making worries and miseries overt by bringing them out into the open. Utilising statistics as valuable aids. Compiling, as it were, a black book on the company's situation. In the case of NS we did do this in the beginning phase by outlining what we termed the 'departure situation'.

2 The language of management is the management of money. It is of great value to select certain objectives as quickly as possible and to investigate them regarding, for instance, prevention costs, estimation costs and failure costs. If it then appears, as one instance at NS showed, that for one objective 60 per cent of the turnover went on pure failure costs then one starts thinking. Traditional book-keeping administrations are generally not designed for revealing quality assets and charges.

3 Another element that tends to appeal to managers is that of assurance. Quality control teaches how to assure processes. It is quite revealing to simply pose the question: 'How much time do you spend improvising?' The fact that all forms of improvisation carry in them something of 'That was not intended' and 'It means extra money', is a stimulus to improve control.

Let management have its responsibility! Never, as quality adviser, take over the managerial position. The management is very busy and is glad if there is another to relieve it of its work load. Didn't a famous quality adviser say recently that management has to spend 30 per cent of its time on quality control? It is the task of the quality adviser to ensure that the manager knows what quality control is.'

What can be learned

1 Create expertise in service quality

One of the reasons that NS made service quality a programme and created a separate working group to manage the introduction of service quality was that none of the existing managers in the company had the necessary expertise to implement service quality alone. By creating a separate unit, the company permitted the group's members to develop a certain expertise in the area which in later years they could pass on more easily to other managers and staff.

2 Know what's most important to your customers

NS ranked its service standards according to what customers said mattered most when it came to good service quality. As a result, the company could concentrate its resources on improvements in those areas and, thereby, achieve the greatest possible improvements in overall customer satisfaction.

3 Start with customers to set standards

The company's service standards relate directly to the moments of contact between the company and the customer. They are statements of what the customer expects at that moment of contact. By relating all service standards to what it brings to the customer, NS avoided the white elephant syndrome, i.e. the creation of a set of standards or norms which have no relation to what the customer really wants.

4 Don't make your service quality absolute

Service quality is relative. NS's standard for queuing of three minutes may be acceptable when the queue at the post office and the cinema is five minutes; it will no longer be, when the post office and the cinema's queues decline to two minutes. There is, thus, a 'market level' of quality which is always moving and which a company should respect if not improve upon.

OK SERVICE

What we appreciated most about OK Service was its simplicity. Only one thing counts – raising the customer loyalty rate. Salaries are paid, bonuses are given, investments are made all on the basis of this one number, produced and published every month for every agency. The best part of the system is that it really does mean that customers are well served!

History

OK Service was not created with the private consumer in mind. It was created in 1956 to assist in the nationwide changeover from 'village gas' to natural gas and from 110 volts to 220 volts. Its sole client was the French gas and electric authority and the principle challenge of the job was to co-ordinate the many teams; each household had to be converted individually and there was no question of changing entire districts before every house had been prepared.

It was quickly apparent, however, that once the nationwide conversion was completed, the company had to have another form of business and, more important, another client. The majority of its personnel were experienced electricians, plumbers or handymen. It was decided that the company would provide urgent repair and light handiwork to individual households.

In France, particularly in the large towns, this is a rather disreputable business for such a reputable company like OK Service. The average Parisian apartment dweller receives one brochure per week from small businesses pressing their services. It is said that many are ready to work on a non-declared basis (so as not to pay taxes on the income), regularly overcharge for their work, overbill for materials and show up late or not at all for appointments. To sum up, it is a sector which inspires little confidence.

Not being overly daunted by sectoral difficulties, OK Service established its operations and pursued its new business with more zeal than the average entrepreneur. Rather than accepting that it must function in the midst of consumer distrust and apprehension, it chose an approach which helps increase customer confidence in its services. In 1981, the company began offering a subscription formula which gives the customer the right to be serviced as often as he likes as long as he continues to subscribe. It has been the unique approach of the company ever since.

OK Service today has over 40 offices located in major cities throughout France. It is the largest service provider of its kind in the country and has recently introduced a franchise option, 21 of its agencies function on this basis.

Service strategy

The subscription approach is at the heart of the company's service strategy. The strategy is designed to provide customers with greater security of purchase, with greater ease of purchase and with a guaranteed level of service quality.

The subscription service works as follows: customers pay a flat fee per month. This entitles them to use the company's services as many times as they wish. The first two hours of work on any job are free of charge, i.e. covered by the subscription fee. If they are dissatisfied with the work done or simply decide that they no longer need the services, they can cancel their subscription with just a month's notice.

The company has a hot-line available and is generally able to meet the needs of its customers with only a very short delay. In addition, the company has committed itself to meeting certain standards of service quality; they act as a kind of guarantee. They are presented in the form of 12 engagements to customers. They are:

to be at the aid of its customers with the least delay possible;
to provide a service six out of seven days per week from 8 a.m. to 8 p.m.;
to inform the customer of the prices charged before beginning any work.
to prepare an estimate and a work order for any jobs which exceed FF1000;
to have the work performed by qualified specialists;
provide a detailed bill that permits the client to verify the time passed, the price per hour and the materials employed;
permit the client to refuse to have certain material replaced;
not bill if the repair is not made;
in the case of a justified complaint, award the customer one month's free service;
pay for all damage done to the apartment during the repair work;
agree to have its work checked by the Synadep (a union of repair companies);
constantly improve its service quality by consulting continuously its customers.

On the one hand, the document sets forth the basic operating terms of the agreement between OK Service and its customers; on the other, it represents an assurance that the bad experiences which clients have previously had with repair companies won't be repeated with OK Service.

The OK Service approach makes it possible for customers to benefit more regularly from repair or handyman assistance. As a general rule, a city dweller calls in an urgent repair or handyman service, on average, 1.8 times per year. Customer loyalty is extremely low, partly due to the infrequency of the call, partly due to the lack of differentiation between the various service providers. At OK Service customers use their service on average four times per year and customer loyalty is more or less guaranteed through the subscription system.

The subscription system appeals most to three groups of clients. Nearly 50 per cent of the company's customers are elderly couples or individuals, another 20 or 30 per cent are couples in which both the husband and wife work. The remaining percentage is made up of small businesses.

The company is gradually developing an adapted approach to meet the different needs of its different customer groups. For the present, this is limited to changing the discussions between the repairman and the client in a face-to-face contact. Studies have shown, for example, that the elderly client group are in general less rushed and for a major repair prefer to have time to consider the problem. The working couples, on the contrary, take rapid decisions and want the work to begin immediately. Repairmen have adapted their sales dialogue accordingly.

The repairman's contact with the customer is not limited to a discussion of the repair at hand. He assists the customer with general questions about maintenance and other necessary repairs. In this way, he is able to sell additional services to customers which fall under the category of small handiwork. This includes the installation of a water heater or a washing machine, the painting of a room, the building of shelves etc.

Sales realised in this second way form the other leg of the company's revenues and provide even greater reason for employees to provide good service; the customer only orders additional work if he has been well served in the past by the repairman and by the company.

Service strengths

OK Service offers a nice neat formula. But what does a customer receive from OK Service beyond that formula? Perhaps the first question is what should any customer receive from a company in the rapid repair and handiwork business other than a job well done – technical advice, a learning experience, peace of mind?

One of the major complaints of customers for so-called 'technical services' is that technicians treat customers like children or idiots. The most blatant example is that of the unfortunate car owner who goes in to have his car fixed, only to be spoken to by mechanics who insist upon using terminology incomprehensible to the layman and then ignore one's efforts to elicit the most basic bits of information about the state of the car.

In the rapid repair business the situation is much the same. Most repairmen are incapable of telling you in simple terms what exactly is wrong with your water heater! Is the pilot light off or is it not; can it be repaired by tomorrow or not – and if it can't, why not?

At OK Service, the frustrated customer can at last find relief. He can receive a simple answer to a question like 'Why are the parts of my dishwasher strewn over the kitchen floor?'.

The company invests heavily in the training of its repair personnel to conduct a comprehensible dialogue with the client. Highly technical terms are broken down into series of simple phrases. The repairman is trained how to explain to the customer each step of his work and why it is being done. As the head of the Paris agency put it, 'Today's customer needs to be treated like an adult. We try to make sure he is.'

OK Service's broader objective is not only to make the customer understand what the repairman is doing, but to make it possible for the customer to 'participate in the decision' about what should be done.

To do that, the repairman must be more than just a technician, he must also be a teacher. The company wants its repairman to pass on a bit of its wide expertise to the customer. A visit becomes more than a simple repair job; it becomes a learning experience for the customer and a job-enriching experience for the repairman.

Implementation

The tool with the greatest impact on service quality at OK Service is the monthly subscription cancellation rate, i.e. the customer loyalty rate. Because customers can cancel their subscriptions on such a short notice, the rate is a very reliable indicator of existing customer satisfaction.

The rate is not only an indicator of customer satisfaction; it is also a direct reflection of the revenues of the agency for the month. Because the two are so closely linked, managers follow as closely the evolution in the monthly subscription cancellation rate as they do the profit and loss statement.

OK Service uses the rate as an active management tool. They have broken the rate down into two parts – the controllable and the uncontrollable. The uncontrollable are those cancellations due to address changes, death etc. They amount to 1 per cent a month. The rest is considered controllable. Agency managers are paid a fixed salary with a 'commission'. Part of each managers's commission is gauged to the 'controllable' loyalty rate. They are not the only ones.

Other than the manager an agency has administrative employees and the staff of repairmen. The administrative staff centralises the information on customers having cancelled their service. When a client cancels his service, the administrative staff can try to recoup a client and are encouraged to do so. Each month headquarters fixes a maximum number of clients that can be lost during the month – should the number rise above that number, no commission is given; should it fall below that number, then the administtrative staff receives a commission which increases as the number of customers retained is greater. Presently the number runs about 3.75 per cent per month. The recovery rate is good, however, with nearly 80 per cent of clients cancelling being recouped by the administrative staff.

The remuneration of the repairman is tied to customer loyalty in three ways. First, he receives a commission every time that he sells a subscription to an unsubscribed customer. Secondly, he is given a bonus on additional work commissioned by customers he worked for. Thirdly, he is given a 'quality' bonus which reflects customers' comments on his work in the form of subscription cancellation and through the customer satisfaction survey which is handed out to each customer with the bill.

Providing repairmen with the correct system of motivation for service quality plays an extremely important role in the company's success. The recruitment market is such that most of the individuals applying for jobs with OK Service previously worked in the construction sector. On the whole, the construction sector pays much better than the quick repair and handiwork sector and the hours are more regular. Many workers regularly hop from one to the other. With the bonuses for quality, the repairman can easily top a normal construction salary, however, he must learn skills which permit him to improve his general presentation, his sales dialogue with the customer and his service quality orientation. OK Service thereby succeeds in preserving those employees with the greatest customer service orientation.

Having established this framework of management and motivation for its employees, the headquarters' role is primarily one of resource provision in terms of training, marketing support and investment in development.

Marketing research is centralised, although each agency manager can have studies done on his particular region if he feels the need. Customer satisfaction is measured through the returns sent direct by customers to the headquarters. The customer has the opportunity to indicate his satisfaction on each of the 12 commitments of the company (see above) as well as his pleasure or displeasure with, for example, 'the telephone answering system, the delay before the repairman arrived and the physical appearence of the repairman'.

The form also permits the customer to confirm that the amount listed on the receipt is the same as that which was paid to the repairman at the end of the visit. Many clients are particularly appreciative of this latter item, as it permits them to verify that the work was all declared and paid for according to the official rates.

A certain percentage of training is also centralised. Each new employee is trained at the headquarters in Marseilles on the basics of the company and about the importance of customer satisfaction and customer fidelity.

The bulk of the training provided at headquarters, however, is conducted in order to teach agency managers how to manage and motivate their teams using the tools available to them. Sessions are held every month for one full day. The sessions are mandatory and every agency manager is expected to attend, 'unless he is in the hospital with a broken leg *and* a 40° fever'.

What can be learned

1 Managing service quality doesn't have to be complicated

The example of OK Service shows that sometimes it is enough just to find one or two very good tools for motivating people to provide good service. The customer loyalty rate provides the key at OK Service.

2 Hit them where it hurts

When trying to get employees focused on improving service quality, don't hesitate to use financial incentives. Practically no employee is immune to the attraction of increasing their revenues at the end of the month. It also demonstrates the company's own commitment to improving service quality.

3 Create a challenge

OK Service lets customers cancel their subscription on a month's notice. Some would say that is too short. The advantages are that it creates a greater challenge for employees and convinces customers that the company will do its utmost to keep their business.

4 Set the parameters, then let them go

Managers at OK Service are not the kind that send out piles of memos dictating to employees to do this or that. It is enough that they have established the conditions for success and made the resources available for employees to operate on their own.

QUELLE

Good service when it really counts – that Quelle believes in. They provide their best service after the sale when the customer has a problem and needs Quelle to be there to fix it.

'When a customer calls, he has a problem; top service is absolutely necessary in order to satisfy their expectations,' says Rolf Beckmann, manager of Quelle's after-sales service operation.

Background

Quelle is in the mail-order business. It is Germany's largest mail-order house with over DM10.6 billion in revenues per year and Europe's largest company in the business. Through its catalogue operation, Quelle sells a full variety of clothes, textiles and household goods, including white and brown goods. The company even offers pre-fabricated houses for sale.

Quelle was started in the 1920s by Mr Gustav Schickedanz. Originally the business consisted of selling textiles to travelling salesmen who then sold the products door to door. Very soon after the company began distributing the same products by mail. Quelle, the name adopted by the fledgling company, means source in German and it quickly became a success. By 1934, the company already had 250,000 customers. By 1939, that number had risen to 2,000,000.

Shops were added to the Quelle network after the Second World War when the postal system had become less than reliable and somewhat complicated due to the post-war conditions. Shops also gave customers the chance to 'touch' the products they were buying.

Electrical and mechanical products were particularly a success and the number of Quelle stores handling these items increased. During the same period the after-sales servicing of the parts was added to Quelle's offering to customers.

In the 1950s the company began its European expansion. This boosted the company's revenues to over DM1 billion by 1961. Today, Quelle is a household name in Germany and has a strong position in the market. Its market share for some products, sewing machines for example, is up to 30 per cent. In addition to an enormous catalogue containing all the products, Quelle also has separate catalogues for its major line of products – clothes, electrical goods etc.

Forty-two thousand people are employed by Quelle, 2,600 of which work in the after-sales service division. The after-sales service division provides repairs and parts replacement for all kinds of electrical and mechanical products sold by the company in addition to products sold by other companies.

Service strategy

Service at Quelle is, by design, particularly strong in after-sales repairs and parts replacement. 'It is our chance to reach out to the customer,' explains Mr Beckmann.

Service prior to after-sales service consists primarily of providing the right selection of products for the target market and delivering those products quickly, and according to the agreement with the customer. Quelle management believes, however, that the real difference between mail order houses comes in only after the customer has purchased. With a top-quality after-sales service operation, the company can differentiate itself as compared with its competitors. It also permits the company to come face to face with the customer and to demonstrate the company's commitment to serve the customer well.

While good service before the sale represents primarily 'hassle-free' service for the customer, good after-sales service represents more. It gives the customer confidence in the company. The customer is relieved to receive rapid and attentive service, and he feels secure in relying upon them in the future.

Quelle's service strategy for its after-sales service is not only to offer a reliable repair. It also means adapting the speed of service to the particular requirement of the customer. Families with children whose washing machine has broken down are given priority for example. The company has also created a special high-speed repair service for televisions during special media events such as the Olympics or big football matches. Customers who express a need over the phone for a fast repair are also given top priority. There is also a special weekend repair for freezers and deep freezes.

A second aspect of Quelle's after-sales-service is to provide the repair as close to the customer as possible. Customers are not required to bring their goods into a service centre; Quelle prefers to send its people to the customer's home. It represents a more convenient service for the customers. As a result, 100 per cent of white goods products and 50 per cent of brown goods are serviced out of the home. The other electrical or mechanical products are brought by the customers themselves to the service centre.

To bring it as close to the customer as possible, the company has established an extensive network of 101 service centres throughout Germany and believes that 'a complete regional coverage of Germany and a solid training of their employees makes the strength of their service'.

Quelle's service centres are not only intended to service products sold by Quelle. Each of the service centres operates as an individual profit centre with managers from the centres operating their centre as if it were an entrepreneurial activity. The long-term objective is for Quelle's service operation to be independently recognised as a top after-sales service supplier for products sold by any company. At present the division represents an excellent demonstration of Quelle's commitment to top service quality. 'The after-sales service operation represents a marketing tool for Quelle; it is to be run as a profit making profit centre,' says Mr Beckmann.

Service strengths

One of the nicest things about Quelle's service is that it is not something which is forced upon the customer. A customer who calls to ask a question is not immediately sent a repairman and then billed because the machine wasn't plugged into the electric socket. Quelle's service technicians are trained to make a diagnosis of the problem over the phone. While not all problems can be identified with a discussion, the technician can often identify if the problem is a worn-out filter or a blown-out television tube. In such a case, the customer simply thanks the service centre, buys the replacement filter and fixes the machine him or herself.

If it's Sunday afternoon and the freezer breaks down with 10 kilos of prime beef in it, Quelle has a hot line. Customers can call and have their problem treated immediately over the phone and then in person by a service technician on call.

In most cases, one visit from a Quelle technician is enough. Junior technicians are never let out to service a customer alone before having at least six months' experience and training. In any case, there are not very many inexperienced technicians working for Quelle. Employee turnover is extremely low; a large percentage of the service technicians have been with the company for 10 or more years. To make sure that one visit is enough and that the quality of the repair is not slipping over time, Quelle monitors, on a monthly basis, exactly the number of service calls taking two visits.

For the customer who doesn't receive satisfaction from the service centre, Quelle offers recourse to one of the company's 24 main subsidiary centres that are acting as support stations for the 77 service stations. In the support stations there service consultants who report directly to one of 6 regional managers and who are given the complete responsibility for solving the customer's problem. Such individuals are immediately available to the customer with a phone call.

It is unlikely that customers will fall upon an unresponsive manager in Quelle's after-sales service business. Over 60 per cent of Quelle's managers have worked on the frontline and, having been trained on how to work with customers, they understand very well the kind of problems customers can have with their products.

In the event that a customer expresses his dissatisfaction in writing, Quelle does its best to respond rapidly and to the client's satisfaction. Complaints are read by the managers, as well as by the complaints department. All letters are responded to within one week. Complaints are very important to Quelle and all letters received are analysed very carefully to know what are the major problems facing the customer and to know which regions are encountering the greatest number of problems.

Complaints are also important to the personnel. The monthly reports which are done once the letters and complaints have been analysed are sent around to all employees to see. Bonuses for all of the employees in a given centre are impacted by the number of complaints letters received. Too many letters mean fewer bonuses. To date, Quelle has the extremely low rate of complaints to customer visits of 0.05 per cent or only 700 complaints for 1,500,000 visits.

Implementation

One of the keys to good customer service at Quelle is the fact that managers and staff alike are all committed to the level of satisfaction of their customers. Quelle has been conducting customer satisfaction surveys for 15 years. On a quarterly basis, the company's central marketing research unit selects customers of a certain week in a quarter to which the questionnaires are sent. The questionnaire covers every phase of the customer's contact with the company for a repair, starting with the first contact by telephone. The questionnaire ends with the question: 'Would you recommend our after-sales service?' The results are centrally processed and communicated to every employee in the repair station. Over 96 per cent of its customers indicate that they are satisfied with the service.

Employees are committed to customer satisfaction, first because the results of the satisfaction survey have a direct impact on their salaries. Employees can receive bonuses of up to 30 per cent of their fixed salary if customer satisfaction is high and if the economic results for their station are good. If customer complaints are too numerous they represent negative points in the bonus calculation.

Managers are encouraged to run their stations as if they were their own company. They have the authority to do their own recruiting and their own programmes for boosting customer satisfaction and sales. If the results of the customer satisfaction surveys are low it is the responsibility of the manager to take measures to improve those levels of satisfaction. The managers themselves are judged according to the profitability of their unit and according to the level of customer satisfaction.

Both the customer satisfaction survey and the customer complaints highlight problems in Quelle's service which should not only be addressed at the station level. To deal with these issues, the company organises problem-solving groups at the regional level in which station managers and personnel participate. The objective is to look at the problems from a broader organisation-wide perspective. Results are almost always implemented because groups are not formed until a precise problem has been identified.

Quelle believes that one of the major reasons why it is able to offer customers good service is because of the quality of its training. 'Our policy is "Don't let them go to the customer before they know how and what to do".' That means that no service technician is permitted to work on his own at the customer's premises until he has undergone six to nine months' extensive training, both in technical and customer handling skills in Quelle's own training centre.

There is one entire period of the training devoted to dealing with the customer over the phone. This includes as much on how to answer the phone and identify a customer need as the technical aspects of diagnosing a customer's problem. There is also a training session on how to handle customer complaints. The most important aspect of the training, however, occurs while the new employee is in the company of an experienced technician. Once a visit to a customer is complete, for example, the employee receives a complete debriefing on what he has done right and wrong. Mr Beckmann and all of the management at Quelle are convinced that the dialogue between the customer and the technician, while the technician is on-site, is vital to customer satisfaction. In training, therefore, a great deal of emphasis is placed upon this aspect of the service.

What can be learned

1 Give your customers the ultimate in service: the opportunity not to be served

Quelle offers customers the possibility to diagnose their problems over the phone. It's the best service they can provide. The customer pays nothing and his problem is solved. The advantage for the company is that this gains the customer's confidence. When there really is a serious repair problem, Quelle is the first place he will come to.

2 Don't be in a hurry to let youre employees out on their own

Quelle keeps its new staff in training for over six months. It's a good way to ensure that the customer gets the best service possible and a good way to ensure that the employee truly understands the business and the customer service principles of the company.

3 Hit hard with customer satisfaction figures

By tying bonuses to customer satisfaction and customer complaints, Quelle is sure that employees understand how important customer satisfaction is to the business. It is also a valid justification for demanding the best out of the company's service technicians.

ROBECO GROUP

In today's society a person takes a lifetime to set aside a small pool of money – security against old age and the hope of ensuring a slightly better future for one's children. The minor satisfaction that one can gain from such an achievement is generally destroyed by the arrogant behaviour of bankers or investment managers who look down their noses at the small sum presented to them. In general, they are not only arrogant with small investors, they are also careless – your account and its profitability represents little or nothing to an account manager whose livelihood depends on the performance of the large accounts of the very wealthy. Let's face it, you don't count for much . . .

. . . except at Robeco. Robeco has a reputation for also caring for the small accountholder. It not only cares about him; it has created a special service which does nothing but work for him and his investments. He is advised; his questions are responded to rapidly; his buy/sell orders are executed promptly and he receives the basic consideration which he is due. If all this happens over the phone, so what, the service is the same or better.

Background

The Robeco Group is a consortium of mutual funds each of which has been established as a separate company. Robeco, a Dutch-based entity, has existed for over 50 years and is responsible for managing each of the mutual funds and for promoting the sales of shares in these mutual funds to private and institutional investors. Assets under management of the Group amount to US $25 mm, of which one third comes from institutions and two thirds from private investors.

The Robeco Group consortium is made up of four major mutual funds/companies whose shares are sold independently in Rotterdam, Geneva and Paris, and 10 other entities, each of which deals with a specific financial service – Ro-total (mixed investments), Roparco (savings accounts), Rotrusco (discretionary capital management), three Regional Funds etc.

Each of the mutual funds/companies (Robeco, Rolinco, Rorento and Rodamco) has a specific mission for its investments. Rolinco, for example, invests internationally in the stocks and shares of companies showing good opportunities for growth. Rorento invests internationally in fixed income securities (mainly bonds). Robeco invests internationally in the stocks and shares of financially sound companies, and Rodamco invests in commercial property worldwide.

The Robeco Group shares are sold through intermediaries or direct to investors through the company's own sales network. For direct sales, the company manages its relationships with customers entirely by phone and by mail. Because of the group's structure and its marketing approach, it can offer considerable cost savings in terms of management costs per mutual fund; in 1989, they ranged from 0.21 per cent to 0.32 per cent of the average total net assets of each company. The approach is particularly attractive to small investors who would otherwise find it difficult to find the same conditions of investment elsewhere.

The company has sales offices in three locations – Rotterdam, Paris and Geneva. In addition, they have operations in the US, Belgium, Germany, Luxembourg, the UK, Uruguay and The Netherlands Antilles. Besides these offices, the company communicates widely to the investing public through print advertising in international magazines and newspapers, and through direct mail promotions.

Robeco is recognised for its achievements in customer service. In 1988 it came out in first place in the Biannual Customer Satisfaction Award and came out fifth in the same Award in 1990.

Service strategy

Robeco offers its customers a choice – the choice not to use an intermediary to invest their money in mutual funds of the Group. Investments in most mutual funds are made through an intermediary, such as a bank or an investment management institution. The customer pays transactional fees and sometimes management fees to the intermediary for acting on his behalf. The smaller the sum of money the customer has to invest, the more expensive these fees become as a percentage of the total earnings on the account. In some instances, the fees can be so important that they wipe out any earning on the account. By selling direct to the public, Robeco can offer customers relatively low transactional fees.

Robeco is not the only company to offer this kind of possibility. Other companies encourage investors to approach the company directly by phone or by mail. Like Robeco, they do heavy advertising in business journals and newspapers. The advantage which Robeco has, as compared with its competitors, is the added-value it offers in terms of investment advice and administrative ease, efficiency and low cost.

Robeco is an investment advisory service by telephone. Because of the depth and degree of expertise demonstrated by the investment advisers, Robeco's role exceeds that of a fund manager. It not only offers customers the choice between a variety of well-defined investment alternatives, it also provides general advice and information on financial markets and specific investment opportunities. To reinforce this image, it also ensures that transactions are executed with exceptional efficiency and that any written communication the customer receives is extremely user-friendly.

Robeco customers fall into one of three categories. In the first group are customers with under G100,000 to invest. They are handled by one of the company's three central offices in Rotterdam, Paris and Geneva. In the second group are private investors with over G100,000 and up to G1 million to invest. These accounts are handled by a separate department; each client has his own account manager. In the third group are institutional clients; they also have a private account manager. Together, the company has over 400,000 customers.

The segmentation of the company's customer base by customer size has permitted the company to target the small investor and to focus on creating a value-added service package for this market. While a small investor doesn't have his own personal account manager, he does have access to a qualified investment adviser any time he calls. There is no waiting and he doesn't have to skip work in order to receive financial advice.

From the Robeco investment advisers, the investor can obtain leaflets on specific products, know the status of earnings on his account, be given information on market trends or on particular companies – practically anything that one could obtain from a personal account manager. In addition, he receives regular publications produced by the company, and extremely prompt and reliable handling of whatever transactions he undertakes. As compared with the service provided by many banks and investment companies to small account holders, Robeco's service represents a notable difference. 'The customer can ask us all kinds of questions, "Should I sell my stocks?" "What happened on Wall Street today?". We're trained and we do our best to respond.'

Service strengths

At Robeco, the customer has access to a large range of information via his investment adviser. Many Robeco customers are constantly in touch with the company. They use the Robeco advisory service to its full extent. These customers can call and ask for information on a daily basis. For example, in the Rotterdam office, the company receives over 350,000 telephone calls per year.

In most companies, the amount of information provided to the investment advisers by the investment management departments can be very scarce. At Robeco, the company makes a point of arming its investment advisers with as much information as possible.

Every morning each investment adviser receives a package of the most important newspaper articles of the day (worldwide); every week they each receive an update by the portfolio manager of each fund on developments during the week. For major trends and major developments, the investment advisers are given books of information on political, economic and financial developments by country and region.

Minute by minute information is available from the adviser's computer terminal which links the adviser to data providers, which gives interest rate movements, the status on the world's stock and bond markets, and important developments affecting the financial markets.

Together these measures ensure that every time a customer calls, the investment adviser is in a position to provide him with new and different information on Robeco's funds, as well as on the financial world in general.

The investment adviser is also able to provide the customer with up-to-date and complete information on his own account. The return, by month, by year, is available at the push of a button. The adviser can have all the information pertaining to the customer's account for at least two years instantly on his screen. If the customer has a question or a problem, the investment adviser is in a position to respond.

The customer has access to information as much as he wants and over a large time span. The company is open from 8 a.m. until 9 p.m.. As the client is not assigned to one particular investment adviser, any of the investment advisers on hand are prepared to answer his questions. To ensure that the telephone is promptly answered, Robeco has installed a red/green telephone monitoring system. When the system lights up red, a customer is on hold and an investment adviser must pick up the line. If it's green, no one is on the line.

The accessibility of information doesn't stop with the telephone. Robeco provides the customer with a bi-monthly magazine called *Safe* which gives financial information and general information on developments within the Robeco group. They also provide customers with detailed information on each of the Robeco products, including information about what is to be done in the case of death, accident or other extraordinary situations.

All responses to specific enquiries are noted in the computer on the person's account. The letter is sent out by the person who received the call and sent out the same day by another department which handles the stockage of brochures and financial data.

In general, the philosophy is to ensure the customer receives all the information he needs in order to feel confident in the professionalism of the company. 'When someone asks for information, it's nice to have a good conversation on the telephone, but if he doesn't receive the information he asks for, he's not going to be happy.'

Robeco also takes care of the little extras in order to personalise its service. If a new customer comes to the company on the recommendation of an existing customer, Robeco writes a thank you letter to the existing customer.

Some customers communicate only in writing. It happens, for example, that one of these might write in to withdraw an amount over the non-penalty limit of G25,000 per month. To help the customer avoid the penalty, the investment adviser would try to call the customer and propose that he spread his withdrawal over a two-month period. If they cannot get the customer on the phone within two days, they carry out the order anyway.

Other customers move and forget to leave a forwarding address. In The Netherlands, rather than waiting until the customer contacts Robeco again, Robeco goes in search of its customer by contacting the mayor's office in the previous town of residence to obtain the new address. (The Dutch must register whenever they change residences.)

Implementation

There are two crucial aspects to the provision of good service to customers at Robeco. The first involves ensuring that the customer's contact with the company is always uniformly courteous and receptive to customer needs. The second involves ensuring the efficiency and accuracy of any work carried out for the client.

Robeco ensures the first primarily through the use of service standards. The first thing that investment advisers are taught upon entering the company are the standards to be observed concerning how to interact with customers, how to talk over the phone, how to present investment information and how to respond to different type of question. 'Investment advisers need to have an enormous amount of information. They have to know more than just the financial background of a transaction because the conversation does not stop there. The customer might ask questions about return rates of different funds or "What do you think about developments concerning Rolinco?".'

Basic standards concern the way the person should answer the telephone. In the standards for France we find, for example, 'When answering the phone, one should give the name of the company, one's own name and a polite greeting.' There are other standards concerning the delay in which requests for information must be responded 'within three days' and requests for information on opening accounts 'within one day'.

More complex standards concern the way in which the adviser deals with the client. All investment advisers are evaluated on the way they handle clients and specifically on different aspects of that – accuracy of the response, flexibility, knowledge of the products, general knowledge, telephone manners, etc. A new employee is evaluated every two weeks for the first six months.

Performance on some standards is followed by the computer. Each incoming letter, for example, is stamped with a date and registered in the computer with the nature of the request. The investment adviser must then answer the letter within the standard delay set for that type of request. Should that not be possible, the adviser must send out a little note to the customer indicating that they received the letter and will answer it as soon as possible. An ultimate deadline is also set for each type of correspondence, 'for letters asking for information on fund performances, the outside delay is five days'.

Because of the importance the company places on the customer-responsiveness of its service, Robeco has a precise way of handling customer complaints. All customer complaints or comments are registered by the investment adviser who receives them. Many are received over the phone; they are all noted down by the adviser in the computer. The entire list of customer comments and complaints prints out at the end of every week for the department manager. The list is then published in the form of a document for circulation and, together with comments received from all of the Robeco investment centres are circulated from top to bottom throughout the company.

The objective of this measure is to ensure that all employees are clearly aware of what customers think about Robeco's service and of the areas which, from the customer's perspective, need improvement.

This does not mean that the complaint itself is not handled without the greatest consideration. All complaints are dealt with the same day or within two days. 'We make a lot of effort to answer the complaint as soon as possible because as long as the complaint is not answered the customer is unsatisfied. We try to find a solution which is satisfying, although we cannot always give the client what he wants.' They cannot, for example, compensate the customer for the poor performance that was realised on one of the funds; they can and do, however, try to propose alternative investments that might better respond to his requirements.

The second area which the company emphasises in order to ensure service quality to its customers is in the exactitude and precision with which the transactions of the clients are handled. All transactions are handled by a separate department from the customer services department. In one location, they handle over 4 million statements every year, 200,000 forms concerning applications and changes, and a few thousand letters. In terms of financial transactions, there are over 1.5 to 2 million per year. This is done with a staff of 45 people.

It is a standard part of company policy to effect every financial transaction on the same day it is received. The next day, the confirmation of this transaction is sent out to the client. The manager of the operations department monitors the maintenance of this standard on a daily basis – he receives a report every evening which shows what percentage of the transactions were made.

To make sure that the mail gets to the operations department as fast as possible, the mail is sorted by the mail room upon arrival and is immediately brought over to operations.

To avoid entry errors, the forms sent by the customer are checked prior to entry; their computer system helps them add information which is missing, i.e. the customer forgets to indicate his complete address. The data entry of financial transactions is done twice – the system compares the two – if there is a difference, the computer system signals the employee who then makes the correction. 'Once a year at most there's a mistake; there is almost a 100 per cent guarantee for the customer that the transaction is handled correctly.'

When a mistake is made in the information provided by the customer, 'We analyse why it has occurred. We try to know why a certain type of mistake frequently occurs; maybe our forms are not clear enough in that area.'

To avoid errors in the entire process, the operations department was reorganised so that they might 'cover everything, from the incoming mail to the outgoing mail. We also handle the management of the statements, including putting them into the envelopes. The total chain is complete; it's the only way you can influence people to do things the way you want them. By managing the whole chain, I can guarantee quality at each step.'

The efficiency of co-ordination between the operations department and the information department is dealt with in a weekly meeting between members of the two departments. They talk about the problems they have and the ways to solve them.

What can be learned

1 Use the telephone . . . to add value and save money

Robeco offers nearly the same service to large and small investors as other companies offer only to large, important clients. They do it by using the telephone, a tool which permits them to maximise resources and offer more to small investors than their competitors do.

2 Hearing it straight from the customer

Being told by your boss that customers are not satisfied is one thing; hearing it direct from the customers is another; it leaves a lasting impression. Robeco publishes all customer comments by month and by country, for all to read and make note of.

3 Focus on the customer/company points of contact

Robeco has a limited number of points of contact with its customers. The customer's impression of the company is entirely based on the outcome of these contacts – over the phone, in responses to requests for information, account statements, confirmation of execution and advertising (direct mail or mass). As such, Robeco does its utmost to ensure that those contacts are 100 per cent error free.

4 To 'responsibilise' employees, let them control the whole process

Robeco reorganised its operations department in order to permit the department to control the entire process of customer transactions from start to finish. The result is that employees feel more capable of guaranteeing the level of quality provided to customers.

SAAB

Good customer service is not a determining factor when a customer first sets out to buy a car. He imagines the prestige value of the car, its performance, its price, its colour even. The importance of service quality is something which grows on him; he becomes aware of it only gradually over the course of his contact with the dealer and with the company. Bad service is something that infuriates car buyers, enough to make them leave and never come back again.

At Saab, they want to make customer service a reason to choose Saab and a reason to stay with Saab. Their objective is to make customer service good enough to bring the customer back again, and again and again.

Background

Compared with many other car manufacturers, Saab has had to overcome certain handicaps. First of all, it's based in Sweden: at the present time, in the present economic world situation that is not necessarily a good place for a car manufacturer to be. Second, it is relatively small. With practically all of its manufacturing in the Nordic countries, Saab has been hit by the comparative rises in production costs in these countries which cannot be offset by increases in car prices in most of their markets. Despite recording gains in market share in some countries, sales which since 1988 have been relatively flat because of the slump in the world car market, have been accompanied with losses. In early 1990, General Motors purchased 50 per cent of Saab Automobile which is now permitting the company to source its goods using 6m's purchasing leverage as well as areas of the world where material and labour costs are more favourable.

Saab began as and still remains a very Swedish company. It was never uniquely a producer of cars. It began its existence as a producer of aircraft. Just after the Second World War, Sweden's principal aircraft manufacturer, Svenska Aeroplan Aktiebolaget (or Saab), decided that would be a good idea to apply its skills and its now unused manufacturing facilities, for the production of cars.

A Mr Gunner Ljungström, with a staff of 20 people, began this impressive effort in 1945. 'Since Saab had no experience in car construction, nor any traditions in this field, it became a matter of common sense and the ability of those involved to think and design technically, analytically and innovatively. But, if one could design and manufacture advanced aircraft, why not cars?' (*The Saab Way*, Gunnar A. Sjögren).

By 1949, the Saab 92 series was rolling out of the newly converted manufacturing facilities. Despite its flaws, the car was very well received and permitted the company to believe that it had found a niche in the automobile market. Following from the Saab 92 was the Saab 93, then the Sonett, a sports car, then the Saab 916 and so on, until today's 900 and 9000 series.

For the most part, Saab had never sold more than three Saab model lines at any one time – a Saab is a Saab. It has retained its distinctive character and its distinctive looks throughout its over 40-year history and despite various options or improvements which have been made on the car.

In terms of the comparative advantages of the car, they lie principally with the car's road-handling ability and its safety features. Just as with some of the first Saabs, today's Saab is recognised as being one of the safest cars in the world. Both the Saab 900 and the Saab 9000, the two Saab cars presently on the market, have rated first and second best for the last five years by insurance companies rating cars for accident damage. In Sweden, the Saab 9000 won the Folksam Insurance Company award for being the 'safest car of the year' in 1989 and 1992 – the only time that the award has been given twice to the same company.

In the period ending 1989/92, the company has gained recognition for its breakthroughs in turbo-powered engines. The Saab Turbo 900 was the first to carry this technology and 'most of the press reports were so laudatory that Saab people were afraid of repeating them for fear of being accused of excessive bragging' (*The Saab Way*, Gunnar Sjögren).

Service strategy

The Saab car is positioned in the premium sector of the car market. A Saab car is for the individualist. It is for the customer who wants an exclusive car which surpasses its competitors in terms of safety, road-handling and performance. It is for the customer who wants quality in an original package.

With this marketing approach to their market, Saab moved from being a relatively insignificant producer in the 1950s and 1960s to gaining a solid reputation on the major world markets in the 1980s. Over 73 per cent of Saab's cars are sold to the export market, the principal of those being the US and Middle Europe.

In the 1970s and early 1980s, the focus of the company's efforts was on gaining new customers. Today, the company has a strong customer base which it would not like to lose. While it is still looking to draw new customers to the mark, it is increasingly concentrating its efforts on keeping existing clients loyal to the company. 'One of the marketing goals is to retain the loyality of Saab owners at least at the present level' (Saab marketing guidelines).

'Saab's goal is to get Saab owners to repurchase a Saab when he buys his next car. To do this we need to take such good care of our customers that they come back and buy a Saab next time. And by that we do not mean [only] when he trades in his car for a new one, but also when he comes in and comes back for service and repairs. It is much more expensive to find new customers, so it is more important to care for old customers' explains Mr Arne Höglund, Service Manager.

It is in Saab's efforts to retain the loyalty of customers that Saab's service strategy plays a major role. The present service strategy was developed in 1986. 'It is a customer oriented programme for the handling of service, parts and accessories.'

Saab's service strategy could be simply called its importer/dealer strategy, because Saab's aim is to work entirely through its importers and dealers to deliver good service to customers. 'In the parent company, we are working through our importers and our dealers, they have the most contact with the customer. We have to make the weakest link stronger. The importers should support the dealers and we should support the importers.'

The programme goes under the name of FAST which means forming after-sales together. It focused first upon communicating to dealers and importers that customers buy more than just a car, they buy parts and servicing as well. 'We must have a holistic view.'

It has then targeted areas for action by the importers and the dealers. Saab wants to position its dealers as exclusive providers of sales and service assistance. 'We want a distribution network which is exclusive – personalised customer care, not a super-market type sales process.'

The FAST programme therefore starts by talking about reliability. 'We must have special tools and workshop manuals sent on time if we expect them to do their job well.'

The more exclusive one's service is, the more personalised it becomes and the more need there is for dealers to manage relationships with finesse. Another part of FAST puts an accent on a strong customer orientation. 'This is a key element. It enables us to reinforce our relationships with all of those on whom we depend – the importers, the dealers and the customers. By customer orientation, we mean:

Take people seriously;
show respect;
be intuitive;
show consideration;
display insight;
be prepared to produce 'customer-designed' solutions;
always demonstrate a positive attitude.'

Finally, Saab doesn't intend to lose sight of its Swedish heritage. 'Our Swedish heritage is important to Saab – to distinguish us from the Germans and Japanese. We want to emphasise all the good things of being a Swedish company – safety, concern for the environment, technological advance.'

By putting all of this together in the showroom, Saab is enhancing its image as an exclusive car dealer with premium, personalised service for the individualistic customer; it gives customers a good reason to come back again.

Service strengths

In terms of what goes on in the showroom and after-sales servicing area, the focus is on 'doing the right thing'. Saab has provided its dealers with guidelines on what must be done for customers in order to meet the company's standards of customer service. 'There are standards that must be met for one to become a dealer and service quality standards that must be followed once they become a dealer.'

Perhaps the most important area of focus is on providing trained and capable staff on hand who are prepared to work exclusively for Saab cars. In most dealerships, Saab is not the only make of car which the dealer handles. Yet, it is vitally important that the dealer demonstrate an expertise in Saab cars.

In any dealership with which the customer comes in contact, he will meet at least one salesman who handles only Saab cars. By policy there is also a second individual who is 'sufficiently familiar with the Saab products to handle enquiries professionally in the Saab specialist's absence'.

Likewise, in the Saab garage, there is a chief Saab technician who, 'fulfils all the international and national requirements for a Saab master technician'. He also has an assistant who is trained and prepared to work in his absence.

Both the salesmen and the technicians have not only been trained on-site, but also participated in training organised by Saab to prepare Saab dealers' employees all over the world. 'When it comes to winning the battle in the market place, we are sharing the possibilities with the product itself, the salesman and the after-sales service.'

Most Saab dealerships have a quick service facility for customers in addition to the normal repair shop. Whenever possible, customers are loaned cars while their cars are being repaired. Their car is also washed and when delivery or collection of the car occurs out of the standard delivery times, Saab delivers the car directly to the customer's doorstep.

'We see the customer for services, for repairs, for buying parts, etc. We see the customer an average of 12 times between his car purchases. If we do that well, we have a positive influence on the customer. Every time we meet the customer we have to satisfy him.'

Customers can also count on hot coffee, the use of a telephone and up-to-date and interesting Saab brochures on hand to read about the company. Everything should be professional, clean and comfortable. 'We don't want to become too big; we want the customer to feel that they have a unique car and unique service to go with it.'

Implementation

For Saab ensuring that customers receive good service doesn't just mean ensuring that dealers respect certain service standards; it also means helping them to run their business better so that good customer service comes more easily.

'We have a mission to assist the management of the importers – commercial, administrative, technical guidance and support in the after sales area and as well as by marketing parts.' The FAST programme not only means reliable and customer oriented service; to dealers and importers it also means 'business know-how, skills and target awareness'.

1 business know-how: Saab must keep importers informed about developments within Saab and the industry.
2 Target awareness: together with importers, targets must be determined and communicated to dealers; progress must be monitored.
3 Skills: Saab must provide training.
4 Reliability: importers must perceive the parent company as a reliable supplier.

'Targets are developed at the group level for each of the goals. For example, with reliability we have to see that the technical literature is delivered on time to the importer, the importer has to see that it is delivered on time to the dealer, and the target is described in customer terms: "when I get my new Saab, I need complete instructions on all technical parts, I need an owner's manual and a demonstration from the salesman and from the service manager".'

In addition to setting internal goals for the chain from the Saab company on down to the importer, Saab has also established a dealers operating standard guidebook which sets service and operating standards for the dealerships. They are presented in the form of a booklet which is designed for use by importers, as a monitoring tool (with a checklist) and by dealers as a reference tool.

According to the book, Saab dealers should 'accept all major credit cards', 'use seat, floor and wing/fender covers at all times', 'maintain customer records including vehicle service history linked to the dealer sales department'. They should also have 'one person responsible for Saab related tools, literature and training' and 'a gross sales follow-up on Saab parts and accessories divided into: workshop, retail and wholesale'.

The objective of these kind of standards is to go right down to the dealer level to ensure that the basics in good management and customer service are being respected. They are divided into basic standards and others; 40 basic standards are, 'the ticket of admission . . . and are as such compulsory for all dealers, regardless of their size and location'. 'The other standards – 170 in total – represent progressively more important goals in operations management and service which the dealer should meet.

The dealer's success in meeting the standards is measured as part of the overall dealer assessment process. Dealers are assessed on the results of a scoring on a checklist of the standards and on the results of a customer satisfaction survey.

The customer satisfaction survey is carried out by the importer or by an external organisation. Dealers are tested primarily on customer service aspects such as, skill and behaviour of the salesperson, condition of the car at the time of delivery, availability of Saab parts at the dealership, the dealer's handling of the warranty process etc. The survey can be conducted either by contacting a new car purchaser just following his purchase (using this method some questions cannot be asked) or as part of the Dealer of the Year Award process, i.e. once a year.

In the dealer assessment, greater importance is given to the results of the customer satisfaction survey – the weight factor is 60 per cent. For dealerships whose score is very low, a complete audit is performed by a field representative from the importer using the dealer operating standard as a guide. The objective is to help the dealer improve his score for the future.

The dealer with the best score per country wins the Dealer of the Year Award, which is a recognised title within the company; the winner receives an award plaque for display in his dealership.

What can be learned

1 Create a chain of support

Saab works with dealers in 41 countries worldwide. It must rely exclusively on those dealers to deliver the kind of service they believe their customers need. Saab has chosen to create a chain of communication and support through which its messages can be passed. Importers, whom the company can influence directly, are trained, motivated and provided with the necessary tools to help them help dealers in their country improve service quality to customers.

2 *Make service quality a concrete goal*

It's one thing to say to a car dealer that he should be more customer oriented; it's another to ask that he have refreshments on hand to provide to customers. Saab doesn't wait for dealers to interpret for themselves what it means to be customer oriented; it's done it for them by providing concrete and tangible standards of customer service. That way, there is no room for misunderstanding, and no room for error.

3 *Make customer satisfaction measurably important*

Saab's dealer assessment system permits customer satisfaction with dealers' service to be measured. Its importance is underlined by the company whose dealer assessment system is 60 per cent based on the results of the satisfaction survey.

SAINSBURY'S

Sainsbury's can be a bit surprising. One imagines the old-fashioned, friendly, corner gourmet food store with a modern, spiffed-up interior. The reality is a chain of supermodern, impeccably clean, efficient self-service 'department store' food markets. What surprises is the extreme professionalism, the clockwork precision and the army of behind-the-scenes staff which keeps Sainsbury's a calm, pleasant and easy place to shop.

History

Sainsbury's is the biggest supermarket chain in the UK. It employs nearly 100,000 people in 315 stores (at last count). Forty per cent of the entire population shops or has shopped at Sainsbury's in the last year.

The origins of this highly successful group go back to the nineteenth century. In 1869 John James and Mary Ann Sainsbury set up a modest dairy on Drury Lane, London. Seven years later they established a second and soon diversified into ham and bacon. The showpiece store on London Road, Croydon in 1882, with tile and marble, brought real success and provided a model from which the business grew to 106 stores by 1910.

Centralised production of meat pies and sausages was added at the turn of the century and was expanded in the 1930s. The key change in the after-war period, however, has been the conversion from full service to self-service, a switch which began in 1950.

Sainsbury's is still in the hands of the Sainsbury family. The present John Sainsbury, knighted in 1980 and created Baron Sainsbury of Preston Candover in 1989, has been company chairman since 1969. He is a recognised public figure and spends considerable time promoting the image of Sainsbury's in the community through his own charitable activities.

Sainsbury's is a household word in the UK. It has a strong image with the public and is recognised for the quality of its products, the quality of its service and its leadership position in the retail food industry. As it was put to me, 'We pursue excellence in every aspect of our business. We want to be the best; if we get to be the biggest, that's the icing on the cake.'

Service strategy

Sainsbury's service strategy and positioning in the market is founded upon the results of its marketing research. The modern-day Sainsbury's performs all of the market research it feels it needs to understand its customers well – and that's a lot. As the director of the department explained to me, 'Sainsbury's feels comfortable operating with a large backlog of information. It's like the difference between trying to cross the room with the light on and trying to cross it with the light out. With no light you may get there, by chance, but it's a lot surer and smoother with the light on.'

The research that has been done divides Sainsbury's customers into two groups, the 'main shoppers' and the 'secondary shoppers'. Main shoppers shop at Sainsbury's on a regular basis and would choose Sainsbury's above any other store if given the choice. Secondary shoppers are occasional shoppers. Sainsbury's main shoppers have higher expectations than the average shopper in terms of service and product quality. They tend to be more upmarket in terms of their socioeconomic category and the company's core offering, including Sainsbury's branded products, are attractive to them.

The Sainsbury's offer is enshrined in the company's slogan, 'Good Food Costs Less.' The company advertises offering value for money and maintains high standards of service and product quality to back it up.

The company's service strategy focuses on providing an exceptionally attractive and functional shopping environment to match the expectations of its main shoppers. Secondly, any transaction with the company – at the check-out counter, at the information desk, in the aisles, by letter, by phone, should make the customer feel appreciated and important. In addition, Sainsbury's is positioned as the company with a social conscience. It is in this respect that one finds the company heavily committed to major social concerns of the population, such as the green movement, assistance to the disabled and the development of derelict land.

As concerns the shopping environment, the company puts emphasis upon the functionality, attractiveness and cleanliness of the environment in which the customer shops and circulates. Strolling around a Sainbury's store, one of the first things one notices is the wide aisles; they're practically twice as wide as in other supermarkets and there is plenty of room for three trolleys to pass at the same level.

Another thing is the cleanliness. There is not a spot on the ground – no dead lettuce leaves, no sugar sprinkles and no broken yogurt pots. Sainsbury's has at least three staff working full-time in the store doing nothing but cleaning. (While explaining this to us, Sainsbury's store manager proudly wiped his index finger across the top of the 5-ft-high dairy case to prove that no spot was left untouched.) Customers also appreciate the parking facilities which most stores have, the toilets (a must), the no-runaway trolley catchers and the clear, daylight quality lighting which is also standard in all of the stores.

Beyond the pleasant shopping environment, there are the friendly staff. Sainsbury's staff are trained to respond politely and with a smile to customers; they're trained on how to answer enquiries and how to assist customers in their shopping. Upon joining the company, their initiation training includes an entire section on customer service with typical questions and answers, and support videos showing life-like situations.

Any contact with the customer is intended to finish on a positive note, even complaints. Complaints registered with the staff at the customer service desk are handled with the greatest consideration possible. Eggs broken on the premises are exchanged, goods brought back to the store for product quality problems are refunded on the spot and then sent to the lab for analysis.

Sainsbury's differentiates itself, not only on the basis of the shopping experience, but also by pursuing goals with a broader social conscience which appeal to the majority of its customers. The company doesn't just champion these goals with lip-service and financial backing; they choose goals in which the company can take an active part. Two which the company has emphasised in recent years are the renovation of derelict property and the green movement.

In the former case, the company has consistently made an effort to build on land which is earmarked for renovation. A complete team of in-house architects are assigned to the site and asked to preserve, to the greatest degree possible, the original attributes of the building or property. The result is that over half of Sainsbury's stores built between 1985 and 1990 have used derelict or run-down urban sites. Sainsbury's today can incorporate old churches, factories, taverns etc.

More recently, the company has decided to put an enormous effort towards the environmental conservation movement. In 1989, it created the Environment Affairs Committee. The committee's mission is to 1) ensure that Sainsbury's conducts its business with a real consideration for environmental issues, and 2) gain corporate leadership in the consumer's perspective in terms of environmental issues above and beyond its competitors. In addition to the environment friendlier landscaping programme and the recycling that the company has been doing for some years, the company has introduced an environment friendlier line of products. 'Greencare', the company's line of environment friendlier cleaning products is, today, the number one 'green' brand in the UK.

The decision to become an environmentally conscientious company reflects the wishes of Sainsbury's customers. In the numerous studies performed by the company, concern for the environment became an ever more important issue. Mr Mike Samuel, head of the environmental department, summarised the logic, 'Sainsbury's does things either because they are right commercially or right socially – in this case it's both'. Today, the company is continuing to study customer expectations in terms of 'greenness'. They just ran focus groups to identify how the expectations of the committed green consumer differ from those of the average consumer in order to better target products and services to meet the needs of both.

Service strengths

An adult in a Sainsbury's store is like a child in a sweet shop – he doesn't know where to turn, it all looks so good. The minute one enters the store, there's the smell of freshly baked bread – that's not by accident, the ventilation pipes from the bakery are piped all the way across the store. Next, there's all those crispy green vegetables, fresh and restocked all day long. There at the end of the corridor is the white-tiled fish counter with the specials for the day and a new recipe in an attractive dispenser on the counter. To have a view of the delicious pastries and bread goodies which tantalised your nose on entering the store, you pass by the refrigerator section with its three different settings – one to keep the ice cream at $-23°$, frozen veggies at $-18°$ and meat, just at $0°$. At long last, there it is, the bakery shop with cakes, breads and pies galore. There's a new one practically every week, thanks to the inventiveness of the bakers who are given free rein by the store manager. And, don't worry about missing the hot fresh bread if you can't get there early in the morning – there are three baking cycles a day. Sainsbury's is truly a gourmet's delight.

It's also a delight for the practical shopper. There is plenty of parking for customers with cars. If not, transportation to and from the store is assured by the community (there's generally a bus stop just in front), by a Sainsbury's 'shopper hopper' miniature bus or by taxis from the free taxi phone installed just at the store exit. There are also free bags for your groceries in bright colours or designs and, better yet, staff who help you pack them.

Every Sainsbury's store uses the same layout. The fish counter is always in the far left-hand corner and the bakery in the far right-hand corner. Pasta and rice are just after the veggies and the customer service desk is next to the check-out counters. In case you get lost or can't find something, there are clear signs hanging from the roof which can be read, not just one or two aisles, but five aisles away.

If you are a 'green' consumer or just looking for low prices, it's all marked – with little coloured plastic tags hanging directly in front of the items on the shelf. Because everything is so clean and neat they don't get lost in the mass of product labels, like they do in other supermarkets. Discount price tags are of only three types (that's clearly indicated too). There is the 'everyday low price' offer which is a long-term (six weeks to three months) special low price, the 'special' offer which is a two-week discount, and the 'multibuy' which gives you a discount if you buy in bulk. With the multibuy, discount is made automatically when the relevant number of items have passed through the checkout.

Sainsbury's wants to make sure its customers have a choice. As such, it stocks over 15,000 different commodities. For most major products or for prepared foods, there is a Sainsbury's brand available which complements, not replaces, the offering of other name brand goods. You don't have to worry about them being out of your favourite strawberry jam; the 'gaps', as they call it, are filled every night or sooner if necessary. Delivery schedules are rigidly observed and stock levels are controlled by computer which links the check-out stand to central store ordering. Out of 15,000 lines controlled regularly, only 30 are ever out of stock. Sainsbury's depot guarantees to the stores 99.8 per cent relability.

It's apple season and you've decided to bake an apple pie – a new adventure as you're not a born cook. There you are in Sainsbury's in front of the apple display – there are no less than seven types of apples from which to choose and the're not at all the same! In desperation, you ask the 18-year-old fellow filling the lettuce counter to tell you which one to buy. Barely the question is out of your mouth when you're sure you're made a fool of yourself – how is an 18 year old boy going to be able to advise you about the right apples for apple pie. 'Well, sir, [here it comes] the Bramley there is very tart and has lots of juice, so is the Granny Smith, although it has a little less juice and might dry up your pie. I wouldn't recommend the Golden Delicious, as it is a dessert apple as is the Red Delicious. According to the information we've been given, the Bramley is best for a pie with a couple of Granny Smiths mixed in for good measure.' You are flabbergasted and go away forgetting to buy the apples.

So that you won't be caught off guard the next time, it's handy to know that all

Sainsbury's staff are trained on the different types of products – the care and handling, cleaning and preparation. Just behind the pretty walls of your supermarket is the staff room with walls lined with descriptions of new products, their growing season (if there is one) and their pictures. The product knowledge rule applies for all of the goods in the store, including those at the fish and meat counter where the shopper can receive all kinds of advice from experienced butchers and fishmongers.

Implementation

At the beginning of our description of Sainsbury's, we said that Sainsbury's was a bit surprising; it was surprising because of the level of sophistication of their management functions. One way in which we found the company very sophisticated was in their store development policy. Sainsbury's does not pursue growth just for growth's sake. While building over 20 new stores per year, the company increases total stores managed by only two to three stores per year.

Its objective is to have a chain of the most modern, energy-efficient and best located stores in the country, providing the best possible service to customers in a particular area. This may be achieved by refurbishing or extending an existing store, or by building a completely new store – either to replace an existing, out-dated one or in a new trading area. In this way, Sainsbury's has expanded – organically, rather than by acquisition – and now has a total sales area of nearly seven million square feet, compared with just over three million square feet ten years ago. The prodct range stocked has grown similarly – from an average of 7,000 lines to 15,000

More square footage and good location favours a high turnover. Sainsbury's stores record the highest sales per square foot of any supermarket chain in the country. A good store can take well over £10 per sq ft, which is the average for the retail industry. Around 25,000 customers a week shop in such a store with Thursday, Friday and Saturday being the busiest days. To handle the volume, Sainsbury's has installed scanners at the check-out counter and accepts most credit cards, as well as debit cards for automatic payment which permit the customer's account to be automatically debited for the purchase. It also has a check-out counter monitoring system for each store which permits it to schedule enough staff on the tills just when the demand is the heaviest; the target standard is no more than 3 customers waiting per till.

All new stores incorporate the most modern techniques available for the preservation of energy and premises management. The concept of the 'low energy supermarket' was developed in 1984. There are now over 100 low energy Sainsbury's stores. The principal advantages from the customers' perspective are that these stores improve the shopping environment, are ecologically conscientious and permit cost savings which are passed on to the customer in his food bill.

Such a store permits a reduction in energy usage of over 40 per cent as compared with a similar store built 10 years earlier. The main feature is the computer operated environment controller which has entirely eliminated the need for a boiler heater. The heat thrown off from the refrigerator units is recycled and used to provide hot water and heat the store and its offices in winter.

The temperature in the store, as well as the temperature in each one of the refrigerating units, is controlled and monitored by computer. Any change of more than 3° in the cold freezers sends up an alarm signal: the food can be immediately transferred to another cold storage, with no loss of merchandise. The temperature in the store is kept at 20°. Studies showed that this was the temperature which was the most agreeable to the average shopper. After store closing time, the temperature is allowed to drop. Prior to opening the next morning, however, the store temperature is brought back up to 20°.

The lighting is also controlled by computer and is adjusted according to the season and to the time of day. As the sun sets, the lighting gradually increases in order to maintain the same overall level of brightness. High frequency fluorescent lighting is used rather than the standard version; it flickers less and is 10 per cent more efficient. Even the heat which is generated by the lights is controlled – it is sucked away by the ventilation units to be recycled for store heating.

The latest addition is the 'CFC sniffer'. Sainsbury's uses R22 version refrigerants in all new stores, the only one which is not controlled by the 1989 Montreal Protocol. Even so, R22 CFCs could escape, so Sainsbury's installed a 'CFC sniffer' in all its new stores which regularly monitors the level of CFCs in the air and sends out an alarm if anything is amiss.

To manage a Sainsbury's store, the company uses a heavy concentration of management resources. In the average store 40 per cent of the staff have supervisory or managerial status. Out of 407 people in the store we visited, there were 47 department and assistant store managers; this is double the industry average. Roughly half of the management staff is on duty at any one time – most of the time they are on the shop floor. Sainsbury's give their managers a good deal of autonomy in the management of their stores. As Norman Lake, the manager of the Streatham Common store explains, 'The company sets the standards and management must maintain them.'

The staff itself is multifunctional – all of the staff are trained to perform three or more functions. They are initiated into one function when they join the company. Within three to six months they have been trained on a second; the third they acquire within the year. As such, staff scheduling can put one member of staff in one post in the morning and move him to another in the afternoon. The scheduling is computer based. Staff can also jump positions as necessary if a customer requires assistance.

Each store has a training room and there are set limits as to how much training each employee should receive. Referring to the training log which is keep in each store, regional directors check that the prescribed amount of training is being organised for staff. Each employee also has a personal workbook in which his or her own progress is recorded.

When an employee joins the store he receives induction training, regardless of his position or his status (part-time, full-time). Over two-thirds of the staff in a store are part-time. Every employee receives a minimum of three days of introduction training to the company. A part of those three days includes a half-day customer service exposure training carried out with a video on customer service and a follow-up of questions and answers by an instructor. The session focuses on examples of life-like situations within the store which the employee is likely to encounter. In addition the employee is given an introduction to the company history and the standards which it expects the employee to uphold – particularly in the area of dress and hygiene.

A check-out counter operator, for example, subsequently receives three additional days of technical training on how to operate the machines. He/she is tested before he/she can assume the function – bringing the total of her pre-job training to six days. A manager generally receives even more extensive introductory training. One manager we spoke with said he had over one month of training before he even entered his office. All managers are required to spend time in a store as part of their training – the minimum is three days, the average is one week.

Sainsbury's has one of the lowest turnovers of customer contact staff in the industry; they're in the top 1 or 2 per cent in the industry. A recent count showed that 1,300 staff have been with the company for over 25 years and 30 for over 40 years. To keep motivation and job stimulation high, management staff is circulated fairly frequently between functions. Employees identified as having potential are rotated once every three to four years. Prior to assuming their new post, each employee has a period of doubling-up with the individual still occupying the post. They call it a 'structured handover'. At the store we visited, for example, there were 47 manager posts, but actually 54 managers on the job because 7 were doubled-up for training. The doubling-up period generally lasts from between two to three months.

Sainsbury's believes in closely monitoring quality in the stores. Perhaps the most important way this is done is through 'hands-on' management. All the directors make regular tours of the stores. Colin Harvey, Head of Retail Operations, is visiting stores two days per week; in total, he makes over 250 store visits per year. His five regional directors are doing likewise. The buying division and other central functions are also expected to make regular tours of the stores. At a minimum, a given store will get at least two visits from directors per year. The norm is three or four. For each visit a report is completed and handed in to Colin Harvey.

In addition, there is the staff of 'specialists', 11 for every area director for a total of around 55. Each is responsible for a given aspect of store management – fresh foods, systems, audit, security etc. Their job is to assist the store managers to improve their management in that specialised area and to ensure that the standards set by the company are being observed. Their visits yield a completed checklist on each store which indicates strengths and weaknesses. It can also give rise to a report, if there is a specific problem which needs to be addressed. Both the checklist and the report are turned in to Colin Harvey and the district manager.

The company also uses mystery shoppers to monitor their service quality. In general, the mystery shoppers are ex-employees. They are given a checklist and asked to monitor items such as stock shortages, the appearance of the staff and the quality of service provided by the staff.

Store managers also control quality within their own store. Automisation at the check-out counter permits the company to know exactly how many items pass through the counter per minute. The targeted standard for the company is 21 items per minute; in general, the staff do a little better. The number of people waiting at the check-out stand is also monitored and the schedule of personnel adjusted to anticipate heavy business hours. To make sure that the advertised price on an item is the same as in the store, all prices are double-checked on a weekly basis.

To be sure that no stone is left unturned, the company even monitors progress on its savings account programme on a weekly basis. This is a savings scheme offered to customers which permits them to invest whenever they like in small amounts. The amount coming in each week is surveyed by the store manager.

During our store visit, we had a small demonstration of how important it is for a store manager to have a quality conscience reflex. When we saw the savings plan, we were intrigued by the concept, which is presented to the consumers as a box attached to the wall in which the individual deposits money and receives a receipt. We asked for a demonstration. Unfortunately, the machine had just gone out of order; when Norman Lake (Store Manager) saw that it wasn't working, he didn't hesitate a second; the store repair staff were there in two minutes and the box was fixed in five.

We had our demonstration. A little old lady followed us and popped a £1 coin in the box.

The company's quality consciousness and its overall objectives are summarised in the company's statement of objectives. This statement hangs in the office of every manager and appears in every financial statement and annual report. We have reproduced it for our readers below.

Company objectives

- To discharge the responsibility as leaders in our trade by acting with complete integrity, by carrying out our work to the highest standards, and by contributing to the public good and to the quality of life in the community.
- To provide unrivalled value to our customers in the quality of the goods we sell, in the competitiveness of our prices and in the range of choice we offer.
- In our stores, to achieve the highest standards of cleanliness and hygiene, efficiency of operation, convenience and customer service, and thereby create as attractive and friendly a shopping environment as possible.
- To offer our staff outstanding opportunities in terms of personal career development and in remuneration relative to other companies in the same market, practising always a concern for the welfare of every individual.
- To generate sufficient profit to finance continual improvement and growth of the business whilst providing our shareholders with an excellent return on their investment.

What can be learned

1 Make the entire community your customer

Sainsbury's community service programme gives the company an alternative way of reaching customers and demonstrating the company's commitment to them. In practical terms, it is low-cost advertising and a good motivation tool for employees – who feel better about the company they work for.

2 Flow with consumer trends

If your customer is concerned about something you can do something about, then don't wait, act! Sainsbury's policy of building on derelict land for new stores was initiated when the issues of property and economic development were beginning to emerge. Sainsbury's present green policies reflect a topic of major customer interest at the present time. Can you do something that your customer will applaud you for?

3 Keep service quality aims in the forefront of every policy

Sainsbury's store development policy is a key success factor for the company. It permits it to keep its promise to customers by providing an attractive and environmentally friendly shopping atmosphere.

It also permits it to locate its stores in the most commercially attractive locations and to follow constantly demographic population flows. Because of the high loyalty of its customers, a change in location within the same community does not necessarily lead to a loss in clientèle.

A more short-sighted, though less costly, solution would have been to renovate the existing buildings. This proposition is less interesting to its target customers who appreciate the Sainsbury's shopping ambience and is, perhaps, less interesting commercially.

4 Keep your head office staff field oriented

Do this by not closing them in their offices, and by sending them out in the field. Sainsbury's keeps its headquarters staff in the stores as much as possible. It also rotates staff, taking them off the field for a stretch to fill a head office post and then putting them back on.

SCHLUMBERGER WIRELINE & TESTING DIVISION

A 1 cm thick stack of 12 by 20 cm paper had been pushed across the desk. 'This is it,' he says. 'This is our service at Schlumberger. That (very thin) stack of paper is worth around US $50,000 and represents between 10 and 50 hours of work.' 'He' was the quality manager, responsible for controlling the quality of 'log' reports for all of the non-US operations. The stack of paper he had shown to us was a 'log', the only directly touchable outcome produced by Schlumberger's Wireline & Testing Division.

A 'log' has nothing to do with a tree and has little relation to logarithms. A 'log' or a 'Schlum', short for a Schlumberger, as it used to be called in some parts of the world, is a way of estimating the earth's subsurface. It is a key source of information for the estimate of hydrocarbon reserves, generally those of gas and oil. Schlumberger is the originator of the technique and remains the leader in the industry. Its clients include all the major oil companies in the world. It is a company dedicated to the quality of its service and to the satisfaction of its clients in all aspects of its contact with them.

History

Schlumberger Company was registered as a company in 1927 by the two brothers, Marcel and Conrad Schlumberger. Conrad was a professor of physics at the Ecole des Mines de Paris (Mining School in Paris). Marcel Schlumberger had studied engineering at the Ecole Centrale à Paris and had worked in the automobile and mining industries.

Over the 15 years prior to the creation of the company, Conrad and Marcel had perfected a method for exploring the substrata of the earth using electric current flows sent from the earth's surface. The concept was based on the theory that different rocks or substances conduct electricity at a different rate. By studying these levels of conductivity systematically, one can determine the location of certain types of minerals.

The first major opportunity to use the Schlumberger technique for oil exploration was in Romania in 1922. The success of this project gave the Schlumberger brothers greater credibility and increased their penetration in the oil industry of which they would later become an inseparable part.

The company went into the USSR in 1929. Over the period to 1940, it had projects in the US, Venezuela and Indonesia. By 1954, Schlumberger was established in the US, in the Far East, the Middle East and in Africa, in addition to Europe.

Schlumberger was multinational early, not only in terms of its activities, but also in terms of its personnel. One of the first employees of the company was a Swiss engineer, Mr Poldini; another was Vahé Melikian, a Russian. Everywhere the company worked, it hired nationals of that country and trained them. These recruits stayed with the firm, travelling like their French counterparts to all corners of the world.

Technological innovation has always been a cornerstone of Schlumberger. Over 40 patents were registered by the Schlumberger brothers before 1927, a research and development department had been established and '. . . when it came to tightening the belt, the research department was always the last to be affected' (Anne Gruner Schlumberger *La Boite Magique* 1977, Fayard Press, Paris, p. 224). Today, the lab originally located in the centre of Paris has expanded and others have been built. In Connecticut, US, the company set up a large facility as early as 1947. Today, there are also facilities in Houston, Texas, in Cambridge in the UK, in Fuchinobe, close to Tokyo, as well as in Clamart and Melun, France. Together they employ over 3500 researchers.

Schlumberger has always exuded an air of adventure. Accepting a job with Schlumberger means agreeing to live the Schlumberger adventure. Travel and perpetual change are just the backdrop to a lifestyle demanding complete mobility and an unerring devotion to one's work and the company. As one Vice President puts it, 'One has to desire to do the impossible to achieve the task at hand.'

One only has to look at the nature of the work to understand why. A logging engineer is required to be on-site to manage the entirety of the operations from start to finish. The work cannot be delegated because the quality of the data being recorded by the surface equipment must be constantly controlled and the machines adjusted immediately, if necessary. A job can take up to 50 hours non-stop. Each minute counts because a drilling rig, for example, cannot drill while the measurements are being taken. One day on a drilling rig costs roughly US $100,000 or $70 per minute.

Wells can be located anywhere in the world – in the middle of the North Sea, in the Saudi Arabian desert or in the Papua-New Guinea jungle. Engineers and their families are similarly distributed throughout the world; in total, a vast majority of the engineer/manager population is expatriated. There is very little to do 'back home'. In Schlumberger's Paris office for Wireline and Testing there are no more than 90 persons; in New York corporate headquarters, there are just over 100.

On-site, there has always been the challenge of overcoming physical and technological barriers in order to achieve the objective. Certain situations can be hazardous and the workforce is constantly trained and prepared to handle any situation. As one manager put it, 'This job is never predictable; no two wells are the same.' Each has its own peculiarities and creates new problems to be overcome. Despite advances in technology and increasing use of computers, the challenge of responding rapidly in difficult situations remains an essential and, by some, a very sought-after part of the job.

Intercom, the in-house journal describes a recent mission to an island in northern Norway, 1300 km from the North Pole,

'Longyearbyen, the capital of Spitzbergen, is 60 km to the north-west . . . a four-hour trek by sno-kat . . . The rig and its associated equipment were brought to the well-site on sleighs towed by two D-8 caterpillars. Accommodations were small wooden huts linked together about 200 m from the fully enclosed rig.

A large part of the island is designated as a National Park, . . . There are approximately 10,000 polar bears on Spitzbergen, and no one was allowed to leave the well-site unless accompanied by a guide armed with a rifle, radio and flares.

On bright, clear days with an average temperature of about −30°C, the well-site is a glorious place to be.

Service strategy

The Schlumberger service permits oil companies to have a more precise idea of the characteristics of the earth layers which are being examined. It is a service for the collection of information. Costly decisions on whether to drill or not drill, more wells, continue to prospect etc. are made based on the information provided by Schlumberger. The reliability of the information provided is, thus, of crucial importance.

Reliability in a business which involves reservoirs of gas or oil over 5000 m underground is not an easy thing to achieve. Even with modern technology, a logging company can only guarantee a relative degree of accuracy. Perhaps more important is the degree of confidence which the client feels that he can have in the information.

Schlumberger has always been the technological leader in its business − the trail-blazer. By assuring its level of expertise, the company increases the confidence which its client can have in the information it provides.

Its eight large research centres help, as does the work of the company's full-time quality control manager. He travels the world verifying first hand some of the work done by the engineer on-site. His personal level of expertise is illustrated by the fact that he has written an industry textbook on log quality, *Log data acquisition and quality control*, 'designed to assist engineers to improve the quality of their logs'.

Providing its clients with the most accurate information possible is not enough. Schlumberger knows that clients need to understand the information given to them and be able to use it to its maximum potential. 'Full-use through interpretation' is what they call it at Schlumberger.

The technology behind logging is laid out on a platter for Schlumberger clients. Through seminars, training courses, free publications and personal exchanges, it is the policy of the company to provide the client with whatever he needs to understand and use Schlumberger data to its maximum capacity.

The company has prepared a book called *Log Quality Control Reference Manual*, to be used by both clients and employees alike in order to verify the accuracy of the work performed.

The company is not concerned that the communication of their technology will give competitors information that could threaten their lead in the industry. They feel that it's more important that their clients understand what they do. As they explained it to us, 'What is the use of having a leading technology if no one understands it enough to use it?.'

Schlumberger would never have become what it is today without the special care given to the quality of the relationship which is developed between the client and its engineers. Its approach is to provide engineers who are competent, ethical, available to the client and culturally adaptable. The company has pursued this aim to such an extent that, today, the quality of its engineers is a key point of differentiation between itself and its competitors.

A Schlumberger engineer is trained for over three months before he sets foot in the field. He has another five to six years of training before he can handle all available services.

He is also expected to be highly ethical. Few clients understand the entirety of the technology used and they rely upon the Schlumberger engineers to tell them what that technology is doing for them. It would be too easy to cloud over data or ignore poor data on-site just to 'please the customer'.

A Schlumberger engineer is always available. He is on-site with the client, he is available at home by phone and he comes over at a moment's notice. He is, according to the Schlumberger client philosophy, someone who is and likes 'to be at the service of others'.

He is also multicultural. Moving around the globe, he is able to adapt rapidly, to communicate easily and simply, and to socialise and work with all classes and types of individuals. From his work, he has also developed contacts worldwide in the 'small world of oil' which will help him be more effective and useful as he progresses in his career.

The Schlumberger engineeer is a service in and of himself – at the service of the client. To quote one top manager with whom we spoke, 'He [the engineer] is a quality product'.

Service strengths

Schlumberger has a major share of the world market for logging services. Clients are loyal to Schlumberger despite the efforts of competitors to break into the market and despite the somewhat higher prices which Schlumberger charges for its work. Such devotion is not solely explained by Schlumberger's technological prowess.

What clients appreciate is the continuity of the relationships which they establish with Schlumberger people. Schlumberger engineers are not 'here today, gone tomorrow' type people.

Schlumberger engineers are both accountable and traceable. There is no 'That guy left and so did his boss. Can I help you? I'm new here' situation at Schlumberger. If a client can't be put directly in touch with one person with whom he worked, he will shortly be found, even if he's now working on another continent and it's five years after the fact. One engineer told us about a client which he called back three years, to the day, after the completion of a project, 'to find out how things were going'. It was no coincidence that he didn't miss the date, he had noted it down in his agenda.

Once you are a Schlumberger client, you are always a Schlumberger client. Just because you go over to the competition for a while doesn't mean that Schlumberger writes you off or forgets your existence. On the contrary, they treat former clients just as if they were active clients. In fact, they told us that there is no such thing as a former client at Schlumberger, so 'Why treat any client differently than another?'.

If you've been a Schlumberger client at some time, then most likely you are on the mailing list to receive invitations to attend information sessions, lectures and presentations of new products or technological developments. The 1991 programme of scheduled 'educational seminars' included 136 events. They are available on all six continents and in six different languages. Most are offered free of charge.

In addition, clients are regularly approached by Schlumberger engineers to give their input on new product developments and on how best to use new technologies to create products desired by their clients. Over 130 different products are presently offered by the company, most if not all of which have been developed and tested with the help of clients.

A friend made is a friend kept. Clients can run into Schlumberger engineers they know anywhere in the world. A client who worked with a Schlumberger engineer in Norway will find him once again in Dubai or Jakarta. One engineer met two of his former clients in the same minute, as they all checked in at the Dallas airport. And so on.

Schlumberger engineers know that these relationships count and they do their utmost to make sure that no old contact is given lesser importance and that any new contact is a good one. One manager has received a postcard every year for the last eight years from a former client in Taiwan, and he returns the same. Contacts are important, not only for their professional value, but because they improve the quality of life at work for everyone concerned. In the spirit of Schlumberger engineers, it is infinitely more agreeable to work with a client-friend than with a client-enemy. 'A client is not the person you argue with, it's the person you're living for.'

Another thing which clients appreciate about Schlumberger engineers is their cultural flexibility. For a start, Schlumberger is not under the influence of any one national culture. Over 80 nationalities are represented within the company.

Moreover, Schlumberger engineers are comfortable in almost any situation. For them, a dinner party at the oil ministry is as easily managed and enjoyable as a camp fire on the open prairie. Likewise, it can be as much fun to work with an Omani government official as with a Texan rancher.

Schlumberger engineers are not only easy guests, they are also well-informed working associates. They know the names and backgrounds of their principal counterparts. They are familiar with the customers of the country and with the particular needs of each client. Upon his arrival, each engineer is briefed, not only on the technical aspects of his work, but also on the important cultural, social and political considerations to take into account.

Sometimes, a client can be surprised and pleased when an engineer knows the brand of his favourite drink. This is thanks to one of the most useful tools which the manager of a Schlumberger post has at his disposal – a book called the 'Client Book'. A 'Client Book' exists for each location throughout the world. In it are recorded all the names and backgrounds of the individuals the engineer is likely to meet in that location.

Implementation

In the words of Schlumberger managers, 'The engineer is everything.' He is the major point of contact between the company and the client, and his actions stand out in bold above all others. He must be mobile, culturally adaptable, competent and capable of operating independently. Being all of these at once is as much an acquired skill as it is an in-bred trait.

It starts at the recruitment phase. Over 200 graduates are recruited every year. They come from the top engineering schools and are chosen on the basis of their personal traits, as much as for their achievement record in university. In some cases quotas are used to ensure the cultural diversity of the group.

Do they test a candidate for his customer service orientation? The answer is, 'No, we make them [customer oriented].' That takes three months of intensive, make or break training. Thirty per cent don't make it and drop out during the training or within the first year. Besides the massive amount of technical information engineers are expected to absorb, they are also trained on how to handle critical situations and what to say to a client when things go wrong. To make the training environment more real, Schlumberger has built five training centres with real life drilled wells.

The philosophy that is drilled into the engineers from day one is the same as that which appears on the cover of the company recruitment brochure, 'The clients, that's all that counts. We provide them with technical services, not just any services, but those which we believe in.'

Only at the end of the three months does an engineer actually step out into the field. This doesn't, however, mean that his training is over. For another nine months, the engineer is considered an apprentice and works closely with an assigned superior who follows the junior field engineer's progress along a part book, part practical training programme. As the junior engineer completes a phase, he passes a test which qualifies him for advancement to the next phase. Only at the end of this one-year process, does the engineer receive the nomination of 'Field engineer' and be considered ready to work on an independent basis with clients.

Almost everyone has been a field engineer at Schlumberger. Most will always be field engineers, at least at heart. Managers who now run the company were once pulling cables and leaning over plotting recorders in the Saudia Arabian or Sahara desert. It's said that no organisation outside the Army has a higher concentration of managers with hands-on field experience. And, field experience means experience with clients, because the client is always right there at the rig with the field engineer.

It is not reasonable to suppose that once engineers are trained that they will always perform perfectly and that nothing will 'slip'. Schlumberger doesn't suppose so and instead has a system of quality monitoring which permits it to monitor the number of failures which occur and help everyone learn from them.

A failure at Schlumberger can be of two sorts. The first sort concerns the measuring activity itself and the result thereof. The second sort concerns the management of the relationship with the client.

To manage the first sort, Schlumberger publishes a monthly report which gives the results of all the operations occurring in that month. An entire section is devoted to service quality, in which is listed the number of 'log failures' and 'MOF's which occurred during the month. For the lay reader, a 'MOF' stands for major operating failure and occurs when the rig is incapacitated for more than seven hours. A 'log failure' occurs when the results of the measurement are not up to the standards set by the operating standards book. With these simple figures, the entire organisation has a good indication of both the frequency and the gravity of the failures which are occurring worldwide.

The monitoring activity does not stop there. Once a failure has occurred, it must be analysed. A failure/maintenance analysis report is then submitted. This is a short, two-page document which permits management to identify the exact causes of the failure and the circumstances in which it occurred. The form uses a modified Ishikawa fishbone system which allows the failure to fall into one of three categories – organisation, people or equipment.

Managing the second sort of failure is handled in a more delicate fashion. Taking advantage of the close relationship which Schlumberger maintains with most of its clients, it has created 'service quality meetings'. A service quality meeting brings together the individuals responsible for managing a project together with their counterparts on the client's side. The aim is to discuss the evolution of the project over the past month and to bring out into the open any problem which might have occurred. Most often, clients begin by citing technical problems, but Schlumberger managers readily admit that a key objective of the meeting is to let clients air their more sensitive complaints about the relationship in a co-operative, non-threatening environment.

A more ancient, but very reliable system of getting feedback from clients is through the 'old boy network'. Any manager at Schlumberger has from 50 to 60 people he can call at a moment's notice to have feedback on his own company's performance in various parts of the world. If there is a serious complaint, it's just as likely to be heard through a personal contact as through any official method of communication.

Schlumberger managers don't neglect this method of quality monitoring and they foster it on a daily basis. A manager 'stationed' at headquarters in Paris or New York actually spends 15 days out of every month on the road visiting those clients and his own operation sites.

What can be learned

1 Make your people a differential advantage

Schlumberger has refined the system of selection and training of its staff to such a point that the quality of their engineers has become a major point of competitive advantage for them.

2 Don't underestimate the power of the personal relationship

In our efforts to create new and better tools to monitor and control service quality, it is easy to forget that one of the most effective is the use of personal contacts. The 50 to 60 people known to most Schlumberger managers amount to a small survey panel of experts. Because they are long-term working partners with an interest in the future of the firm, they are sensitive to changes at Schlumberger.

3 Don't be shy, tell customers what you do

Schlumberger makes it a policy to expose their technology to its clients. One might think that this would leave them open to competitors' imitations. The fact is that the technology is seldom the unique factor in a business relationship. For Schlumberger, the benefits gained by working openly with clients far outweigh any potential dangers. In the end, the Schlumberger's approach had made it possible for them to move ahead ever faster with technological developments as customers feed back ideas for new applications.

4 There is no such thing as a lost client

Schlumberger does not distinguish between former clients, active clients and super-active clients. All clients are created equal and have the rights to receive the associated benefits, be they special training courses or visits from engineers. This is a powerful approach and one that can help ensure that Schlumberger never does lose a client.

SIXT BUDGET

Sixt Budget is about making wishes come true. Wishes of nearly every little boy and a good number of little girls, like 'I want to drive a red convertible Porsche 911 when I grow up'. When people grow up, their wishes don't change very much. But, most people don't pay very much attention to wishes, they are too busy trying to make the everyday essentials become reality.

Mr Erich Sixt cares about people's wishes. He may be in the very unfairytale-like business of car rentals, but the success of his business is due to his imagination and his concern for people's wishes and not to an inordinate preoccupation with boring realities.

Background

Sixt Budget is Germany's number two car rental company and is specialised in the rental of exotic and luxurious cars, motorcycles, planes and trucks. It has not always been known for being the Disneyland of the car rental business. Sixt has a very long history of more traditional car and limousine renting in Germany which goes back to 1912.

Martin Sixt was the founder of the company and set up business in Munich in a former Franciscan monastery. He had just one car to rent, a 'Deutz'. Mr Sixt had two cars in 1912 and finally four cars in 1927, three of which were Mercedes. At that point, Hans Sixt took over the business and began the successful development of the limousine service side of the business which he called, 'The Bavarian Traveller'.

Hitler put a stop on the growth of Sixt's business in the early 1930s; finally all of Sixt's cars were confiscated by the army to be used in the war effort. The Sixt family didn't let that deter them; their determination to continue in the car rental business was reaffirmed in 1946 when Sixt reopened to do business with one car in what remained of the company's bombed-out premises in the former Franciscan monastery.

Sixt-Limousine Service established in 1950, Auto-Sixt in 1951. Auto-Sixt was the family's first step towards serving the general public – it rented primarily VW Beetles. The first 'rental stations' were established in the Munich–Reim and Frankfurt airports in 1966.

Erich Sixt, grandson of the company's founder began working for the family firm in 1969. In 1973, Auto-Sixt created the first 'Fly and Drive' system with Pan American World Airways. Finally, in 1977, the company signed a contract with Budget Rent-a-Car, the third largest car rental agency in the world, which led to a change in the company name to Sixt Budget.

In 1983, the company had 50 rental offices throughout Germany. It was at this point that the company launched the 'Rent a Mercedes for the Price of a Golf' campaign which was the first step to the company becoming recognised as the luxury car renter of Germany. Over the next eight years, up to the present, Sixt Budget experienced tremendous growth, bypassing all of its competitors except Hertz.

Today, Sixt Budget has 171 rental offices in Germany and a fleet of 20,000 cars. It has the largest fleet of Mercedes in the world and a large selection of Porsches, BMWs, Harley-Davidson motorcycles, Ferraris and other luxury sports cars. In addition, it has a truck and trailer rental service, and an aeroplane rental service which rents Lear jets and other small aircraft. One-way rental of cars and trucks is also available, as are leasing services.

Service strategy

The Sixt Budget service and marketing strategy was developed in the early 1980s. A look at the German car rental market at this period showed that the industry's primary customers were businesspeople. The price charged was relatively high for what the businessperson was receiving – a standard, boring car – because it was not the customer who was paying, but his company in the form of business expenses.

There was also little customer loyalty in the market because there was very little difference in either the cars or services provided by the major car rental companies. The major rental companies were (and still are) closely tied in with the car producers and, in the case of Hertz, for example, have to purchase 50 per cent of their cars from Ford. Avis is tied to General Motors in the same way, and Interrent to Volkswagen.

For the customer, that meant very little choice and not much excitement. Customers going into Hertz, for example, could have had the choice between a Ford Escort and a Ford Fiesta at the lower price range and between a Ford Sierra and a Lincoln Mercury in the upper range.

Sixt had basically two options: he could offer the same cars and services as the others were offering at a more cost-reflective price, which, by the way, is the strategy Budget used in the US, or he could offer his customers more products and services at the same price.

Sixt believed that a large stake in the German car rental market could be taken by giving the customers what they really were dreaming of – the possibility to drive a truly suberb vehicle. Because Sixt wasn't tied to any car producer, he didn't have to buy a certain percentage of average cars and could stock his entire business with cars that fitted the wildest dreams of his customers.

In 1983, he began offering Mercedes 190s at the same price as Hertz, Avis and Interrent asked for their standard VW Golf. The businessperson's business trip was suddenly transformed; the customer who could not, by company policy, normally afford to rent anything but a car in the simplest category, could now look forward to driving his 'dream car'.

Higher volume more than made up for the higher cost of the cars and Sixt rapidly grew, enlarging both its fleet and its business; the company defines its business as 'fulfilling customer dreams while keeping them mobile'. Indeed, Sixt was the first car rental company to offer the BMW convertible (3-Series) at the price of a three-door Ford Escort from Hertz!

Erich Sixt's strategy of fulfilling customers' dreams has now been extended into every part of the business. In addition to expanding into planes, motorcycles and trucks, Sixt is now offering dreamlike add-ons to their luxury cars. Today, Sixt has a reputation as one of the most creative and innovative companies in the German service industry.

Service strengths

Being a Sixt Budget customer is a bit like having a touch of Christmas every time you rent a car. There is a new, clever little goody available every time.

The first happy discovery of Sixt's more talkative customers is that Sixt supplies most cars with telephones free of charge. The customer only pays the units consumed. If the customer prefers hard copy to chit-chat, he can rent a fax machine which he hooks up to the telephone unit. The car – say a Porsche – becomes an office on wheels.

If it's play and not business that the customer wants, Sixt offers that too. Free music cassettes are supplied and the customer can choose his preferred sort at the rental counter. The newest entertainment gadget is the joke hotline. Customers in a traffic jam or just plain bored on the *autobahn* can telephone into a 'joke' service and hear the joke of the day.

Sixt makes travelling more luxurious, but it also makes travelling easier. Every car is equipped with a book of flight schedules with all of the major airlines, street maps to a host of major cities and a guide explaining how to find your preferred radio station in each region. Sixt is also the only company to provide safety air bags as a standard feature in their cars.

The good fun service doesn't just start when you enter the car; it starts in the lobby of the airport lounge. Sixt has installed its Rent-o-Mat in the departure lounge of major German airports. With a major credit card or Sixt Budget's own card, the customer can reserve and rent a car before he even gets to his destination. The machine prints the rental contract and has a diagram of the destination airport's garage in which is marked the exact location of the parking space where the customer can find the car. Upon arriving, the customer goes directly to the spot where the company's employee is there waiting for him with the keys.

For those who pass by the rental counter for their contract and the keys, Sixt has streamlined things. Tourists (slow as they sometimes are) are in one queue and businesspeople (impatient as they sometimes are) are in another. Sixt caters its counter service accordingly. Tourists get good explanations from 'A' to 'Z'. Businessmen get the abbreviated version and more information about time-saving services like the night-time drop-off option.

The attitude of counter staff reflects the happy, creative spirit of the company. In a pack with the competition, they really stand out. Helpful, friendly and ready to share in the fun, Sixt staff are all trained in customer service and how to keep the spirit of the company alive and active.

Sixt also wants to make sure you don't get disappointed, so they provide 'availability assurance'. If the car you reserved isn't there waiting for you, you get one from the higher class upwards. Like that, a customer who reserves a Mercedes 190, could easily find himself behind the wheel of a Ferrari, all for the price of a VW at Hertz (is Hertz still in business?).

It probably comes as no surprise, but Sixt Budget customers are a very loyal bunch. The company has an estimated 600,000 rental contracts each year. But about 150,000 of those customers are using Sixt, on average, three to four times a year.

Implementation

Erich Sixt believes that one of the key success factors for Sixt has been their personnel. The company attracts young people, who have an entrepreneurial spirit and are able to work autonomously. Most of them have little previous experience and are 'not spoiled by working in a heavy administration'. This makes them capable of taking initiatives on the frontline for the customers. 'We prefer it if they've never worked for another car rental company at all.'

To make sure that they have the right people, Sixt puts a great deal of emphasis on the recruitment process. They pass through a three-stage process. At one point, employees are put on the frontline for a day and then asked what they think should be improved. (See Chapter 8 for more details.)

Company policy fosters the taking of initiatives by employees; for one thing, the price of renting a car from Sixt is not fixed by management. There is a suggested rental price and a break-even price for each car which is known to every employee. The employee is completely free to give discounts to customers whenever he feels it necessary or he can provide the customer with an up-grade; whatever best satisfies the customer.

Employees are free to use their imagination and take initiatives for the customer under normal circumstances; when there is a problem however, the company has fixed minimum service standards which must be respected. For example, when the car reserved is not available, the customer gets a car from the higher grade at the same price. If the customer has a mechanical problem with a car, he is automatically given a certificate for a free rental in the future. The employee is, of course, free to do more than that for the customer if he deems it necessary.

Unlike most of its competitors, Sixt Budget is not very 'top heavy'. It has a flat management structure. There are 700 or so employees, 500 of whom have daily contact with the customer. Only 130 people are at headquarters. That compares with 200 at Avis whose revenues are less than Sixt.

To keep tabs on what Sixt is doing as compared with the competition, the company has a 'mystery man' who shops at Sixt and shops at the competitors' premises as well. He is equipped with a checklist of what Sixt considers to be 'service minimums'. In addition he notes what he likes and doesn't like, be it an employee attitude or the lack of choice in cassette tapes. Mystery shopping is done twice a year, sometimes by employees from another station. This gives them the opportunity to see at first hand what it's like on the other side of the counter.

A different form of mystery shopping is done by Mr Sixt himself – in fact it's not being a mystery shopper, but a mystery employee. In order to experience what is happening on the frontline, Mr Sixt goes down on the desk and works the desk for a day in one of the agencies. His favourite stomping ground is the Munich airport where he joins the work force about every three months or so.

As a company that appreciates initiative, Sixt rewards initiative. Champagne parties are a frequent occurrence at Sixt when it comes to celebrating a job well done. When the work is really extraordinary, employees – either individuals or groups – are sent on trips; the last one was to the US.

What can be learned

1 Give the customer what he really wants

Sixt Budget is a success because it gives customers what they want; not what a bureaucrat thought would be financially interesting. The irony is that by giving the customer what he wants, Sixt has not only attracted more business, but he has created a more profitable operation.

When it comes to considering costs and profitability, it is worth while keeping in mind, for example, that the value of a second-hand Mercedes or Porsche after two or three years diminishes by perhaps 20 per cent, whereas the value of a Ford or an Opel shrinks by as much as 40 per cent.

2 Go for the fantasy

Another reason for Sixt Budget's success is that the company has had the courage to do things differently; to dare to offer outrageous extras like a joke hotline. The visible difference which this creates in the mind of the car renting public is more than enough to compensate the company for its cost. Besides this, the joke hotline is a lot of fun!

3 Set standards on the downside, but not on the upside

Employees need to know the lower minimum level of service to be provided to the customer; beyond that let them exercise their imagination. Sixt Budget sets standards for when there is a problem. Otherwise each employee can express his concern for the customer in his own way. The result is a high-quality, highly personalised service.

SUPASNAPS

The spirit of a family-owned enterprise with the professionalism of a large corporation, is an attractive combination which describes SupaSnaps well to those who know it best – its customers. In its short, 14-year history, the company has become a mainstay in the High Street retail scene in the UK and has distinguished itself from its competitors in the photoprocessing business by its sincere concern for satisfying its customers. 'For us, giving good service quality is as fundamental to our business as having someone in the shop', says Colin Glass, Managing Director.

Background

SupaSnaps is a nationwide chain of over 360 branches selling photoprocessing services and related products. It was started in 1978 by the Gratispool International Holdings group. The impetus behind the business and its early growth was a growing need of consumers for a low price alternative to photoprocessing by mail. The postal strikes of the late 1970s accentuated this trend and led to a switch of 8 per cent from the mail sector to the retail outlet sector of the photoprocessing business.

In 1981, Gratispool sold SupaSnaps to 3M, one of whose primary objectives was to become a fully vertically integrated company. The blending of a strongly retail-oriented company into a product and industrially-oriented company was difficult, and the association was discontinued with the sale of SupaSnaps to the Dixons Group in 1986. Dixons is the world's largest electrical and photographic retailer.

When Dixons purchased the company, SupaSnaps primarily had two assets: an enthusiastic and customer-oriented staff and over 340 locations throughout the country. In each shop, however, space was frequently underutilised. In addition, the service and product line was limited, and little had been done to define a target group of customers or create a SupaSnaps image with the public.

One of Dixons' first steps was to conduct a thorough study of SupaSnaps customers . . . and not just in terms of their socio-economic profile. The research was sufficiently detailed enough to permit SupaSnaps to construct a profile of their four primary customer types. These were diffused to the sales staff with graphic descriptions of what each might prefer in terms of photoprocessing advice and the style of support products, such as frames or albums. To keep the approach coherent, the marketing department developed four separate lines of support products with these customer groups in mind.

The company then launched a series of co-ordinated advertising and promotional sales effort, each with a separate theme and each with their own point-of-sale support tools for use in the stores. The advertising was designed to do two things – one, to promote a consistent image of SupaSnaps with the public, and two, to bring customers into the stores where salespeople could present to the full range of the company's new products and services to them.

Behind the scenes, the management team worked with suppliers in order to bring delays on photo processing times down to a guaranteed overnight service in all stores and one hour in 50 stores. The company guaranteed that overnight time to customers, but had had difficulties sometimes in meeting it, which had lost the company money and customer confidence. Dixons also launched a major internal communications programme and an enhanced training programme designed to bring all branches up to the same level of service quality to their customers.

By 1989, SupaSnaps was once again making a healthy profit which continues to increase. In 1990 the market was worth 105 million rolls of film. By Spring 1992 that figure had fallen to 84 million. SupaSnaps is the only major film and processing business which has grown in volume and at the highest retail prices. According to Glass this is primarily due to the quality of their customer service.

Service strategy

Prior to Dixons' involvement, SupaSnaps outlets were acting principally as deposit sites for photoprocessing. The exchange between the sales staff and the customers was agreeable, but limited in time. The stores offered little, either in terms of products or presentation, to keep customers in the shops more than the time it took to leave and collect their film, and pay.

SupaSnaps' chosen objective was to keep the loyalty of existing customers, and to increase revenues per customer by offering a greater selection of services and products. Customer loyalty was already very high with 50 per cent of the company's customers using only SupaSnaps for their development and another 25 per cent using SupaSnaps for most of their development.

This could be mostly attributed to SupaSnaps's sales staff who were recognised for their friendly attitude to customers. Ninety-five per cent of the staff are women, who enjoy discussing with customers and advising them whenever possible. Moreover, three of the four directors are women and 75 per cent of the senior management is female.

Today, the key success factor in SupaSnaps's strategy is their excellent relations with their customers which keeps customer satisfaction high and creates opportunities for additional sales. The customer-oriented sales staff ensure that the exchange between them and the customer passes in the most agreeable fashion for the customer. Through the conversion, the (now) well-trained staff can identify opportunities to offer additional products to the customer. The customer is also more likely to stay in the store to browse, to look at the products displayed and, eventually, to make an additional purchase.

In order to make the most of SupaSnaps's good relations with customers, they increased the number of services and products offered in order to offer the customer enough choice, and position the company as a complete provider of photography-related services.

The research conducted into SupaSnaps's client base showed five categories of photoprocessing clients defined by their 'level of interest'. Out of the five categories, snapper, hobbyist, amateur, semi-professional and professional, SupaSnaps chose to target the first three.

In the market for complementary products, five main segments of clients were identified according to their 'lifestyle' – the traditional, the classic, the fashion, the high-tech and the avant-garde. The company decided to target the first four segments and designed a line of products to meet the profile of each group – 'Windsor', 'Balmoral', 'April' and 'Index'.

The company subsequently defined three categories of product and services upon which the company would concentrate. The first is 'images', meaning photoprocessing work as well as enlargements, reprints, posters, puzzles, coasters, tablemats etc. The second is 'image-related' products including frames, albums, carry bags etc. The third is 'event-related' products which includes products and services related to times of the year or events in which photos make up an important part, for example, weddings and holidays. Products in this last category include carry bags for children to take on holiday, a currency calculator (for travelling), a sewing kit, a teddy bear with a frame (for Christmas) and special Christmas stocking-sized photo albums. However, only the photographic related products have been successful.

Today, SupaSnaps offers a full package of services and products tailored to meet the specific needs and service expectations of its customers. The point of differentiation remains the quality of the advice and the personal exchange between the customer and the sales staff with the possibility of this exchange leading to additional purchases of new items in the range.

Service strengths

SupaSnaps service strategy is to offer customers superior advice on photoprocessing and photography, and provide them with excellent assistance in their purchase decision. The SupaSnaps customer today benefits fully from this approach.

Fundamental to excellent customer service is the company's approach to training. SupaSnaps staff are given on-going training via the Success Through Sales and Service programme. This course is designed to help the staff achieve the fine balance between effective selling skills, after sales service and excellent customer service.

SupaSnaps staff do not advise customers just on the basis of their own personal photographic experience. SupaSnaps ensure that their staff are trained to handle questions and provide valuable advice in the basics of photography. In the store, each employee has, within reach, a short reference guide giving tips about how to take care of cameras and associated material, and how to take good pictures. The guide includes examples of bad photos with detailed explanations of what went wrong. The staff are not only trained to identify photographers' errors, but also those of the developers, which permits them to be responsive in the case of problems with the quality of the photo or film developing.

For each product in the store, the sales staff are also thoroughly informed. Not only can they give the primary features of the item, but they can also describe exactly what benefit that gives the customer when he uses it. This is again thanks to another handy guide, available in every store, which describes each product or service in very simple and customer-friendly terms, and simultaneously explains what the advantages of that product or service are for the customer. For example, the SupaSnaps cameras are described as having the following.

Features	Benefits (to customer)
• double exposure prevention lock	• stops you forgetting to wind on
• fixed exposure	• no settings to make, ensures good photography in good lighting conditions
• direct vision finder	• easy to frame your subject

The training is based on the need to discuss a product in terms of its benefits because customers want to know what it will do for them. According to Glass that is the key aspect of customer service.

Excellent customer service must extend into handling complaints effectively. The value of photographs is far greater than the cost of raw materials. Photographs embody memories, which for customers, are precious. For SupaSnaps dealing with a customer's complaint may go beyond a refund and if a member of staff cannot deal with a problem, it will go up the line, even to Colin Glass if necessary.

Implementation

When Dixons took over SupaSnaps, one of the first things he concentrated on was ensuring that the staff in the stores had all they would need to service and sell well to customers. One of those was complete knowledge about the company's marketing and sales strategy.

The strategy was communicated and explained in detail to all of the staff and to every store employee.

Vivid descriptions of target customers were given so that employees would remember the different customer types and their possible likes and dislikes. There was also an explanation of the hard sell versus the soft sell and a visual presentation of different store layouts showing what SupaSnaps should be trying to achieve – friendly, clean and crisp – as compared with other well-known shops (Marks & Spencer, Body Shop, Mothercare etc.). At each stage, the message was supported by data and sales figures from the marketing studies done, as well as with statistics for the industry as a whole. The information was also put into a handbook for managers.

The next move was to ensure that the strategy was being implemented in the same way, with the same care, in all of the company's stores. The sales operations and marketing teams devised a 'kit' which ran on the stores' computers and explained in meticulous detail the exact way in which the window and the store should be arranged and decorated. The display of items on the shelves was specified and was changed on a regular basis to reflect seasonal fluctuations or to make the most of promotions. Because of the different square footage in each of the stores, items are prioritised with priority one items being given display space in preference to lower priority items.

A 'housekeeping list', which is a checklist of all of the duties of the store manager and the store staff was also devised. The store manager, regional managers and district managers monitor activities in the store using this list. A dress code was also established and uniforms were made available to staff.

As a quick reference support tool for ensuring good customer service, SupaSnaps created the 'SupaCards', a set of plasticised cards, printed on both sides, which hang next to the cash register. SupaCard 1 gives the features and benefits of the most popular cameras, Card 2 gives a chart of the most popular camera features and the cameras which have them, Card 3 lists the most important factors contributing to good customer service ('Start with a smile', 'Use the customer's name', 'Make eye contact when you speak' etc.) and lists the company's procedures for handling complaints, Card 4 lists the most common problems with prints and what causes them, and Card 5 presents common questions and their answers. Each SupaCard is a short handbook of good service 'in a nutshell'.

A 'day book' in which employees write down all the important activities of the day was introduced. There are four columns. If a customer calls with a question, the employee notes down the time (in one column), the nature of the call (in another column), the action to be taken (in the third column), and the initials and date when the action was taken (in the fourth column). The employees themselves, or the store manager, check at the end of every day to ensure that the 'action taken' column has been completed for each of the items. 'It's then up to the shop manager or whoever is in charge to go through that page and check that things have been done. And, for anything that hasn't been done they can highlight it and bring it forward.'

If, for example, a customer calls with a question that can't be answered immediately, the question, and the customer and his number are noted down. If the customer hasn't been called back the same day, he will certainly get a call the next day, because his call will have been noted down in the day book.

The company also created a system of store support. That meant that there was always to be help immediately available to store staff in the event of questions or a problem. As a first step, the schedule and home and office telephone numbers of district and regional managers and all the directors are always known by each shop every day. In the case of their absence, a base store for each district was identified and the manager for that store was given the authority to assist employees from other stores in the district. In addition, an 'action desk' was established at headquarters and this is empowered to resolve problems up to certain limits.

Tools are not the only means of support given to the frontline staff. The regular presence of managers is another. District managers visit their stores at least once every four weeks; regional managers are in touch either by phone or in person at least every four weeks. In addition, head office staff, including the managing director and the marketing and personnel controller, make regular tours of the stores. 'But we believe in more than just state visits'. SupaSnaps insists that all senior managers and the directors of their suppliers spend a number of days working behind the counter each year. 'This is the only way to ensure that we and our suppliers really understand our customers' needs.'

What can be learned?

1 Make the most of your staff's good attitude

SupaSnaps' employees care about serving their customers well. Dixons didn't try to change that attitude, they reinforced it and, at the same time, showed how good service could be combined with good sales in order to improve their own performance as well as the company's.

2 Back up what you say with tangible reminders

SupaSnaps employees don't have to remember everything their managers say . . . because it's all written down. SupaSnaps created a large number of practical, quick-reference tools for the entire staff – like the SupaCards that hang next to the cash register or the SupaSnaps product reference guide that gives a quick summary of all the benefits of any product the company sells.

Keep it in mind that studies show that people only retain 10 per cent of what is said and only 30 per cent of what they have only read once. Quick-reference tools are a good idea.

3 Don't undersell in order to overservice

Good sales is good service. Although the word 'sell' has a negative connotation to many people which implies that a product is being 'forced' on to a customer, a good sale has little or nothing to do with 'forcing' a sale.

At SupaSnaps, selling is described as giving the customer the advice that will help him make a choice. The objective is to bring greater satisfaction to the customer with what he has purchased, because he goes away with greater knowledge about the product and greater security in his purchase decision.

SUPERQUINN

It was the scissors hanging over the grape stand that caught our attention. They were there to help customers cut off the juiciest morsels to weigh and take home. Then there was the play area for children with a real playhouse and toys and games, and someone there full-time to keep track of the children. And, the friendly, happy – yes, happy – faces at the check-out counter.

We came away wishing we lived in Dublin or, like one former customer who moved to England, we wanted to ask, 'When are you going to open up over here?'.

Background

Superquinn is a chain of Dublin-based grocery stores; it is a large chain – at least in Irish terms. There are roughly 3.5 million people living in the Republic of Ireland; over one million of them live in the Dublin area. Superquinn does business with about 350,000 of them or, if you like, with 10 per cent of the entire population of the country.

There are 13 Superquinn stores of about 2500 square m each, spread throughout the Dublin area. According to tradition (which is now policy), there is not more than half an hour's drive between any two. By 1992, there might be a 14th store, but growth is not a primary aim of Feargal Quinn, the chain's founder and energetic manager. 'I'm not trying to be the biggest. I would like us to be the best. What would really make me happy is if everyone in Dublin would say, "I'm proud of having Superquinn in Dublin".'

The Dublin market is fiercely competitive. In the last 19 years, 16 large stores and chains have gone out of business. Even with fewer companies in the market, competition is still stiff from Irish and foreign-owned companies. All of the big UK chains are still represented, including Safeway and Sainsbury's. Superquinn's biggest competitor is Dunnes Stores, an Irish company, that competes primarily on price.

And the profits to be made are not astronomical. Profit margins are in the range of only 1 to 2 per cent of sales, compared to 5 or 6 per cent in England. 'This market is basically over-served.'

Despite the tough business environment, Feargal Quinn and Superquinn are thriving and healthy. 'Feargal Quinn has always believed that you can make money by putting the customer first.' He first expressed that belief in 1960 with the establishment of the first Superquinn store in Dundalk, a small town 50 miles north of Dublin. It was one of the first 'self-service' stores and had to overcome people's initial reaction that self-service meant poor service.

When trying to explain to newcomers and researchers, like ourselves, how he achieved initial success, Feargal Quinn talks about the holiday camp where he worked each summer as a teenager. The most important thing to the holiday camp owner (Feargal Quinn's father) was that his customers were satisfied enough to come back the next year. 'He sold satisfaction.'

Feargal Quinn made customer satisfaction Superquinn's *raison d'être* and the company has grown ever since. It went from 8 employees in 1960 to over 2000 today, from 250 square m of selling space to 2500 (per store). Superquinn is considered to be the leader in the Dublin market and Feargal Quinn is today a celebrity in the community.

Service strategy

Superquinn's service strategy is the same one as that of the holiday camp where Feargal Quinn worked as a teenager. 'Our objective is not to sell more, but to bring the customer back again,' says Feargal Quinn, '. . . quality service is service that brings the customer back and even does a little bit more.' So, Superquinn aims for service quality.

Service quality is the goal, but not one to be obtained at the expense of price. Ireland is not a rich country and most of the people are, by necessity, very price conscious. Feargal Quinn is convinced that he can offer quality service without higher prices, and the proof is that he does it!

'Come for the prices and stay for the service' is the Superquinn slogan and it expresses well the company's approach to its market. Feargal Quinn and his team would prefer to cut their own margin rather than charge high prices to customers. In fact, he hasn't had to do it very often. For the most part, the extra services like the children's playhouse 'pay for themselves' by increasing the average total purchases of shoppers. Customers are happier being in the shop, they are happier with what they see and so they buy more at Superquinn.

Another way that Superquinn stands out from the competition is by being the innovator. Let's face it, who has ever seen scissors hanging over a grape stand in a supermarket? It's a great idea and it's a Superquinn idea. Feargal Quinn and his staff are constantly searching for new ideas. They get some of them from customers; they get others from their travels. Superquinn middle and top managers travel to the US, Europe and even to Japan to collect ideas about ways to improve service to customers.

Some of the most popular ideas have been tissues at the fruit and vegetable stands to wipe off dirty fingers from handling dirty fruit. Another has been the home-made sausage counter. If you are not a Dubliner, you may not know it, but Superquinn is renowned for having some of the best tasting fresh sausages in the whole city!

Superquinn strategy is also to be the store that serves 'people' and not 'consumers'. 'Picture every customer as though she is your mother or your wife on a day when she's under pressure,' says Feargal Quinn. If that doesn't get the message across, he tries another, 'The next customer you see is somebody who's already been to four different shops and knows that her husband's coming home with the boss for dinner.'

Feargal Quinn doesn't just talk about being people oriented, he also does something about it. There are more staff on the shop floor at Superquinn than in other stores and that, he says, 'is intentional'. Feargal Quinn is also right down on the shop floor with the customers on a daily basis. He's not there just to chit-chat, he's there to help customers. 'The "young boy" packing grocery bags could be me!'

Service strengths

Superquinn's most important customer service practice is listening to customers. 'Listening to customers is preached all the way up and down the line.'

'Our real secret weapon in our listening campaign is our consumer panels,' says Feargal Quinn. Every week, there is a consumer panel. Every time, it's held in a different shop and Feargal Quinn chairs every panel himself. Around 10 to 15 shoppers generally attend. They are all volunteers and they have responded to the signs in the stores which invite them to come and 'talk to the boss'.

'We don't make the agenda, they do.' Customers are free to speak their mind about anything – to complain, to compliment, to suggest new ways of doing things. 'Most of them are long-time customers and they feel good about being able to contribute to improving the shop.'

'At first staff were defensive; that is where management plays a role. We convince employees that they should go out and look for complaints – that complaints are fun.' The report of the panel appears in the form of a series of quotes and is distributed widely in the company. Many of the company's new ideas for services in the shops are now coming from these panels. Management says that it helps them 'spot consistent wishes' and 'identify patterns or trends'. 'It's a wonderful crystal ball.'

Listening to customers doesn't just happen at consumer panels. Superquinn's customers can say anything they like right when they walk in the door. There, in front of them, is the customer service desk, manned on a continuous basis and ready prepared and willing to hear whatever the store's customers have to say. The clerks at the check-out counters are also trained, ready and willing to take notes on what the customer says. 'Feargal is always saying, "Listen carefully and open your eyes".'

Listening to customers helped Superquinn to develop a whole series of customer services. Elderly people told Feargal Quinn and his team that sometimes they would like to buy half a portion; living alone meant that they could never finish a whole one. Superquinn then decides to split the portion on request. It means a loss for the company, but it means a whole lot greater gain to elderly customers.

Superquinn packs grocery bags for customers, they help them carry them to the car and, if it's raining, customers can borrow an umbrella to get to their car without getting wet.

On Mother's Day women receive flowers and on any day of the week, dogs get free bones. Children doing shopping for their mother get to carry big signs saying, 'I'm shopping for Mum', which entitles them to a good deal more attention.

And, there's much, much more. When he finds out about a new service idea, Feargal Quinn doesn't hesitate to try it out. He believes that customers' expectations change more rapidly than we realise and that to stay ahead, one has to always be ready to adapt – fast.

Pizzas were a really new thing to Ireland when they appeared on the market a couple of years ago. First, there were the frozen kind. They sold well – the Irish tastebuds developed a liking for pizza – but the topping never seemed to satisfy. There wasn't enough variety; everyone wanted something different. Superquinn heard this through their customer panels and, so, they developed a pizza stand inside the store. The pizzas are made to order right in front of the customer, but it's not cooked, it's taken home and put in the oven to bake just as if it were homemade.

'It's a big success! Suddenly, we find ourselves in the food preparation business rather than the food sales business.' There aren't only pizzas being prepared in Superquinn stores; there are also 'the best sausages in Dublin', delicious cakes, baked goodies and salads. Feargal Quinn doesn't mind as long as it pleases the real 'retail experts', his customers.

Superquinn's reputation as a store providing top service quality is well established in Dublin and the company goes to great lengths to guard that reputation, particularly when it comes to dealing with customers with a problem. Most complaints come into the customer service desk and, like the following example, are dealt with in a way which exceeds the expectations of practically any customer.

'Mrs Smith' bought a chicken at Superquinn. The next day she went to cook the chicken and discovered that it was bad; she brought it back the same day. At the customer service department, they took back the chicken and asked her by what time she would need to have another chicken to begin her dinner. At 6 p.m. the same evening (that was the time she gave), the chicken supplier showed up at her doorstep with not one, but two chickens ready to pop in the oven.

Implementation

At Superquinn the store manager is the really important person. 'We have a totally decentralised approach. The power resides with the store managers; everyone in head office is just support.' The management commitee or, as they call it, 'the

Monday morning meeting group'. They do not see themselves as directing business, but rather 'guiding it along'.

'The assumption is that the managers are very responsible individuals.' As such, they are given a great deal of freedom to make decisions and act on them. One time, a new store manager asked Feargal Quinn what kind of 'capital authorisation limit' he had. Feargal's response was, 'Go ahead and spend it and then I'll tell you if you spent too much.' One manager recently spent £1 million redoing the exterior of his store, using non-budgeted funds. 'Store managers have that kind of discretion.'

To keep up on what is happening, Superquinn managers like to practise the American management method of 'managing by wandering around'. Feargal Quinn has his own way of putting it and believes that, 'you can't do business by sitting on your armchair' (YCDBSOYA). So, a good deal of management's time is spent in the stores. Area managers, of whom there are three, do not even have offices. They work alternately between the four or five stores that they are responsible for overseeing. Feargal Quinn himself is in every store at least once a week, if not twice.

At Superquinn, one of the great management principles is that information is there to be shared. 'You must be open with employees, disclose a huge amount of information. Everybody should sees the figures. They enjoy working more if they see how they are doing,' says Feargal Quinn.

'This process of involvement is critical, not just to the development of the culture and the spirit of customer service, but also to the level of commitment. It makes it possible to reach a level of agreement about costs – more than if the figures were imposed. For new employees, it helps them gain an understanding of what profit is,' explains the Marketing Manager.

Every Thursday morning, a member of the management board goes into the store and meets with everybody to go over the financial results of the store. Practically every department is present – the check-out stands, the store rooms, the cleaners – 'everybody sees the figures' and has the opportunity to ask questions. The figures are also broken down into profit centres which permits each employee to know what his group's contribution was to the results. 'The focus is on problem-solving. If there's a problem, we discuss how they are going to put it right.'

A good customer orientation is still at the heart of the Superquinn culture. 'In the 17 years I have been with this company, customer service has always been a daily topic.' 'Service is the topic discussed more than any other topic.'

Recruits are judged on their spontaneous customer service orientation. As Superquinn's managers put it, '90 per cent of the training is done in recruitment. Our people are natural; we just let them do it.' When new employees enter the company, one of the first things they are told is that they may spend time on the shop floor dealing with the customers. What they are judged on is how they deal with customers. 'The important thing is the customer; how you handle the customer is really important.' Feargal Quinn says, 'The litmus test is the smile. An employee should know the value of a smile.'

What can be learned

1 Let your customer do the talking

Superquinn's customer panels are not designed as a way for managers to explain the store's shortcomings to customers. They are an opportunity for customers to speak their mind. Managers say that it's a fabulous 'crystal ball' into the minds of cus-tomers. The whole effect would be ruined if Feargal Quinn would speak his mind instead.

2 Remember details – again and again

What is good service if it isn't a flower on Mother's Day, a free day care centre so that mothers can have one hour of peaceful shopping, or a split package for elderly people who don't need a whole one? It's the little things that really show one cares.

3 Go with the flow

And so, your customers have decided that they no longer want frozen pizzas, they want fresh ones. Don't look on it as a nuisance; it's an opportunity. If it means changing your business from food selling to food preparing, then change. As Feargal Quinn would say, 'It's the customer that is the real retail expert.'

4 You can't do business by sitting on your . . . armchair

Feargal Quinn believes that success in the retail business depends upon being out there on the floor, where the action is. Everyone in his company is expected to pass time on the shop floor and all of his managers have worked in the stores before moving up.

SVP

Ring, ring. 'Hello, this is SVP, Mr Bridges speaking, can I help you?'

'Yes, can you give me the names of all the cello manufacturers in Paris, please?'

'Indeed, hold on just a moment. . . . I have the list right in front of me. There's about 10 and they're a varied bunch. . . . If I might, can I ask what it's for?'

'We want to do a photo for our company journal and I need to have a cello in the picture.

'Ah, if I might suggest, the best thing to do would be to call the publicity and theatre props company; they have that sort of thing ready at hand. I have some names right here . . .'

'Wonderful, thanks very much.'

SVP is in the business of providing advice and information by telephone to management. It is practically the only company of its kind in the world. The public library, the chamber of commerce and government authorities are all able to provide only some of what SVP provides. SVP stands out by the quality of the advice provided and by the immediate availability of the response. 'Our job is to provide the information that is necessary for management in order to take decisions,' explains Madame Brigitte de Gastines, CEO of SVP.

Background

In 1935, the name SVP – the abbreviation for 'if you please' in French – was approved for the name of a company whose goal was to provide a service of information by telephone. The first clients were individuals and the first questions answered concerned household or personal concerns.

Maurice de Turckheim took over the company in 1937. He redefined the business of the company as an information service to businesses and launched the company aggressively into the market. By 1960, the company had 210 telephone lines and 200 researchers and operators.

Brigitte de Gastines entered the business through sales. SVP, in its fourth decade of existence as a virtual monopoly, had begun to lose touch with the market place. 'I decided to try to make things change by pushing from the outside; so, I attacked from the international market.' Mrs de Gastines's first step was to go to Belgium to set up SVP Belgium.

One thing that the company had learned in its international expansion was that franchising was not something for SVP. 'SVP is not just a marketing concept, it is a whole organisation and way of approaching the provision of information,' says Mrs de Gastines. Those who bought franchising rights rarely succeeded.

When Madame de Gastines took over the direction of the company in 1976, she began a systematic development of the international network. Today, SVP has an owned and managed international network of subsidiaries in 24 countries.

Business, both in France and in the international markets has been excellent. In 1990, SVP could claim a total of 150,000 subscribed users throughout the world for whom its 1000 employees resolved one million problems or questions.

Service strategy

SVP offers a full range of information services designed to meet the needs of the small and medium-sized business. It splits those services into six departments: technology, products and markets, economy and finance, human resources management, general legislation, accounting and tax legislation, and social and cultural information. A good 32 per cent of the activity comes from questions on economy and finance, tax and accounting. Seventeen per cent comes from social and cultural enquiries which include anything from recommending a suitable restaurant for a business meeting in Bordeaux to providing 'Who's Who' type information on a minister.

Their target client is the CEO and members of top management of small to medium-sized firms that don't have the resources to set up their own information centre. 'I cannot say whether we are more or less expensive than the others – there are no others directly comparable.' The essential is that the customer is satisfied.

SVP offers its services on a subscription basis. The company pays a one-time subscription once a year and has the right to call the company as many times as he needs or wants during that year. SVP has a 90 per cent fidelity rate. 'My objective is zero-depart [to have none who leave],' says Madame de Gastines.

Her strategy for achieving zero-depart is to be sure that the service her company provides, both in terms of the way customers are treated and the advice her consultants give, is of a very high standard. 'The originality of SVP is in its capacity to treat information, to advise customers well and to be always available and always at the disposition of the customer.'

As regards 'treated information' versus raw information, SVP consultants are experts in their domain. Their job is not just to take information from a database to which they subscribe and recite it over the phone to the customer, SVP has researchers on staff whose unique function is to compare information from various databases, analyse it and package it in a form which can be used readily by the consultant speaking to the customer over the phone.

Next comes 'to advise clients well' versus 'throwing' information at the customer over the phone. Advising means to interpret the information for the client. Information is put into the context of the problem which is facing the customer. If a customer wants to divorce her husband and asks to know the divorce regulations pertaining to the various types of marriage contracts, the consultant provides the information that is relative to her type of contract. Not only that, they go beyond – by trying to find out the situation the customer finds herself in and finding the particular information adapted to her needs.

'To be always available and at the disposition of the customer' means two things. First, it means being open from 9 a.m. to 6 p.m. without a traditional French lunch break. It means not having to wait 10 rings before someone picks up the phone and it also means not having to wait 10 minutes on hold until a consultant is available.

Secondly, being available and at the disposition of the customer means answering the phone with a smile and being prepared to listen with interest and patience to the customer's questions. It means not cutting the customer off in the middle of his explanation and it means asking the right questions to clarify what information the customer really needs. 'What is the most important is for our consultants to understand that success in this business depends upon service.'

Service strengths

SVP implements its strategy well; customers get all of what is described above and much more. Where SVP really excels in serving its customers is in its ability to go to the heart of the customer's questions and find the question behind the question. 'My job is to find the real problem behind the question.'

Only by going to the heart of the question can the consultant really add value to the information they communicate. The process of bringing the customer to expose his problem is a science at SVP; it's a technique which is refined and perfected every day, by every consultant.

In its most basic form, SVP compares its approach to that of a doctor. 'Our job is a bit like that of a doctor who receives a customer. It begins by a dialogue; the doctor's job, like the consultant's, is to listen and to ask questions in order to try to identify the specific disease troubling the customer. He then makes a diagnosis which he announces to the customer. Lastly, he gives a prescription.'

'Like the doctor, only through the dialogue can the consultant truly identify and resolve the customer's problem.'

An SVP consultant stays, on average 16 minutes on the telephone with a customer. His objective in that 16 minutes is to do a very good diagnosis of the customer's problems. All consultants have university degrees and additional experience in the specialised fields in which they work. 'But, for us, they must be consultants, able to communicate and advise a customer, before they are jurists.'

There are customers asking to know what the various legal forms of a company in Germany are. If the consultant didn't try to find out why the customer needs this information, he would never be able to advise him on exactly which forms would be the best for his type of business.'We must always go beyond the question to provide good service.'

Each customer is seen as an individual and each problem is a case in and of itself. 'We have customers calling for the names of lawyers; through the discussion, we try to know why. Most of the time we cannot only give them the same information that the lawyer would give, but also the same advice,' explains Mrs Cazaban-Peyre, head of the legal department.

'Often our competitors are our biggest customers,' says Mrs de Gastines. In the legal department, 30 per cent of the biggest users are lawyers who have neither the time or the inclination to do the necessary research for a customer's question and call SVP.

All SVP's advice is provided in the best conditions possible. A sophisticated telephone answering system can handle 1800 calls per hour. Automatic monitoring systems ensure that a customer's call is being answered before four rings and that he is in contact with a consultant in less than 30 seconds after having spoken to the receptionist: an enormous monitoring system with green and red lights lets consultants know whether a customer call is waiting to be picked up.

Eighty five per cent of all enquiries coming in are handled over the phone within the 16-minute average; SVP is connected on-line to over 2000 databases worldwide. The remaining 15 per cent of the enquiries are generally handled the same day. If not, they are answered in writing within five days. These exceptional cases generally relate to questions for which the consultant must contact SVP's foreign subsidiary.

'When they call, our customers are facing a problem; when they hang up, they should have the answer to that problem,' says Mrs Cazaban-Peyre.

Implementation

The most important factor for the provision of good customer service at SVP is the quality of the consultant. 'He must be three people in one. He must be a good technician in his field, he must be a professional in communication and he must be a good salesman.'

The first step in the making of a top consultant happens in the recruitment phase. Just to be interviewed, all candidates must have a university degree and experience in the field. They pass two interviews: the first is designed to test their skills and their experience. The second tests their understanding of SVP's business. 'The most important thing for me is that the candidate has understood that this is a customer service business.'

Next and perhaps most important is the apprenticeship phase. A consultant is rarely prepared to work completely independently before three months. After an introduction to the company as a whole, the new consultant is assigned to a godfather or godmother. Working with a telephone with two receivers, the consultant learns how to speak and respond to customers. He never actually speaks over the telephone before one month's service and then that's only with the godparent listening on the other end. (See chapter 8.)

Training is also a continual process and it's offered not just on how to work with customers, but also for the advancement of professional knowledge. Seminars, conventions, lectures, outside research – anything and everything is permitted as long as it is useful to the consultant and is approved by the department head. 'I don't have any restrictions concerning my training budget. The criteria is whether it relates to a concern of our customers. There are very few requests for outside training or research that I have declined; it's just not an issue.'

To keep consultants in touch with the market and to know what a customer looks like when he isn't on the other end of the phone, consultants are required to visit customers with the sales staff at least once a year. 'It's so that they hear direct from the customer their needs, their expectations. . . .'

SVP consultants appear to enjoy their work. It is motivating due to the variety of the questions and the continual contact with customers. 'There is a continual intellectual exercise in this business; I learn something every day.'

To keep abreast of the standard of quality being provided by the entire company to the customer, SVP performs customer satisfaction surveys. Once a year, the sales staff personally delivers the questionnaire to the customer and asks him to fill it out. The quality manager, who reports directly to Mr Bodmer, general manager, follows progressions in the report. For the last few years, they've been continuously on the upswing. 'The new telephone system has helped us improve our speed and accuracy of telephone responses.'

The quality manager 'investigates any problem that a customer can have'. He looks into specific problems and handles complaints which are not handled directly by the departments.

Quality is constantly monitored by the department directors. Each director has, at the end of the day, a report which presents exactly the activity of the day. Specifically it lists the average time spent by each consultant on the phone, the number of questions handled by each – a good average is 18 – the area in which the question was asked, the number of letters that have not been answered in the proscribed limit of five days etc. It permits the director to identify trends in questions, to spot problems being experienced by consultants and anything else detrimental to the proper functioning of the department.

Perhaps one of the best monitoring tools the company has is a self-monitoring tool. Once a week, consultants randomly choose a customer with whom they had contact during the week. They score their performance on that contact and send a copy to the customer with a nice letter asking him to score them as well. The respone from the customer permits the consultant to evaluate for himself whether his conception of the service he or she provided matched the preception of the customer.

What can be learned

1 Strive for excellence in just one thing

SVP doesn't have any direct competitors. It's been doing well and making money for over 50 years. It does just one thing and it does it very, very well. The greatest barrier to entry into the market against SVP is not the investment in databanks and information systems; it's the degree of expertise SVP has developed for itself in advice by telephone.

2 Know your key success factors

SVP knows that the quality of the dialogue that the consultant has with customers is key to customer satisfaction. A tremendous amount of effort is therefore made to ensure that this dialogue achieves its purpose – diagnosing the customer's real problem and solving it.

3 Give your employees a tool to compare their conceived quality with the customer's perceived quality.

SVP has a lovely system which allows consultants to have their work evaluated once a week by a customer they helped in that week. Because it first requires the consultant to evaluate his own performance and then send that evaluation to customers who return it with their comments, it is an excellent self-learning tool for the consultant and a way to compare his conceived quality with the customer's perceived quality.

TETRA PAK

This is a company which knows where it came from, what it does, what it stands for and where it is going. Tetra Pak develops, produces and markets complete packaging systems for the distribution of food products; milk and juice or juice-based drinks being the most common.

'Tetra' comes from the word tetrahedron, the Greek term for a four-sided object – a good description of the company's first product, a flexible carton for milk or cream developed in the 1940s. Today, the company has seven individual packaging systems with registered trade marks. It is entirely specialised and, as the creators and only large producers of these systems, is the world's leading supplier of aseptic packaging systems but has its sights set on the global market for non-carbonated foods, of which it holds a mere one per cent today. In terms of service quality, this makes them no less vigilant and, to the contrary, ever more anxious to prove that their success is merited.

History

Following eight years of intensive development effort on the product concept, AB Tetra Pak is established in Lund, Sweden by Ruben Rausing. It was, at first, a subsidiary of Akerlund & Rausing. The product, today referred to as 'Tetra Classic', featured new techniques for coating paper with plastics and was produced by machines which permitted the sealing of the packages below the level of the liquid. The technique was a considerable improvement in terms of practicality and hygiene over the prevailing method of distributing milk in glass bottles.

In 1951, the first Tetra Pak machines were up and running in a Lund dairy, Lundaortens Mejeriförening. Tetra Pak delivered packaging material and packaging machines to the dairy, which carried out the packaging. The machines were leased to the dairy, but were maintained and improved by Tetra Pak.

Growth was rapid in Sweden and, by 1959, production capacity of packaging material represented one billion cartons annually. In 1960, the company established its first production facility for packaging materials outside Sweden in Mexico. Tetra Pak was already selling in Europe and the US.

In 1961, the company introduced the first machine for aseptically filling cartons with bacteria-free milk, a development which contributed considerably to the industry and to the company's subsequent growth. Aseptic packages now account for over 70 per cent of total production.

Today, the company has over 6500 machines producing packaging materials in over 100 countries worldwide, including China and the US. As from September 1

1991 Uno Kjellberg is President and CEO of the Tetra Pak Group, reporting to Dr Hans Rausing, Chairman and CEO Tetra Pak Alfa-Laval Group. Tetra Pak forms part of this Group since July 1991 with the formal acquisition by Tetra Pak of the Swedish Alfa-Laval Group.

The emerging world pattern of strategic economic groupings – in Europe, Americas and Asia/Pacific, which results in increased call for decentralisation, has provided the impetus for Tetra Pak's recent regionalisation of its operations.

Tetra Pak Europe, Middle East & Africa operates from Lausanne, Switzerland, Tetra Pak Americas is based in Atlanta Ga, and Tetra Pak Asia/Pacific is located in Singapore.

This regionalised operating structure will permit the company to act on market signals even more swiftly and sharpen its competitiveness, thereby securing its leadership position in the liquid food packaging sector in the future.

Service strategy

The Tetra Pak range of products is the result of a highly technology-bound series of innovations. Its successful performance lies with the interdependence of specially developed packaging machines and packaging material. Selling a Tetra Pak package is not then a matter of selling an object, but rather a whole packaging system. What is mostly billed to customers is the price of packaging materials. What is actually bought is over 60 per cent service content.

This is the first key point in their service strategy. It permits the company to provide an excellent product/service package without having to bill for each individual service offered. The services are essential to the product which couldn't be sold successfully without them. The customer benefits because his packaging needs are provided for from 'A to Z'.

A second major tenet of their service strategy is the emphasis upon a partnership relationship with the customer. For the most part, Tetra Pak maintains long-term contacts with its customers which makes the establishment of a good rapport with the customer essential. Along with the good rapport come many of the support services highly appreciated by Tetra Pak's customers. Tetra Pak provides assistance in the choice of product image and packaging: Tetra Pak relationship managers are regularly brought in to assist in the discussions with their customers' advertising agencies. Tetra Pak also provides marketing support: it conducts market research for the dairy and drink sectors and makes the results of these studies known to its customers.

In the technical areas, in addition to providing customers with expertise in aseptic know-how and in the use of modern packaging technologies, Tetra Pak assists customers – well beyond its specific responsibilities as a supplier of packaging systems, but when it is within the range of its competence – for instance in the design of the customers' storage and distribution systems and on bacteriology matters.

A third element of their strategy is the transfer of technology. This is primarily done through training. Tetra Pak trains customers to understand the technology behind their products, training customers' employees to operate the machines which are used to produce their products, how to maintain them, if the customer so desires.

Tetra Pak has 22 schools for technical training spread across the world. The oldest and most advanced Tetra Pak school is in Lund, together with the company's research and development facilities. While many of the students are Tetra Pak's own staff; some courses put customers, staff and Tetra Pak employees together in the same classroom. Additional training and assistance is provided on-site by Tetra Pak technical staff.

Additional technology transfer is achieved through the regular provision of information. Information comes from Tetra Pak in the form of brochures, audio-visuals and house magazines, which are small books of information devoted to a specific topic of potential customer interest. There are also seminars, exhibitions and study tours for customers, as well as access on request to regularly updated information stored in Tetra Pak's database on technical and market developments.

Service strengths

Tetra Pak representatives are accepted as being true experts in their field. Their advice is of top quality. The fact that customers permit Tetra Pak representatives to participate in discussions with other outside companies demonstrates the kind of confidence which customers place in their professionalism and their know-how.

Representatives' expertise is not limited to the production process. Customers can consult Tetra Pak on a wide variety of issues related to their business; in addition to the range of marketing, logistics and technological information provided, advice is available on political and economic developments in countries where these are an issue.

Tetra Pak is exceptional at making the information they provide user-friendly; they are specialists in the packaging of information. The house magazines are a perfect example. They are full-sized brochures, attractively packaged and presented with full-page glossy pictures. Each one deals with a separate topic. Each topic addressed is dealt with in depth. Over 25 full pages, excluding photographs, are devoted to the topic. Number 49, for example, deals with product design, and gives numerous explanations and examples of key points to keep in mind in the developments of packagings for milk or juice-related products. Number 69 deals with changing lifestyles and presents the results of research done on lifestyles for the year 2000, including eating, working and buying habits in various major countries.

Another example of good information packaging is in the presentation of their products. Brochures are available on each product line. Even for the novice, the technology and its use becomes blatantly clear. Tetra Pak avoids extensive use of technical jargon and concentrates on the end result for the customer. Diagrams and simple drawings support the text at every stage of the explanation.

Another aspect of service in which Tetra Pak excels is in 'availability'. By availability, we mean the readiness with which the company is prepared and equipped to come to their customer's rescue. Downtime in packaging means a loss in productivity and eventually a loss of product due to spoilage. Problems must be dealt within hours, not days. Customers are provided with round-the-clock telephone access to managers prepared to respond in the case of a problem. Tetra Pak's technical staff are trained to respond rapidly and are equipped to deal with most technical problems on the first visit. In addition to the staff on hand in each of the 50 technical service centres, an international technical service pool is available to intervene and resolve technical problems, at any time, in any location.

Implementation

Managing service quality at Tetra Pak means managing where people are going. Tetra Pak relies upon the clear and unambiguous presentation of the company's goals and general standard of service to motivate and direct its employees. In a booklet given to employees joining the company, the company's goal, strategy, technological policy, standard of customer service, standard of product quality and the nature of its relationship with suppliers is all set forth in very simple terms. In most communication tools used by the company these goals and *modus operandi* appear again and again.

Additional reinforcement of the company's mission is received from each employee's manager. Most managers have been with the company for many years and are familiar with the company's objectives – even if they didn't participate in their elaboration, which many did.

Once understood, the company's goals have an influence on the way each employee does his job. Most successful employees adopt the objectives of the company as their own and make decisions which promote those goals. This method of management by the osmosis of goals is particularly applicable to a company like Tetra Pak where a large portion of employees have management-level jobs and need to make on-the-spot decisions which reflect company policy, sometimes in remote locations. Narrow directives on dos and don'ts are not enough. Good decisions are only possible if the employee has fully understood and adopted the company's mission.

A second crucial element in the management of service quality at Tetra Pak is the system of recruitment and integration. Beyond meeting basic requirements for levels of education and skills, employees are chosen on the basis of their fit with the company rather than any particular achievement or skill they may bring to the company. All employees pass through a rather vigorous interview process in which only those who are universally liked and appreciated are hired. Any doubt or hesitation on the part of an existing employee regarding a recruit means the likely rejection of that candidate.

Once the employee is hired, he is integrated. For most major positions, employees are sent to Lund to see the facilities and to be instructed in the technology and services. Newly employed marketing/sales and technical staff visit a customer plant as part of their introductory training course. Before they can represent the company to the customer, however, an employee receives several weeks' training.

What can be learned

1 Ensuring your customer's future ensures your own

Tetra Pak has clearly understood that their survival is dependent upon the survival of their customers. As a result, the company does practically everything they can to foster the development of their customer's business. Most of the support services they provide have been created with that aim in mind. They will even go to the point of helping one customer compete against another, if necessary. The packaging business is not the only business in which this can be applied.

2 Remember the strength of the written word

Tetra Pak relies extensively upon written communication materials, both within the company and with their customers. It is an extremely effective tool for them and prevents them from becoming a forbidden temple of knowledge to their customers.

3 Service is essential to single product or service companies

Tetra Pak has chosen a strategy of concentration. It does one thing and only one thing. Its exposure to the competition would be 10 times greater if it had not protected its product by the provision of a vast array of complementary services. The company remains a world leader in the aseptic packaging sector because its services cannot be matched.

4 Bill a product; sell a service

Services, like consulting on packaging design, are hard for a product or technology-based company to bill. Customers don't know how to evaluate the value of the services provided and are reluctant to pay for intangible items. The customer is more comfortable paying for a product – the packaging material – even if he knowingly pays more for that product in order to receive the associated services.

3 M

It is innovative, market driven and quality oriented. Known worldwide for its ability to translate customer ideas into tangible products, 3M has built its success on listening to its customers.

As is stated on the front page of the company's annual report, 3M's 'success is due to the rigorous application of a simple principle established early in its history: stay close to your customers, listen to what they tell you and meet their requirements.'

It's something every manager and employee at 3M believes in completely and tries to implement every day throughout the world in 50 countries.

Background

The Minnesota Mining and Manufacturing Company, as 3M was called in its early days, was created in 1902 to mine abrasive minerals and manufacture sandpaper. Today, the company is involved in over 100 technologies, of which coating and bonding, technologies related to its original activities, remain one of its strongest.

3M today is best known for its 'Post-it' notes products and those who do a bit of cleaning around the house, 'Scotch' and 'Scotchgard' products. But, these form only a tiny tip of the product iceberg that is 3M. The majority of 3M's products are actually used in industrial applications or as ingredients in other products. 3M's products are used to fight fires, protect metal rods from rusting, sand crystal glasses, protect rugs and curtains and protect valuable paintings; the complete list is incredibly long and varied, and even in small print is probably extensive enough to wallpaper your office.

3M's worldwide sales now exceed US$13 billion and the company employs over 83,000 people in its various locations. Despite its size, it also remains one of the most innovative companies in the world. Twenty-five per cent of the company's revenues every year come from products that didn't exist five years before.

3M has been in Europe since 1929. Today, it is completely committed to the European market. It manufactures, distributes and creates products in Europe for Europe. Twenty-one thousand members of its staff are located in Europe. There are

20 plants and 13 technical centres for the European market.

To ensure the efficient co-ordination of its various European operations in the new unified commercial environment, 3M has formed European management action teams with group managers from all of the European operations. The teams discuss evolutions in the European market and develop strategies designed to position 3M correctly for the future.

In the last year and a half, quality has become an ever more important topic of discussion for the company. With the same enthusiasm with which the company has approached any major technological innovation, 3M is now attacking the quality issue. It is using the Malcolm Baldrige award guidelines for its quality push and no matter where one goes in the company today, the quality issue is a hot topic.

3M's rationale for looking at quality is that the company believes that, in the future, its success will be ever more determined by the things that are peripheral to the products – customer advice, logistics, support materials, aid in installing or using products. The total quality approach is designed to help the company develop ways to identify and improve all types of non-quality, be they in delivery, telephone answering or product quality.

Service strategy

For 3M, the best service it can offer its customers is to create products that really meet their needs. That doesn't just mean designing a product which the market likes, is easy to manufacture and can be sold by 10,000s per year.

What it really means is one man visiting the customer, discussing with him, discussing with him yet again . . . and again, coming back to a 3M lab and telling them what the customer wants. The lab, then, creates for the customer. The product is tested endlessly, both by 3M alone and with 3M and the customer. Only then is the product actually sold – sometimes two to three years later.

Because in most cases, 3M's products are not actually products, but technologies, and once they are developed, they can be sold for a large number of applications. For example, the same abrasive that is used for the finishing touches on crystal glasses might be used to treat computer disks without damaging the contents.

Once again the key man is the technical services engineer who goes out to the customer. He knows that a technology has been created for another customer and what its basic attributes are. His job is to ask customers the right questions so that, together with the engineer, the customer's needs are fully expressed. The engineer is tuned in to identify those needs for which an existing technology might apply. If he finds one, he comes back again to the lab and finds out whether the lab can't adapt the technology to this new customer need.

3M's definition of good customer service is 'doing what the customer requires . . . delight the customer'. The philosophy behind this approach is to create a primary demand for products; in business circles it's known as a pull-through sales approach. '3M's founder always claimed that the last person you wanted to sell to was the purchasing agent.'

The principle points of this strategy from a service perspective are:

- the dialogue that occurs between the customer and 3M, which gives the customer the feeling that he is contributing to the development of a new technology (which he is);
- the emphasis on the identification of customer needs, rather than on the actual

sale, which occurs sometimes years after the original contact has been established; and

- the trust and commitment to the customer demonstrated by 3M's willingness to 'customise' for the customer.

Up to now, 3M has concentrated primarily on executing this strategy very, very well. New technologies are known as 'Oh, gollys' in the lab and the focus of the entire company has been upon developing and selling new products developed from 'oh golly's' to end-users. 'In the future we feel that there may be less "Oh, gollys" coming from the labs and we now must look at differentiating on the basis of service.'

For 3M Europe, good service is going to be, above all, good logistics, good 3M-customer relationships, good customer problem and complaints handling, and good technical service, which is the support provided to a customer to put the product into application.

To find out what it should be concentrating on in terms of service, 3M went direct to the customer. In late 1989, the company conducted a very extensive and thorough survey of 3M's service and product quality on a Europe-wide basis. Forty thousand customers participated in the survey. Customers included distributors of 3M products as well as end-users.

In addition to discovering the present level of satisfaction of customers with various aspects of the company's services, the study permitted customers to compare 3M against its competitors. For 3M, the most useful part of the study was to be able to find out where it was weakest. 'We found gaps in our service, important gaps which we intend to work on.'

Service strengths

3M's founder also said, 'Know your customer'. To this day, that continues to be a vital element of the company's service approach. By knowing their customer – who he is, what his situation in the market is and what he wants, 3M is now developing ways to serve him better.

3M's commerical office supply and home stationery products division in France identified three types of clients: the large hypermarket chains; the large distributor of office products; and the retailer of paper products. 3M's approach has been adapted to meet the expectations of each. The large hypermarkets purchase a very narrow range of products, particularly those that sell well. Their primary requirement in the paper products area is that there is a high turnover.

3M is focusing on providing merchandising assistance and top quality information to help the client make his purchasing decisions. As a first step, 3M developed a special brochure with only top-selling items just to appeal to the hypermarket chains. The brochure provides all the information necessary to large-scale purchasers of these products – the number of units per carton, the number of cartons per delivery, and the weight and the height of the packages. The booklet also provides information about promotions, and advertising which is scheduled for the year.

The company has also recently developed a computer program which permits it to advise its customers on the best way to organise their shelves in the paper department. The program allows other products than 3M to be included in the arrangement. The information is personalised for each shop according to its overall size, the sales that it has had in the past in the paper department, the present structure of the shelves (their height, width etc.) and the number of different types and brands of products the client wishes to be selling. The result is the optimum merchandising layout, complete with measurements, product names and the location of signs.

For the second group of clients – the distributors – yet another approach has been developed. 3M has positioned itself as the 'partner to the distributor'. These clients need access to a large range of products and efficient service in terms of billing and delivery. They also need to be sure that they are offering the right balance of products in their catalogue to the end-user. 3M provides them with information on the end-user market, and advice on how to order and compose a selection of products according to the market demand. 3M is also putting greater emphasis on its logistics capacity and its ability to respond rapidly to immediate demands. The company schedules appointments for delivery and bills using a very efficient EDI system.

In its role as a partner to the distributor, 3M has organised a 'board of distributors'. There are 15 representatives on this board which changes every two years. They include clients from companies which together represent around 40 per cent of 3M's revenues in the distribution sector. 'This group serves as a sounding board.' At each meeting a theme is chosen and the members work in sub-groups to discuss ways to meet the end customers' needs better.

Also for distributors, 3M organises 'study trips'. Each client visits, with his 3M representative, four clients in other countries in Europe. The objective is to compare what the two companies are doing the same or differently, and to pick up tips. Once the tour is completed, the entire group of clients gathers in one site and each presents what they have learned to the entire group. Around 100 people attend this event every year.

For the last group of clients, the paper and office products store owners, 3M offers a proximity of access to the client for restocking and advice within his store on merchandising, as well as financial considerations. The emphasis is on a more personalised relationship with the store's supplier.

In the future, 3M sees the paper and office products market becoming more and more service conscious. 'A few years ago, 3M was above market expectations in terms of what it was providing to the distributors; today, we are going beyond the present level in certain areas because of what our competition is doing,' explains Claude Denais who is the manager of commercial office supply and home stationery products. 'One has to be capable of following the rising expectations of our customers.'

'In some cases, based on what we know about our clients, we actually create an expectation. Otherwise we can't have the edge on the competition.' Creating expectations means, for example, giving customers the opportunity to make an appointment for a delivery of goods. This new service creates expectations by customers for the same level of service from other competitors.

Implementation

Keeping in touch with the customer and creating products and technologies for the customer is 3M's key to success. They are made possible by an intensive direct contact with the customer, by regular market research studies for every customer segment, and by a regular and continual exchange between the customer contact person and the labs.

With greater focus on quality and service, the company is now developing other ways to ensure that it's providing customers with all of what they really need. The service quality programme initiated by 3M France is a good example of how a quality process is being implemented throughout the company.

3M calls it its 'Quality for the 90s' programme. The first phase of the programme was called the self-assessment phase. The customer satisfaction survey conducted on a Europe wide basis was part of this phase (*see* Service Strategy, above).

In addition to the satisfaction survey, there were internal meetings on a regular basis, most of which demanded the participation of 3M's top managers. 3M France calculated that it spent 17,000 hours, between 16 individuals, doing the assessment phase. The company identified 25 major gaps which had to be worked on.

The company has now entered the plan of actions phase. The objective of this phase is to devise action plans for how to address each one of the 25 gaps. This phase also means planning the introduction of a process for continuous improvement. By April 1992, all of 3M France's supervisors will have been trained in 'continuous improvement techniques', which they will then be expected to pass on to their employees.

A detailed action plan will also be ready by April, 1992. There are five categories of goals for which actions will be scheduled: employee welfare, customer service, quality, financial, and citizenship. For every single objective, there will be a way of measuring progress; there will be an analysis of tactics and systems available, and an analysis of the gaps to be filled before that objective can be reached.

Already, it has been decided that the plans will include the scheduling of regular customer satisfaction surveys (including lost customer analysis) for every business unit, and the establishment of cross-functional teams which will brainstorm on customer service issues – 'throw it over the wall' – and report progress and ideas on a quarterly basis.

The human resources department is already well advanced into phase two and has defined objectives for their division in four of the five quality areas. Mr Hammer, head of the division, defines the department goal overall as, 'to optimise the efficiency and motivation of the company's people in order to achieve 3M's strategies'. In the belief that 'people respect what you inspect', his division has already introduced indicators for monitoring the quality his service is providing the rest of the company with.

One indicator is the average time it takes for the company to recruit a new employee. Another is the qualifications which people are hired with as compared with the specified need. A third concerns the quality of the recruitment process – each new employee is asked to complete a questionnaire on the way 3M treated candidates. Yet another is the rate of mobility of personnel within the company and of departures.

3M now has 23 training courses dealing with customer service issues. Overall, training represents 5.1 per cent of total salaries and charges for the company; that is nearly four times larger than the legally required rate in France. All sales and customer contact staff receive customer service training of three to five days per year. Choosing who gets what kind of training at 3M is 'almost mathematical'. The personal skills of the individual are evaluated against the requirements of his or her job and the gaps are filled with training. There is also a consideration for the future advancement of the person; training is also given to prepare employees to take over certain posts in the future.

One area where the company hasn't waited before taking improvement measures is in the telephone response at their facilities. A few mystery customer tests carried out by 3M's CEO Mr Richelsen were enough to convince him that 3M's speed of response and speed of transferring had to be improved. Today, virtually the entire company has received training on how to answer the telephone. The company also installed a system which now monitors, on a monthly basis, the average response delay. Last, but not least, the company occasionally uses mystery callers – like the CEO – to check up that things are still running smoothly. 'It's like they say, if you can't measure it, you can't manage it.'

What can be learned

1 Involve your customers in the product and service creation process

3M's 'panel of distributors' that serves as a sounding board is an excellent way to get customers involved in what the company is doing and a good way to increase their commitment to the company.

2 Go beyond what you do to meet customers' needs

3M is not a company that designs computer programs, but that didn't stop them from creating a program for their hypermarket chain clients that meets their need for good merchandising advice. By listening to customers, a company can obtain a wealth of ideas about services they can provide that will help sell their products better.

3 Use internal indicators and get 'people to respect what you inspect'

3M's human relations department developed a concrete way of measuring its service to the rest of the company. They call them indicators and they help draw people's attention to problem areas or identify improvements when they occur.

TNT

Practically anything, 'anywhere, anytime, anyplace'. It has a great ring to it and what's more, it's true. TNT, a good solid company from Australia, is the UK's leading express transportation company. After 13 years of spectacular growth, today TNT is equipped to deliver customers' mail and packages by air, land and sea to 190 countries and to practically every destination in the UK. Reliability is the company's byword; customer service quality is its motto.

Background

TNT in Australia was founded by Ken Thomas, an energetic, dynamic individual committed to the advancement of his business on a worldwide basis. TNT entered the UK market in 1978 with the acquisition of Inter County Express, a company with 6 depots and 500 staff.

The first major expansive move of the UK company occurred in 1980 when it launched TNT Overnite, the first door-to-door nationwide guaranteed next-day delivery service in the UK. A year later it launched TNT Parcel Office which today has a network of more than 450 retail parcel delivery acceptance points. In practically every year in the decade of the 1980s, TNT launched itself into a new business – each time with astounding success.

While every business it has entered has been a success, some of the most notable are TNT Express – the company's core overnight and same-day small package delivery – TNT Newsfast – delivery service of daily newspapers throughout the country, and TNT White Arrow Express, a joint venture project with Great Universal Stores to deliver mail order goods directly to the home. In all three cases, very optimistic provisions have been exceeded and the services provided have obtained the leadership position for the company in those sectors in just a few years.

'In 1988, for its 10th anniversary, TNT celebrated the opening of the 600th TNT location in the UK. The awards for excellence, which would later shower the company, had already started to come in. In 1986, TNT won the Motor Transport Award for the 'Best Marketing Campaign' for its TNT Express Service. The following year, the TNT Contract Distribution division won the Commercial Motor Livery Competition for Cow and Gate [a firm producing baby food] contract vehicles. It has since won many more awards, more than one a year, including being named as one of the 100 Best Companies to Work for in the UK' (published by HarperCollins).

As it stands today, TNT is the leader in the UK for most of its businesses. Alan Jones, who strives to emulate Ken Thomas in his dynamism and determination, is the managing director of TNT UK; he plans to push the company to even greater heights in what he believes to be a mature industry. 'After years of market innovation and consequent massive growth, express distribution is a maturing business in the UK. . . . Service is the major competitive battleground,' says Alan Jones.

Service strategy

When it came to asking TNT what their 'product' was, the answer was clean and neat, 'Our product is service; we transport anything, anytime, anywhere.'

In fact, TNT does even more. Starting from a very basic market need – the need for express delivery of parcels and small packages – and from a very basic company skill – the efficient handling of quantities to be delivered – TNT has developed an impressive number of delivery and delivery-related services.

There are presently around 35 separate services offered by the TNT group. Each of TNT's services is established as a separate 'divisional company' within the umbrella structure of TNT. Each divisional company is expected to pursue its own marketing and sales policy and to manage its own sales force. It is a separate profit centre within TNT.

Support services such as data processing and despatching are frequently operated as profit centres as well and are free to sell their services to outside companies as well as within the Group. TNT Data Processing, for example, has developed tailor-made distribution computer systems for major customers such as British Home Stores, House of Fraser and the Volkswagen Audi Group.

Overall, the company divides its services into three categories:

front door services – which consist principally of deliveries of letters or small packages for business and individuals;
back door services – which is delivery of larger items primarily for business and industry;

special services – including the company's delivery services for bulk fluids and liquids, its 'just-in-time' delivery system (for customers using 'just-in-time'), and its TNT Taxitrucks which are 24-hour vehicle/driver rental services.

Before any new service is launched, the marketing and service strategy of each is considered very carefully. Particular care is taken to evaluate the new service against potential competition in the market. The company's differential advantages *vis-à-vis* the competition generally fall into one of the following slots.

TNT is selling something nobody else yet does

TNT's Overnite service is a good example. It was the first door-to-door nationwide guaranteed next-day delivery service in Britain. TNT Sameday is another example. When it was launched, it was the first to offer same-day delivery.

TNT is selling its expertise in the logistics of fast delivery to be used in something other than delivery of parcels and letters

Its activities in the garment industry are an excellent example. TNT launched TNT Garment Express which provides rapid and reliable movements of hanging clothing stock. TNT Brewery Distribution designs and sells tailored distribution systems for the brewing industry.

TNT sells reliability and customer service by providing a guarantee

A large number of TNT services come with a guarantee. They are the assurance that TNT will meet their promise to the customer and, if not, 'your money back'. All of TNT Express delivery services for letters and packages, except for offshore island service and its same-day service, carry guarantees.

Because of maturing in the industry, Alan Jones believes that the days when TNT can bring out one service after another that are 'firsts' is largely over. His strategy for the future is to concentrate on the second two options – selling TNT's expertise, and its reliability and excellent customer service.

The focus will increasingly be on reliability and customer service as the number of new businesses the company wishes to enter declines and the need to increase the loyalty of the present customer base grows. 'Better service standards means higher levels of customer retention, and that is the key to building a business.'

The emphasis on quality and customer service first becomes apparent in TNT Express service's divisional companies. 'As the market settles down with a balance between major companies with a global reach, and smaller companies in niche markets, customers are looking at an increasingly standardised market place. Quality is the one major advantage that firms can have and maintain over the competition.'

Service strengths

'Our market intelligence clearly identifies reliability as the central concern of the customer. Delivery is our job and customers expect us to deliver on our promise to deliver.'

Reliability is indeed the first stopping point on the way to customer satisfaction.

And TNT knows that it's not just a question of being reliable; it's also a question of providing tangible references and assurances to customers about that reliability. 'It is not just enough to do the job, we have to tell our customers. In their eyes, we are only as good as the last consignment.'

TNT has created a broad range of tools which help employees improve reliability and give customers greater assurances about TNT's reliability. Infobot is available to customers over the phone and is a robot answering system which answers customer's questions about the status of the packages. Infobot can tell the customer whether or not his package arrived at its destination and who signed for it.

TNT's BMS system makes sure customers get calls just often enough and not too often. BMS is a database which automatically produces daily call programmes for sales personnel and customer service staff.

Another system automatically displays the customer's account information up on a screen the minute that the call comes in on the switchboard. For customers that means that there is no delay while the customer service and sales personnel look for the customer's account in the computer. It also means that the customer doesn't have to recite his or her account number over the phone every time he or she calls.

In-Cab is a system by which drivers can receive hard copy of customer delivery and collection requests. This cuts down on communication errors from phone communications and makes sure that the drivers never have to ask to use the customer's telephone. It also allows drivers to pass on delivery confirmations extremely rapidly which can then be made available to the customer.

Drivers also use 'Gizmo', a computerised check weighing, labelling and routeing system. It's an excellent example of a 'get it right the first time' system and has greatly reduced errors and improved accuracy and operational efficiency.

The kind of reliability that these TNT systems permit have brought the company tremendous success. One of the most notable examples is with TNT Newsfast, where TNT has moved in just five years from being a newcomer to the market to being the market leader in newspaper and magazine distribution, hauling more tonnage than any other UK carrier.

The greatest demonstration of reliability by the company occurred in 1986 during the so-called 'Wapping' labour dispute. TNT gained a nationwide reputation at that time for the "must get through" attitude of the drivers which permitted many TNT handled papers to be delivered when others were blocked. Numerous letters of thanks received from publishers are proudly displayed by the company in its entry hall.

From the *Sunday Scot*, 'Could I personally thank you for the extremely hard work that was put in by TNT Newsfast which enabled the first Scottish popular Sunday newspaper for 72 years to arrive at all wholesalers and retailers on time.'

From Rupert Murdoch, '. . . I must say I have been very impressed with the quality of service and consistent reliability which your company has provided during the last five years. Your people have got the 'must get through' attitude which I need to get my newspapers delivered on time.'

And they are not the only customers to say the same thing. TNT has gained an excellent reputation for reliability, but not just for reliability. TNT has also made an effort to be close to the customer and to provide the kind of friendly and personalised service customers appreciate.

In terms of getting close to the customer, it was TNT Newsfast's customer-friendly practices that won over many customers. 'Live News' is a report produced for each publisher every morning no later than 8 a.m. giving a report on the status of delivery operations that day. For time-sensitive magazines, customers receive on-line information on daily performance. Weekly summaries are also available.

During 1990/1, the entire company merged two of its biggest operations in response to customer comments that they preferred to deal with only one person for all of their TNT business. TNT Overnite and TNT Tristar (three-day delivery) are now one division. Customers not only deal with just one person, they also have only one set of tariffs to understand and work with a simplified subscription system. Studies following the changes showed that customer loyalty increased.

Also to bring it closer to the customer, TNT reorganised its operational and sales territories. The split-ups are now done on the basis of postal codes instead of by counties. Now all the sales, customer service and delivery personnel work in smaller, better co-ordinated teams which have made staff more available to the customer and more efficient.

In the TNT Supamail operation, an innovative approach led to an increase in customer loyalty rates. From the start, one of the four main objectives for the service was to 'ensure that once customers are persuaded to try the TNT Supamail service, repeat business is obtained.'

TNT Supamail is an overnight delivery service aimed at the commercial express delivery market place for users largely located in offices and town centres. Its only major competitors on entering the market were public carriers.

Supamail launched a new method of selling consignment notes called 'subscription ordering'. Users are encouraged to buy prepaid blocks of 10 subscriptions to be used for 10 deliveries. The subscription rate gives the customer a slight discount over the standard rate. The customer is invoiced for the notes.

The subscription notes are preprinted for the customer which makes parcel or document preparation extremely rapid for the customer. Because use of the notes is recorded by TNT, the customer receives a call from a salesman just as his book is running out, which saves him from calling.

Studies after introduction of the subscription system show that 90 per cent annual customer loyalty rates are being achieved with customers who use subscription books as opposed to 50 per cent loyalty rates with those who don't.

Even job candidates at TNT benefit from the company's customer oriented attitude. When TNT refuses candidates who apply, they don't just say 'No, sorry we aren't hiring', they receive a full and valid explanation. 'As you will be aware the Kuwait crisis and the recession have created considerable uncertainty about future economic prospects. As a result, we have decided not to take on additional staff for the time being.'

And that doesn't mean that TNT isn't ready to discuss. 'However, I will be pleased to see you for a discussion if you feel that I may be able to help you in any way.' The letter is signed by none other than Alan Jones, himself.

Implementation

While service quality has been a key point for TNT ever since its establishment in the UK, it is even more so since the launching of its service quality programme in 1988. The programme is independent of, but is inspired by, actions taken at the worldwide group level to raise quality still further through a total quality programme. In the UK, the company has concentrated on two aspects – an operations programme for quality and a company-wide programme for the establishment of service standards.

The TNT service excellence campaign, as the operations quality programme is called, was the first to be introduced and went out under the slogan, 'Who Cares – Wins!'. Service excellence squads were created at all TNT locations with volunteers. They are responsible for coming up with ways to improve quality and have been behind some of the major computer and system-based quality improvements in the company. The Gizmo system described above is one of these, which came out of a Service Excellence Squad chaired by Peter May, Northern Regional General Manager.

More recently, 'Driving for Quality' has begun and is focusing on service standards, 'not only in internal operations, but also in our customer contact'. As a very first step, standards were introduced concerning the telephone. No customer has to wait for more than six rings and he is never asked to call another number.

Other sets of standards have been created for drivers including: 'he must be in a clean, undamaged vehicle and he must wear his uniform'. Most of the standards for frontline staff have been completed. TNT's approach is to move from the customer contact staff positions and from the lower end of the hierarchy, inwards towards the support functions and upwards.

Standards have now been established for the financial administration department which are called the 'five fives'. One of these is that invoice queries are not to represent more than 5 per cent of the total number of invoices; another is that the 60-day debt should not exceed 5 per cent of the ledger balance. Mr Jones would like to turn these into the 'five fours'.

TNT isn't just creating standards, it's monitoring them on a weekly basis. Now, there's a saying within TNT that, 'you're only as good as your next week's figures'. Telephone standards are monitored by computer and the figures for each location are communicated for everyone to see; there is a competition running to see which TNT office can get the best. 'Copynotes' or problems that were resolved the first time around are also being monitored.

TNT has employees who regularly 'mystery shop' the company at different locations. Mystery shoppers produce what are known as 'Big Brother' reports every Monday morning which are communicated to the whole staff.

The results of all of the reports and the results for the week are discussed at the 'Friday Bleaching' personally by Alan Jones.

Above all service quality at TNT is due to strong interest and commitment by management to achieving improvements in every single area of the organisation. TNT is a very marketing oriented and a very competitive organisation. It is not the intention of this very competitive company to be bypassed and certainly not in the area of service quality. 'We have a culture of quality and dedication. It's team spirit, but it's not for everyone.'

What can be learned

1 Give your company achievement units

By creating separate divisions for nearly every new product launched, TNT created an extremely market oriented and combatant spirit inside the company. Marketing plans for each unit are finetuned to the last detail. Staff, encouraged by management, go all out to make their product a success in its market. No product is ever a follow-on, because it's the responsibility of a whole new team. Their job is to draw customers to the product and keep them loyal to it. It is 'their baby' and they are totally committed to it. In the end, it's the customer who benefits.

2 Don't just offer 'quality', tell customers what kind of service quality

In the past, companies that differentiated on the basis of service quality were few and far between. Today, there are an increasing number that are claiming to offer top service quality. Companies that offer real service quality generally tell the customer what kind of service quality they offer. TNT guarantees reliability and it works for highly personalised customer service. As a customer, you know what to expect.

3 Develop tools to build customer loyalty

TNT subscription notes are a good way to get customers to repurchase their services. That in itself is no guarantee of loyalty if the service delivered is bad. In the case of TNT, the advantage is that a customer who tries TNT 10 times will see 10 times over how good the service really is and want to keep coming back for more.

VERGÖLST

'A company turned around by service', Vergölst underwent a massive change in its way of viewing its customers and its market strategy following the implementation of a dedicated programme of service quality.

The results were quantifiable. Revenues grew by roughly 25 per cent in four years in a slow growth market. An operational loss was turned into a profit and the investment made in the service quality programme is being paid back from the profits from revenues of the new services introduced for customers.

Vergölst today differentiates itself from its competitors by the quality of service it offers customers.

Background

Vergölst is in the business of selling new and re-tread tyres direct to the customer through its own point-of-sale outlets or on a wholesale basis to garages or speciality shops. It is a 100 per cent owned subsidiary of Continental AG of Hannover and 70 per cent of all new tyres which the company sells come from Continental. The remaining 30 per cent come from a variety of other quality tyre producers.

The company's turnaround began in 1986. At that time, the company was a product and industry oriented company. The primary objective was to achieve full capacity in their factories of re-tread tyres. There was a corresponding lack of interest in the company's retail operations. With heavy price competition in the German tyre market, the company found itself selling increasingly on a discount basis to the wholesale market and less and less on a direct retail basis to the end customer.

Vergölst had also diversified into selling a whole variety of different products which had resulted in a dispersion of the company's efforts and resources.

The management team's response was to propose the adoption of a strategy which focused on the sale of tyres through the retail outlets, to re-centre the company's efforts on the sale and servicing of tyres and closely associated accessories, and to differentiate the company from its competitors via the quality of the service provided – in short, to become more than just a tyre dealer and become a service company.

'Management was looking for a differential advantage that would make Vergölst stand out from its competitors in the German tyre distribution market. The vision that was developed was that of a service oriented company which was close to the final customer.'

Service strategy

The company's strategy for service is contained in what is now the company's slogan. Vergölst is, 'the most customer friendly service company around the wheel'. The company's objective is to increase customer satisfaction through efficient and friendly service, and to increase sales through the offering of complementary tyre services.

With 160 point-of-sale outlets and roughly 75 per cent of the company's sales coming from its direct retail operations, Vergölst was well placed to increase its business to consumers. The company already had a reputation in Germany for selling high-quality products. In addition, they are recognised experts in the handling of specific tyre-related problems, such as balancing, brakes or alignment.

The company's primary target customers, who make up roughly 40 per cent of the company's sales, could be described as middle to upper-class buyers. They are quality- and value conscious. For re-tread tyres, Vergölst has a large percentage of ecology-conscious buyers.

To find out specifically what needed to be done to make these customers more satisfied with the service they were getting from Vergölst, customer focus groups were organised by region. Dissatisfied customers were invited to come and voice their opinions about how the service could be improved and explain what their own experience had been.

The company also established a customer satisfaction survey which is available in the outlets for customers to complete and send in.

Managers of the outlets as well as the staff were involved in the focus groups. In some cases, employees participated as listeners; in other cases the results were communicated using verbatim quotes from the groups.

One of the most important techniques which was used was 'do-it-yourself market research'. Each employee would make an assessment of the outlet's service quality. They would then ask customers for their views personally. The results permitted the employee to compare his perception of service quality with that of the customer's.

The survey results led to two things. First, employees on the whole became more conscience of the importance of making efforts to treat the customer with extra consideration. The message being passed was that customers expected Vergölst staff to be friendly and helpful.

The second outcome from the surveys was the creation of a whole new set of services for the customer. Rather than just sell tyres, Vergölst outlets were turned into true tyre service centres in which the customer could expect to receive maintenance and repair services, as well as auxiliary services such as insurance. The revenues generated from these new services alone covered the cost of the service quality programme.

Customer surveys and focus groups have not stopped. The company's present CEO, Burkhardt Köller, who joined Vergölst in 1988, has continued the process and is constantly refining and adding to the technique. The company now uses mystery shoppers as well to test Vergölst services and report back to the outlets on ways to improve. Each shop is 'mystery shopped' three times per year. The company also uses the surveys and mystery shopping as a way to identify each new customer needs.

Service strengths

Once the new strategy was in the first stages of realisation, Vergölst customers began to discover a whole series of new services being made available to them. One of the most important is a hot-line for truck drivers. On a 24-hour basis, truck drivers can call for assistance if they have problems with the tyres. Vergölst provides repair for any tyre brands and not just those sold by the company. A hot-line is available for every region which means that the drivers have assistance on hand and not thousands of kilometres away.

Another major service development was the offering of tyre insurance. Vergölst began offering insurance against theft or damage. For the company, the insurance operation reported a loss for the first year but after 18 months it represented a profitable activity for the company.

In addition to tyre insurance, Vergölst extended its guarantees on re-tread tyres and created a guarantee on balancing work done for customers. Vergölst's guarantee on re-tread tyres is now two years as compared with the standard one-year guarantee for the industry.

Balancing work is guaranteed for 24 hours after the work has been completed. If the customer has any doubt, he is free to come back in and get his money back and have the work checked as well as re-balanced for free.

One of the most popular services developed by Vergölst is the stockage of tyres on behalf of customers. Summer tyres are stored during the winter and winter tyres during the summer. Maintenance of stored tyres means checking them, balancing them, cleaning them, etc. which makes the service more than just a stocking activity. The service was introduced in 1987 and has had growth rates of nearly 30 per cent per year.

A special central department was also created to handle complaints or any customer problems; something that had not existed previously. The objective is still to have complaints handled at the local level; headquarters receives only 60 complaints or so per year.

The complaint department is also responsible for analysing customer complaints, including those that are handled at the local level. Even verbal or walk-in complaints are measured and analysed. Vergölst wants to know exactly why customers complained and have the opportunity to respond in the best way possible in order to keep the customer.

Employees are now trained in how to handle customer complaints, as well as in other customer-handling approaches. As a first step, a new training centre was built which provided training to every employee designed to change employees' attitudes towards service provision. DM2.2 million was invested from 1986 to 1989 and the number of days of training increased from about 800 to 2289. The centre was used to capacity to achieve the objective of making employees more friendly and helpful in the customers' eyes.

Over the same period, the company invested DM25 million in revamping all of the outlets across the country. The new image of the company was promoted more heavily in external communication and a figure – a tyre with two hands and a friendly face in the middle – was created to represent the company's new service oriented approach to its customers and its employees.

Top management wanted Vergölst to 'forget about being dominated by the product and start being dominated by concern for the customer.' With all that was done over the four years of the programme, management achieved its goal. Vergölst today has a customer loyalty rate of 70 per cent which is quoted by the BBE Institute as being the highest in the industry.

Implementation

The key to success in converting Vergölst into a customer-conscious company was the systematic introduction of different service quality management tools, together with an active internal sales and communication programme designed to convince managers and employees alike of the need to change the company's approach.

Top management started with methods of identifying customers' service expectations to know their level of satisfaction with the service presently provided. Customer satisfaction surveys, focus groups and the 'do-it-yourself' market research were all different methods used to obtain information on customer's expectations. With this information they showed the gap between what service customers were expecting and what they were receiving.

This information was a powerful tool for convincing reluctant managers or hesitant employees. The next step was to show what needed to be changed within the organisation to become more customer oriented. Top management presented the new strategy to the entire team at headquarters. In the presentation the message was passed that management for good customer service basically means good people management. Top management explained that it required a reversal of the hierarchy, putting the customer on top and that an enormous investment in people was required at the frontline.

Top management subsequently visited all 160 subsidiaries to pass the message personally and convince each and every employee. This was part of a personal communication effort on the part of the management team to get everyone's commitment to the new vision. (See Chapter 3, for further details.)

Top management then launched a large internal and external promotions campaign. Articles appeared in the company newspaper about good service deals. Complaint letters were also published in their entirety. A Vergölst song was written and a special service award was used to decorate administrative and customer contact staff for good customer service. On an annual basis people were recognised at dinners and get-togethers. Employees from the outlet receiving the best mystery shopper report won a paid weekend trip.

Following the renovation of 160 outlets, there were a series of service and sales competitions between different Vergölst outlets in order to promote the new customer service approach internally and externally. Participating teams could win prizes. During these competitions, record business was developed as employees went all out to win customers' confidence and satisfaction. The service and sales competitions coincided with the introduction of new customer services which helped employees to change their focus from selling tyres to selling service.

Once employees were convinced of the need to make changes in their customer approach and were shown via the competitions that better service could yield tangible results for the company, the company introduced a method which tied outlet managers' bonuses to the revenues realised on services provided by his outlet. Thirty per cent of the variable part of a manager's salary is tied to the point score obtained in the annual Vergölst service league. The service league ranks the results of each outlet's service-related revenues.

Training was introduced, designed to increase the administration and management staff's understanding of work on the frontline. A special training film was developed for the purpose costing DM40,000. Everyone in the company is now expected to be able to perform at least one frontline task such as tyre balancing.

In addition, every employee in the company was given a training course designed to increase their customer awareness. The course lasts between one and a half and four days, depending on the position of the employee within the company. Frontline staff and managers received more training in customer handling.

All managers are expected to spend at least one week a year working on the frontline. They help load trucks, receive customers or accompany drivers in order 'to know what is happening at the front'. Already, 90 per cent of Vergölst regional managers have worked on the frontline before assuming their positions. At the director and managing director level, roughly 50 per cent have had prior customer contact experience at Vergölst. The policy helps keep former frontline managers in tune with changes and increases the awareness of those who have not.

Last, but not least of the new methods was the introduction of service quality standards. A 'Service Bible' was designed for all employees and is handed out to each and every employee when he enters the company. In this document, customers' service expectations are related to norms of service which the company should be attaining. On the left-hand side of the page, there is what Vergölst asks from its employees in terms of service; on the right-hand side of the page, there is the desired customer reaction. The 'Service Bible' ends with a two-page picture which shows what service means to everybody for every single function in the company.

All of the service management methods introduced by the company continue to be used on a regular basis. The present management recognises that the process of service quality improvement must be kept going. The methods are being continuously refined and expanded better to identify customer expectations and better to monitor the service delivered.

What can be learned

1 Give managers a taste of the frontline

Top management established a policy for managers to spend one week a year on the frontline. In this way, managers have a better feeling for what the day-to-day working conditions of employees are and the real problems that face them when they try to offer good service to customers.

2 *Involve the back office in the frontline*

The importance of increasing every employee's awareness of the end customer was emphasised. Administration staff were not only trained for customer awareness; they were also trained how to perform specific duties at the frontline.

3 *Let your customer convince your employees*

The most powerful weapon for selling service quality internally was the results from the focus groups and customer surveys that were being done. Top management communicated not just the results; employees were given verbatim transcriptions of what customers said about their services. In other cases, employees heard for themselves what customers said when they participated in focus groups themselves.

INDEX